YANKEE TEACHER

The Life of
WILLIAM TORREY HARRIS

BY
KURT F. LEIDECKER, M.A., PH.D.

THE PHILOSOPHICAL LIBRARY
NEW YORK

William Torrey Harris

FOREWORD

William Torrey Harris, whose intimate friendship I enjoyed for a long generation, was an outstanding mind in the history of our American life. His contributions to philosophy and to the theory and practice of education were not only numerous, but of commanding importance. He was so fortunate as to add to the mind of a scholar and statesman the ability to make clear and simple the doctrines which he taught. It was this which gave to Dr. Harris his commanding influence over the teaching profession during his long years of active leadership in all which related to its thought and work.

The history of American education and of our American contributions to philosophical thought cannot be understood or estimated without knowledge of the life work of Dr. William Torrey Harris.

Nicholas Murray Butler

PREFACE

But there are deeds which shall not pass away,
And names that must not wither . .
— BYRON

A long time ago, they tell us, Zeus assembled around him all men to give immortality to the one having done the worthiest deed. One by one they came forward, recounting their deeds of valor and distinction, till only a kindly old man was left. "And what is it *you* have done?" inquired Zeus. "I am a teacher," he replied, "and all these men here before you were my pupils." Then spoke Zeus: "Thou art the greatest among men and deserving of immortality before all others." If the contest is repeated, as they say it is every hundred years, that humble follower of Socrates may well have been the subject of our biography.

"With the death of Dr. Harris, there came to its earthly end the activity of one of the greatest philosophical minds of modern times," writes Dr. Nicholas Murray Butler.[1] But in order that it may no longer be a pity "that so few can ever know how distinguished an ornament he was to his nation and his race," this biography has been written.

William Torrey Harris, a mastermind in his profession, did not shoot across the American horizon like a comet. Slowly he rose, a satellite at first, a sun later, making good each trust put in him and doing his full share of the duties attached to each station in his life.

As far back as 1888, when Frank H. Kasson[2] weighed the question: "Who is the most potent influence upon the public school system and the teachers of America?" he was forced to eliminate E. E. White, John W. Dickinson, Larkin Dunton, John Eaton, J. E. Pickard, F. Louis Soldan, G. Stanley Hall, and Wm. H. Payne, to give first place to W. T. Harris.

Those who know the history of American education cannot insert between Horace Mann and John Dewey any other man so influential and generally known as Harris. "Officially and unofficially" he was, as A. E. Winship wrote, "for a third of a century" "the public school leader of the United States" and "the best-known American educator in foreign countries." His position was established long before he became United States Commissioner of Education. It was his zeal, his vast knowledge, and above all his shining qualities as a man that made him an "equal to kings," as someone said, or the "spiritual father to thousands" as C. P. Cary has put it.

In 1899, *New York Education* acknowledged that it honored itself by putting his picture on its title page; for from New England to California Harris was acclaimed and from Minnesota to Kentucky he was respected as no one else before in the educational field. Friend or foe had to concede that they were dealing with a philosophical giant. "He is the most commanding figure in the educational field today" said Ossian Lang in the *Nation* of July 5, 1906. "Neither England nor France nor even Germany, the home of pedagogy, has as great an intellect at work in the philosophical elaboration of the fundamental problems."

But if the American eulogies of Dr. Harris should be taken as prejudiced opinions springing from national pride or personal favor, let us go to Europe. A young man from Webster Grove, a soldier in the army, but interested in philosophy, met Henri Bergson not many years ago in Paris. In the course of conversation he mentioned that he came from St. Louis. "Oh," said Bergson, "that is the city Dr. Harris made famous by his great insight into philosophy!"

Cloudesley Brereton of the London County Council, Educational Department, stated in a letter to Mrs. Harris after the death of her husband: "His name was known in every civilized country outside his own, in none better than in England where it stood for all that is real and substantial and thoughtful in American education. We felt in Dr. Harris here is one who has gone down below the mere froth and flux of things and has brought us up permanent and abiding treasures in the art and science of education that can never be forgotten." Sir Michael E. Sadler would have concurred in this most heartily.

What the Cairds, what T. H. Green and Hutchinson Sterling did for idealism in England, that Harris did for it in America, and more yet, in that he had access to the vast educational machinery of the country to drive idealism home. New England idealism became transcendental, Harris' became operational in thousands of schools and wherever people met to discuss philosophical and pedagogical problems in America. As G. P. Brown said, Dr. Harris will go down in history as the philosopher in education.

Not as literary genius and creative philosopher, but surely as versatile and profound thinker he could be placed second to Emerson among American philosophers, as Dr. John J. Tigert wants it. Without doubt, around the turn of the century he had attained the position of the greatest philosopher America had produced, and the pertinent remarks of Susan E. Blow, his great devotee, are not exaggerated. His life was work, expounding, administering, and creating the forms as a sort of conditioning for insight.

In a worthy tribute by the late Dr. Walton C. John, of the United States Office of Education, the remark was made that "in many respects his contributions were not spectacular." True, a gentle philosopher's seldom are. Nevertheless, no one was "so popular in a fine way," if we may trust Dr. Philander Priestley Claxton among a throng of others. Anna Tolman Smith wrote in 1890 that Harris was personally known to almost every teacher, school officer, college professor and president, and if you chanced upon a company of philosophers absorbed in intricate problems of time and eternity, ten to one, they would be quoting Dr. Harris.

"Such a record . . . so diverse, so pregnant in great influences, so profound in its principles, was never before made by any American educator. It is doubtful if, under all the changes of educational and literary conditions, another is even possible." Thus Charles Franklin Thwing. And while this statement emphasizes the greatness of Harris, it implies at the same time the reasons why Harris' name shone dimly after his death until the centenary of his birth. All who knew him, never forgot him; nor did any true historian of education and philosophy by-pass him. However, he has not yet become, as Dr. Elmer Ellsworth Brown so beautifully expressed it, the historic character with mellow tradition gathering like autumn haze about him, but he will, just as surely as Jefferson and Hamilton have emerged in their full stature, for he had a wise and fruitful conception of true democracy.

* * *

It was in 1935 when the celebration of the 100th anniversary of his birth drew the attention of many to Harris as a great educator and philosopher, that some members of the American Philosophical Association gathered in St. Louis definitely characterized the biography of Harris as a desideratum. Soon, educators also joined in the expression of the belief that a good service might be rendered by writing such a work.

To these vague suggestions and statements of the desirability of a biography, the author responded almost immediately with enthusiasm, for he had been convinced for some years while working on the influence of Oriental thinking on leading Americans, that here was a virgin field for investigations of a highly significant nature. Being familiar with much that had been written about Harris' educational theories and the like, he had been struck in his researches by the fact that all writers, including the authors of dissertations, had labored under a decided handicap: They knew practically nothing about the personal life of the man who, in a sense, had symbolized American education for nearly half a century.

However, as soon as work was begun, it became evident from the tremendous amount of material to be gathered and studied, that the contemplated biography would require years to finish. This impression was borne out by the facts. With many interruptions, including service in the Army Air Forces, the work progressed slowly until 1944, when Dr. Dagobert D. Runes, Editor and Publisher, Philosophical Library, Inc., urged the writer to press on to the completion of the book. Since a one-volume work was planned, many chapters that had already been written, had to be condensed severely or left out entirely, while a large section of the work had yet to be worked up from the sources. The task was finished in six months, despite other duties that claimed the major portion of the day. While the questions as to who Harris was, asked so many times by friends and acquaintances who learned about my absorbing interest, were a bit disconcerting and had a slightly frustrating effect, continued inspiration was derived from the solid conviction as to the importance of the life and work of Harris in those who *did* know, as well as from the personality of Harris himself who, whatever may have been his limitations, was a comprehensive, deep and persuasive thinker, a thoroughgoing American and a great man, and one of the best.

Kurt F. Leidecker

Wright Field,
Dayton, Ohio
July 12th, 1946.

TABLE OF CONTENTS

ACKNOWLEDGMENTS

With selfless devotion, Miss Edith Davidson Harris, daughter of the subject of this biography, has assisted the writer in the preparation of this work. Without her generosity in supplying personal data, letters, documents, copies of published and unpublished writings of her father, transcriptions from his shorthand and many helpful suggestions throughout, the book might never have been. It is with pleasure and profound gratitude that I think back upon the voluminous correspondence which has contributed so much to the authenticity and documentation of the material that has been presented here.

To Doctor Nicholas Murray Butler, President of Columbia University, the great friend and admirer of Harris, I owe thanks for many kindnesses, not least that of placing at my disposal his entire correspondence with Harris. His constant interest in the progress of the work which he manifested despite the pressure of multifarious duties, and his unalterable belief in the greatness of Harris, have been a source of encouragement and inspiration to the writer.

Many are the persons who have read portions of the manuscript and helped with friendly, if sometimes severe criticism. Let them be assured here also of my thanks and my obligation to them. Among those who knew Harris personally, and in some instances intimately, I name but the following: Mr. W. J. S. Bryan, of St. Louis, Mo., who at one time taught under Harris, has for years collected his writings and made valuable suggestions on the pertinent chapters of the biography; Dr. Henry Ridgely Evans, who was Harris' personal secretary for three years and was associated with him closely all through the Washington period; the late Mrs. Lucia Ames Mead, of Brookline, Mass., whose husband was one of Harris' most intimate friends; the late Miss Lilian Whiting, of Boston, who had a deep and sensitive appreciation of the person of Harris; the late Dr. Thomas B. Ford, sometime Dean of Lincoln Memorial University, and a Harris enthusiast; my teacher, the late Professor James Hayden Tufts, of the University of Chicago and Santa Barbara, California, who had pleasant recollections of Harris extending back to the Concord Summer School of Philosophy; the late Professor James B. Pratt of Williams College who spent many days in conversation with Harris at Glenmore; the late Miss Lucy F. Wheelock, Principal of Wheelock School, Boston, whose interest in the Kindergarten drew her close to Harris;

and a number of close and more distant relatives of the biographee in New England, New Jersey, and in the West.

In the U. S. Office of Education, at Washington, the author would like to acknowledge with many thanks the help received by the late Dr. Walton C. John, Senior Specialist in Higher Education; the late Miss Sabra W. Vought, Chief of the Library Division; Miss Edith A. Wright, Reference Librarian; Dr. Willard O. Mishoff, Specialist in Public Libraries.

Among librarians in and out of our colleges and universities I mention with gratitude the assistance given me by Miss Harriet R. Peck, Rensselaer Polytechnic Institute; Dr. Arthur E. Bostwick, St. Louis Public Library; Professor Andrew Keogh, Dr. Charles E. Rush, and Miss Anne S. Pratt, Yale University; Professor Winthrop Holt Chenery, Washington University; Dr. Harold L. Leupp, University of California; Mr. Richard G. Hensley, the Public Library of Boston.

Apart from all these, pleasant and profitable correspondence has been enjoyed with the following persons whom I likewise have to thank for suggestions wisely considered. The late Professor Charles M. Perry of the University of Oklahoma; Dr. Joy Elmer Morgan, Editor, National Education Association; Dr. Floyd C. Shoemaker, Secretary, State Historical Society of Missouri; Professor Daniel S. Robinson, Lt. Comdr. ChC. U. S. N. R.; Professor emer. Edward Parmalee Morris of Yale; Mr. S. H. Paradise, Phillips Academy; Mr. Harold Hamilton Wade, Headmaster Worcester Academy, and Mrs. Gertrude L. Houlihan, Secretary, Alumni Office; Professor Odell Shepard, Trinity College; Dr. Carl A. Lohmann, Secretary, Yale University.

Very special thanks are due the publisher, Dr. Dagobert D. Runes who, with singular insight, recognized the importance of the figure of Harris in American education, philosophy and history, and has been kindly indulgent in many ways.

The book went to press while the author was overseas on a special mission to England and during his absence, as well as after his return, Professor Herbert W. Schneider, Chairman of the Department of Philosophy at Columbia University, took it upon himself to read the manuscript and the entire proof, making most valuable suggestions. Professor Schneider may ever be assured of the author's deep gratitude.

K. F. L.

YANKEE TEACHER

Part One

NEW ENGLAND PERIOD

CHAPTER ONE

ANCESTRY

FIRST SETTLERS ALL

IN William Torrey Harris met the cross-currents of blood from well over a hundred sturdy American settlers. He himself attributed much of his personality to his ancestors, and eagerly expanded his own notes by study of the genealogical material at the Congressional Library.[1]

In 1631 the good ship "Lyon" brought a number of Harris' ancestors to America, disembarking them on February 5th at Boston from where they dispersed into the "wilderness of wants." Winter storms had whipped the waters to a raging sea and made the passage an exceedingly uncomfortable one. In fact, the same sea retarded two weeks the ship which bore John Winthrop, son of Governor John Winthrop, who brought with him the original charter.

His lineal ancestor, Thomas Harris,[2] in 1637, followed his brother William to Providence, R. I. William had a colorful career as lawyer, large landowner and associate of Roger Williams. Three times he went to England on business and was captured the fourth time by a Barbary corsair, sold in the markets of Algiers as slave on February 24th, 1680, and ransomed a year or so later for the sum of $1200.00. After that he did not see America again, but died three days before he reached London on his route through Spain and France.

Roger Williams himself, another passenger on the same

1

boat, was destined to play an even greater rôle than any of his fellow-travelers. He left Boston for Salem; from Salem he went to Plymouth, only to return to this hotbed of self-righteous fanaticism and be ousted, in 1635, by the General Court of Massachusetts for his belief in freedom of conscience and religious conviction. Helped by the Indians to whom he had always shown understanding and kindness, he founded the place to which "Providence" had led him. To have become First President of the Rhode Island Colony is an imposing achievement, but to be looked upon as father of the principle of liberty of conscience inscribed in every heart on the Western continent, is a greater satisfaction still. Harris naturally felt proud that he was descended, through Mercy Williams, from this man whom Bradford's *History of Plimouth Plantation* (1632) called a "man godly and zealous, having many precious parts, but very unsettled in judgemente." Roger was supported by Thomas Harris and several others through whom the Harris line can be traced, including Richard Waterman.

This Waterman, a Colonel in the militia, had come to America as early as 1629 and settled at Salem. He associated with the Quakers, but distinguished himself enough to have a monument erected to him at Providence.

The Mowry branch of the family likewise was closely associated with the venture of Roger Williams whose kins-men they were. In 1631, Roger Mowry was entered as Freeman in the Plymouth books, went the same year to Salem and later followed Williams to Providence. Both his grandson and great grandson became captains, and in the fifth generation there appeared Judge Daniel Mowry who was a member of the Continental Congress during 1780 and 1781.

Another of the early settlers of Providence, R. I., was Captain John Whipple.[3] He lived there about 26 years and was present when the Indians burned the town. Many of

2

the political offices were entrusted to him, as membership in the Town Council, the office of Town Clerk and Deputy to the Rhode Island General Assembly. As proprietor of the "Whipple Inn" he became even more prominent in public affairs, for it was in this inn that the Town Council, and once the General Assembly convened. His son, Eleazer, became a member of the General Assembly in 1670.

In the ship "Lyon" came also Thomas Angell, a lad of about thirteen years and apprentice to Roger Williams. First he stayed at Boston, then in Salem and later we find him a "cunstabel of Providence," taking part in all the major operations in that city.[4]

As a young man of 22 years, the Rev. Obadiah Holmes had come with his wife to Salem, Mass., around 1629. His whole temperament and Oxford training had made him love discussion a bit more than the Pilgrim Fathers thought wholesome. Consequently, they excommunicated him, and finally he settled in 1650 or thereabout at Newport, R. I., where many honors were conferred on him, such as Commissioner to the General Court of Rhode Island and member of the Governor's Council. He became even more a martyr to his religious conscience when, on a visit to Massachusetts, he attended a private religious gathering. Religion, in the State, was to be carried on only in designated places, and so he brought back from his vacation a black, bloody and swollen back, mutilated by 90 stripes.[5]

It is probable that Capt. John Johnson came "from England with Winthrop's large fleet which arrived in Salem, Mass., June 22, 1630."[6] He was "Surveyor General of all ye armies;" his house was an arsenal and it was the explosion in his house, on February 6th, 1645, that not only shook Boston and Cambridge like an earthquake, but robbed us of the early town records of Roxbury, Mass., much to the distress of many a pedigree seeker. It was furthermore in his house that Anne Hutchinson was confined after banishment, but

3

enjoyed all the privileges of the family except on her walks which she had to take escorted.

If Thomas Low was the son of John Low, he did not follow in the footsteps of his father who was Master of the ship "Ambrose" and Vice-admiral of Governor Winthrop's fleet. He did not go to sea "to be lost," as was Capt. John Low, but settled at Ipswich, Mass., about 1641 and established himself as a "maltster."

The Aldriches, remarkable for their longevity, hail from George Aldrich who arrived in America on Nov. 6, 1631, landing at Dorchester, Mass. He became one of the first settlers of Nipmugg, which later was incorporated as Mendon.

William Almy was in America as early as 1631, went back to England and re-appeared in 1635, assuming the posts of juryman and Commissioner.

John Newgate came to Boston in 1632 and, true to tradition, became one of the largest property owners in this region.

A veteran of 60 years, Edmund Hobart came to America in 1633. Though he held several important posts, a good deal more is known about his son, the Rev. Peter Hobart.[7]

The Rev. Zechariah Symmes was a graduate of Cambridge, England, before he came with wife and seven children to Boston in the ship "Griffin."[8] This was September 18th, 1634. Though rather liberal-minded, he became in due time the staunch opponent of the Antinomians. Perhaps his wife, Sarah, also contributed to the fact that he sailed well on the rough waters stirred up by the Quakers. Edward Johnson described her as a godly woman, a "virtuous woman, endued by Christ with grace fit for a wilderness condition, her courage exceeding her stature," etc.

Two half-brothers, William and Thomas Arnold, made their way over, in 1635, on board the ship "Plain Joan." William went with Roger Williams to Pawtuxet in 1638 and

4

became one of the thirteen original proprietors of Providence Plantation. Thomas, after a stay in Virginia, went to Watertown, Mass., leaving for Providence not until 1661. He served as Deputy to the General Assembly intermittently for five years.

John Greene, the surgeon, sailed from Southampton, England, in the ship "James" and arrived at Boston on June 3, 1635. Once he was fined in Providence because he had spoken contemptuously of the magistrate. This was by no means the only time that his tongue and free thought got him into trouble. Once he wrote a letter which he addressed to the Court of Massachusetts charging it with usurping the power of Christ over the churches and men's consciousness.[9] He even had to barricade himself in his house against the soldiers who wanted to apprehend this unruly subject of the King. In 1644 he went to England and obtained redress. Then he became Commissioner and Freeman. He belonged to that group of physicians who are always in the front rank of intellectual progress. With ten others he bought Warwick, R. I. He married three times, his last wife having the unusual name of Phillip. His son John rose from Freeman, Solicitor, Attorney General and Warden to Deputy Governor of Rhode Island.

In 1635 arrived Stukeley Wescott, or, as he is sometimes recorded, Westcote.[10] He was 44 years of age when he tried to settle at Salem only to be soon after ordered, together with Richard Waterman, Thomas Olney and Francis Weston, from the jurisdiction of "The Governor and company of the Massachusetts Bay." Thus, he became one of the twelve associates of Roger Williams. Jointly with the others he founded at Providence the First Baptist Church and lived through the raid of the Massachusetts Bay authorities, one of the most infamous acts in Colonial history committed by liberty-seekers against liberty-seekers.

It might have been better if William Towne who came

5

about 1635 and settled in good faith in the Salem community[11] had stayed in England and endured the persecution there. Two of his daughters, Rebecca and Mary, had to mount the scaffold to satisfy the religious craze of Cotton Mather and the rest. "Fire brands of hell" was the comment of the Rev. Mr. Noyes when he saw the bodies dangling. All his subsequent sorrow did not restore these two innocent women to their heartbroken parents.

George Parkhurst came about 1635, bringing his daughter Phebe, who married Thomas Arnold.

The Rev. John Fiske, born in St. James Parish, South Elmham, Suffolk County, England, had earned his degree at Immanuel College, Cambridge. In disguise he sailed for America in 1637 together with his brother William and sisters Anne and Martha. In Wenham, Mass., he would have gone out immediately to preach the Gospel had he not been "hindered by Satan" in the shape of the Conformity Act. At last, at Chelmsford, Mass., he was esteemed as a "beloved physician" by the whole community.

Chad Brown put in his appearance with his wife and one or more sons in 1638, when the ship "Martin" cast anchor at Boston. But he did not relish the atmosphere and was driven the same year by his "conscience" to Providence where he signed along with the others, including William Harris, the document that sealed their town fellowship. In 1642 he was ordained as the first Baptist preacher. The College of Rhode Island whose name was changed to Brown University stands on part of the home lot owned originally by Chad and given to the institution by two of his descendants who re-purchased it after it had gone into other hands.

It was the Rev. James Fitch,[12] another ancestor of Harris, who married Brown's daughter Abigail. He had set foot on American soil in 1638, when only 16 years of age, and was ordained as first minister at Saybrook, Ct., in 1646, after finishing his theological training in America. Much is

6

known of this eloquent divine whom Cotton Mather called the "holy, acute and learned Mr. Fitch."

John Lippitt established himself in Rhode Island about the year 1638.

When, in 1639, Guilford, Ct., was settled,[13] the Rev. Henry Whitfield, a man of independent means, was the leader. The solid stone house which he built and which is yet to be seen, symbolizes even better than the 10 children he raised and the successful marriages he arranged (ministers were eager to marry his daughters!) the solidity of his character and the soundness of his business interests. As a matter of fact, he was equally skilled in the use of holy rhetoric which we are assured "lingered so long in thousands of hearts," and in the language and ways of business. So absorbed was he in business transactions of the "plantation" that four years elapsed before a regular church with the requisite seven "pillars" was incorporated.

In 1639 the London merchant Matthew Cradock sent to Charlestown, Mass., as his agent Nicholas Davison, who was to become one of Harris' ancestors. He then went on business to Barbadoes and England, but returned to America in 1656.

Edward Jackson[14] came from White Chapel, London, to America in 1640. He deserves special mention, for he seems to have been present at every lecture which the Indian apostle, John Eliot, delivered in the neighborhood of Newton, Mass., taking notes on all of them.

In Richard Tew who came with his wife in 1640 to America, Harris had Quaker ancestry. He lived at Newport, R. I., and Maidford, in Northampton County, and was elected Deputy to the General Court. He is named in a Charter of Rhode Island that was granted by Charles II. Business interests sent him to England where he died. His son Henry, however, rose to the position of Deputy Governor of Rhode Island, in 1714.

Harris was always fond of the Torrey branch of the family. Capt. William Torrey[15] came from England in 1640. His ancestral home was in Combe St. Nicholas, Somerset. At Boston he commanded as Lieutenant the Royal Artillery, and he further distinguished himself as a land-owner, prominent business man and Captain of the militia. Edward Johnson tells us he was a Latin scholar and a "good penman". In fact, we have his *Brief Discourse Concerning Futurities or Things to Come*, written in 1687, as the title page says, by William Torrey, "a very old man, in continual expectation of his translation into another life and world."[16]

Then there was the Rev. Samuel Torrey[17] who had the enviable reputation of being able to say prayer for two hours without wearying his congregation. Conservative Puritan, twice elected President of Harvard College (which office he declined on both occasions), a successful man in real estate dealings, he preached Election Sermons for the General Court, which a contemporary called "very pungent." The Rev. Joseph Torrey was a M. D.

William Davis we find in Roxbury in 1643, or perhaps earlier, playing a prominent rôle there.[18]

Laurance Wilkinson was a Lieutenant in the royal army against Cromwell. He had been taken prisoner at the surrender of Newcastle, October 22, 1644, and his estate had been sequestered and sold by Parliament in 1645. The same year he came to America, bringing with him, it is believed, his wife and child.[19] His son Samuel and his great grandson Benjamin fell in with the military spirit of Laurance, both becoming Captains. His grandson held all of the town offices at Scituate, R. I., and was once Deputy of State for the General Court.

John Smith, the mason, refused to serve as President-elect of Rhode Island Colony in 1649, was consequently fined ten pounds, but exempted from paying. Three years later he did accept the Presidency of Providence and Warwick, R. I.

8

Thomas Stafford was a millwright who came to America about 1626. He was the first to construct a grist mill driven by water at Plymouth, Mass. At Providence and Warwick he later constructed others.

Clement King was the son of a first settler, but of which one is not at all certain. Roger Burlingame we meet in Stonington, Ct., in 1654. Sergeant Christopher Smith arrived before 1655. In Providence, R. I., he gave his name to "Smith's Hill." A latecomer was John Steere, whose name appears on the town records of Providence for the first time in May, 1660, and who must, therefore, have immigrated a few months before that.

And Royalty To Boot

Our Harris' brother Edward once related how upon someone's interested enquiry his brother William told that, just having begun the study of genealogy, he had found only thirty among his ancestors who belonged to royal families. He remembered that among these were William the Conqueror, Charlemagne, and Queen Eleanor. "He was telling my family with great glee," so Edward went on, "about this correspondence and the number of our royal ancestors when one of my boys, six or seven years old, who had been having English history read to him, suddenly piped up and said, 'I don't like it, they were a bad lot'!" Graciously and affectionately Edward continued: "Of course there are all kinds of Royalties, but my oldest brother William Torrey seemed possessed by inheritance, and otherwise, of all the highest and best that is implied by the word royalty."

Indeed heraldic families by the dozens we find among Harris' ancestry. Through the Wilkinson line Harris was 25th in descent from Edward I, King of England, and his wife, Eleanor of Castile. Imposing are the names of this affiliation: Humphrey de Bohun; James Butler, Earl of Or-

9

mond; General Sir John de Talbot; Sir Henry de Grey; Sir John Conyers, and others.[20]

The Fiske line he traced through the Rev. John Fiske to the Houses of Laxfield and Stadhaugh, especially Lord Symond Fiske, who died in 1464, and his grandfather Daniel who must have been born about 1300. The Fiskes go back to about 1200 in extant records.

The Arnold line also was worth being proud of. Was not Ynir, the first of the family, King of Gwentland, Wales (A.D. 1100), and himself descended from Ynir, second son of Cadwalader, last king of the Britons who built Abergaveny, Monmouthshire and its castle which was afterwards rebuilt by Hamlet, son of the Duke of Balladon in France and whose ruins are still visible?

Benjamin Child, the American ancestor with his illustrious name, too invokes memories of tales from Norse-land replete with strife and chivalry.[21]

Back into the dim past of kings and myths reaches the name of Morgan, meaning "the one begotten by the sea." For it was to a place by the ocean (now Glamorganshire) that King Arthur is said to have brought his queen for safety and that she bore him a son there.

Roger Williams' mother, a born Pemberton, could look back to Sir John Pemberton of Stanhope, England, as her great grandfather.

Another aristocratic lineage goes back to the Tattersalls, through Joan Tattersall, the wife of surgeon John Greene. Still another can be traced through Lieutenant Laurance Wilkinson.

The name of Newgate, though not of royal taint, is found already in 1400, and through the centuries we now and then hear of landed gentry by that name.[22]

Jane Haviland, the second wife of Capt. William Torrey through whom Harris is descended, had among her ancestors mayors of Poole and Bristol. Her line goes back at least as far as 1470.

Divines and scholars in number are among the forbears of Towne who run far back into English history, but had apparently no royal blood in their stream.

There seems to be no German blood anywhere, except very thinly in the Fiskes far back. But French blood poured in more directly, for instance through the Devotion line. Edward Devotion came from a family of Huguenots, originally from La Rochelle. The people of Muddy River were well pleased with him as constable, "perambulator" and tithingman.[23] But his ancestors with their motto *"Toute pour Meilleur"* can be followed back to the 15th century in France.

The Steere family too may have been of Huguenot origin and settled in England and Ireland. In the 14th century the name was already common. Clergymen are very much in evidence in this branch, while in America the profession of law seems to have been especially favored by this line.

The Staffords link their name with Roger de Tonci, a Normandy standard-bearer whose son was given the castle of Stafford by William the Conqueror. The dukes of Buckingham, among others, are descendants of this family.

Further French influence is to be noted as coming through the Parkhursts. This family name we meet in the Doomsday Book of 1086. It is associated with William the Conqueror and there are a number of well-known clergymen and scholars by that name in English history.

The Torrey family itself probably originated in Normandy and perhaps came over with William the Conqueror to settle in the South of England. There was a barony and castle de Torre in Normandy in 1180. The name is also common in Spain and Italy. Their arms are: Sa, a tower or within a bordure barry; crest, a griffin, passant per pale or, and argent. The Motto is: *Turris fortissima Deus.*

CHAPTER TWO

SCHOOL AND HOME

THE EDUCATIONAL PATTERN

THE life of an educator fittingly begins with his education.

It is a curious fact that very early in New England history an ancestor of William Torrey Harris, William Torrey, who was Clerk to the General Court of Massachusetts, signed, in 1659, a grant that should insure the continued existence of the first American public school. It was that of Dorchester, Mass., which in 1639 had passed a law whereby through taxation of property on nearby Thompson's Island a school was to be maintained, thus setting a precedent for the American free, public and tax-supported public school.[1]

Connecticut had the perfect tradition for the rise of an educational genius. As far back as 1650, the parents of that State were obliged either to educate their children themselves, or have them educated, and the selectmen were to see to it that the law was enforced. The 18th century saw the formation of so-called school societies, made up of those qualified to vote within the confines of a town.

More than a hundred years before William Torrey Harris was born, 637 acres of Connecticut land were donated to the cause of education by Col. James Fitch, son of the clergyman of Norwich through whom the Harris family was descended. His generosity went as far as glass and nails for a college hall.

12

Not until 1795 were the schools regularly supported by the State which had realized from the sale of Ohio lands the sum of $1,200,000 to be "forever appropriated" to the support of Common Schools. To this was added, in 1836, a portion of the surplus fund belonging to the United States.

The first of the Fellenberg Schools was established in 1819. The Bible, to know which the Pilgrim Fathers had considered the birth right of every child, was not used as a regular text-book. The State Constitution neither forbade nor prescribed the use of the Bible at school. Religious instruction had already become a matter of Sunday Schools. Fellenberg's views on the use of the Book of Books in school had not been accepted generally though they were discussed now and then.

The year 1827 marked the founding of the Society for the Improvement of Common Schools which attempted to stir the somewhat dulled sense of public responsibility in the matter of schools.

About 1840, a more persistent and conscious influence of foreign educational theories and practices had made itself felt even in the smallest schools. For every school master or mistress and every "visitor" read Henry Barnard's *Connecticut Common School Journal* in which they were offered much useful information not only about domestic affairs, but also experiments in Prussia, France, Switzerland, Holland, England, and some other countries.[2]

When William Torrey Harris went to school at North Killingly, not all the reforms suggested by Henry Barnard, the great Connecticut educator born at Hartford, had become effective or even adopted throughout the State. There were still some who thought of education as too costly an expenditure the returns of which they vainly sought on the credit side when it came to efficiency and interest in farm work. To be able to read, write and count they held to be the upper threshold beyond which schooling should not

13

pass under penalty of disturbing the peace of the family.

Nevertheless, the Common School convention was held regularly on the 10th of October, at 11 a. m. Each county had its own convention to which flocked teachers and parents, clergy and laity, officials of the School Board and "visitors." Windham County usually met at Brooklyn, Ct.

According to a report by Henry Robinson and Thomas Dike,[3] school visitors at North Killingly during 1840-41, the number of parents or voters who attended the meetings of the School Society and districts was usually small. The money that had been raised in 1840 amounted to $245.50, in addition to public funds. They praised the desire to obtain good teachers, but discountenanced the fact that there was a little too much regard for the amount of public funds in determining the length of time during which school should be held.

School Boards went shopping for teachers as for merchandise. The cheapest offer usually decided the choice of instructor. The North Killingly district, it seems, was more fortunate than other districts, if we can believe the Robinson-Dike Report. Most of the teachers in 1840 were young, and some had enjoyed "very good advantages for education." Their success was various, "but in most cases very respectable."

The average salary for male teachers was $15.48, for female teachers $8.33 per month,[4] exclusive of board, so that in rural districts, for instance that of North Killingly, the rate even fell much below this. It took a good deal of idealism, ambition or economic necessity to sit through 20 weeks of teaching two dozen or more children of varying ages, all huddled together in one classroom with stuffy air and uncomfortable seats, at $5 to $6 per month.

The teacher boarded "around" (board, however, could be had anywhere for $1.00 a week), and amusing stories were circulated about stingy farmers who would look forward to the last day of their turn to feed the teacher. One of them, it is said, reminded the teacher after the course of soup that she was to receive board only up to that point, but that he had no objection to having her stay for dessert. It so happened that the number of pupils in the school did not divide evenly into the number of days school was held.

The masterly essay by the Rev. Noah Porter "On the Necessity and Means of Improving the Common Schools of Connecticut," which deservedly won the prize of $100.00 in 1847, helped tremendously to alleviate conditions. With subtle rhetoric he whipped up the pride of his fellow citizens by telling them that at one time Connecticut "on account of her system of public education, was the brightest spot in all Christendom." But at the time of his writing, Connecticut had landed in "Sleepy Hollow." Europe was awakening to her duties and Massachusetts, New York, Georgia and Rhode Island made great efforts in behalf of their schools. With noble gesture he pointed to the church collections for missions in Ceylon, Burma and China to teach the children there, while right at home children went without that education, leaving them "hopeless subjects of religious truth."

These voices of the prophets, however, cast a gloomier picture than was actually the case. According to the census of 1840, Connecticut compared very favorably with the other 29 States of the Union. There were universities or colleges with 832 students; 127 Academies and Grammar Schools with 4865 scholars; 1619 Primary Schools with 65,739 scholars; 10,612 scholars at public charge; and only 526 white persons over the age of 20 years who could neither read nor write.[5]

FIRST DAY OF SCHOOL

It was one of those days on which the sun was destined to keep up his torch triumphantly during his appointed

time, wafting the early mist and vapor through the under-
brush. Upon the operatic performance of the birds had
followed the chorus of insects which could be heard even
deep in the woods. The more taciturn appeared the evergreen among the gnarly oaks. On such a summer's day
nature swells with hope and pursues its course with confidence. It could not be otherwise with the two human beings on the path below the leafy roof.

A bit more pensive than usual walked little William
Torrey Harris beside a pretty young woman just emerging
from her teens. September last, they had celebrated in
Puritan simplicity his fourth birthday, there on the farm
which now lay basking in the morning rays of the sun that
had cleared the tree-tops.

Was the girl beside him—it was his aunt Catherine, the
school mistress[6] — aware that she was ushering in the education of a great educator? As so often in the lives of great men,
there stood at the gateway to their spiritual awakening a
woman who guided and, secretly, and often unwittingly,
inspired. Read Emerson's *Social Aims* and find the answer
to "who teaches manners of majesty, of frankness, of grace,
of humility."

At the end of the mile, they arrived at the little school
house, one like many others in New England. It would
easily be mistaken for a garage today, remodeled for ten-
ancy.[7] Just a box made of weatherboards once painted red,
gable roof with a protruding chimney, a door and a few
windows, all essentials of a house,[8] The entire temple of
learning itself probably covered less than 500 square feet of
ground, set against a background of dense forest.

Some scholars were waiting, sitting on the steps or the
rocks. It was the first day of summer school. Hence it
augured well for a 100% attendance which in those days of
insufficient school-funds, lack of transportation and a certain
indifference habitual with some of the parents, was never

attained later in the summer. Teacher and pupils filed in through the aisle at whose other end was piled the wood for the winter. The older scholars immediately went to benches placed along three walls of the room under windows so high above the floor as to afford the pupils, when seated, no view of the outside world. They knew them well, for they had occupied them during the winter session. The newcomers, introduced by their parents, gathered in the center. How many there were of William's age we do not know, but we do know that 2% of all admissions were less than four years of age. These little ones were assigned the low benches in front of the desks of the older pupils sitting on the farther side of the room.

The teacher's desk stood on a platform at the fourth wall, while the center of the room, some eight feet square, was empty. There the scholars would stand when it was their turn to be quizzed.

On the first day, "registration" took up part of the time, the division into "classes" or grades and the important matter of text books the rest. Old pupils were kept busy by putting them to the first lesson in the book, no matter how often they had covered the same text. It was no easy matter to classify the handful of pupils who ranged from four to sixteen years of age and over.[9] "Grades" existed only in name, and classification was resolved into ascertaining how many could be grouped together in reading the identical texts, recite and be quizzed on the same, provided there were identical texts. One of the two pupils of a certain grade might have brought the book his father used thirty years before, the other might have big brother's which he had read a few years before.

There was the blackboard in the corner which held little William's interest. There was the inevitable sharpening of the older pupils' quills. The atmosphere was one of propriety and polite deference for the teacher. Fortunately,

William did not hear threats of bleeding, hanging, and "shivering the top timbers" which were among the favored designs of male pedagogues.

Intently he listened during the period of recreation to the counting-out of the older boys and learned the "ee-ny, mee-ny, mo-ny, mi, es-ky, lay-ny, bo-ny, stri, hul-dy, gul-dy, boo" — reminiscent of a savage custom for determining the victims among the captives, but now part of the game they called "gool tag," properly, "goal tag."

The first day of school, replete in the mind with pleasant incidents and palpitations of the heart over trifles, drew to a close for little William. It was the opening of a chapter of his life never to be closed—the great experience of learning. Indeed, sixty years later he acknowledged that this little red school house had had a unique influence on him, "unlike that of all other educative agencies which came later."

Through the woods fell thinly the long rays of the evening sun. The homeward journey was shortened by the view of the farm, a peaceful ensemble of seven buildings.

The main building was a frame house with a gable roof, a story and a half high. You entered by a door in the center of the broad front. There were four rooms, two with windows to the front, two looking out in the back, and there was an "el" kitchen. The up stairs was divided into two rooms.[10]

The lowing of the cows signalized the end of another day's work. Soon the family would gather around the big table and discuss the day's harvest of news and experiences. Without the daily paper, this "poor man's college," as Emerson called it, family life was much more abundant and congenial than with it, for no member could enshroud himself in silence while monopolizing the scant candle light. News came by word of mouth and reached them quickly over the fence, though the next neighbor was a mile away.[11]

The Torrey-Harris Home

Neither the Torreys, little William's grandparents, nor his parents were original settlers in these parts. They were newcomers to North Killingly which was the name of a collection of farms in the North-east corner of Connecticut until they were voted incorporated into Putnam June 8th, 1855. To be sure, their New England lineage went back 200 years; they were, as we have seen, of the blood and moral fibre of the earliest settlers in Massachusetts and Rhode Island, which States were then more strongly connected with Connecticut than by mere geographic proximity. Movements in search of land, intermarriages, trade and the facing of common dangers had made these people forget their differences long ago. Especially the War of Independence had brought home to them their *raison d'être* in this part of the world — the love of liberty.

The *pater familias*, Capt. William Torrey, was now approaching his 78th year, but his wife was only 59. The Captain had married her after his first wife, Hannah Plank, had died on August 5th, 1809. There was but one offspring from his first marriage, a daughter by her mother's name. From his second marriage, to Zilpah Davison, there were two daughters, Zilpah and Catherine, five years apart. Zilpah, at the age of 20, had married William Harris. The little bushy head of auburn hair whom we accompanied to school, was their first child, born September 10th, 1835. Catherine was his first teacher.

Captain Torrey, besides owning a farm of several hundred acres, was also a goldsmith and a banker, or, rather, money lender who carried on these occupations in a desultory manner, as would be the case in a scattered community. But he was an honored and esteemed citizen and had a wide yet limited clientele. He spent his time principally in overseeing a colony of several laborers whom he employed. He was remembered by a granddaughter, Miss Katherine Fenner Peckham, as always wearing a swallow-tailed coat and a tall beaver hat, according to the custom for gentlemen of those times, as he went about superintending his workmen. His father, the Rev. Joseph Torrey, occupied the South Kingston, R. I., pulpit for sixty years, truly a notable record. His mother was the daughter of the Rev. John Fiske, first pastor of the church in Hull, Massachusetts.

His son-in-law, William's father, was born at Scituate, R. I. He is said to have been a manufacturer of woolen cloth in Providence, until he removed to the farm of his wife's parents. He was dark, smooth-shaven, of average size. A venture with a drygoods store in East Killingly, about 1841, was unsuccessful. A chronic impatience and restlessness drove him West. The business which he established there, together with a relative, again proved a failure. Eventually, the young son-in-law, a sympathizer of the Whigs who later joined the Republicans, became a well-to-do farmer and a deacon of the Congregational Church who, according to the *Biographical Record of Tolland and Windham Counties,* "commanded the esteem and respect of his neighbors and friends."

Zilpah Torrey Harris was a fond mother. Intelligent, keen eyes were set in strong and regular features. William was much attached to her, and in later years never failed to visit her at least once a year.[12]

In these pre-suffrage days the patriotism of the American mothers manifested itself in teaching with tender care the sons whom they expected to have an equal chance in the democracy. In contrast to the sterner he-man's universe they taught the gentle virtues of true piety, love, respect, and courtesy. Their contribution to American life is inestimable. It made possible the idealism, such as William developed, which is so deplorably lacking in a prematurely disillusioned generation. "Men are what their mothers made them," says Emerson in *Fate*, and John Cowper Powys calls women the aristocracy of America. This was even more true in the last century than in Colonial days.

Mother Harris was a great reader. Much of the intellectual acumen of William was doubtless derived from her and the long line of Torreys, many of whom were notable divines in their day. Arthur Mathewson, a Woodstock neighbor, described her as a rare woman with high ideals of life and duty. She did not need to write of love to her son. He must have known she loved him dearly; her sacrifices proved it more plainly than words.

Great minds on this continent have all been suckled close to the famliy, and in comparative isolation. But it was only during the first four years of William's life that the "eloquence of solitude" was to teach him; yet she taught him enough so that he retained his calmness of vision and insight throughout his busy life. Finding playmates at school, was, indeed, a great event, as he acknowledged later.

However, William was not to remain the only child of William and Zilpah for long. A brother, John Wilkinson, arrived two years after William. The Harris branch of the family was in the habit of having nine children per household, witness Thomas and Elnathan, and Richard and his first wife. Eleazer and Alice Whipple with their seven offspring, or John and Sarah Pray and William and Deborah Torrey with their eight, fell short of the ten of the Rev. Henry Whitfield, the eleven of Capt. John and Sarah Whipple or of Joseph and Ann Greene. Nathaniel and Johanna Mowry had twelve children for certain, but about the Rev. Zachariah Symmes and his wife the chronicler said they had "about twelve." As to Benjamin Child with his full dozen, he made the laconic remark: "An example his descendants have satisfactorily emulated." However, the Rev. James Fitch had fourteen children by two wives, William Davis fifteen by three wives, and Joseph Wilkinson fifteen by his

21

wife Martha. By 1853, William and Zilpah Harris were to have their share of nine offspring.

We know little about the home-life in the Torrey-Harris household. There is no indication, however, that it was not a happy one. In this region the women, even those fairly well-to-do, would operate a loom at home, but they bought the yarn that was manufactured in the mills and sold cloth to the nearby factory at Pomfret. The flax raised on the farm was also spun at home and the young mothers would make their boys' clothes.

EARLY TEACHERS AND LESSONS

For William, Noah Webster's primer and first reader were to become the sole text book during the two or three summers that he went to the little red school house. Within twelve weeks he could read.

William gradually became fond of grammar and "parsing." The English grammar by Roswell Smith, of Hartford, he long remembered without regrets. Among other things, he read the Rev. John Pierpont's *National Preceptor* on which he whetted his intellect, the book being a bit above his head. Having surgeons and clergymen among his ancestors, as well as physicians and metaphysicians, he thought later, accounted for his fondness of abstractions.

Two or three times during the winter an evening spelling-school was held, to which not only the day pupils but also the elder brothers and sisters and parents from the neighboring district were invited. Two leaders were appointed by the schoolmaster, who chose for their respective sides, alternately, one after another, until all the persons present were ranked on one side or the other. Then began the match. The person who missed a word left the line and took a seat on the front bench. The side which spelled the other

22

down had gained the victory. After the spelling-match came recitations of poetry, oratory and dialogue. Byron's "There was a sound of revelry by night"; Campbell's "On Linden when the sun was low"; Halleck's "Marco Bozzaris," the first lines of which are

At midnight, in his guarded tent,
The Turk was dreaming of the hour;

or sometimes "Webster's Reply to Hayne," and Patrick Henry's "Give me liberty or give me death," were favorites with the more intelligent class. There was, however, a tendency to buffoonery in the dialogues.[13]

These were adventures in social living, of greater value and reality than the wealth contained in the geography book by Roswell Smith to which William was put at six, in the third summer of his school career. He long remembered it as "a stout volume with logical definitions as strict as Noah Webster's." One evening, the whole class was kept because none of the pupils remembered the definition of a city. William, usually good at memorizing, could scarcely mumble amid tears and sobbings: "A city is a large town containing many inhabitants incorporated with peculiar privileges and governed by a mayor and aldermen."

The educational theory in back of all this learning by rote was that what could not be understood could yet be committed to memory. Under this category fell the technical terms and definitions of accent, cadence, emphasis and the rest, as given in Noah Webster's *Elementary Spelling Book*. "Not only did these sentences fail to convey their meaning . . . , but they received no illuminating application from the teacher." And the publishers of this best seller sold nearly a million and a quarter copies annually, printing the entire book at each revolution of the press.

The book was rightly called "a sort of juvenile introduction to Webster's *Unabridged*." It was much more than a spelling book. The sentences illustrating the words conveyed general information and were designed to further knowledge in science, economics and civics, aside from teaching a moral.

Mr. Paine, among his teachers in that early period, William held in highest esteem.

One day he brought to school a copy of Walter Scott's *Lay of the Last Minstrel*, and after reading some lines of it, lent it to the three or four oldest and most advanced pupils, requesting them to select passages that pleased them most, giving each the opportunity to carry the book home with him for one night. No one of us had ever before seen a volume or even a single poem of Walter Scott, but we never forgot the description of the night visit to the tomb of Michael Scott in Melrose Abbey, and probably we all purchased Walter Scott's poems when we came to own books later in life.

System, in the small school house, was notoriously absent. Education was, beyond the rudiments, haphazard. One day, William brought along a Latin book he had found among his grandfather's books and which he had handled for years. When on visits to his father's people in Rhode Island, he had attracted the attention and commendation of his aunts and uncles by producing from memory Latin phrases snatched here and there from its contents, such as *adeamus scholam, emi librum duobus assibus.* Somewhat timidly he put the volume on the edge of the desk so it had to catch the eye of the teacher. It worked; Mr. Paine who knew both Latin and Spanish, picked it up and said: "That is right. You may begin on this page and learn by heart the declension of *penna.*"

Latin grammer was not exactly to the taste of William and he wrestled long and hard with inflections. But somehow he contrived to read Andrew's *Latin Reader* which Mr. Paine lent him. The first selection, Aesop's fable "The

Kid and the Wolf" he once construed word for word to the clergyman of the North Parish, who happened to be also a school visitor.

The Robinson-Dike Report mentioned above called attention to the fact that the evil of neglecting primary studies and attending to the more advanced was, to some extent, found in the schools under their supervision. This was doubtless true in the little school to which Harris went. Mr. Paine apparently was a young college student who taught in order to be able to continue with his studies. He naturally favored the higher studies and tried to raise the children to his own level. As a consequence he was extremely stimulating and created a deep and lasting impression on all the pupils.

William was well-behaved at school so that he never or only rarely received punishment of any nature. Only a very strict school-ma'am — not ill-esteemed among the farmers who had the greatest respect for anyone who was able to "beat knowledge into the heads of her pupils" — had it "in for" William, as we would say, and once struck him with a ferule on the hand. It happened as follows. Studious William apparently roused the sudden disgust of his neighbor on the bench, an older boy who forthwith thrust a pin into his side. William winced, but the big fellow snickered. William bore the tale and was punished together with the culprit, unjustly, he thought, because the strict mistress did not usually punish such an offense.

Good scholar that he was, our little hero never committed the sin of truancy, quite common in those days, even though he felt a sort of represssion in the schoolroom, particularly after experiencing "a sense of freedom in the presence of untamed nature" on the pleasant stroll to school when the many different kinds of trees, bushes, herbs, birds, insects and small animals that inhabit the woods of Northeastern Connecticut were encountered and watched with interest.

CHAPTER THREE

EARLY ENVIRONMENT

THE RELIGIOUS BACKGROUND

THERE was a time, then already a century and a half past, when the good people of Connecticut enjoyed the reputation of out-poping the Pope, out-kinging the King, and out-bishoping the Bishop, all in spite of the fact that they called vicars, rectors, deans and priests wolves and anti-Christian tyrants, sprung from the devil. One early traveler sarcastically remarked that they would have exorcised the whippoorwill (they called it at that time the Pope), had it not been for its "whip-her-I-will" which was more in keeping with the spirit of the Blue Laws.

The church had become a place of worship, such as it should be. At first, of course, it was considered an infringement of the fundamental American right to free speech when the Colony put a curb to the unlicensed revivalist preachers who thought themselves unsuccessful unless people howled and fainted at the realization of what would be in store for them as sinners. "New lights" appeared and shone less boisterously. They even came to wear a halo for having been unjustly persecuted after Connecticut adopted the policy of toleration which should have prevailed from the first on the continent.

People had become generous and charitable in spirit. "Loathsome haeriticks" enjoyed comparative freedom. Bundling, perambulations with their quota of liquor, and the mortal fear of Quakers, were things of the past. It was said, the Connecticutensians "loved the house of prayer, loved to leave it too." The vulgarity which accompanied the French Revolution, had had its counterpart in the State also. The young folks, unaccustomed to discipline, revelled in and drank to the death of the old church regime, coupling with it that wrong sense of liberty which leaves only sorrow and disgust behind.

In 1818, the State Constitution of Connecticut had been adopted. To the consternation of the clergy it separated church and state, thus striking at the heart of Puritan tradition. The revivals that took place immediately like a reflex mechanism were of short duration, however, and fizzled out into nothing more than a clamorous drive for church-membership or a loyalty campaign. Even the "election sermon" before the Legislature ceased to be preached in 1830. A modern era had been ushered in, together with a new piety which gave the politician his own, but prayed for his soul and divine guidance. The perfect state no longer became associated with visible institutions, but with conditions of spirituality.

Connecticut had favored the Congregationalism of Pilgrim memories, since before 1650. In a more dilute form it was able to stem the onrush of Episcopalians, Baptists, Methodists, and Universalists. Catholics[1] there were extremely few and the Unitarians had been successfully rescinded, thanks to the energetic Lyman Beecher.

But the old piety would not die so easily. In William's boyhood days the Sunday laws were still strictly enforced, rather to satisfy that inborn religious urge than to appease ecclesiastic authority. The dire lack, in this State, of amusement provided by shows, theatres, dramas or the circus, reinforced by the relative isolation on the farm, of necessity fostered a sense of harmless pleasures and preoccupation with nature.

The school had become a supplement to the church in

that it initiated the community into the common objective of improving and furthering spiritual values, aside from cementing people together in friendly social union. No longer was there a preacher vested with authority from "the great God" to hear whom one rode miles on horseback, as a hundred years earlier when messengers would inform the settlers of a sermon to be preached by a Whitfield. No longer did people come out of church hypocritically humble thinking themselves elect, nor distressed because of the certainty of impending judgment which would write every sin in burning letters upon raw flesh. People had become sober and settled, even in religion, but by no means indifferent. Still, every evening at nine o'clock the church bells were tolling. Fundamentalism was rampant, but it had become somewhat volatile. Religious upheavals sublimated into intellectual stimuli which contributed, no doubt, to moral enthusiasm, but not to ecstasy or frenzy.

Of seven clergymen in Killingly four were Congregationalist, and three Baptist.² The Torrey-Harris household was staunch Congregationalist, and even though they were comparative newcomers, they felt that the community still honored the memory of the Rev. John Fiske, the great grandfather of William's mother. Grandmother Torrey herself was a bit fundamentalist in her beliefs, quite in keeping with Torrey tradition.

William was little affected by religon, for it was an unobtrusive piety that was the custom at home. The family Bible was holy book and family register at the same time. In 1847 it recorded the death of grandfather Torrey. For the rest, "giving to the heathen" and visiting church regularly on Sundays were the principal outward religious duties. We do not know whether grandmother Torrey and mother Harris belonged to the Missionary Society of Connecticut which, founded in 1798, was the oldest in America, or to the Female Tract Society of Killingly and Thompson;

28

but we do know that both women gave freely to all good purposes, even though they were in moderate circumstances. They went to meetings regularly and contributed their share of bed-quilts which were annually disposed of by lottery under the sponsorship of the local sewing society. Sending the boys to academy, financing their first venture into life, putting aside for rainy days, these objectives they pursued, even at a sacrifice, thus spending a selfless life in the interest of the things their little circle held noble, quietly contributing to the spiritual and material progress of the real America.

ECONOMIC AND SOCIAL CONDITIONS

The Torrey-Harris household had been reared in the spirit of the founders of Providence to whom, as we have seen, they could trace their lineage. In moving to Connecticut, they were transplanted into an industrial neighborhood. From Old Killingly Hill on which their farm was located, now Putnam Heights, one could barely see the "vales lined with factory villages."

Windham County had been a welcome hinterland in the troubled years following the Stamp Act of 1765. For it was along the seaboard that the fury of the Americans and the reprisals by the Tories had vented themselves and eventually made the whole vicinity of Boston the center of the imbroglio culminating in the War of Revolution. Not only from Boston, but especially from Providence had come families who wanted to bring up their children in quiet surroundings, without the continual fear of the fulminations of the god of war.

At the time of which we are writing, the stories were still circulating of how the community helped in boycotting England, of how the simple life was lived even simpler and without imported tea. Weddings were attended in homespun, toasts were given with good domestic apple-cider. The excitement fully repaid the privation. The yoke of liberty was easily and gladly borne, Killingly had sent her full quota of militia men for the impending conflict, and had contributed liberally to the sinews of war. And when a local man, Israel Putnam, became the hero of Bunker Hill and of many a battle later, heaping new laurels on old, everyone in that community became the prouder and basked in the prospect of historic glory. But the price of history is always dear. When the war dragged on and was fought away from home, in New York and in New Jersey, the sacrifices became almost unbearable.

Peace after the Revolutionary War meant increased industry for the North-eastern towns of Connecticut. Cotton factories were established, stimulating another wave of immigration, this time not of farmers of the old stock, but of laborers drawn from the most varied types of Eastern city population. Incipient industrialization always spells prosperity to all concerned — the manufacturer who could earn dividends from his investments, the laborers who were assured a fairly steady income, and the farmer who found a ready sale for his produce.

Prosperity, of course, meant not much more than a decent homestead, sufficiency of food and some money to spend on things the farm could not supply. The tax on one dollar was 2½ cents. The salary of Samuel A. Foot, Governor of Connecticut, was $1100.00 in 1835, and that of the Lieutenant Governor only $300.00. The Windham County Bank held a capital stock of $100,000.00. Windham was one of the thriving counties of the state, and the Township of Killingly with its 120 square miles had a major share in the development.[3]

Hartford, in 1835, had started the first silk-factory, and all of Connecticut entertained the hope of competing with China in raising cocoons. It was a short-lived dream, but

30

the silk-mills continued to produce on the Oriental raw-material.[4]

Putnam, in the valley, which later was to swallow up North Killingly, was not a city, though it had all the ear-marks of one. William, in his youth, knew this factory center full of the nameless people who had forgotten or had stripped clean of what the New England stock was ever so proud: their tradition and lineage. For two years he worked in a cotton mill, 14 hours a day.

Killingly had barely three and a half thousand inhabitants. It was the birthplace of Manasseh Cutler, preacher, botanist, soldier and politician; of Amasa Learned, student of law and theology and representative in the national government; and of Joseph Howe, teacher, orator and idol of Boston churchgoers — "he in refined, pathetic sermons shone."

William and his parents had become attached to their farm. Heavily wooded hills alternated with fertile fields rich by an admixture of clay. In olden times the farmers in this region had concentrated on butter, cheese, hemp, Indian corn, and horses. Now Indian corn, wheat, oats, and rye were grown. Apple trees would do exceedingly well on rocky hillsides worth nothing otherwise, and the woods would yield an abundance of blackberries, blueberries, huckleberries, raspberries, gooseberries, and currants. One of the greatest blessings was the pumpkin, or pompion, which was put to a hundred uses — custards, bread, molasses, vinegar, beer, and pies as a substitute for what the Blue Laws termed "unchristian minced pies." The butternut and walnut had delicious meat and the maple sweet sap. Partridges and rabbits were caught in snares. Nature was liberal in these parts, and even when she withheld some blessings, as in 1839, when corn and rye failed, disastrous consequences were not bound to follow. The barns were well-stocked with horses, cows, sheep, hogs, chickens, turkeys, geese, and ducks.

In all, the first settlers had not made a mistake in acquiring the land for wampum and cloth, taking it into possession with the simple, yet impressive and appropriate ceremony of breaking a twig and cutting the sod as symbols of title to a portion of mother Earth. And the benefit was reaped by our industrious and thrifty family who once again was destined to produce an intellect of which America may well be proud.

BOYHOOD ON THE FARM

Life on the farm was not drab. Of his own accord, William read and re-read the pieces in his school texts till he had full command of them. There were things to see and do. He liked to plant vegetables, hoe corn and sow popcorn. If one could not ride on the stage-coach, at least one could watch it whizz by on the pike road, pulled by stately horses and carrying who knows whom? — perhaps the Governor or some lady fair. In 1843, they watched the great comet, in 1848 they went to Putnam to see the first iron horse, perchance to board the clumsily moving choke-a-te-choke from which all living beings kept a safe distance.[5]

Even today, boys from Putnam walk ten miles to picnic on the oak wood hills above the wolf's den made famous by Israel Putnam and listen with a throbbing heart to his daring exploits among the wily Indians and the wary French. Torch in hand, this stout soldier had entered the cave alone, shot and killed the she-wolf and thus started off on the road to history. Such were his deeds of valor that the Indians dared not kill him when they were fighting on the side of the French. Though they had tied him to the fatal post they would not take his life lest they insult Hobbomockow whose immortal son they perceived in him. They sold him into captivity, instead. Not far away was the peaceful homestead of this famous General, "Old Put," as everyone called him affectionately.

Every boy was acquainted with the stories of church feuds, inspired by the proximity of the house which Justice Cady had built. They shuddered over Tory terror. What's a Tory? one would ask, and receive the reply: "A Tory is a thing whose head is in England and its body in America and whose neck ought to be stretched."

With his smaller brothers William would occasionally visit the ancestral Harris homestead at Scituate, R. I. There was a large apple tree on the farm, a historic tree for the family, whose stump in later years was carefully preserved and round which they had periodic gatherings — William and his family, Edward and his, sister Mary Jane and hers. For it was on that tree that great-grandmother Mowry one fine day saw a large black bear shaking down the apples which were very choice and highly prized by the whole family. None of the men-folks being near to punish the beast, she seized a loaded gun, rushed out and gave the bear a shot which brought him down to the ground dead, so they said, of apple-plexy.

They thought fondly of their great-grandmother and many another tale was spun around her. For instance, on one occasion her daughter who lived twelve miles away, was dangerously ill in mid-winter and not expected to live. The snow was so deep that teams could not travel, but great-grandmother put on her snowshoes, walked the distance and brought the patient through all right.[6]

At Scituate also was the home of great-grandfather John Wilkinson who had the reputation of being the greatest teller of stories in Rhode Island. He had been a regimental surgeon in the Revolutionary War, a charter member of the Rhode Island College and had helped to establish the Rhode Island Medical Society. Besides that he had been a town treasurer and held other important public offices.

When William and his brothers romped about on the farm, Indian alarms, if any, were given only by them, not real Indians. As a matter of fact the redskin had disappeared entirely from Connecticut. It had cost the life of 20 Indians for every Englishman to pursue happiness on land he never had a title to, and it took the larger part of the remaining aborigines to make room for Christianity à la Hooker.

The land in the environs of the Torrey-Harris farm had, indeed, been a great theatre of the Indian tribe of Nipmuck who used to hunt there and raise the beans, corn and malt which, together with the acorns they had gathered in, saved the life of many a settler in the Bay region during the bleak winter of 1630-31. Several paths led through this region where deer, bear, and wolf were tracked down by swift feet before they could flee to the fastness of the forest beyond. It was dangerous then to pass through here, and only "forts" and missionaries trained by John Eliot, the beloved Indian apostle, offered sufficient protection, the one by prowess, the other by peaceful entreaty. In time, Indian fought Indian, regardless of whether they had been taught to pray or not. The Mohegans dealt savagely with Nipmucks, only to play into the hands of the white man who acquired the territory from the remaining Nipmuck or his drunken conqueror. Before that, Indians were wont to come in throngs to visit the homes of the Yankees to trade in hemp and beaver. So thoroughly did they enjoy their stay that not seldom fifty or more would encamp on the settler's lot.

Amid the quarries, slate rocks, and mill streams of the Killingly region, many another legend lived on. There were the oddities connected with the rigor of the Blue Laws, the story of the "frog panic," the battle with the caterpillars, the burning of the witches, echoes of thundering sermons, and tales of dainty young ladies who hoed their patch of onions before dressing beefsteak for breakfast.

CHAPTER FOUR

THE BEGINNINGS OF THE PERIPATETIC

FROM FARM TO CITY

W ILLIAM'S ante-mundane soul-wandering, as he himself termed his youthful experiences, was still in its early stages. Those twelve, and later 25 weeks on an average per year in the little red school house outwardly meant mastering the three R's. Esoterically, they signified an initiation into civilization, a sharing of all that man was, is, or harbors as a seed in his innermost self. This confession is of importance in its social consequences:

The school excelled in giving an opportunity through plays and games for each pupil to learn the motives and principles of action of his fellow pupils. He there learned his most important lessons in human nature. He measured the intellectual forces of his comrades when they struggled with their lessons in the schoolroom. He learned their goodness and unselfishness, their directive power and their trustworthiness, through their behavior in the sports of the schoolyard.

The little red school house was eventually exchanged for a larger, white one, at the central village of Killingly. There, education was carried on much in the way already described. When, on May 29th, 1936, educators and residents of Putnam, Ct., and surrounding communities gathered with relatives and friends of William Torrey Harris at the invitation of the Connecticut State Board of Education to honor

35

the memory of their distinguished citizen, this same white school house held a central place in the ceremonies. Scenes were enacted which, with infinite variations, had been daily enacted there nearly a century before.[1]

Everybody in the Torrey-Harris household was aware that William had the makings of a scholar. His mother and grandmother were delighted and sought to give him every opportunity of education. When the Harris branch of the family removed to Providence, R. I., probably in the latter part of 1844, such an opportunity seemed to present itself, for William could now enter an urban school. As was the custom, he wore tightly fitting long trousers and a jacket the tails of which were flipping as he walked. The collar of the coat was rebent, to expose the neck.

At least three or four terms were spent in the city schools. There prevailed quite a different regime from the Killingly schools. The teacher refused to take that personal attitude that William had been accustomed to heretofore. Teaching was done in a business-like fashion. Instruction was by the clock, something William could not immediately get used to. Punctuality was considered a serious matter. In particular, he disliked the "martinet" system intensely and in general had nothing good to say about the city school:[2]

Much more pains was expended in causing pupils to mark time with precision than in marching forward toward any definite object. I came to detest city schools very bitterly, because I loved individual freedom and hated mere forms as such. I desired to come at the substance of the study, and grudged the time which seemed to me wasted over the mechanism of it. For a long time we were required to commit to memory the questions of our catechetical geography, and repeat them word for word in their exact order, as the "analysis" of the lesson. Little or no time was spent on the

36

answers to the questions, and there was no discussion whatever of the real subject. Moreover, there was frequent corporal punishment, and sometimes it reached a degree of cruelty that I shudder to remember. The high school of that city imposed on the grammar schools a severe standard of preparation in those studies that were required for admission. This kept back the pupils of the classes in the lower schools in order to make them more "thorough," as it is called. The direct result of this was the "marking time" system, in which mechanical memory was almost the only faculty acquired or much cultivated.

THE RUN OF ACADEMIES

With the year 1848 William resumed his peripatetic education, this time making the round of five different New England academies within five years. His younger brothers later also went to several private academies. It was the thing to do, especially when the boy was to enter Yale College, as all his brothers did, John Wilkinson, who died very young, excepted.[3]

The second academy William attended (we know the name of neither this nor the first one),[4] stood out in his mind because it employed Milton's *Paradise Lost* as a text in the study of syntax. "Entranced with its sublime poetic form," he appreciated also its religious message.

At these academies, William initiated the practice of supplementing his education above the desk by another below the desk. Having recited his lesson, which he always knew well, he would slyly reach for the book on natural philosophy which he had borrowed from a friend and read in it while pretending to be studying above the table.

Woodstock Academy, the third academy to be visited by him, was conveniently located, as one could take a stage which regularly ran the five miles between Putnam and

Woodstock. The family would occasionally come over when the school put on its theatricals. William's brother Edward took part in plays, while William presumably never did.

We find him registered in 1850 as a scholar in the classical *and* English departments, paying $4.50 in tuition per term of eleven weeks and sharing his room with a certain Napoleon B. Jennings from Mannahawkin, N. J. Board, with room rent and laundry was $1.75 per week. Here he met a dear friend of his and his family, Arthur Mathewson, whom he was to have again as chum at Yale. This young lad served as surgeon in the U. S. Navy during the Civil War. At one time, this Mathewson confessed[5] that, though only a boy, he was at once attracted by William's

> genial and kindly manners, his purity of character, his high ideals, his eagerness in search for knowledge and truth in all things. He was already at the age of fifteen a philosopher — a lover of knowledge — and not content with surface knowledge, but anxious to get at the foundation of things, and to go as far as the human mind is capable of pentrating.

Already the 1850 catalogue calls Woodstock Academy a venerable institution which has survived more than fifty years. It was a school for ladies and gentlemen. The teacher boarded with the pupils and endeavored "as far as possible, to exercise over them a salutary moral influence." The equipment too seemed commendable: "A good chemical and philosophical apparatus" and a large hall where the young ladies could exercise "when the weather or walking excludes them from the open air."

On May 7th, 1851, there was the "Students' Exhibition." With its five plays, the musical numbers, the many orations and the prayer, it must have lasted from 7 p. m. till the wee hours of the morning. William read an essay on a weighty subject, "The Faculties of the Mind," betraying

thus his philosophic bent.[6]   He was also extremely interested in a students' play called "Spiritual Manifestation,"
a burlesque, which he thought was composed by E. R.
Osgood. As late as 1897 he asserted he could rewrite it from
memory, having done so once in 1863 when he had his
St. Louis pupils recite it with huge success at a public exhibition.

From William's correspondence with Charles C. Baldwin we gather that he had in mind attending Normal
School. But, in the fall of 1851, William entered, along
with 81 other students, Worcester Academy which celebrated its centenary in 1934. This renowned institution[7]
became known as an Academy in 1847. Previous to that
time the name was Worcester County Manual Labor High
School. Since William intended entering Yale college, his
course was the classical one. Not only did they endeavor
at Worcester to instruct faithfully "in all matters appertain-
ing to the grammars — the structure and idioms of the
ancient languages — but every effort" was made, as one of
the early catalogues says, to awaken the enthusiasm of the
students "by introducing them gradually to the history,
geography, literature, usages and mythology of the ancients."

We have part of the detailed financial statements of
William, according to which it cost him 80c to travel from
home to Worcester. An extra 5c covered handling his trunk.
Tuition was $7.00 per term. Being inclined toward vegeta-
rianism, he was fond of fruits, particularly raisins (he put
them down as raisons), peaches, figs, pears, plums, dates,
filberts, oranges, and cocoanuts. Candy he purchased several
times. Aside from these articles of food he acquired a fluid
lamp for 33c, fluid with a wick, a mirror, soap, a comb,
pins, blacking, matches, a penknife for 17c, a portemonnaie
for 6c, wallets, an inkstand, pens, paper, collars, handkerchiefs, gloves (25c), suspenders (12½c), neckcloths (8c and

15c) and a pair of boots for $2.25. Spectacles he also needed surprisingly often, but they were only 30c.

It may be surprising to learn that already at this tender age William wore glasses. No one ever saw the teacher, the lecturer and the Commissioner Harris without his spectacles, and not even his nearest relatives knew that he did not wear them to correct stigmatism or relieve a myopic or hyperopic condition. but — to conceal an artificial eye. It all happened on July 4th, 1851, when he tried to pound the percussion cap of a fire-cracker with an axe on the door-step of their farmhouse.

At Worcester he joined the Legomathenian Society, a debating club, founded June 5th, 1834, with dues to the amount of 25c. They took their debating very seriously and once expelled an honorary member for being "an un-principled scoundrel." The Society was convened by the ringing of a bell, fifteen minutes before the appointed time. It tolled five minutes. After that, the doors were closed except to members.[8]

In this Society, William came in close contact with Walter Scott Alexander, of Killingly, the Recording Secretary, and Robert Roberts Bishop, of Medfield, Mass., Vice-president. Lasting friendships developed with these students. Robert Bishop in particular came to have a decisive influence on William in that he possessed a copy of Andrews and Boyle's phonographic *Class Book*. William who borrowed it, was immediately intensely interested and had his friend promise that as soon as he got to Boston at the close of the term he would buy and send him a copy. Robert Bishop, later Judge of the Superior Court of Massachusetts, kept his word and William was able to begin his study of shorthand from the *Class Book* and the *Reader* in the summer of 1852. When, a little later Andrew J. Graham brought out his *Universal Phonographer* he subscribed to it. Here were the beginnings of a life-long interest.

His budget, the spelling in which did not foreshadow the mind of an editor of Webster's, disclosed, furthermore, that he bought a lot of mirrors, convex and concave lenses, lozenges, pincers, tweezers, a hammer, a kaleidoscope, compasses, a tin tube, etc., all things that he would need for astronomical and geodetic observations.

Most of these things he acquired from the spectacle maker. The lenses of 1 and 30 inches focal length he fixed in the tin tube, and soon succeeded in making several achromatic telescopes. Even later in life he was very fond of his telescopes. The one he constructed in these academy days he exchanged for a real one which he would lug about with him wherever he went. On visits to Putnam he would train it on Woodstock and the scenes of his youthful exploits. The family remembers how, on one such visit, he was a long time puzzled where to locate the wolf's den, until he struck the happy idea of using a large newspaper which he hung in the fashion of the pirate's skull in Poe's *Goldbug* up on a tree near the cave. This was, of course, an easy object to spot with the telescopic lens and thus the den was located.

Among the books he bought was Kühner's *Elementary Greek Grammar*. The preceding summer he had spent reading one of the six volumes of Edward Daniel Clarke's *Travels through Greece, Egypt, and the Holy Land*. Even more than by vivid description he was intrigued by the quotations from the Greek. Having no Greek grammar he consulted the derivations given in Webster and made out, unaided, but correctly, the sound value of each letter of the Greek alphabet.

A revolt against the too intellectualistic studies may be seen foreshadowed not only in the interest William displayed at this age in optics, but also in his first attempts at engineering, for in his spare time he would make force-pumps and fire-engines on a small scale.

Some time was spent by William in one or more academies

at Providence, R. I. The last one was University School. When there, he lived with the Peckhams, and after more than eighty years, his cousin Katherine,⁹ five years younger than he, recalled his gentle nature. She noted that he was very studious and not boisterous like the other lads of his age. He was "tall, blue-eyed and fine-looking."

It was grandmother Torrey, as we intimated above, who contributed liberally to his education. Her own daughter she had sent to Mt. Holyoke Seminary. Believing in modern education, she was also a Christian. Her grandson had not yet come in contact with the Hegelian interpretation of Christianity and hence was not restrained in voicing the results of his youthful meditations on religion. But that was heresy to grandmother and she forbade him ever afterwards to mention such views again.¹⁰ While at home during the summers he would, of course, visit church regularly with his parents. Besides, he was a member of the choir. They went to the Congregational Church, still standing on Putnam Heights.¹¹

English composition was, apparently, one of the strong points in the Providence preparatory schools.¹² One such theme, written in class, is especially noteworthy — not for the theme itself, which is Hercules, and a description of his twelve arduous enterprises, nor for the fact that in the midst of the lengthy final passage in which our William tells excitedly the story of the garment dipped in the Centaur's blood, he forgot the name of the lady whom Hercules finally married. No. In pencil his neighbor had scribbled on the last page: "Do you know someone in West Killingly by the name of — —?" And William had added: "I am not personally acquainted with him, but I have heard of him. He is a *damned scoundrel*. I used to go to boading [sic] school with him. I don't know anything to the contrary."

Studying Under "Uncle Sam"

An important period, intellectually, began April 20th, 1853, when, after a winter spent at home helping his father, William entered Phillips Academy, at Andover, Mass. Completely swept off his feet by the rigorous discipline prevailing there, his capricious will was finally overcome by transmuting the pulpy substance of impulse and inclination, and the haphazard nature of his intellectual exploits was changed in earnest study to become "directive intelligence that can reinforce the moments by the hours, and accomplish something in the world."[13]

His training at the other academies and his self-instruction enabled him to enter the last term of the "middle class" in the Classical Department. This class of 1854 was noteworthy in that it started a Students' Educational Fund, thus laying the basis for the much-needed endowment provisions of the Academy which was and is a preparatory school for college.[14]

William roomed in Academic Hall with John Albee, the poet, and Harrison Everett Chadwick of Bradford, Mass. His friendship with John was to last 60 years. The atmosphere was almost monkish. All that was provided was a bedstead (*with* an underbed) and a table. The members of the English Department fared better, for they had even such a luxury as a looking-glass. All other necessities the boys had to provide themselves. Expenses were very low, one dollar per term for the room, $1.50 per week for board in Commons, and $7.00 for tuition during one term. The thorough instruction placed every pupil under a debt of gratitude which Harris was not loath to acknowledge many years later.[15]

On Sabbath Day there were "biblical exercises" in the morning at the Academy, and regular church later in the chapel of the Seminary. There were but six instructors, including much-feared, much-respected dictatorial "Uncle

Sam," Principal Samuel H. Taylor,[16] greatly looked up to by William at the time, but perilously indifferent to reforms in education. It seems William also made the acquaintance of Peter Smith Byers who acted as an Assistant to Dr. Taylor[17] but resigned the very year in which William arrived. He was a most stimulating instructor who was idolized by all his students.

On August 2nd, 1853, William witnessed the Commencement exercises with Latin salutatory, prayer, class ode and benediction, 14 orations in English, Greek and Latin, two dialogues, one discussion, one dissertation, and a colloquy, relieved by four musical offerings.

Among those giving an oration was Addison Van Name, whom, together with others, William was to meet again at Yale. Of his own class particular mention ought to be made of S. W. Abbott, A. T. Jones, G. B. Knapp, E. G. Porter, B. S. Snow and William A. Mowry on whom Harris made a deep impression, so much so that he confessed after his death that although Harris was his junior by five years he had considered him as his elder brother.

William had come to Phillips upon the recommendation of a friend of his, Robert R. Bishop, Hon. R. R. Bishop in his later life, who had transferred to that school and had given him a glowing account of it. Indeed, William was never able to rid himself of a certain romantic feeling about the place.[18] In a letter to his brother John[19] he called Andover "one of the pleasantest places in New England, all things considered" and commented on the fact that a good many great men lived in the village or visited it frequently. Mrs. Harriet Beecher Stowe lived there when at home. Her son was William's fellow student at the Academy, and thus William became acquainted with Mr. Stowe.

What impressed William most was that everybody was imbued with the desire to "discipline the mind." Mornings he would get up, sometimes at three o'clock, and as he gazed out upon Andover Hill he would see lights burning in the students' rooms. Practically everyone studied seven, eight, and even ten hours a day. So he too worked "patiently and ploddingly" emulating Benjamin Franklin. "Dry, uninteresting books, written with old fashioned s's," from the library of his great grandfather Wilkinson, he read for the sake of mental discipline; and as a continuation of this same drive he later read Kant's *Critique of Pure Reason* without understanding what it was all about.

To the tune of "Doo-dah" the boys went occasionally over the hill and practiced elocution in the open air. Debating, elocution, anything reeking of the scholastic, attracted William. He attended the United Anniversaries of the Porter Rhetorical Society and the Society of Inquiry of the Theological Seminary of Andover, on September 6th, 1853.

With the reading of Humboldt's *Cosmos* which expanded his vision beyond the narrow class-room, he intuitively felt, however, the tardiness of the progressive spirit in education. Nature and her conquest by man seemed more and more to outweigh in significance the contributions of the ancients which were studied with a vengeance at Andover.[20] In the summer of 1853 he wrote an essay on "Steam: Its Influence upon Society," which rings out in a truly Phillippian note.

In all, William stayed only 28 weeks at Andover, that is, during the summer and fall terms. Once he was called away for two weeks, probably to help on the farm, as a treasurer's refund indicates. He left to teach school at Thompson, Ct., in the winter of 1853-54. According to all standards of the times, he was well qualified to teach. His records of attendance, which cannot be called neat, show the pupils on a folded sheet, boys on one page, "females" on another. Presence is indicated by a perpendicular stroke, absence by a point or a short stroke. He did not employ the horizontal bar through four vertical bars, so helpful in keeping count, and the whole record is a sore trial for healthy eyes: 87 strokes on a space 3½ inches wide. Here becomes manifest for the first time that Harris had, indeed, method, but method without too much clarity in presentation. There were twenty-odd boys and about the same number of girls, all ranging in age from 9 to 17, most of them from 10 to 13. He taught them for 18 weeks, or 89 days, to be exact.

After this, he did not return to Andover, but prepared himself for Yale, thus following in the footsteps of the average Phillips graduate. Whether he went, as was usual, with the recommendation of "Uncle Sam," we do not know. But, at the age of 16, he had mastered geometry and trigonometry. At 17, he had acquired and read Locke's *Essay on the Human Understanding,* because Franklin somewhere proudly states that at exactly that age he had read this work which set modern philosophy on its course. Once more he applied himself to the whole of Virgil and Sallust. Cicero's *Select Orations* he did in shorthand while at home. We still have them, with his signature: *Translatum et scriptum est a Guillelmo T. Harris.* To satisfy Yale entrance requirements, he had to review his Latin grammar, prosody and the first twelve chapters of Arnold's *Latin Prose Composition,* up to the passive voice. In Greek, they required knowledge of a reader and grammar and of the first three books of Xenophon's *Anabasis.* A review of Thomson's *Higher Arithmetic* and Day's *Algebra,* up to the quadratic equations, of English grammar and geography, completed the stiff assignment for the summer.

CHAPTER FIVE

THE NON-CONFORMIST YALE SCHOLAR

THE BEGINNING OF A STRANGE COLLEGE CAREER

WILLIAM, his mother and his grandmother had set their minds on his going to Yale. And he did. But little did they realize how quixotic his connection was to be with that college. He entered in the fall of 1854, got this Master's degree, *honoris causa*, in 1869, was voted enrolled in his class of '58 in 1888, which was equivalent to receiving the Bachelor's degree, and was given the LL.D. *honoris causa* in 1895, twenty five years after receiving his first LL.D. from the University of Missouri.

The day after his 19th birthday, William left for New Haven.[1] His sister Sarah rode with him as far as Danielsonville. He was very excited, had a violent toothache, and developed a fever in the room he had engaged in the hotel opposite the depot. However, his "distemper" left him after thirteen hours of sleep. The following day he was examined with 50 others in Latin, Greek and mathematics, and did not think the examination hard at all. Now he felt more light-hearted and stopped off at the New Haven Hotel. While making arrangements for his room at the school, he met a tall "gentleman from Maine" with broad shoulders, large head, good disposition and good morals, who became his room-mate. His name was John Dennet Frost, of Eliot, Me. Their room was located in the North Middle College, and they moved in the next day. The boys had to get their own furniture, bedding, lights and fuel. Much could be bougth at second hand from the previous occupants. William immediately began to fix up a book case and spread the rug he had brought from home. The room was about $10 for each boy. Tuition amounted to $39, or $13 per term, and extras for sweeping and the like totalled another $10. Board, for which they charged $2.50 per week in the "clubs," and $3 in private, was too expensive for William and he therefore resolved to live on baker's bread and apples, a fare he had already been accustomed to. But even apples were dear in New Haven, and at 80c a bushel they were not even good. William had to economize even if father Harris had not approved of the warning in the Yale catalog that parents would not contribute to their sons' happiness or respectability by making their allowance too liberal.

Two days after entrance examination, college routine was in full swing.[2] William rose at 4 or 5 a. m. Prayer was at 6, followed by breakfast and the first recitation. Half an hour of the morning was given over to exercise in the gymnasium. Study until 9 a.m.; after this a meal of rice, "raisons" and syrup; study again till 11, and recitation till noon. Upon this followed an hour of relaxation in which he did nothing in particular. From 1 to 4:30 p.m. further study, interrupted only by his second and last meal of bread and apples. At 4:30 there was a third recitation, after which they prayed once more. William then did his shopping between 6 and 7 and studied till 9, when he was off to dreamland.[3]

Yale, at the time, was under the Presidency of the Rev. Theodore D. Woolsey. William's certificate of admission was signed by Denison Olmsted, for the Board of Examiners. There were 137 Freshmen in all in the class of '58. Among his classmates were Walter Scott Alexander from Killingly, and Arthur Mathewson, Professor Silliman's nephew, his old Woodstock chum whom he had met again in the cars when travelling to New Haven. There were some fellow students who attained distinction later in life: Josiah Willard Gibbs of New Haven, who became famous for his *Equilibrium of Heterogeneous Substances*, published by the Connecticut Academy, and later translated into German; Frederick Charles Hewitt who, as multimillionaire, donated two million dollars to the New York Postgraduate Medical School and Hospital, one and a half million dollars to the Metropolitan Museum of Art, and half a million dollars to Yale; Daniel Garrison Brinton of Thornburg, Penna., the anthropologist; Samuel Henry Lee who was called to the presidency of the American International College at Spring-field, Mass.; Frederick Alphonse Noble, the well-known pastor of the Union Park Congregational Church in Chicago; George Edward Street, another Congregational preacher who became known beyond the town of Exeter, N. H., where he preached; Addison Van Name of Binghampton, N. Y., who later so ably headed the library of Yale.

In the first two years of his stay, the curriculum comprised Greek, Latin, mathematics, rhetoric, and one short term of history, which again was ancient history. It was a classical and mathematical education, relieved in the Junior year when Denison Olmsted lectured on Natural Philosophy. Homer, Herodotus, Xenophon, Euripides, Aeschylus, Isocrates, Sophocles, Plato, and Thucydides; Livy, Horace, Cicero, and Tacitus — none men of the hour. Euclid, algebra, geometry, logarithms, trigonometry, isoperimetry, differential and integral calculus, navigation, and surveying — but no survey of the times that were brewing with vital problems. Declamations, compositions, rhetoric in all its branches — artfully constructing and reproducing language not of today, but of yesterday.

William felt that he had come to get something else. This feeling, inchoate at first, grew stronger and stronger. There was something not in order with that education for which he had been so eager all these years. Beginning with the red school house and then again at the academies his views had been broadened, he had become accustomed to larger perspectives. But here, at Yale, they were narrowed down again and focussed in the past. He reached out, only to find himself continually hemmed in by the rigor of tradition and formalism. Gradually he began to find fault with the subjects that were being taught. More and more he realized that education was a talisman for the present life, not a magic screen to show up the past. But time was not yet ripe.

His teachers at Yale were James Hadley in Greek, Thomas A. Thacher in Latin, Denison Olmsted in Natural Philosophy (which included mechanics, hydrostatics, hydraulics, pneumatics, acoustics, electricity and magnetical phenomena), and the Rev. William A. Larned in rhetoric. None of these seems to have left a lasting impression, except the more colorful lectures of Olmsted. Whether he met the great Whitney is doubtful, but he did hear at least the weekly religious lectures by Professor Chauncey A. Goodrich, son-in-law of Noah Webster. Little did he dream then of his intimate connection with the great work of Webster, nearly half a century later. He became acquainted with Theodore Parker who made a deep mark on his youthful mind which the years should not blur. Secretly he emulated the industrious, virile thinker and acquiesced in his philoophy which had such dynamic power in the New England of his day. He also met Amos Bronson Alcott, whom he admired greatly. Of this, however, later.

At grammar school he had never crammed. At Yale he learned it and later acknowledged the usefulness of thus performing a large task within a brief space of time. Of languages he wearied more and more during this period. As regards mathematics, he fell into lax habits, being far in advance of the class. Natural science, of which he was taught nothing in the first year, held his interest throughout.

He visited the mineralogical cabinet at frequent intervals to gain a knowledge of geology. His sister was promised a detailed account of the wonders it contained.

Christmas 1854 was spent at home.[4] The whole first year at Yale passed without major events, except those having to do with college life. On June the 13th was the great class Pow-Wow with the customary singing, music, orations, and final procession. William took no active part.

But he did take advantage of the prize problems in mathematics that were offered the Freshmen with their examination in July. We still have the neatly executed paper with the solutions of all ten problems. At Yale one paid particular attention to two things in the examination papers which it were well to print on every "blue book" today:

> In estimating the merit of the student's work, two points will be regarded. — 1, fullness of learning; exactness in translating; extent and accuracy of information on the subjects proposed. — 2, perfection of form; neatness, perspicuity and elegance in the exhibition of that learning.

BROTHER, SELF AND SWEETHEART

In the summer of 1855, William's brother, John Wilkinson, who was a year and a half younger, decided to go to California, the country with possibilities practically unlimited. The autumn term at Yale did not begin until September 12th, and so William accompanied John to New York to see him off.[5] It was William's first trip to New York. Broadway in particular impressed him. He looked up Andrew J. Graham, the publisher of the *Universal Phonographer*, on Bleecker Street, and almost missed the boat on which John was sailing. The time between seeing his brother off and the beginning of the fall term at Yale, William spent in New Haven, much to the suprise of his friend Charles C. Baldwin[6] who was afraid that he might overtax the one eye left to him in studying too hard.

During the summer, if not long before, William's boyhood acquaintance with Sarah Tully Bugbee, of Thompson, began to develop into deeper friendship. She was a little over a year younger than he[7] and was the youngest of five children of James and Elizabeth (Dorrance) Bugbee. Her father was bookkeeper for Harris Bros., Twine Manufacturers and owner of a Variety Store in Woodstock. There was a sister, Mary Ann, who was 22 years older than Sarah. Another sister, also by the name of Sarah, had died as an infant. Her older brother, James Henry, became a Captain, her younger brother a manufacturer, while the sister was married in Warren, R. I. When Sarah became acquainted with William, she was the only child at home and on occasion visited her sister Mary Ann who had married Charles Jenkins Harris. She showed an interest in what he was studying, less the Classics than the occult and the mystical sciences, including phrenology. She also learned shorthand with him.

A passage from a letter he wrote her on October 25th, 1855, from New Haven, told her of the death of his brother John:

> My dear friend,
> ... I received news a day or two since from California, that my brother John who went out there last August, had just lived to get there. 200 passengers died of the cholera on the trip from the Isthmus to San Francisco. My brother was one of the twenty who lived to be carried to the hospital where he lived two or three days. Such sad news to me, as almost unfitted me for study. He was only a year and a half younger than myself and we had grown up together, so that almost all my early recollections are connected in some manner with him. I went down to New York with him when he sailed. I felt that it was the last time I should ever see him and

it has not disappointed me, although to my sorrow. If spiritualism were true I suppose that there would be opportunity to [have] intercourse with the departed spirits of friends with whom I should like to commune, but the teachings of science and facts forbid any such thing . . .

The death of John was a serious blow to the family. The ship on which William had seen him off had unloaded the passengers at the Isthmus. Some political trouble had made the natives remove their mules on which the passengers for the Pacific usually were transported (the Panama Canal was, of course, not in existence yet), and thus many or most were compelled to walk across. This was an exertion in an un-accustomed climate which weakened those of a less robust physique. And John never was very well, even at home. When they finally embarked on the "Uncle Sam" the voyage was "one of the most uncomfortable and boisterous ever experienced upon the Pacific side." According to the *San Francisco Transcript* cholera broke out and spread rapidly and savagely. Within two to six hours after the first symptoms the passengers died and their bodies were thrown overboard. With a loss of no less than 106 passengers, including 8 children, the "Uncle Sam" pulled into the wharf at the foot of Jackson Street, San Francisco. But the cholera was not subdued and the Sisters of Mercy came to care for the patients that had been handed in to the State Marine Hospital. John was among those that were in very bad shape, and he died soon after.

The memory of John lingered long in William's mind because John was a piece of himself, and reflection on him turned into an autobiography:[8]

NEW HAVEN, *Jan.* 15*th*

. . . I was somewhat gloomy last Sunday — John comes into my mind every time I get lonely and how can I feel otherwise than sad. Every time I go down to the bay and look off on the blue Sound stretching far away in majestic silence broken by rippling waves rolling ceaselessly against the beach; every time I look over to West Rock raising its snowy side into the cold wintry sky, I feel a sense of bereavement — it recalls all the scenes of my life in childhood: the old farm; the red school house and the route through the woods, over fences and among rocks.

The snakes and the squirrels — the butterflies and tumble bugs that we watched with childish curiosity. The times we used to have in the winter are called up: what snow forts we used to (help) build! How fast John used to run when we played "Goal tag." There was not a boy in school could catch him! Danforth Chase and a whole host of boys were the inhabitants of all our thoughts at that time. How I used to revolt at the idea of manhood!! I shrank from combat with earnest life. I used to wish that childhood with its sunshiny gladness and sportive enjoyment might be perpetual. It was a grand lack of character — a want of combative "get out of my way" spirit.

John was more energetic and less cautious — anything that was bold he was always on the alert to perform. I could not stand the cold as well as he; not because I was not as tough, as people said, but because I lacked spunk or determined opposition. It was for this reason that I sometimes turned back from going to school through drift and storm while he pressed on and reached the school house. When any one spoke severe to me it cut me to the heart and I writhed under the blow; but John only resented it and grew fierce — I hated to do any kind of business that required me to come in contact with the rough side of society. As for instance to sell apples by peddling them around at

THE NON-CONFORMIST YALE SCHOLAR

houses, I was so sensitive that I felt it keenly to inquire at a house and be told *"no!"*

I have found it exceedingly difficult to overcome this in later life and I am quite sure that I never should have made any advances if it had not been for phrenology. This shows me that I am lacking of combativeness and destructiveness and consequently I am apt to feel things different from what I ought to. So bearing this in mind I rush ahead when any duty, before unpleasant, occurs, and finally take delight in meeting such obstacles and overcoming them, and 2 organs are growing fast on the back side of my head. I am led to speak more on this point because combativeness and destructiveness are lacking in our family as a rule . . .

EXTRACURRICULAR AND OCCULT INTERESTS

The second year spent at Yale College was infinitely more important for the mental development of William than the first had been. His talents unfolded, and, although rather retired, he endeavored hard to make come true in his own case what he later postulated of education in general:[9]

The great object of all education is to fit the individual to combine with his fellow-men. His intellectual training should enable him to master the arts of intercommunication and give him the conventional view of the world.

However, the conventional view was not what William wanted at the time. As a matter of fact, he was very much dissatisfied with school which, while teaching, did not advance him in the direction he had hoped for. The result was a feeling of loneliness in spirit which he tried to relieve by corresponding with Sarah and keeping a scrap-book.

Even though a good student, he never was a "high stand" man in college. He frequented the library when others engaged in extracurricular activities of a non-scholastic nature, and strayed considerably in his reading from the standard college course.

All the colleges were then accepting the idea that the purpose of education was to discipline the "faculties" — memory, imagination, reasoning — and this was, therefore, the period of the disciplinary college. It was the manifestation, in education, of the same spirit that produced Federalism in public affairs and orthodoxy in religion, and all three may, perhaps, be traced back to the reaction against the turbulence of the French Revolution. More than half of the four years went into the three subjects that could be made disciplinary, Greek, Latin, and mathematics.[10]

In the fall of 1854, William had bought himself Ollendorf's *German Teacher*. Studying such an abstruse and nonclassical language as German, he ran the risk of being looked at askance. But to top it all, Mesmerism, hydropathy and spiritualism made inroads upon his mind. Eeagerly he studied John B. Dodd's *Spiritual Manifestations Examined and Explained*, and J. R. Buchanan's *Journal of Man*. He professed to distinguish between genuine spiritual phenomena, "spiritual telegraphing," and fake mediumistic appearances. The latter he denounced freely and vigorously, but he was intensely interested in any investigation that was carried on scientifically. At times, as in the letter to Sarah quoted above, and in a little article written for the New Haven (Ct.) *Journal and Courier*, February 24th, 1857, he seemed to the superficial reader entirely averse to spiritualism.[11] Yet, he continued to study it all his life, as his subscription to the publications of the Society of Psychical Research prove.

Many more forms of occultism were studied and, if possible, tried. Graphology became his hobby, as is evident from the collection of famous signatures in his first scrapbook. As time went on, he leaned more and more toward vegetarianism. Bread became his staple food, and he stocked rye flour, wheat and rye bran, rice, syrup, popcorn, honey, graham bread and the like, apart from melons, sweet potatoes and divers fruits, nuts and raisins, preparing a frugal fare in his room.

At the time, the phrenologist Orson Squire Fowler[12] toured the States and Canada, lecturing in all larger towns and many of the smaller ones, selling all the while his own books and subscriptions to the *American Phrenological Journal,* which he had established with his brother Lorenzo in Philadelphia in 1838 and for which William had an abonnement. By 1856, William was thoroughly familiar with all the Broca convolutions and bumps on his and other people's heads.

The ambitious program of his studies, quite outside Yale perspectives, was confided to Sarah in a letter. It was a sort of New Year's resolution:

NEW HAVEN, *January 3rd,* 1856

MY DEAR SARAH

. . . .

I have come back this term with the design of studying considerably on the regular college studies; of reading considerable metaphysics; of investigating Swedenborg's writings and reading his Principia; of writing several essays and keeping up a numerous correspondence; of spreading phonography by teaching it and disseminating phonetic principles. Perhaps I also shall have a little to do with studying German. Perhaps also all these things will take my time up pretty extensively!

I have been reading Life Illustrated just now; it is my favorite newspaper. It pleases me too and charms [?]. I want you to have it so much that I think of sending you the back numbers of the present volume and continuing it to you. You can save the papers after reading them and keep them filed to bind sometime [in the] future. It seems to me that it will be as worthy of binding as anything ever published. Fowler and Wells publish many works that have a very salutary influence upon society. If I get an opportunity I will send you three works that form a series called "Education Complete" embracing "Physiology Animal and Mental," "Self-culture," and "Memory." If you meet with ideas that you do not like in Fowler's works, of course you can think for yourself. I imagine that they are more free from errors in the vital principles than most works. While they have the merit of making people think for themselves.

We do not suppose that any man can write a work free from imperfections, all that we can ask is that he shall set us to thinking in the right vein and develop principles that have their foundation in truth.

Knowledge of the human mind and constitution is of the utmost importance. Nothing is so valuable as "to know one's self." "To know one's self" includes the knowledge of the methods of developing your present capabilities to a state of perfection. We can *improve* ourselves, at least. If we go to work blindly, we shall be apt to grow worse instead of better. "Prove all things and hold fast to that which is good." . . .

Although a Sophomore, William attended, on April 2nd, the Junior Exhibition, on June 16th the "Presentation of the Wooden Spoon," also of the Junior class, and in July he joined his own class in the Biennial Jubilee for which some fine songs had been composed by his classmates. The Wooden Spoon ceremony deserves some notice, as it was the most humorous event. A wooden spoon was presented to the greatest glutton in the class,[13] a matter that was somewhat hard to determine inasmuch as not all students ate together in Commons. Whately's rule, however, came to their aid, to the effect that if a student eats a great deal he cannot be a good scholar. *Ergo,* the poorest scholar must also be the biggest eater. Of course, he had to be inclined to be jolly in order "to take it," which excluded any man that was "lean and hungry." To make the spoon acceptable, it was bought at the price of $30.

From July 10th to the 25th were held the biennial examinations of the Sophomore class. All of the examination questions were rather stiff, and some formidable. As in the past, William participated in the prize problems in mathematics. Did he also participate in the following event? He did preserve the printed program.

On the 15th of November, 1856, Euclid was burned as was the custom of every class at Yale. The program bore, somewhat incongruously, the class motto: *Fortiter, Fideliter, Feliciter.* The *Gaudeamus igitur* became *growleamus igitur.* The geometrical progression was formed by a parallel o'pipe (d)s, with Ana Tommy and Theo'Dolite as children mourners and the friends (*in tuo oculo*) of the deceased.[14]

EXERCISING BODY AND MIND

The impression which William made on those who knew him at college is well summarized by W. P. Bacon and Samuel H. Lee:[15]

The undergraduate community, always conservative in its point of view, thought him odd because he was a vegetarian and "affected Graham bread, gymnastics, stenography and German." But some of the quiet, thoughtful men in the class were attracted to him. He was in a group of students who

Spent not their time on toys or lust or wine,

But wisdom, wit, philosophy divine,

and were in earnest to try to make the most of their opportunities. His poor physique led him to much walking about the hills of New Haven, and to excercise in the gymnasium. It is probable that this early period of his life was not a very happy one, partly because of ill health, partly because he cared little for the curriculum, and even more because he was passing through a period of religious doubt and difficulty, from which he did not emerge for many years.

His classmate Perkin[16] had this to say about him:

To me from the earliest days of our class life in 1858 there was something in his face reminding me very strongly of one of the angels in Correggio's "Holy Night."

The reference to gymnastics which William is said to have affected is, indeed, interesting. It is somewhat at variance with the other impression he conveyed of not enjoying good health. Was it that these sophisticated lads looked upon walking as improper for a Yale man? The fact is, William exercised his limbs as well as his wits according to the implication of the Latin dictum: *mens sana in corpore sano.*

With but a very few picked friends who recognized leadership and sought to benefit by his readiness to divulge his acquired wisdom, he set out for the hills and dales in the neighborhood. A mere hike, however, was not to the taste of William. He made an excursion of it by naming and observing the wayside flowers, studying the geologic formation of the country, and watching the rise of the constellations when night overtook them before reaching home.

There was, however, a more strenuous exercise in which he engaged and which he persuaded others to enjoy with him. It even seemed to warrant making one of his first ventures into business. For $250.00 William rented, on the first of September, 1855, the City Gymnasium, on High Street, New Haven.[17] How profitable this venture was we do not know for certain, but there never was a second lease signed, and the records of receipts and expenses which William kept — cents below dollars, and dollars below cents — show it to be a non-profit one, if not worse. But the records are hardly complete.[18]

However, success met William from other quarters. In June, he had been elected to membership in the Delta Kappa Epsilon Fraternity, exoterically known as the "Divine Knights Ethiopian." Scholastic attainments and good fellowship were requirements, and the motto was "from the heart forever friends." At the meetings they read poems and essays and engaged in hot debates.

It soon became evident to all that William's was a formidable mind that abhorred trifles and had a distinctly philosophical bent. The words of his classmate, Arthur Mathewson, are too plainly a eulogy,[19] yet they describe the essential seriousness that he lived and inspired in others, when he said that William "was a marked man, as with such a character backed by an intellect of such penetrating power, he was sure to be, and soon became the leader of such a following as Plato must have had in the groves of the Academy . . ."

Serious debating was done in two debating societies on the campus, the "Brothers in Unity," and their rival organization "Linonia." William joined the Brothers, probably at their annual meeting of July 30th, 1856. Strangely, they report that he was not very active. In all likelihood his other interests prevented him from taking too forward a part. Yet, there are some papers that emanated from his den at 65 North Middle, which attracted more than ordinary attention. We are thinking especially of the prize debate on the subject "Do the Signs of the Times Indicate Degeneracy in the American Character?" He wrote on both the affirmative and the negative side of the question.

Another major debate in 1856 had to do with the abolition of capital punishment. William probably did not take part, as the first draft ends rather abruptly without developing the theme. The later draft of 1858 shows a distinctly Kantian influence in its ponderous method of proving that, as mankind progresses, capital punishment loses its justification.

There were some other debates, toward the end of 1856, in which he joined issue, probably after he was released from his duties in connection with the gymnasium. One of these bears the title: "Is it True that Man is the Architect of his Own Fortune?" William's treatment is suggestive particularly in the last paragraph, which is an admirable piece of confession. The whole foreshadows his main contention as a philosopher that infinite possibilities lie ahead. He seemed fully conscious of the fact that he was building into an ideal world, that such a world necessitates man as a free agent. Splendidly he set aside all mechanistic, behavioristic and materialistic interpretations of man's destiny and told his listeners that even if these were true, it would be better to keep them out of sight. He probably had little opposition at that point, as Yale was rather untouched by the materialism of the age, even though the traditions of Jonathan Edwards, a Yale man, and that of Samuel Johnson, the disciple of Bishop Berkeley, were no longer so strong as they might have been. Besides, with Noah Porter in the chair of professor of moral philosophy, these principles were safeguarded.

A debate of another type was that on the question: "Is Rotation in Office Politic?" It was a luscious piece in which we see William rising to a righteous indignation and subtle irony on that 11th of October, 1856, carried along by the heat of political discussion. References to Kansas were fraught with much importance in these months, not only at Yale, but throughout the nation. The Honorable Charles Sumner had hurled his historic speech at the Senate on May the 19th and 20th, culminating in the plea to admit Kansas, "where the very shrines of popular institutions, more sacred than any heathen altar" had been desecrated by compelling this virgin Territory "to the hateful embrace of Slavery," into the Union. His acrid exposure of the Slave Power, garnished with classical learning, met strong approval among the Yale scholars, for less than 15% of them came from the slave-holding South. Debates among them upon this topic were on the order of the day. Did William at the time realize what honorable rôle his Principal at Worcester, Eli Thayer, was playing in the Kansas turmoil?

Whately's rules were once again put to the test on the 3rd of December when William matched wits in this problem: "Is the Existence of Political Parties Beneficial to National Institutions?" Still another debate dealt with the question of immigration. To lock the gates of this country against the human tide from Europe seemed utterly selfish to him and inconsistent with his conception of the government of the United States as the most liberal on earth, not perfect, but the best that has been formed. He maintained he had no sympathy with any patriotism that is not subordinate to philanthropy, predicting a future in which all institutions tending to cause nationality, sectarianism and seclusion will be swept away and "every man be cosmopolite."

Into that period fall some other essays and scraps which were collected in a book of *Early Writings* kept in shorthand and comprising a period of nine years, from 1851 to 1859. We notice a growing tendency toward a deification of reason which was exactly the cause of his clash with grandmother Torrey. As a matter of fact he had written, in the early fifties, in the essay "On Eternity":

Since the Bible does not teach us that matter was eternal we may justly appeal to reason and decide according to the preponderance of evidence . . . . We are not to rush into absurdities, but to use our reason where we do not have clear revelation on the point. God

made the constitution of our minds and they tell us
that matter could not be created out of nothing.

The theme was developed philosophically and psychologically. In the essay entitled "Attention" he wrote about
his observations in the schoolroom. It was a topic which he
later, as a pedagogue, made into a cardinal school virtue.
In this paper he called attention the chief thing which a
teacher should endeavor to cultivate with courage and per-
severance. *"Sat scito, si sat bene"* enjoins the teacher to be
a man of extensive information, rather than a man of one
idea; for, a variety of knowledge and human attainment he
considered essential to the gratification of one of the deepest
instincts of our nature.

There were also papers on "Association of Ideas," "Energy
of Character," "Early mental Culture essential to the Man
of Letters," "The Supremacy of Laws," "On Hasty Judgments," "The Analogy between the Life of the Individual
and that of the Nation," "The True Manly Spirit," "The
Inquisition," "The Different Judgments of Contemporaries
and Posterity," and "Athens." Things written while at Yale
are undoubtedly mixed with later writings in the *Commonplace Book.* Thus the title: "The Adaptation of Nature to
the Mind of Man," though brief, seems maturer. Interesting in this connection are the "Reflections on the Limitations
of Human Knowledge." The essay "On Knowledge" pur-
ports to have been written January 22nd, 1856. William's
intellectual adjustment and essential course along which he
steered later, were definitely charted here. He counseled
digesting and applying facts and things rather than merely
acquiring them. Not perceiving, but employing the reasoning faculties is what everyone stands in need of. Again he
drew a distinction between originality, which is well enough
in its place, and real knowledge that absorbs the experience
of the past.

THE NON-CONFORMIST YALE SCHOLAR

Knowledge then should be the object of our earthly ambition. Knowledge of God in his works, knowledge of man in all relations, knowledge of ourselves, knowledge of history, literature, science, philosophy, religion, and most especially natural theology, and in fine, knowledge of the truth wherever and whatever it may be. Observing of course to obtain the most useful first and that which pertains more closely to man's welfare. Our minds are immortal and will never be full of knowledge till we become infinite which can never be. Although we may approximate eternally to the infinite mind we never strictly speaking can approach any nearer to it than now.

THE START OF A LIFELONG HABIT

The end of 1856 was spent at home. On the 21st of December a little sister had made her debut in the Harris household. There were now eight brothers and sisters: William Torrey (*1835), Edward Mowry (*1841), David Henry (*1844), Charles Joseph (*1853), John Wilkinson, the only boy close to William's age (*1837), having died in San Francisco; Sarah Lydia (*1839), Anna Rebecca (*1847), Mary Jane (*1851), and that year Ellen Elizabeth.

Early in January William had to report again at Yale. But before leaving he delivered a Sunday evening lecture "On the Progressive Element in the History of Mankind," in the Orthodox Church of Dayville in the town of Killingly. The lecture was read from the longhand manuscript.[20] In reading it we look, as it were, up and down the lanes of his experiences, the things and the sciences that stimulated him and catch a glimpse of his philosophy, which is full of righteous vigor, burning love of liberty, and a keen appreciation of a provident hand even in those institutions that are outgrown and appear cruel and meaningless to us from our point of vantage. One hundred people attended.

A blizzard that had been blowing all day had kept three fourths of the congregation at home.

Somehow, William did not return to Yale College with the same enthusiasm he had had the year before. Something was on his mind, a vague restiveness which had gathered momentum. He had given his class-mates the impression of ill health and, perhaps, he was overworked during the eventful year of 1856.

We do not have his journals from those early days of 1857, but his *General Scrapbook No.* 1 reflects somewhat his state of mind. While in his second year of college, William acquired the habit of collecting articles, poems and the like in a scrapbook for further reference. The first scrapbook was compiled from accumulated clippings and perhaps was started conjointly with Sarah. For the purpose he used the *Reports and other Documents relating to the State Lunatic Hospital at Worcester, Mass.* (Boston, 1837), the printing of which is rather neatly covered by pasted-in clippings.

The first item is an inspirational article "Look Aloft" with a quotation from Walt Whitman at the head: "Long have you timidly waded, holding a plank by the shore, Now, I will you to be a bold swimmer." Walt Whitman was not often to be his guide again, though *Leaves of Grass* was among his first collection of books.

The scrapbook abounds in poems suggesting shades of the same mood — a somewhat melancholic nature love intermingled with reflections on death; dreams of longing, bright with the nearness of the beloved, yet not without an undertone of sadness; thoughts on the miracles and joys of love. No doubt, the lady of his heart sent him such poems with lines underscored:

Mine! God, I thank Thee that Thou hast given

Something all mine on this side heaven.

or

I watch for Thee! — Hope of my heart!

or

. . . 'tis sweet to feel
Thy soul shall blend with mine forever.

Where else but from Sarah might he have obtained poems
from Godey's *Lady's Book* and similar sources? A good deal
of what remained unsaid in letters could yet be conveyed
in the clipped poems. A picture of the Oread Institute on
Goat Hill, Worcester, Mass., carefully mounted in the scrap
book, reminded him of his own stay at Worcester Academy,
directly opposite, but more particularly of Sarah who had
studied there in 1852.[21]

More in the nature of a soliloquy, and for his own consolation, in his state of bachelorhood, are poems like "The
Frantic Lover in Search of a Wife." There is hardly a heroic
poem. They all convey some thought or idea. Emerson
is represented by "Dirge," "Two Rivers," and "Brahma"
(including two parodies), Charles Dickens by "One by
One," John G. Whittier by "The New Exodus," Bayard
Taylor by "The Song of the Camp," its last line running:
"The loving are the daring".

William did not lack humor, yet he despised frivolity.
Firmly convinced of the truth of phrenology, he nevertheless relished a poem entitled "Use of Phrenology". Despite
the charms in Jane, Nancy, Mary and Helen, phrenology
revealed to the eager bachelor serious deficiencies rendering
them ineligible till at last he finds a skull so intricate and
involved that

'Twould take a whole age to decipher
The bumps upon Emily's head —
So I said, I will settle for life here,
And study them after we're wed!

William could laugh about a good joke, even at the expense

of a serious minister from Mississippi or the Dutchman with two feet and a half of pipe in his mouth.

Among the rest of the items in this first *General Scrapbook* we discover anecdotes, true stories, some fiction, speeches and lectures by Horace Mann, Thackeray, Theodore Parker and less known clergymen and doctors, as well as articles on — farming in the West.

PROSPECTS OF HAPPY FARMING

Fifty-two bushels of wheat per acre was reported from the West, and "no gas about them." Chicago was going through a phenomenal boom. The *Freeport Journal* gave a glowing account of a visit to an Illinois farm. William's father had gone into these parts to seek a new homestead, and had sent him these clippings on farming in Illinois, Minnesota and Wisconsin. There were distance tables for planting from which you could read off the exact number of plants per acre; statistics of wheat culture proving that the "newest States" produce most, having rich, virgin soil; computations of the cost of pork per pound, if corn fetches 12½c per bushel, or as high as 50c, or vice versa. While studying Pliny and the unburnt portion of Euclid, William poured over descriptions of the ideal farm and read and reread the poem "The Happy Farmer."

Was his academic career to come to an abrupt end after those years of promising toil? Was farming to be William's next venture? It seemed so, for he cast about in earnest to raise funds. The rather non-academic gymnasium exploit could not be relied on to supply the needed capital. So, why not commercialize the knowledge one already possessed? Teaching school was not remunerative, to say the least. If a tie-up could be made with business, if people could be shown they actually profited by additional knowledge or ability, then the ideal situation would be realized. And what would be more suitable than phonography?

William considered himself expert at shorthand. He had kept notes in class, had taken down lectures, as the one by H. B. Storer, or sermons like the one Dr. Bacon delivered of a Sunday, had used shorthand for every purpose in which it was essential to catch thought and time on the wing. He advertised in the papers: "Phonography taught in ten Lessons by Mail. For terms address W. T. Harris, Box No. 73, New Haven, Conn." The scheme did not work as well as expected. However, a little teaching of phonography was done in classes formed by Yale students. Sunday sermons were reported for the newspaper. Professor Chauncey A. Goodrich's lectures to students every Sabbath were taken down. Later he exhibited with pride several volumes of work of that nature.

In the meantime, William's connection with Yale had become most delicate. He no longer participated in class-events, perhaps he no longer visited classes regularly. Debating ceased to hold interest for him. Lecturing was tried, but abandoned, realizing he did not have the qualities of an orator. He was too dilatory and philosophical and could not hold the audience interested because he read his lecture off. But he was to earn more success with writing.

To the 1857 Beckwith's *Almanac*, for instance, he contributed a reply, on pages 56-58, to an article by the editor and publisher in the previous issue entitled "Is God or the Devil the Author of Death?" Beckwith did not see his position refuted by the Yale youth who exhibited a trend towards theologizing. William's assumptions, dictated by orthodox ways of thinking, were almost Spinozistic, with a dash of optimism and a show of logic. However, the article found response and permission was granted to reprint it in the *Boston Investigator*.[22]

CUTTING LOOSE FROM YALE

Cataclysmic changes were predicted for 1857. The world

was to come to an end on June 13th, for which astronomers had calculated the appearance of a comet. Odd bets were the order of the day. Most people were composed, until they learned that not one but several comets were to be expected. It put a damper on the humor of the rest when one fine night another faint comet was spotted by the Harvard Observatory near Theta Draconis, making it the sixth comet for that year.

For William a crisis was impending. He loved Sarah, wanted to make a home for her. He was looking out into the future while the college demanded devotion to the past to learn about which put him under deeper financial obligation to home.

As early as 1856, he had definitely decided for the new and progressive, as he wrote to Edwin H. Bugbee who, in the meantime, had been elected Representative of Killingly in the State Legislature. The world of which our tyro had got a glimpse in virtue of his wide interests, did not use algebraic or trigonometric formulas, it did not employ Latin or Greek, except in speeches, and then only with loss of popular approval. This world could use the memory training which a Fowler recommended, and it did use those mechanical "toys" which he had constructed while going to the Academies. The situation called for a choice, and school learning lost.

The reason which William gave for leaving Yale was that Yale had taught him all it could teach him. It was certainly not religious doubt that prompted his action. He began to disparage the study of Latin and Greek as dead languages. They were devoid of the spontaneity and exuberance of nature which he had come to love dearly ever since his walks to the little red school house. Grammar seemed, in comparison, so artificial, so dull, so inferior a product of human intelligence. Science, on the other hand, described and explained a cosmos far more interesting than the Yale curriculum suggested. He saw history in the making in the political turmoil of the times. The world expanded Westward, whereas the eye of the scholar was fixed on Athens and Rome long since faded. A magic wand had touched William in the metropolitan atmosphere of New York, Providence, Hartford, and New Haven. The spell was irresistible, the sense of direction was yet inchoate. Even Yale could not endure the strain much longer. Its formalism was eased soon after by an elective system with greater emphasis on history and natural science.[23]

The fifties of last century were still packed with golden opportunities. But William was not tempted so easily. A slow gestation was going on inside him. The call of the modern world was offset by a natural piety toward the old and a philosophical outlook on the new. He could not shake off history and tradition as so much dead weight. The emigrant could do that, a scholar of the type of William, never. The West lured him, to be sure, now as never before. When his brother John had left, he had not yet experienced this attraction. As a matter of fact, he had once curbed in John that urge to go West by counselling him to stay and get an education in an Eastern academy.[24] The West did not attract him even now so much for the opportunities it offered for entering the maelstrom of the birth of a new civilization, as for the occasion it offered for gratifying his reflective mood and thoughtful temperament by finding a home in deep solitude. Though patriotic passions swayed him and the pulse of modern life was throbbing in his veins, he wanted to retire, become an anchorite in the Western woods! What a perfect picture of a day-dreamer suspended between extraversion and introversion!

A world of destiny finally came to fruition with the decision to quit Yale and go West with Robert Seney Moore, of Hudson, N. Y., his classmate and by two years his junior, with whom he had nothing in common except the interest in shorthand. An honorable discharge was obtained on January 15th, 1857, signed by President Theodore D. Woolsey and stating: "Wm. T. Harris, a member of the Junior Class, in good standing is hereby honorably dismissed at his parents request."

As late as May, a letter arrived from father Harris, containing a friendly warning:

LAWRENCE, K. T., May 17, 1857

DEAR SON:

. . . You say that you and Moore have made up your minds to go west to locate yourselves and wish some advice. I hardly know what to say — it was rather my impression that it would have been better for you in the end to have graduated. But I may be in the error. You say you want to go into the fruit business. I suppose you will have to consider the climate some for that business. I suppose the middle or southern part of Illinois would be well adapted for fruit raising. Southern Minnesota and Northern Iowa has been recommended to me as an excellent tract of country well wooded and watered and healthy land in that section rises in value very fast. Dubuke and other places is growing up rapidly on the Mississippi, which might be good places for your reporting business in the winter. As it is getting too late in the season to get in crops, I suppose you want to lay out your money in land and then get into some business that will pay best. I think Buck may be well posted on what point to locate as his is on the great thoroughfare to the west. The expense of living in the west is very great this year if people have to stop at public houses, it has been all speculation and no crops raised in Iowa and in some other parts of the west the past year. . . .

PASSAGE TO ST. LOUIS

Midsummer 1857 came around.[25] Back on the Killingly farm William, now close to his 22nd year, made plans for a non-academic future somewhere in the West. The West had claimed his brother John and a cousin, Albert Harris, who had returned in the last stages of consumption just about the time that John started out. The West had taken his father to an uncertain destiny. He was still away, unsuccessfully searching for farming country and business opportunities in Kansas Territory and Illinois. But to William the West would be kind.

"The folks begin to think that it is a sober reality that I am going," he wrote in his diary. His mother did not approve very much. Grandmother Torrey, who thought the East healthier than the West but would not interfere in his plans so long as he would not forget to read the Bible, let him have $100.00 which he got the day before his departure from a Norwich, Conn., bank. In return, he gave her a note for $125.00 payable the following year. Sarah was in a bad state. The last night William spent at her home. It was the 21st of July. Both she and her mother were consoled when he told them he would be back in October. In his heart of hearts he doubted his own statement. He knew very well: "I have not yet arrived at definite ideas enough with relation to what I shall do."

The following morning he rose early and Sarah, "sorrowful that she was to lose for some time her companion, moved about moodily." She would doubly feel her loneliness, for she had neither brother nor sister of her own age. Time came for parting, and in the confusion William forgot his journal and the extracts he had made from Alcott's *Orphic Sayings* when he had heard him in Boston. His brother David, now thirteen, went down to Putnam station with him. The trunk containing his clothes and books, some

73 ·

from Sarah, was put into the wagon, he picked up his carpet bag, and soon waved good-bye.

Through Plainfield and Hartford he travelled to New Haven. In the afternoon he bought Cousin's *Course of the History of Modern Philosophy* in two volumes, and in the evening went with his friend Charlie Chapman to see Etta, Charlie's friend and an acquaintance-to-be of Sarah to whom he sent her daguerreotype. The following day he "saw some fellows," made arrangements with Daniel Tertius Potter, a senior at Yale whose beautiful handwriting he later admired so much, to have his own daguerreotype taken for his class of '58, and in the evening he went with Charlie to Etta whose head he examined for phrenological purposes.

That same Friday night he took the boat for New York City in the company of several Yale fellows, among them his classmate Alfred Otis Delano, who was going home to Brooklyn at the close of the third term of the year. William did not join his former fellow students in conversation; instead he read Carlyle's *Hero-Worship*,[26] seeking his berth by and by. He awakened when the boat edged her way into the dock. With Delano, he went around the city, visiting again Andrew J. Graham and calling on Fowler and Wells, publishers of *Life Illustrated*. This was the magazine which he had read since 1854 and to which he subscribed for Sarah. He took along some books on how to write, talk, behave and do business, which were intended to be put to good use. Mr. Graham was glad to see him, of course, for he always left money and "promised more." Indeed, he had an ardent disciple in William. He invited him for dinner the following day, but William had to decline. He passed the day, having an ambrotype taken of himself, visiting with Delano the Brooklyn navy yard and going aboard "some large concerns," having his trunk transferred to the Hudson River and boarding the steamer. It was late in the afternoon when the boat slowly steamed up the river to Hudson. Beautiful scenery accompanied him on the West shore, and he read Carlyle till the sun set behind the highlands. A young man came up to him and they talked, with little profit to William, for the fellow "thought he knew about as much as Theodore Parker".

Next day was Sunday. William rose from a sound sleep. They had been lying in Hudson for some time, and so he hurried off the boat and ran all over the city to locate the home of Robert Seney Moore and thus make good his promise to stop by for him. When finally using the simple expedient of asking, he learned that the Moore's lived three miles out of the city. The walk was pleasant, he drank in deeply the scent of hay and extolled the beauties of nature.

The Moore residence was a "magnificent large one situated on the highest part with pillars and a cupola." A large flight of steps led up to it. Robert was at home. Mrs. Moore was different from what he had imagined her, and Mr. Moore was nervous, cold, calculating and pessimistic, his original genial enthusiasm having long since dried up.

It was a hospitable house; William enjoyed the luxury of a bath. But over it all lay the deep shadow of Robert's departing. William thought best to be conservative in order not to oblige Mr. Moore to put the damper on too hot an enthusiasm. For he had been in California during the gold-rush, and returned disillusioned. He evidently was also not quite successful in the management of his farm.

The following day the boys left, well provisioned for the journey, Mrs. Moore asking William to take care of Robert, which he promised in a fit of generosity, seeing how badly she felt. Robert's brother brought them to the train, and for $17.50 they bought each a ticket to Cincinnati. At 55 miles per hour the train sped to Albany where they ferried across the river and boarded the train to Buffalo, skirting the Erie Canal. Moonlight lay on the water. William wrote letters to Sarah and Mrs. Brooks.

About 9 or 10 in the morning the train pulled into Buffalo. The trunks were re-checked to Cleveland and a letter hurriedly written to Sarah. For the first time the boys got a glimpse of wild country and the log-cabins of pioneers. Except for occasional views of the Lake, the scenery did not change much in the afternoon after they had transferred at Cleveland to cars for Columbus and Cincinnati. At Columbus, night overtook them and they slept in their seats as well as they could. When S. T. B.[27] would come out with him, William promised himself he would make better provisions for a comfortable trip and take two seats, a blanket and an easy dress.

That very night they left the train and spent the remainder of the dark hours at the Walnut Street Hotel in Cincinnati. In the morning William looked up Elisha A. Buck, a schoolfriend of his on Killingly Hill, who served as General Freight Agent of the Cincinnati, Hamilton and Dayton Railroad Company, at $30.00 a month. He had written William as early as November, 1854, that the West would be the place for him and father Harris had recommended getting in touch with him. William stayed for dinner. He found him cordial, but changed, so that he would have hardly known him. He and Robert bought round-trip tickets to Dayton from him. It was there that William wanted to see his uncle George Harris. In the afternoon they started for Dayton. But when William had finally located the house of his uncle it was night, and the uncle was just retiring. His wife and daughter came downstairs to greet the visitor from the East. At first they took him for his father. Glad to see him, they put William up for the night, while Robert stayed at the Hotel. The next day the boys changed to a cheap boarding house after eating their three meals on the "American plan."[28] They had

76

planned to make Dayton their *pou sto* until they had learned of the whereabout of William's father. Letters were sent home and to Sarah, as well as to uncle Stephen, another brother of William's father who had married a Missouri lady. He was to send some more money.

All seemed to go well, especially as there were two letters from father Harris which seemed to suggest that he had left Kansas Territory and was already in St. Louis. So, the next day William celebrated by having a haircut, a bath, and eating some new pears and ice-cream. Over at uncle George's the letters were read once more and plans forged. They decided on the strength of these letters that Kansas was not a desirable place, but that the thing to do was to buy land around St. Louis. William went wholeheartedly for the idea: St. Louis "was a great place for business as it was the center of business and migration to the West and surrounded by a rich country". Indeed, everyone thought it would become the metropolis of the nation. In imagination he had the land already:

Perhaps we may go into the grocery business or that of raising cattle or something, perhaps we can return to Kansas. It seems that money can be made some way. I am bound to do something that will pay. I want to go back to take my "lamb" . . .

The following forenoon the boys drove with Peter, a neighbor, through the city, up to the hospital and to the brickyard nearby, where William's brother John had worked before he had gone on his fateful trip to California. It was Saturday. In the afternoon William packed his things and went by train to Cincinnati. There he dropped in on Elisha Buck once more, helped him in "casting up accounts," and then went with him and some others on a spree "over the Rhine," a district north of the Miami Canal, where most of the German population resided. The lager beer and wine agreed well with the ice-creams they had, and William slept soundly after his return at midnight.

On Sunday he took breakfast with Buck at an inn and drove by carriage around the residential part of the city on the hills overlooking the broad Ohio valley. Then they walked to the southern part, crossing over into Kentucky where they called on a young lady whom William described as "a pleasant creature, but not very stocked with knowledge".[29]

Monday came around and William covered the last lap to the frontier in a second-class railroad car, leaving Moore in Cincinnati. The ticket to St. Louis was $6.00, but "the road appeared no more than half done" and consequently he was jolted about the worst that he had ever been. He slept all night "in a kind of dreamy way." Sarah was not forgotten all the way. Whenever the train stopped, he picked a weed to send her. Past rich cornfields and through extensive prairies rushed the train to halt at one o'clock in the afternoon at the Mississippi. With the rest of the passengers he took the ferry over to the city of St. Louis.

Part Two
ST. LOUIS PERIOD

CHAPTER SIX

PIONEERING

REUNION WITH FATHER

IMMEDIATELY on reaching St. Louis, William went to the Post Office. To his surprise he found no letter from his father, but his own letters to his father unclaimed. He did not worry greatly as yet. He left a note with the postmaster for his father to the effect that he had arrived, giving directions where he could be found. It was the fourth of August, and the heat was oppressive. The mosquitoes and bedbugs were extremely troublesome and he awoke "with vermin thick about" him. The lodging place had many boarders at $6.00 per week; but William decided to change. After writing letters to Sarah (enclosing the flowers) and to Moore, he went uptown to look for better boarding places and settled on one. But as he was preparing to leave with his things from the old place, he was suddenly seized with cholera and had to stay, bathing his stomach all night with cold water. Though weak in the morning, he escaped with his life. He managed to remove his belongings, paying the woman $2.00, and settling down in his new place which he got for $5.00 a week, and liked it very much. His fourth day in St. Louis approached. The effect of the suspense in which the continued silence of his father had put him, coupled with his illness, now made itself felt in nervous apprehension. On top of it all, he read about "mysterious disappearances."

81

Suddenly it occurred to him that there might be more William Harrises in the city. Forthwith he looked them up in the city directory and went to everyone, asking whether they had received any letters that did not belong to them. Though unsuccessful, he "felt better satisfied after this." His ennui was now growing and he wished he had some of his "deep works" that were in his trunk. He got himself some German books and read again Carlyle's *Hero-Worship,* an excellent book, only it is not long enough."

The ensuing day found him wandering about the business-like city in streets covered by dust and rubbish, mainly from the many new homes that were going up. An effort was made again to reach his father by letter in Kansas. Anyone familiar with border raids between Kansas and Missouri and the precarious situation of the new State in those days can well understand William's anxiety. His nervous strain became well-nigh unbearable, but somehow he did not lose faith and was able to concentrate on study and reading. So passed this day and the next and many more.

The long-expected father did arrive one day in August. It happened like this. One morning while studying or writing upstairs in his boarding house, the landlord came up and informed him that a man was waiting for him downstairs. His heart, he wrote, leaped into his mouth and he hastened down and was delighted to meet his father, safe and sound.

He looked worn out and his eyes were red like a drunkard's which was caused by the winds and sand of Kansas. There was the story of hardships in his countenance. I thought I would not lose him again very soon when I saw him. A gentlemanly, fine looking man was with him; he had also come from Kansas. They had been together down to the southern part of the state looking at Missouri lands. They had seen some great lands there and Father [had] bought a little.

Father and son now took a long walk. They talked about every conceivable thing. William heard that he had not done very well in Kansas and in the South. He had been unlucky. Plenty of people owed him money, but he could not collect.

It is not very easy to imagine what things a man has to go through with in settling a new country. Perils from robbers, the climate, the government, and everybody else. Sharpers by the thousand have flocked to Kansas and have made it their game to get a fortune by cheating everybody.

Harris Junior gave up the idea of Kansas for good and decided to stay in St. Louis. Harris Senior went to Illinois and from there back home to Connecticut.

LIFE IN REVIEW

September was a difficult month. One day, it was the fourth, William was in a humorous mood and wrote a description of himself, in shorthand, addressed to Sarah, a sort of second proposal.

I am now 22 years old or shall be on the 10th of this month, about the time this letter will reach you. It will be on Thursday and I was born on Thursday, Sept. 10, 1835.

I am about 5 ft. 10 in. in height and have blue eyes and auburn hair which is said to be very fine. I have some hair where a beard ought to grow that begins to look like a philosopher's beard. In the course of five years it will be developed into handsome proportions. I am rather strong and weigh in the winter usually about 160 lbs. . . . I am a vegetarian and have been for three years and a half. I have eaten some meat on several occasions, however, since I came into Missouri, principally to test its effect on my system, which I find to be rather bad than otherwise. I am a freethinker and actor. I believe that there is some truth in almost everything that has an existence and yet I doubt that there is anything that we can come in contact with which has all truth or contains all truth.

I am an eclectic in philosophy and read Cousin with great relish. If anything I lean towards idealism in my tenets. To me there is no system so universally discarded [?] by mankind as that there may be some valuable ideas in it.

I am somewhat of a spiritualist. Nay, more, I am an entire believer in the spiritual nature of man and in the communication of man with the spirits who have put off the flesh. I totally disapprove of the sensual philosophy that ignores the intuitions of the soul. I love music, poetry and painting and sculpture. I love natural science, metaphysics, and above all theology. I am a phrenologist and moreover I write shorthand at the rate of about 100 words per minute. Shorthand I suppose you will understand to mean phonography. Phonography is a system of writing by sound. . .

I am somewhat of an astronomer and moreover a geologist. I am no believer in the pretended powers of fortune-tellers and yet I think that there are natural intuitions in the human soul called "premonitions." I think that the human soul is so great and its powers so mysterious that we scarcely know anything of it as yet.

I am not an atheist and yet I believe in no God as the popular mind does.

I have lately read in Cousin a method of proving the idea of a God which I do not fully comprehend, perhaps you may.

It is this. We have an idea of infinity from finite bodies and things. Everything which is finite or imperfect implies something infinite and perfect.

I have not finished reading Cousin and my course in philosophy, but am progressing rapidly during my spare moments. I shall be able to settle some of my ideas before long. I have been waiting for sometime to read up till I became satisfied on some points. I read Andrew Jackson Davis's autobiography through, which Moore brought with him, this week. It was the most interesting of anything I have read of the kind. I am a believer in Davis to a great extent. I think that he is very progressive and that each succeeding volume published by him assumes a higher tone. I shall have his volumes that he issues after this I think. In his autobiography he calls his Penetralia his best volume.

I am studying German and practising reporting with Moore now. I have an advertisement in the newspapers for phonographic pupils, but it has not been long enough in the papers to excite much attention. I shall expect to make my living and perhaps a pretty good sum besides by teaching phonography. I intend to give phonography a fair trial. I shall see whether there is money to be made teaching it or not. I expect to get an opportunity to report sometime this fall if I do not succeed teaching phonography. I want Father to send me some money from Uncle Stephen and I shall need it for capital in my phonographic business. I shall want you to come out with him when he comes again if I am ready to support you. My sister Sarah must come also. She will be company for you on the way and also after you arrive here. . . .

IN SEARCH OF A PROFITABLE BUSINESS

In the early part of September, William remembered his

academic qualifications and took and passed an examination
for admission to teach in the Public Schools along with
fifty others only one of whom outranked him, a graduate of
Harvard, who had taught eight years.[1]   Superintendent
Divoll recommended the Yale scholar to Dr. Charles A.
Pope, a member of the Board:

DR. CHAS. A. POPE.   ST. LOUIS, *Sept.* 10*th* 1857
Dear Sir:
   The bearer Mr. Wm. T. Harris is the gentleman of
whom I spoke to you yesterday.   At his examination a
short time since, he showed rare and critical scholarship and great familiarity with the practical and
theoretical questions pertaining to teaching.   I think
him admirably qualified for teaching in any department
of English or classical education.

                          Yours truly
                          IRA DIVOLL
                          Superintendent of the Public
                          Schools in St. Louis, Mo.

   During November, William was persuaded by some
"rascal" to come in on a magazine that was to be started,
the *People's Magazine*.   As usual, William brought his
enthusiasm to the matter — he acknowledged himself that
he was insane on the subject — and thought he had hit upon
the very thing he would have liked to do best, editing. Here
is his own story, in part:
   I wrote to my friend Albee to contribute to it and
he answered me favorably.   Saying "Use me."   George
Washington MacCord [?] was the fellow, arrogant and
inflated [?] and dirty, who thought himself capable of
planning out a people's magazine.   For many a night
and day he thought of it and we all did.   I did not commit myself on the subject to any one out of it.   He
tried various individuals to get patronage and they re-

86

fused and thus it fell through. So it was a great delusion and I am so happy that it did not succeed. If I only had been tied up to such a thing I do not know what I should have done.

Other difficulties presented themselves. Robert Moore, who had joined him in September, had become more and more unmanageable. William and the would-be promoter of the magazine played cards together. At first, Robert would not join them, then he became such a fanatic at it that William was glad when the cards were burned up. All the while he did not receive money enough from home, so that he ran into debts and owed William and the boarding-house keeper. As a matter of fact, when father Harris had raised $50.00 in gold, William paid $22.00 for Robert's back-board. He never called him Robert in his diary, but always Moore. William's almost ascetic attitude toward eating made him look upon Moore as a glutton — "altogether too much in favor of his stomach." Moore could not stand so well as William the inconveniences of their living. At one time they had neither washbowl nor washstand in the room and only two sheets apiece. These nights even William tried to blot from his memory, as he did not wish to accustom himself to looking at the dark side of things.

William advertised himself as a reporter or amanuensis in the dailies, but without success. Phonography, or shorthand, seemed more and more to be the thing that promised at least some income. The ad which William mentioned in the biographical sketch to Sarah was this one:

PHONOGRAPHY. — Everyone who has much writing to do will find this art invaluable. It saves three fourths of the time and labor required by long-hand, and is easily acquired, owing to its philosophical simplicity. Terms, $5 for course of 15 lessons with instruction book. Apply at this office, or through the Post Office, to WM. T. HARRIS or ROBERT S. MOORE.

As a direct result of this ad they got one pupil, Joseph B. McCullagh, who was to become the inventor of the "interview" and editor of the *St. Louis Globe-Democrat*. This McCullagh, William related later, "was at that time learning the printer's trade, a very bright young man, and he soon learned Phonography much better than I knew it, and became one of the best reporters in the West."[2]

The firm Harris & Moore published a two-page folder advertising their Phonetic Institute at the South East corner of Green and Third Streets which extolled the many virtues of shorthand, its educational, time-economical and financial advantages by profuse quotations. The Pitman system was eulogized, also Graham's brief longhand, and samples were reproduced, the shorthand one unmistakably in Harris' writing, the longhand ones in Moore's.

William went to the Second Agricultural and Mechanical Fair and got a medal for his phonographic writing which he exhibited. Robert also practiced, but he used up too much paper for the thrifty William. Robert's debt to William was an economic bond between them, but spiritually they drifted apart. At last, on October 14th, they moved to a room at 35 Pine Street, a building in which some lawyers and others had offices, one of them being Ulysses S. Grant who was then in partnership with two lawyers in the real estate business.[3]

In making this change, William gave up one of his business ventures which had been a total failure, the Phrenological Institute. Practically nothing was ever mentioned by him either at the time or later, concerning this, and only a yellow leaflet advertising the Institute is preserved. Nevertheless, phrenology remained long his hobby.

Their new office was also study and living quarters. Ten dollars were spent for a carpet, and one bed served for a lounge. From here, William carried on operations, more or less with the co-operation of his partner. As an instance, when a $40.00 consignment of books arrived from Andrew J. Graham in New York, Moore promised to go around and sell them, but "he backed down and would not sell any of them."

There was another matter that made William furious. Rev. H. B. Storer, a spiritualist whom William had known in New Haven, came to St. Louis to give some lecture-sermons. The first one he delivered was not well received, to his and William's dismay, but the following ones drew a better response. One of these lectures netted about 14 dollars. He was generous enough to take both of our young pioneers to the theatre on occasion. William was much impressed, particularly by a play "Richelieu" in which Forrest played the rôle of the Cardinal under Louis XIII. Another time they saw the "Fall of Pompeii." William liked the play immensely, but in his reflective mood he formed a different opinion. He rejected scenes of cruelty. "Such plays do not leave a good impression on the mind. I could wish that there were no occasion for such things to be written, in other words that all cruelty were banished from the earth." Such salubrious effect was not to be noticed in Moore. He fell into a theatre-going mania and could not be restrained. The worst feature of it was that William had to lend him the money.

Through Rev. Storer, William got acquainted with a man who had made a large globe and wanted him to lecture on it, but William had no faith in it. Through Storer, however, he got in on the groundfloor, as it were, of a philosophical society which was then being formed, probably the first society of that nature in the West. William took part in the debates. In one of the earliest he took the affirmative on the issue whether the world had existed for longer than the Bible stories would imply. Anticipating considerable activity in this society, perhaps as secretary, he joined the

Mercantile Library at a fee of $2.50 semi-annually. Affiliation with this library, which had been established only about a dozen years before and was growing by leaps and bounds, saved William many a dollar which he would have otherwise invested in books. He used it often in preparing for the meetings of the society. One of the essays he read at these meetings was on the "Unity of the Races."[4]

The eventful year of 1857 was about to close, and the new year did not hold much promise. The idea of teaching school had, indeed, occurred to our pioneer, but how subordinate it was to other schemes! The great number of applicants for a teaching position had made him despair of ever getting into a school, for vacancies were very few. He reasoned: "If I received 10 dollars a month for teaching public school besides teaching my pupil and getting 30 dollars per month besides it would make $400 besides my expenses." A farm in Illinois still looked very good at this juncture with a possible teaching position on the side; but then he had not made up his mind at all as to whether he should get married and bring Sarah out West, or go back home, or stay single for a couple of years, make money, and then return East.

BUSINESS FAILURES

They were writing 1858, and destiny was wiser than William thought at the time by steering him away from the thought of becoming a farmer near Farina in Illinois and frustrating a hundred desires and plans to guide him gently into the profession that he all along appeared to be trying to avoid or think little of.

A diary tells all about this strange development. It is a story intensely human and genial in parts. Like Cicero, or Samuel Pepys, or Charles Dickens, William Torrey Harris used shorthand for this intimate record.[5]

The address was still 35 Pine Street, St. Louis, Missouri,

from where William T. Harris and Robert S. Moore endeavored to conduct a Phonographic Institute. It had more the aspect of a student's den than of a place of business. The books about were certainly not those seen usually in offices: Kant's *Critique of Pure Reason,* Carlyle's *Sartor Resartus,* works by Emerson and others in that category. The ad now run in the daily papers was boldly phrased:

☞ Harris & Moore, the celebrated phonographic teachers and reporters have established their office at No. 35 Pine Sreet. Any one desiring reporting done, should by all means call on these gentlemen; they have a new and very superior style pen, that holds ink enough to write all day. Call and see them, and examine for yourselves.

On the second of January a gentleman called and paid some money for a few phonographic works. He complimented and encouraged the young men by saying that in his opinion the Phonographic Institute should pay well. However, disillusionment had already settled on the mind of William. Would he, the stranger, by any chance go around to private homes and get pupils to learn the "beautiful science"? William was sure that he himself could not. But there was Moore who probably had not yet done all that could possibly be done on that score. Alas! he too had not the slightest talent for any such thing. William would have to do something in earnest, and that very soon!

St. Louis in those days differed remarkably from the city of today.[6] It had a population of about 160,000. Progress was not reckoned in years, but in days. Streets in this brick-built city could not be macadamized with limestone rapidly enough. The mud was horrible. It was difficult to find persons, new streets springing up over night and neighbors never knew each other. In vain did William at one time look for Andrew Jackson Davis; at another time Moore was not able to locate a prospective customer. Nevertheless, there were hard times in the city. The period of 1857-58 was one of the worst. There were bank failures galore. People would accept gold only. Paper money became valueless. One had neither time nor money to learn shorthand, nor short longhand.

The second of January shed a ray of hope. For also on that day a Mr. Hayden called who was "a friend of the phonetic cause." He took William to Mr. Spaulding, a tailor and a keen phonetician. They talked about phonetics and phonography. Someone else had established a school of phonetics and English for foreigners. William then made a firm resolve. It was on a Saturday. Monday he would go into the business with gusto and visit as many teachers and lawyers as he could. The firm had to manifest some activity. "Phonotopy," in whose favor such men as Sir John Herschel, Horace Mann, and many other eminent persons had spoken, deserved to be spread with the zeal of missionaries, for aside from its material value as a source of income, did it not have a decided cultural and ideal value?[7] In his own family, William had created an interest in phonography. On leaving, he had given his mother a phonographic note for the $10 which she had loaned him. His sister Sarah and brother Edward, in their letters, scrawled a few lines in shorthand. Sarah, his fiancée, he thought would be sufficiently interested to dictate to him Plutarch's *Lives*, were she to come out to St. Louis. His courtship of her, had begun with an offer to teach her phonography, which she accepted, and their early correspondence was carried on in phonography.

Benn Pitman's *Reporter* became William's as well as Moore's constant companion. Every night at least one page was written out for practice of the phonographic reporting style. More pleasing forms were substituted for improvised, awkward and slow ones. William became very desirous of being a good reporter, as it would have been one of the most lucrative professions, paying from $1500 to $2000 *per annum.* He knew he could master it. At the same time, he entertained no doubt that he would get business *eventually.*

Monday came around, but neither teachers nor lawyers were contacted. On Wednesday, the intention was voiced again. Indeed, an opportunity offered itself when Andrew Jackson Davis, the spiritist, lectured in St. Louis. William reported these lectures. In the meantime, plans were laid for visiting high and common schools in the city, also private schools, to interest the teachers in phonography. A point of diplomacy and subtle salesmanship was not neglected: "I can mention what a beautiful accomplishment phonography is to them and present the lady teacher with a brief longhand book to gain her graces." He got twelve pupils, by dint of this effort — but only in imagination, for the scheme was never tried. Instead, new projects began to pop up, but doubt lurked in everyone of them. "I think that there can be one hundred pupils raised even in this city and 500 dollars would pay well for a year's receipts besides teaching other things which I might do if I was energetic and enterprising."

At last, one school was visited during January, the Commercial Academy, whose Principal was a certain Mr. Harts or Hortis. He was quite sympathetic and allowed William to speak to his class one Friday evening. He spoke of the advantages resulting from the use of shorthand and explained its formation. They asked him to put a sentence in shorthand on the blackboard, and he left $1.50 worth of books. The Principal was impressed and promised to influence his students to form a class. But nothing developed. Instinctively sensing his failure in this direction, William postponed his seeing Mr. Hortis again. At one time it looked as if the Principal wanted him to teach mathematics at the Commercial College, but it turned out to be a will-o'-the-wisp.

In spite of all these troubles and tribulations neither William nor Robert lost courage altogether. Doggedly they tried to improve their speed, accuracy, neatness, and form. William's library of stenographic, phonographic, phonotype, common type, corresponding and reporting type or style items comprised about 40 titles, all classed under *Phonetics*. In due course of time, he amassed a collection of about 100 works, a great many curious and rare.[8] Outstanding among authors were the names of Benn and Isaac Pitman, Andrew J. Graham, E. Webster, Andrews and Boyle. The multiplicity of systems suggested by these names is reflected in the shorthand which Harris wrote.[9] Being of a reflective bent of mind, William wrote more slowly and meticulously than Moore, carefully shading all the differences, highly critical of forms coarsely executed.

Lectures, or the meetings of the Literary and Philosophical Society were attended on Sundays and an attempt was made to report them, but William failed miserably because he was intensely interested in the subject and could not bring himself to be an automaton which a rapid reporter must be. This was especially the case one Sunday morning when Mrs. Mary E. Davis lectured eloquently on the "Ministry of Angels," and he admitted having lost, to a large degree, his power of verbatim reporting. Immediately he applied himself to writing verbatim from dictation, giving up improving himself by mere copying.

It so happened that William was charged with tutoring a solitary pupil in the three R's, five times a week, at $50 per month, a position for which he had to thank superintendent Divoll and Dr. Chas. A. Pope. It was Henry O'Fallon, one of St. Louis' most prominent citizens whose name "became a synonym through the West for enterprise. liberality, and benefaction."[10] Could not Henry be utilized

94

for improving his verbatim reporting? Happy thought! While he was reading aloud out of a book on the history of Europe, William would follow in shorthand, and teacher as well as pupil enjoyed this practice very much. The plan worked so well that it seemed worth a dollar a week to hire a boy to read. As it was, William deemed himself fortunate to be paid instead. It was the best idea he had ever had, and it put him well on the road to beat Moore considerably by getting up to 150 words per minute.

Now he could report nearly verbatim a lecture by Andrew Jackson Davis. Every week brought new experiences, and it was not long till he discovered a very fundamental principle in reporting, to write in a small hand. Money went for phonographic paper, a chart and other things needed in shorthand, such as a reporting cover. He sent to Cincinnati for these things. He wrote to Graham in New York again for more lessons after having sucked all the good out of his manual. Always he entertained a warm friendship for the man. He would ask his forgiveness "for being a broken reed to lean upon" when he could not immediately pay for the books which Moore failed to sell from house to house.

About February, there was a general disappointment because the total number of phonographic students registered with the Harris & Moore Institute was exactly zero. Moore, who was reporting for lawyers, once managed to get $10 in gold which went to William who had heavy claims on his purse. But it found its way back to Moore almost immediately to enable him to assert his "unwarrantable right" to go to the theatre. In revenge, William also went and saw Charlotte Cushman in *Macbeth*.

Through a clipping sent by Moore's parents, William learned about a subscription racket which offered to every $3-subscriber to their magazine "a copy of the celebrated 5-dollar engraving of the 'Last Supper' " and, in addition, a chance on drawing a prize up to 1000 dollars. Those who would get 24 subscribers, would obtain a "library of 40 large volumes of the popular works of the day in the market." This last offer was, of course, almost irresistible to William, but in the end he was persuaded that it was too good to be "on the level."

A serious situation developed when Moore began to think in earnest about leaving St. Louis. Robert was doubtless worse off than William who could always fall back on his earnings derived from tutoring Henry O'Fallon whom he was obliged to teach for ten months, or till July. What would become of the Phonetic Institute in that case? That was William's main concern. Someone had to be around if there were enquiries, and Moore thus far had at least attended to this aspect of the partnership while William had to be away at his pupil's house for two hours in the forenoon, and two in the afternoon. Besides, William acknowledged that Moore was the better reporter and therefore an asset to the business. As a reporter he might eventually line his pockets in gold and silver. His faults, consisting in lack of energy, theatre-mania, and gluttony could be forgiven him. With his leaving, the end of the Institute seemed inevitable. The very prospect of such a happening had a paralyzing influence on William. In the fourth week of February he recorded that he had forgotten to practice phonography, and exonerated himself by a philosophical attitude to the effect that he really had no disposition to be tied up, that he would not be tied down to anything, and that the soul anyhow will not be otherwise than spontaneous.

However, the diary, begun in shorthand, was a constant reminder and gave him daily shorthand practice even though not systematic. A fresh impulse was received from Andrew J. Graham who at the time was working on a new book of improved writing. The delayed publication of this work William, in his exaggerated sense of obligation, laid, erro-

neously no doubt, to his failure to pay for the large consign-
ment of phonographic books. Hence, $25 of the monthly
$50 for teaching Henry went to Graham on account. The
next draft for a like amount was to come out of his next
salary check.

From this may be seen that William's despondency was
not entirely due to lack of energy or day-dreaming. In a
confidential letter to his father[11] he even spoke of suicide:

> I would just as lief be dead and make an end of it as
> to live as I have lived the last three years. I have been
> miserable almost ever since I went to school at Andover
> 5 years ago. The only pleasure I have rec'd has been in
> the intellectual pursuits which helped me forget the
> present . . .

But duty was ingrained in him: "I do not enjoy life much
but shall not commit suicide or get married till I have
discharged my obligation to others." To board oneself is
a kind of "slow suicide," and a "hermit life is not the best
one for a man." The high cost of living coupled with the
depression was but one phase. His clothes were well-worn,
and new ones were expensive. Already at Yale, where appearance was rated an asset, he was sensitive to his need of
a good overcoat "for handsome," yet did not wish to put his
folks back home to unnecessary expense. Sometimes he
would dismiss the idea that he was so badly off when he
pictured to himself the situation in the country at large.
In the East they had "soup houses" for the unemployed, as
his father wrote.

There was another business venture that was doomed to
failure from the start. Early in January, William, in answer to an enquiry, received a letter from T. G. Stearns,
262 Broadway, New York City, an agent of Prince's Protean
Fountain Pen Manufactury. He was invited to become
their Western agent by selling from three to five thousand
pens a year. Investment was from 50 to 100 dollars, but

on looking over their catalog, William found that $21.60 would get him a sample of each of their eight different kinds. (The final bill was $24.99, including the 15% discount). Should he think of nothing better between the present and the time he got his monthly payment, he would indeed become their agent! After all, being an agent "is not a very bad" business, provided one is energetic. Perhaps he would realize $10 a day. "Eight or ten pens would bring more than that. For $500 worth of pens sold they take off 25 percent from the trade price which is a dollar off of each. So after I have sold $500 worth of pens, I shall receive $50 worth gratis."

The plan, to his mind, merited much consideration and that the pens would sell was *a priori* so certain, particularly if he could, on his calls, take along some phonographic circulars and sell phonographic books and Graham's *Brief Longhand*. Thus, he would not wait for his next monthly payment but immediately wrote Elisha Buck enquiring whether he could let him have $20 for a month, to be paid back at 5% interest.

Almost daily after that he braced himself for the impending business. On January 22nd, the pens came by express. The morning after, when he should have tested his salesmanship as grandiloquently advertised in his diary the day before, he entered in his diary:

This morning I did not get up till 9 o'clock. I sat up in bed and fixed my pants and sewed some buttons on my shirt first. I did not feel like going around and selling my pens. In the afternoon I felt still less inclination to do any selling.

That week he started Charles Dickens' *Martin Chuzzlewit* and it engaged his attention to such an extent that the pens were nearly forgotten. The following week he frankly confessed that he was astonished at his own indolence, that he had no courage to undertake anything whereby he would become rich. It was the prospect of being rich that he was interested in, for he had other plans. There was S.T.B., his fiancée back East, and a farm in Illinois. Thus, when an opportunity seemed to offer itself through the good offices of Mr. Ira Divoll, the Superintendent of Schools, he penned these lines in his diary: "The opportunity to teach school is not a very agreeable thing, I must confess. I could do better selling Protean pens it is possible."[12]

Now Moore was to canvass the city with the pens, but the poor fellow was so bungling that he not only did not sell any in several days and weeks, but brought back the one he had left on trial, broken. The case of Moore became "abominable vexatious," and when William's own gold pen failed him at the end of March and not a single person had bought a pen, his patience was exhausted. The business was definitely a failure. Customers had taken the free shorthand lessons, had spoiled the pens in trial, and even made off with them without paying.

To vary his business experience, William then took lessons in penmanship at Jones' Commercial Institute as a sort of reciprocal arrangement with Mr. George B. Hayden, writing master, to whom he read and expounded Kant. There he practiced till his arm ached.[13] He also wrote back home asking to have his books and earlier journals sent on. Would reading his diaries pay him? He was not sure, but one thing he knew, that in this way he might improve in reading phonography. He "should be interested and perhaps instructed by the various shades of thought" that had passed over him these past years.

When Moore owned defeat by the glorious West in March and went home, William gave up all thought of selling Protean pens and books of brief longhand, and invested what money he had in the classics of English and American literature. Pens and books could be returned at a loss. Better still, by disposing of the books in bulk he would

save expressage. No more business transactions like that!
"I believe that when I embark on another such speculation
I shall sign over my property and assume a false name as
well as change wits and give up writing in my journal!"[14]

The Phonographic Institute had *eo ipso* vanished after
a languishing existence of about eight months. Only a possible reportership held out hopes. His capacity as a reporter
should yet serve him in the world, he thought for certain.
It was a position with the largest paper in St. Louis. To it
Moore had aspired, and now with his aspiration cropped
up the desire to be an editor, so long suppressed since the
still-born *People's Magazine*. Would not his knowledge of
German and French and his thorough acquaintance with
English qualify him more and more to become not only a
reporter but an editor of some journal?

However, first he had to cut the coat after the figure. On
March 27th he took up his carpet and his books of which
he had a great many now, and prepared to move to a smaller
room in the same building. The room was hot and oppressive, not at all conducive to study and thinking. Dust in the
carpet, dust in the air, dust in the whole of St. Louis. And
if there was no dust, there was mud. "The Western country
is a very dirty and dusty and muddy country," he wrote to
his father in disgust, probably longing for a neat Connecticut farmstead.

His insolvency did not improve, but he found comfort in
large sums:

> If money can be let here on good security at 25 per
> cent it would pay to earn money and let it, it seems to
> me. Supposing I put a hundred dollars out at interest
> and it brought me in 25 dollars per year, then if I got
> 4 hundred dollars in the course of a year and let it out it
> would bring me in 100 dollars per year. In 5 years . . .

and so on until he had accumulated at the age of 55 the

sum of 1,500,000 dollars, provided of course that he would give his whole attention to getting rich.

But I do not forget that money increases slow after one has a hundred thousand.

Oh money, money what a fool-maker art thou! For thee thousands and millions will destroy their happiness here and hereafter, nay, even barter their hopes in immortality. Let me never be carried away by an inordinate lust for such lucre. I hope that I shall have neither poverty nor riches. Riches, I mean so much that it takes from my time, which I should devote to development, to take care of them. I can be temperate in eating and drinking, and clothing, and devote my time to spiritual and intellectual growth.[15]

A little business was yet to be wound up, as collecting some bad debts owing the firm Harris & Moore, but with little prospect of success. Having had all this experience he did not really regret, for it had saved him from greater extravagance. He knew he was

. . . as extravagant as a March hare!

Money slips through my fingers as fast as water. It is so lucky that I do not get any very often! Well, I must shut down on my extravagance as soon as I have spent my next 50 dollars. But hold, there is Andrew J. Graham, my friend, who will want some money and I, in justice, should pay him some too. If Moore will pony up, he shall have some money too.[16]

SCANT LIVING AND HIGH THINKING

The beginning of spring brought on a touch of homesickness. William's thought turned to his sweetheart and the "beautiful hill countries" where he was born. There he had seen such fine spring weather; at St. Louis it rained fiercely, turning the countryside into swamp. In the middle of March, spring had burst forth with splendor and William feared he was being hurried into Summer without much notice.

Living expenses for a month in the Harris economy figured at $10, of which $4 went for the room, $4 for board, $1 for laundry, the rest for "burning fluid" and miscellanies. Until his departure Moore, who had become ill boarding out, eating too much meat, had joined him in his self-prepared board and was made cook. It did him good to superintend the management "of one department." For weeks they lived on porridge made of meal and flour, with cheese and sugar. Boiled rice and cream diluted with sugar water was rated delicious, and likewise rice and milk with either raisins or plums. Even though Moore was to be blamed for much of the situation, William thought that this slim fare would be of benefit to himself and that his stomach would "get the better for it." The book *Fruits and Farinacia* by Smith and Trall, and one entitled *Fruits, the proper Diet of Man*, were consulted frequently.

But even with good-will good food will become tiresome and the "stomach's health tone" remained but a wish image. Thus they bought turnips and changed off with apples. At home, William's father manifested a concern for his son's health:

PUTNAM, *Febr.*, 23, 1858

Dear Son:

Your letter to Mother has just come to hand, it being very cold to day and not much to do we concluded to answer yours forthwith. You write you are very poor and I see by the tenor of your letter that you are very nervous. I think I can prescribe a remedy that will help, if not entirely cure you, if you will adopt it. The remedy is to change your course of living altogether, eat meat, drink coffee, cider and occasionally a glass of Dayton ale. So much for diet and now for the most important of all. Leave off reading all works upon metaphysics, spiritualism, and like subjects. Hold no arguments nor have any correspondence with any spiritualist. Sleep 8 or 10 hours out of every 24. Read nothing of a grave nature and but little of any kind. Try to compose your mind as much as possible. If the golden stream does not flow as fast as is desirable, keep cool. The times are hard, not one half of the inhabitants of N. E. are making their board this winter. Thousands are depending upon the charity of soup houses for their daily subsistence. Teaching school is the best and surest business that I know of at present. . .

The advice of father Harris was not heeded. A baker on Greene Street was engaged to bake graham crackers or pilot bread at 6 cents per pound in 25 pound lots. That and apples[17] at $1 per bushel, or free, when Henry O'Fallon's mother would supply them to practice arithmetic with, was a fare cheap enough. It cost almost nothing to live that way. The dyspepsia left him, but chills appeared, probably the "Missouri malaria," which was cured with wet cloths. William longed for vegetables, however, for oysters with vinegar, for eggs instead of cheese, good butter and beer. But these things were expensive and he could indulge in them only after Moore left. Arrangements were made with the janitor to have plenty of eggs boiled in advance. Mr. Freeman would get 36 for 25 cents and sell them to William at 25 cents per two dozen.

After long experience and watching himself, William came to the conclusion

. . . I perceive that vigor of mind is so closely allied to body that I can study only if I am very temperate and I cannot exercise either unless I am healthy in my stomach and my vigor of body literally then rests solely on my stomach. Well I can be, if I try hard enough, temperate in eating, I think. What a great ocean of temperate things there are which I have never done![18]

The ill consequences of his mode of living showed themselves all too frequently. To his reporting ill twenty times he mentioned only twice that he was feeling well. His sour stomach he treated with soda. To stimulate his appetite he thought seasoning would do. He was getting weaker all the while and thoughts of suicide returned. There were headaches, liver complaints attributed to eating natural or toasted cheese, colics and colds. He thought himself extremely susceptible to colds, but the main trouble remained dyspepsia, physical as well as mental. The two were interdependent, he was convinced. Once he noted that his mind was entirely worn out. His glass eye also troubled him now and then. A keen self-analysis was made on February 13th:

Now I expect that there is something radically wrong in my system which works by fits and jerks. I know that when my dyspepsia is cured that I shall be an altogether different man from what I have been for the last three years. It is dreadful to think of how many years I have spent that were spoiled entirely by this horrible dyspepsia. There is no counting them. My time at college was little better than wasted by this awful scourge which came on me by reason of Pond's confectionary store. What one does, that also must he reap, is a truth that I shall not dispute. So I suppose that I must reap what I sowed then. I planted dollars in Pond's store and dyspepsia in my guts. Had it not been for the gymnasium, I should have been a dead man. I know that my muscles being developed as they were saved my life. It may be saying considerably more than I have warrant in saying, but I believe my case is not a rare case among collegians. But it is horrible to think of. The blues come to students frequently and it seems to me that whenever the blues come, indigestion must be a remote or approximate cause or effect of it. I know that when I am joyous and light-hearted I seem to digest well, but when I feel

gloomy, my food, let it be ever so light and easy digested
in itself, will not digest, but lays on my stomach hard
and heavy.

Often he would marvel at his fundamentally good constitution by nature of which he could endure all the physical
and mental strains.

What an idea it is to suppose that man has only a
certain amount of life force, that it is limited, in short,
to a certain quantity. Does it not make one tremble
when one thinks of it? I expect that I have used up
much of mine foolishly. It can never be helped. But
I can spend the remainder more carefully.

That is true reform. It will bring back health to my
bones.

I do not know whether I should be healthier if I were
married than I am now or not. It seems to me that I
should have some reasons, among which I think of these.
I should have my food prepared for me well. I should
not have to live in a dyspeptic sort of way. I should
enjoy the society of one of the best creatures in creation. I should feel much happier. I should be regular
in my habits. There would not be so much care on my
mind as there is now.[19]

When he could not sleep and was in a "horrid state,"
mentally, he tried to apply cold water, being a believer in
the curative powers of it. In his library he had Dr. R. Y.
Trall's *Hydropathic Encyclopedia,* Trall's *Hydropathic
Cookbook,* the *Watercure Journal* for 1856 and 1857 and,
oddly enough, *Watercure in Pregnancy and Childbearing.*
The water-cure mania gradually subsided and became dis-
placed by a greater emphasis on exercise. He devised a
whole set of gymnastic exercises which he elaborately described in his diary and carried out in his room. Some he
had Moore do, to improve his health. Later comments
suggest that he felt "pretty well" if he conscientiously fol-

lowed them, which he did not. Walks in the fresh air did him good. Once he walked out to Bremen to see the Indian mounds and was invigorated by the exercise and the new impressions.

Standing up while reading he found beneficial also, but complete health he thought would come only when working out of doors at least four hours a day. In his opinion nothing but life on a farm would do. He remembered his own gymnasium at Yale and would have welcomed another opportunity to exercise, as then. It presented itself in April, when Mr. Hayden introduced him to the German gymnastic club, the *Turner Bund*.[20] Every day he was looking forward eagerly to exercising in the gymnasium. It gave him the buoyancy he needed, and he aspired to becoming a trainer or leader, and eventually a first-rate gymnast. He found, "there is no need of being like the Vicar of Wakefield's family." He must have combativeness. It had served him to good purpose in times past whenever he had been inspired with a little of it.[21] One wet and rainy night he went up to the place and exercised with the rest. When one of the men complimented him by saying he was the strongest in the class, William denied it, knowing, however, full well that he was.[22]

All the while William was trying to keep to a regular routine thus to improve his health in addition to exercising. Getting up depended on going to bed, going to bed depended on whether what one was reading was absorbing or not. He would find himself waking up in his chair over *Martin Chuzzlewit* at four o'clock in the morning. The life of John Sterling was finished "late, very late, in the night," and Carlyle's *Goethe's Helena* kept him awake till two, writing by candle light or "burning fluid," with home-made ink. Often Moore would keep him company over Goethe's *Faust, Wilhelm Meister* and *Goetz of Berlichingen*. The mornings were devoted to writing in the journal.

Sundays, William would take a bath and then hear lectures both in the afternoon and evening. Church also was attended, probably a spiritualist one. Satisfaction was derived from hearing spiritualist discussions and philosophical debates, as well as from music. "What a pleasure Sunday might be if people only knew how to bring together useful things at that time. . . I could have some music every day of this life. It would be a paradise if we only could have what we need to gratify all our senses."[23] He was charmed by the voice of a woman singing during one of Mary E. Davis' lectures. Sometimes he would play the flute, perhaps at a friend's house. Among his books were the "Songs of Zion" and "Social Orchestra."

"That is the way for me, I must be pressed with something else and a strong desire to do the thing that I ought to put off, and then, pressed between two fires, I can work like a hero!"[24] And work he did. He made it his motto to "*toil terribly.*" But as to orderly living, it simply could not be done, for the soul is spontaneous and it "will not be a machine to suit the little bump of order situated at the corners of the Iberius."

To get a laugh at himself, for it fitted his situation so well, he clipped this verse for his scrapbook:

Money goes, no one knows,
Where it goeth, no one showeth;
Here and there,
Everywhere,
Run, run,
Dun, dun,
Spend, spend,
Lend, lend,
Send, send,
Flush to-day, short to-morrow,
Notes to pay, borrow borrow.

So it goes, no one knows,
Where it goeth, no one showeth.

On January 5th, the pawn broker was paid $11 with the intention of *trying* never to patronize him again, for interest was very high, at 10% per month. But in order to satisfy Moore's love of the theatre, this had to remain a pious wish. Among other things, his watch was there, which made him come late for lectures, and when it was finally redeemed it did not keep time so well as before.

Luckily, January was mild in 1858, so mild that fire was hardly required and only $2.55 needed to be allocated for coal which was bought by the bushel, in the January-February budget. Twenty dollars would have bought a new coat in February, but by waiting till the 15th of March a double-breasted frock coat was had at $14. After all, one had to look "better than shabby." Shoes, socks, and collars had to be bought out of slim earnings. Sarah, back East, was making shirts. "She could take off my mind all thoughts of victuals and drink and many other things as well as my wardrobe. I am now puzzled with all such things that I have no business to meddle with."

The farm in Illinois became resurrected and bathed in a halo of peace and happiness with his dark-eyed, dark-haired maiden. The whole necessity of money-making seemed to have this objective. It had been one of the principal reasons for his leaving the East and immersing himself in the expansive West. But his mother wrote with little sympathy:

I should advise you to keep school a few years. I think you will make more money that way, and make it easier than you would by farming, as you are not used to outdoors labor. But I could write all night on the subject if I thought it would be useful to you. Farming is hard work and needs much care and attention to succeed. But I hope you will decide upon something that you will succeed in.[25]

Later she even counselled William to come home to live and build a house on the farm near her, while father Harris was thinking of Missouri or Illinois.[26] Perhaps she knew that it was more or less a gentleman's farm that William was thinking of. The "Latin farmers" in the neighborhood of St. Louis may have inspired him to write:

I suppose that if my health was good — in other words if I lived on a farm and worked gently 4 hours per day that I could read and digest more literature in 5 years than the majority of the literati.[27]

I am sick time and again of this life. Why is it? I want to get on to a farm. Conscious happiness, conscious health. I do not like it. My happiness should be so full and deep that I should be totally unconscious! I see folks self-conscious. It spoils them entirely. It is vanity. I am disgusted with a man who is conscious of his own excellence or benevolence or esteem or anything else.[28]

The Record of the Gain

William kept more than one notebook, but the diary or journal was by far the most important one. The 1858 one was the fourth journal written in shorthand. The New Year's resolution was, to all appearance, a simple one: *"Never to neglect this Journal let come what may*: I have found that whenever I keep my Journal up vigorously it has been like a brother to me and indeed ten times better than a brother or any other friend I have had." To us it is valuable as it was to him: "My Journal is valuable in as much as it records my daily life and that I may live it over again as biography and see how much I have gained."[29]

Every evening, the activities during the day were reviewed; later he wrote his page or two of shorthand in the morning of the following day because he was persuaded that he would thus have more vigor. At the end of January he had to remind himself of his resolution, and in February he censured himself: "It will never do to omit one page. I have experienced the disastrous effects of that in my other Journal." In Edgar Allan Poe he had read that if you make a memorandum of anything, it will surely escape your memory. Was there some truth in that? Perhaps, — and he did keep neglecting his journal sometimes for days on end. Occasionally he would read his "cold" notes of his earlier diaries which his folks had sent him. Unfortunately, not much of these is preserved.

At the bottom of a good many pages of the journal room was left for entering extracts from various sources, such as Emerson's essays, Carlyle's works, Shakespeare's *Cymbeline,* Goethe's aphorisms and the like, or for writing in an original essay. The first one thus projected was to be on the many-sidedness of truth. We also find abortive attempts at reporting a lecture.

In the journal he wrote little essays, some only partially developed, dealing with such topics as "Culture," "On Great Men," "On Humanity," "Virtue and Interest," "The Autonomy of Will," "On Good and Evil," "Against Socialism," "The Haughtiness of Scientists," "On Sleep and Dreams." There were also various fragments, some very terse and suggestive: "What is skepticism but despair?" and "A lie is a punishment in more ways than one only."

To keep a commonplace book beside a scrapbook and a journal was an idea which he owed to his Yale chum Potter. While scrapbooks were made by Harris throughout his life, the journals or diaries were few in number, and the commonplace book was even more ephemeral. At the beginning of the 1858 diary, the idea was evolved to copy daily the best passages from the philosophers so as to have a nice collection of quotations and references useful in the writing of papers. The plan was to put the name of the philosopher at the head of each page and to read up on him, topically.

Even before the first commonplace book was started enthusiastically on February 7th, William, in a very characteristic manner, aspired to *whole series of commonplace books.*

In the first commonplace book, 26 pages were to be devoted to the index, an idea carried out only partially. On page 27, and continued on page 85, the first topic, "Spiritualism," was started, which was immediately followed by its antithesis "Sensationalism," *without* quotations under it, then "Greatness, human" (inspired by Emerson), "Mysticism," "Tobaco" (cf. three essays on the subject. by Trall. which he owned), blanks under "Sensational Tendency of the Age" and "Kant," with a shorthand reference to the *Critique of Pure Reason.* After this, but not consistently, he started his quotations and references to Greek philosophers, an attempt at a systematic study of philosophy. The sources were carefully noted in the margin in long and shorthand, while the quotations were all in shorthand. The philosophers included Thales, Anaximander, Diogenes of Apollonia, Pythagoras, Xenophanes, Parmenides and Zeno of Elea. Apart from 1859 entries, starting on page 95, there were, moreover, some blank and meagerly represented topics, many of Alcott's *Orphic Sayings,* extensive extracts from Richter's *Levana,* quotations from Goethe's *Faust* and Lewes' biography of him, 16 phonographic reporting rules, and a catalog of his books comprising 368 (minus 1) items.

At the beginning of March, the commonplace book was filling up rapidly, but not without great labor. S.T.B. could make herself useful in this connection! She also would make him independent of the opinion of others. Effort was relaxed and by the middle of the month the idea was abandoned despite the fact that he hated incomplete things. Even while the commonplace book was thus surrendering to the exigencies of time, another idea was conceived for keeping "a place full of themes." But where was the place to be? For

111

a long time past he had written down notes on slips of paper without any sort of system.

The ideas captured in diary and commonplace book were to be used as nuclei for articles for publication, aside from serving as lecture notes. He was dismayed at his indifference and indolence in the matter of developing his essays and persuaded himself that he should write more. But there was the infernal dyspepsia! Summoning his energies, he would get off a pretty good essay and felt as if he could write several more. A few days afterwards, however, he was unable to "get up steam," no matter how he tried. He worked by fits and jerks.[30] He did manage to write essays for the Philosophical Society which were not intended for publication, because writing for publication he considered a different matter altogether.

These considerations, after all, must be rated as of great credit to himself, for he did not want to be a superficial writer, but a scholar. Thus, he felt the need of being better mounted in history, perhaps following out Emerson's suggestions, and to begin his studies with Herodotus and Xenophon, working up to the present. Edward Gibbon, David Hume, and Macaulay, along with William Hickling Prescott and George Bancroft, were on his reading list and, in part, in his library. Nevertheless, the hope of accomplishing this large assignment remained unrealized for a long time; likewise the articles projected on the basis of this historical survey remained in limbo.

For *Life Illustrated* he contemplated what would have been an interesting piece by his hand on the "standpoint which men assume in looking at things." Presently he dismissed the idea from his mind for lack of time, and only the sketch on the many-sidedness of truth, mentioned above, was written.[31] He decided he would not disgrace himself by producing "miserable writings for low papers," and *Life Illustrated* appealed only to a superficial taste.[32]

When sitting down to write for publication, his usual equanimity failed him. "I must write in my essay-book or journal and afterwards copy, I think. Let me get in a habit of writing for myself alone and then copy out whatever pieces I think good ones. This is the true way, I believe." There was no lack of ideas, to be sure. They were budding forth all the time: The relationship of phrenology and transcendentalism,[33] dialogues between atheists and theists, and a general one on phrenology which eventually did take shape as a paper for the Philosophical Society. But the perpetual wrestling with ideas that were to be adequately conveyed in words often made him despondent and morbid in a realization that he might not be "talented enough," that he had "no faculty for it." In other words, the idea did not burn him up as yet. He was at times too much dominated by other minds, too dependent, too receptive, and too much swayed by foreign logic. Hence, he sacrificed his writing to his reading. If he could have but established his own position more genuinely, he would have felt his obligation less and ventured more boldly on his own. He was still waiting for inspiration, and frequently admitted a realization of the insufficiency of his knowledge. It was not yet a year since he left the tutelary wings of Yale, and his self-education was not yet adequate.

Eager to amass learning, he would carry books along in his pockets wherever he went. Carlyle, for instance, he read in the theatre. But he was out of patience with himself for so doing. It never did him any good to read either at meals or at public places. "Just as if there was not one moment to be lost from out my time but that I must have a book with me. Now it is altogether a great mistake to suppose that a moment is lost because it is employed without visible means in my hand. For it is absurd to make such a supposition." The mind needs rest as does the body.[34] But of all places, he carried *Martin Chuzzlewit* along to church to write his report on and "read out of between services."[35]

Unlike his friend Moore who tore through a book, William read "slowly without hurry, without rest." In a novel or a drama he would pause, observe the characters before his mental eye, and philosophize upon them. His daily capacity of substantial works was 100 pages. In the Mercantile Library supplementary reading was done, mainly in reference works and such books as could not be taken out. No notes were taken, but he trusted his memory, often digesting what he had read on coming home.

Omnivorous reading he considered good up to a certain point, but it was liable to cause an intellectual nausea, particularly if too many authors were tackled at the same time. Reading was varied enough not to weary. After reading metaphysics, novels were found to be refreshing. He followed the rule never to read an inferior writer so long as a deeper one can be understood. Having read some criticisms of John Sterling he was convinced the writer belonged to a lesser category. "There is no need of reading many books if one knew exactly *what* books to read. Goethe, Shakespeare, Plato and Homer will be of service to me."[36] This is genuinely Emersonian, even to the employment of the "algebraic formula" in which the names of the great are strung together as simple reminders of the wealth of their ideas. The popular slogan, "Reading with a purpose" was changed by William to "reading with the proper attitude." Thus, to the reading of Plato one should bring a devout spirit. However, in a fit of overindulgence in reading he sometimes would acknowledge that experience is better than knowledge derived from books which give us merely opinion.[37]

THE END OF THE PARTNERSHIP

Few were the major events in the first quarter of the year 1858. The slight earthquake that rocked the city of St. Louis in the morning of October 8th of the previous year was long forgotten. A great fire broke out between 2 and 3 a. m. on February 20th, in the Pacific Hotel, corner of Poplar and 7th Streets, with a loss of 40 lives. The funeral of the victims was on February 24th, with William watching among a crowd of 20,000 people the procession of the seven hearses that formed on 5th Street. He decided that henceforth, when in a hotel, he would always seek a room that is not too high for him to jump out of in case of fire. Once he heard an Irish wake and commented on the awful howling of the women. But nothing touched him so deeply as the departure of Moore, his owning defeat by the West and leaving him to carry on alone.

It happened this way. One day, Moore received a letter from his father in which he was "not very kind in his expressions" about his son Robert's progress. William sympathized with the downcast Moore. Often he had felt "mean" toward him because he had contributed unreasonably to aggravating their financial straights. Moore's father had recommended that Robert sell everything off and come home, but William dissuaded him from the idea. "It will never do for him to leave St. Louis till he has paid his way."

Middle of March, Mr. Moore wrote again asking how much money it would take to get his son home, and he offered some prospective business with a brokerage firm in New York. Now Robert was no longer to be held back. His father sent him $25 toward a first class railroad ticket via Buffalo to Albany (it cost $27), and William gave him an additional $7 so that he would have enough "to carry him safely." He realized that Robert needed a mother's care very much. He thought he might do for a scholar or teacher, but never for a business man. He himself would be very lonely, as lonely as he had been before his father arrived, and, in order to keep Moore, even thought of giving up his mainstay, the only solid money he was earning teaching Henry O'Fallon: He would talk to Mrs. O'Fallon and recommend a young man, that is Moore, "who is of good morals and of some experience of teaching young scholars" to take his place.

When Moore packed his trunk on the 22nd of March, William was angry and called him a scamp in his diary. As a sort of farewell supper he had bought some cheese with William's money. The cheese was excellent, better than the monotonous diet of apples and crackers. The St. Louis dream was finished for Moore. They burned the basket with which they had brought out provisions from Moore's parents' house. It made a great blaze. The day of parting came. It touched William deeply. "I talked to Moore in such a strain which may have seemed to him like sense or nonsense, I don't know which. It was nonsense anyway." Books which Moore sold to William reduced his debt by 10 dollars, leaving still 52 dollars to be paid.

On March 31st, William received a letter from him,

. . . which is very refreshing, he feels just as nice as can be, just as though he had escaped from wild beasts. He says that when he was walking up home Thursday evening that his feelings were as follows. "The mud beneath his feet was the past, the old scenes around him was the present, and the stars above were the future!" Pretty good for Moore. Thus it should be. I am not surprised that he should feel pleasantly to get rid of the care of being out here. Home is a blessed place no doubt. . . . Moore feels splendid. It is good to receive letters from those who feel hilarious.

The two friends never met again.[38]

Letters, Facetious and Otherwise

With Moore gone, letters were the only concrete bond William had with home and the East. But ever since he had come out West he had received mail not only from his fiancée, his parents, brothers and sisters, but also from his college chums and other acquaintances. They sent him clippings and news-sheets, such as the *Windham County Telegraph* and New Haven papers. The Yale fellows kept him informed about his *alma mater*. Among these it was particularly Daniel Tertius Potter with whom he had some correspondence about his daguerreotype. William had delayed having it taken and sending it to him because of lack of money. He meant all of his friends to have his picture.

His letters to Potter, who was a disciple of David Hume and a student of German, occasionally turned out very long, for he endeavored to give him first lessons in Kantian philosophy. "I want to make as many idealists as I can. It will be a splendid thing if I can open their eyes to the new life of the soul that appears. The pure reason has in store for them such rich treasures that they ought to come out of the poor understanding and arise into the regions of the truth of Plato and Emerson."[39] Potter took it gracefully. Some letters, and very long ones at that, he wrote entirely in German, even using the German script. He said he was longing to sit now and then with William and hear him wander off *"ins Leere,"* into the regions where there are neither space nor time and from which William was in the habit of bringing back thoughts full of beauty and meaning. He endeavored to read Hegel, but decided to wait for the American genius who could make him readable.

Potter was always very complimentary to William. From hearsay he once reported that William had gotten over the shallow conceits of phrenology — which was not entirely the way in which William would have put it. As a matter of fact, he had sent Potter a year's subscription to the *Phrenological Journal*. In a later letter, Potter criticised William's stand against popular theology, influenced no doubt by Kant and then by Agassiz. He kept William apprised of everything that might have been of interest to him, as the difficulty the Yale fellows had when they were engaged in a fight with some firemen and one of the latter was killed by a shot.[40] William did not think him a good scholar, but a smart business man who overworked himself with college duties. The last of March brought a long expected letter from Potter's brother who was working with the railroad in Charleston, Missouri, and intended to visit William that summer.

With Daniel Garrison Brinton, one of the editors of the *Yale Literary Magazine,* likewise letters were exchanged. Brinton seems to have possessed a versatile mind and he publicized William among the Yale fellows. Hence William was very careful how he composed his letters to him. He corrected and slept over them and tried not to write pedantically. The major theme of the letters was Kantian metaphysical ethics, with Cousin's views on the matter and Jouffroy's lectures on ethics which William had delayed reading because of lack of time.

Walter Scott Alexander studied theology at home after a brief stay at the Theological School in New Haven. William thought that he himself had something to say in the matter of theology. Alexander was friendly and chummy and told about a visit to Boston, wanted to know something about William's friend Charles Baldwin, and was likewise deserving of a present from William of the *Phrenological Journal.*

Long letters were written to Henry Andrew Pratt who was "a good fellow" and from whom William hoped to hear oftener; to Miles Beardsley who had his letters routed via William's parents but wrote nothing of importance; to Alfred Otis Delano, whom he liked "pretty well' and who seemed to be interested in coming out West to teach; to Arthur Mathewson of long acquaintance; to his old Worcester friend, Robert R. Bishop, who wrote facetious, cheering letters; to Edward Waters whom he criticized as the shallowest correspondent and whose letters contained fewer ideas than those of his 14–year-old brother David, in fact, "not one-half"; to Abner Weyman Colgate, William Russell Frisbie, the poet, and George Arba Dickerman. Often it was difficult for William to muster enough courage to write, and days intervened between start and finish of a letter. For he was exceedingly sensitive to the fact that thus far he had not been a success in the West. For this reason he did not give them encouragement to come to St. Louis. "I do not want any of the Yale College fellows to come near me out here. I would rather build myself up alone."[41]

The correspondence with John Wesley Albee, his one-time roommate at Phillips Academy, who was now at Cambridge, was kept up faithfully. Knowing John's deep interest in poetry he wrote about Emerson's verse and the philosophers he was studying. A good letter was composed, but he wondered what effect it might have on John. "Let it take its course. Flattery is almost always good when not too open. I have reasoned out my belief that he is a first rate poet and equal to Emerson. Well, he is to me."[42] William was not very wrong in his judgment and he was drawn toward Albee by a mutual love of high minds. It was John who had persuaded him that it takes a pure and good person to understand the ancients, especially Plato.[43]

Strong ties of friendship connected William with Charles W. Chapman. He was, perhaps, next to Charles Baldwin, his dearest friend — so at least he thought at first. In his letters Charlie addressed him in various ways, sometimes Guilelmo, Lehrer, and Wilhelm, in German script. When William saw him and his sweetheart, Etta,[44] last, they probably had planned to settle together in the West. Even now, both of them were thinking strongly of it.

Chapman will want to do something before many months, I mistrust. If I mistake not he is tired of waiting in New Haven for the wind and waters to come around favorably. His father has been pressed for money to buy a new piano with, I suppose. Perhaps, too, he does not want Charles to come out with such wicked persons as Moore and myself.[45]

William carefully weighed the advisability of his and S.T.B's living together with Chapman, alone or with Etta. There was "much to be feared" if they had a colony, "less privacy, and less inward growth too." William could be happy when within himself "and flow strongly and surely.[46]

When William made practical proposals in his letters to Chapman and his friend realized that not all was rosy in St. Louis, the erstwhile most intimate friend put a distance between them by his dignified writing. By 1861, vivacious, modern Etta was out of the picture, and Charlie wrote he could do without friends and would not love anyone again very much, but guardedly put a question mark to that sentence. In 1864 he married her.

Charles Clinton Baldwin he valued highly, being "as constant as the hills, a true friend indeed." They would correspond about such matters as immortality. Charlie moved from Cambridge. On a visit to the Harrises in Putnam, William's oldest sister, Sarah, caught his fancy, but he married William's cousin Ella Peckham.

A worth-while correspondence was carried on with his fiancée's brother, Edwin H. Bugbee, a well-educated and thoughtful person who had a real gift for expressing himself well on different subjects. He was a firm believer in spiritualism, yet thoroughly rational and no less sensitive to a true, inward recognition of God, which made him rebel against the formalism and the canonized superstitions of the Church. He loved Theodore Parker dearly for his frankness and range of mind.

Some plan had been discussed with Rev. H. B. Storer who had visited with William and returned East. And now, William anxiously awaited his letters. When the Utopia was not to be realized in the near future, William was some-what relieved. Were they thinking of giving lectures illustrated by slides, as the magic lantern mentioned in the letters seems to indicate?[47]

Letter writing, when in the mood, was as great a pleasure to William as was letter receiving. If they would burn his letters, let them, but keep the knowledge of it from William![48]

TOKENS OF AFFECTION

The effect which William's letters had on his folks at home was somewhat disheartening. When there was a likelihood that his uncle Stephen was coming out West, William was afraid that he, being of an excitable nature, would, on finding him so poor, tell his folks "such a story."

Continually he was thinking not only about repaying the small loan to his mother, but, in addition, doing "some good things" for his friends at home. His mother was always in his mind, along with his sweetheart when his pay-day came around, and whenever possible he sent at least $5.- from his meagre earnings. He knew that his mother "who has to work so hard is troubling herself" continually about money. Finances, indeed, were in a bad state at home. The unsuccessful attempts on the part of his father to establish himself anew in the West during these hard times had swallowed up all savings. Sometimes William thought it would be better if he were not another mouth to feed, but his folks had the deepest concern and affection for him and would have gladly had him back in their midst, all difficulties notwithstanding.

With the approach of summer the prospects darkened. For whoever was able to, left the hot city. The possibility of getting pupils for private tutoring became exceedingly slim. Anxious letters were exchanged, therefore, toward the end of March and the beginning of April. Father Harris gave sound advice to his son. He realized that, after all, William was not born and trained to be a farmer, and he pleaded with him to go into teaching. It was "the best business" he knew of. William reacted in this way: "I am inclined to agree with him. School-teachers make the most money in the East now and they are surest of getting what they make."[49] Though the temptation was very strong at times to emulate Moore and return East, William became firm in his decision to establish himself in St. Louis. On March 31st he wrote his father that he could not come home, even for the summer, as it would cost too much and that he would have to stay another year.

William showed himself not only in his correspondence but in the intimate notes of his diary as most affectionate to all his relatives. His attachment is most charmingly illustrated by his relation to his grandmother. Together with S.T.B. he felt the greatest concern for her health. When she was taken with a numbness in her limbs, S.T.B. rubbed her limbs and she became better. She tore up the note for 125 dollars William had given her, handing to Sarah only William's name as a keepsake.

> It was a kind act in her to remember me when her life was in such peril. My dear, dear Grandmother, when shall I find another such a friend! Never, I fear. Well, she is better, God be praised! I feel thankful that she is still on earth. Although I believe in immortality yet I want my friends with me in this life as long as possible.

> I dislike to have anything so sad come upon me. I am chaotic enough now without having any such thing happen. I shed tears as I read about my grandmother and thought of her. My grandmother will stay with us a long time yet, I hope. I want to soften her old age with my care for her. I have received all the good

things from her hand. All that I am, I owe to her agency.[50]

Great tenderness on the part of William was, moreover, apparent from his relationship to his brothers and sisters. He being the oldest they all looked up to him. His sister Sarah was a good correspondent. Together with her mother she was making clothes for him, for which he sent occasionally some money. She was almost nineteen and now was contemplating going to Mt. Holyoke. "She has not yet reached her bloom though, for she is not one who matures early, but one who will look better at 25 than at 20 or any time before it. She matures very slowly, I think that she will be quite a handsome woman." Anna was now 11 years of age. She was sure to become a scholar. "Anna was made with a love for knowledge. Acquirement is her end." Next was Jane, or Jennie; she would some day be a beauty. In March she had become 7 years old and in her brother's eyes she ever had a "nice womanly nature." Both, Anna and Jennie, were prettier than the rest, he supposed, because they were young. Ellen, the baby, or Nellie, as he called her, was not forgotten. Instead of a letter he sent her a pictorial paper.

Edward, then about 17, begged William to send him pieces "to speak." David, 14, was given a blank book by William to use it as a journal. The whole family was remembered at Christmas and with his presents he gave "universal satisfaction," as his mother wrote him. Charlie remembered his big brother often and William longed to see again the boy whom he had so enjoyed carrying about. When he was leaving for Yale, the little fellow had repeated over and over, ruefully: "William gone to Haven." Now, with his 4½ years he already printed letters for William, in fact, wrote once "quite a letter." So, William printed one in turn for him. There was a wonderful spirit of devotion and regard that was mutual in the whole Harris family.

That there were, however, occasional frictions is intimated in the reference to the two natures that William found in himself and which he sought to trace back to his father and mother.

My father, I recollect, used to talk to my mother all the time about having things go like clockwork. But I am thankful now, though not then, that my mother had a stronger instinct in her for freedom untrammelled than to submit to any such thing. She was extremely unsystematical though, and there was a fault on the other side.[51]

To his father[52] he acknowledged that he took after his mother more than him, though mother "would contest such a hypothesis."

The Dark-Haired, Dark-Eyed Maiden

Till the middle of January, 1858, Sarah T. Bugbee was in Providence, R. I., as she was wont to visit her married sister Mary Ann. Later she went to Putnam Heights (North Killingly) to which place her parents had removed a few years before, and where she was close to the Harris family. Fluctuating between hope and despondency about being united with William soon, she took to making shirts for him, and pants, and wrote letters, "pleasantly" when in "a very cheerful humorous strain," reproachfully and sulkily when she realized too keenly that he had not yet come back to her nor brought her out to St. Louis. But her stern "where there is a will, there is a way" failed to have the desired effect on William who wrote back equally sternly to make her think, hoping that she would not take everlasting offense at it.

William had to reject the thought of having her come out during the summer because he was faced with the difficulty of perhaps not earning a cent during these months. The diary rings out with the firm determination to "stick it out" in the West, though he knew how hard it would be on her to wait, possibly two years or longer, when first she could not wait from one vacation to the next, or at their parting thought their separation would be a matter of only a few months. He wrote her cheerful and re-assuring letters, while she took up Spanish, with his encouragement, and contemplated going to Mt. Holyoke, because she felt the need of company. William thought it an excellent idea and figured how he could pay for her tuition.

Whenever feasible, William sent money, from three to five gold dollars at a time in the hope that "it will be pleasing to her doubtless." It would have been to him, he reasoned. But did he think in earnest that she would give it to her mother to spend it on the household? He was vexed to think that she was buying "foolish things for the purpose of spending the money."[53]

Except for those little clouds that now and then appear in the heaven of lovers, William had a very tender love for her. His thought of her was of an even temper, almost philosophical, never of a passionate type. She was *his* Sarah (in distinction from his sister Sarah), his girl, his darling, his dear Sally, if she was not plain S. T. B. In his Puritan outlook he probably went as far as he dared to go by calling her in his intimate diary prematurely "my dear little wife," "darling wife," "dearly beloved wife," "dearest wife," and *Frau*. She was the "darling creature," the truest being he had read of in romance or history or had seen with his own eyes. He was thinking of her as a real companion. Pleasantries and frivolities apparently never entered his mind and his romantic urge spent itself when calling her a "bewitching creature." Love was a serious matter with him. His library contained these somewhat odd titles: *Nervous Diseases of Women, Lectures to Young Women, Parents' Guide* and *Teacher and Parent*.

Etta, in her letters to Sarah in which she sent a "huge

piece" of her love to William, had advised Sarah to be like
a bird, flitting from flower to flower and tree to tree to lure
her lover on if she would have him continue to love her.
But William, though accepting and returning the huge
piece, refused to be inveigled into loving his dear little
creature more by virtue of such tactics, were she to adopt
them. He might even have loved her less and Etta more,
but he prided himself on possessing free will and choosing
the higher motive.[54] Discussions of libertinism and free-
love were then greatly in vogue, fanned by Mrs. Julia
Branch's dynamic personality. Her speech in support of
free-love, given at Camp Rutland, Vt., on June 26th, 1858,
was quoted widely and reached even St. Louis where William heard of it.

When in the theatre, William thought of his dark-haired,
dark-eyed fiancée "way off alone longing" for him.

There were some rather beautiful women among the
witches in Macbeth. They had their long black hair
hanging down around their shoulders just as she did
one night I remember long ago. It adds wonderfully
to a black-haired maiden to let her hair be loose. But
not to a flaxen haired one I think. There is a certain
look of youth about it that one cannot help loving.[55]

Then there were Cleopatra, Miranda, Octavia, Desdemona, Imogen, Thaisa, Dionyza, and Mignon. They resembled Sarah in more points than one, especially innocent
and loyal Desdemona, not highly gifted in intellect, but most
richly so in affections.

SOME PERSONAL REFLECTIONS

William left us some very candid snapshots of his inmost
states which were often in a worse condition than his bodily
states. He described them as awful and horrid. When
not directly dominated by a "sad feeling of unrest," "a
mournful feeling" and downright blues, usually caused by

bad news, cares on his mind, ill-health, and occasionally by the weather, he had a sort of "half-way feeling."

By nature he deemed himself optimistic and given to cheerfulness. Dark fears of the future he tried to dispel as well as he could. "I am an optimist and have a desire to make everybody else the same for it is a blessed faith. There is nothing in the whole range of philosophy or religion that gives so much satisfaction as does the confidence in the infinite God, which is optimism."[56] The day before he wrote: "Oh dear. I do not know where this curious world will bear me to. I am going most nowhither. I am borne on the wings of the time-spirit, but have but little to say about what is to be done with me."

Fortunately, he prescribed his own medicine. When he lacked the power to work creatively and felt the need of greater vigor and combativeness, he took to reading classical literature. By this means he "regenerated" himself, "rejuvenated his mind." Then the period of despair and gloom was over and calm came over his soul. "I have learned what is to heal me when I am mentally sicklied o'er with the pale cast of thought. I am to read something that will combine all my sentiments as well as my mind,"[57] and he took to reading Shakespeare's *Pericles* after which he felt much better. Shakespeare, anyhow, did him "heaps of good."

But the conflict due to his introverted nature was not so easily settled. Gazing inwardly with more intent and retiring within himself would not do. The other method of getting himself to read something brave and then run out among men and *be* brave was better—if he would but follow it! That he required a little egotistic increment is seen from the fact that, when he was recognized in company or by important people, he became self-satisfied. Study progressed, not when the will was applied, but when inspiration was upon him. He knew full well that he was splitting himself, that he had too many things on his mind, and that it is better to concentrate one's energies and to digest during periods of respite from work; he was aware that thinking too much about what is not useful is not practicing mental hygiene. The adolescent feeling of unrest never left him. Let us follow him once to the library:

> I went up into the library to-day, but was not particularly benefited, for the "yearning of my bowels" to read everything I see that is good came upon me. No sooner does this take me than I immediately have anything that is in my stomach become sour. It shows what a morbid sympathy there is existing between my brain and stomach. I master myself in this way. There are, I say to myself, certain heights which I may wish to obtain. For instance the plane on which Carlyle thinks, the plane on which Goethe sees things. Now it is the end and aim of all study and reading to reach higher and higher planes, or, at least, it should be the aim of everybody. Now I can best attain that degree by reaching upwards to the geniuses and walking with them till they communicate to me some of their greatness, or attract out of myself my own world. That is, I may be furthered by them. A writer who but pleases the ear and does not make me think is not of value to me.[58]

Shall it be humble subordination to greater minds, or a journey to the very Olympus of genius? Thumbing the leaves of his shorthand journal, we come upon these passages which tell his story:

> There is a kind of grand harmony, a kind of calculus that will solve the problem before long. I wonder if I am to be the person who shall solve it? I laugh at the absurd idea of my solving anything of the kind. But soberly would it be a strange idea? I am born for something. I take that as a logical deduction from the fact

that I am born. Now I at least can solve it for my own soul's satisfaction, can I not? No soul can ask a question of itself which it cannot at some period of its existence solve. Now this must be true. (January 16th)

I feel more than ever my lack of genius, that is, the fact that no inspiration pours through me. I am no poet. Well! Shakespeare will do for me what can be done. He *shall*. (January 19th)

I find I oscillate a little. I have more of a disgust for natural science than is healthy. Yet I think that I will give my genius its own rein, being at the same time conscious of my latitude and longitude. . . I shall be up in the literary atmosphere where I cannot be frightened by people coming down upon me from above. No man shall think any deeper than I do if study can make me understand and comprehend the great thoughts of all thinkers. (January 22nd)

I am not sure that my course does not lie in the direction of the literary life. I have no power of expressing myself is one trouble. But habit will get me over that in some measure. (January 31st)

Be excellent in your sphere whatever it may be is the doctrine of Socrates. Now I suppose that is excellent. I will be a philosopher and no-one shall surpass me, say I. I wish to understand the deepest man. Well, I shall have to grow immensely before I can get upstairs. (February 21st)

I feel that I am on the eve of a change in my external circumstances. I do not know what makes me, but I cannot help it. I have noticed and suppose that such was the case on former occasions. When I have become immersed in any great book I have returned to my usual life a different man. (March 12th)

What do I wish to be able to read Goethe for? I read him that I may rise up to his standpoint and see things from the elevation on which he stands. Now if I can rise up by reading Kant it is best for me to read Kant. Read that which lies nearest to you in a figurative sense. The mind you can interpret easiest. You will progress if you study and that easily. You pass on from Parker to Carlyle to Emerson and Goethe and Plato. Shakespeare gradually becomes distinct. Now it is the influence of these upon yourself that you seek and not a mere selfish pleasure. If you can become like Goethe, or rather, think like him, your task is accomplished. I reach up and take hold of these great men and thereby draw myself upward. I wish to become strong by wrestling with those great geniuses. By and by I too shall become a great man, or, rather on a high standpoint. The culture of mind that can live on an elevated plane is what is requisite. He is great who lives out away on a plane which others rise to with difficulty. On the high elevated plane we still aspire for a higher. I shall not be satisfied with seeing things from Kant's standpoint in philosophy, but shall push on to a still more profound standpoint. What a world I have to learn. I know nothing as yet. But still I am inflated with a ridiculous notion that I have got profounder than most men into metaphysics. Absurd! (March 14th)

I lack ambition. It is the fault of my life. I wish to be brilliant and understand anything all at once and I have more than half a notion that I drink in philosophy and education when I am in the mood. (April 1st)

I do not suppose that people think my productions of much value. Well and good, perhaps they are not of much value. I mean to go on learning and raise myself up to a point where I shall *be* — *be* and not seem. (April 4th)

My inspiration is drawn from wide sources. Now what is there to hinder me from taking courage and going steadily on without swerving either to right or to left? Nothing. (April 7th)

I must get inspired in some way so as to drive my tasks before me. There is nothing like inspiration. When I feel positive and energetic, how little seem the tasks that loomed up in mountains before me on other occasions. Well, I have got tasks before me that would make some giants tremble, I know.

I no sooner commence a great course of things which would be heroic could I only finish them, than, lo, something, quite unexpected turns up and I am left, or rather the projected things are left, in the lurch. Well the only way is to have enthusiasm and diligence and a heap of things will be accomplished after a while and all that is truly worth being performed may be performed, I expect. (April 8th)

Perhaps I can be a seer in some measure. A theory of influx [?] is not so difficult to learn if there were only one that could teach us to prepare the conditions. There must be a way in which the influx can come in and there must be, it is true, also a certain grade of intellect before one can appreciate this way. Well, it is comfortable to believe that you are the one who can appreciate the knowledge and so I may as well. (April 9th)

Less than a week[59] before the last observation was recorded, an untoward event happened to William. He was fixing and washing the windows, and while looking up to see what was the matter with the upper sash, a piece of glass came down and hit the side of his cheek within an inch of his sound eye. Had it been struck, his eyesight would have been destroyed forever and he would have been blind:

> I felt thankful that I was preserved. If it had been so, I think that I should have never lived to cause my friends much trouble, for I would have destroyed my life by taking poison, or a cold bath in the Mississippi! Oh dear! It makes me feel bad to think of it. My dearest one would have mourned for me and then pined away and died, I suppose, and my father and mother and brothers would have sorrowed over me. My grandmother would have died soon. I know that my brother John made very sad hearts when he went before, but for the reason that I have been more in the family and am older, I should have made a much greater grief.

TRAINING FOR CAPACIOUS THOUGHTS

In order to understand fully how Hegel got into the Mississippi Valley, we must accompany William to the library and to his room and watch to what his *amor philosophiae* attached itself.

His systematic study of philosophy dated from his purchase of Victor Cousin's *History of Philosophy*, just before he left for the West, in July, 1857. At first he did not make any definite attempt to read methodically in order to supplement this history; but the attempts he did make in his commonplace book remained abortive. He confined himself to excerpts from the work of Cousin, as well as from George Henry Lewes' *Biographical History of Philosophy*,[60] and the histories by Schwegler and Morell. The title of Lewes' work he resented, for it sounded to him as if philosophy were defunct, and, he objected rightly to its dogmatism. The Greek philosophers were to be understood first, for the moderns only explain the ancients. But that was a difficult beginning. Plato "had not yet spoken" to him, nor Aristotle. This he tried to remedy by studying some of the dialogues, *Phaedo, Sophist,* and *Protagoras.* Emerson was his chief interpreter. The Socratic argument he did not comprehend as yet, but he hoped he would. Did not Emerson say that there are only a dozen men in a generation who read and understand Plato? He would be one of them; he would nestle with the Concord sage into a corner of Plato's brain!

William did not have a mind to sacrifice breadth of learning to system, and so he was lured on by the brilliance of the French eclectics and the challenge to his logical powers in Kant. At this stage he knew little of David Hume; but Locke's *Essay* had been read two years before. With Cousin as guide, the latter appeared in a somewhat different light. Gradually, Hume also emerged from being merely the author of a six volume history of England to being the author of the *Enquiry Concerning Human Understanding.* The Emersonian prejudice cleared away, and a better appreciation than even his Yale friend, Daniel Tertius Potter had, was gained, especially after the *Critique of Pure Reason* had been tackled. Kant's great work was studied "somewhat profoundly," together with Moore, on the first of January, 1858. Like thousands of other students of the Koenigsberger, he experienced the difficulties of style and depth of thought. Wisely he withheld forming an opinion. He expected that one day he would have it appear clear to him whether Kant is right or wrong. In the meantime, reading him developed "most acute powers of analysis and abstraction." In the morning of January 4th, he had finished the Transcendental Esthetics and anticipated "something harder than anything before attempted" by commencing the Transcendental Logic. Discouragement set in. He thought he would rest satisfied by absorbing Cousin's philosophy and just continue to study the history of philosophy.

But he returned to Kant to "acquire a talent" that would enable him "to read through deep works with acceptation and profit." "Suppose I struggle through with Kant's *Critique of Pure Reason,* then I shall be able to call myself a better philosopher than most people are who live in America."[61] Potter, Brinton, and Baldwin were now instructed by letter in the *Critique.* Things appeared by and by in the light of Kant's logic. The sensationalists and the French materialists were pitied. The weapon for defeating the non-spiritualists had been forged and, being in possession of a master technique of dialectics at the age of 22, they were defeated in the person of Mr. Hayden and the members of the St. Louis Literary and Philosophical Society. Could he not, perhaps, be appointed professor of philosophy to some college?[62] There was a great metaphysician in the city in the person of Dr. Holmes. Thanks to Kant, he would now match his intellectual powers with him, yes, even with the best of them.

In the early part of 1858, William had not made the firsthand acquaintance of Hegel, though he possessed his *History of Philosophy*[63] and his *Logic* in the three volume German edition.[64] In Fichte he appreciated the "wonderful clearness and subtleness" of the idealism which Kant left undeveloped. In Schelling he saw the teacher of Cousin; he was "the most correct," Hegel "the most profound." Though these opinions were gathered from the histories of philosophy, his insight was remarkable: "It seems to me very strange that a man of Hegel's depth should produce such a ridiculous system as Mr. Lewes represents him doing. Thereupon I conclude that it is not so. I must come to the conclusion that Hegel has been misunderstood."[65]

The French encyclopaedists impressed him less and less the more he studied Kant and Emerson and Theodore Parker. Their facts he considered barren, and the same applied to Comte. Maine de Biran he valued for his spiritu-

alistic outlook, and there was, of course, Victor Cousin,
of whose works he owned, besides the *History, The True,
the Beautiful and the Good; Elements of Psychology;* the
Lectures on Kant; and some other treatises on the Scotch and
Sensational Schools. A fat stenographic notebook was nearly
filled with copies of the lectures in the introduction to the
history of philosophy, comprising altogether 308 pages of
shorthand. Moore filled the rest of the book with transcriptions from *The Healing of the Nations.*

With the French eclectics he was soon done, with
Theodore Parker never. His speeches, sermons and addresses were read and re-read. William approved of his
siding with the slave, his having joined the thin ranks of
honest politicians, his heading a small group to study the
classical German literature which was still considered by
most people in America as having sprung from the devil
himself. He also was a theologian after William's heart, not
rabid, but informed and broad. He dwelled "upstairs,"
and William feared he might never equal him in all his
literary attempts.[66]

It pleased him that Carlyle spoke of Parker favorably,
though with courteous reserve. For, Carlyle was likewise
his man ever since he read *Hero-Worship.* However, he had
his ups and downs with the Scot. He complained at times
that he could never more than half understand him, that
he slipped from his comprehension. The *Characteristics*
contained truths deep and profound, though the thing
seemed to have been carried a little too far.[67] He was glad
Carlyle had a peculiar style, he could read him all day,
whether it was the *Sartor Resartus,* the *Life of John Sterling,*
the *Miscellanies,* the *Life and Speeches of Cromwell,* or his
Popular Delusions, or *Heroes.* In general, Carlyle influenced
him in many matters of literature, as in his destructive
criticism of Coleridge. But not for long, because as soon
as he studied the *Aids to Reflection* more thoroughly for

himself he had to confess that the English Plato had received less than his due from Carlyle, who dismissed him so contemptuously.

It was not merely for recreation that *Oliver Twist, Martin Chuzzlewit* and other novels were read. They yielded a wealth of information about human nature. They seemed to put a broader foundation under experience than the Kantian thing-in-itself. William loved and hated the characters; he ached to thrash Mr. Pecksniff, he was enamored with Tom Pinch's little sister, just as John Westlock had been. That Dickens had, some sixteen years before, visited the very city in which he now was, held considerable interest for him, since doubtless much of the scathing irony was based on observation in this raw frontier town.[68]

In April, William started Oliver Goldsmith's *Vicar of Wakefield,* in which the family reminded him very much of his own. "It was gloomy enough and it seems as though they were going to be always miserable, for such harmless people as they are never get along well . . ."[69]   He felt very, very gloomy, yet had to read it through before giving up. Walter Scott he liked and revelled in the wealth of his imagination.[70] Would that he could travel "among the hills and heather braes," to sun himself and "muse the live-long days."

There were projects in the journal to read Thackeray, Dryden, Cowper, Beaumont, Fletcher, Ben Jonson, Spenser, Chaucer, Farquhar, Smollett and a number of other musts. Milton's *Paradise Lost* he knew from reading it under the bench when studying in one of the academies, but now he tackled Philip James Bailey's *Festus* which he called wordy, cumbrous, and "too thick reading," especially when one's head was full of other things, above all Shakespeare. From this bard he would draw some of his genius, for he seemed to have enough of the beautiful and the cheerful to satisfy one's "most eager nature." Being such a comprehensive mind, he seemed to William still external to him. But with Emerson he was on more familiar terms and he held him in the highest esteem. In philosophic depth and literary polish he compared him with the greatest. Edgar Allan Poe was found somewhat lacking in the profundity of the idealist's standpoint, while Longfellow was not difficult to like because he shared his affections for Goethe, Richter and men of that type.

Shakespeare, however, met his rival in Goethe. It was Carlyle who had long stimulated William to read the *Altmeister*. With his background of Kant, William had no difficulty in comprehending an "Oversoul" or "Spiritual Laws." But now, *Faust,* in A. Hayward's translation, presented other problems to the understanding. He found the book in the Mercantile Library and brought it home, and before the evening was over, it was half read through, — not by himself, but by Moore. Such reading did not satisfy William. *Faust* was quite different from *Festus*. At first he called it a curious work. He could not comprehend why Faust wronged "the young female, named Margaret, who loved him passionately," though he himself loved her in turn. Her leaving open the bedroom door was certainly not proper. As a matter of fact, "there are many strange wild things in Faust. Many things said by the devil . . . are disgusting and vulgar."[71] The ending of the first part made him sad, but the finale of the second part, Faust's union with Margaret "in the land of the hereafter," was most pleasing to him. Something, however, had caught. He bought a copy with two out of five dollars he once earned, to delve again into this "wondrous poem." Of all books, *this* ought to be read in the original. He frankly acknowledged he had failed to understand it completely in his first reading. It dawned on him that it was not so much the narrative that made this classic significant, but the cosmic and broadly human sweep of conceptions. Now he had aspirations to become another Goethe.[72]

Other works of Goethe's were to follow, particularly *Wilhelm Meister*, which he carried with him to read at his pupil's house and wherever there was a wait of a few minutes. Letter-writing was postponed on many an occasion, because the story could not be interrupted. Even Kant took second place. He had to confess: " . . . This book is the truest book that has yet appeared in the world."[73] "The wise sayings and expressions that slip out on all subjects, particularly upon art, etc." enchanted him. Goethe was, indeed, after the idea of Emerson, most modern of moderns.[74] He was not aware until later, that *Wilhelm Meister* was the perfect book for frontier life.[75] The story of Mignon, apart from the Confessions of a Fair Saint, were by far the most fascinating to him at the time. "I know of nothing equal to this in sublimity and pathos. It touches a chord which vibrates in the inmost soul. I feel a different sensation from anything before."[76] After finishing the *Lehrjahre*, parts of *Faust* and *Wilhelm Meister*, "the most 'delicious book' of the age," were re-read. Overjoyed at having discovered one day a German bookstore, he acquired, though lean of purse, the following day for the price of $10 a six volume edition of the works of Goethe. This set finished off his bookshelf, with Schiller complete also. He knew Goethe's *Helena* and *Märchen* (*The Tale*) through Carlyle, but now he added to his reading the conversations with Eckermann, and planned on reading the rest of the works. He could find the time only for Goethe's lectures on art, which he considered "very fine." Other writings, he thought, he would peruse in time and "get through with them," but Schiller and Goethe, together with Shakespeare, Emerson, and Plato would have to be food to him "for a long time."[77]

Before immersing himself in Goethe, William had read Baskerville's *Poetry of Germany* and George Henry Lewes'

Life and Works of Goethe. The fact that he found the latter weak and addressing itself to a plain understanding had contributed to his studying the original. Friedrich Schlegel's *Lectures on the History of Literature*, though pretty good, he did not consider very brilliant and attractive; they were "too Roman Catholic" to suit him. August Wilhelm Schlegel's *Lectures on Dramatic Art* endeared themselves to him mainly because of his keen analysis and defence of the plot in Shakespeare's plays. When one day in the library, he was attracted by Johann Paul Friedrich Richter's *Levana*. Nothing remarkable was discovered on first reading, but since Carlyle had given an appreciative account, he returned to it later and found "some splendid things" in it. However, it became a cumbersome duty to finish the lengthy *Levana*. Little could he gauge at the time the influence Jean Paul would have on him beyond the fact that it made him curious to know Rousseau's *Emile*.

All this reading, formidable as it seems for a span of only four months, from January to April, 1858, did not by any means comprise the intellectual diet of young Harris. At Yale he was known to "affect" a knowledge of German. He had stopped half-way, as he said, and now he would go all the way. Accordingly, he studied, programmatically, Heinrich Gottfried Ollendorf's German text and key,[78] then the New Testament in German, and, finally, parts of Schiller's and Goethe's works. The daily lesson in Ollendorf sometimes comprised as much as 20 to 30 exercises. He would have to know German which lends itself so well to expressing metaphysical ideas, even if it took him two years "to read it off glibly." Once he had in mind studying languages for a week — he was also interested in French — and literature the next, thus by alternating to rest his mind. It did not work so well, for he was anxious not to let his Kant and Goethe and Shakespeare gather dust. The German "common newspaper" he was able to read very well. What was it then that hindered him from reading the literary German equally as well? English! Should he continue to live, he would read it even better than English.[79] By reading Racine and Corneille, he intended to learn not only French but acquire a wider knowledge of the drama. Thus, by mastering French, German, and English, he thought he would realize one of his life's ambitions and be "capacitated more and more to become an editor of some journal."[80]

To relieve the heavy diet of philosophy and literary criticism and the strain of learning German language lessons and French dramas while preparing papers for the press and lectures for the Sunday meetings of the Philosophical Society, writing letters and having a rather full-time tutoring job on hand — one must have *some* diversion! Then, why not study Spanish, and read *Don Quixote* in the original? That really proved a little too much for William. and he contented himself with reading Cervantes in English and filling in the serious study of Kant and the rest with some wholesome jokes. Snatching stories here and there, of course, did not finish the book. When will the everlasting *Don Quixote* be done? he asked himself. " . . . It will serve as dinner reading for a century."[81]

At the end of the first quarter of 1858, William had classified his 367 books according to an original, yet little perspicacious system.[82] It was creditable nonetheless, in that he had not merely taken it over from *The Theory of Human Progression.*

ACTIVITY IN THE FIRST LITERARY AND PHILOSOPHICAL SOCIETY

Almost as soon as William became acquainted with the members of the St. Louis Literary and Philosophical Society through Rev. H. B. Storer, he made a place for himself as Recording Secretary. While it was not an organization entirely to the mind and taste of an idealist, it yet gave him a chance to whet his wits in discussions and debates with those whom we might consider the intellectually alert in the city of St. Louis at the time. The full story of this society cannot be told here,[83] but it antedates the famous Harris-Brokmeyer combination which so greatly influenced the development of American philosophy for many years.

The membership of this organization was made up of physicians, lawyers, teachers, principals and others, representing a wide variety of opinions and convictions. There were liberal Christians, skeptics, infidels and atheists, phrenologists, spiritualists, "metaphysicians", and advocates of slavery as well as abolitionists. Occasionally, some uninvited "screwball" like Elija, the Tishbite, would throw the assemblage into a turmoil. They had regular Sunday afternoon meetings and often forgot the time over hot disputes in a congested room that was quickly drained of oxygen. Sometimes they would stay till after gas light. There was much cavilling, and once William called them a parcel of unbelievers. They all had more or less an interest in the natural sciences which William shared, of course, but which he came to regard as responsible for a materialistic outlook on life which most of the members professed. Still, he did not give up his own interest in the sciences. As a matter of fact, his imagination was greatly stimulated by natural phenomena, particularly those of a spectacular kind, and the scrapbooks abound with clippings about astronomy, Franklin's comet, arctic phenomena, solar eclipses, meteors and related topics. He wrote an article on "The Comet", the meteor that appeared at the end of August in the skies. This article was copied by some 200 exchanges all over the country and was praised highly, especially by the *Philadelphia Inquirer* which called it "a pleasing and really learned chronological notice from the columns."[84] It was the comet Donati which was confused by him and many contemporary writers with other comets, notably those of 1264 and 1556.[85] He also wrote a scathing and ironic review of George Brewster's *A New Theory of Matter*[86] to the tune of 600 lines in 6-point print, and in it he incorporated, probably by way of contrast, a notice of Alexander von Humboldt's *Cosmos, Entwurf einer physischen Weltbeschreibung.*[87] That Humboldt, then in his 89th year, had laid a deep foundation for his superstructure by studying Kant's critical writings, was to William sufficient evidence of the excellence of his work. The same "wonderful obtusity" which he criticised in Brewster, he found among the members of the Society.

The Bible often was the topic for discussion. but even the superficial observer could detect the undercurrent of resentment and heresy occasioned by the growing belief in the up and coming natural sciences. One of William's first lectures dealt with the Bible versus all other influences, which earned him the criticism of "benevolent shoddyism" of which he swore he would not be guilty again. He was too much under the influence of Theodore Parker to suit his friends who were unmoved by this paper. Once they asked him to "take the side of the infidels about the Bible", but William neatly sidestepped the issue. There were other topics, such as the Bible and civilization, immortality, the free agency of man, capital punishment, and Christianity and the printing press. The latter theme was particularly relished by William who wrote his discussion under the title of "Which has done the more for Civilization, Christianity or the Printing Press", under stress of inspiration.

At home, William was considered a free-thinker, if not an infidel, while at St. Louis among the members of the philosophical group he was looked upon almost as a protagonist of orthodox Christianity. In reality he had gotten off on the tangent of spiritualism, even while at Yale. His grandmother who had heard of his interest, had begged him not to let her or anyone else know that he was not a believer in the Bible. His mother also, who was ordinarily quite matter-of-fact but had come under the influence of a religious revival in Putnam, had begged him not to become an infidel and to continue in the Christian faith so he might die in peace. With Moore he had often visited spiritist meetings. They listened to a poet spiritualist preach and took down the words in shorthand. William bought *The Spiritual Age* and the *Banner of Light;* he read John B. Dods, *Immortality Triumphant, Spiritual Manifestations Examined and Explained,* and *Electrical Psychology;* Robert Hare's *Spiritualism Scientifically Demonstrated;* Joel Tiffany, *Spiritualism Explained;* Buchanan's *Journal of Man;* Fowler and Wells, *Life Illustrated;* and the *Spiritual Telegraph.* When someone borrowed a book on spiritualism by Charles Beecher, he was most anxious to have it back and even went to retrieve it. When Andrew Jackson Davis. a mutual friend of Andrew J. Graham, came with his wife Mary E. to St. Louis, William went regularly to their lectures and complimented them in no uncertain terms. He appreciated Mr. Davis' keen interest in and understanding of Emerson, his favorite for some time, while Mrs. Davis appealed to him because of her florid language and deep spirituality. Her lecture on "The Ministry of Angels" he called an exceedingly eloquent and beautiful production. Gradually, however, his disappointment over Mr. Davis grew, because he soon found out that he did not have that philosophic background which he himself could bring to bear on these issues. It was the sublimity of the sentiment in spiritualism that had caught his fancy in the beginning, and when he no longer saw it borne out by the somewhat haughty Davis who often lacked ideas as well as inspiration in his lectures and showed little knowledge of natural science even though excellent in the *a priori* faculty, William's enthusiasm became dampened. It must be admitted that he was caught up in a movement that swept the country in the fifties, a movement that was so powerful that in 1854 the U.S. Senate was unsuccessfully requested by 15,000 adherents of spiritualism to support a commission to investigate all occult phenomena. William's address on "Do Spirits Communicate", which also appeared in the *Spiritual Telegraph*, summarized his philosophic position in regard to the doctrine. He never returned to the subject with the enthusiasm he had shown at first, although he never lost interest in psychic phenomena. Despite the earnestness with which he viewed these things, he could derive some fun from the more sensational claims of downright spiritists such as "'Spirit-rapping made easy."

The Literary and Philosophical Society likewise showed signs of interest in phrenology into which William had delved by now rather deeply. They raised the question as to whether it is a science. William drew fire immediately, for he was not only familiar with Johann Kaspar Spurzheim's *Phrenology* and *The Natural Laws of Man;* Combe's *Lectures on Phrenology, System of Phrenology* and *Constitution of Man;* O. S. Fowler's *Illustrated Instructor in Phrenology,* his *Phrenology* and other writings on self-culture and improvement; but also Andrew Boardman's *Defence of Phrenology;* Joseph R. Buchanan's *Outlines of Anthropology as Discovered, Demonstrated and Taught in* 1841-42; and *The Phrenological Journal.* The debates on this subject were of particular interest to him and he wrote reports on them to his Yale chums.

In time, William developed a certain scorn and aloofness toward some of the members of the Society. They thought him rather orthodox in his beliefs and he was, in a sense, but he refused to go the whole length in condemning the ideas of the past and yielding to the impact of modern skepticism. He transformed the ideas of the past in the alembic of a metaphysical interpretation which, of course, was far above the heads of his average hearers. They told him so after his first talk. Still, he stuck to his guns. "I think that I must be more careful than ever of making a fool of myself. I

must be more secretive. Although as I am a growing fellow
I need not be scared about reputation among others. It
is altogether a morbid feeling that leads a man to think
much of the opinions of others."[88]

In Mr. S. D. Hayden,[89] William met his spiritual antithesis. He regarded him as "a specimen of what atheism
makes a man." He had absorbed all the superficiality of the
French authors. He would read to William, and William
read certain other things to him, trying to lift him out of
the mire of materialism. It was somewhat puzzling to William
that this atheist-materialist did recognize any sort of morality at all, that he would acknowledge even ideals in Diderot,
and impute virtuous traits to Voltaire. After those strictly
professional meetings in which Le Système de la Nature
of the German-French encyclopaedist Paul Heinrich Diet-
rich Baron von Holbach and Victor Cousin were debated
and read, which lasted often two hours or more, William
would fly back to his room and read his Kant or Goethe to
rid himself of the strain of converting the man from the
"blackness of atheism." Some weeks they met as often as four
times; finally they took to reading Kant. It was exceedingly
difficult to convince Hayden of the a priori origin of some
pure ideas or to have him acknowledge the infinitude of
space and time, but William had to admit, in the end, that
"his head cannot contain the philosophy of Kant as yet."[90]
However, the young philosopher owed more than he knew
at the time to this Hayden who died five years later, for it was
on him as a stubborn subject that he practiced his logic and
argumentation and thus groomed himself for the job ahead
as a master of debate and one of the greatest defenders of
idealism. He wrote a tribute to Hayden in which he praised
his sincerity. The atheist's last words had been, probably
to William himself: "I have lived for truth; I have no re-
cantation to make: I wished to make my mark on the world
in favor of justice, but I am dead now." He had ruffled

145

many a discussion and had carried his arguments for dethroning God and the devil forward with animosity. But his enlightened selfishness had ever stopped short of denying his frank cordiality the day after the argument. He resembled Heraclitus, William stated later, in that he despised mankind "for the most part."[91]

William's function as Recording Secretary of the Society was not carried out with too much conscience. He was late, he was absent; he mislaid his record, he forgot it. Once he even started in delivering a lecture on a certain topic when they stopped him and called his attention to the fact that the topic for the day was quite a different one . . .

RASCALLY PUPILS OF THE SMALL FRY AND OTHERS

On January 4th, William noted that his pupil, Henry O'Fallon, was "very glad to get back to his studies after the holidays." If he would keep after him for a year or so, Henry might be able to drive some skilful bargains for apples, William thought. Perhaps he might never "see into the hidden things of mathematics." Our young teacher felt discouraged and tried to make it up by strengthening his pupil's memory of history and dates. In this he did very well, indeed, and William made the fine observation that he could learn processes, but not principles. At all events, his and his mother's courage had to be sustained. Two weeks later, Mrs. O'Fallon, — it was the Colonel's second wife, the née Caroline Scheets (Schütz) of Maryland — made one of her periodic visits and William "displayed" what her son had learned. He did not do so well, though his writing was improving constantly. Now William decided to "get some of the show" into his pupil so that his pupil's friends and relatives would know he had earned his money. "It is not in me to make a good teacher," he wrote in his journal, for he became "wearied with long botheration over a small thing." He could not beat anything into the head of another.[92]

There was one other boy who was tutored by William, Warren Outen (or some such name), who was not so regular as Henry O'Fallon. He had been taking lessons from Moore whom William credited with being, perhaps, a better teacher than himself. Since about the beginning of 1858, William had taken him over. He was not so satisfactory a pupil and William intended to be more energetic with him.

If William could have kept both pupils during the summer, he would have earned a monthly $60. Even with a reduced schedule, he thought he might have gotten some $30 which would have been as much as he could have earned teaching school East. Whether he actually went to see Mrs. Outen and Mrs. O'Fallon, we do not know, but it seems unlikely, for pretty soon something else was to come up. He continued teaching Henry through June, having him practice arithmetic tables, addition, subtraction, multiplication and division to groom him as "a prodigy to astonish his mother with."[93]

It would have been an easy matter for William to teach shorthand and mathematics at a commercial school, as well as other subjects, such as English history in which subject he once coached a school-teacher successfully. He was aware that the abstractness of mathematics and metaphysics had contributed to making him more proficient also in other directions.

When he made the acquaintance of the retiring Superintendent of Public Schools, John Howard Tice, and the new one, Ira Divoll, and had passed his examination that earned him a recommendation to teach in the schools, he still had in the back of his mind offering his services as teacher of phonography and mathematics. Mr. Tice seemed very sympathetic, and his opinion, expressed in the *Annual*

Report of the Public Schools for 1854, was quoted by Harris & Moore in their leaflet to the effect that "an education that does not embrace a Knowledge of Phonography must be regarded as incomplete, and short of the wants of the age, and I would therefore recommend its early introduction in the Grammar and High Schools, as one of the regular branches of study." Harris had gone to both superintendents well prepared to show how in England shorthand had been introduced into the schools, or at Philadelphia, Penna., and Waltham, Mass., and what in particular were the great educational advantages. But the School Board could not be induced to share this point of view.

The teacher whom Harris had coached advised him at one time of the need of another teacher in the Public Schools and mentioned that Divoll had enquired for him but had not been able to find him. The prospect of teaching grade children, however, was not joyously received. The principal reason was that he would earn only $70 per month to be paid quarterly, while he stood in immediate need of cash. Nevertheless, if the opportunity presented itself, he held himself in honor bound to accept it from Mr. Divoll. However, it did not materialize even though the very next day a Mr. Reed (or whatever his name was) informed him of an actual vacancy in the schools.

Not only would teaching in the Public Schools have failed to increase his earning capacity sufficiently; it would also have rendered impossible, so he thought, having his fiancée come out West that year, which would have made the separation one of two years' duration. Again he reasoned that his teaching schedule would not allow him to keep up his phonographic writing, nor his reading literature. Thus, from more than one point of view, he did not feel eager to become "involved in a common school". His objections to becoming a teacher would not have been so strong if he could have kept the pupils he tutored. The possibility of doing something like this he envisaged, nevertheless, for the coming fall. His heart, at this time, was assuredly not in teaching Public School children.

It was a letter from his father that made him re-consider it as a means of livelihood. He himself would have preferred almost anything else if remunerative, be it business, farming, or merely tutoring. Had it not been the desire "to do better" that had "controlled" him in St. Louis? With the approach of summer, however, William stood ready to accept even a Public School job.

In the meantime, he had an experience with Washington University which was promising but turned out to be fruitless.

It was on a Saturday afternoon, March 13th, 1858, to be exact, when Mr. Spaulding, the tailor, who had made the acquaintance of William some time before because of their common interest in shorthand, brought a gentleman from Washington University to William's room. In all likelihood it was the Professor *emeritus* of Greek. The regular Professor of Greek, Sylvester Waterhouse,[94] had been taken ill with the mumps, and someone had to take his place during his absence. Superintendent Divoll had recommended William for the post and an appointment was made for the following Monday. William promised to call. He thought he could study Greek with enthusiasm if he were appointed professor in the greatest college this side of the Mississippi River.

One of the first thoughts William Harris, the scholar, had was, that teaching Greek would give him an opportunity to study Plato, Xenophon, Herodotus, Homer and Aeschylus in the original. In other words, teaching would benefit him more than the pupils. The taste for reading the tragedies of Aeschylus and Sophocles had been instilled in him by Goethe's *Wilhelm Meister*. But as yet he knew

149

neither them nor Euripides nor Demosthenes, and he had never read the *Odyssey* and *Iliad* all the way through. Dressed in his best, he interviewed[95] Mr. Tirrel, Mr. Luke and another gentleman who "chattered away in an agreeable strain." The students were in the 4th chapter of the 1st book of the *Anabasis*, and were studying the Greek lessons of Crosby. He was to go there from *drei viertel auf zwölf* to *drei Uhr*, and his pupil Henry he would have to put off till about 4 o'clock. He was to study by himself in the meantime. His earnings, he thought, might be at the rate of $100 per month.

On coming home he prepared himself prodigiously to have a good lesson the next day. One of the classes was of small boys. They bothered him considerably "in his spirit," for he hated to govern small boys: he would rather go in with Rev. Storer in whatever scheme he had than teach in the Public Schools! He was convinced he would make a poor teacher. "As for those little boys", he was "going to exercise some control over them if there is such a thing." He regretted he had no stick to manage them.

The second day went more smoothly. He puzzled them with questions about derivation so that they were quite astonished. The following day, however, he "passed through," as the journal states, laconically. He got along shabbily with the little boys and "felt mean in consequence." He would have to show more manliness of character to "those little wretches." "I am provoked to think that I can find nothing better than school-teaching. Perhaps I shall, if I try. A place in the Commercial Institute would be better. Even reporting would be better if I could get business."[96]

Even Henry, poor as he was, was a good sight after teaching the scholars at the University. However, during the rest of the week, teaching was done in as pleasant a manner as possible; still, at the beginning of the second week he had not discovered a way to teach his "rascally pupils of the small fry", and he probably never did, for before the second week was over, his term was finished. He was introduced to the teacher, Mr. Waterhouse, a short man, lame, with squint eye, a plodding, commonsense fellow. He thanked Harris for carrying out the same thoroughness that he wished to introduce among the Greek scholars.

He never said a word about paying me anything. I had laid out 14 dollars for a new coat to go up there with. I had put out my pupil somewhat to attend to them up there and they did not even offer to pay me. Well, I did not complain. I have renewed my acquaintance somewhat with the Greek authors and experienced somewhat the trouble it is to teach school. I think that I could survive it if I could only govern the scholars. If I could not, I should have to leave the school, that is certain.

I wish I had some other way to earn money than by teaching.[97]

That the professor "forgot" to pay William, "fits in so well with the Waterhouse legend" which Professor Winthrop Holt Chenery, Librarian of Washington University, recalls. "Waterhouse was famous for his closeness. Although he always posed as a very poor man, he died leaving the University an estate valued at more than $200,000. The property was invested in railroad securities which were not to be touched until their value had increased to a stipulated sum. Unfortunately their value has decreased and the University has had as little benefit from the money as Waterhouse himself."[98]

Thus, William once more had lived on false hopes but, as always, he took his defeat gracefully and, like a true idealist and optimist, searched for the small good that could possibly be eked out of the adverse condition. "It will not do to let anything discourage me," he jotted down the very day the disappointment came over him. "I must not grow dark, but look up in the world. There is no other way than to keep on learning all I can."

With renewed vigor he built castles in the air, "perhaps too high", as he acknowledged, "for they will tumble down on my head likely enough." He was ready now even to teach in the Public Schools for whatever money was to be had. Thursday, April 22nd, 1858, he wrote in his journal, at the top of the page:

"I commenced teaching in the public school this morning."

CHAPTER SEVEN

CAREER

William Torrey Harris was appointed to teach in Franklin Grammar School in the afternoon of Monday, April
19th, 1858, at a meeting of the Teachers' Committee.[1]
He had qualified for the position many months before,
in fact three weeks after his arrival at St. Louis, at which
time he had presented himself to the members of the School
Board. One of the dignified gentlemen later told President
Canfield of Yale his own impression of the young man with
his gold-bowed spectacles. He seemed thoughtful and very
scholarly, rather older and maturer than his years indicated. Quiet, almost to the point of bashfulness, he made
no show of his knowledge. The impression he made was
extremely favorable, because his ways and manners were
genuine.

The Franklin School consisted of three sections, the Primary No. 1, the Primary No. 2, and the Grammar Department. It was located on 17th and Christy Avenue, had been
built in 1857, and was the largest school in St. Louis with a
capacity of nearly a thousand pupils. The school children
in the primaries had an average age of 8 years, those in the
Grammar department 11.8 years. When Ira Divoll, who
had just been called that year to the Superintendentship,
had in his rounds come to Primary No. 2, on April 7th,
he found that another assistant was urgently needed in this
department which held over 180 pupils. He thought imme-

153

diately of Harris, and at the next meeting of the Teachers' Committee, with Messrs. Samuel H. Bailey, John A. Leavy and G. M. Fichtenkam present, he proposed his name. A certain Miss Virginia D. Rickman, who also was appointed that same day was installed in Franklin Primary No. 2 the following day. On the 21st, the Superintendent went again to the Franklin School to straighten out a difficulty between Mr. Charles F. Childs, who was the Principal there and a certain Master Bryan "whose father felt aggrieved towards Principal Childs for taking his name from the roll book on account of 5 days absence." The following paragraph in the *Daily Record* of Superintendent Divoll tallies with an earlier statement in William's 1858 diary to the effect that Mr. Divoll was looking for Harris but could not find him. It reads: "Found Mr. Harris, and requested him to go to Franklin School to-morrow morning."

Thursday, April 22nd, was a day "pleasant enough", noted Divoll, and in his book he made the further notation: "Mr. Harris took place 1st Assis't Fr. Gr. Sch." The unusually large letters in which this is written in at the end of the day's record might indicate the significance which Divoll attributed to his new acquisition. Evidently he thought much of Harris, which is proven by the rapid advancement he gave him, making him eventually his right hand man.

On May 21st, the annual Public School Picnic Holiday, 3000 children were guided by their teachers, doubtlessly including Harris, on their excursion to Jefferson Barracks. Ira Divoll described the scene of this May morn which started gloomily but turned out to be a pleasant, fair day:

As early as 7 o'clock the schools which were to go in the first trains at 7:30, began to assemble at the Plum St. Depot. At 10 minutes before 8 the cars, 17 in number, being filled to overflowing, moved off for Jefferson Barracks, with their precious freight. The deafening

154

shouts of the assembled thousands, and the enlivening strains of music rendered the occasion one of thrilling interest.

Examinations started as usual in the middle of June and lasted till the 1st of July. Divoll conducted them mainly himself, going from school to school with his committee. The teachers, and Harris as one of them, merely assisted.

The St. Louis Public School system had undergone some changes towards expansion and liberalization. It was not merely the building program that exhibited that trend, but a change in pedagogic attitude. To be sure, a certain stern-ness was still stolidly adhered to. All teachers had to be in their respective class-rooms 15 minutes before the time of opening school. If not present 5 minutes before, they ran the risk of being reproached for being tardy. There was to be no sectarianism in the schools and, according to one resolution, all those teachers who were most successful "in controlling their pupils without the use of corporeal pun-ishment (other qualifications being sufficient) shall be awarded by the Board a higher degree of appreciation, and receive preference over all others in promotions and ap-pointments."[2]

Principal Harris

The *Fifth Annual Report of the President, Superinten-dent and Secretary of the Board of St. Louis Public Schools,* published on the 23rd of August, 1859, lists Wm. T. Harris as Principal of Clay School. This is an earlier date than that of the meeting of the Board of Public Schools which convened Sept. 13, 1859, and at which the official recom-mendation was made to the Teachers' Committee, to have Harris transferred from Franklin Grammar department to the Principalship of Clay School. Under him he had five Assistants, Orilla Howard, the former Principal of the Old Clay School, Emeretta A. Waters, Sylvia Blake, Virginia A.

Clarke, Julia M. Musick, and Mr. C. H. Green, a music teacher, whose services were, however, claimed by other schools also. With the new set-up, the greater authority entrusted to the Principal, Harris' position was, in the words of Superintendent Ira Divoll, almost from the start equivalent to that of a local superintendent because the Clay School was considered a model institution in every way. Principal Harris occupied room No. 1.

The New Clay School was the latest addition to the family of two dozen public school buildings in the proud city. At the time of occupancy only the second and third stories were finished, while the first was still to be finished and furnished. Apparently, the $1000 needed were not forthcoming so readily as desired. When completed, the building was to seat 672 pupils, while the old Clay Primary held only a little more than a hundred, and was meant to accomodate the pupils not only of the old Clay, but the Fairmount Grammar, Fairmount Primary and Natural Bridge Schools.

The brick and quoined stone structure with its tin roof was located on Bellefontaine Road and Farrar Street, in North St. Louis.[3] The rooms were wainscoted, and a particular feature was that they were separated from each other by movable panel partitions, suspended on pilasters with double axle pulleys. This arrangement permitted fusing the two rooms to form an Assembly Hall. The total cost of the building was figured at $12,400. Ira Divoll had to concede that it could not be called ornamental, though it was a model building, "finely located, well ventilated and lighted, easily warmed, with large, airy, comfortable, pleasant rooms, a play ground 100 feet by 250 feet, and such pieces of gymnastic apparatus as are required for the healthful physical exercises and recreation of the pupils."[4]

The salaries of St. Louis School Principals ranged from $1100 to $1250 per annum; Harris' salary was fixed at $1100, at least for 1859-60. The highest paid female principals received only $750. From 1859 on, the policy of the Board was to have but one principal for a school instead of one for each floor, as was the custom in the Lancasterian system.

The finances of the School Board, as was somewhat loftily recorded, were in sound condition. Revenues exceeded expenditures, even though education in the city cost more than elsewhere. The increase in population was so rapid that it was nearly impossible to keep pace with the children of school age. Places of worship, dwelling houses and even bar-rooms had to serve temporarily for school purposes. The bar-room was found better adapted than the old type schoolhouse, and when transformed into a school it was far better supported than when it catered to the thirsty throats of the neighborhood.

The Public Schools took care only of two-fifths of the whole number of children that ought to have been in school. Private and parochial schools sheltered about one-half of the remainder, leaving three-tenths, or at least 8000 children without schooling, roaming the streets and presenting quite a danger to society. The pressure on the Public Schools was, therefore, great.[5]

It was a wise economy to build larger schools to consolidate organization and thus save in principals' salaries and overhead. To educate a pupil in the Old Clay, for instance, cost $17.82 during 1858, while the 1859 figure for the New Clay was put at $10 to $13. Even though a still lower cost could have been effected by adopting the policy, followed for instance in New York City, to build schools holding thousands of pupils, the St. Louis plan at that time was to make schools not larger than 700-800 capacity.

Efficiency and thoroughness in teaching ran parallel to these developments. According to the *Annual Reports* this was due to "a better classification of the pupils throughout the schools, a reduction of the number of studies to be pursued at any one time, and a greater and more general effort

157

to soften down the harsh features of school government." Samuel H. Bailey, the President of the Board, who wrote this, was indeed a progressive thinker, one who in his own phraseology had left the old stagecoach mode of doing things behind. His defence of the first St. Louis Normal School for teachers is almost classic in its vigor.

A most significant resolution of the Board gave the Principals permission "without interference on the part of any member of the board, or the Superintendent" to exercise a free hand in the government of his school, to use his own methods as long as they were not inconsistent with the general regulations of the schools. This, indeed, was fostering the initiative and enthusiastic co-operation, particularly of Harris who came to his job equipped with a working acquaintance with pedagogic theories grafted on a much broader general education than any of the other Principals could command.

Little need be added in regard to the duties which were incumbent on our Harris as Principal. Record keeping, supervision of Assistants, inspection of all school grounds and properties, dispensing of the school books to indigent pupils, giving account of the activities of his school to the Superintendent, such and similar routine work kept him busy, except Saturdays and from the middle of June till the last Monday in August, the 25th of December to the 1st of January, Thanksgiving and Fast days and a picnic in May. We should also mention a teacher's Festival on July 1st.

The total number of weeks school was kept was 44, a period of time divided into 4 terms of 11 weeks each, with two daily sessions of 3 hours each. If the weather was stormy, the pupils were not sent home for lunch but were kept in a double session from 9 to 2:30, whereas ordinarily the first session ended at 12, and the second began at 1 o'clock during the winter months, at 2 o'clock the rest of the year.

When examinations were held many visitors and friends

attended. The school managed to hold the interest of the community it served, witness also the annual spelling match in June. The members of the Board of Education were present at the examinations, as were "a large number of gentlemen disconnected with the schools" who acted as a special examining committee. Not all the schools held examinations on the same day, so as to allow persons interested or commissioned to make the rounds.

The popularity which the school enjoyed even in a metropolis such as St. Louis was due to the fact that the Educational Department of St. Louis was not a branch of city administration. It maintained its independent organization since its incorporation in 1833, with due Charter, By-Laws and Rules. The Board was a self-perpetuating body with full and absolute powers to hold and control lands and properties ceded or granted by the Department of State of Missouri, after the United States had relinquished all rights and titles in 1831. In actuality, provisions for financing education in the territory of Missouri through income from certain "town or village lots, outlots, common field lots, and commons," had already been made by Act of Congress on June 13th, 1812. Since then, the Commissioners of the General Land Office had made further assignments, till in 1865 the quota of one twentieth of the area of the city of St. Louis was reached. Real estate holdings exceeded in value two million dollars in 1860, but were somewhat less in the years of the rebellion. The small yield was due to the fact that much of it had been leased on 50 years' terms. John F. Darby[6] asserts that the grant of lands from which St. Louis Public Schools derived their income "did not originate in Congress, but emanated from and was started by Thomas F. Riddick, of St. Louis." On the basis of documents, Col. Riddick is credited with having conceived the idea and having carried it out. Since 1849 a School Tax was levied and collected in the City of St. Louis, amounting to one fifth of one percent in the 1860's.

The members of the Board were drawn two from each Ward and chosen by the Ward voters. They held office for three years, one third going out every year. In 1833 there were in existence three Wards in the city, yielding six Board members. In 1859 the number of Wards was ten, and consequently 20 members sat in deliberation. There were no local trustees or inspectors.

During the first years as Principal of Clay School, Harris had a book in which he kept a record of the weekly exercises, consisting of normally 10 questions in the fields of geography, history, mathematics, English, and civics.

The first entry was made under September 21st, the last under April 26th, probably 1859-60. Some of the examination questions were entered in handwritings not his own. Usually the number of papers was noted at the bottom of the page, together with the average marks attained by the pupils. The rest of the book was taken up by outlines of history, dates, places and persons, words to spell, the workings of the U. S. Government, an analysis of the French and Indian Wars, lists of Spanish and English discoveries, the early history of Virginia, Massachusetts, Connecticut and a few other States, and the colonial history of some European powers, and an outline of the causes of the American Revolution. On the last pages were registered pupils' grades and the whole book was pasted up and stuffed with printed Examination Questions of all grades of the St. Louis Schools, from 1859 to 1867.

That Harris was a popular teacher is evident from a little letter which six of his "affectionate pupils" sent him on December 23rd, 1859, along with a gift for Christmas, the nature of which we cannot ascertain.

The new Clay School combined at first the three lowest classifications according to the new grading system introduced in 1859, the Primary, the Intermediate and Grammar, but very soon the primary department lost in importance.

The method of grading in the New Clay School which served as a model for all other schools, called for classifying and distributing the pupils by fifties, depending on their advancement. The groups of 50 were then subdivided into two classes according to their attainments or standing. Hence you had a first and second class in each room; while the one was reciting, the other was preparing the lesson. They all used the same textbooks.

The lowest division was made up of newcomers, for the most part those who were just beginning. The ones in the highest divisions were under the immediate charge of the Principal. The lower classes were usually overcrowded, while the upper classes were decimated because of the withdrawal of the pupils when they reached an age when it became expedient for them to earn money. The Principal was entirely responsible for the deportment of the pupils during recess and intermissions, also while assembling and when leaving school.

The scale of marking used in those days was: *e* for excellent, *g* for good, *a* for average, *m* for moderate, *p* for poor. The same system applied to instruction as well as discipline, so that there were always two letters; for instance, *ap*, meaning average in instruction and poor in discipline.

The Clay School, situated in a district that had a rather transient and changeable population, had its vicissitudes during the early Civil War period, as can be judged from the *Reports* of Harris, as Principal, extant in copies from Nov. 11th, 1859, to June 14th, 1866. Harris started, as already mentioned, with 5 Assistants and a Music Teacher. In 1859-60 he had six Assistants, during 1860-61 only two, 1861-62 three to four, 1863-64 seven, 1864-66 nine to twelve.

The number of children in his school also fluctuated a

great deal, not only from year to year but from quarter to quarter. One sometimes wonders what became of the children during the Civil War, because there was a great drop in enrolment lasting a year or two when tuition was charged. Considering the number of seats available in the unfinished building when Harris moved in, he operated to capacity, which did not happen again till 1864 and subsequent years; in the period of 1861-2, the number went even below 200. His school did not receive the furniture for accomodating the number of pupils it was built for, till September, 1864, when there was a great pressure for admittance into the schools. Neither the *Quarterly* nor the *Annual Reports* convey a clearcut picture of the number of school children. Their attendance was highest in the last quarter of 1862, but fell as low as 85% in 1865.

This percentage in Harris' school was not very large, taking into account the entire school situation. Superintendent Divoll estimated for the year ending July 1st, 1859, that of 10,111 names registered in the Public Schools, 2000 were discharged, and re-admitted, once, twice or even three times. The Principals' reports accordingly were difficult to keep, but the worst feature was that the classes were tremendously hindered in their progress. In accordance, Divoll sought to inculcate a finer sense of duty on the part of the parents and spread the motto: "The place of business for children is in the school room." There were truant officers who scouted the city streets for truant and vagrant children during the hours school was held. Seemingly they did not pursue their office very conscientiously if from 8000 to 9000 children went without any schooling whatsoever. The State appropriated school money for all children between 5 and 20 years — but in the absence of reliable statistics, how could one ascertain their number correctly? Harris' own records of tardy children show a large number of offenders. When once the cases reached unusual proportions, he felt called upon to state in explanation that the district had been extended that year, i.e., 1864-65, beyond the old limits and that many more young children were attending.

Teachers also were marked for absences and tardiness. If they were tending the tables at the Fair, that fact was noted. So conscientious was our Principal that he put down the cases of his own tardiness into the Record that went to the Superintendent. It amounted to thirteen times in seven years, of which three cases totalled exactly 14 minutes. His absences counted up to three half-days for the same period of years, one half-day of which was taken because of the death of his friend C. F. Childs. Truly a remarkable record reflecting his sense of duty and sterling character. During the year of greatest retrenchment, neither he himself nor any of his Assistants were absent or tardy, a fine proof of the co-operation he received.

Superintendent Divoll took occasion to comment on the "deservedly acquired great popularity" of Clay School and the fact that it accomplished the high purposes of a public school "in a most satisfactory manner",[7] and referred personally to Harris several times. A most flattering report of the examinations in the Clay School appeared in the papers on June 23rd, 1860:

This school was opened not quite a year ago. We men of the world can hardly appreciate the labor of putting it in running order. Just think of taking from 300 to 500 children of all ages and sizes, from hovels and from palaces, from public streets and from private schools, and bringing the heterogeneous mass into a house where order, precision and promptness are indispensable! Labor, patient, constant and long continued, alone can bring any order out of such a chaos. We were astonished, therefore as well as pleased to see the Clay School so well regulated, and making such fair promises of future success.

Too much praise cannot be bestowed upon Mr. Harris, the Principal. We believe him equalled by few, and surpassed by none, of the young men of this city, or other cities, in high culture and extensive learning. He is a worker, too. He has the spirit of a working man; and we all know how quickly children catch the life and imitate the example of such a teacher.

At the beginning of each academic year it was the duty of the Principal to make out the program of teaching. Harris kept a record of his in the 1860 diary as follows: 9:15 Geography, both divisions; 10 History, first division; 11 Mental Arithmetic, second division; 11:30 Grammar; 1:40 Written Arithmetic; 2:15 Reading; 3 Reading; 3:25 Writing. The teachers would all meet on that day to discuss which textbooks to use, and they decided, it seems, by vote. From day to day the number of registrations would increase. The first day 230 scholars were present. Two weeks later they had increased to 306. Harris himself was teaching, probably the most advanced students.

Indigent children needed free books, and they were referred to Superintendent Divoll. There were changes in discipline to be made, and new ways to be tried. Now and then, Harris would pay a visit to his teachers' classes and go to other schools to keep himself apprised of different methods. When he related to his own Assistants that Mr. Wallace C. Willcox, who had charge of Washington School, tried to encourage his teachers by offering a book prize to the most successful one, moral effort, regularity of attendance, punctuality and other items being weighed, they were utterly amazed and, in his own words, he "never saw a more astonished and indignant set of people." He apparently had the devotion of his colleagues, and did not have to resort to incentives.

CAREER

While still an Assistant, for some reason or other, Harris was not often present in the beginning at the meetings of the Teachers' Voluntary Association, since 1859 called the St. Louis Teachers' (Monthly) Association which assembled at 10 o'clock in the morning at Benton School every second Saturday of the month.[8] Later, however, he was more regular and presented papers now and then. These meetings were carried on in strict discipline. Absence was equivalent to half a day's absence from school duties. The Association even had a tradition behind it when Harris became acquainted with it.[9] Efficiency and uniformity in methods throughout the school system were, in part, attributed to it by Superintendent Divoll. He was *ex officio* Secretary, and any member of the Board, if present, became the presiding officer.

The two hours of meeting were taken up with the "reading of essays by both ladies and gentlemen, an oration and criticisms, by persons previously appointed by the executive committee. When time allowed, a lecture was given, or an extempore discussion took place upon some practical question connected with education."[10] There was also singing.

For the *Sixth Annual Report* the Association voted to offer an account of their activities for publication. From it we infer why Harris appeared no oftener than he did on the program: Every teacher was to have a chance, and veterans were called on only to help out. Suggestions to the Board were also brought out in these meetings. They enabled many instructors to correct faulty teaching methods in that occasionally the whole gathering was used as a test class. There was also an *esprit de corps* well characterized by the Executive Committee in these words:

But we do not believe that work and study, that grammar and the multiplication table are the chief end of man . . . Who has wit? Humor, who? Whom did God baptize with mirthfulness? Bring him here. Let us have the lessons of his forceful art. Show us his side-shaking power. Brush away the cobwebs of our care. Let him illustrate one high and peculiar attribute of our nature, — for man is the only laughing animal.

These teachers were astonishingly progressive in asking for greater liberty in determining the subject-matter of their meetings. Could they not have a monthly summary of educational news? They wanted to be informed about what was going on in other schools inside and outside their own state. The Executive Committee was desirous of having also non-pedagogic matters discussed. Thus, a "Mr. H." was asked to read an essay on "Idealism".[11] It was, of course, our Harris who, in December, 1858, read his paper on "Practical Idealism."

The Saturday classes which Harris referred to in a diary kept during 1860 are, no doubt, identical with the meetings under discussion. The diary stated in different places that Haven's *Mental Philosophy* was studied. In connection with this, Harris once spoke about the principle of association in empirical psychology, which drew a rather interesting discussion from James A. Martling and another person, but must have been far above the heads of the audience. By 1866, Harris visited the Saturday classes quite regularly, and his presence became almost imperative as a directing spirit in the discussions of higher literature.

A close co-operation existed between the various educational agencies in the city and those outside. For example, Edward Wyman, President of the City University, would invite the members of the Board of Public Schools to attend an academic exhibition; Chancellor J. G. Hoyt, of Washington University, would be requested to make a speech; the Evening Schools linked the University with the Public Schools. Principals and Superintendents from other

cities visited the St. Louis system and a stimulating exchange
of views was always the result. Special conventions were
called, as the one in September, 1858, to consider the subject
of Agricultural Education. St. Louis was ever the focal
point of such gatherings.

There were also special meetings of the Board to which
the Principals were admitted. In this manner, valuable
contacts were made by Harris who, by now, had gotten over
his shyness. Chancellor Hoyt became an intimate friend of
his. It was still in the fifties when Harris was sent as delegate from the Missouri State Teachers' Association to the
Illinois State Teachers' Association meeting, thus enabling
him to extend his personal and professional acquaintances
beyond State lines and, perchance, reconnoiter the territory for a farm . . ?

THE CIVIL WAR AND EDUCATION IN ST. LOUIS

In August, 1860, when the Superintendent of Public
Schools in St. Louis, Ira Divoll, proudly reviewed his three
years in office, the spectre of the Civil War had not yet raised
its ugly head and there was reason to be optimistic. Every
statistical table showed an upward trend. An efficient management and supervision had saved thousands of dollars
in the vast construction program. Mr. Samuel Robbins,
Chairman of the Building Committee, had watched the
contractors with eagle eye. The comfort of the pupils had
been cared for in that 5000 new seats and desks had been
provided, unhealthy basement stories eliminated, and play-
grounds laid out. Actually, the number of pupils had increased from 4750 to 7233, that of the teachers from 110
to 168.

The Lancasterian system had largely been supplanted
by the Graded System. Greater leniency and milder punishment had been recommended and practiced. Records
were kept more uniformly, punctuality on the part of pupils

and teachers had improved, and tardiness and absenteeism greatly diminished. Recently introduced singing exercises and musical drills had contributed to the usefulness of the schools, socially and physically. The Public Schools were ranked superior to private schools in point of discipline and instruction, so that hundreds of the most wealthy and influential St. Louis citizens sent their children to be instructed with the sons and daughters of mechanics, laborers, and others. This was the greatest tribute that could be paid to any school system, and Clay School, situated in the Northern part of the Tenth Ward, with William Torrey Harris as Principal, was considered by the Superintendent's report the model school.

The St. Louis schools were, indeed, fortunate in having started their work of expansion and perfection before the great conflict. The financial depression hit them in 1861. The fiscal year was operated with a deficit of about $30,000, because the special school tax, called the mill tax, netted only $53,185 for the current year, compared to $83,070 the year before. In addition, rent of real estate had decreased proportionately, making for a delinquent rent roll of $10,000. To attempt to enforce a collection by forfeiture of the leases would have worked "a distress tantamount to confiscation", giving at the same time no immediate relief to the treasury. To make matters worse, a bill was passed enabling the State to appropriate the public school money for military purposes. Efforts were made to repeal the laws under which the bulk of the school money was derived, luckily unsuccessfully.

The pay-roll due the teachers on April 14th, 1861, was still unpaid in the middle of May, a total of $25,000. Harris wrote to his uncle on June 26th: "A considerable portion of my salary for last year is yet due and cannot be paid till September at least." The Board saw itself forced to dismiss nearly 200 teachers and with them more than 8000 children. It was near the end of the spring quarter, anyway, and examinations were held before closing so that the advancement of the pupils was not to suffer; re-examinations for those who failed were provided for. The Board pledged to re-open the schools in the fall, calling on the public to co-operate. Harris shared their optimism and wrote to his friend, Judge Jones, expressing confidence that he would have a "good living" after all.

During summer, a special Ways and Means Committee, charged with the investigation of finances, was busy and finally reported on August 13th, 1861, to the Board. The majority report was adopted recommending a 40-week scholastic term instead of the 44-week one in force till then; a 27% reduction in salaries; quarterly tuitions, payable in advance, in Normal and High School amounting to $7, in the others $1.50; no instruction for those unable to pay; all appointments to be *pro tempore;* schools to be kept open only when full; and a drastic reduction in the teaching staff. As a result, Harris retained his Principalship of Clay School at about $700, with three Assistants under him, Misses Orilla Howard, Julia M. Musick, and Emma Mumford.

When General Halleck asked the Missourians to renew their fealty to the National Government, the members of the Board of Public Schools in St. Louis came forward immediately to express their loyalty, as did all the teachers. The State Convention of Missouri then drew up a teachers' oath to prevent disloyalty and made it obligatory for all. In essence the teachers had to swear that they would support, protect, and defend the Constitution of the United States and the Constitution of the State of Missouri.

The Public Schools flew the Union flag, though not every building possessed one. Harris' school, the Clay building, was given one in 1863 (?) by Robert Barth, of Angelroth & Barth, whose two boys Harris was tutoring.[12] The educational interests of the city were not swayed in the least by economic or moral considerations of slaveholders. The city population was far removed from such problems, because their field of activity was inspired by the needs of a purely urban, commercial, and industrial environment. That the secession could not have been possible if the South had established a Public School system as liberal and free, was the generally accepted axiom. It became a great propaganda slogan later on. Also the influx of poor whites, fugitives from the South, gave a great boost to education. They were mostly illiterate. "Their ignorance," said Galusha Anderson, "was so dense that we are in no danger of exaggerating it."[13] Many of them sent their children to Public School.

But while the financial situation had been prudently and, under the circumstances perhaps successfully handled by the Board, it had been done at a price — education was no longer *free*. Hope was abandoned, at the moment, of ever making it free again. However, the lack of wisdom which dictated the drastic cuts in salary (some up to 50%) was acknowledged in the 1862 *Report*. Comparison with other cities showed that St. Louis had in almost every respect the lowest salary scale. When the salaries were voted in June, 1862, to be increased,[14] many valuable teachers had left, including Calvin S. Pennell,[15] Richard Edwards,[16] and Thomas Metcalf.[17]

Tuition was soon reduced from $1.50 to $1. More than a third of all pupils, however, had to be admitted without tuition, for no one wished to assume the responsibility of turning them loose in the streets to add to "the uneducated that swarm in our large cities and mingle in our riots and mobs."[18] The population of the city which at the outset of the War had regressed, was advancing right along, increasing for the entire duration of the War by 40,000. While rummaging through Harris' papers we came across

170

a bunch of Free Permits to the Public Schools, all signed by Ira Divoll and held together by a big black hair pin, doubtless Mrs. Harris'. The young Principal also kept the tuition receipts of his own school on which were usually marked the averages of scholars per teacher. Registration increased markedly between November, 1861, and June, 1863. When the doors of the schools were opened in September, 1862, there was a satisfactory attendance, contrary to all expectations. As a matter of fact, there was somewhat of a rush on each succeeding term, so much so that schools closed till then had to be re-opened. Four of the Evening Schools were re-opened in December, and High and Normal Schools enjoyed popularity.

In July, 1863, the English and German papers carried for days the announcement of the unanimous decision of the Board no longer to charge tuition, but to make the schools, except the High and Normal Schools, free again. During 1863-64, 12,349 pupils were registered, over four thousand more than in 1862-63, and nearly seven thousand more than in 1861-62. Even the peak year of 1860-61 was exceeded by nearly two hundred. Rooms were rented in the different parts of the city.

Practically everywhere in the State of Missouri the public and private schools had been destroyed or suspended. In the country which was "frequently overrun by marauding and guerrilla bands" and "occupied by armed forces now by one party, and now by the other,"[19] people could not turn their attention to education. St. Louis was fortunate in that the heavy clouds of war had merely cast their shadows. Even the temporary relapse could have been avoided if the Board had not become panicky. True, often drastic ways and means had to be found to keep the schools operating. Thus, benefit performances were given by the pupils, while the participation of the Public Schools in the Great Western Sanitary Fair in May, 1864, put $5711.87 into the treasury of the Board.

"At the beginning of the war", Ira Divoll wrote in his 1863-64 *Report*, "alienations of friendship took place between many who had long sustained the most intimate social relations toward one another. Children partook of the feelings of their parents, and the schools were affected by the *madness* of the age. For a while, the bitter animosities came near breaking out into open rebellion . . ." But these difficulties were soon overcome by the level-headedness of the teachers.

At the beginning of the War, the Board gave permission to Dr. R. W. Oliphant optionally to vaccinate schoolchildren against smallpox, because an epidemic was feared in the city, due to the presence, in large numbers, of soldiers who were in constant touch with nearby camps in which the disease took its toll all the while. Even though no purely military operations affected the schools, the horrors of war were brought home to both teachers and pupils, nevertheless. Harris, for instance, was among others who were called as witnesses in a riot in St. Louis, on the 4th of July, 1863. The order, dated July 8th and issued at Headquarters of the Post St. Louis, to appear the next day "to witness in regard to the riot at Hyde Park" reached him in the official yellow envelope on which he wrote the word "massacre" which suggested the seriousness of the "riot." The *Daily Records* of Ira Divoll disclosed something of the proximity at least to the class-room, of warlike operations. Thus, September 15th, 1864, Divoll jotted down:

Saw authorities about the execution of the two bushwhackers in the neighborhood of the Washington School, to ask that in case of more executions another place be selected. Wrote to Col. Sanderson Prov. Mar. Gen. on the subject.

On April 15th, 1865, he wrote:

Pay day for the Teachers.

Arrangements had been made by the Board to give a Festival to the Teachers this p.m. The same is indefinitely postponed in consequence of the terrible gloom cast upon the whole country by the murder of Abraham Lincoln, President of the United States. The anticipated day of rejoicing is turned into a day of deep mourning.

Five new schools in rented houses were opened during 1865, but the salaries were not raised, as there was still a large deficit. A new, partially unforeseen problem arose, that of educating 3000 Negro children in free schools, as directed by the State Legislature.[20] In spite of all efforts, two thousand white children had to be turned away for lack of accomodations. Divoll put it strongly in his 1865 Report: "*The people must build school houses or prisons.*" By 1866 the total enrollment in the schools was 14,556, over two thousand more than in the pre-war peak year, but pressure at the school doors mounted incessantly.

Superintendent Divoll still published the school reports over his signature, but ever since the year ending the Civil War, his contributions had become less, and the bulk of the reports also decreased. The fighting vigor which he had so eminently displayed was no longer in him. He was almost ready for his demise. He had created a framework in the *Reports* to show up the almost phenomenal progress of education in the metropolis of the West. Already another hand could be discerned in the arrangement of the details bearing on the progress of the schools in a more graphic manner, the hand of William Torrey Harris . . .

RECONSTRUCTION AND NEW ISSUES

The Civil War had come to an end, but something else replaced it in the beaten South which had given its last and had nothing left when surrendering at Appomattox. Economic and spiritual ruin had settled on it. The Whites were without objectives. Indolence and resignation became rampant, squalor and wretchedness robbed many of their moral fibre. When Superintendent Divoll went down to New Orleans in 1866, he found the people conquered, yet with rebel spirit. When he returned in 1869, he found them subjugated. So it was throughout the land below the Dixie line. Beneficent nature covered with green what the hand of Mars had withered. Yet, not so easily could the blotches be removed from people's hearts. The North could well revel in rising business curves. Business may have been a sign of economic recovery, but it was not an indication of health. To repair the damage to the South, to reinstate the other half of Americans, required more than selling; it required educators.

Once more St. Louis became a frontier. From her proceeded much to reconcile North and South, for she had been a mother to them both. The problems of the South demanded solution even within her borders before they became national problems. Reconstruction in St. Louis began before national reconstruction. Order was the element most needed. There was then no far-fetched connection between Harris' admiration of the German system of philosophy and the groping for a way out of the confusion.

How perfectly did Hegelian synthesis apply to this very city of St. Louis! Harris and his friend Childs revelled in visions of the future: "The East produces the elements of opposition: it is for the West to unite them in the deeper unity." Childs believed that the West needed a Horace Mann, and the South several of them. He wanted everyone to become a Francke of America. Millions of black men had to be adapted to the civilization as interpreted by the North, poor White trash had to be raised into self-esteem.

Harris appreciated all these problems and burning zeal

174

filled him. On January 1st, 1866, he wrote in his notebook that the national problem had entered upon a new stage: that of the riddle of the Sphinx, in application to the United States. With the achievement of freedom for the individual, new problems in connection with the intellect, described under the title of "The Piety of the Intellect", were awaiting solution. Above all, one needed understanding for the new tasks, and to understand one had to comprehend, to "take together", to see life whole. And in the Hegelian system the world in all its aspects was one such whole.

In that same year, Harris spoke and already expounded a doctrine of "unfolding" with respect to the child which had to attain the standpoint of the nation through civilization. He was not blind even then to the disadvantage of America as compared with the paternal and less corrupt and cheaper European Governments. He knew full well: the Old World drove men to goodness with the stick, the New World let the good grow, if grow it would. Anticipating great events he penned this:

Who knows what poetry and statesmanship and philosophy will one day get done in this Mississippi Valley?[21]

The grimace of war was banished, the work of reconstruction would be joy. And, as if freed from a spell, even Harris became romantic. In lyric mood he described the spring of 1866, with its throbbing and swelling and blowing in every bud of humble weed and stately tree. Still, the eternal dialectic pursued him even in this mood and showed him the ground littered with the fallen blossoms, scorched by summer's heat, and finally blanketed in white.

If as early as 1860[22] he had felt that the Public School system was a prime necessity and should be the best in the world, how much more did he feel it in 1866? If good government even then seemed to him to depend on realized

175

intelligence, how much more now? Six years of turmoil had not only strengthened him in the conviction with which he challenged his fellow-teachers, but also brought him nearer to a position from which he could more rigorously apply the type of education that seemed ideal to him because it held great promise, the education that is comprehensive, the education that has a meaning, a purpose and engenders the realization of the whole.

If we sink our importance into that of mere preceptors of Grammar, Arithmetic, and Geography we shall, although those departments are necessary in their way, most dangerously misapprehend our position.

We shall thus put in peril the cause entrusted to us and thus be responsible for rottenness in the State. It is the Public School Education that is the essential element and it should comprehend all grades and be the best in the world.

It is our business to appreciate the importance of our position and to act in full view of the same.

The place is now open for us and since we stand at the vestibule it is for us to enter, for who shall stand outside and bid us go in?

It is here that we distinguish between such teachers as Socrates who taught the universal, and the Gradgrind who taught simple facts.

One was a true Teacher and comprehended his calling, the other a charlatan and did not — The one assisted the birth of the Soul out of ignorance into intelligence, the other smothered the same with insignificant rubbish.[23]

Assistant Superintendent Harris

It seems that everyone in the schools of St. Louis knew already in April 1867, that Harris was to become Assistant to Superintendent Divoll whose continued ill health made a younger force indispensable to him. This letter which revealed the character of Harris as fully as the esteem of those who worked under him, proves by the date that the significant development in the organization of the Public School was iminent before it became officially known:

ST. LOUIS, Mo. *April 8th/67*

To the Assistants
of the Clay School
Ladies

I cannot do less than express my profound gratification upon receiving a mark of your esteem which is at once so elegant and so useful.

The agreeable memories that I bear away from the eight years' connection with the Clay School are due chiefly to the kind cooperation and sometimes I may say forbearance of my assistants.

I beg that you will accept my sincerest thanks for this most welcome present and allow me to express my heartfelt wishes for your future prosperity and happiness.

Very truly yours,

WM. T. HARRIS

The present was a writing desk[24] which they gave their Principal with a brief note dated March 26th, 1867. That the pupils likewise honored him with presents is proven by a note that reads in faulty spelling: "Mr. Harris, Beloved Teacher, Please accept the accompaning as a token of our esteem for you. Scholars of No. 1. — April 1/67." The present was, probably, a scrapbook.

The official appointment of Harris came on May 1st. In the beginning, he was designated Superintendent English Department to create a parallel position to that held by Francis Berg, Assistant Superintendent German Department. This fiction, however, was not long maintained as

everyone knew that Harris was the right-hand man of Divoll.
Harris was, thus, the first person in the St. Louis Public
School system to hold the office of Assistant Superintendent,
an office specially created by the Board. It had been made
necessary when, toward the end of March, 1867, Divoll.
on whom the ravages of time and the effects of yellow fever
began rapidly to tell, sailed with his wife down the River
to New Orleans for rest and recovery. It was March 13th
that he notified Harris in one of his usual formal, dry notes.

Dear Sir:

If possible I wish you would meet me at my office
this evening at 6½ o'ck, to help work up some of the
office business and other matters. I expect to leave the
city on Saturday or Monday, and you will have to run
the concern.

Very truly

IRA DIVOLL.

The hope of recovery proved illusional. The weather
in New Orleans was damp, rainy, and disagreeable, not
meant to cheer the spirit or stimulate health. He stayed
with a wealthy friend, G. Q. H. Fellows, whose residence,
"one of the finest of the many splendid ones", occupied
a whole square, and was executed "in the highest style of
taste." The season preceded that of St. Louis by a month.
The flowers were out and strawberries were on the table.
Mrs. Divoll was perfectly delighted over the change.

Divoll took it easy for a while. All he did was to send
up North a few professional observations and pamphlets
on the New Orleans School System. Harris was entirely
in charge at St. Louis. In practical, and only practical
matters,[25] Divoll and Harris were of one mind, both being
Yankee. Now and then this fellow-feeling could be seen
to crop out in the correspondence. For instance, April 2nd,
1867, Divoll wrote about a report he was preparing: "If

it is read at all I want you to read it, or someone who can read English so that it can be understood."

Harris had been well groomed for the position. He had often mediated between influential persons, such as Judge Carr, and Superintendent Divoll in the naming of members for Visiting Committees. Mr. Barlow, President of the School Board, had sent for him occasionally to discuss matters of some importance. Divoll, as early as 1862, had asked him to write the model examination questions for admission to the High School, and in 1864 had requested his co-operation in a new scheme of studies on the basis of seven grades instead of six, in order to prevent cramming and the withdrawal of discouraged pupils. He had visited with Divoll parents who had failed to send their children to school, to change their minds. By 1866, Divoll discussed with him the transfer of Principals. Outside the city, Harris had gained for himself a reputation also. It was his brother David who found out that William's name helped him in getting ahead with the School Board in Macon.

From Harris' own notations when he functioned as Assistant Superintendent we learn that his multifarious duties led him to look into the matter of discipline, corporeal punishment, punctuality and stealing. He had to investigate the condition of the school-yards, some of which were unpaved; the effects of the absence of play-grounds and of playing in the streets; the detrimental consequences of city noises on instruction. Notes had to be written to teachers, Principals, and to Divoll; resolutions had to be formulated for special meetings and lectures had to be given on discipline and the behavior in colored schools. The matter of native pronunciation demanded explanations and advice, the teachers' oath assumed large importance and required a stand in 1867. Journals required reading, the Catholic schools had to be watched, German teaching had to be supervised, and Washington University be kept in

179

touch with to examine new methods of teaching. The minutes of teachers' meetings had to be drawn up. He had to teach the upper-class pupils and inspect the schools the city over, periodically.

Divoll had left Harris with a number of administrative difficulties and given him a long list of items to attend to. Harris had long before instigated the mimeographing of such questions as were sent regularly to all Principals and bearing on the condition and management of their schools. They covered such matters as seats, blackboards, a checkup on Assistants, records, class visits, cellar and outhouse inspection, the work of janitors, and many more. Serious problems soon arose that were really lying outside the routine work of the Assistant Superintendent. For instance, a Mr. Smythe had introduced a bill into the Legislature proposing to vest the appointment of St. Louis Public School teachers in the hands of local ward committees. Ostensibly this was done with a view to political control, a thing which the schools had to a large extent been free of. Promptly, Harris wrote to Judge J. G. Woerner[26] and persuaded him to block the bill.

Divoll had been a stern Superintendent who wished to hire only the best teachers and Principals. His influence with the Teachers' Committee had been large, and even while Harris had taken over he wrote a vigorous memorandum to the Acting Chairman[27] in which he bared his expectancy of Principals in general. They were to be made entirely responsible for the conditions of their schools, "and I do not hesitate to tell them so", was his after-thought. He expected them to do two or three times as much work as their Assistants, "they are paid for it." It may thus be seen that he dealt brusquely with his personnel. Harris, on the contrary treated them in a more personal, friendly manner.

Gradually Harris became introduced to problems of

finance and the like. To mention only one in passing, in August, 1868, the Polytechnic Institute Building was to be sold to the School Board at the very tempting figure of $260,000 with a $100,000 bequest, the O'Fallon library, furniture and fixtures all thrown in, provided the polytechnic department were kept up. Divoll counselled Harris strongly to persuade the Board to accede to the offer, though the buildings were ill constructed and hinges might have attached to the use of the bequest.

With the erection of new schools, the duty of planning the dedication exercises devolved on Harris' shoulders, and Divoll, writing from St. Joseph, reminded him of it.

During his first half year of Assistant Superintendentship, Harris commenced, at his superior's suggestion, a general examination of the conditions of the schools "with respect to the mode and proficiency of teaching reading." St. Louis had to cope with a situation peculiar to herself in that the great mingling of nations there produced many defects of speech, and foreign idioms and provincialisms were constantly introduced and rapidly acquired by the pupils. It was thus a continual fight to preserve the American language. Harris made a thorough study of the subject by personally visiting all schools and making recommendations. One in particular may seem odd in that he advocated having a pupil suffering from a weak and inaudible voice read the lesson backward.

The widespread "modern" tendency of that time to use, in the reading texts, material which the pupils could understand thoroughly, analyze fully, and which was simple, straightforward throughout just like the lessons of science, he opposed vigorously on the ground that without elevation of style, without aspiration or knowledge of "the sacred treasures embalmed in literature," the child's education had to remain deficient. "Such instruction is, as Goethe says, 'like baked bread savory and satisfying for a single day, but flour cannot be sown, and seed corn ought not to be ground'."

English grammar was to be taught with due regard to English genius, rather than by taking some classic "dead language" as model. Mathematical reasoning he considered of too

abstract and mechanical a nature to be of much service as a mental discipline when we compare it with grammatical analysis. The pupil who can analyze and perceive the relations of thought expressed in a sentence, has far more practical acuteness of mind than the one who can solve an intricate problem in arithmetic. To decide points of law, statesmanship, morality and other essential interests, we must have *qualitative* culture. The comparison of quantities involves merely the perception of equality *or* inequality, while qualitative reasoning involves both in one, and thus cultivates *comprehensiveness* in the pupil.

With history teaching in particular he was dissatisfied, looking forward to that historian who can write history in the spirit of our future nationality. "As yet we have not even a dream" of what history thus written "may be." As to geography, Harris pleaded that it be written and taught in the interest of *civilization*. What significance a region has for *man* is the important thing. There should be more object teaching. Show the pupil the mound[28] in the neighborhood and thus make him understand a mountain.

After touching on many other phases of the curriculum, Harris lastly turned to the subject of textbooks for which he was so grossly misunderstood in some quarters. The American idea of education he saw based on this principle: not what the teacher does for the pupil, but what he gets the pupil to do for himself, is of value. The texbook he thus regarded superior to oral instruction in attaining this end, because he looked upon it as not only containing the carefully digested results of research freed from the idiosyncracies of the author (?!), but as a thing to which the pupil may return again and again. Reading intelligently books on different subjects rather than giving exhaustive information was to him the American way. This led him, finally, in his reports, to making some statements about the value of the Public School Library.

Harris had worked vigorously on the *13th Annual Report* which yet appeared over Divoll's signature. It was highly praised in many quarters and none of the reviewers failed to make complimentary remarks on those sections of a philosophical-pedagogical nature for which Harris was entirely responsible.

The *14th Annual Report* for the year ending August 1st, 1868, was the first for which Harris assumed entire responsibility. Although covering the year of his Assistantship, it was published in 1869, the year after the close of the academic year to which it referred, and in which he became Superintendent. The practice of dating the *Annual Reports* one year later was established by this precedence.

CHAPTER EIGHT

LIFE DURING THE CIVIL WAR

THE PURSUIT OF HAPPINESS

IN portraying Harris, the educator, we have neglected Harris, the man, and it is time to pick up the thread once more.

As soon as his teaching position in the Public Schools was assured, William went East at the first opportunity. During Christmas recess, 1858, he took the train to New England, and on December 27th he married Sarah Tully Bugbee, the dark-haired, dark-eyed maiden at Providence, R. I., and took her back with him to St. Louis.

We know nothing about the honeymoon. Was it romantic? To be sure William used to write verses when he was at Yale. His mother praised him at the time for his talent, so did his father, and Grandmother Torrey called his poems very flowery. Let us sample them, for we may never catch William in the same mood[1] again.

Summer Evening Musings

'Tis even now, the day of toil is o'er,
And silver moonbeams fair illume the sky.
The air is calm, and stiller than before,
The streets, deserted, tell the time is nigh
Of needful slumber, to restore the power
In labor spent through many a tedious hour . . .

Slow tolls the clock, its echo dies away,
A mournful sound, as when a solemn chime,

184

Of mortal man proclaims the funeral day.
Sad requiem! It wails departed time:
The joyous hours of youthful sunshine fled;
Those golden dreams so soon forever sped . . .

Now music soft and sweet the charmed air fills.
'Tis as the fairy notes of mermaid's lyre,
And now mingled murmurs of the rills
With warbling birds and zephyrs that inspire
The forest trees, low sighing, measure time
To keep among their leafy tops sublime . . .

And now borne on the gentle breeze it swells,
And seems a plaintive dirge played o'er the sea
By naiads fair upon their stringed shells,
A dirge for ocean's dead now sleeping free
From all life's troubles, care and pain . . .
Thus slumber they who rest beneath the main . . .

The strain, first soft and sweet and then awhile
Like music of the woods, soon changed to slow
And solemn measures such as oft beguile
The aching heart o'ercome with grief and woe . . .
Now bolder sound the notes, the air they fill,
Now thinner grow, and now 'tis hushed and still . . .

The insects blithe are singing in the trees,
The cricket chirrups, the katy-did we note
In turn responsive silence break and please
The listening ear. While from the city float
The softened hum of voices blending sweet
The sound of wheels rough rolling o'er the street . . .

How often boisterous glee dissembled vain
Betrays an empty heart devoid of joy . . .
The mind consumed within by secret pain
Avoids itself. For memories drear annoy

185

Its musings, thronging from a bitter source
And effects of conscience follow in their course . . .

Thus revel they who in convivial song,
And jest and story pass the night away . . .
Their din incessant often they prolong
Till midnight darkness passes off and day
Steals on them unawares and bids them cease,
Their drunken riot leave, and keep the peace . . .

Harsh on the air amid the silence
The shrill unnatural tone of railway steed . . .
As o'er the track it rolls and earthquake seems
Along our vales in fiery haste to speed . . .
Thus flies the train propelled o'er land by steam,
Reflection's train aroused takes up the theme . . .

Of progress well may steam the emblem be;
For art was long in shackles bound, but when
The age of steam brought power, then art was free
And onward progress made. 'Twas blest of men.
For upward as its rays from earth ascend
The star of science human weal shall blend . . .

But hark! Once more the clock proclaims the hour,
And midnight reigns. But Luna still is queen.
Now sleep holds young and old within its power
And naught but stillness here may intervene,
Till morning gray comes from the East and fills
The world with smiling vales and sunny hills . . .

'Tis time to close this weary waste of words;
And barren desert where no cooling fount
Beneath green shades melodious with wild birds
Invite the way-worn stranger to dismount.
Meanwhile may moonshine mesmerize my muse,
So soothing silence shall soft sleep suffuse . . .

In St. Louis, the newlyweds settled down to domestic life at rooms on the corner of Orange and 18th Streets, later at 187 Christy Avenue. They were a bit pinched, for William sent for the tablecloth which he had used at Yale and which was now "on Grandmother's round table in her chamber." The advent of little Theodore, "without any trouble", on the 12th of September, 1859, and William's promotion to the Principalship of Clay School occasioned their moving to the corner of Salisbury and Ninth Streets where they stayed till late in 1863. They then moved up a block on Salisbury, to the corner of 10th Street. After that, they changed apartments frequently, in conformity to the custom of the times, at least once every two years, to be in style.

Domestic life was one of normal happiness. William had sought and found a spiritual companion in Sarah who would share his adventures into the realm of literature and even philosophy. They read together and worked over their scrapbooks, — until the burden of a household and the care of children divided their interests, though not their affections. Late in 1863, in the midst of the Civil War, William complained of his spiritual loneliness. "I miss very much some person whose society I can seek to stimulate to an atmosphere of higher elements", he wrote to General Hitchcock. That, after all, was the price he had to pay for a life devoted to the pursuit of the deepest thoughts of mankind. But as the clouds of war dissipated, so cleared away his loneliness and he soon found himself once again at the centre of a company of like-minded persons, such as he had enjoyed in those who had studied together with him and Brokmeyer the Hegelian philosophy.

School took up a considerable portion of the day. Phonography was taught now and then to a pupil or an interested class of six or eight. There was some tutoring to be done. Yet, study and reading remained William's cherished occupation. He sat up till two o'clock in the morning, reading and drinking coffee. All his books that were still back East, had been sent to him by now. He not only patronized L. Bushnell's bookstore in town, but sent off to Philadelphia, New York and even Germany for books. Luck favored him, for he was able to amass a large library before the drastic reduction in salary during the war. He liked his books bound. One day the binder sent up forty. Then again he found that a new bookcase could not hold two hundred new volumes. Thus he decided to wait till he had two hundred more and then got another bookcase. One Sunday morning in September, 1860, he spent in the Mercantile Library, looking through the catalogue, checking his books and adding up their value. The total amounted to $851.60.

While thus a good deal of his money went into books, the cost of living rose steadily. He reproached himself that he was living extravagantly, spending $75 in a single month, not counting the $40 for board, nor his expenses for books.[2] Sometimes he had to borrow. But the price of the higher life was worth all of it to him. Before he was married, he had written to his brother Edward[3], who wanted to go into business at their father's advice, but later came out to St. Louis to enter Normal School: *"Culture,* at your age is worth more than all else. An ounce of that article now will bring a pound of valuables by and by. It always pays good interest, you may depend upon that."

As if possessed by the philologic demon, William studied language after language. He tackled Sanskrit with the help of Oppert's Grammar; he bought a Hebrew Lexicon, coached two professors from Washington University in Greek, studied Danish, read Dante's *Cantos* in Italian with C. F. Childs. One Sunday he re-read Matthew in Spanish, Mark in Portuguese, Luke in Italian, John in old Greek, *Acts* in Modern Greek and part of Romans in Dutch. Spanish and Italian he thought he could manage without first studying grammar. The *New Testament* was represented in his library by editions in Chinese, Hawaiian, Russian and Irish, the Bible, in addition to some of the languages mentioned, also in Welsh, Gaelic, and Swedish. Comparative philology was studied in the works of Bopp, Dwight, and DeVere. He pored over Grimm's work on the origin of language. All this not without receiving public recognition, for he made good use of his knowledge in his articles on Phonetics and Philology. The last mentioned even got him a very flattering letter from a "distinguished German philologist in the East" who called it a "remarkable article."[4]

Often he applied his mechanical talents at home, be it in making a stool to reach the top-shelf of his bookcase, or constructing a telescope. He wrote his friend, Judge H. M. Jones, about the latter, describing it as magnifying from 18 to 120 diameters. The rings of Saturn were plainly visible by it and it had power enough to separate the double star of Ursa Major. Had he bought it ready-made, it would have cost him $75, but the parts were only $15. While thinking out a problem or preparing an address or article, he would do some "tinkering." Making a new bookshelf or some special contrivance for rendering work among his books and papers more convenient, was always a preliminary to some big mental task.

This interest in practical appliances and inventions, a true Connecticut trait, was of advantage especially later when, as Superintendent, he was able to check and order the tools and machinery needed in the schools. He kept every circular which the manufacturers sent, circulars advertising heating units, steam engines and pumps, "Flour Bolts", filters, wall paper, paints, spinners, sewing machines, ventilators, hydrants, wire fencing, well augers, weather strips, patented inkstands and pantographs. He admired every gadget that meant convenience and saving of time; adjustable bed tables, granite iron ware, Holcomb's "Acoustic Speaking Telephone", which came out in 1878 and worked efficiently for lines of one mile or less, without magnetic or electric current. He possessed one of the first typewriters. Lenses of all kinds were his weakness, whether in telescopes, "spy-glasses" or microscopes. His grandmother had been given a thermometer by him; now he wanted it back if she did not use it. Being fond of shooting, he studied in detail the various types of rifles, particularly the Peabody Breech-Loader. On his desk he fixed a revolving mechanism for his *Webster;* a slight touch would swing the heavy volume in position or send it away.

The 1860 diary tells little about the intimacies of family life, but the Fair in September is mentioned. Almost daily it was attended by William, Sarah, and their little "gift of God". School had been dismissed as always on such occasions, this time already on the last Wednesday of the month, and on the following day, Albert Edward, then Prince of Wales, arrived for a visit. About eighty thousand people were present. On Saturday, the famous trotting horse, Ethan Allen won the $1500 prize. The family watched it drinking from a silver bucket. No doubt there were occasional trips to the big mounds on the opposite side of the Mississippi.

With the approach of 1861, the most distressing circumstances of the political, military and financial conditions made themselves felt. Much of the 1860-61 salary remained unpaid as late as June. The outlook was gloomy. William's father was still prospecting for a farm, not in Illinois any longer, but in Nevada. The whole idea of a family farm had not been allowed to lay dormant even during 1860 when there were some preliminary dealings with the land agent in the Jackson district. Judge H. M. Jones wrote William in July from Phoenixville, Penna., that he was going by steamer to California and thence to Nevada, where he expected William eventually. From the tone of the letter it may be inferred that William was thinking some of removing with his whole family to that far Western country which had just been separated from Utah and had not attained Statehood as yet.

The prospect of crops in 1861 was unusually good but no-one had foreseen that most of the wheat would never be threshed, nor most of the corn gathered. By June, the St. Louis Harrises deemed themselves safe from the danger of war, living as it were "in an orchard with plenty of fruit." Everything was cheap, new potatoes selling at 25 cents per bushel; land became the cheaper the greater the number of war-scared people who left the city. Property was selling at almost a fourth of its assessed value. Lots, ordinarily fetching $2500, could be bought for $500. But money was very hard to get.

While William and Sarah kept in good spirits and borrowed money, the folks at home worried about them. The fratricidal war was assuming larger proportions by the week. Hence, they had Dr. Fenner H. Peckham, William's uncle, write a letter urging him to return East with his family.[5] To this William replied with a long letter[6] in which he made clear his and his wife's determination to stay in St. Louis. They would have come East to visit, had not the State put them in financial embarrassment by confiscating the School Board's money. The exodus from the city and the cheapness of property made William bold to anticipate for fall "a great revival of business."

Now it is an important principle for a young man to adopt, not to change places frequently nor capriciously. Let him go far enough away from home to secure fair-play, for you know that it is rarely to be had in one's own native hamlet, and work to build up his character and work out a reasonable deed. The friends at home should not judge too harshly if there is an apparent apathy or even neglect on his part. For the doing of anything of consequence requires intensity . . .

During July and August, William, Sarah and Theodore took a three weeks' trip "into the interior of Missouri," more for a change in scenery and to accomplish some work on Hegel, than for rest and recreation. William wrote to his grandmother:[7]

. . . My wife and child accompanied me and we enjoyed the country as well as city people usually do, who go out into the woods in the heat of the summer and put up in one end of a log cabin with gnats and mosquitoes and ticks and grandpa-longlegs as thick as can be imagined.

One may see through the roof in numerous directions, and when it rains (as it did one night) hard, there is quite a smart shower in one's face when he lies in bed asleep. There is a difficulty, too about getting any thing to eat that in the city would be thought palatable; bacon and corn bread are not good except for woodchoppers.

We were all glad to get back to our nice home in the city where we had things at least convenient, if not extravagant.

Great changes have gone on since Frémont came here. There is nothing but military movement and bustle. Thirty or forty thousand men will be encamped here within a week. The barracks which are 700 feet long and ten rows of them are a sight to see. Everybody feels downhearted at the death of the brave Gen'l Lyon who was a Connecticut man.

We shall have considerable war in this state to drive out the rebels, as they have got such strong hold again. St. Louis is under martial law now. I hope the East will keep their shoulders to the wheel as they have begun for this land will never again be a fit place to live in, if the North does not come out first in the contest. We shall be no nation but a mere dependency that will be spit upon here and elsewhere. School matters have finally taken shape for next year . . . I have my old place and can live off of my salary and thus get along till better times. Everything is much cheaper here now. Meanwhile I shall keep up an unwearied industry which will make every term as good to me as a year in college, as it has done ever since I came out. I believe that is the best assurance I can give you of myself: that I never waste any time. This I can say with considerable pride . . .

I should like to have you see our little boy Theodore who has now got to talking some. He is very strong and vigorous and has very bright eyes and of course I have a right, (being his father) to think him a leetle smarter than any other one of his age around here. You may be certain his mother does . . .

The Harris and Bugbee families in the East had gradually become reconciled to William's unshakable decision to stay on in St. Louis. And it was not a bad decision. Perhaps there entered also something of the spirit of venture into his determination, which is reflected in a letter[8] by his friend Charlie W. Chapman: ". . . And Will, haven't we always had a boyish hope *that something would happen* in our day?" The New Englanders all had long been eager for war. Now that the war was here they dreaded it. As Charlie said, nations have moods. They get tired or sated with peace. Like a flock of wild ducks — one will fly, then another, until the whole fly . . .

To be sure, of money worries in St. Louis there was no end. Had the whole money-exchange been a complicated business before, with Illinois bills in favor, others in disfavor, this bank failing, another refusing payment, there was now even a shortage of coins. All the silver 5-cent pieces had vanished and postage stamps were used for car-fare. Finally, the Government issued "postage currency" in March, 1862. Lucky the one who had any money at all.

In the summer of 1862, the President of the St. Louis & Iron Mountain Railroad Co. invited the teachers of the Public Schools on a pleasure excursion to the Iron Mountain and Pilot Knob. The teachers were to provide their own refreshments, except coffee. They would start on a Friday night at 10 o'clock and return about two o'clock the following afternoon. The Board accepted, and the teachers made a day of it. Harris headed the Committee who drafted resolutions thanking the Railroad for the kindness. They expressed their gratitude for having received an "opportunity of viewing a locality, which, furnishing an element so essential to civilization, must eventually play an important part in the future prosperity of St. Louis and the West." Moreover, they remembered with gratitude "the kind and cordial attentions of the patriot soldiers stationed at Pilot Knob." The distance from St. Louis to Pilot Knob was 86 miles.[9] The trip held an added interest to William because a parcel of ground not far from the Iron Mountain, "on the ridge West of the Mt." had been acquired by William for his father three years earlier. Harris Senior held, indeed, a number of pieces of ground from Rhode Island (Scituate) to Missouri, probably for speculation. Two years after the school visit to the Iron Mountain, a crucial battle was fought in the vicinity, with St. Louis at stake.

The Harris household kept cheerful. William's sister, Sarah Lydia, who had come out to teach school, and to help her sister-in-law who was expecting another baby, wrote to their father:[10]

... We are all well. Theo has got to be quite a large boy. I like living in St. Louis very much. It is very pleasant where we live, have a fine view of the Missississippi River ...

194

Monday was William's examination. I went to it. He has a good school, but it has not been so large since the trouble, for each has to pay tuition, the school money being taken by the Governor. He used to have seven teachers, now there are but two besides himself. He is liked very much as a teacher and will probably have a large school next year.

Six weeks later, a little daughter by the name of Charlotte was born to William and "his" Sarah, on July 27th, 1862, to be exact.

There was a general conscription of Missouri Militia in the latter part of the year, but on the basis of Ira Divoll's and Robert Holmes' certificate (as Superintendent of Schools and President of the School Board respectively) that he was the principal teacher of Clay Public School, Harris was declared exempt from service on September 11th, 1862. This exemption was eloquently and pertinently justied by Principal C. F. Childs, William's fast friend:

You and I have not gone into the field with our fathers and brothers to hazard our lives in defence of our country, and we feel a blush of shame at the thought of confessing to coming generations that we, being of martial age and in full health, enjoyed the luxuries of home through these dark days of the Republic. But be of good cheer. We may yet wash away the foul reproach— not on the tented field . . . Not on the tented field, but in the turbulent struggles of civil life, is the service to which we are called, and for which we must renounce all the follies and pleasures of sense, and, like the wise that have gone before us, give our days to toil and our nights to thought.

School matters and a heavy teaching schedule somewhat slowed up Harris' voluminous reading and literary productions during the years of the Civil War. However, he had time to follow events closely and publish his opinions. He

also devoted himself to civic improvements in the Tenth
Ward to which he belonged. There he lent his support, as
secretary of a committee, to the conversion of Hyde Park
"into a respectable place for the use of citizens and their
families". The Committee was composed almost entirely
of Germans and they deliberated largely in German. Brokmeyer was present. They resolved to put an end to the
bawdy entertainment, the bars, the dancing and the public
shows, and make the place into what it was meant for, a plot
with well-kept gardens for decent people to congregate in.

The War dragged on. St. Louis was a bee-hive. She did
her share in alleviating the suffering of the wounded and
the needy. Yet so great were the demands that the means
of the Sanitary Commission were exhausted. The Western
section, accordingly, opened a Fair on May 17th, 1864,
called the Mississippi Valley Sanitary Fair, to replenish its
empty coffers. It extended along 12th Street, from St.
Charles to Olive. People bought, ate, drank and made
merry, netting charity over half a million dollars. It was
inaugurated with a huge procession in which right after the
military and the members of the City Council, the Western
Sanitary Commission, and the Central Finance Committee
rode the Board of Public Schools in five carriages. The
whole affair could only be compared with the celebration
of Grant's victory at Vicksburg.

Gloom, however, spread over the Harris household when
little Charlotte died on the 22nd of May. Many were the
expressions of sympathy by friends and neighbors, but especially touching were the resolutions passed and signed by
Harris' pupils in which they called him their kind friend
and teacher. The sadness was only partially allayed by the
birth of a second boy on July 20th, who was called in
honor of William's personal friend, General Hitchcock,
Ethan, but who, too, was to die at the tender age of six and,
most pathetically, on his birthday.

Beginning of 1865, there was great excitement in the city when the State Convention required of everybody in responsible position, first of all the teachers, the oath already mentioned which was so phrased that no person could take it without mental reserve, except those who had always and ever embraced the Union cause. Cruel in that it barred even those who had experienced a change of heart, it became odiously known as the test-oath, and was repealed only by the Superior Court of the U. S. three years later as unconstitutional. Harris, as a consistent and faithful Lincolnite was able to take it without scruples, for he had always favored the Union.

Just four days before Lee surrendered at Appomattox, Harris was enrolled in the State Militia of Missouri, on April 6th, 1865. The celebration over Grant's victory was, however, of no long duration; for on the 15th news reached St. Louis of Lincoln's assassination.

THE DIALECTIC OF THE CIVIL WAR

St. Louis was a frontier city during the Civil War, and Harris took issue immediately on the side of Lincoln and the Union. Not being in the fight — the nature of his position and his glass eye preventing him from active service — he watched the development of the conflict as the unfolding of a Hegelian dialectic. Already while at Yale, he had felt the clouds gathering, and the experiences of his father in Kansas had added something of the real to the issue.

On July 17th, 1858, he had gone to Springfield, Illinois, to report a speech by Senator Stephen Arnold Douglas on the Lecompton Constitution for the *St. Louis Democrat.*[11] When this Douglas of "Old Sangamon" had mounted the platform and was not quite finished expressing his inability to show his profound joy over being received so enthusiastically home after his battles in the U. S. Senate in behalf of Kansas, the platform gave way under a roar of laughter.

But he mounted a table and continued his speech which bore the liberal message that "you have no more right to force a Free State Constitution on the unwilling people, than you have to force a Slave state upon them against their will."

Carl Schurz who believed that the large German element in St. Louis might serve as a nucleus for an effective emancipation movement in the State,[12] came to the city to thunder a great and defiant speech at the Southern slave-holders who, sitting in the audience, refused to be moved by his sarcasm. Dressed in white, and a bit inebriated, the Hon. Thomas Marshall, of Kentucky, argued with choice words the Union cause in 1860-61, while about the same time the Hon. Joshua R. Giddings, a well-known lawyer, lent his support to the abolitionists in his Mercantile Library Hall talks. Nevertheless, "My Country, 'tis of thee" and "The Star-Spangled Banner" were not sung in St. Louis between 1860 and 1861, but Harris had them in his possession.

Almost all the votes for Lincoln in Missouri came from St. Louis. There was wide-spread disappointment, gloom and fear over his election. The "Minute Men" and the "Wide Awakes" armed themselves underground. St. Louis had always been fond of the military, due to its heavy quota of Europeans. When, for instance, a crack battalion of Zouaves from Chicago, imitators of the Algerian *tirailleurs,* visited at the Fair, every train, car, or horse-drawn vehicle poured the crowds on the Fair grounds to see them go through bayonet and other drills with their customary admirable precision. St. Louis was simply Zouave-struck.

Missouri was in a peculiar position when the issue of slavery became acute. As a slave-holding State it was completely surrounded on three sides by people of different sentiments. Officially she was within the Union, but the ever present Father of Rivers symbolized the ties with the South. Missourians caustically remembered 1818, when they were subjected to an ordeal similar to Kansas, now her neighbor, and the Missouri Compromise was fresh in their minds. St. Louis, however, could not help but develop a peculiar psychosis, because in virtue of her industry she was deeply in debt to the North. Eventually, Missouri was laid waste, but St. Louis stood.

Harris, the Yankee, could not emotionally appreciate the feelings of native Missourians: The slave *had to* be freed; industrial progress *had to* be made; the Union *had to* be preserved; feudalism *had to* go; the influence of foreign powers *had to* be eradicated. Yet, Harris the philosopher conceded that in the ensuing strife a decision was to be reached between an ethical principle and an ideology embodied in the concept of democracy. Both seemed worthwhile ideals, both originated ultimately from the same ubiquitous, speculative, and still largely untested idea of an equality of all those "that human features bear." In the one case it branched out into the problem of human dignity, in the other it asserted itself as rugged individualism. And when both were taken advantage of by unscrupulous politicians, all principles became obscured and only fundamental human passions remained. War became inevitable, and thus the ideals of equality, freedom, and democracy created their own antithesis.

Now, all this was comprehensible to Harris on the basis of Hegelian dialectics which he had mastered as fully as his friend Brokmeyer. But as a *Realpolitiker,* Harris could not help but believe with General Harney that the Unionside held all four aces.[13]

St. Louis, during the Civil War, was really not a part of Missouri.[14] It was a land and a law unto itself. At odds with her Governor at Jefferson City, she was controlled by Brigadier-General Lyon of the U. S. Army, in charge of the Arsenal, while the people cast their lot with either the Union or the Secession, and the city government played a pitiable rôle. There was as much sympathy with the Rebels as there was with the Loyalists, and the only reason why the latter impresses us as stronger at the beginning of the War was that the Federal Government had, much to the chagrin of the underground, sent a formidable army corps right into their midst.

With General Lyon at the head, it was St. Louis against the State, and when Governor Jackson left the memorable meeting with the General on June 11th, 1861, the railroad bridges between Jefferson City and St. Louis were burned, and St. Louis was charged by the Secessionists within the State as a traitor, because she was giving succor to the "invaders of the sovereign State of Missouri", that is, the troops of the U. S.

The Rebel yell, that "penetrating, rasping, shrieking, blood-curdling noise that could be heard for miles on earth, and whose volume reached the heavens"[15] was never heard in the city of St. Louis, but Union flags and Rebel flags, the latter mainly in the shape of decorations on ladies' bosoms or ornaments for carriages and the like, were shown for more than a year, side by side. The only large Confederate flag that flew from a building near where Harris used to have his Phonographic Institute, was taken down after the surrender of Camp Jackson, in 1861. It required a good deal of pluck to show one's true color as a Secessionist, or even trample upon the flag of the United States, but it was done.

Harris wrote East that the Secessionists were the bluest set of men you had ever seen. Why? because they regarded their political ruin equivalent to the ruin of the whole country. "In proportion as they leave the city and state, a buoyant feeling manifests itself among the remaining portion." He said there were some 50,000 persons less in the city in the summer of 1861 than there had been in 1860.

But it would be wrong to infer from Harris' impression

that Secessionists had abandoned the city. With undaunted vigor Southern sympathizers continued to believe in a Confederate victory, to which the wrangles of the Northerners and their oftentimes dubious victories lent semblance. An accurate picture of the sentiment in the city was in so far difficult to get in that even the Secessionists talked about the Union, but, of course, in a different sense from the followers of Lincoln. General Frémont, in his defense presented to the Joint Committee of the two Houses, testified emphatically that St. Louis was a Rebel City and that the wealthy and influential citizens were friendly to Secession.

Although she furnished soldiers for both sides, St. Louis was less affected than the rest of the State by the dual governorship after the State Convention at St. Louis had appointed Governor Hamilton R. Gamble. Governor Jackson had been driven by Union Troops from the capitol and into the Southernmost part of the State from where he, at first, continued to issue orders and proclamations through his Lt. Governor until he went to Richmond, Va., from where he directed Secessionist activities. Through this double appeal to loyalty, and the continual harassing of bushwhackers, the suffering of the Missourians outside St. Louis was indescribable, for safety could not be had, whichever party you chose. Enlistment in one of the armies was still the best policy. At least you recognized your enemy — provided he did not wear your uniform.

But while life was comparatively safe in St. Louis, she had troubles peculiar to herself. Less than three weeks after his arrival, Major-General John Charles Frémont had declared martial law at St. Louis. That was on August 14th, 1861. Newpapers were suppressed, editors imprisoned, slaves freed, all without proper authority and often with the certain knowledge of President Lincoln's disapproval. Nevertheless, Frémont was probably justified, for everyone knew that thousands of Secessionists were ready, waiting for their chance to attack the city from within if the grays should show themselves outside. One danger-spot had already been eliminated by farsighted Capt. Lyon when he took Camp Jackson, a creation of Governor Jackson with the design of training State militia for use of the Confederacy.

Those who thought Frémont was procrastinating, paying attention to unessentials, and holding himself incommunicable, were partially right; he was of a certain Teutonic heaviness and circumspection that made him over-cautious and slow to act, which proved fatal in the case of Lyon who asked in vain for reinforcements and was killed on Wilson's Creek when charging a superior force in self-defense, as well as in the case of Mulligan at Lexington. Yet, Frémont was successful in all his operations afterwards and if he had not been called away he might have terminated the campaign in Missouri three years earlier in virtue of his stringent measures.

It is very characteristic that Harris came to the aid of Frémont and defended him in an article in the daily papers against adverse criticism and abuse from almost every quarter except the Secessionists. He had prepared himself by studying Frémont's *Life*. The objections of the War Department dealt with provisions and the costly acquisition of war material. Harris dismissed them, stating that the War Department itself rather than the General was to blame if, failing shipments from the East, purchases elsewhere and express shipments had to be made in the face of an emergency.

Most serious, however, he deemed the charges directed at Frémont's military tactics. As a firm believer in organization, authority, and centralized planning, he went to metaphysics for support: "We have no instance of a successful General who did not give unity to his circumstances." He quoted the Napoleonic sentiment that incidents ought not to govern policy, but policy incidents. The point of it all was that a General must *comprehend, that is, know the whole in its parts.* Weighing the various probabilities of the rebel movements and designs, Harris came to the conclusion that the Chief of the C.S.A., "if he be politic", would decoy troops in the interior of Missouri and Arkansas, away from railroad and river communications, in order to cause the greatest possible inconvenience and expense to the Union forces. As he saw it, the tactics to be employed in counteracting such stratagems would be to compel the enemy by procrastination and the avoiding of guerilla warfare, to draw their men out of hiding, gather them to a head, and afterwards deal them a decisive blow.

From this point of view he considered the campaign of Lyon after the battle of Boonville as ill advised. While he did not wish to tolerate even "a breath of blame" against Lyon, he localized the fault in the War Department which issued orders to pursue the enemy without making provisions for adequate supplies. At the close of the article, he expressed complete faith in Frémont, "our most experienced General."

Harris' friends back East appreciated his stand. To them, as to his brother-in-law,[16] Missouri affairs were a great enigma. They could not understand why the rebellion had not been completely crushed months before.

When Frémont was discharged, Nov. 2nd, 1861, he was followed by General Hunter who virtually abandoned Missouri to the Confederates by retracing his steps to St. Louis. Frémont had, after all, made considerable progress upon leaving the city and Zagonyi had wrested Springfield from the Southerners. General Hunter was succeeded a fortnight after by Major-General Halleck. What had been resented at first from Frémont, it was imperative to accept now at the hands of Halleck. A Commandant of St. Louis was appointed and later a Provost-Marshal in the person of

Major J. McKinstry who exercised a close vigil. The morale of the troops, which had completely broken down for lack of confidence in the leaders and any sort of organization, was restored by stern measures, while the hopes of the Secessionists were dashed. Union sympathizers never had to fear anything, while the Rebels and their sympathizers were hunted down and their weapons confiscated. General Samuel R. Curtis, successor to General Halleck in the Department of St. Louis, made abundant use of the increased bitter feeling against those who still professed Secessionist leanings. They were considered co-responsible for the entire War and as much money as could reasonably or otherwise be extracted from them was raised by taxes and compulsory contributions to help relieve the dire social conditions arising from the great influx of prisoners, Southern poor Whites, and Negroes. The Western Sanitary Commission was not able to meet the demands upon it in any other way, and it seemed absolutely just to assess those who sided with the foe. St. Louis became the refuge of all those who suffered misfortune, whether in battle or through the fact that they were in somebody's way. In they poured by land and by river, on foot, on stretcher, on conveyances of different types, from as far as Arkansas, Alabama, Kentucky and Tennessee. Most churches were turned into hospitals, a better use than they were put to in the rest of the State where they were converted into "forts of ashes."[17]

In the opinion of the nation, there was not only one bungling, incompetent General in these parts, but many. Thus, from the vantage point of philosophy which showed him both thesis and antithesis, Harris felt called upon to write a letter to the editor of the *Missouri Republican*, that paper of somewhat doubtful loyalty, which appeared October 8th, 1861, under the title of "Philosophy of History." What formerly in theological language was called Providence, modern philosophy he showed to have discovered as

204

Ideas in the history of mankind. History is not a cropping up of quite heterogeneous, wholly disconnected and totally unpredictable events; with Harris and Hegel it is the distinct working out of a plan or idea to which all happenings, however remote and seemingly antagonistic, are tributary.

The Civil War was the logical result of a dialectic which ordinarily exists between nations, but in America developed into one of North and South. Industry and machinery in the North, passivity and slavery in the South. The North required everyone to be self-determining and established a universal democracy, the South could not allow the majority of the subject race to rule, and hence favored aristocracy.

Here was, indeed, an attempt to interpret in as detached and philosophical a manner as possible the great conflict. The perspectives may have been wrong, to be sure, for Harris saw with Hegel's spectacles. Nevertheless, calm and understanding had changed Harris within a few months from a Yankee among Compromise Missourians to an American as true as there ever was one. Have we become any wiser since he penned the closing paragraphs of this article?

Meanwhile there has been a superficial observation current that our Government was founded on public opinion. Were mere opinion its basis, it would long since have ceased *to be,* for opining is the opposite of knowing, in that the former grasps one side of the subject and that generally the *unessential,* while *knowing* must grasp both sides of the subject; i.e., *comprehend* it. One-sided views develop opposition and may produce disaster. The wonderful increase of opinions in this country over the sober, cautious habits which characterise the Anglo Saxon, is one of the most dangerous signs of the times. The flippant sensation dispatch of the reporter, who believes himself capable of judging at sight of the movements and qualifications of Generals and armies, is having a terrible influence on the cause for which the patriot is contending. If "the self-swallowing eddy of opinions wherein the time is wallowing", shall prevail, instead of "Vox populi, vox Dei", we shall have to repeat the words of one of the wisest of our time, "Vox populi, vox Diaboli."

In conclusion, the hope of the country is now, as always, in the patient, conservative element of the people, who serenely work on, while the loud mouthed hours are refuted and silenced by the ages.

The year 1862 was making history. The military control of Missouri was completely in the hands of Union Troops, all Secessionists having been gradually driven from the State. Price in the South was defeated and Grant had embarked on his victorious career scoring a victory at Fort Henry. Some tangible results were showing at long last in favor of the Union. And as a symbol and a release of nervous tension a huge celebration of Washington's birthday on February 22nd was staged in the form of a colorful, enthusiastic parade in which all favorable to the Union took part. All denominations of troops were there in dress uniform, gaily attired ladies rode in carriages, floats followed upon floats representing the businesses of the city from the oyster bar to the printing presses. Civic organizations were marching, including the Jaegers and the Total Abstinencers, while the trades, down to butchers and draymen followed in close formations. Even the slightly cynical *Missouri Republican* had a float in the procession for, after all, the honors went to the Father of the Country!

The day of the parade had been cold and misty, foreboding the fading of enthusiasm in the weeks that followed. Wounded Union soldiers to the total of 8000, reached St. Louis after the battle of Pittsburgh Landing. None of the victories, if there were any, were decisive. The

Confederacy was still alive and stirring. But worst of all, a guerilla warfare had developed, writing the saddest chapter in the Civil War history of Missouri. St. Louis had become an asylum, reflecting the gruesome, ghastly happenings throughout the State.

A feeling of futility and despondency crept over the citizens of St. Louis. There was wrangling, nagging, and fretting. The Unionists split up into parties which fought each other bitterly. Not even Lincoln could appease them.

The precarious, slow, and disappointing maneuvers of McClellan's before Richmond, in June, 1862, were being watched keenly by the entire North. Everyone had hoped for a great victory when discouraging news made headlines. Harris again picked up his pen. Taking to hand a map and with faith in the General who, to him, seemed desirous of accomplishing his objectives with as little loss of life as possible, he clearly outlined the state of affairs and sent his conclusions to the *Missouri Republican.* "McClellan's Position before Richmond" took into consideration all his operations in and around a difficult, swampy country, up to the last day of June, 1862. The article displayed, indeed, a good deal of insight into military tactics and discredited alarmist reports that visualized the Northern Armies on the retreat. Boldly he praised the move that had evoked public disapproval as one of the most skillful in the war, "rivaling even the capture of New Orleans," late in April that year.

Now, it is certain, that Harris did not have an accurate map of the Potomac and James River region; the General Staff itself did not possess even a passable one. Yet it seems he was essentially right in putting trust in McClellan's mildness as a prime motive of his procrastinations. The verdict of most historians is still against the General, although there are some voices that give him credit and discount some of the wild tales of fantastical warfare.[18]

Quietly Harris watched further developments, reading much and clipping all significant articles and speeches for his scrap books. In the meantime, other and greater dangers had reared their heads. The spectre of war threatened St. Louis once more in 1864, when all available soldiers were sent to the front to reinforce Grant in his famous campaign. Seemingly out of nowhere, small bands appeared even in the neighborhood of St. Louis, the very city which they had avoided thus far, for good reasons. They pillaged and burned and killed, while in secret another, deadlier poison was brewed by organizations that had sworn the end of Unionism. With nationwide ramifications these "Knights of the Golden Circle", or by whatever other names the conspirators went, prepared a final death blow to the Union, and would doubtlessly have been successful if it had not been for the vigilance of General Wm. Starke Rosecrans, then head of the Department of Missouri, whose informers had kept him apprised.

It was, however, in September, 1864, that St. Louis really trembled. The last of the Confederate Troops in this region were advancing under General Price from the South on Pilot Knob. All the Home Guards in St. Louis were immediately called out, Smith was recalled, and Illinois implored for help. But already the backbone of the valiant fighters in Gray was broken. They were stopped, with heavy losses, by General Ewing and his Home Guard, though not effectively. But instead of marching on St. Louis which they might easily have captured, they turned North and West, leaving St. Louis to wonder why she had been spared. It was one of those strange happenings that defy rational explanation. Thus, St. Louis, the key-city, practically at the mercy of the Confederate Army, escaped because the Southerners did not see their opportunity, and the secret organizations who were to strike from within, failed to come to their aid, probably having been neutralized by the ever watchful Rosecrans.

But now the Secessionist force had spent itself completely. The South had fought gallantly as well as savagely. In deeds of chivalry and atrocity neither side held monopolies. Sherman's March to the Sea in its various phases certainly equalled the punitive raids into Missouri by Pillows, McCulloch, and Price. The North had the trend of economic development on its side, the South had aligned itself with conservatism and wished to perpetuate its way of life. At Appomattox, the Confederacy was but a shadow: it had given up its spirit and its substance long before the formal surrender.

While sojourning in New England in the summer of 1865, Harris learned that the New Englander had a totally different "slant" on the origin and conduct of the Civil War than the Missourians. His impression was that the New Englanders thought *they* were the ones responsible for the winning of the war. Accordingly he made several sketches in his diary (such as "Politics of the Present", "National Ideas", "State Forms", "Civil Society"), in which he tried to arrive at an objective evaluation of the great conflict. Industry would have transformed the South peacefully, had it been permitted to enter. The war would then have been unnecessary. The South unfortunately sneered at the mudsills and greasy mechanics of the North. She precipitated the war before the North had an opportunity to put across its ideas of industrialization in a sermon without words.

In writing the "Theory of American Education", in 1870, Harris thought back to the Civil War which illustrated to him the close relationship between educational theories and practices and the spirit of the times as it expressed itself in social and political institutions. Both sides of the nation, he explained, were really in the same stage of humanitarianism, "but one had preceded the other in discovering the true and proper instrument for its realization," that is, productive industry, instead of serfdom.

In an address before a Peace Society, in 1873, Harris looked into the causes of war and found them not in the plans and purposes of single individuals, but in national relations "of such a character that neither of the two parties could act in an untrammelled manner without limiting the freedom of the other." War, he said, is a cruel thing, a terrible ordeal; yet great political principles are being discovered through it which may become valuable in human progress. Harris was no sentimentalist or wishy-washy pacifist, for he believed and professed that war is "the divinely appointed means by which mankind ascends into a higher consciousness of its rational principles, and it is only to disappear from the earth when civilization has discovered and realized other methods of attaining to this all-essential knowledge."

Harris spoke rarely of the Civil War. But again in the year 1878, during one of the country's greatest depressions, he alluded to it frequently in his lectures. He then elaborated on the cerebral effects of the war, its strain upon the nerves, and also its disastrous economic effects. "There is no waste like that of war. It is conflagration heightened by the assistance of human fury." Since, with the exception of the Crimean War, there had been no great war either in Europe or America prior to the Civil War, some had already predicted the millenium. "Philanthropy", he said in the 1878 address[19] before the Spelling Reform Association, "could 'sit under its olive, slur the days gone by, and prate of the blessings of peace', unmindful of the slowly gathering rust of corruption which ensues when the epic spirit of devotion to a national cause dies out in the mere spirit of individual gain. For then

'When the poor are hoveled and nestled together,
each fed like swine,

LIFE DURING THE CIVIL WAR

When only the ledger lives, and when only not *all*
men lie;
Peace in her vineyard—yes! but a company forges the
wine?' "

A General, a Mystic, and a Friend

Sometime in 1860, Harris made the acquaintance of an
interesting and stimulating personality who at the same time
attained considerable importance during the Civil War as a
close adviser to President Lincoln. It was General Ethan
Allen Hitchcock, whom Harris described to his uncle, Dr.
Fenner H. Peckham, as "a man of eminent literary tastes and
who had time in the leisure of the camps to master the secret
of Plato and to absorb the mystics." That he possessed
300 volumes of the mystics alone endeared him to Harris
beyond measure. He wanted Harris to assist him in the
proofs of a new book, and on that account Harris intended
to go East in August, 1860, a plan that did not materialize.

General Hitchcock[20] hailed from the Green Mountain
State and was the son of Samuel Hitchcock and the grandson of Ethan Allen, the hero of Ticonderoga, on his mother's
side. At the time of his correspondence with Harris he
was in his 63rd year. He had come to St. Louis in 1840,
after having taught at West Point and fought in the Sem-
inole War. In 1842 he had gone once more to Florida,
but on returning was put in command of Jefferson Barracks, St. Louis. After several promotions due to distinctions in Mexico and California, Col. Hitchcock resigned
in 1855 from active service and established residence in
St. Louis where he devoted himself to study and literary
activity. At the outbreak of the Civil War he put himself
immediately at the disposal of General Harney as an adviser, writing the proclamation of September 15th, denouncing in strong terms the Missouri Legislature's "Military Bill" as Secessionist in character. His service was such

211

that President Lincoln called him to Washington, March 17, 1862, as a special legal military adviser to himself.

Always mystically inclined he had studied Spinoza, Swedenborg, books on alchemy and occult subjects in general. By the time he repaired to Washington he had published five books, one on the identifications of the doctrines of Spinoza and Swedenborg, two upon *Alchemy and the Alchemists*, another on *Swedenborg, A Hermetic Philosopher*, and, in 1861, the 2nd edition of *Christ the Spirit, being an Attempt to state the Primitive Views of Christianity*. These productions were followed from 1866 onward by *The Red Book of Appin: A Story of the Middle Ages; Remarks on the Sonnets of Shakespeare;* Spenser's poem *Colin Clouts Explained;* and *Notes on the Vita Nuova and Minor Poems of Dante*. Of fugitive essays there were a great many apart from the writings on military subjects.[21] His collection of hermetic books, given to the St. Louis Mercantile Library, was one of the finest in the country. Though a soldier, his biographer described him as of "almost child-like simplicity and womanly tenderness." He revelled in art appreciation and loved music.

Now, Harris was distinctly influenced by his thought. He had in his library practically all of Hitchcock's published works which seemed to fit right into Harris' intellectual development as a transition from the "ante-mundane soul-wandering" to Hegelianism. In order to discharge a debt of gratitude, Harris published in a January number, 1862, of the *Missouri Republican,* a review of the General's *Remarks upon Alchemy, Swedenborg,* and *Christ the Spirit*. Prefacing his discussion with the sarcastic remarks of Carlyle's about book-reviewers into whose haughty airs Harris refused to lapse, he exhorted the reader to get these "wonderful books" and study them.

The alchemists, he acknowledged, were philosophers in disguise. Their subject, esoterically, was always man. It is up to us to "look through the letter" to perceive the spiritual implications of what otherwise would seem futile chemico-metallurgical experiments. Eight reasons were then isolated by Harris why such an interpretation is not only plausible but correct: The alchemists themselves claim to be philosophers. They warn against a literal interpretation. Their terminology would be absurd if applied to anything else but man. The philosopher's stone is spoken of as already found, not as something still to be discovered. They were otherwise intelligent men with reputation for practical wisdom, such as Roger Bacon, Geber, Albertus Magnus, Thomas Aquinas and many others. "The deep principles, that they refer to, to prove their position, is indicative of a subject that contains within it universality, e. g.: 'Nature is a whole everywhere'." The colors they describe must refer to man's condition, the outer, or the body, being subjected by the inner, or soul. Symbolism, in the days when they were writing, was considered the highest form of popular exposition of things of an infinite character. If the symbolic interpretation were rejected we would be forced to look upon smart men as dupes of a monstrous delusion.

Harris concurred in the General's opinion that if the alchemists had used familiar words to express their thoughts, these words would have suggested familiar trains of thought and images, a thing they wanted to avoid, because they were speaking of spiritual things, whose essence and nature could be conveyed by adjectives to a whimsically chosen symbol. The reader would thus not be misled in associating popular fancies with such words as God and be able to concentrate on the meaning-content.

A direct relationship was to be discovered, according to Hitchcock, between the older alchemical writers and the highly speculative and spiritual poets and thinkers of more recent times, such as Shakespeare, Dante, Goethe, Spinoza,

Swedenborg, who only chose a varied phraseology. The same was applied to the Holy Scriptures, and Harris became enamoured with some of the revealing interpretations of the Bible that may be constructed if the central theme of the gospel stories is taken as the inter-relation of body and spirit. The Fourth Gospel in particular lent itself splendidly to such an exegesis. To those confused by Biblical criticism or stumped by the letter, he recommended Hitchcock's *Christ the Spirit,* of which he had at least three copies in his possession. The Church, he thought, would also benefit even if the reconciliation or re-conversion was in spirit only. Hitchcock himself did not go so far as to deny the historical Christ. He was even credited by our young philosopher with having found the very philosopher's stone: Never had he "read any books written so thoroughly in a spirit of truth". His admiration for the General was genuine, and when, in 1864, a second son was born to the Harris family, he received the General's first name.

The ascendency of Hitchcock over Harris made itself felt particularly in one field: the appreciation and interpretation of art and music. Having read in the writings of the General, Harris composed short treatises in his diary which leave no doubt about the fact that he was consciously making use of the symbolic method. For example: Trinity, aside from its theological significance of the triune character of Father, Son and Holy Ghost, wishes to express also a philosophical truth with its triune character of Pure Thought in itself, Nature, and Reconciliation: or, it may symbolize God in himself, God out of himself, and the union of both, their union being organic, each implying the other. All religions asserting only unitarianism must be wrong. But such differences as Roscellinus and St. Anselm represented, could be made to cancel out. Harris out-philosophized the good General, however, when he asserted that Trinity is also the highest philosophical Idea. For, Hegel said in essence in the third volume of the *Logic*: "The Pure being or the *Universal limits itself* and *cancels this limit,* or the Universal becomes individual by means of the *Particular . . .* Now the Pure universal in itself cannot be distinguished from the pure particular. Hence both = o. They only exist in union and therein truth is their identity."

On how different a plane all this speculation of Harris' was from what he professed before he studied Hitchcock and Hegel so deeply, can be appreciated if we compare with it his earlier dogmatism, philosophically grounded though it was, with which he defended himself only a year or so before against the charge by his grandmother that he was a lover of Voltaire, just because he had quoted one of his witticisms. He averred that it was "a most unjust conclusion", for he had not read *one* of his works, that he despised "him and his class of writers for the superficiality of their reasoning." "My attempt has been to find a positive ground to start from and build up a system of philosophy. I have found it. Christianity is based on the immutable nature of Spirit and can be the only result of a development of Humanity. To convert *beliefs* into *truths* is the province of a philosopher. You must acknowledge yourself that it is better for one to *know* than to believe."[22]

The hostility to mysticism and Church ceremonial, so natural to New Englanders, if it was ever present in Harris, vanished completely on absorbing Hitchcock. The association with him brought out a side of Harris' nature which is not generally known. The essay on "Mystics," written in the early part of 1861, shows Harris in a rare mood of appreciating and acknowledging the veracity of the mystic insight into the problem of man and the universe.

There was a frequent interchange of thought between the educator and the general, the former delving deeper into the meaning of German idealism, the latter continuing to speculate about the obscurities and incomprehensibilities of mystics, scholastics, and poets. When General Hitchcock removed to Washington, his delicate health and continued occupation with problems of diplomacy did not permit a too frequent correspondence. With most of his philosophic friends dispersed due to the Civil War, Harris felt lonely. Some of his letters to the General became 1300 words in length, veritable essays in mystico-philosophical interpretation. In one of these long letters[23] he informed Hitchcock of how he had applied his method to solving the mystery of music and related his impressions and conclusions on hearing a cantata. This episode of the Philharmonic rehearsals Harris later retold in an article, "The Pilgrimage of the Rose", which was published in 1877.

A year later,[24] a letter was sent to the General which made explicit reference to an essay which was written nine months before[25] and of which there are two versions. It deals with an interpretation of Frederick Edwin Church's famous painting, "Heart of the Andes." He suggested to him that his "method of investigating the Hermetic writings would yield the same happy results if applied to painting or indeed any other province of art whatsoever." The province in which the General's method seemed most fruitful, was that in which we are dealing with works "which form the transition from religion to philosophy." If we bear in mind the many later writings and lectures of Harris' upon the subject of painting, sculpture, and music, we can in some measure fathom the substantial contribution of General Hitchcock to the intellectual development of Harris.

Psychologically interesting is a dream which Harris had on March 11th, 1863, and which testifies to the subconscious occupation of his mind with a far-reaching symbology.

A Dream

I had a dream last night about the beautiful. I was passing a picture window and my attention was arrested by a picture of some Greek hero overcoming a dragon. The immediate elements of conflict were the dragon snorting flame, the horse attacking him with his teeth. The Grecian hero in sublime beauty stood erect on his chariot while his horses attached to his chariot were rushing on towards the dragon and snorting fire like the dragon. The hero used means, the horses, but did not disturb his graceful attitude in the struggle. The horses were not so serene in their attitudes. The background was full of Grecian temples — beautiful outlines. I remember that I made a lecture on the spot, treating of the beauty of the outlines and showing that it was owing to the fact that self-determination was the thing represented . . .

ı
In the first volume of the *Journal of Speculative Philosophy* Harris reviewed Hitchcock's *Alchemy and the Alchemists* in an unsigned little article in which the author's view is briefly stated that not the transmutation of metals was the object of the alchemists, but the regeneration of man. Likewise in the second volume, Hitchcock's *Notes on the Vita Nuova* was appreciatively referred to.[26]

The method of allegorizing and symbolizing, however, lingered on. It was tried in the 1866 *Notebook*, on Longfellow's translation of Goethe's "The Wanderer's Night Songs." The poems which his friend John Albee sent him on occasion, were forthwith subjected to the same symbolic and musical analysis. Into this transition period from the occult to the metaphysical belongs also the profound impression created on him by Emerson's short poem "Experience". Many years later he called it[27] a condensed epic of human life and confessed that he was "elevated and inspired by this poem more than by any other" because, he presumed, "Emerson has transfigured the fact of life as a whole at once into a poetic trope."

Pedro Caldéron de la Barca became Harris' favorite author for a time, since he blended so successfully theology and nether morality in his plays. Likewise the comments in his 1866 *Diary* on the *Divine Orpheus* and *The World Theatre*, in their allegorizing tendencies, plainly reveal the influence of General Hitchcock. In the Shakespearean studies of Hitchcock, which appeared under the title of *Remarks on the Sonnets of Shakespeare; with the Sonnets*, Harris searched deep for new meanings. Long he had been familiar with most of the bard's dramas and had learned to appreciate them from the point of view of language and depth of thought. It seems he even developed an outline for a system of the historical plays before the appearance of Denton J. Snider's essays. However, Harris was becoming more and more wary of Hitchcock's interpretations. Eventually, the intellectual spheres of both minds became divided, the General withdrawing into the mystic, Harris into the Hegelian spirit. Nevertheless, a fine personal relationship continued to exist between them.

Harris' loyalty and attachment to General Hitchcock was tested and proven beyond a doubt when, probably at the suggestion of the General himself who must have supplied him with the data which he might not have easily obtained otherwise, he went as far as criticising publicly the Secretary of War, Edwin M. Stanton, in an article for the St. Louis papers, published on or about September 9th, 1863. It was an audacious move, the Secretary receiving a very vigorous rebuke for dissolving the General Court Martial at Washington, D. C., of which General Hitchcock had been President, and appointing another one with men of inferior rank in its stead, probably in the hope of receiving decisions from that body that would be more subject to influence by the War Department. The occasion was a judgment against a certain Hazel B. Cashell, a citizen of Maryland, who had given intelligence to a Rebel cavalry squad about a herd of cattle belonging to the U. S. It seems the information was not volunteered with an animus to aid the Confederates, but under personal danger, and that the information, after all, had netted little to the enemy. The verdict of General Hitchcock's Court was, guilty on three points, but the case was dismissed with a warning in the future to be more cautious in answering questions put by the enemy. The War Department was of the opinion that it was a case in which the supreme penalty would have been in order, and hence dissolved the Court, recommending that the case be prosecuted again under a different section of the act to suppress insurrection, etc.[28] Harris commented on this as follows:

The enormity of this deed will appear if one reflects on its bearing as a precedent. It, in fact, makes null and void the whole judicial element in the army. If the Secretary of War, or one of his clerks, can decide offhand what is military justice, and execute it without hindrance of what use is the *form* of a Court Martial? Or of what use are any of the so-called "safeguards" of Anglo-Saxon liberty — such, for example, as "Nor shall any person be subject for the same offense to be twice put in jeopardy of life or limb" — when a citizen can be "handed over to the civil authorities" to be prosecuted again? Why not at once go back to the plan of the Turkish justice, who said, "Would you have me try the criminal before I pass sentence? That were a waste of words and time, for if I should condemn him after examination, why not before, and so save the trouble of looking into the matter?"

As represented by Harris, the verdict returned by General Hitchcock not only disclosed great leniency and kindness of heart, but also discrimination, understanding and justice. In regard to the General's character he gave this testimony:

The President of the Court, Major General Hitchcock, is well known, especially in this vicinity, as one of the purest and most incorruptible patriots this country ever afforded. For forty years an officer of the regular army; Inspector General of Scott's army in Mexico, and frequently called to sit on Court Martial, he is, perhaps, the best read in military law of all our officers. It is a Court Martial of such members and with such a head that is treated like a pack, of delinquent schoolboys by a man "clothed with a little brief authority," a blustering lawyer.

CHAPTER NINE

POST BELLUM LIFE

Sojourning Among the Concord Brahmins

L ATE one afternoon in June, 1865,[1] William, together with his Sarah and their two children, Theodore, age 5, and Ethan, just a year old, went aboard the steamer "Peoria City," bound northward. William relaxed and felt very pleasantly the movement of the riverboat which was pushing a barge on either side of her. A few miles above St. Louis, night came on and for the first time in many years William observed the stars of the Scorpion's tail down near the horizon. They passed the mouth of the Missouri at dark, and Alton, Illinois, rose to view with a bright light which his telescope revealed to be a burning building.

There were showers the next morning. The Illinois River which they had entered the night before, seemed like a wide canal, very level and straight. The countryside was wooded and they passed some hills and cliffs on the North shore of the river. There were frequent stops, and ever so often the turnbridges of the railroad had to be swung out of their way. The fare aboard was good. The air and the water seemed fresh and pure and bracing to the four who had breathed limestone dust and coal smoke for years. Some soldiers that were their travelling companions, were home-bound and seemed to be in a hilarious mood.

The following morning at 9 o'clock the boat docked at Peoria after a trip of 240 miles. The last 60 miles to Chicago, where they arrived at 5 o'clock, were covered by railroad.

Geologic observations were made on the fact that Lake Michigan at one time must have poured into the Gulf.

While the family was left to wash up and rest at the Sherman House, William joined a friend K. and walked up Michigan Avenue on wretched sidewalks. The buildings were fine, and there was much activity. The turnbridges in the middle of the city again caught William's fancy. They visited a Grammar and a High School, both of which left a good impression. But while the two friends were walking, K. suddenly had the nose-bleed and they turned into a house to get some water. The place was neat and clean, kept by a Negress who was ironing. There was a fine carpet in the front room, a piano, rosewood furniture and a marble-top table with books and an album on it. The walls were hung with pictures, one being an allegorization of the Emancipation Proclamation. What a change had been wrought in the life of Negroes! Machinery and the division of labor had made culture among them possible. All labor shall henceforth be intelligent labor! "Producing the raw material without machinery produces raw men. Mere animals."

The stay in Chicago lasted only a day. On Thursday evening they took the Propeller "Potomac" out of Chicago at 6 p.m., and sailed into Lake Michigan with a considerable breeze which rocked the boat severely. William was not a good sailor, he soon "felt the qualms of seasickness, but not seriously." He slept well, had breakfast and spent most of the forenoon with his spyglass looking out over the lake. Sails could be seen in all directions, and land was near, at times. However, after dinner William took seasick "in good earnest." He was glad of the experience thinking thus to get over it once and for all.

Grand Traverse Bay came in sight on Saturday morning. They put in, took on some passengers, and soon after sailed through the busy Straits of Mackinac. Ever watchful for anything of interest, Harris, the student of natural science, watched the loons on the water through his telescope and noted the latitude and the time of setting and rising of the sun. Toward evening, on Sunday, they approached the St. Clair River with the huts of Indians along the Eastern shore.

They stopped but half an hour on Monday morning at Detroit and steamed out into shallow, windy Lake Erie. The green water appeared like emerald in the sun, quite a change from the blue waters of Lake Michigan and Lake Huron. The waves began to rise up to 20 feet, but the boat, being loaded down with 700 tons of grain, did not rock much. During the night, someone tried to work the pumps, but no water being below, the result was a tremendous noise which made the ladies give loud expression to their regret of ever having come by such an old boat. William, however, slept soundly after the hubbub.

On Tuesday morning the wind blew even more fiercely; they were having "quite a gale." But at 11 o'clock they reached Buffalo harbor which was well protected by a breakwater. The afternoon was utilized in looking around the city: There were many fine churches, many elevators; copper cents were in use; cherries and strawberries were cheap, the cheese was good. At 6 o'clock in the evening they went by sleeper to New York.

In the big town they put up at an up-town hotel conducted on the European plan. William rode the street railways for six miles, took in upper Central Park with its tunnels, bridges, arches, Swiss cottages, fishponds and other attractions, and returned to the hotel elated, thinking it the "finest place imaginable." Unlike the practice in St. Louis, in New York a gentleman would not rise for a lady in the street railway. Thinking it odd, he made a remark to the girl in front of him and she curtly retorted that she would not take a seat offered her by a gentleman. The following day he was shopping at Pike's Optical Store for an object glass, 2⅝ in. in diameter, and with a friend[2] who had come from Buffalo on the same train, visiting Astor Library and the Mercantile Library.

Once more a steamer was boarded at Pier 39, in the North River. It was the "City of Boston". Men-of-war and gunboats were sighted in number in the Sound; a stiff breeze was blowing, but the boat was making rapid progress while William jotted down his observations on the corrupt political machinery of New York City. On Friday noon, June 30th, the steamer entered Thames River. "The sea breeze from the Atlantic smelled the most grateful of anything" to William and he developed an enormous appetite for shell fish. Formerly the boat had stopped at Allyn's Point, but now it discharged its passengers at New London. They boarded the train and soon were on their way to Danielsonville. Arriving there at 3 o'clock in the morning they got a carriage after some difficulty and were driven to Williamsville, just in time to awaken Sarah's parents from sleep.

Mother and Father Bugbee had grown old and they, in turn, found Sarah and their son-in-law changed. Sarah's brother Edwin came home at night to greet the visitors. Sarah, William and the children stayed only a single night and joined William's parents, on Putnam Hill, the following day. Somewhat sadly William noted in his diary: "Mother, Grandmother and the children looked very strange." Few of the old people that William had known were left. On Sunday they all attended church and heard the sermon by the Rev. J. P. Watson. Very few people were out to church, and the sermon dealt, in the main, with backbiting in the community. Dr. Peckham came up from Providence to welcome the guest from the West. On Monday William brought Sarah and the children back to Williamsville, while he himself left them on the Fourth to go to Brooklyn, Ct., to the Windham County celebration.

There he met Theodore Tilton and Henry Ward Beecher who appeared peacefully side-by-side on the platform. Also Ex-Governor Chauncey Fitch Cleveland, Governor William Alfred Buckingham, and others made speeches. William reported that of Tilton for the *Windham County Transcript*.[3] He met again many of his old acquaintances and friends, among them Arthur Mathewson who had become a surgeon in the Navy. The toastmaster at the celebration was Edwin Holmes Bugbee, William's brother-in-law. The gathering was estimated at from 5000 to 20,000 people, and they served a kind of Westphalian ham which William relished very much. The tone of the whole celebration was that New England laid claim to the victory in the Civil War.

On the 17th of July[4] William travelled from Providence through Boston to Concord.[5] The interim was probably spent with Dr. Peckham. When William arrived, after some difficulties, at noon at Amos Bronson Alcott's house in Concord, he was welcomed very heartily and took dinner with him and his wife. Alcott was really only paying back in small part what William had tried to do for him out West. In the evening, William met Louisa May Alcott and Ralph Waldo Emerson who invited him to call the following afternoon. In Emerson he admired his "fine voice that makes it pleasant to listen to him." He got into a discussion with him about Goethe, whom Emerson really never understood fully. William, of course, defended the great poet. Before they turned in that night, William read to Amos and Louisa his article on "Emily Chester," which was a criticism of Anne Moncure Seemuller's book published by Ticknor & Fields[6]. They expressed great pleasure in it and suggested that he write a criticism of Louisa's *Moods* in the same spirit, the novel she had published in 1864.

The greater part of the following day was consumed in discussions of the theory of pre-existence (William reading into it a Hegelian construction, Alcott regarding it as a myth) and readings from and critical remarks on a new book which Alcott was planning but knowledge of which he had kept thus far even from Emerson. It was the *Oracles*. Louisa was busy meanwhile finishing a novel. "She is like many young writers", William observed, "who affect genius when complimented on their productions, saying: 'I don't know how it is; I wrote it as it came.' They are dreadfully unconscious creatures — mere unconscious organs, of the over-soul. She disclaimed any idea of treating the problem of Affinities in her work."

As planned, Alcott and his young visitor made their way to Emerson's house. The Brahmin had put off an engagement to see them and it seems he tried to make William think that it would be difficult to establish a sympathetic relation with him. Thinking that he might hit something anyhow, William "blazed away right and left." Soon they got on to East Indian Literature and Emerson drew fire. William asked whether he had ever seen any place in that literature where self-determination was recognized as the absolute. The poem "Brahma," he alleged, was capable of two significations, pure being and spirit. The former he thought was meant by the Hindus, the latter was the development of Socrates and Plato. Thereupon Emerson took down the *Bhagavad Gita* and read some "pantheistic" passages, such as "I am the doubter and the doubt." Listening intently, the voice of Emerson struck William "particularly sweet and manly." He could appreciate that his bewitching manner had made him an idol among his friends. William divulged that he had read the *Vishnu Purana*, the *Hitopadesa*, and the *Sakuntala*, among other things, and that he had studied Sanskrit a little. "Brave man! Brave man!" Emerson exclaimed, while William laughed and added: "Not enough to hurt, it had only been of philologic use." Then they talked of Hegel, and Emerson expressed eagerness to see his *Aesthetic*. William mentioned some translations.

Johann Karl Friedrich Rosenkranz came in as the critic of Goethe, but Emerson spoke of James Elliot Cabot as the greatest scholar in that department.

Rapidly notes were compared on old Norse literature, the Cid and other types of literature. Then Emerson read a letter which he had received a short while ago from Carlyle and which commenced: "You will observe with sorrow that my hand now trembles with age." The writing was scarcely legible. A photograph accompanied it, exhibiting a grisly face which seemed to William much like Walt Whitman's last picture. Being on that topic, Emerson said that Whitman had got out a new book on the War and that "it was a clean book", for a wonder.

Emerson kindly offered letters of introduction to Dr. Frederic Henry Hedge and James Elliot Cabot, He sent them to Alcott's house the following day, sealed. But in them he expressed surprise, at least to Dr. Hedge, over receiving "from Missouri so sharpsighted a philosopher," and otherwise gave a very favorable opinion of William.[7]

On their way home, Alcott and William were still discussing the theory of the immortality of soul, started at Emerson's house. At home, Alcott got out a copy of Proclus and found a mathematical demonstration of the fundamental philosophy. William unfolded it all in Hegelian terms which pleased Alcott so much that he said the book ought to belong to him as the rightful owner. He himself had taken it from Emerson's bookshelf, saying that the book was intended for him, because the legend went with it that a certain Mr. Lane, an English Platonist, had owned the copy and bequeathed it to him who is able to understand it.

The two stayed up till 2 o'clock, Alcott reading from his new book and William half asleep. The next day they walked and talked all forenoon and Alcott confided that William had made a better impression upon Emerson than any young man for sometime. At noon, William took his leave with the understanding that he was to come back. Mrs. Alcott also had become fond of William who reminded her of her husband when she met him at Brooklyn, Ct.[8]

At Boston, William stopped off long enough to visit with his old chum, Robert R. Bishop. He reached Providence in the evening. While in that city he called with his uncle on various persons and read Henry James' work on *Substance and Shadow*, noting good thoughts covered up by a dull style. From Providence he eventually returned to Putnam, where he found letters from Ira Divoll who had written him from New York and Vermont, in which parts he was vacationing.

On the 26th of July, William celebrated the first reunion of his class of '58 at Yale. He was welcomed by Charles W. Chapman and Bailey, a mutual friend, and together they went to Bailey's house where they joined George M. Smith. William "talked enough" "to come to a tolerable understanding with them." After dinner he read his criticism of *Emily Chester* and bored them with it unconsciously, "the only reading of it" that, he believed, ever really had bored anyone.

Most of his classmates, and he met over fifty of them, were not very sympathetic. None of them seemed to have struck a rich vein. Against their achievements he was able to pitch his, that is, having "had eleven assistants and ten hundred and 23 scholars the past year." "Outside of school duties" he had "been engaged in Literature and the study of Philosophy and History" and had "made considerable progress in the German Schools of Philosophy, and in Plato and Aristotle", and "studied Goethe constantly."[9]

Van Name was pursuing Sanskrit and Arabic. Walter Scott Alexander told him that he had made his M.A., and counselled him to do likewise. The class supper, at $4 per plate, with drinking, toasts and sentiments, lasted till 3 o'clock. William "went to bed in a parlor of a hotel and slept three hours." Breakfast was taken at Chapman's who played for him Beethoven's Sonata in C minor on the piano. William thought it needed criticism. At 11 o'clock, and after visiting as many of the old haunts in New Haven as he could in the time, he took the cars back to Providence.

As at Yale, at Putnam he took delight in visiting all the scenes so familiar to him. It seemed like a dream to see the house in which he was born, and the rude chambers and low roof made him feel strangely. As if enchanted, he went through the woods to the old farm. It all seemed so far removed from his "actuality" that he forgot his present state and position and became satisfied with the immediate. His telescope went out of order, and he would not leave before it was repaired. Then he went to Scituate, R. I., to visit with his grandmother and grandfather. They looked very old to him. At their table he luxuriated on huckleberries and milk. When he left he felt that he would never see them again.

Along in August, William prepared a second time to go to Concord. This time he stopped off one night at Robert Bishop's new home in West Newton which he had built on a hill that had been cleared. William thought it one of the finest houses he had ever been in. They spoke of many things, and William was able to convey to him what he "was about, perhaps to his slight surprise." Was it his philosophic ambitions that he meant? . . .

At Brookline, Mass., he wanted to present Emerson's introduction to Dr. Hedge, the great student of German philosophy, but he did not find him at home. He likewise missed Cabot, and thus contented himself with writing them both a little later. Jas. Sumner, whom he saw again, looked ten years younger than when he had seen him last in St. Louis. One evening he spent with Captain Copp, at his residence in Roxbury. The Captain who had been in

China offered him some very fine black tea which was so strong, however, that it affected William's nerves for several days.

While in Boston, he visited, on the advice of Ira Divoll, the Public Library. Presenting letters of introduction to Edward Capen, Librarian, and Frederic Vinton, Assistant Librarian, he was treated politely and given all the information he asked for, no doubt to use it in the building up of the St. Louis Public School Library. While in Boston he heard the Great Organ, and was surprised at the completeness of it. They played an Ave Maria. The *vox humana* stop seemed as though a Soprano solo could be heard far up an aisle in a Gothic Cathedral, accompanied by an organ, and anon the full chime. John S. Dwight, Editor of Dwight's *Journal of Music,* was then contacted with a view to his accepting for publication William's criticism of Mendelssohn's "Song of Praise."[10]

At Concord, he was once again welcomed by the Alcotts. The *Oracles* were gone over thoroughly, and this time William was able to see their method. Samuel Joseph May, Mrs. Alcott's brother, came in for a visit and he talked of many things that interested William who noted that he was a co-worker of Wm. Lloyd Garrison and Phillips. F. B. Sanborn also put in an appearance of a night and was entertaining and cordial. Both he and Mr. Slack whom William had met in Boston, seemed very willing to undertake the publication of anything William might send them. Miss Elizabeth Palmer Peabody called and was very much interested in the writings of General Hitchcock. William also met Thoreau's mother.

Time passed quickly in discussions and more discussions. They talked of this and of that, how Emerson's article on Christianity was refused by the *Atlantic,* what conversations Alcott was to give when a hundred dollars could be found to bring him once more to St. Louis, and a number of other things. William took with him eleven numbers of the *Dial*, promising to send Alcott $10 for them. The Proclus volume he did not take with him, after all.

The time to go back to St. Louis was now close at hand. At Worcester, on the Nashua Railroad, William made another stop with his old friend Charles C. Baldwin who had just completed a translation of a work by Renan on Oriental Literature and was making "very learned notes" from Bunsen's point of view relative to it. They played chess together.

Back at Williamsville, with his in-laws, William relaxed for a short time and read *Reason in Religion*, by Dr. Hedge, who had written him a letter to Putnam and which had been forwarded to him at his wife's home. It was now too late to visit the good Doctor, for they were in the midst of preparations to return to St. Louis . . .

GUARDIANS OF THE FAITH

"I set so much by you that I expected to have you when you got to be a man very near perfection . . ."

The one who wrote these words to William,[11] grandmother Torrey, closed her eyes forever on January 10th, 1866, at the age of 85 years, one month, and seven days. Dearly beloved by William and Sarah, she was deeply mourned. In her letters she had called William her son, the one person that seemed to be nearest her. He was to write his mind to her as to a good friend. She acknowledged that she had been the feeble means of William's education, buying him books, and fortifying him in his trust in providence. In every letter she would admonish him to think of and fear God, to "do well and above all to be prepared for death." Of course, she never heard of Kant, nor of Hegel . . .

Rev. J. P. Watson, Acting Pastor in the Putnam Heights Church, had written William under date of November 27th, 1864, as neither he nor his parish had had any communication from William relative to his "religious state and experience." He considered it his duty to make himself known to William and inquire after his "hopes and spiritual welfare," and, since the General Association was urging "the churches to be more faithful in recommending, and arranging matters, in cases of absence," to arrange a transfer of his membership to a St. Louis Church. In truly Christian spirit he signed: "With christian cordiality, your Bro.: J. P. Watson."

While at Putnam in the summer of 1865, William talked with the good man and, casting caution to the winds, mentioned his philosophical interests. Nevertheless, the name of Rev. Dr. Truman M. Post was mentioned, and his church suggested as one that he might join. It was the First Trinitarian Congregational Church, at Locust and 10th Streets, built in 1858 of brick, with a stone basement and broad stone steps leading to the three entrances. Six fluted columns supported the frontispiece, giving a rich appearance to the edifice. However, no agreement was reached, and the pastor wrote again on December 4th, 1865, this time a little more strongly, addressing William as brother, but signing merely "yours very cordially." The letter was a sort of ultimatum. Harris was either to be dismissed, lose his ecclesiastical connection and be cut off as a delinquent, or he would have to be transferred to the St. Louis church. The papers of transfer were enclosed, containing a statement of his present relation to the church, but William's "late religious walk and piety" was neither endorsed nor vouched for.

Again, William did not make any move. The charitable pastor's patience was exhausted and he wrote on June 29th, 1866, addressing his letter "Dear Friend" and signing "yours etc." This time, William made answer in a long letter:[12]

1866, St. Louis, Mo., 16th July

Dear Sir:

Yours of the 29th ult. is before me. I have to ask

pardon for delay in answering this and the former letter of December 4th, 1865.

I have never used the letter referred [to] although I have had some thoughts that I might on some future occasion. I shall return it herewith at your request and beg leave to make the following statement with reference to my present and past religious views.

After I joined the church in 1853, my experience for 3 years and a half was one continual fight of faith against intellectual conviction. On the one hand was my belief in literal dogma without any grounds, and on the other hand was the mental tendency to consider grounds for and against. I read much in the way of defences on Christianity and outside bolsterings [?] by scientific men (Hitchcock e.g.) and had no rest — it was a one-sided matter; their faith without intellectual conviction, or the latter without the former. Finally in 1856 I got off on to that current that takes the historic side and exhibits development (call it progress or simply change, if you please) in the history of the church or even of all religion. Its procedure with reference to religion is precisely like that used by latter day sceptics, Compte, Lewes, etc., against philosophy. The different statements prove that none of them are true. "One refutes the other and it is all here refuted." Thus they contend that the different religions prove that there is no absolute religion. Then they undertake to show [the] resemblance of certain points in Christianity, e.g. the Indian Trimurti with the Trinity. To be brief, in the summer of 1856 after an extensive reading of what I had not dared before to read, I all at once decided that there was no doubt at all that the popular theology was very imperfect and no more binding, at least upon me. I at once felt great relief and commenced now in earnest my search for what is true on my own hook; looking eagerly to all sides for something that should most fulfill the conditions. First I fell in with quantities of spiritual literature and the Andrew Jackson Davis publications; soon after that Theodore Parker's works, which gave me a strong impulse towards German philosophy and literature and a moderate one back toward Christianity, thus checking the tendency towards Voltaire and Tom Paine.

About this time I began to study Cousin and history of philosophy and Critique of Kant. I began to see glimpses of a rational order in the universe corresponding to reason in me. And more important still, I began [to] see that reason is not my particular property, but rather the universal light of personality into which I rise through consciousness, and hence the talk about Emerson I was obliged to consider mere unfounded assertion. At the same time I got many partial insights into the rational foundations of society, family and state, etc.

My protest had been against all institutions and not religion alone. I challenged them all to make themselves valid to my intellect or else hold their peace. As mere conventionalities they contained nothing intrinsic and must give way to other forms of man's choosing. But with this insight into the universality of reason I began to see a substantial basis outside of mere caprice and individual humor. I saw that truth is the objective and that reason exists independent of my consciousness as an individual and thence institutions proceeded, thence therein religion. From Cousin I went into Emerson and Carlyle and found this view much elaborated by them. In 1857 I went into Goethe and found far deeper questions in the same direction. It is only with renunciation properly speaking a life may be said to begin, says he. This doctrine he elaborates profoundly and hints in no obscure manner at Christianity. So I got an insight into what St. Paul calls the two natures at war within us. The one of them is our finite individuality as a particular being of passion and desires, and the other is our universal individuality or reason which makes immortal beings. It was clear that we must renounce the fleshly self for the universal self. This looked to me very much like the central doctrine of Christianity at that time and as such I accepted it. The crucifixion seemed a deeply significant symbol of the crossing of our two natures in conflict. I began to find great pleasure in reading Thomas à Kempis' Imitation of Christ and such works. And the reading of Dante's Divine Comedy at that time showed me how clearly Dante saw the intellectual side of the religion he professed.

I worked into Kant who is the great rock of philosophic scepticism (Hamilton and Mansel) and in December 1858 I got my first philosophical insight and this lifted me above and beyond the Kantian scepticism. During the next year I got another insight and was really beyond the Fichtean standpoint though I mistook the true results of his system at that time. For 2 years longer there was a streak of pantheism in my view of things, I did not like it but could not see around it and was determined to accept what is and let it work. I saw that reason is the substance of the universal and that time and space are only results of it and hence all that is in time and space is subject to reason as to ultimate design or purpose and that it is perishable. But it was clear that as conscious [beings] we were partakers of the Reason and thus elevated above time and space. The form of insight was not definite enough to settle clearly the question of immortality of the individual, nor of the personality of God, although it seemed that

God is person and that we are persons because we partake of him through consciousness. After studying Hegel sometime I began in the summer of 1862 to get hold of the nature of the difficulty. The article in the *Bibliotheca Sacra* for April 186.) (LXVI by Rev. C. C. Tiffany, Derby, Conn.) on Rothe's *Ethics* gave me much. I saw that the form of the Absolute could not be a becoming, but must be an eternal reality. The relation of this eternal one to the changeable multiplicity of time and space seemed to take this form: there is an eternal self-contemplation (reflection[?]) and thus chaos or pure space is posited and cancelled through time — the form of time including a complete return to the self-thinking one which is the goal. Thus man arrives at immortality while all below him is finite and perishable. — Further development brought out the result very clearly that man is immortal individually, that God is a person, nay more, 3 persons in one and that although man by nature is totally depraved and is only saved through Christ, or the 2nd person of the Trinity, the mediator, and that all the dogmas of Christianity are slightly symbolical statements of the inevitable philosophical results, they follow a purification of the thinking from the stage of mere reflection or sensuous imaging. It is moreover evident that religion is a perennial form of the relation between the historical man and the absolute. The Christian religion has all the ideas in their speculative intent. And it is also very evident that the so-called liberal sects of Christians which revolt at some misunderstood dogma, but state it however to suit themselves, do in fact fall away most woefully from the speculative intent spoken of. Take, for example, the Unitarians who revolt at what I now see to be the deepest and truest dogma, that of the Trinity, of 3 persons in one God, the class who with

Beecher deny the doctrine of the understanding, reflection. rightly called finite (or human), for the speculative one of the reason.

The Trinity is the last point I have got a glimpse into
last winter.

I only wish to say that now I feel an immense and
infinite value in religious expressions in vogue where
I once felt nothing but empty contradictions. I think
that I may describe my experiences as the coming out
of negative scepticism through the piety of the intellect
and arriving again at the standpoint of unity and harmony with the dogmas I professed at first. I do not
know what you, or most preachers of the Gospel would
say to my experience and I by no means recommend it
to others — I only say that if one finds himself in doubt
or scepticism (which always results from the intellect)
that he will most certainly find the intellect to heal the
same scepticism if he will pursue it faithfully and deep
enough. I think the ideal Christian should not only
live Christ in his life, but also see with Christ in his
beholding.

Whatever you make of my case, my own individual
preference is to remain connected for a while with the
church which I first joined and as it is a Congregational
church I trust that the Presbyterian rules do not press
so hard [as] you seem to think in your letter. Please
write me again.

Yours truly,
(Signed) William T. Harris

There is no letter in reply in existence. There probably
never was one. William's epistle, it seems, left the good
pastor breathless and unable to frame a letter which he
might have had to end with due regard to his Christian
conscience with less than "yours etc."

TAXES, CHOLERA, RAILROADS AND WOMAN SUFFRAGE

The year 1866 was important for Harris in many respects. On January 13th, he wrote in his *Diary* with satisfaction that his name was in the property tax list, being assessed to the total of $900, of which his books alone amounted to $500, clocks and watches $50, and the rest, constituting household furniture, $350. His income now was $1350, his income tax exemption $915, leaving a taxable balance of $435 on which the tax of 5% amounted to $8.70. The frugal days of the Civil War had now been weathered and the major part of his loans on which he had to pay as high as 10% were paid back.

Correspondence with friends and acquaintances could now be taken up with a feeling that he was making his mark on the world. The *Report of the Public Schools,* of which he truly could be proud, was sent to his Eastern acquaintances as a token of his progress. New friendships were entered, some with generals who served in the War, and social functions were attended a little more frequently. Above all, 1866 must be noted as the date of the founding of the Philosophical Society and the making articulate a series of definite plans culminating in the publication of the *Journal of Speculative Philosophy* the following year. But of this in another place.

His brother Edward Mowry graduated in 1866 from medical school, receiving his M.D. from Harvard. William looked forward to great things from him.[13] Aside from losing their grandmother that year, William had to mourn the death of a very dear friend of his with whom he had been in daily contact, Charles F. Childs. He died on February 15th. The evenings seemed lonely now, for either Childs had been at William's, or William had gone to Childs' place. Together they had revelled in Dante and taken to studying Italian. When not reading, they used to go to the gymna-

238

sium, and William would compete with the weaker Childs in throwing dumbbells.

Childs was four years William's senior,[14] and was Principal of Franklin School when the two got acquainted. He rose to the Principalship of the High School three years before his death. His nature was gentle, and he shared with William the ideal conviction, but mellowed some of his ardent educational theories. He knew his child psychology, and though William could not note "so good order, in the sense of being still and sitting up erect" in his class-room, he could see that his pupils were alert and enthusiastic.[15] His lectures were always applauded. There was a throng present at the funeral, held in Dr. Post's Church. William was selected to give the eulogy on March 23rd, at the High School, to an assembled 200 persons, because he had been his most intimate friend and was "a teacher like him."

It was in 1866 that the cholera was raging in St. Louis and school opening had to be postponed. William consumed large quantities of quinine. His sister Sarah Lydia had her life insured for $1000 when she finally returned from Putnam to teach in St. Louis after the cholera had subsided. Grave concern for William was expressed in these times by all his friends, including Defonfride who left the city for reasons of health and was then dividing his residence between France and Italy. He knew his friend's habits and warned him not to work "with quite an American rashness." Napoleon studied and poured over his books of strategy at night; Milton found his gems at midnight; Erasmus never ceased his labors — why should not William Torrey Harris do likewise? Who could tell but that one day fame might be his also? Hence, another cup of coffee, but not too strong, and yet another and a third, to whip the tired brain back to animation! William simply would not lend ear to any advice that implied curtailing his activity.

The problem of the cholera was not a new one, for the

plague had raged in St. Louis in the early years of the War. William was much interested in its etiology and prophylactics and filled his note-books with clippings from the daily papers dealing with all aspects of the problem, from statistics to the wildest guesses at its origin and cure.

The *cholera morbus* claimed its victims principally during the month of August. Although 1866 was a very bad year, the last really furious outbreak in St. Louis had occurred in 1849, due to the influx of dirt-infested immigrants from the yards of New Orleans.[16] Then it had actually decimated the St. Louis population. In 1866 it was observed that the greatest virulence came not during the moist and almost tropical weather, but during the following dry and hot period. It made its appearance once more to a lesser degree in 1867. That time, it seems, William was taken by fevers and chills, to judge by his correspondence with Amos Bronson Alcott during January and February, 1868. Yet, it did not seriously impair his prodigious activity for the time being. He did succumb in 1870 when, in the beginning of the year, another epidemic broke out in St. Louis which caused a good many problems in keeping and managing school. From San Antonio, Texas, Ira Divoll wrote him *à propos*:[17]

> . . . I am very sorry but not at all surprised to learn of your illness. You are injuring your health by overwork. No man on earth can endure for many years the enormous amount of labor you perform. No one can have any adequate appreciation of the troublesome nature of the questions you have to deal with — ("killing negations", as you forcibly express it) — except the party who fills or has filled the office of Superintendent. While you would do good, evil is present with you. — While you would spend all your strength on positions, you are compelled to battle with negations. The troublesome question of taxation which I nearly wore out

my life on, it seems you have to fight over again. I wish
I were there to help you . . .

Since such advice militated against William's ambition,
it fell on deaf ears. In the eulogy of Ira Divoll, William
made this statement: "To live for the sake of living is base:
life is but a means given us in order that we may achieve
with it a rational purpose."

On October 19th, 1867, William was a member of a party
of the U. S. Commissioners, Dr. W. N. White, of New
Haven, Ct., Maj. Gen. N. B. Buford, of Rock Island, and
John B. Drake, of the Tremont House, Chicago, who were
on an inspection tour of the Union Pacific Railway which
was then completed as far as mile post 290, just beyond Fort
Hayes, 573 miles from St. Louis, which point they reached
the following morning. It was beautiful autumn weather
and the country, especially around St. Louis, was at its best
in color hues.

There is nothing surprising in the fact that there was such
a close connection between the schools and railroads. Hundreds and thousands of teachers used the railroads to go to
conventions; the railroads bought property from the School
Board on several occasions. In both cases, personal relations
with railroad magnates and officials were established. Thus,
General Buford, engineer for the Union Pacific Railway,
became a close friend of William's. State Superintendent
John Monteith[18] once said: "The railroad is the friend of
the common school."

William's relation to Monteith seems always to have been
friendly. When he was put up for renomination in 1874,
and violent attacks were made on his integrity by some section of the press, Harris was aware that it was nothing but
a phase of the general conspiracy against the schools motivated by the advocates of sectarianism, combined with forces
that sought to rid the school administration of even a moderate church influence.

In 1866 appeared William's article "The Female Protest in America: As Exhibited in 'Emily Chester' ".[19] He had sent it, a manuscript of 6000 words, together with a letter dated April 20th, 1866, to Mr. Slack, editor of the *Commonwealth* (Boston), according to an agreement made the year before when William was visiting in the East. The beginning reads like High School oratory, but with the fifth paragraph we are ensnared in the deepest of metaphysics. The writing of it may have been occasioned by discussions with some German friends centering around the problems of American womanhood, women's rights, free love tendencies and the sentiment prevalent in this pre-suffrage age of woman "wanting to be a man." However, it contains also something else, a description of two types of persons which William identifies with two characters known from Goethe's writings, *Wilhelm Meister* and *Faust*, who symbolize two ways of attaining culture, ways which William himself had travelled, and thus are autobiographical in nature:

First, the prose character, or the ordinary mind, which begins with the narrowest objects, and finds therein his satisfaction. He is the man of hobbies. "Thou shalt have no other gods before me" is the command of Spirit addressed to Spirit. But this man finds the all in some pitiful puppet-show or some science of phrenology, or scheme of universal philanthropy. The inherent negativity of such an object carries him to another hobby, but of a more general character. He has seized the part for the whole, and his development goes on through a long series of widening grades until his thought has dissolved one after another the institutions of the organism of civilization in which he is. He now appreciates all, and apprizes all at its true value; his "other gods" have vanished and given place to the true absolute.

The second character (whose problem is solved in

Faust) is the opposite of the first. Wilhelm Meister the prose character, Faust the genius; the former the passive, the latter the active or creative. The genius has an instinct or feeling of the totality, — he has an ideal. His problem is to unite this with the real. He at first finds himself at war with the real, and this is his negative period. The result is that every contest against the real which he initiates ends not only in his discomfiture, but he finds himself subsumed by it. He finds his ideal in the actual moving spirit of the time. This is inevitable; the rational is the actual; but the actual is never the dead result, but the energizing spirit.

The "female struggle" of his time, William interpreted as the unrest that follows upon the desire for culture in the true sense. Mere sentimentality is laid aside, and the intellectual becomes separated from the emotional, a state of mind necessary for the appearance of consciousness as the medium of culture.

William's interest in woman suffrage and co-education was not at all superficial. His scrapbooks abound in clippings on this topic. However we look in vain for the name of his wife in a list of those who subscribed to the movement, though we find Mrs. S. H. Bailey, Mrs. Wm. T. Hazard, Mrs. Geo. H. Howison, Mrs. C. F. Childs, and Miss Anna Brackett, the last a most vigorous suffragette, and all friends and acquaintances of the Harrises, belonging to it. To be sure, there was a "Mrs. Harris" who signed the petition to strike out the word "male" in the Constitution, but whether it was William's wife is more than doubtful. In the fall of 1869, Mrs. Julia Ward Howe, a personal acquaintance of William's, made a great speech before the Woman Suffrage Convention at St. Louis. William was always fond of mentioning his contributions to some of the issues that produced the movement and referred to the school *Report* for

1872-73, in which he discussed the basic factors of woman's participation in politics, industry and education.

Another visit to Yale occurred during the summer of 1868, when William saw again his '58 class-mates at their Decennial Meeting on July 22nd. With spirit he joined in the fun of the sumptuous dinner and the songs, particularly Isaac Riley's one, "I tell you, Old Yale's Around," reputed to have been the last words and perennial testimony of Jesse Andrews, late sweep of North College.

On August 12th that year, William returned to St. Louis with renewed vigor, for heavy tasks lay ahead of him in the administration of the city's schools . . .

CHAPTER TEN

THE SCHOOL'S THE THING

ASCENT TO THE SUPERINTENDENCY

T HE Board of Public Schools, under the Presidency of S. D. Barlow, had been most appreciative of Harris' work in the capacity of Assistant Superintendent. His suggestions along various lines, such as school management, instruction, methods of engaging attention, exciting interest, and effecting economy in the time and powers of pupils, the judicious selection of textbooks, and the use of apt and comprehensive illustrations, were believed to be of great value and afforded "great satisfaction," generally.[1] Thus, at the May, 1868, meeting of the Board, William Torrey Harris was elected Superintendent, over the other two nominees for office, John A. Gilfillan and Francis Berg.

Harris had not yet reached his 33rd year when he assumed the highest office in the educational system of the Western metropolis. Doubts that had been expressed on account of his youth, were dispelled gradually and his popularity grew year by year. At the next elections, Harris received 15 votes, his opponent, Wm. B. Fielding, nine, and in 1870, at the usual nominations, Harris scored 23 of a total of 24 votes in his favor.

With this decided victory Harris obtained practically the unanimous approval of his policies which even a year before he had become Superintendent were considered questionable by a number of Board members. He continued to hold the respect and loyalty of the Board members till his retirement. With a salary fixed at $4000, on June 21st, 1870, he was the highest paid public official in the school system of the State, excepting the State Superintendent.

The public also gradually became aware, as someone expressed it in the papers, that Harris gave "to his practical duties, as immediate director of this great city's system of schools, the utmost of wisdom and tact and enthusiasm and detailed application." All who knew Harris only as a philosopher and abstruse thinker and had anticipated a visionary in office, were agreeably surprised. Only those who did not derive any benefit from a free, public, and non-denominational education, continued their opposition.

Harris assumed the duties of Superintendent of Public Schools exactly 30 years after the first Public School had been established in the City of St. Louis in April, 1838. This school, at the corner of Fourth and Spruce Streets, accomodated 175 pupils. The first English school established in the city was that of Geo. Tompkins, in 1808, who became later a Supreme Court Justice of Missouri. But the first regular school was held by the Rev. Dr. Salmon Giddings, Pastor of the First Presbyterian Church, oddly enough also a native of Connecticut who had set foot in the city in 1816, arriving on horseback.

Before the first free public school had been organized, education was a matter of the family, or, someone who knew how to write and "cipher" was engaged as teacher. Keeping school was not an "honorable" profession, such as law or divinity; at the most one had sympathy for the philanthropic endeavors of teachers. The Hon. Edward Bates said in 1859 that before schools were established in St. Louis, pupils had to be sent to Danville, Ky., as the nearest place where instruction could be had. Several private schools, of course, had always been in existence, some dating even from before the 19th century. Jean Baptiste Trudeau is said to have been the first school teacher in St. Louis, and Marie Payant Rigauche the first school ma'am.[2]

From 1838 to 1868, the Public School houses had changed considerably. In the words of Barlow, "formerly the schoolhouse was distinguished for its frigid and dilapidated exterior, its cheerless apartments, and crude furnishings; these being generally in terrible harmony with the scowls of the school-master and the discipline of the rod within."[3] An even greater change for the better was now ahead with Harris at the helm.

Since 1848, it had been the custom to designate schools by names rather than numbers, and the names chosen were those of distinguished citizens from the early history of Missouri or St. Louis. Chouteau School, for instance, commemorated Auguste Chouteau, one of the founders of St. Louis who was a very young man when sent by Pierre Ligueste Laclede to mark out and clear the spot for a trading post. This Laclede, after whom another school was named, was the founder of a famous fur trading company that established itself in St. Louis in 1764. Benton School reminded the pupils of Thomas Hart Benton, Missouri's most distinguished statesman, a man of national renown, soldier and far-sighted publisher and industrialist; Clark School was named after George Rogers Clark, the first to establish a fort on the Mississippi River. Mullanphy School bore the name of an early pioneer, Stoddard School, located in a fine residential section and very aristocratic in character, that of Major Stoddard who received Upper Louisiana from Spain for France and later was the accredited agent to deal with the United States. Some schools were named after famous personalities who had visited St. Louis, as Baron de Carondelet, Henry Clay, Daniel Webster. Others again were named in honor of St. Louis benefactors and philanthropic businessmen, such as O'Fallon and Carr. The history of the Public Schools themselves furnished names from among Board members, administrators and teachers whose services warranted such, as, for instance, Shephard School, Penrose, Divoll, and Blow Schools. Pestalozzi, the famous educator, doubtless was commemorated at Harris' suggestion, as was Alexander von Humboldt after whom one school in a purely German section was named.[4]

William Torrey Harris was the 10th Superintendent. His predecessors were, in order:

George K. Budd, 1839-1841, whose salary was "thanks."

Henry Pearson, 1841-1842. Salary $300.00. The following six years show no record of a Superintendent, but it is stated that the Board was financially embarrassed.

Edward M. Avery, 1848-1850. Salary $900.00
Spencer Smith, 1850-1851. Salary $1000.00
John H. Tice, 1851-1852. Salary $1500.00
A. Litton, 1852-1853. Salary $1500.00.
Charles A. Putnam, 1853-1854. Salary $1500.00.
John H. Tice, 1854-1857. Salary $1500.00.
Ira L. Divoll, 1858-1868. Salary $2000.00-$3500.00.
Wm. T. Harris, 1868-1880. Salary $3500.00-$4000.00, reduced to $3600.00 the last two years.

CAMPAIGNING FOR A FRIEND

Harris had fully proven himself even as Assistant Superintendent. The outgoing Superintendent, Ira Divoll, could now relax, relieved of his duties. Down the Mississippi he journeyed again in 1869; still his restless nature could not fully enjoy the leisurely pace of river steamers, even though floods and a great storm made the voyage exciting. In his mind he was forging more ambitious plans all the time. He revealed them first to his trusted friend and former associate, Harris.

Born in Orange County, Vermont, and an 1848 graduate

of Burlington University, Divoll had come West soon after receiving his diploma. At New Orleans he became the Principal of a Grammar School, then opened a private classical school for boys, which apparently was very successful, pecuniarily. He studied law besides and was admitted to the courts of Louisiana in 1852. Then he practiced law for a while together with his friend, G. Q. H. Fellows. But having contracted yellow fever and been very ill, he saw it advisable to seek a more Northern climate and came to St. Louis where he arrived in May, 1855. In June he was admitted to the Bar of Missouri and went into partnership with Hugh Ewing. During his leisure time he wrote educational articles, and in 1857 was elected Superintendent of Public Schools.

Upon his retirement, a very appreciative resolution had been passed by the Board, honoring him as gentleman, scholar, and educator, and ranking him "high among the noblest promoters of free education in our time." Now he expected to run for State Superintendent of Schools, in 1870. Full of confidence he wrote to Harris from New Orleans, January 15th, 1870: "Suppose I should wholly recover my health and take a notion to run for State Superintendent of Schools, next summer, what would be my chances of success? Has the question been agitated at all by the State Teacher's Association or otherwise?" It was his desire to run on pure merit and on educational, not political grounds. Accordingly, he outlined a course of procedure in a letter of January 23rd. In addition, he sent Harris "private letters" on the school situation in New Orleans, which were really intended for publication. Divoll had a disposition to leave no stone unturned to accomplish his objective, and Harris labored in his behalf, writing, speaking, and interviewing. Especially one person had to be won over to the cause, Major J. B. Merwin, editor of the *Journal of Education*, temperance advocate, and eloquent speaker.

In February, Divoll left for San Antonio, Texas, where he found the atmosphere very dry, so dry you could almost touch it off with a match. He returned to New Orleans and, after a brief stay in St. Louis, went North to Baraboo, Sauk County, Wisc., where he expected Harris to visit him. After a prolonged delay of the visit, it had to be given up, however, for little Ethan Harris died in July that year. Although Divoll's personal attachment to Harris is rarely apparent from his cool and businesslike letters, on this occasion he wrote rather tenderly:[5]

I am pained to learn of the death of your little one and do most sincerely sympathize with you in your great loss—the loss of a child that has become endeared to you as well on account of trials of patience and suffering, as on account of its prattle and playfulness, and its promise of future comfort to its parents. 'Tis sad, inexplicable to mortal vision, that such little ones should be taken from those who are willing to spend and be spent in trying to rear them to usefulness in life, but such seems to be the order of providence.

From Baraboo, Divoll conducted his campaign for the State Superintendency by correspondence, living through some anxious days from July to October. Parker seemed to be a formidable competitor, and the campaign was waged by all means — letters, press releases, and gossip.

Divoll had, at first, a good many competitors. There were at least three candidates by the name of Matthias, Smith, and Laughlin, that had to be reckoned with, but Divoll, with his Yankee determination, was confident that they had no more chance of being elected State Superintendent than of becoming Emperor of China. He persuaded Harris to combine with Merwin and Sutherland to force the withdrawal of some of the weaker candidates.

He never knew such a word as defeat. His marriage was like that too. He had seen the lady of his heart only once,

but six months after that she received an offer of marriage,
which she declined. Two more offers were made, which
were likewise rejected — but he did marry her eventually.
Now he utilized Harris for his ends, and Harris profited
much in that he gained an insight into politics and made
worthwhile connections which worked for his own good and
without conscious efforts on his part.

By September, 1870, Divoll was back in St. Louis. Everybody he knew in that city was made to campaign for him,
either directly or indirectly. Harris was excessively busy
getting endorsements for him from teachers, the Board, the
Principals, the staff and Directors of the Public School
Library, and others. Besides, a number of matters needed
consideration, such as the appropriate phrasing and timely
publication of campaign papers. Merwin's *Journal of Education* had to be handled most diplomatically. A pamphlet
was to be printed, with the original call, important endorsements and extracts from the *Missouri Republican,* the St.
Louis *Democrat,* the *Western Educational Review* and the
Journal of Education. Harris acted as Chairman of the
Nominating Committee and the announcement had to contain his statements too. From 5 to 10 thousand copies were
circulated throughout the State, particularly among the
township clerks, "most likely a pretty intelligent set of fellows", as Divoll called them in one of his letters. This cir-
cularizing he considered his last card and he was not mistaken in its effectiveness. By a majority of 40,000, he was
elected State Superintendent of Schools, running on the
liberal-Republican ticket of B. Graetz Brown. By January,
1871, his letters emanated from Jefferson City on official
stationery.

However, with this promotion, Divoll did not disappear
from the sphere of Harris' activity in St. Louis. State Superintendent Divoll relied on Harris for many, often petty
things, such as getting him a lock and key to hide his docu-

ments from prowling officials, drawing up questions to test ability and character of new appointments for Principalship (he recognized Harris' questions as "always exhaustive"), and like services. A weary invalid, he suffered from his old malady, "night sweats" and swollen legs and feet, and overwork, so that almost every letter to Harris carried a complaint and appeal for help.

Divoll's condition had been so low even at the time of his receiving his appointment, that he was seen but a few times in his office. He worked at home and his main problem was the perfection of the State school laws and the appointment of the Board of Regents for Normal Schools. Two or three weeks before his death he sent his resignation to Governor B. Graetz Brown, and it was granted. The Rev. John Monteith was nominated in his stead.

On June 16th, 1871, Divoll's wife wrote from Baraboo, Wisc., where they were staying with her brother, Mr. Rich, that Divoll was growing weaker and weaker, but that he was always "wonderfully gratified" when receiving letters. A few days after, he died of tuberculosis. She wrote Harris an account of his last hours, believing that he was as dear to Harris as Harris was to him.

The trip to Wisconsin had done him good, visibly, but soon after, a change had set in. He became delirious and for a day preceding his death was conscious only at intervals. To quote Mrs. Divoll[6]:

He suffered for a while but died at last in the utmost peace and calm. He spoke of several of his friends and a little while before the end raised his right hand and pointing with his finger exclaimed distinctly, "I see Harris".

Just before we left St. Louis he told me that he *trusted* you as fully as he did his *wife.*

Even on his deathbed, Divoll could not do without Harris and asked his wife to confer with him as to his interment.

When the railroad to Baraboo was finished in the fall, the heavy casket was transferred to St. Louis.

Thus were rent asunder the earthly ties between two educators. It had been an unceremonious friendship which, as Mrs. Divoll admitted, was unselfish and "without much demonstration on either side," "a mutual feeling of trust and confidence such as can exist only between liberal minds."[7] As late as January, 1878, she wrote Harris, expressing great pleasure in his success, but urging him not to wear out his life, thinking, of course, of her late husband.

"Very few can know, as the writer of this article knows," were Harris' words a few years before about Divoll, "the amount of toil which that man expended in overcoming obstacles to the practical working of the schools". The lifesize portrait of Ira Divoll, painted by Weigandt, was hung in 1869 in the Hall of the Polytechnic building, with S. D. Barlow presiding at the meeting while Harris made the presentation speech in "a few neat and appropriate remarks."

Now Harris was free to steer the destiny of the St. Louis Public Schools according to his own conceptions . . .

THE NEW OUTLOOK IN SCHOOL ADMINISTRATION

William Torrey Harris was a successful teacher, but he was an even more successful administrator.

His two Assistants in office, in 1869, were Wm. D. Butler for the English Department, and Francis Berg for the German and English Department. For his personal and routine work he employed amanuenses to look after the interschool correspondence which was sharply on the increase. They charged him with extravagance when his staff included a chief clerk, two assistant clerks, and one supply clerk in addition to a stenographic reporter when the Board was in session. Yet, Harris could not have done with less.

The office of Superintendency took on an altogether new feature. Harris became the link between the Board, the entire school staff, and the public. He had to explain the ways and means adopted by the Board, had to keep abreast of the problems of taxation, political organization, elections, and educational legislation in addition to the problems of pedagogy and Public School administration.

In his report to the Board for the first quarter of the school year 1868-9, Harris stated the fact that, counted by the different departments inspected, he had made over 400 school visits, and Mr. Butler, the Assistant Superintendent, about the same number. Later, F. Louis Soldan assisted in school visits, but the records show that, for example during 1870-71, Harris visited each one of the 48 schools at least once during the first three quarters, and some as often as 12 times, making a total of 187 visits. Until he proved that it would be cheaper for the Board to buy him a horse and buggy, he would, on these visits, use a hired one. His expense account for this item, from April, 1874, to April, 1875, totalled $517. Extensive notes were taken of the difficulties, the quality of work, and the general condition of instruction and school property. Just one of the notes from the year 1876, may illustrate his full schedule of school visits:

P. M.

Pub. School Library	12:05
High	12:30—1:00
2nd Br. High	1:05—1:25
Webster	1:35—2:00
Douglas	2:00—2:30

School organization became one of the most important considerations in the year 1870 when the city limits were extended and the school system grew by leaps and bounds. A change in management became advisable and Harris recommended the giving of greater authority to the Principals. They were to act as local superintendents,[8] thus making the government of 400 teachers easy.[9] By 1871, the Principals had been "emancipated." The promise of no interference was given them, as far as the government of their schools was concerned, but they were held responsible for the results they obtained. It was democracy at work, and a good deal of Harris' success may be ascribed to this policy.

Even good teachers, Harris maintained, could not be expected to secure good results if unassisted by organization. And, conversely, Principals were expected to be good teachers as well. To himself, as Superintendent, he reserved the right to evaluate the work of the schools by the standards he had set. The system worked smoothly by 1872 when the reorganization was practically complete.[10] Later, the Principals of first class schools were elevated to the rank of "Supervising Principals." This office became more or less rotating and carried with it a 10% increase in salary. Late in the seventies, Harris nominated his two Assistant Superintendents, and selected 14 of his ablest Principals to further assist him. All committees of the Board had to work in close contact with him.[11] Philbrick, of Boston, characterized this system as a complete, centralized, responsible hierarchy. By many, the St. Louis plan was called un-American because it lacked a multitude of counsellors in whom democracy seeks safety. The Boston papers[12] pictured Harris on the throne of state, ruling with royal hand the schools as well as the School Board. But Harris himself attributed the fine co-operation of the Board to the absence of a domineering city council or some other municipal authority that might, in a whimsical mood, withhold appropriations or meddle in revenues and appointments.

As early as May, 1869, Harris served as Secretary *pro tem* to the Board, and there was never a meeting when he was not present. He never had to fight with the Board who was always sympathetic toward his ideas, but he did have to fight unenlightened public opinion which freely, and often maliciously, voiced its dissatisfaction, or tried to justify every grumble as a right in the taxpayer who, it might have been owned. paid very little for the protection against ignorance.

Often, Harris had to serve as a spokesman for the Board and, on not a few occasions, supplied the public with statements about school-finances, thus halting inquisitiveness at the gates of the Olympus in which the Directors dwelled and which they succeeded in removing farther and farther from the public gaze as time went on, not without the help of their efficient Superintendent.

The members of the Board did not have an easy time of it, however, as all their proceedings were published in the papers. One of their number[13] was actually struck with a cowhide by a disappointed applicant for a position as engineer, who in addition "used a great deal of offensive language."

Many suggestions were made to the Board by Harris, even in regard to their parliamentary procedure, for which they were thankful and which they adopted because of their practical nature. For he would never make a suggestion before acquainting himself fully with every aspect of the problem. The published letters to the Board in which observations were made on scholastic and administrative progress or deficiencies, and the regular *Annual Reports* give only a partial view of the almost herculean labor done by Harris.

The *Reports* in particular, representing a distinct departure from the run of dry compilations of mummified pedagogues, served many a school board as model and were highly praised in all quarters. And rightly so, for they not only rendered account of school activities and costs, but made the taxpayers take pride in their schools because Harris would reason with them and make them partners in the establishment of the finest Public School system. Beyond that, the citizen of St. Louis was given to realize that he was making a substantial contribution to American democracy by supporting the school; indeed, he was made to feel that he was contributing to the development of humanity, as Dr. Philander P. Claxton[14] has said. The discussions which these reports evoked all over the country and in Europe, especially in Germany where C. L. Bernays advertised them in all his contacts with Gymnasiums and universities, swelled Harris' correspondence to uncommon proportions. And yet, these *Reports* were by no means the only ones he furnished. There were the never ceasing Committee Reports. The State Education Department also had stirred to new activity and required information more frequently and more detailed than ever. The U. S. Bureau of Education was awakening from slumber and depended to a greater extent on the co-operation of the Superintendents throughout the nation for statistics.

To Harris, statistics were fascinating. While they seemed to indicate the "control of an inexorable fate or necessity", "a kind of iron destiny" that could reach even into the circle of human caprice and design, he could as readily see that they revealed freedom as well. The statistics he collected ranged from school furniture to calisthenics, from ventilation to attendance and eye-sight of the pupils. He initiated regular headache statistics which were compiled on a yearly basis. The *Journal of Education* at one time commented on the fact that census statistics were usually dry reading, but that Harris, by the alchemy of his philosophy, got a world of inspiration out of the fact that Americans numbered more than 50 million people. Add to all this the innumerable forms and blanks for teachers' reports, guide sheets, standard definitions and what not, the heliographing machine was kept busy and, with the introduction of the Kindergarten, the ink never dried on it. Harris' head was full of ideas which he jotted down on hundreds of slips of paper of every description and which he never disposed of but filed away even though they showed but a word or two. He supervised the placing of blackboards at a certain angle, the purchase of regulator clocks, the planning of sycamores;

he laid down rules and regulations for janitors and published guidance sheets for teachers and principals; he composed syllabi of physiology and other studies; he watched fire-drills; he kept records of the proceedings of the weekly, later bi-weekly and finally monthly meetings of the "emancipated" Principals and attended the conferences of the Teachers' Association which followed them.

Harris showed great concern for his teachers who were underpaid. They earned considerably less than policemen, and after 20 years of service got less salary than a clever clerk. Out of the $500 which they earned during their first year, they were expected to pay $2 monthly for carfare and stationery for notifying parents of the fact that their children were truant, $9–10 for laundry, and $32–40 for board. At one time the *Missouri Republican* wrote:

It must indeed be regarded as a great honor, that, after a teacher's exit from this *mundus*, that august assemblage, the Teachers' Association, shall put on elongated faces and, with the Board of Education, pass a vote of assent to a parcel of formal and false resolutions of intense grief concerning one of whom half of them had never known. It would be more fitting that the public sit in sackcloth and bewail those victims whom their penuriousness has murdered outright.

This was the responsibility of the School Board, and it must be said to the credit of Harris that as early as 1871 he made a strong plea for increased salaries. He maintained the doctrine of equal pay for equal work, regardless of sex, and that the pay attached to the position, not the person or sex. Women, however, he preferred for teaching children between 6 and 12 years of age. His efforts did bear fruit eventually, and he showed great shrewdness and alertness in drawing new talent to St. Louis. Thus, George B. McClellan, who received in Virginia $900 a year, was called to St. Louis at $1500. Anna C. Brackett had taught in Charleston, S. C., on a salary of $800; she was paid $2000 in Harris' schools.

Harris ran into considerable trouble when he required his Principals, by action of the Board, to be re-examined in 1877. Some absented themselves and, when held to account, openly expressed their resentment at having been insulted. Denton J. Snider, of the High School, was one of them, and his letter to the Teachers' Committee had this sentence: "I therefore declare with as much emphasis as I can utter, that an examination after so many years' service especially, is a professional degradation to which I shall not submit."

Poor teachers and those who had lost enthusiasm, Harris tried to encourage in his pep-talks at the St. Louis Teachers' Association meetings. They were to sustain the fine reputation of the schools in which they served. These meetings were often elaborate affairs with music, and if the public was invited, would often draw an audience of 1000 people. The programs then were multigraphed in an elaborate and artistic style by electric pen. Collections were sometimes taken up for benevolent purposes, mainly for sick and homeless teachers, as well as city charities.

Illustrative of the broad educational thinking of Harris was one of the talks he gave at the quarterly meeting of this Association, in April, 1878, the year which witnessed one of the worst depressions in the history of the United States. Never before had such restlessness, inattentiveness, impatience, crossness and faultfinding been experienced by him in school teachers. Salaries had been reduced, to be sure, but the financial condition of the school was in no way comparable to the straights in which they were during the Civil War. Thus he chose as topic "The Proper Care of the Brain." The lecture was criticized unjustly by the *Globe-Democrat* reporter as "a psychopathic homily in two parts— part one transcendental, lasting an hour, and part two practical, about ten minutes." Yet it was an interesting discourse during which he admonished the teachers to study

259

up on all forms of mental derangement and watch for symptoms in the children as well as in themselves, from insomnia to hypochondria and general loss of tone.

Harris had a wonderful understanding of the hardships and problems of teaching:[15]

> Of all vocations, that of teaching children is one of the most dangerous for warping and cramping the mind, and demands the strongest safeguards to protect the teacher. We therefore shorten the hours of the day's work to five or six, make five days a week's work, and cut off nearly one-fifth or one-sixth of the year for vacations.

And how much vacation did he have? Mr. Lippman or another member of the Board had to offer a resolution before he could even think of taking one for not more than four weeks at a time. It was, indeed, a life of arduous and faithful labor which Harris enjoyed as Superintendent. Even his trips East, West, South and North, when he spread his educational wisdom and gathered new impressions, were business or professional trips for each one of which he had to ask permission of the members of the Board. This they gave him readily and often enough, for they were also in his debt to no small degree.

Ever did Harris stand ready to shoulder the responsibility of advice, research and active propagandizing in matters of tax and income problems. While the population, wealth and industry had increased tremendously in St. Louis, the assessed value of property had maintained a "marvelous sameness." In 1874, a much criticized transaction took place which involved the sale of a portion of the so-called Grand Prairie common fields, in the County of St. Louis, school lands the income of which had been utilized for educational purposes in county and city since 1851. The schools in St. Louis received three-fourths of the money realized, or somewhat more than $150,000, while the county schools received the rest. Harris had to serve as general arbiter between those who thought it best to sell and those who questioned the legality of the procedure. Many were the voices that denounced this transaction as an "unrighteous schoolfund grab."

At the bidding of the Committee on Legislation of the Board of Public Schools, Harris visited, early in February, 1875, the State Capital to bring back valuable information concerning a contemplated redistribution of school funds, a complication that had arisen from the sale of "Section 16." And when in the following year, it had been suggested to abolish all school offices, except that of State Superintendent, and to consolidate all county and township school funds into one to be invested in State bonds, each person to be allowed to draw from it in proportion to the number of his children which he could send to school wherever he pleased — then Harris and the Board had to exercise extreme vigilance, for the passage of such a bill might well have spelled the end of the State school system, the consequences of which St. Louis could not have escaped.

Many were the dangers which threatened the St. Louis Public Schools from within in the mechanical, routine, and commonplace methods of instruction by teachers who were mere laborers in the school that provided a dumping ground for their intellectual dross. And from without they had to withstand a campaign for ignorance. Education was berated as a disease producing mental alertness and exertion. The question was asked: The mind being hidden from view, what will be the ultimate result of the slow pyogenic condition in the gray matter? Does anyone know? Well then, it would be better to take the poor children out of the hands of school masters and school ma'ams, and that as soon as possible! Some feared that education would interfere with civilization. "Brown-stone fronts do not spring up like mushrooms after a shower. Nor do the roads that glitter with liveried equipages furnish their stylish turnouts." Not to forget, there was the eternal complaint: "Here is a boy who has been to High School and cannot even . . ."

Harris was, in nearly every *Report*, able to report "evidences of continued and increasing prosperity" in his schools. It was most gratifying to him personally that the ratio of children in school increased faster than the ratio of the population, which could mean only one thing: that the schools were meeting a popular need and demand. There was a constant cry for more schools in that city of a hundred churches and more than nineteen hundred grogshops, no matter how many schools were built. There was no doubt, despite religious wrangles, Harris had made St. Louis thoroughly school-conscious.

There was only one thing that amazed both friend and foe: How could a man with such "speculative" interests as he possessed, manage such a vast organization as the Public Schools represented, so efficiently? They were in the same predicament as this writer in the *St. Louis Globe-Democrat*:[16]

> Mr. Harris is a transcendental philosopher, and when he gets hold of the Philosophy of the Conditioned he can puzzle a spelling-class; but when he takes hold of a plain question of fact, or explains the management of the public schools, he can satisfy the dullest intellect that his dealings with the abstruse mysteries of Kant and Hegel have not unfitted him for his practical work as a Superintendent.

His Majesty, The Future Citizen

It is a wrong approach to gauge Harris' contribution to education by his theories alone. Let us ask, what did he do for the pupil, the American boy and girl that were some day to direct our national destiny.[17]

Now, there is the poor student. What shall we do with

him? Let him receive a minimum of discouragement. And the good and brilliant pupil? He should get a maximum of encouragement, said Harris. How? Through frequent promotions, four times a year, at least. Let each pupil "fix his status by his own efforts." The student with little ambition, yet some ability, let him be burned twice, like a clinker, in the system of frequent promotions. His own experience in the little red school house and at Phillips Academy had given Harris more insight into what went on inside the pupil who was either held back or pushed ahead too far by a faulty system of grading and promotion. He was not so foolish as to believe that classification of students could be made fool-proof. But co-education he considered a powerful ally in arriving at a *better classification*. The teacher also benefitted by the scheme, for he or she was now able to teach with greater vigor and effect to a more homogeneous group. The brilliant student could no longer become lax and disinterested, the poor student would make progress in his own, slow way. The only trouble was that with a transfer to another school, the pupil had to walk sometimes a mile or so. This was especially the case when Harris advocated the transfer of pupils of the grammar grades from the district schools to the Branch High Schools.

Next, what were the boys and girls to study, according to Harris? That which had always been taught by school masters and school ma'ams? Certainly not, for the introduction of science had changed all that. Each subject was to be visualized as a window of the mind opening toward the cardinal points of the world of intelligence. How, then, could a course of study be forced into a Chinese iron shoe, or "nailed to the calendar"? The trouble was that the course of study had grown up, instead of having been planned with psychological insight — the very thing that vociferous opponents of Harris charged him with not possessing!

Obviously, all studies were either disciplinary or informational. The elementary branches consisted of reading and writing, the mastery of letters; arithmetic, the mastery of numbers: geography, the mastery over place; grammar, the mastery over the word; and history, the mastery over time. Thus conceived, arithmetic "quantifies," geography localizes, grammar fixes and defines speech, history deals with human processes, while reading will eventually lead to the comprehension of literature and all that is deposited by man as a heritage to his fellowmen.[18] So much for the foundation which everyone should have.

What right did the higher educational institutions, the colleges and universities, have to isolate themselves? Or even dictate to the common schools to have them cater to the type of specialized education *they* were giving? Let the Public School system be firmly established and it will force the colleges to adjust themselves. If there was any yielding to be done, it had to be higher education.[19]

In consequence, the course of instruction in the St. Louis Public Schools differed "materially from that pursued in most of the cities of the Union," but it also "won the admiration of educators all over the United States, on account of its philosophic breadth, thoroughness, and the perfect system maintained through the whole."[20]

In geography, not mere names and places were to be learned by the pupil, but he was to be instructed orally in all matters pertaining to the produce of a country, its political economy, and the sociologico-historical factors to know which produces political insight. History, too, was to be taught orally to hold the attention and interest of the pupil, and if taught rightly and understood thoroughly would eliminate all labor strikes which destroy the institutions that gave labor more power than it had ever possessed in the past.

Mathematics was to be vitalized. In the lower stages it had to deal with "the motives of men, their actions, and their life as a whole." No dead and lifeless fixed quantities here! One of his examination questions given to Principals[21] was: "May the teaching of mathematics be made to assist in the development of moral character? If so, how?" The study of mathematics should begin with the number 1, and the pupil was to know all about it before advancing to 2. Artihmetic lessons were not to be studied out of school. With the introduction of the Kindergarten, all of the arithmetic required in the first grade was to be taught in it.

St. Louis had a conglomerate population which was reflected in the speech of the school children. An ardent spelling reformer, Harris introduced Dr. Edwin Leigh's phonetic system when he was Principal of Clay School. His Assistant, Miss Helen H. Smith, did not make him feel as if it should be successful, but he stuck to his guns and had it taught with good results throughout the schools. Children would improve in articulation and uniform pronunciation. Bright children could learn the alphabet and cover the primer, the first, second, and often the third reader in their first year.

In life, the sexes are mixed, why not during the highly important period devoted to education? If co-education was not successful in such a frontier city as San Francisco, that was no proof that it would not work in St. Louis. Art, religion, philosophy have no sex, neither are ideas male or female. Americans were to be emancipated from rose-pink sentimentalism, they had to be weened from snobbishness and hypocritical attitudes. Discipline would improve with co-education. Rudeness and abandon in boys he saw replaced by self-restraint in the presence of girls. The silliness and frivolity in girls disappeared largely in the presence of boys, making room for a quiet self-possession. The female tendency toward learning-by-rote became balanced by the masculine tendency toward formalization. Girls would advance more quickly in mathematics, boys in the study of literature. He once mildly shocked the New Englanders when he expressed the view, in a lecture at the residence of Ex-Governor William Claflin, on Mt. Vernon Street, in Boston,[22] that the sphere of women was bound to enlarge with the advance in industry. Withall, co-education was also economical! Let sex remain the important concern of animals; in the social combination of human beings there takes place an approximation of the female to the male nature, as was the belief of Goethe, and "the special fitness or unfitness arising from sex is a *vanishing element*" in a world that approaches the ideal "wherein a concrete identity of spheres and vocations is to be found."

The test of humanity, however, lay in the treatment of the Colored. The State had decreed in 1865, that they were to be educated. St. Louis was a step ahead of this measure and had allowed them to conduct schools among themselves previous to that. The story of the education of the Colored in St. Louis is a long one,[23] but it must be said that Harris never shared the common opinion that if you gave the Colored the Bible in one hand and the ballot in the other, you had done your duty. By no means! During 1877-78 he established Kindergartens for them, and would participate in the dedication of the Colored schools which were a sort of house-warming. In 1879 he even had to testify to the advantages of an education in a case involving Alice, a colored girl. She had been adopted by Cornelius Lynch. She would not go to school, played truant, and, as her sister who found time to make pies, bake bread, and cook the meat, said, wouldn't learn nothin' nohow. She just went promenading to captivate beaux. When she got married to one, a J. J. Ryan, her husband had a belle to be sure, but one so devoid of the treasures of booklearning, that he was greatly shocked and disappointed and finally sued Mr. Lynch for $6200, of which $5000 were for the loss of educational advantages. Lynch promptly put in a counter claim, charging for Alice's night-gowns, drawers, hats, and other articles of clothing, and a $7 prayer book. Education not being compulsory in Missouri then, how could a guardian be made to pay damages for neglecting to do what a natural father was not obliged to do?

When Harris retired from office in 1880, the editor of the *Freeman's Journal*, Charles Newton, expressed himself in terms of sincere regret saying that Harris had been "an especial friend to the colored teachers of this city," and an advocate for their employment when the question was under discussion.

Harris had an implicit trust in the forward development of economic and purely human conditions. He took into consideration that we moderns live faster and accomplish more. We also exercise our brains more, expecting all the while the same of our children. The school would have to reflect these tendencies, but compensate them by a 40-week school year, a 4¾-hour study-day, short but intense periods, at most an hour of home work, and like measures to safeguard the pupil's health. There was, thus, no foundation to the rumor that in the schools the children were "slain by study" and that many graduated for the tomb. Odd as it may seem, such criticisms would appear periodically, inspired by political and Catholic opposition. By statistics Harris would prove to the parents that children who were overworked had been compelled by them to take lessons in music, languages, dancing and what not. He condemned home-coaching, for a child thus tutored would never learn to rely on himself, and its mind would always remain an unknown quantity to the teacher.

There was much profanity and obscenity among the pupils coming from the lowest strata. Harris stopped this evil by suspension which he found most effective. Matters of hygiene were ever his concern and he kept abreast of all findings and recommendations.

It was his friend Charles F. Childs who introduced punishment American style into the St. Louis schools in which the pupil was made to feel that he was the cause of his pain, the teacher the unwilling instrument. This doctrine Harris made his own.[24] Frank A. Fitzpatrick, of Boston, once delighted a gathering of educators in a hotel lobby preceding their serious conference by telling the story[25] of how he was punished by Harris. Harris was standing at some distance and someone had remarked on his broad shoulders and deep chest. Fitzpatrick related how he attended the school in which Harris was Principal. He was a husky lad who would defy any schoolmaster in the land to lay hands on him. The teacher had threatened him, following some infringement, to get Harris who would bring him to terms. That, however, evoked only a chuckle, for he was sure that Harris, like many a teacher before, would have to retire from the room, red-faced and gasping. Harris arrived after a suspense which hung heavy over the class, eyed Fitzpatrick and before he could gather his thoughts and get his legs and arms into fighting position, lifted him on to the top of the bookcase by his coat collar and the seat of his pants. "There, young man!" said Harris calmly, "you will sit up there until you know how to behave yourself." That cured Fitzpatrick for all time and he was a good boy ever after.

The athletic build of Harris impressed the boys very much. The fact that he could lift two 40½-pound dumbbells with ease, could swim well and shoot with accuracy was common knowledge among the boys. He showed them how to use the apparatus which he had installed on the playgrounds, the ladders, horizontal bars and the trapeze. He himself did not have to resort to corporeal punishment, and he warned his teachers not to flog, pull ears, cuff, or have the pupil stand in the corner wearing a fool's cap or holding a piece of wood in his mouth.

The school is there to develop self-control in the pupil. The police are engaged in the prevention of crime, while the teachers are engaged in the prevention of criminals. There should be strict discipline, but a child must not be "chilled" with too harsh measures. To give him too much rein would be equivalent to paying "that respect to his ignorant, immature, irrational individuality that is due alone to his ideal perfected manhood". The American school should build up American character; control by others instead of self, he reiterated innumerable times, is unworthy of Americans. While thus in the East the cane was still being used, in St. Louis corporeal punishment was nearly non-existent, except during the years 1877-78, for reasons already stated. The few cases in which such punishment did occur during Harris' administration are noteworthy particularly for his handling of them. Suspension he regarded as the severest form of punishment and a lever by which the parents were compelled to share the responsibility of supervision over their children and reinforce the feeble moral powers in them. Moral suasion by the teacher he approved of most; strict government, but by the mildest means. His own experience had convinced him that pupils are "naturally inclined to do right when they see it as right" and that misconduct mostly "proceeds from carelessness, error of judgment, or from a denial of just rights, and not from a demoniac depravity with which children are too often credited."[26]

> Boys and girls are no worse than the rest of humanity; they have not yet learned that pitiful philosophy which considers all men rascals and ascribes the victory to the shrewdest; they have not yet learned to stifle all generous impulses and settle every act by considerations of immediate and personal profit or loss. . .

LEGACIES TO THE SCHOOL SYSTEM

The graded Public School Harris considered the very pivot of democratic education. In that he organized and articulated it at St. Louis, from the Kindergarten to the Intermediate, High, Normal and Evening Schools he showed American educators the continuity and interrelationship of all levels of education. It is safe to say there was no other example of a school system so methodically worked out anywhere in the country, or one that had as much influence upon our conception of an education that is complete in itself at every stage and yet possesses the germs of the next higher stage of which the pupil may want to avail himself, including college and university.[27]

One of the greatest contributions to American education was Harris' establishment of the first Public School Kindergarten. Under his Superintendentship, 55 Kindergartens had been established when Boston was not yet able to support a single public one.

As far back as 1867-68, Francis Berg called Harris' attention to the German Kindergarten, the *Kleinkinderbewahranstalten,* and Harris was not slow to recognize the value of such an institution. The school life of a child could thus be extended profitably, and he forthwith suggested small primary schools, "founded more or less on the Kindergarten." But in the meantime, a practical, though private Kindergarten, was being conducted by Mrs. Felix Coste at 1336 La Salle Street; and Miss Susan Blow, also enthusiastic over the Kindergarten idea, had seen Thomas Richeson, President of the School Board, who referred her to Harris.

Now, Harris was somewhat reserved at first, knowing full well the great number of problems, including financial ones, that would have to be faced and solved before a Kindergarten could be affiliated with the schools. However, Miss Blow went to New York where she studied a year with Mrs.

Kraus-Boelte, and in the meantime he prepared himself by a thorough study of Froebel for the impending task. Finally, at the December 9th, 1873, meeting of the Board, Harris was glad to report the establishment of "a genuine Kindergarten" in connection with the school system, and he credited Miss Blow for all she had done. He urged her to write a report in which she particularly commented on the atmosphere of happiness, and on the fact that all objections to the Kindergarten had been disproven in practice. This first Kindergarten, at Des Pères School, with Miss Mary A. Timberlake as the first Kindergartner, was followed the next year by one in connection with Divoll School. When the groundwork had been laid, and the Kindergarten had emerged as a practical pedagogical undertaking, Harris instructed all Principals to institute a vigorous propaganda for the new member of the school family. It was to cater not merely to the children of the wealthy, but to those of the poor and indigent as well, and perhaps with greater benefit to society.

Many young ladies would volunteer to learn Kindergartening, and for a long time it was only the "Directors" that received a slender salary of $500. It was sufficiently strenuous work so that no one was willing to take $800 and do the work of two directors. By 1876, a charge of a dollar per child was made. All the while, Harris became more convinced of the wisdom that had made him select Susan Blow to carry the work forward. She advocated instruction in addition to development, and not development *or* knowledge, but development *and* knowledge, and not subjective *or* objective knowledge, but subjective *and* objective knowledge in a harmonious relationship. In Harris' view, the Kindergarten effects the subtle conversion of play into work, and it was important to give it the right direction. He had taken the precaution to familiarize himself thoroughly with the findings of experienced Kindergarteners. For the purpose he had attended the Third Convention of the German American Teachers at Hoboken, N. J., in 1872, and asked the Fourth Annual Convention to come to St. Louis. He was fully aware that the Kindergarten had to be Americanized in order to insure its success in an American school system. During 1877-78, the first Colored Kindergarten was in operation, with Colored teachers. Despite the great enthusiasm of Kindergarteners, the institution might have suffered shipwreck, had not Harris been able to keep its cost at a minimum in a number of ingenious ways, without impairing its effectiveness and quality of instruction. He himself was in the habit of calling his economic measures an adaptation of the Lancasterian system to the use of the Kindergarten.[23]

In his last St. Louis report he sounded a parting warning to all those who approached the problem of the Kindergarten from a sentimental predisposition or the point of view of a philosophy that stressed unduly the individuality and freedom of the child. He assured the mothers that they did not have to abdicate in favor of the Kindergarten, and he condemned the excessive cultivation of self-activity as leading to pertness and conceit.

Even after Harris had left St. Louis, his wise counsel was sought, and every Kindergartener studying the subject even now should know the work of Harris[29] alongside that of Susan Blow . . .

However much Harris esteemed German philosophy, his sole aim in education was to give America the best, wherever it was found. No nation holds the patent on ideas that advance humanity. One nation may have the honor of having created a certain institution, but the form it took within that nation may not be the form it will take in another. Hence he rarely if ever was apologetic about his adaptation of the Kindergarten to the American school, for only a petty mind would reject the Kindergarten because it was a German who first conceived it. Yet, Harris was not spared hostility because of it; but he maintained his philosophic calm: "There are deeper grounds than merely national ones — important though the latter be. There is human nature in general and the law of its unfolding — common to all civilized nations . . ."[30]

His partiality to America cannot be better illustrated than by his decisions in regard to the teaching of German in the Public Schools and Public School courses conducted entirely in German. The history of the latter dates from about 1843,[31] not to mention private instruction by Germans for Germans in St. Louis. Tice and Divoll, as Superintendents, both regarded it as an act of justice to the strong German element to have German writing, reading and grammar taught in the Public Schools. In 1860 there were some 60,000 Germans in the city, and the Public Schools would have lost a good support had they not provided for German instruction. The Germans were education minded, especially the "Latin farmers," the '48ers and the '49ers. They believed they were entitled to some consideration, having fought valiantly on the Union side, perhaps having saved St. Louis for the Union by the early capture of Camp Jackson from the rebels, for Capt. Lyon's troops consisted mainly of German volunteers.

In the fall of 1864, German classes were taught at the Clay and other Schools by German teachers, after the Board had sent Divoll on a trip to Cincinnati to contact some good German teachers. The following year seven schools taught in German; Francis Berg, Assistant Superintendent German Department, was much gratified, and so was the German population. Harris justified the existence of German instruction by saying that the Germans were paying the school tax. By giving them the benefit of the Public Schools, all distinctions of caste and nationality would be obliterated. But this apparent concession was not at all an expression of any Germanophil tendencies on the part of Harris. Harris was first and foremost an American, looking out for American interests above all others. Throughout his tenure of office he was able to steer the interests of the German pupils toward English, and thus ween them from any German bias that their parents may still have shown. English remained at all events the main language. The children were really taught only one-fifth of their time in school in German,[32] the rest of the instruction was in English.

The delicate position which German instruction occupied, became very soon apparent. The Germans, aware of Harris' interests, hailed him as a great scholar, and expected him to side wholeheartedly with them in their demands for thorough instruction in the German language. Harris acknowledged the justice of their demands in so far as being able to master the German language would enable children of German descent to "partake of the social privileges of those who speak" German. But he gave them to understand that their home and community was America, and that they would have to adapt themselves in all other matters to American ways.

The Germans sensed that they were waging a losing battle. Only with difficulty did Harris succeed in preventing the wholesale withdrawal of German pupils from the Public Schools. He made some concessions, but they could not forestall the general dissatisfaction in both camps. Political pressure was brought to bear on the School Board to continue as well as to eliminate German instruction. At last, in 1878, the Board, by a *viva-voce* vote, adopted the majority report of its special committee to continue with German instruction. Court action followed, but the courts declared themselves powerless to say what should be taught.

Dr. John C. Christin, who had come to St. Louis in 1869 to teach Latin and Greek in the High School[33] and had succeeded Berg in 1872, was often the unhappy victim of

vituperation. His scholarly nature was not attuned to such
a fight. Ill in body and mind, he went to Denver, Colorado,
where he shot himself in June, 1878.

By retaining German instruction in the St. Louis Schools,
Harris' principle of Americanizing the children of the for-
eign-born, without alienating them from their parents and
others dear to them, found tacit recognition, and his wisdom, and shrewdness, in bringing it about, constitute one
of his legacies to the American Public School.

Another branch of study which Harris fostered and reared
while at the helm of the Public Schools and which had some
slight connection with the influence of the German element,
was music. According to the sentiment of Seume's lines:

> *Wo man singet, lass dich ruhig nieder,*
> *Böse Menschen haben keine Lieder . . .*

music is a first rate moral force, and Harris set great store by
it, endeavoring, through instruction in singing particularly,
to change the mere external regularity of school routine, into
an inner appreciation of regularity and symmetry. Singing is
most important, he held, in humanizing a school[34]. Morality,
religion, love of country and nature, home and family, are
brought together in song in a most powerful form. No religion need be taught where the song reminds the pupil of
these higher things, and there would be no danger of sectarianism in such a direct experience. But scribblers in the
newspapers would deride such noble efforts by recounting
that "the chronometric and anything but melodious cater-
wauling" cost the taxpayers annually $6000; indeed, the
author of a piece entitled "Do, Re, Mi" figured out the
grand total as $28,000. And if Harris assured the skeptics
that music nevertheless pays, they suspected huge profits by
the Board on the sale of the music books. They tried to in-
volve the chief music teacher in the Public Schools, Henry
Robyn,[35] a German, who had written one of the books, the
Classical Singer, which was used in the schools. But unlike

Christin. he was a fighter, it seems, and he died not by his own hand but on board the S.S. Pomerania, when she sank in Dover Straights.

Friday was made Music Day in the High School, when musical and rhetorical exercises were held. The pieces studied were nearly all classical, and embraced Haydn, Mendelssohn, Mozart, Beethoven, Wagner, Kreutzer, von Weber, Rossini. Meyerbeer, Knecken and Abt. The proceeds of school exhibitions went toward the purchase of an organ for the High School.

Until Harris defended drawing as a subject to be taught expertly, it was called an ornamental, useless study. He himself could not draw, but he had a keen appreciation of line and form which may be traced to his phonographic practice in which delicacy and pleasing execution of forms contributed not only to a satisfying appearance of the written page, but to readability and usefulness at the same time. He detailed the teaching of writing longhand in the schools and stressed particularly the esthetic qualities. When Professor Walter Smith was called to direct Art Education at Boston, under the Hon. John D. Philbrick, Superintendent of the Boston Schools and a personal friend of Harris, he adopted his system of teaching drawing for the St. Louis schools. St. Louis acquired the loan of drawings done by the school children in Boston. They evoked such an interest that other cities could not benefit by them, for eager St. Louisians had thumbed, torn and dog-eared them beyond presentability. Conrad Diehl was put in charge of drawing, in all the schools, and the choice was good, for he was an artist of some note.

To satisfy the esthetic needs of the pupils in the schools completely, Harris advocated gymnastics and calisthenics, but warned that both demand as great an exercise of the will as mental arithmetic. Attention being a common element, he did not recommend the passing from one to the other as likely to provide relaxation. Here again, Harris' ideas were not based merely on an abstract, theoretical familiarity with the subject, but on firsthand acquaintance which made his advice and his orders the more valuable.

Probably one of the greatest contributions to the St. Louis Public Schools and ultimately to the intellectual life of the City itself, and one that is perpetuating itself beyond the present day, was his efforts in behalf of the library. Divoll conceived the idea of a real library in connection with the schools; we say real, because Section 59 of the *Rules for the Government of the Board of President and Directors of the St. Louis Public Schools* did make mention of a library committee. Had it been active, the cumbersome duties of its members would have consisted, as late as 1860, in supervising 42 volumes of the *Annals of Congress,* and a collection of miscellaneous books, "worth perhaps $100."

From the first, Harris took a deep interest in Divoll's endeavors. Indeed, Divoll could not have found a more ardent disciple in this his life-long interest.[36] In 1862, when he pushed his library scheme, the Board was financially embarrassed; in 1864 he tried for legislative authority for the "Public School Library Association" for which he relied on Charles F. Childs to draw up By-laws and on Harris for a "motto, device and form for a Seal," also an engraved form for life membership certificates, and the like. In February, 1865, the Legislature granted the Act of Incorporation. Harris served as a member of the Board of Trustees of the Public School Library Society from 1865 to 1869, steadily moving up in rank, to be second only to Felix Coste, the President. He retained his place on the Board of Managers beginning with 1869, when the Library was transferred to the Board. He also served as Vice President, and throughout was a donor of cash and eventually of a great many books and pamphlets to the number of over a thousand.

While in the East after the Civil War, both Divoll and Harris made contacts with publishers to obtain books at a reduced rate and study various library methods. Henry C. Brokmeyer, then a prominent attorney-at-law, added his influence to the appeal to the public. "Incipient operations" started off on December 9th, 1865, in a large session room of the Board. Subscriptions and life memberships in the Association made possible rapid progress. Pageants, such as the ".Allegorical Representation of the Great Rebellion,"[37] campaigns among the teachers and students, and plays with a humorous slant, gradually put money into the library scheme. An appeal to "the Friends and Patrons of Learning in Europe" was sent out in 1866, particularly to the German universities: "In 1865, this city contained 51,000 Germans against 46,000 from all other foreign countries. It is to this German element that the Mississippi Valley is most largely indebted for its wealth and progress. The Germans, coming from a land where education is fostered to an extent unknown in any other region of the old world, bring with them to their new homes a desire to afford their children advantages equal to those they left behind in the mother country . . . We appeal . . . to aid us in this great undertaking."

When the library moved to the Polytechnic Building, thus increasing its facilities, a number of scientific bodies in the city would apply for concessions to use a room for their meetings. Often their whole libraries were acquired in exchange for life memberships in the Association. It seems that Harris had Thomas Davidson, who later compiled a number of reading lists, scout around to find out how many volumes the various organizations could muster. The big geological library of Benjamin F. Shumard, M.D., Harris was able to bargain for at $1850. He managed to acquire part of the library of Professor Rossmaessler, of Leipzig. The Henry Ames library of technical subjects and the books of the Franklin Library Association were absorbed, likewise the collections of the German Institute, the St. Louis Academy of Science; the St. Louis Medical Society; the St. Louis Architects; the Engineer's Club, and many others. By March, 1870, classification of all books was reported as nearly complete. A catalogue of 384 pages, classified and alphabetical, was published by the Library. It was prepared by Jno. Jay Bailey, the Librarian, and had an essay by Harris on the system of classification.

Lecture series, to which flocked the *crème de la crème* of the city, were held to replenish the funds. Harris usually introduced the speaker. Emerson spoke in Philharmonic Hall on "Success;" Wendell Phillips on "The Times" at Mercantile Hall; Bayard Taylor gave readings from Schiller. The moving spirit behind all this activity was Harris who was convinced that "the library is the temple dedicated to the communion of man," that it is "the museum for the preservation of the results of human labor and experience as embodied in language." There were difficulties, of course, such as business depressions, boycotts when the Board at one time showed an anti-novel-reading attitude, and lack of funds for upkeep. The engineer who had paid $4 down and heated the library on Sundays, was given life membership. It was a truly democratic institution to the heart of Harris, for through the portals of the library entered the "proud lady, wrapped in her costly, and we might add countless, robes, and also the man of but a single shirt . . ."

In 1884, the St. Louis Public School Library became the "St. Louis Public Library," one of the great libraries in the country.

It is doubtful that Harris foresaw the magnitude of the enterprise when he first became interested in it. He had the intellectual advancement of the students in the schools in mind, and it was they who benefitted perhaps most by membership in the Association. The Evening Schools were a most valuable adjunct to the day schools and interest in them was promoted by Harris by offering free membership in the Public School Library Association upon satisfactory attendance.

Harris knew that in a democracy education was of importance, and the more education each could get, the better the schools were serving democracy. For that reason he gave much thought to the "Intermediate School" which was in operation since 1869, and represented in some fashion the modern Junior High School. It formed the link between the District Schools and the High School, and was meant to give those who, because of poor grades, could not enter High School, a chance to do so after a satisfactory examination.

A practical course of studies, without overstressing the classics, had been devised for the High School, and Harris taught some courses there regularly. He did not believe in elective studies at all at that stage of education. "That course which lays the best foundation in discipline and insight for a future 'liberal education,' is doubtless the best to give the pupil strength of mind and practical ability to grapple with the details of business."[38] For the convenience of pupils living too far from Central High School, St. Louis had Branch High Schools which they could attend during the first two years of their course.

At one time, it aroused the ire of some citizens when Harris, as School Superintendent, was appointed upon recommendation of Wm. H. Stone, Member of Congress, Third District, Mo., to act as Chairman of a committee to select from among the High School students a candidate for appointment as cadet to the Naval School at Annapolis. Other Congressmen had chosen candidates from among "the flower of the land"! Under a similar appointment, Harris was instrumental in determining a candidate for West Point.

The graduating High School class of 1878 was shocked

when an examination was suddenly announced shortly before the exercises, due to a change in the wording of the rules of graduation, recommended by the Teachers' Committee upon some allegations of inefficiency. Harris had to make a public announcement to appease the young ladies who, anticipating the sheepskin millenium, had already purchased their dresses for the occasion. and now were running the risk of being embarrassed, should they not pass the examinations.

At the St. Louis Normal School, Harris would offer a course in the "Theory and Art of Teaching" which was marked by breadth of vision and philosophic insight. He personally made out the examination questions and officiated at the Commencement Exercices. He was ever open to new suggestions and put them into practice, such as a school for practice teaching and a school for observation. With the Normal School functioning smoothly, the system of education established by Harris in St. Louis became self-perpetuating and complete. . .

EDUCATION RELATES TO THE FUNCTION OF SOCIAL
DEVELOPMENT

This phrase was a favorite one of Harris', and one that reveals the scope of his thinking which never remained in the stage of pedagogy and speculation. As a matter of fact, he treated pedagogy as a branch of social science.[40] His Hegelianism never stood in the way of social reform. Thus, the Kindergarten he considered as playing a most important rôle in society in that it teaches artistic skill which will enable the laborer to rise from the manipulation of a mechanical tool to the level of inventions, ideals and the cultivation of the power of expression as a necessary in an industrious, wealth-producing country.

The school, in teaching punctuality as the *sine qua non* of all virtues, contributes to that quality of character which sacrifices ease and pleasure of the moment in order to gain reasonable ends, and thus is a moral force *par excellence.* In view of the indulgence which parents grant their children, Harris looked upon the Public Schools as the greatest safeguard of the morality of the community. Of course, he was criticized by those who did not care whether society would some day be ridden by the excrescences of untutored infant genius.

He understood the school to be a preparation for life, not a preparation for a job. It was to be a foundation on which the individual could build, remaining at the same time the master of his own fate, while yet recognizing social obligations by force of habit. The school was to prepare not for work and toil, but for participation of the individual in the life of the whole.

In surveying the field of social relations, Harris could not find any investment that paid so well as a good system of schools. Education is wealth-creating. Wealth creates activity, industry. People concentrate at centers of industry, real estate doubles and trebles. Thus education becomes one of the moving forces of economics. The schools, in turn, being "good enough for the best and cheap enough for the poorest" alleviate the social ills following upon industrial expansion. Since the end of the Civil War, poverty was conspicuous in St. Louis. There was unemployment and social vice. The solution, Harris found in education. In a little article on "The Identification of Capital and Education," published probably in 1871, he stated that an educated laborer will add, on the average, a thousand dollars *per annum* to the wealth of the State. Integrated with the creation of wealth are land and people with institutions.

From the fact that America does not possess a titled nobility, Harris deduced that in America all are and must be laborers. He even put a Vanderbilt and an Astor into that class. But democracy demands not mere manual labor from all, it also requires directive power. The cure of labor strikes, Harris saw in proper education and the elimination from that education of abstract ideas, by which he meant the dissociation of certain problems from others; as he would say, we should see the situation in its dialectical development, or, as we would say, see it whole.

While keenly interested in the socialistic Workingmen's Party which had its Executive Committee at Cincinnati and which spread rapidly among the Germans in St. Louis who kept the movement on a rather high social and cultural level, Harris sided strongly with all powers that might be termed progressive and capitalistic. He prudently overlooked the element of exploitation inherent in industrial expansion and became somewhat of a mouthpiece for the bankers, railroad men and industrialists of the city whose gospel was a bigger and better St. Louis. Chicago was a thorn in their eyes, and Harris chimed in on the prophesies that pictured St. Louis some day bigger by far than Chicago. He succumbed, as so many with him, to the Great St. Louis Illusion, and lectured far and wide on the "Commercial Geography of the Mississippi Valley" and related topics, to business men and educators, picturing the great American bottom as a region that was to develop harmony and unite differences, a "very happy circumstance for the strength and stability of our nation."

Meanwhile, slavery had been outlawed, but financial and political slavery was something to be endured. "Rings" of every description had cornered the market and cheated people out of their rights under the very aegis of a democratic government. Bankers were tried, fraudulent transactions were on the order of the day, political scandals made headlines. It was the era of boss Tweed. The farmer, never remembered, was still forgotten. Millions had evaporated in railroad "privileges." The State bought the defunct road and taxed the people on what they had lost.

Harris watched and tried to understand it all as a logical development of thesis, antithesis, and synthesis. He confessed by 1878 that the times were passing to the nadir, yet he could not help believe in the miracle America, that always rose like a phoenix from the ashes, if but for a while. Was there not the Public School that was ever improving in quality and service? Did not the Centennial Exposition give the lie to that tremendous mire created by corrupt politics?

His philosophy had room for understanding social and ethical phenomena. Thus, property he interpreted as the great invention of the human mind by which man elevates himself above the mere brute, in a sort of reflected existence. In his affiliation with the American Association for the Promotion of Social Science, he had many an occasion to occupy himself not merely theoretically but practically with such problems. The first convention of the Western Social Science Association was held at Chicago, in November of 1868. The following January, Fred H. Wines, Corresponding Secretary, sent Harris the Constitution and History of the Association, asking him to join. Harris was elected Vice-President in the national organization when the Western set-up became obsolete in 1872. He once declined the office of President; after 1877 he served as Chairman of the Committee on Education. There were sporadic meetings of an offshoot of the national organization which called itself the St. Louis Social Science Association. In the spring of 1877, Wm. Greenleaf Eliot and Harris called a meeting to discuss the formation of a Missouri branch of the A.S.S.A. Harris served as Secretary *pro tem,* and became a Director of that branch,[41] continuing in this capacity till he left St. Louis. He went to nearly every meeting, and also attended the national ones. His addresses and lectures in almost every case centered around the idea of education and its influence on the community. He sometimes tried out his papers first on the St. Louis audience, as the one on "Methods of Study in Social Science," which he subsequently delivered at Saratoga Springs, N. Y., September 10th, 1879.

THE GOOD FIGHT FOR DEMOCRATIC SCHOOLS

There was no ground for assuming that Harris tried to engraft a foreign educational theory and practice on the American schools. He was a New Englander, a Yankee, not a Puritan, in outlook. St. Louis education was thoroughly impregnated with the New England virus, witness himself, Ira Divoll, J. B. Merwin, Anna C. Brackett, Susan Blow, and above all Wm. Greenleaf Eliot at whose instigation many teachers were imported from New England during 1848. Harris did not even believe in borrowing outright: he was re-creating in conformity to the spirit of America. Said he:[42]

It is very difficult for a citizen of one country to form any adequate idea of the true political value of an issue raised in another country. Likely enough what seems to him the cause of progress and enlightenment — measured by his own standard — is in reality a deadly attack on the most rational phase possible in the institutions of that foreign State. It is still more difficult to judge correctly of the merits of social customs and usages . . .

He believed that the American government had developed only one of its essential phases, that of "brittle individualism." To be sure, the development of individuality is the prerogative of America. The chief use of organization is that the individual derives a sense of security from the feeling that the whole is backing him up.

All the evils which we suffer politically may be traced to the existence in our midst of an immense mass of ignorant, illiterate, or semi-educated people who assist in governing the country, while they possess no insight

into the true nature of the issues which they attempt
to decide. If in Europe, and even in China, the directive classes are educated at public expense, how essential is it that the Republican State shall before all insure universal education within its domain![43]

Harris never tired of stating that one of the principal
functions of the American Public School is to break down
caste-distinctions. He wanted to educate a free American,
and whatever ideas could be utilized, whatever there was
of pedagogical wisdom adaptable to the American scene in
Froebel, Pestalozzi, Herbart, Benecke, Hegel, Kant, Rosenkranz, Ziller, and Diesterweg, Harris, like Philbrick, made
use of despite F. W. Parker's cry of "mediaeval absurdities."
Whoever claimed that Harris wanted to educate to any other
end but that of a free, American citizen, was either ignorant
of his ideas or misconstrued them intentionally. For, there
is no other fact so outstanding about his good fight for the
schools than that he wanted that education which alone
would safeguard democracy, freedom and individuality,
which, after all, he understood as the essence of Americanism.
"Better not so cheap, better not so wisely governed, provided
the people be self-governed. Monarchies are doubtless
cheaper, doubtless not so corrupt, as republics: but the great
end of all government is the elevation of mere individuals
to the dignity of self-directive *persons*: the concentration
of the realized products of *all* in *each*. Hence the self-determination of the individual is the object of all government."[44] In this he was consistent throughout his life. It
was the burden of almost every lecture; it was the central
theme of "A Statement of the Theory of Education in the
United States" which he was asked, in 1872, to draw up in
conjunction with Hon. Duane Doty for use at the Vienna
World Exposition and which was recognized officially until
about 1926 when a reformulation seemed necessary; for this

end he planned the course of instruction for the Public Schools to which the colleges and universities eventually tacitly acceded by making their curricula contiguous to High School education; it was for this reason that he opposed vigorously any move to de-liberalize the Public Schools, to make them places of instruction for technical subjects, science, religion, or what not, thus leading the individual into an intellectual, moral, political and economic *cul-de-sac*, narrowing down his initiative, his will, and his understanding which should be as free and wide as possible in every citizen that has the privilege of living under a democratic form of government. The earlier the specialization, the greater the political domination over the "well-trained" pupil.

Granting Harris his initial assumption of the feasibility of an American education, very few could refute him despite his interest in what they considered abstruse theories. If he did interpret American ideals correctly, he was but the mouthpiece of freedom and democracy, not the "chief mogul" of American education, as some maliciously suggested. His failing, as an American, was that he reduced everything to principle and thus *seemed* to limit that freedom for which he stood. But just criticism of Harris always confined itself more or less to methods and interpretations of the educational data. How Harris did visualize the application of his theory of American education under penalty of persecution by party interests, may be shown, in passing, on a few examples.[45]

Even though Harris was the last speaker at the dedication exercises of O'Fallon Polytechnic Institute, on February 11th, 1869, his speech was lauded over those of Felix Coste, Dr. Wm. Greenleaf Eliot, Dr. Richard Edwards, and Ira Divoll, because it was "characterized by learning and original thought, expressed in a graceful and polished diction." This Institute, at first a Department of Washington

287

University and a liability to it in that it competed with the Public Schools, had been acquired by the latter after some legal and other tangles involving, for a short time, the status of the University as holding the Institute in academic trust for the Board. It was incorporated into the school system — at the suggestion of Harris — as a more advanced school than the Evening Schools, offering classes in arithmetic, physics (natural philosophy), line, machine and architectural drawing, English grammar, geometry and the Spencerian system of penmanship to which Harris was always partial. When it opened on October 29th, 1868, the enrollment was about 100, at least double of what it had ever been under Washington University. C. M. Woodward was appointed Principal.

With the acquisition of O'Fallon Polytechnic, St. Louis was way ahead of other Public School systems, possessing a real people's university. The Public School Library was housed in it, the office of the Superintendent was transferred to it, the Normal School occupied the top floor, and there were rooms for the Board, the Historical Society, scientific academies and art associations.

As Thomas E. Spencer[46] pointed out, perhaps with some justice, that Harris damned the Institute with faint praise, or, rather, praised it with faint damn, it should be remembered that Harris judged the venture on whether it was consistent with the principles of American Public School education. Throughout his tenure he kept it on the level of a High Evening School and concurred with those who were opposed to turning the schools into apprentice shops due to its influence. For, in training for a vocation during a period when a broad foundation should be laid, do you not limit and ultimately enslave the individual who has not grasped the fullness of life, nor is decently equipped for the venture for lack of the rudiments of education for freedom . . . ? O'Fallon Polytechnic, under Harris' supervision, was not to take the place of the Public Schools, but was to supplement them.

By insisting on the mastery of the printed page, Harris likewise applied his principle of American education. The printed page he thought of as cool and dispassionate. Light and warmth come from the pupil: it should not come from the teacher who, through oral instruction, might foster prejudice and exercise suasion which are incompatible with democratic education. Having been taught to read, the pupil is capable of reinforcing himself with the power of the race, calling on all thinkers from Plato to the present. The *How* is to be taught in the democratic school; the *What* is up to the student. Let him go to the library and feast on the treasures of the world! The American system is based on the principle that only what the teacher makes the student do for himself, not what he does for the pupil, is of value. The printed page is an Aladdin's lamp by means of which the humblest citizen can pronounce a spell over space and time.

When he formulated his position as having in mind mastery of the textbook and contrasted this, as the American method, over against the method of oral instruction in the German schools and universities which he characterized as medieval and mere mechanical workshops for memory exercises, dictating and copying, he brought down a flood of criticism from the German element in St. Louis, and had to retract and correct his estimate to some extent. The Germans had come to regard the textbook as a *Mordwaffe gegen den Verstand*, a deadly weapon against intelligence, while Harris made it the very foundation of education! There were misunderstandings on both sides, of course; the Germans charged Harris with inventing plausible theories to cover up a lamentable practice, and Harris acknowledged that he had emphasized mastery of the printed page only because the school life of the average pupil in the Public Schools was exceedingly short, and he was anxious to give him what would prove most likely of greatest benefit to him later.[47] In view of some recent tamperings with the American Eagle, the suggestion was interesting that it be given a couple of textbooks instead of those ugly thunderbolts!

However, also with educators Harris clashed seriously over the textbook method as the American method. At first he merely charged them with misunderstanding the function of the textbook. He himself was singularly blind to the fact that even a textbook may most powerfully prescribe the course of future thinking and thus run counter to his own contention that it would make the individual free. By 1875 he had revised his opinion to the effect that the new method of "verification of book learning by independent experiment and true scientific investigation" was "all-worthy of adoption", but that the old method which was contemptuously spoken of as the cramming textbook method, had not been sufficiently valued.[48] His textbook method received somewhat of a lift when the *Anschauungsunterricht* was considered by some a tendency in the wrong direction. He himself, however, could discern much good in applying this method within limits, but continued to advocate the textbook method for the elementary school.

One more, and possibly the most important phase of education which Harris deduced from the American ideal of democracy and freedom, was his defence of the non-denominational character of the schools. In this he was most successful even though he had to fight the hardest for it and endure some of the most underhanded attacks.

An article in the daily papers, appearing in the year 1868, heralded a most vicious attack on the Public Schools in the name of religion. It was charged, children were educated to be radicals in politics and infidels in religion and trained for the brothel or the jail as well as to become enemies of the social order and good government. The Hon. Dr. Charles R. Smythe, a Democratic Member of the Legislature, likewise published damning articles in the *Missouri Republican* in which he called the Public Schools immoral and dangerous pest houses. He even charged that infanticide, demoralization, divorce, despair, and prison were the consequences of girls visiting the schools.[49]

The *Western Watchman* sounded the fanfare of Catholicism by saying: "We will have a share in the Public Schools, or they must have a very disagreeable share of us." Harris met the attacks graciously, with political philosophy and facts. He familiarized himself thoroughly with all phases of Catholicism, particularly as relating to St. Louis. He acknowledged that the schools were anti-religious, if they meant by that anti-sectarian; but if they intended to mean atheistical or anti-Christian, he repudiated it fully and completely.[50]

Harris had called the separation of State and Church the cardinal principle of the United States. Was this to be given up? In 1870, the denominational forces brought a tremendous pressure to bear upon the House of Representatives of the General Assembly of the State of Missouri, to reduce the income of the Public School Board, charging extravagance and inefficiency and the use of garbled figures. But this was only the beginning. The move was supported by Senator M. H. Phelan who introduced a bill in Jefferson City which was unanimously adopted and the purpose of which was to encourage teachers in St. Louis to pick up poor children from the streets and organize them into schools which were to be under the surveillance of the Board. The Board then was to be compelled to appropriate yearly to every private school, existent or to be established, ten dollars for each pupil receiving free tuition. At one time, Phelan proposed that the $10 go to the teacher who would pick up one of the 16,000 waifs outside the school walls. He styled himself a friend of the friendless. Divoll, then at San Antonio, was fuming, but sighed with relief when Harris took a stand against the Phelan scheme.

Now the *Western Watchman*, the mouthpiece of Phelan, issued the call: ' We must gain control of that Board at all hazards." The Catholic members that were on the board they called wishy-washy. Through a loan of $200,000 in Philadelphia, in 1867, the Board had placed itself somewhat in difficulties when it matured in 1872, and the Catholic opposition made the most of it. The Board was charged with unscrupulousness, oppression of the poor and robbery. The stately O'Fallon Polytechnic was denounced as a "temple of science and snobbery" and the poor taxpayer was inveigled into admitting "that the poor are now supporting the rich in sumptuous style." But, Father Phelan in urging the cutting down of the salaries, the reduction of the grade of instruction, the making of public education rudimentary so that the poor as well as the rich could profit by it, had overstepped his bounds and created a widespread impression that the Catholics were conducting their parochial schools for the sake of the very poor and ragged children. Their criticism acted like a boomerang, and Father David J. Doherty tried to soften the blow.

A controversy on a somewhat higher level was carried on in the daily papers by a writer under the pseudonym "Catholicus" and another who called himself "Hermes" in whom we rightly suspect Harris. The latter claimed that "as a reformer of immoral conduct" education "is out of its sphere, and powerless. This is the sphere of religion." He could not see eye to eye with "Catholicus" that Public School children should not be denied the right to be instructed in the faith of their parents, enjoyed by the robber and murderer in jails and penitentiaries.

However, there were also other religious factions undermining confidence in the schools. The *Christian Advocate* waged war against the "Public School Brahmins". The

Presbyterians alleged that Harris and his subordinates taught irreligion and made infidels. The Rev. W. M. Leftwich, a Methodist, carried on a vigorous, mostly one-way correspondence with the *Missouri Republican* and the St. Louis *Globe-Democrat* to have the Bible taught. In all this, Harris stood out like a giant. His oft repeated lecture on "Church and State" showed with wonderful lucidity and candor the distinct provinces of each. Religion, dealing with absolute value and regarding man as totally depraved, would disrupt the function of the state completely. Likewise the State would bring about disintegration in religion were it to apply its design for the finite needs of men to the realm of spirit. Did the denominational groups realize how un-American their reactionist activities were in that they claimed the benefits for themselves which they denied to others?

The fight of Harris in St. Louis had its reverberations throughout the country, particularly in the East. The New York papers supported him, while the State of Massachusetts would have gladly accepted him as their Superintendent. Harris was called an infidel, a free-thinker, a skeptic, but also a believer in the Orthodox faith. Few understood his philosophical position, fewer had his grasp of the meaning of democracy in relation to Church and State, and religion to education, and still fewer knew how he personally felt, that "the undevout philosopher is mad."[51] He ever held out the olive branch to secular as well as ecclesiastic institutions, and his article in the *Atlantic Monthly*[52] bears re-reading even today for some of its cogent arguments.

Once more, in 1878, a crushing blow was aimed at his schools under the guise of deference: 15,000 children were to be released from the Parochial schools and left in the care of the Board of Public Schools wholly unprepared for such a flood! While but a ruse, it would have meant the complete disruption of the school system as built up by Harris . . .

CHAPTER ELEVEN

MAN WRIT LARGE

COLLEAGUES OF MANY COLORS

M AN attains his fullest stature in the institutions with which he affiliates himself. According to this his view, Harris, as soon as he had entered the educational field, aligned himself with all organized pedagogical interests that had not as yet become so specialized, as the Herbart Society was, to represent an antithesis against his own theories.

The first society he joined was the Missouri Teachers' Association. It was a sultry July day, in 1858, when this body, convening for the third time, was addressed by our young educator from St. Louis on the Phonetic System, "discussing some of the reasons for a change in our orthography and the adoption of a simpler one based on Phonetic Laws." He argued against "learning a mass of unphilosophical rubbish", but did not wholly support etymological iconoclasm. He served as Secretary but with the same nonchalance, it seems, that we know from his association with the St. Louis Literary and Philosophical Society.

The next meeting was held in St. Louis in preference to Independence, Mo., as one felt more secure against the border ruffians in a larger city. This convention may be noted for Harris' presentation of his paper on "Comparative Philology." Language he considered the fountain head of national consciousness, and he showed himself completely dominated by Hegelian thinking.[1]

The Fifth Annual Meeting was held also in St. Louis, in July, as usual; but only five months later, in December, 1860, the Sixth "Annual" Meeting was called to the same city, and Harris tendered his resignation as Recording Secretary. He did serve, however, on the nominating and other committees. In August of the following year, already under stress of the political situation, the members of the Association met once more in St. Louis. Sporadic meetings took place after this, but the Civil War played havoc with the Association so that in June, 1867, when convening again in St. Louis, they dedicated themselves to the re-establishment of a proper union, and Harris served as Secretary in the temporary organization, as well as Chairman of the Committee on Permanent Organization and representative of the First Congressional District. Thus he became one of the founders of the revived Missouri State Teachers' Association.

During the first session, the oath of loyalty was taken by all as required by the State Constitution and Almighty God was thanked for peace, supremacy of National power and the unsullied honor of the flag. An astounding activity was manifested by Harris in this meeting. Among other things he suggested the establishment, without delay, of a State Normal School, and offered resolutions regarding a State *Journal of Education.*

"The Province of Education and its Present Requirements in our State" was the topic of a lengthy paper for the 1868 meeting. Some significant remarks were reiterated regarding the introduction of phonetic reading.[2] Harris was also busy as Chairman of the Committee on Normal Schools. Furthermore, they included him in a delegation to represent the Association at the next meeting of the National Teachers' Association and made him a member of a Committee to memorialize the Legislation in the matter of national schools.

At the informal meeting of the Directors in 1869, Harris offered a paper on "Text-Book Education". In 1870, he held the crowded audience at Sedalia, Mo., in rapt attention for an hour by his address upon "The Theory of American Education."

The occasion of the Kirksville, Mo., meeting of the Missouri State Teachers' Association in 1870, was a rather momentous one in that it realized an ambition of Harris' to have a State Normal School. The brief talk, "Position and Work of the Normal School in a System of Education," Harris wrote on the cars riding from St. Louis. The burden of it was: "The Avatar of Democracy has come in the universal realization of the possibility of each individual to ride on the backs of all." The School to be established should realize the inscription over Fichte's grave in Berlin, that the teacher shall shine as the brightness of the firmament . . . They met again at Kirksville after Christmas, 1872, to hear Harris dedicate the Normal building.

Formally, Harris spoke at subsequent meetings as at Jefferson City, in 1874, on "The Relation of Common Schools to High Schools and Colleges"; at Mexico, Mo., in 1875, on "The Course of Study for High Schools"; at St. Louis, in 1879, on "The Place of Latin in a Modern Education." But he was present at nearly every meeting down to 1880, when the Association convened at Columbia, Mo.[3]

The participation of Harris in the activities of the American Institute of Instruction, dating from 1871 (though acquaintance goes back as far as 1861) infused some of the national scope into the organization which it had always claimed but never enjoyed. Into the rather poorly attended 42nd Annual Meeting at Fitchburg, Mass., July 27th, 1871, Harris brought the spirit of the West and made Easterners realize that New England was not alone in determining educational policies.[4]

Harris had travelled East in the company of his brother David who was teaching at Jacksonville, Ill. The paper which Harris presented was "Prescription — Its Province in

Education". When it was read, there was no comment. After a while, John D. Philbrick, the Boston Superintendent, rose and called attention to a point of order and flatly demanded a discussion. Amos Bronson Alcott immediately came to the rescue and characterized Harris' thinking as the latest on these problems. With this, Philbrick concurred, and when Miss Peabody got up and thought that doing comes before thinking, thus introducing an antithetical thought to that of Harris, he flatly called Froebel whom she cited as her authority, in error on that point. Turning to Harris, he said that the whole country was indebted to a man who could prepare a lecture such as they had heard. Harris had called it the Sphinx enigma of American education, how we could build a deeper and wider freedom without letting it degenerate into licence. He wanted Americans of the future, in which he foresaw density of population, gigantic corporations, an array of wealth and poverty, sansculotism, and despotism, to be educated not for skepticism and selfishness, but for insight and aspiration.

Harris had joined the Institute at the right psychological moment. It was on the brink of disaster and needed new blood badly. When they met again, in the pleasant surroundings of the White Mountains of New Hampshire in the following year, the attendance rose to 1700. The Institute even operated on a little surplus and had gone into the extravagance of decorating the pavilion with festoons of evergreen, flags and 40 large kerosene lamps. In his paper on "The Function of Latin and Greek in Education", Harris had gone a long way since his initial antipathy against the ancient languages which he used to flout openly. What has been mentioned does not by any means exhaust the service Harris rendered in the American Institute of Instruction.

Harris' connection with the National Educational Association was just one long record of faithful service and devotion. As President, Life Member, officer, counsellor, and member of many a committee, often as Chairman, his thought influenced this organization profoundly. He became a member at the Cleveland meeting, 1870, when the Association was formed out of the miscellany of educational agencies that aspired to national recognition.[5] The paper on "The Theory of American Education" which came to be known the country over, was read by him at this meeting.

He brought the Association to St. Louis in 1871, and was elected for the ensuing year a Vice President. He had labored hard to make it pleasant for all the members. He had prevailed upon the President of the Iron Mountain Railroad to invite the members on an excursion to Iron Mountain and Pilot Knob. At Jefferson Barracks near-disaster overtook them in that a mail train, just ahead of the excursion train, was derailed, its cars hanging perilously on the bank of the river. However, it proved a most successful and enjoyable excursion which was personally managed by Harris and J. B. Merwin.

At the Boston meeting in 1872, he read an essay on the early withdrawal of pupils from school. He was nominated a counsellor and was to serve on a committee to "inquire into the form in which Froebel's principles of education may be most efficiently applied to the educational wants of our country." The meeting at Detroit, in 1874, was addressed by him "On a National University." Harris believed firmly in the moral influence of such an institution which would offer training in the philosophy of literature, history, and science, and thus contribute to the general educational scheme which was fraught with certain dangers due to the opposition of the colleges to the continuance of a liberal education, such as the Public Schools offered, and the general neglect of disciplinary studies and their substitution by a smattering of natural science. Harris was elected President, and words of praise were even forthcoming from the *New*

York Times, and both he and St. Louis were congratulated on his appointment.

When, thus, the Association met at Minneapolis, Minn., in the summer of 1875, Harris, who had brought with him his son Theodore, functioned as President, and together with John Eaton, of Washington, he was appointed Counselor-at-Large for the following year.

Beginning with 1879, the Department of Superintendence of the National Educational Association met in close collaboration with the U. S. Bureau of Education, at Washington. Harris was invited, and served on the Legislative Committee, and a Committee to confer with the Commissioner of Education, who was none other than his friend John Eaton.

Many more appointments followed until finally Harris became an incorporator of the Association when it met in 1880 at Chautauqua, N. Y. Once more he was made Vice President and, besides, appointed Delegate to the International Educational Congress at Brussels, Belgium, to represent the National Educational Association of the United States.[6]

In the Thrall of the Muses

The idea and inception of the first *popular* St. Louis Art Society was, beyond doubt, due largely to William Torrey Harris. The first members were recruited from among his friends, acquaintances and colleagues in the Public Schools. The Missouri Historical Society has preserved, in the Jefferson Memorial, the original manuscript of the Constitution in Harris' own hand. It bears 15 signatures in the following order: Wm. T. Harris, Louis Soldan, Wm. P. Heston, H. H. Morgan, Brandt V. B. Dixon, H. M. Faltman, M. W. Miller, Edward H. Long, S. Geo. Fenby, Lewis J. Block, Jno. J. Bailey, Edward H. Currier, Conrad Diehl, Wm. D. Butler, Robt. Rombauer.

The St. Louis Art Society made its début in 1866, with

Harris as the first speaker. The prominence of persons connected with the schools, stamped this venture, from the first, as a sort of feeding organization to the Public School Library. In addition to those named above, there were others in the employ of the Public Schools that were also active in this society, as Denton J. Snider, Thomas Davidson, Mary E. Beedy, Sue V. Beeson, Anna C. Brackett, and Amelia C. Fruchte. Harris spoke on Raphael's "Transfiguration", with a copy of Morghen's engraving of the painting before him. Three months later, in February, 1867, he interpreted Beethoven to the members. First he gave a sort of outline which was followed by the playing of the piece by four hands, with Charles S. Bernays and Mrs. Arnold Strothotte at the piano. More comments were made, and the pieces discussed were played a second time. They represented selections from the symphonies and the Moonlight Sonata.

The Society shared to some extent the vicissitudes of the Public School Library, and hence its activity coincided with the facilities the Library was able to offer. In 1869, Harris presented, in the usual form, a talk on " 'The Last Judgment', as painted by Michel Angelo." When, in 1872, Professor Conrad Diehl presented his painting "Macbeth" to the St. Louis Art Society, he laid the foundation for a noteworthy collection which Harris sought to augment by purchases, especially of autotypes[7] of paintings in the possession of the Vatican. Plans for a School of Design were drawn up, with classes in Composition, Still-life and the study of the Antique.[8] Conrad Diehl, an inheritance from Chicago after the great fire, was most active in guiding the destiny of this School. Jno. J. Bailey spoke in glowing terms about the fact that, in 1874, the newly created School of Art had already "been able, through the products of its pupils, to vie in certain branches with the Academies of our Eastern cities and of Europe."[9] Diehl was eager to place it on a national basis. Steps were taken to offer collections of models, casts, pictures, photographs and other objects of art for exhibit in the rooms of the Public School Library and intensity the study, discussion and interpretation of all forms of art. All collections were to remain intact and become "perpetually the unconditional property of the community." When the Society finally disbanded in 1881 — the moving spirit, Harris, having left St. Louis — it was able to pass on a fine collection to the Library.

The first good-sized exhibit of the St. Louis Art Society was held late in April, 1873, in the large hall of O'Fallon Polytechnic Building, and it was the most unique and pleassurable the city had ever witnessed. When they had acquired the plaster of Paris cast of the huge frieze of the "Niobe Group," Professor Thomas Davidson spoke on the sculptors Skopas and Praxiteles and the philosophy expressed in their works of art, while Harris also contributed philosophical remarks. Sculpture was further represented by the Venus of Milo, the "Torso of Hercules," attributed to Michael Angelo, the "Theseus" and "Ilissus." These colossal casts were ranged at the front of the platform, on either side of the rostrum. Their "magnificent proportions loomed up grandly in the brilliant gas-light." Then there were the autotypes of Michael Angelo's works and those of Raphael, Leonardo da Vinci, Titian, Tintoretto, Domenichino, Salvator Rosa, Perugino and Fra Angelico; Dürer, Rembrandt and Van Dyck were likewise represented.

About the time when rumors were current that the arms of the Venus of Milo had been found, Harris spoke on the "Restoration of the Venus of Milo." But, lectures alternated with musical presentations and interpretations, such as the ones he gave on Beethoven's Sonata in F-Major, on the Pastoral, and on Mendelssohn's concertos. Snider himself and others loaned and presented prints. The Frescoes of the Sistine Chapel were discussed by Harris. Noted St. Louis musicians contributed with their talents. It was the heyday of art for St. Louis. The Society aspired to making the city, by reason of its wealth, the "Art Center of the West." The connection with the Public Schools was a great economical factor and served equally as well for maintaining a large clientele, while high society was also attracted to some extent by the affiliation of the members of the School Board and their friends. Artists who had studied abroad were invited to speak, and wealthy citizens opened their homes to the members for special meetings and entertainments. Exhibits were loaned and the public invited to view them.

Around 1878, the whole country was in the throes of an art mania. Lilian Whiting, who visited the Western metropolis in May, wrote back to Boston: "You cannot sit, you dare not stand, and there is no room to write. Life is a burden, a perpetual sacrifice and burnt offering at the Shrine of Decorative Art!" The "true art spirit" was fostered with a vengeance and expressed itself in China-painting, Kensington embroidery, charcoal drawing, clay modeling and what not, and the Art Society bowed to the spirit of the times. It interested itself in such ventures as that of Miss Halsey, of the Cincinnati School of Design, who was crusading for wood carving; and Mrs. John B. Henderson's short-lived St. Louis School of Design which had such a range of esthetic vision that it included phonography, Harris' long time interest.

Now, Harris was not an artist, but he took every opportunity to learn about art. His scrapbooks were filled with clippings, every advertisement or art-notice was preserved. He would visit every art gallery and special exhibit. Admiringly, and philosophizing, he would stand in front of Albert Bierstadt's six by ten foot canvas "Autumn in the Sierra", or his "Storm in the Rocky Mountains", or Church's "Heart of the Andes." He went to art dealers, interested himself in Oriental bric-à-brac, in miniatures, missals, early printed books and autographs. When the Mary In-

stitute featured an exhibition of these items Harris served
on the Committee, and contributed 17 Bibles in as many
languages, Porta's *Physiognomiae Coelestis* (*Libri VI,*
Strassburg, 1606), Fauvel Gouraud's *Cosmophonography*
(the Lord's Prayer in 100 different languages), Sextus Em-
piricus, *Adversus Mathematicos* (Paris, 1569), Erasmus,
Colloquia (Elzevir, Amsterdam, 1650), the *Sankhya Karika*
in Wilson's translation and a Prayer Book in the Algonquin
dialect.

Harris supported the cause of art wherever he could, sub-
scribing to journals like *The Aldine,* collecting autotypes,
engravings and sculpture. Practically one-third of the first
volume of the *Journal of Speculative Philosophy* was devoted to discussions of art and esthetics. In his 1874 lecture
before the University Club, he spoke at length on the relation of art to philosophy and religion. Art portrays the
infinite in the finite, it manifests the divine, while religion
reveals it, and philosophy deals with the relationship in a
reasoned way. He was conscious of his own limitations in
the matter of creative imagination and made the admission
that the Anglo-Saxon mind does not see so much in art as
do the Italians and the Germans. Charles L. Bernays once
said that, to his knowledge, Harris had never seen a real
classical piece of sculpture or painting in the original. That
was as late as 1879. He interpreted everything, in true
Yankee fashion, through *Vernunft,* never *Gemüt.* Nevertheless, Harris was in a certain sense an esthete. In discussing a book by Walter Smith, he stated:

> What a fine thought to have the furniture of our
> houses, the implements of the household, the table-
> ware, etc., all fashioned with lines of beauty; not such
> cheap and tawdry ornamentations as is common but
> with such lines of grace and beauty as one sees in the
> Etruscan vases, the Venetian table glass, Greek toilet
> ware, or in the works of Benvenuto Cellini. True art

should take the place of the mockery of art which everywhere meets our gaze.

He envied the European who, even though he be a beggar,
could behold "the spectacle of graceful outlines" right in
the market place.[10]

However much a professional artist or art critic may try
to lessen the merit of Harris' art endeavors, it must be remembered that he thought of art as a democratic venture,
or, rather, necessity, like education, and that he wanted to
make it available to everyone. He accomplished what such
institutions as the Western Academy of Art, founded in
1860 and catering only to the wealthy who could afford the
membership fee of $250, or the St. Louis Art Union, also
rather exclusive and interested in helping local talent, or the
Art Department of Washington University which, with its
School of Art and Design that began functioning about
1860, had mainly academic interests, could not accomplish,
that is, reaching the public and thus making art a democratic concern. Harris took great pride in the fact that he
had brought the study of art, architecture, sculpture, painting, music and poetry "into the teachers' life so as to make
each teacher a growing power in the community."[11]

In music, likewise, Harris had no formal training beyond
playing the flute for his own enjoyment, yet he recognized
not only its tremendous power but its social significance as
well. Charles W. Chapman, who had become a Director
of the New Haven Philharmonic Society, wrote him that "all
the music one doesn't *hear* is a lost lift"[12] and Harris agreed
with him. Ever since his "symbolic" period when under the
influence of General Hitchcock, he would let no opportunity pass by of hearing good music. He became a member of the St. Louis Philharmonic Society in 1862 when it
had been in existence but two years or so. Eduard Sobolewski wielded the baton, and he became a friend of Harris'
who gave him an opportunity to contribute to the *Journal*

of Speculative Philosophy. All through the Civil War, the Orchestra, composed mainly of members of the Society, carried on and ventured even into the "music of the future" in the shape of the grand overture to Tannhäuser.

Music is a reflection of the emotions of the soul, according to the philosophizing Harris. It is only secondarily a portrayal of objects. Gluck he credited with having first discovered the intimate marriage of sense and sound, words and music. Meyerbeer's "Dinorah" is symbolical of man's development from loss of self-identity in madness back to sanity. Music saves us from the "night-side" of our nature. Palestrina, Mozart, Hayden, Händel, Bach, Beethoven, Mendelssohn, Schumann, Kreutzer, Schubert and Rossini gave us truly religious works without being sectarian. Psychologically, music is of the utmost importance in that it is the greatest dialectic of feeling, and it should be a necessary branch of education. The German nation loves music and thus has developed an *Innerlichkeit* which also forms the basis of true knowledge.

When Sobolewski retired in 1866, the Philharmonic went through a crisis. For a while, A. Waldauer and Charles Balmer took over. A new leader from Hanover was expected, but when he did not arrive, Froehlich, who hailed from Stuttgart. was offered the baton. Harris interested himself deeply in these developments and wrote the reviews of the activities for the daily papers. The seventh season of the "Soirées" started with social hilarities for the five hundred friends and supporters, and there were "copious libations to the musical god supplied from the products of various vintages, foreign and domestic" which Harris may have passed up in favor of the "zest and pungency" of lively conversation.

Dilettantism was progressively banished, but still the critics charged that most participants were above the years of youthful freshness and censored the young for having all their charms *on*, but none *in* their throats. Through the press, Harris pleaded with the best vocalists for a spirit of self-devotion to the cause of art. For, it seems, they refused to sing except in solo parts, depriving the chorus of its "aroma." The orchestra, likewise, showed defects, but no one dared to offend the musicians who were "so touchy in general." A Monster Concert was planned for the summer of 1868, and Harris served as member of the Executive Committee, but due to various circumstances and involvements it was never given.

How faithful a disciple of Euterpe Harris was may be seen in that he went as far as taking lessons in vocal culture from Miss Currier in the spring of 1868, but his notes required more of his attention than did practice. He gave high recommendations to the Theodore Thomas Orchestra which came to St. Louis in the 1874-75 season. At the Centennial at Philadelphia, in 1876, he waxed enthusiastic about the Women's Centennial Chorus of over 400 voices. He praised the Germania Club that boasted of Vogel's Orchestra, the Liederkranz, and the Arion des Westens. He faithfully attended the Hans von Bülow concerts in 1876. The teaching staff was circularized to make possible the payments on the organ of the St. Louis Mercantile Library Hall. Every week he would attend the rehearsals of the Oratorio Society at Washington University, with Waldemar Malmene as the leading spirit. Sometimes these musical ventures were connected with financial losses, as the one mentioned last and the Monster Concert, but this did not deter Harris from working actively for the cause of music. He philosophized through the performance of "The Messiah" and Mendelssohn's "St. Paul"; he subscribed to the Balatka Quintette Club of Chamber Music and the St. Louis Harmonic Society under Robert Goldbeck, as Director.

The Semple & Birge Manufacturing Co., as agents of the Bell Telephone Company, put on a telephone concert in November, 1877, one of the first to be given, and Harris was

306

among the 40 select persons to listen on one of the earphones at the home of Mr. and Mrs. E. H. Semple to a concert transmitted over a circuit of about 60 miles of wire.[13]

FOR THE ADVANCEMENT OF SCIENCE

It has often been alleged that Harris did not care for science because of his philosophical interests, and was of retarding influence in the teaching of it in the Public Schools. Nothing could be farther from the truth. Not only did he take a keen interest in science, particularly astronomy, optics and physics, but he introduced the teaching of science into the Public Schools of St. Louis, and belonged to several scientific societies in an official capacity.

More than that, Harris made an original contribution to science. He was probably the first to give a comprehensive qualitative explanation of the phenomena observed in the gyroscope, which was correct on the basis of Newtonian physics.[14] His notes on the problem of the gyroscope were made in 1861, on reaching home one day after spending the evening with philosophical friends as he was wont to. "I said to myself on the street car: If one only analyses his problem correctly, he will solve it and I then thought of the gyroscope and exclaimed to myself: Why haven't I solved the gyroscope? The analysis of it by horizontal plane came to me at once. Then the agreement of top and bottom in pushing the disc around the standard." The printed article appeared in the *Standard* for October, 1865, and was reprinted in Merwin's *Journal of Education* for August, 1869. He also gave a lecture on the gyroscope; and throughout his life was quite proud of his solution, collecting material, references and notes as late as September 27th, 1905.

It was, perhaps, even before 1867 that Harris expounded the theory of colors to the teachers in their Saturday class. At another meeting he exposed the fallacy in Benson's theorem of determining the area of the circle. In his reviews of the volumes of Johnson's *Universal Cyclopedia*, which he furnished for the papers, he always paid more attention to the scientific contributions than to the philosophical ones.

Ossian Lang tells us, though with what authority is very doubtful, that "when Spencerian ideas struck America, he forthwith had a laboratory established in the rear of his house, and made a thorough study of biology and related sciences." However, it is true that he was thoroughly familiar with Darwin's theories and often thought in natural science terms. For instance, the Kindergarten was interpreted as a short recapitulation of the experience and culture of the human race up to the stage of alphabet development. He thus showed his familiarity with anthropogenetics. The analogy of substituting the snake or turtle for tadpoles in studying the embryology of the frog, was in his mind when he heard that educators wanted to substitute modern languages for the classical ones in the curricula of the schools.

When Professor C. Gegenbaur, of Heidelberg, sent out a call for Mississippi Valley embryos of turtles, alligators and opossums, as well as fishes, Harris was most anxious to accommodate the German professor. With pride he reported in the same year (1875) that the contributions of St. Louis to the endowment fund of the Museum of Comparative Zoology at Cambridge, in commemoration of Louis Agassiz, amounted to $766.28, or nearly one tenth of the entire amount collected throughout the country. When efforts were being made by many societies and individuals to introduce birds from Europe — the Cincinnati Acclimatization Society had sent a Mr. Schwan to Germany to bring back 1500 songsters — Harris published a circular impressing teachers with the importance of telling their pupils about conservation and the protection of birds. The *New York Tribune*[15] paid tribute to Harris' fairness to science in that he recognized the value of the *Popular Science Monthly* even though it presented views opposed to his own. He recommended highly a popular science series published by Estes and Lauriat, at Boston, in 1874. From his youth he had the greatest admiration for men like von Humboldt and Newton.

New Englanders noted with some jealousy the strides of education on the banks of the Mississippi, particularly with reference to the introduction of science teaching, an achievement due mainly, if not solely, to Harris. The teaching of natural science was formally introduced into the St. Louis Public Schools by resolution of the Board, November 14th, 1871. Even before that, every teacher was to give her class weekly an oral lesson an hour in length on the subject of plants and animals, the structure of the human body, care of health, machinery, heat, light, electricity, the weather, and allied themes. The lesson was to be illustrated by blackboard diagrams and specimens. The Course of Study had to be completely revised due to the innovation. All grades were affected, and all subjects. The Course of Study which Harris finally evolved was copied all over the United States. It took the place of the English-Oswego object lessons because Harris had reduced science teaching to a logical development. As late as 1887, the Committee on Physics Teaching of the National Educational Association incorporated this Course of Study in their report.

Harris assumed full responsibility for science teaching in the schools. All instructions regarding it emanated from his office over his signature. He pored over anatomical and other models that were offered for sale by the commercial houses. He furthered scientific collections, such as the mineralogical cabinet. as well as exhibits of specimens of manufacture. For the Normal School he advocated trips to factories. The examination questions of Assistants invariably included problems of physics and enumerations of the most important plants. The "philosophical apparatus" was to be made available, by his order, also to students in the Evening Schools.

Early in 1870, the Public School Library comprised 2750 books on natural science and useful arts, almost as many as on social and political science, and constituting about one-seventh of the total number of volumes. The percentage of novels in the library was 17, while the general average for the country in libraries of the same standing was 26, speaking well for the scientific interest in the St. Louis schools.

This should be sufficient demonstration that Harris was not opposed to science, but to the tendency to present exclusively facts to the pupil and call it education, or to strive to give him proficiency in the handling of tools. Harris advocated the study of principles in primary education, including methods and tools of thought, on the assumption that life will fill in the factual content, at the same time leaving the pupil the choice of subjects. Were the teacher to make a selection of the "objects" to be studied by him, the school could not be said to foster the principles of freedom and democracy. Harris' Course of Study was at the same time a piece of political philosophy, and it was not a question with him of whether more science and more practical courses should be taught, but how best to preserve the American outlook by an appropriate education. At the same time he had too high a regard for the exact and higher branches of science than to think that they could be taught adequately in the Public Schools. That is evident from his essay "On a National University."

"Not one jot or one tittle of natural science is to be given up; its magnificent results as regards the emancipation of man from the slavery of physical toil are to be counted at their full value," he said before the graduating class of 1877, at the Massachusetts Normal School.[16] To be sure, he called science with its materialistic attitude one of the Sphinx riddles of the age; he indicated the solution which he did not

310

seek in repudiating it but by assigning science its proper place in civilization. If science aspired to dictating in the realm of morals and values, he rebuked it as he did religion if it meddled in the worldly sphere of politics and education. He was struggling with essentially the same problems as we are facing today and he would have fought it as an absurdity to declare a holiday for science.

Leaving out of account his invention of a system of diacritical marks as an aid to easy and uniform pronunciation, his philologic studies, his ardent support of the National Spelling Reform Association, and his connection with social science groups, he affiliated himself with a number of scientific bodies. There was, for instance, the International Academy of Natural Science (New York and Berlin) which, under the directorship of Dr. Adrian J. Ebell had as purpose the diffusion of science and the assistance of teachers. With the American Association for Advancement of Science he was even more intimately connected.

When that body held its meeting for the first time in its history West of the Mississippi, in August, 1878, Harris served as Chairman of the Reception Committee. The meeting was engineered with the co-operation of the St. Louis Academy of Science which furnished the rooms and a hall and took care of the excursions into the vicinity of St. Louis, to Pilot Knob and Iron Mountain, to Cahokia Mount, the Smelting and Silver Reduction Works, and other plants, to Shaw's Botanical Gardens, the "Eden" of St. Louis,[17] and the parks, and by steamboat along the river banks.

Comparatively speaking, the 27th Annual Meeting at St. Louis was poorly attended, because, as Professor F. W. Putnam, of Salem, Mass., the Permanent Secretary, hesitatingly divulged, the feeling had been prevalent in the East that the yellow fever was raging in St. Louis and that the papers were suppressing the facts. The valient torch-bearers of science could not and would not so easily sacrifice their lives. Besides, it was rumored that many deaths had occurred from heat and the "foul germination of the heated atmosphere." Professor Putnam saw himself forced to send a special dispatch through the Associated Press, presenting the true state of affairs.

The meeting was opened on August 21st, 1878, in the chapel of Washington University. When all were seated, in came, a few minutes after 10 o'clock, a procession of eleven gentlemen and quietly seated themselves upon the platform. Among them was Harris who entered with his Honor, the Mayor Overstolz. After the introduction of the new President, O. C. Marsh, and the invocation, Harris, as Chairman of the Citizens' Reception Committee, addressed the assembly. He welcomed those present in the name of the Committee and the St. Louis Academy of Science. He described some of the problems with which Missouri was faced and in which she was most anxious to have the cooperation of entomologists, geologists, meteorologists, and others. "With good reason", he said, "our people prize science; for its fruits in this State will surpass all its harvests in other times and other fields." After mentioning the interest in pure science fostered by the St. Louis Academy of Sciences, he introduced the Mayor.

While on the first two days the sessions had a "mighty slim" audience, they proved stimulating and fertile; but on the third day the number of participants increased (because no one had died yet in the foul air of St. Louis) and Thomas A. Edison was introduced under great applause, presenting three papers. There was an elaborate reception at the Lindell Hotel, with music and an "elegant collation", attended also by the ladies. The excursions were a huge success, and thus the discouragement of the first two days changed into general satisfaction, owing to Harris' efficiency as Chairman of the Reception Committee.

The St. Louis Academy of Science had received its charter on January 17th, 1857. Its library of well over three thousand volumes was housed in the rooms of the Polytechnic Building and is considered by many to have been "the best and most extensive of its kind West of the Allegheny mountains." At the time of the affiliation with the Public Schools, the Academy was receiving regularly the transactions of about 170 foreign and 75 home learned societies. Harris became President in 1874, following the retirement of Capt. James B. Eads. In his presidential address he simply made a few reflections, as he called them, upon the recent achievements and the status of the sciences. Though disclaiming humbly all pretentions at being a scientist or being able to judge adequately the progress of science, he hailed science as the great power of the age. On the subject of astronomy he dwelled at some length, for upon telescopes he could speak with a great deal of knowledge, having been interested in them since his youth. "Science is free and fears no results; the truth alone is its object; and wherever the truth leads it is for the man of science to follow unhesitatingly. But all circumspection and all coolness of temper are here requisite." Nature is the realm of efficient causes, but spirit deals with final causes.

The members of the St. Louis Academy of Science interested themselves in what they called a Sunday Lecture Society which was organized in the second half of 1875 with a guaranty fund of over $300. The sponsors gathered some time in August at the offices of Garland & Green to discuss the unique features of the venture. They intended to bring well-known scientists to St. Louis to lecture before the laboring classes, charging only 10c. admission. The men interested in it included Wm. A. Seely, Wm. H. Pulsifer, C. F. Johnson, Geo. C. Finkelnburg, B. Graetz Brown, R. J. Lackland, the Rev. Drs. Snyder, Holland, and Learned, E. S. Rowse, Professor Hosmer, and Ira Shippen.

Harris appears as Vice President right after Mr. Pulsifer, the wealthy President of the St. Louis Lead and Oil Co., and among a coterie of St. Louis notables.

The first lecture course featured Moncure D. Conway, of London, speaking on "The Devil" (illustrated); Dr. Isaac J. Hayes, the arctic explorer, speaking on his experience in a lecture illustrated "by the Calcium Light"; the English orator, Charles Bradlaugh; Professor Proctor, the astronomer; Hon. Carl Schurz, who needed no introduction to a St. Louis audience; and Robert Collyer, the Blacksmith Preacher.

The second course of the "People's Dime Sunday Lectures" announced a series of eight famous lecturers, at least three of whom dealt with natural science, one by Professor E. C. Bolles entitled "An Evening with the Microscope." The lectures were held first in DeBar's Opera House, then in Armory Hall. The sole object of the Society, as published, was to give the people generally "and working men and their families especially" a chance to hear, at cost price, some of the best platform speakers of the day. This type of presentation was a duplication of such lectures in London, Milwaukee, and Chicago, among other cities.

In addition to these activities for the promotion of science, Harris joined the St. Louis Society of Useful Knowledge, again not merely as an interested member, but as a Secretary of one of its departments. This Society was founded in May, 1876, and completed its organization in the fall. As the prospectus says, it "sprung from the conviction that co-operation may be made to yield large results in the accumulation and diffusion of knowledge." All efforts at self-improvement and toward the improvement of others, were the central aim.[18]

At first, the Society confined itself to informing "many persons, and especially women, young and middle-aged"— anxious to embark on a systematic course of study, of the best method of procedure, supplying references to the latest books, etc. By means of its written communications, the Society was interpreted as "a director of the studies of many persons, at many different and distant places. The teacher, as it were, visits the homes of the pupils however far they may be separated."

In a sense, this was the first Home Study Extension Course in St. Louis.

Lectures and publications were projected. The scientific note was again very prominent. For instance, in one lecture course of six, at least four lectures dealt with science: "Archaeology of Missouri," "The Eye," and "Combustion," the latter in two evenings, with experiments and illustrations.

On June 8th, 1877, Harris talked on " 'The Fates,' by Michael Angelo", and on December 5th he gave his essay on "The Scope and Problem of Dante's Divine Comedy." The latter lecture was given at the meeting of the Society at the residence of Mrs. Jas. N. Norris, 3039 Pine Street, who acted as Treasurer. Most of the later lectures, as also the March, 1878, lecture on Emerson by Dr. Holland, were held at Washington University. There was an interesting lecture course in 1879 to which Harris contributed and which included talks on Fire, the Telephone, Finance, and Propagandism in Art.

With the scientific department of Washington University cordial relations were kept up during all the years of Harris' stay in St. Louis. Their class lectures, whether in Botany, Zoology, or Astronomy, were advertised by circulars as special features of the Polytechnic School. They were regularly sent to Harris, sometimes with the personal note: "Please speak a good word for the lectures." Harris would not only do that but visit some of the courses himself, as that of Richard A. Proctor, F. R. S., on Astronomy, which was illustrated by charts, pictures and photographs. More than that, Harris took copious notes on the interesting course.

Finally may be mentioned the active interest Harris took

in the St. Louis Museum of Arts and Sciences, which had been organized under the auspices of the members of the Merchants' Exchange. and aspired to be the Museum not only for St. Louis, but for the State of Missouri.

THOUGH PHILOSOPHY BAKE NO BREAD

The founding of the St. Louis Philosophical Society and the publication of the *Journal of Speculative Philosophy* are the two greatest single contributions of William Torrey Harris to philosophy in America. These two projects, the history and prehistory of which are long,[19] were instrumental in bringing about one of the most significant movements in the history of American philosophy, the St. Louis Movement in Philosophy, the whole extent of which has not yet been presented adequately, let alone exhaustively.

The pivotal figures were Harris, the thinker, expositor, organizer, without whose energy and financial support neither the Society nor its *Journal* might have been, and Henry Conrad Brokmeyer, the Hegel and Goethe scholar, of great brilliancy of mind, a bit erratic, master of many trades and a self-made man who was at home in the woods or at the bar, yet was able to meet the social élite. An emigrant, not a refugee, from Minden, Westphalia, he landed on these shores with 25 cents in his pocket and became Lieutenant Governor of Missouri, in time. When Harris met him one Sunday in 1858, presumably at a meeting of the St. Louis Literary and Philosophical Society at the Mercantile Library,[20] he had been a currier, a shoemaker, a tanner, but was, at the time, engaged in molding iron pots in the Bridge, Beach & Co. Stove Foundry. Already then he had studied Plato, Aristotle, Goethe and Hegel better than anyone in America. Harris had had his own preparation in philosophy, which was not mean, and he was immediately drawn to him, especially after tasting, through him, some of the depths of philosophy which he was unable to discover in the other members of the St. Louis Literary and Philosophical Society. William would drop in and read his older friend's most intimate jottings of ideas caught on the wing, would go with him on hunting trips into the interior, and became his amanuensis when he had persuaded the German to translate the works of Hegel.

Brokmeyer was really a kind man, a good story-teller, an unusual combination of metaphysician and poet.[21] Unfortunately, students of philosophy know him, if at all, only through Denton J. Snider's portrayal and William James' kind condemnation as the man of one book, meaning Hegel's *Logic*. His Romano-dutcho-scratcho-chirography[22] certainly did not impair his power of expression and literary talent which he proved incontestably in his play '.A Foggy Night at Newport". He exercised such power over Harris, and some others of his philosophic acquaintance, that they wished to give up living in civilization, as he had elected to do when he removed to the Backwoods in the neighborhood of Marthasville, Mo., living in a hut and without benefit of furniture, yet devoting himself, like Thoreau, to the highest pursuits. In the wilds he subsisted on what his gun could procure for him, and he also raised pigs. From St. Louis, Harris would supply him with books and pens, with soap and shoes, with sacks of salt and onions, with sugar and green tea. And while he was thus enjoying for a time his retreat, a circle of friends, with Harris as leader, continued to devote themselves to the study of philosophy, love for which he had kindled among them, sending him money in payment for the copyrights of his Hegel translations, and eagerly waiting for his letters which then were circulated amongst them. Thus, Harris owned the copyright of his translation of Hegel's *Logik* in three volumes,[23] and he offered the copyright of the translation of Hegel's *Philosophy of Right,* which Brok proposed to furnish by February, 1862, for $75 to Judge H. M. Jones, one of the eager members of the philosophical circle who had gone to Phoenix-ville, Penna., to establish himself. It was this Jones who gave them all the idea to pack up their families and belongings and track across the plains to found a new homestead in Nevada, subsisting on farming, teaching and devotion to philosophy. George C. Stedman, a Southerner and a reporter for the papers, was likewise a member of the circle, and his attachment to both, Brokmeyer, whom he compared to "fierce burnt brandy," and Harris, who, to him was "sweet old tokay or the best of 'perfect love' ",[24] was very touching, especially during the Civil War which claimed his life fighting for the Confederacy.

In 1860 Harris had in mind to place Brokmeyer's translation of Hegel's *Logik* with the English publisher, W. T. Bohn. Early the following year he sent a MS, representing the whole introduction and a portion of the *Lehre vom Seyn,* in all 150 pages. In the accompanying letter it was divulged that there was a group which possessed "a complete library of the Hegelian philosophy, including also the most recent developments, such as the work of [Johann Karl Friedrich] Rosenkranz and J. Eduard Erdmann." The translation, done by Brokmeyer and "undertaken at the expense of Harris" and two others "who had been studying the works of Hegel some years," was made from the 1841 edition of Leopold von Henning, which they took to be the latest.

The sample translation was examined by Henry Bohn who rejected it in a letter dated London, November 11th, 1861. The tangled affairs of business with America were given as a reason, and he added: "I have however cursorily glanced at the translation and presume it to be faithful, but the style is insufficient, and I should have to get it revised by a fluent English scholar."

It was during 1861 that Harris undertook a pilgrimage to Brok's hut in the woods and in two weeks took down in shorthand 254 pages of the *Phenomenology* of Hegel as translated by Brokmeyer which was later transcribed into longhand. When they were thus working away, they found "the grades of consciousness" of most of their philosophic study circle, "Stedman, Hayden, Reed, etc." and finally they "pitched on one that unexpectedly described Brok. 'That is me', said he. Pretty quick, however, his negative side was shown up and it turned out that this grade of consciousness which rested on the assumption of everything rational and arrogated to itself a *prima facie* (that is a good use of the term) insight into everything and condemned everything as utter zero that did not square with it, this very consciousness lacked the comprehension." "Ye gods," Harris continued in the letter to Judge Jones, "how I chuckled in my sleeve! Brok did not say anything, but looked as though he was keeping up a devil of a thinking . . ."

The Civil War was breaking up the circle of friends by and by. Brokmeyer had already retired to the Backwoods, Jones had left, Stedman was in Jefferson City and elsewhere and had premonitions of death; only Harris was left in St. Louis, with Childs, the gentle pedagog, and Hayden, the almost renegade agnostic, not to mention the others whose appreciation of Hegel was less keen. It was thus incumbent on Harris to carry on the tradition and the torch of the philosophical circle which inherited the remnants of the St. Louis Philosophical and Literary Society, and was to become the forerunner of the later and better known St. Louis Philosophical Society. In a letter to Judge Jones he said, in fact — it was in 1861 —: "The works of Hegel will prosper so much better that I think better for us all if I stay in the vicinity of St. Louis a year longer."

By spring, 1862, Brokmeyer, however, became very despondent over his inability to earn enough money in the Backwoods and the fact that his "culture" was not rendering him capable of his "highest fitness in the social whole" in

which he thought he was living.[25] Perhaps there was no
social whole for which to be cultivated . . . ? When, in all
this trouble, a son was born to him and almost the very
hour of the birth brought him the bad news of the inac-
ceptability of his translation and hence his inability to earn
cash, his spirits were low. Harris suggested he carry the
mails. Two days a week, on horseback, with plenty of time
to think? Yes, this *did* appeal to Brok, but fate willed
otherwise. Even though his bid was the lowest, his competitor received the contract. But, a trip to town in June
netted him admission to the Bar. From then on his star
began to rise. He was commissioned Lt. Colonel in the
Militia of Missouri, did important work at Headquarters,
went to Washington, returned to St. Louis where he served
on the Board of Aldermen, became a State Senator and
finally Lt. Governor of Missouri, and Acting Governor during Phelps' term, but retired later after having served as
Corporation Counsel for the Missouri Pacific Railroad,
to live for ten years among the Indians of Oklahoma.

The meeting with Brokmeyer was always acknowledged
by Harris as an event fraught with great meaning to himself. Brokmeyer's name was entered in large letters in his
Diary for 1866. This autobiographical *Diary* briefly
summed up his spiritual development beginning with 1857
when he was under the influence of Goethe and Cousin.
Brokmeyer appeared in the company of Kant and Fichte,
and Hedge's German Prose Writers, during the year of 1858;
in December of that year the Objective was breaking
through for William and he reached the first universalization of time and space. He thought it was Fichte's, but was
mistaken. In 1859, it was Brokmeyer again, also Hegel and
Sir William Hamilton. The second universalization was
attained by grasping the category of existence. Landmarks
for 1860 were: Coleridge on Method, the Vishnu Purana,
the Hitopadesa, Sakuntala, Vera, and Rosenkranz, not to

forget Hegel's *Philosophy of History,* and Spinoza. The third universalization, the theoretical method, was now attained.

During 1861, Harris realized the ideas of freedom, ideal and real, as well as the dialectic of time and space, and of Being and Nothing. A new and fateful phase was entered in 1862, when he took theology to correspond to freedom, seized upon Spirit and Personality as ultimate values, and "cleaned up" his pantheism. For 1863, only the publication of the article on Kant and the Absolute was noted, but early in the year the *für-sich-sein* was seized. Nothing was noted for 1864, but a *Commonplace Book* was started that promised to be of significance particularly in that it contained, among translations, short essays, comments and other matter, a dictionary of Hegelian terms as variously translated by Brokmeyer, Stallo, Hedge, Smith and others. Mention of the threefold method of Hegel and studies in essence during 1865 conclude the spiritual autobiography. But the little work is significant for its information concerning the developments leading up to the founding of the constituted Philosophical Society.

During all this time, Harris was the most active member of the group in the philosophical field, although Brokmeyer had worked like a beaver on Hegel during the opportunity provided by his living away from civilization. Harris held the circle together, he even unified North and South as is so touchingly evident from Stedman's last letters. He made propaganda among his friends for idealism; he wrote glowing letters home. His brother Edward Mowry who knew that William had paid Brokmeyer at the rate of $100 for each Hegel translation, during a period when his salary was very slim and continuous employment was at stake, censured him for looking "too much to one side of a question," and thinking "too little of common affairs."[26] Sister Sarah Lydia, who was acquainted with members of the philosophy circle, was pressed into service and made to copy a Hegel translation. She liked to read William's published "pieces", and confessed to being able to understand "now and then an idea in them." But when a cousin read one of the pieces, she told Sarah, "I don't see the point to it or any meaning to it," which Sarah forthwith reported to brother William, adding in her letter: "Don't you feel bad?"[27]

The War of the Rebellion was looked upon by the adherents of Hegel as a grand dialectic which ended with Lee's surrender to Grant. But the principle of development could not be stopped. When the old members of the philosophy study group could finally be brought together, an organization was to be set up which could also foster the cause of philosophy financially. The actual founding of a society was postponed till the beginning of 1866. On the 19th of January, or thereabouts, seven persons, Brokmeyer, Harris, Denton J. Snider, Geo. H. Howison, Britton A. Hill, J. H. Watters, and Dr. J. Z. Hall met at the downtown office of Mr. Britton A. Hill, "for the purpose of organizing a society for the promotion of Speculative Philosophy and its application," to quote from the *Record Book of the St. Louis Philosophical Society* kept by Harris. Brokmeyer and Hill were appointed to draft a constitution which they submitted and which was adopted with a few amendments on January 26th at which meeting Brokmeyer was elected President, Howison and Watters Vice Presidents, Hill Treasurer, and Harris Secretary. The first formal meeting was held on February 2nd, which date was taken as the date of founding the Society.

To trace the history of the St. Louis Philosophical Society requires a volume in itself. The modest rôle which Harris seemed to play was, indeed, only apparent. He was only 30 years of age, but it is safe to say that the spread of the influence of the Society was entirely due to him. Later he would

322

openly acknowledge that he was "an active mover" in the establishment of the Society.[28] The *Westliche Post*, sometime in 1868, conjectured correctly that Harris was the real founder of the Society, and even Snider had to acknowledge that Harris had cultural primacy.[29] There were 18 signers of the Constitution, every single one of whom was a personal friend of Harris. The *Record Book* further contains the names of 39 Associates, among whom Horace H. Morgan and Chas. C. Michel were elected Directors. Out-of-town members and some others, as Henry T. Blow, were called Auxiliaries, and there were 48 of them. They included Amos Bronson Alcott, Ralph Waldo Emerson, Henry James, F. B. Sanborn, J. Elliot Cabot, General Hitchcock, F. E. Hedge, J. H. Fichte of Halle, Johann Karl Friedrich Rosenkranz of Königsberg, Jas. Hutchinson Stirling of Scotland, A. Vera of Naples, and many personal friends as well as relatives of Harris, his uncle, Dr. Peckham, and his brother-in-law Edwin Holmes Bugbee among the latter, R. R. Bishop, John W. Albee, Joseph Defonfride, C. W. Chapman, and Chas. C. Baldwin among the former. With practically every member Harris carried on a correspondence some of which, as with Thomas Davidson with its hundreds of letters, cannot be termed otherwise than voluminous. None of the original founders of the Society, neither Geo. H. Howison, Snider, J. G. Woerner, Charles L. Bernays, nor any of the others, including Brokmeyer, could boast of such an epistolary activity, not to mention the hundreds of articles which Harris wrote and published. He was, beyond the shadow of a doubt, the prime mover in the St. Louis Movement in Philosophy.

There were regular weekly meetings of the Society; there were informal study groups such as the one meeting regularly at Harris' house to read Hegel's *Phenomenology*, or at Adolph Ernst Kroeger's house to read Fichte's *Wissenschaftslehre*; there were special meetings to which the public was admitted, as when the Society promoted Alcott Conversations and Emersonian lectures at St. Louis; papers were read; the letters of Auxiliaries were spread upon the minutes; connection with European, particularly German philosophical bodies and organs was sought; the publication of works was planned, as that of Judge J. B. Stallo who had made some "strictures upon the system of Hamilton and Mill"; memorial meetings were held, as the one for Charles F. Childs; and, finally, the publication of a journal was planned to serve as an organ of the Society whose professed object it was to "encourage the study and development of Speculative Philosophy, to foster an application of its results to Art, Religion and Science, and to establish a philosophical basis for the professions of Medicine, Divinity, Law, Politics, Education, Fine Arts and Literature." This last mentioned project took shape in the *Journal of Speculative Philosophy*, which became America's first serial publication of a professional philosophic nature and in it many a well-known philosopher prepared himself for flight, including William James, Josiah Royce, Charles Peirce, John Dewey, Thomas Davidson, G. Stanley Hall, G. H. Howison and Nicholas Murray Butler. Not only was the *Journal* far more significant than any other of the transcendental journals of the time; it antedated "the founding of any other definitely and significantly philosophical periodical in the English language."[30]

In order to settle all disputes as to whose brain child the *Journal of Speculative Philosophy* was, which even now is a tribute to American philosophy on the shelves of our university libraries, it may be well to quote from the record of the Proceedings of Friday evening, January 4th, 1867, when the St. Louis Philosophical Society met at Mr. Hill's:[31]

A protracted discussion took place on the subject of a Journal of Speculative Philosophy which one of the

Society (Mr. Harris) proposed to publish. Upon the request of Mr. Harris a committee of five was appointed by nomination to make final adjustment of the relation which the Society should sustain towards the projected journal. The committee consisted of Messrs Brokmeyer, Howison, Kroeger, Jones, & Bernays.

The phrase, "which one of the Society . . . proposed to publish" is significant. That Harris wanted to found it merely in protest of his failing to get the *North American Review* to publish his 12,000 word criticism of Herbert Spencer, or even in defiance, as Denton J. Snider seems to imply, is not entirely correct. For, in a letter from Concord, Mass., dated July 15th, 1866, Amos Bronson Alcott wrote to Harris:

> What you say about the desirableness of having a Speculative Journal I feel as strongly as yourself, and wish the thing might be. There is a class of thought for which we have as yet no organ. The Radical is good in its way, but fails to serve the Speculative needs of original thinkers; nor is it likely to command the full strength of the country. We need the scope and volume a quarterly ensures; and if Emerson, James, Cabot, Wasson, will join the men of the West — yourself, Stallo, Brokmeyer, Kroeger, Howison, Tafel, Goddard — we might open with large perspective and prospect. Meanwhile the Radical serves as current advertisement and deserves the best it will take.

Now, Chauncey Wright's letter to Charles Eliot Norton, Editor with James Russell Lowell of the *North American Review*, bears the date of Cambridge, July 24th, 1866, and Norton's letter to F. B. Sanborn who was promoting the publication of Harris' Spencer article, was written July 27th, 1866, while Sanborn informed Harris of the rejection in a letter from Hampton Falls, N. H., August 3rd, 1866.

In the opening paragraph of the first volume of the *Journal of Speculative Philosophy* and elsewhere, Harris spoke of "Editors," possibly making use of a fiction or merely employing the plural of majesty, while in the Table of Contents he invariably put "Editor." Above all it is Harris's payments of the bills for publishing the *Journal* which clinch the argument that it was entirely his creation and must, as such, go down in the annals of American philosophy.

The Society and the *Journal* had a profound influence upon the intellectual life of St. Louis, primarily, but equally as much upon the intellectual life and the philosophical interests at various centers in the United States. As far as Europe was concerned, these two creations "put America on the map," for now America had evolved from its purely theological tradition and attained philosophic stature. Even the daily papers of St. Louis carried metaphysical articles which would spell the ruin of any newspaper in our own day. A Boston correspondent of the *Springfield* (Mass.) *Republican* once[32] dared to affirm and trusted the future to prove it that in Harris America has a philosopher "worthy to be compared with the great Germans."

Even St. Louis society opened its heart and house to philosophy. Lilian Whiting related how, for instance, Mrs. Major Merwin entertained her friends in her beautiful parlor, "a leafy-green, fern-adorned nook, where it always seems summer-time," with bits of talk, music and readings from the German philosophers. A cousin of William who attended the philosophy classes out of curiosity rather than appreciative interest, related what she considered the spice of "an evening with Hegel" at the Harris home: Young Theodore's imitations of his dad's lectures and pantomimes. When Julia Ward Howe passed through St. Louis in the summer of 1877, she was, of course, snared by the Philosophical Society to give a lecture. To the reporter she described Harris as the most gentlemanly of the members, the rest of whom reminded her of the critics that formed the Radical Club in Boston who would pound upon the reader of an essay as on an anvil.

So great was the jealousy of the East with its claim to cultural and intellectual supremacy, that when notice of the international acclaim of the St. Louis Philosophical Society and the *Journal of Speculative Philosophy* had to be made in the *New York Times,* it disclaimed Harris' right to lecture on metaphysics because he lived in St. Louis. Others deplored that inasmuch as many of the teachers were exposed to the cultural influences that Harris was spreading, they were engulfed in intellectual night and, worst of all, were led away "from the God of their fathers and the Christ of the Gospels" . . .

CHAPTER TWELVE

CHIPS FROM AN AMERICAN WORKSHOP

Addresses Mostly Educational

Wᴵᴸᴸᴵᴬᴹ TORREY HARRIS was best remembered by his friends as he stood, tall, erect, on a platform, his head slightly bowed, peering intently through his gold-rimmed spectacles into his manuscript which he held somewhat obliquely in both his hands rather close to his eye, while his lips gave forth each word with a distinctly New England modulation. "Pale, nervously twitching, thin-cheeked and seemingly thin-blooded, with a sharp face and rather pointed nose, he appeared a needle that could prick keenly and deeply into things. A soft silken coverlet of hair at that time spread over his temples, and his features were knit of exceedingly fine and delicate lines; one-half of his face was very regular and showed almost a sculpturesque perfection, the other half was uneven in comparison and more craggy in outline."[1]

To thousands in St. Louis and elsewhere he was a familiar lecturer who commanded respect in virtue of his inherent sincerity, even though his thought was often much too high for popular comprehension. Some of the hundreds of talks he gave while connected with the Public Schools at St. Louis, found their way into print, a good many were reported in the journals and newspapers, many more are still in manuscript and some are irretrievable, particularly his informal philosophical discussions, the multitude of incidental speeches and extended "remarks." Perhaps a little geographic survey will convey the range of his influence from the platform.

328

His talk before the St. Louis Teachers' Association in 1864, might be taken as a sort of confession and self-defence. "Abstraction Considered in its Practical Relation to Life" discussed the popular error which takes a deep man to be an abstract man. While it has its uses, abstraction seemed to Harris not the mark of profundity, but the unfailing accompaniment of shallowness. Abstractions are most dangerous in the political and economic spheres. Society he considered the better half of man for it enables an individual to "achieve a Cosmos," a phrase he probably owed to Brokmeyer.

An organization upon which Harris looked with a sort of paternal affection and to which he contributed talks and lectures as liberally as to the Association just mentioned, was the St. Louis Society of Pedagogy[2] which, functioning somewhat spasmodically between 1872 and 1880, may be considered the continuation of that Teachers' Association. Harris served as an Honorary Member, and by 1880 he had read a number of papers, among them "The American School System", "Tendencies of Educational Systems", "Value of Culture in Education", "Kindergartens", "Sex in Education", "Culture and Discipline versus Information and Dexterity," and "The Novel as an Educator." The Western, which gave publicity to many of the ventures with which Harris was associated, printed occasionally a lecture by him. We need not mention again his many lectures in St. Louis on the subjects of art, music and philosophy which augmented the renown of the city as an intellectual center.

Outside of the city, Harris was also in constant demand as a speaker. It sometimes happened that his insight and philosophic sweep was opposed to the provincialism of mere school masters and ma'ams. Thus, he conducted a close and searching examination in Mental Philosophy, at the North Missouri State Normal School.[3] At Kirkwood Seminary, Kirkwood, Mo., he was called upon to deliver a lecture on "The Facts and Ideas that underlie our Modern Civilization."[4] Drury College, Springfield, Mo., heard him speak[5] on "Relations of the Mississippi Valley to the United States," a variation of an often repeated theme which the students of Columbia University (Missouri) had heard him deliver as a chapel talk six years earlier[6] under the title of "The Elements of Civilization Found in the Mississippi Valley."

In the State of Tennessee, Harris was much in demand and favor, especially after his famous Chattanooga address before the Interstate Educational Convention from June 29th to July 1st, 1875. The South had finally combined in the educational field to remove the pall of ignorance from among its people, and when Harris developed for their benefit his theme of "The Mississippi Valley and the Basin of the Gulf of Mexico, as Related to Education and Civilization," all lent grateful ears. Most of the educators from Alabama, Georgia, Kentucky, Illinois, Missouri and Virginia, had probably never dreamt of the politico-philosophical derivation of their usefulness in the national scheme, and no speech could have been better calculated to instil into them pride and enthusiasm. Harris was looked upon almost as their prophet and deliverer who had shown them the way toward a more glorious and very important future. It was much more than praise Harris won at Chattanooga.

When the Western Division Institute and Convention of Teachers for Western Tennessee met at Union City,[7] Harris spoke on "The Education Demanded for Industrial Arts and for Citizenship." The District Institute and Convention of Superintendents and Teachers for the 9th Congressional District, held at Brownsville, Tenn., heard him on "Organization and Management of Schools." After that, Harris attended a convention of friends of public education at Chattanooga where he met General Eaton, U. S. Commissioner of Education. He prolonged his visit to the South—ill-timed, because there was an exodus to the Northern States to avoid an impending yellow fever epidemic—

and attended educational conventions in Tennessee and Alabama, perhaps also in Georgia and North Carolina. When, at Nashville, he read his paper on "The Press as an Educator," two years later,[8] he was greeted as a friend. Kansas, likewise, esteemed him, and the State Teachers' Association invited him to speak,[9] at their Ottawa meeting. At Pike's Opera-house, at Cincinnati, Harris addressed the Seventh Commencement of the Cincinnati Normal School,[10] acquainting Ohioans too with the educational problems and promises of the great American Bottom. Here, however, he did not receive such a welcome as he had in the other States: The audience left, first in little squads till their number swelled into a "steady column of retreaters," to return only for the music and the awarding of the diplomas to the impatient young ladies on the stage who were wilting among the flowers and foliage. However, they called him back, four years later,[11] to enlighten them on the workings of the Kindergarten.

With Indiana, Harris entertained friendly relations which were to result in important developments. He addressed the Logansport meeting of the State Teachers' Association in 1873.[12] His discussion of the relation between education, government and society, was acclaimed enthusiastically by the progressive organization, which claimed almost a hundred more members than the corresponding New York State organization. At the opening session of the Terre Haute Normal School, [13] Harris again was one of the principal figures, as on many other occasions in this State and in Illinois.

As early as 1868, Harris addressed the Southern Illinois Educational Convention at Centralia, Illinois.[14] In 1871, he told[15] the Illinois State Teachers' Association in special session at Rockford about some school phases in St. Louis. Two years later he addressed the same body at Springfield. He was present, in 1874, at the Commencement exercises of Shurtleff College to address the Literary Societies,[16] and in 1875 at the First Annual Commencement Exercises of the Southern Illinois Normal University, at Carbondale, to deliver[17] the Annual Oration on "The Place of the Mississippi Valley in Civilization and Education." In 1876, he joined J. M. Gregory and S. H. White in addressing[18] the 23rd Annual Meeting of the State Teachers' Association at Champaign on "Centennial Lessons and Report of Centennial Committee." "Education as a Science" was his topic in 1879 when speaking[19] before the St. Clair County Teachers' Association, at Mascoutah, Illinois.

In Iowa, the State Teachers' Association, at its 23rd Annual Meeting at Marshalltown,[20] asked Harris to speak on "The Theory and Art of Education," while in 1879, a year later, he acted[21] as one of three judges at the Fifth Annual Contest of the Inter-State Oratorial Association that convened in the Opera House at Iowa City.

Pennsylvania knew Harris from lectures in connection with the Pittsburgh meeting of the American Institute of Education, in the summer of 1871, and, of course, the Centennial Exposition in Philadelphia. When the Spelling-Reform Association met during July, 1879, at Philadelphia, as a branch of the National Educational Association, Harris gave his little known talk on "The Potency of Caprice, — each man for his own alphabet."

At the time of the Centennial, there occurred his trip to Baltimore, Md., where he also was invited to speak. New York State knew him at least as early as 1873 when he was President of the Department of School Superintendence in the National Educational Association, meeting at Elmira.

New England, Harris' home territory, recognized and honored him on many an occasion, especially after he had made his début at the Boston Radical Club, later the Chestnut Street Club. He became a frequent guest in the East before he settled there in 1880. The Massachusetts Teachers' Association, among other educational bodies, listened to his address at their 32nd Annual Meeting in Haynes Opera House at Springfield.[22] His subject was "The Educational Significance of the Centennial Exposition," but the burghers did not turn out in great numbers, and their town was flayed in the papers afterwards as "characteristically shy of genuine worth" that evening. The famous lecture on the Sphinx Riddle was given by Harris in 1877[23] before the graduating class of Worcester Normal School. It was a tribute to him that he received an invitation to the Annual Unitarian Festival in 1880.[24] At the Boston Music Hall he found himself surrounded by a cotery of notables, College Presidents, Governors, well-known literary men, scholars and clergymen from all parts of the country who were addressed by Charles W. Eliot, President of Harvard.

LITERARY VENTURES, PROFITABLE AND OTHERWISE

Most literary contributions of William Torrey Harris during his student period had been essays on various subjects of a serious nature. Many had their specific origin in debates and class discussions at Yale. During the St. Louis period, a tremendous literary activity was unfolded, but the preponderant number of published articles — and Henry Ridgely Evans' list by no means even approaches the total number of printed articles[25] — were originally lectures, addresses, and "extended remarks" made in pedagogical, philosophical and related circles. There were numerous other contributions that fall outside such a classification, material of a collaborationist type, letters, reviews, opinions and the like. The garnering of this material is, indeed, a tremendous task in itself,[26] but the collating with the manuscript material[27] would require an even greater labor and entail the unravelling of sheaves of shorthand and longhand manuscripts. The research student would discover not one but several drafts of many of the lectures and articles; he would find whole books filled with shorthand copies of chapters from philosophical and educational works; phonographic copies of personal letters; the translation of Hegel's *History of Philosophy;* transcriptions of Brokmeyer's translations as well as the original shorthand copies; projected articles and books; comments; autobiographical notes and related matter in great quantity.

The *Journal of Speculative Philosophy* which Harris founded, contains a good many of his solid articles. The *Annual Reports* of the St. Louis Board of Education were in large measure written or compiled by him. The *Journal of Education* (St. Louis) received a number of contributions by his hand, and so did *The Western,* the *Western Educational Review,* and the *American Journal of Education,* not to mention other serial publications, including the *Atlantic Monthly.* His own statement that he contributed some 40 articles to Johnson's *Universal Cyclopaedia,*[28] needs considerable correction. A patient search through the 12 volumes of the 1908 edition has revealed about 100 signed articles.

This Cyclopaedia had been projected around the year 1871, but serious work was not started until 1874. In a sense it was a revised edition of the 1858-63 work that had been brought out by the same publisher. At the time of Harris' first acquaintance with the work, George Ripley was the Senior Editor, a literary critic for the *New York Tribune.* He was supported by Richard H. Dana. In the later editions, Charles Kendall Adams was the Editor-in-Chief. Harris thoroughly enjoyed his connection with this encyclopaedia, and he became very devoted to it, editing the Department of Philosophy and Psychology in conjunction with J. Mark Baldwin, Professor of Experimental Psychology, at Princeton University. He took great pains in presenting his topics in the light of historical development. His contributions were of a mixed type, including general and broad philosophic themes, such as *Aesthetics* and *History of Philosophy;* con-

cepts of scholastic philosophy, such as *Actus;* universal phil osophical concepts, such as *Apperception* and *Cause;* and names of philosophers, from *Aristotle* to *Nicholas Murray Butler,* in the later editions. He was associated with many distinguished scholars and men in the public eye; his St. Louis friends also contributed, among them Thomas Davidson, A. E. Kroeger, Dr. Geo. Englemann, Dr. T. M. Post, Professors Raphael Pumpelly and C. V. Riley, Gov. B. Graetz Brown, and Hon. Carl Schurz. Harris continued as an Associate Editor.

Another venture which, by the way, proved highly profitable — quite different from the *Journal of Speculative Philosophy* which drained his purse considerably — was his editorship of *Appletons' School Readers.* Appletons' Series grew out of a real need to lay a better foundation for the study of English in the grades with the aid of more efficient methods of teaching pronunciation than any of the existing *Readers* at the time could offer. Their huge sales were made possible by the conniving of varied interests in and out of the schools throughout the country.

As early as the spring of 1873,[29] Harris received a communication from D. Appleton and Company, apparently in response to a personal interview, regarding a set of *Readers* to be prepared by him and J. P. Wickersham, Superintendent of Public Instruction for Pennsylvania. The collaboration of Wickersham was, apparently, not forthcoming; as a matter of fact, after two years, he declined the proposition.[30] Finally, end of 1876,[31] C. W. Brown, Superintendent of the Educational Department of D. Appleton & Co., wrote Harris from Cleveland, Ohio, that Andrew J. Rickoff, Superintendent of the Public Schools of Cleveland, had received the proposition in regard to the *Readers* "most favorably." Inasmuch as Horace H. Morgan, Brandt V. B. Dixon, and Professor J. C. Pickard, of Urbana, Ill., had projected a series of *Readers,* from *Primer* to the *Fifth Reader,* they had to be

persuaded to sell their manuscript and all rights to Harris, which they did on May 25th, 1877. The MS formed the basis on which *Appletons' Readers* were then built by Harris and Rickoff. In 1877,[32] they enlisted the co-operation of Mark Bailey, the well-known and able Professor of Elocution at Yale. That Harris was the originator of the plan, at least so far as the Appleton Series was concerned, is evident from a passage in a letter to Rickoff[33] which reads: "I hope you will write me as freely as if you were the initiator [?] in this entire process [?] and certainly I desire in every respect to have it as much yours as mine."

The burden of the work rested, however, almost entirely on the shoulders of Harris who not only arranged all the material, but looked to some extent also to the business end of the matter and corresponded extensively with the publishers. In the summer of 1877 he went East for the express purpose of supervising and rushing through the press the first four *Readers*. Brown had seen to it that proper permission to include their pieces was obtained from other publishers and authors. A personal letter from Bayard Taylor is an interesting item in Harris' collection. The help which Harris received from Rickoff was rather slight. Rickoff was the author of the Cincinnati Plan and was in the midst of reorganizing the schools in Cleveland. His wife aided him in reading proof of the *Readers*. He complained frequently in his letters of illness and need of rest.

Many problems had to be faced during and after the publication of the *Readers*. The size of the books had to be adapted occasionally to State regulations to make them eligible for class-room use in some of the States. Thus, the *Fourth Reader* had to be cut down for use in Minnesota schools. Brown once wrote[34] that he feared the reference to Don Juan would not be approved because of the "immorality of the poem." "The extract is all right, but by referring to the poem in the foot-note you really invite the

reading of it entire — by school-girls, — an improper thing to do . . ." Later he wrote[35] that it was necessary to take out the Gettysburg Speech in order to make the *Readers* adoptable in South Carolina. Southern business which had suffered by competition in the shape of readers reflecting the spirit in Dixie, had to be revived at any cost, And then there was religion! ". . . I know the difficulty of suiting everybody," Brown confessed, "but will not those who like religious pieces generally concede the necessity of omitting them? . . ." The Catholics of Scranton, Penna., had objected to the Sermon on the Mount in the *Fourth Reader*.

However, it was generally conceded that the method had been gleaned in the class room. Teaching to read was made easier and pleasanter by far through these *Readers*. Though only skilful teachers could derive the full benefit from these books, they were unmistakably the product of varied and concentrated experience. Henry David Thoreau was introduced to the pupil in the *Fifth Reader,* as well as Goethe. Benjamin Franklin would impress the reader, indeed, as the wisest American; Hawthorne, America's best prose writer, and Shakespeare, the greatest poet of the world. People in the West had always objected to the familiar milking scene in *Primary Readers* which pictured the milker on the wrong side of the cow. They had no criticism to offer on that score, as the illustrations were superb and unsurpassed for the period. The whole series, sold for $1.30, was, therefore, extremely reasonable. Before the year was over nearly a million copies had been sold. On June 6th, 1878, Brown wrote to Harris that if he contemplated disposing of his copy-right interest, he should first consult with him. It shows shrewdness on the part of Harris that he never considered anything of the sort. It would be too rash to say he knew how to make money; yet he seized the opportunity when it came to him. During the year in which the *Readers* were published, he did little else in the matter of literary work. Perhaps even then he was looking forward to resigning his Superintendentship and retiring on the money to be received from the sales of the books. They had advanced $4000 on May 21st, 1877, representing the first installment of the sum of $7500 that was to be paid to Harris and Rickoff in part consideration for the undertaking. Before his death, Harris confided to a friend that the *Appleton Readers* netted him more than $85,000. His royalty being but 1 cent per book, or 5 cents per series, about 1,700,000 sets must have been sold within a quarter of a century, a very reasonable assumption. Appleton and Company, indeed, had not made a mistake. Orders by the thousands, yes tens of thousands, poured in almost from the beginning. Their Chicago office alone ordered 50,000 copies the first month of publication. All New England States, New York, New Jersey, Pennsylvania, Ohio, Indiana, Michigan, Illinois, and Kansas were eager to adopt the *Readers*. Kentucky was very favorably disposed. Catholic Schools also ordered. The reviews were for the most part full of praise. Even Father Phelan, the arch enemy of the Public Schools of St. Louis, wrote well of them saying that he failed to discover the slightest unfavorable allusion to the Church and her teaching. And the phonetic press exuded kind words. Their review, however, almost escaped our notice: *"Apltun'z Fifth Reder, bai W. Harris"* was the title, and the reviewer expressed his great *plezhur tu faind a rieder compaild upon a proper plan.*

Being a successful business enterprise, the *Readers* faced serious opposition, and Church interests were exploited to discredit Harris because of his well-known investigations of speculative philosophy which were said to have led him to ignore the existence of God and all religious principles and belief. Excerpts from the *Readers* had to be printed and circulated with rejoinders by Harris who explained his position in regard to religion over his signature. Handbills were circulated which alleged that a conspiracy had been formed for the purpose of preventing the use of *Appletons' Readers,* and that $200,000 had been pledged for the purpose. Rival publishers even wanted to withdraw all their books and substitute copies of a new edition for them. Hundreds of agents toured the State to discredit the work of Harris. There can be no doubt that all this adverse propaganda contributed to Harris' desire to withdraw from the Public Schools . . .

MARSHALLING THE EMPIRE OF BOOKS

Already when very young, Harris had occupied himself with library classification on several occasions. His own book collection, in the early part of 1858, comprised 367 items for which he invented some sort of classification. Librarians, generally, had despaired over being able to cope with the flood of new books that was rushing on year by year with ever mounting volume. Something had to be done, and many people gave it a thought.

Harris conceived his book classification system in connection with the work he did as Assistant Superintendent (later Superintendent) on the Course of Study in the St. Louis Public Schools. This course he characterized as "a voyage of discovery" for the pupil, but it proved to be no less the impetus for the development of a scheme by which to classify the knowledge accumulated in books. This interrelationship was evident from the *15th Annual Report*[36] written in 1869. However, it is certain that the problem arose in his mind as early as 1865, the year of the opening of the St. Louis Public School Library. While most systems were essentially alphabetical and chronological at the time, Harris divided the "empire of human knowledge" into classes. His original scheme he printed during 1870 in his *Journal of Speculative Philosophy*.[37] He acknowledged that the scheme rested upon Bacon's fundamental distinction as developed in *De Augmentis Scientiarum,* Book 2, chapter 1. Inverting Bacon's departmentalization of the faculty of the soul into memory, imagination, and reason, and the corresponding departments of human learning into history, poetry, and philosophy, he established three main classifications: *Science, Art,* and *History,* and an appendix of *Miscellany.*

It was this classification which was discovered by Melvil Dewey, who was studying library classification most intensely. In 1873[38] he wrote Harris for a catalog of the St. Louis Public School Library and other matter bearing on the subject. In 1876[39] he acknowledged that the St. Louis plan and that of the Apprentices' Library of New York resembled his own, but "were not seen till all the essential features were decided upon, though not given to the public." In view of the enquiry mentioned above, this admission is significant and may well be interpreted as an indebtedness of Melvil Dewey to Harris,[40] which becomes apparent when we compare Harris' scheme with Dewey's "Decimal." A simple tabulation may suffice:

DEWEY		HARRIS	
— — — —	0— 99	SCIENCE	1
Philosophy	100—199	Philosophy	2— 5
Theology	200—299	Theology	6—16
Sociology	300—399	Social & Political Sciences	17
		Jurisprudence	18—25
		Politics	26—28
		Social Science	29—31
Philology	400—499	Philology	32—34
Natural Science	500—599	Natural Sciences & Useful Arts	35
		Mathematics	36—40
		Physics	41—45
		Natural History	46—51
		Medicine	52—58
Useful Arts	600—699	Useful Arts and Trades	59—63
		ART	64
Fine Arts	700—799	Fine Arts	65
		Poetry	66—68
		Prose Fiction	69—70
Literature	800—899	Literary Miscellany	71—78
History	900—999	HISTORY	79
		Geography and Travels	80—87
		Civil History	88—96
		Biography	97
		APPENDIX — Miscellany	98-100

Not a few libraries acknowledged their indebtedness to Harris, the Peoria Mercantile Library (later Peoria Public Library) and the New York City Apprentices' Library among them. It was Dr. Walton C. John who once felicitously pointed out that Andrew Carnegie, the great benefactor of public libraries, was born in the same year as Harris. Both men, though widely apart in their main interests, made significant contributions to the domain of books, the one by donation, the other by intellectual assistance to the reader. Melvil Dewey made these contributions generally available to the public.

Harris and Dewey were on the friendliest of terms since the 1873 correspondence. Grosvenor Dawe's biography of Melvil Dewey[41] mentions that there is among his collection of letters a most cordial one from Harris while he was still Superintendent of Public Schools. They came to know each other very closely, not only in connection with library classification, but as zealous spelling reformers. Thus, Dewey spoke at the St. Louis Spelling Reform Association meeting of 1878.[42] He was the Secretary, and Harris one of the Vice Presidents at the time.

Both Harris and John Jay Bailey who was Librarian of the St. Louis Public School Library until 1877[43] and who never denied credit to Harris for the scientific and philosophical construction of the classification, were co-operating editors of Dewey's *Library Journal,* and Harris contributed an article on "The Function of the Library and the School in Education."

IN AND OUT OF THE STUDY

Throughout the country, Harris became known as "a gentleman of broad and liberal views, with a mind capable of grasping those grand philosophic principles, on which popular education is founded," and as "a clear-headed, free thinking, practical, puritanic spirit." He was eagerly sought for as a speaker not only in educational and philosophical circles, but by civic and religious bodies as well. Indeed, he seemed to be without denominational prejudices. He lectured equally as readily in the Methodist Episcopal Church,[44] as at the Mount Olive Temple[45] or Fairmount Church, or before the Free Religious Association at Boston.[46]

Together with F. Louis Soldan he made, in April, 1872, an extensive tour of inspection of different school systems, at the suggestion of the Board. It carried them to Cincinnati, Chicago, Cleveland, Oswego, Boston, and New York. In his report[47] he stated that the school system there could no more be transplanted to St. Louis than bananas from Havana. His full report reached only the stage of a printer's proof, for he withdrew the whole because it was too critical of Eastern systems.[48] Ties of friendship connected him with many of the Superintendents, — Pickard of Chicago, Rickoff of Cleveland, Paul of Milwaukee, Doty of Detroit, De Wolf of Toledo, Shortridge of Indianapolis, Hancock of Cincinnati, Cowdery of Sandusky, Tingley of Louisville, Henkel of Indiana, Bulkeley of Brooklyn, Philbrick of Boston, and many more. They came to St. Louis, or sent their representatives. As early as 1867, Harris served on the Reception Committee of a delegation from the Board of Controllers of the Philadelphia Public Schools, headed by the Hon. Edward Shippen.[49] J. L. Pickard came in the spring of 1871, and in the same year the Superintendents of Toledo, Milwaukee and Detroit arrived on a tour of inspection. Visits of this nature continued throughout Harris' administration. But on September 22nd, 1876, there called M. Ferdinand Edouard Buisson, the President of the Commission which the French Commissioner of Education had sent to Philadelphia for the International Exposition. Earlier Harris had conducted Herrn Sigismund Blum, Attaché of the Austro-Hungarian Legation at Washington, through the schools in St. Louis. The Hon. Fujinero Tanaka, Vice Minister of Education, from Japan, reciprocated for his reception by sending a gift of books and charts on Japanese education. It may have been that this visit by the Japanese Commission was inspired by Emerson who, upon enquiry from the Japanese Embassy, had referred to St. Louis as the city having the best school system, better than Boston. Reference to such an advice by Emerson we find in a letter by Dr. Robert A. Holland to Hon. Judge J. S. Hager, recommending Harris for the presidency of the University of California in 1887. Late in 1879 W. F. Shropshire, the Editor and Publisher of the *American Journal of Education* (Tennessee), paid his visit to Harris' schools, and about this time, or a little later James L. Denton, State Superintendent of Public Instruction in Arkansas, called and carried away fruitful ideas. The Board knew long before this that they did not have to go outside for advice on how to run St. Louis schools . . .

But the price of success is often dear. Petty politicians and feeble pedagogs combined to make Harris' position as Superintendent unpleasant. From 1873, till Harris left the city, a veritable barrage of insinuations flooded the newspaper editors' desks, one more absurd than the other. Probably the jealous mind of an unsuccessful Board member conceived of calling Harris "an absolute king"; a disappointed militant Protestant said, "the Pope in the Vatican is as democratic as the present Superintendent"; a bitter Catholic made the ungracious remark that "speculative philosophy has deceived our School Board and cursed our schools."

Evil things which Harris never did were charged to him, and good things were deceitfully appropriated by other quarters. But stoically he worked. Charles L. Bernays, who knew Harris well[50] and whose letters written while in Europe bear witness to his friendship for him and show how much he did to distribute both the St. Louis School Reports and the *Journal of Speculative Philosophy* to interested persons in Europe, as well as to procure for him the latest books, was not afraid to say that Harris was opposed in education by a number of incompetent and arrogant teachers who believed in rotation in intellect and honesty. The way in which Harris answered the scurrilous letters to the editors of the daily papers, if he answered them at all is worthy of note. Even his enemies had to acknowledge the decent and winning manner in which he treated the anonymous authors of poisoned arrows. Singular, perhaps, is the way in which he pacified J. B. Engelmann and practically won him to his side. He never attacked persons, but he tracked down lies mercilessly.

The New England Publishing Company in Boston was publishing life-size portraits of eminent educators, mounted on heavy cardboard, 20x24 inches, and retailing at a dollar each. The first series included Horace Mann, George Peabody, Barnas Sears, Froebel and Agassiz. They included Harris in the second series, along with John Eaton, the Rev. A. D. Mayo, J. D. Philbrick, and Col. F. W. Parker. This portrait of Harris' was found in nearly every office of Principals and Superintendents in the last quarter of the 19th Century. While Harris was still at St. Louis, Professor Edward Rowland Sill, of the University of California, gave currency to the comparison of him with Horace Mann . . .

CHAPTER THIRTEEN

OF MORE PERSONAL CONCERN

FORTUNES OF FAMILY

A LETTER by William Torrey to his sister Sarah told of the misfortune that had befallen the Harris household in St. Louis:

ST. LOUIS, *July 21st /70*

DEAR SISTER,

A great bereavement has fallen on our family in the death of our little Ethan. He died yesterday afternoon at 3 o'clock. It was his birthday — just six years old.

Scarlatina four weeks ago and followed after an interval of two weeks (in which we tho't him quite recovered) with the dropsy of which he died. We bury him at 3 this P.M. in Bellefontaine near his little sister.

It is a most terrible stroke to us all —

Your brother,

WM. T. HARRIS.

The little sister was Charlotte who had died in infancy. Affectionate letters of condolence were received from many friends. Amos Bronson Alcott wrote:[1]

A bright, keen-eyed boy, I remember he was, and like your surviving son, promising to make his mark, like their father. I trust his mother finds consolation in the thoughts which the event awakens, and is assured that time softens and heals like sorrows for the present loss— translation, I should write rather, to spheres of brighter activity.

You, of course, can meet the event with the manliness becoming the philosophy which you affect and have mastered . . .

In 1873, on March 17th, William's sister, Anna Rebecca died. She had studied at Mt. Holyoke College, and her sister Sarah Lydia had recommended her strongly to brother William in 1866 when she had a mind to go to St. Louis. She thought she would make "a very good teacher", and the two sisters had planned to board together. Apparently, the plan never materialized.

Happiness again made its abode in William's family on August 6th, 1875, when another girl, Edith Davidson, was born who was to give such valuable assistance to her father in his later years and to the writer of this biography. Her name was given her by Professor Thomas Davidson who suggested that it be Edith, the "fair-haired Saxon Edith", to which her parents added the middle name of Davidson out of regard and friendship for "Tom Davidson", as he was called by his St. Louis associates at that time.

Harris' father died in 1876. David Henry, William's brother, who had graduated from the Connecticut State Normal School in 1867, had attended Yale, and then gone West, resided in 1876 as Superintendent of Public Schools at Jacksonville, Illinois, having previously occupied the same position first at Macon City and later at Hannibal, both in Missouri. His sister Ellen Elizabeth, who graduated from Mt. Holyoke in 1878, came to St. Louis where she taught for two years, as long as William was Superintendent, and then joined David Henry at Jaksonville.

Strange, this urge of the Harris family to go West, which had cost John Wilkinson his life. Anna Rebecca was the only one of the four sisters that had not gone out to St. Louis. All of the four remaining brothers sought the West for longer or shorter periods in their careers. For Charles Joseph also had come to St. Louis after graduation from

Yale in 1874, and graduated from the Law School two years later. He did not, however, make his home in St. Louis, but went to Denver. From there he moved to North Carolina where he interested himself in Kaolin mines and many other industries. He was a delegate to many a National Republican Convention and served as member of the Industrial Commission of 1898-1902.

The literary vein of William Torrey was passed on unmistakably to his son Theodore who wrote some stories for the *Missouri Republican* which reveal a poetic gift and a feeling for the tragical-romantic which might have been inspired by an Edgar Allan Poe. In the story "A Hidden Genius"[2] in which he extolled the life and character of Roderick Lyell, the line between truth and fiction is exceedingly delicate. His "Tale of the Moonlight Sonata"[3] is a passionate account, well-written, but in a flowery style, of the circumstances of the birth of Beethoven's wondrous work. In 1879, he married Florence Fairchild, of St. Louis.

At home, William Torrey was an affable but determined father who enjoyed the love and respect of his family circle. There were no ostentations of affection. Compare, for example, the ending of the letter quoted at the beginning of this chapter with its signature. "Wm. T. Harris," quite symptomatic of his almost Puritan restraint. The Civil War had created the fashion of wearing a full beard. In William's face with its youthful lines it only enhanced his dignified appearance, mellowing at the same time his New England tenaciousness. In an "Anthropological Chart" which some phrenologist[4] had made of him, his intellectual capacity had the average index of 5 (7 being very large), but, more accurately, he scored highest in the only propensity classified among the selfish ones, that of firmness. No doubt, Harris was amused by this chart which made such obvious blunders as the underestimation of his powers of concentration, verbal memory and reasoning faculty.[5]

Though his fame was nation-wide, Harris lived simply and austerely. He enjoyed his family and friends yet never relaxed to "take it easy". Such an idea was simply foreign to his mind. The horse and buggy which he owned he did not keep for pleasure. He kept it to be able to visit the schools more easily and to save the Board the expense of cab service. The bill of $500 which he presented to them in 1877 was thus unjustly criticised by the opposition.

One Saturday night — it was in 1878 — horse, buggy and all was stolen. When Sergeant Powell, of the police force, found the whole outfit several days later, the buggy was standing on Gratiot Street, near Seventh, in front of Stolle's Hall. Some fellows had gotten in and driven off. The animal was in a sad state, looking as if it had not tasted grain since it was stolen. The buggy was beyond repair.

OBLIGATIONS AND PLEASANT DUTIES

When the teachers in the St. Louis Public Schools purchased a full-length portrait of Ira Divoll, painted by C. F. Weigandt, for the Public School Library, Harris made the presentation speech.[6] But only two years later, on October 28th, 1871, he read the eulogy at the funeral of this one-time superior, colleague and friend. The only life, Harris said on this occasion, which was to Divoll worth living, was one devoted to work, — a remark, which applied even more to the speaker than to the deceased.

When Adolph Ernst Kroeger, an active member of the St. Louis Movement in Philosophy, was sent to prison in 1871 by some freak of legal-political reasoning, Harris left no stone unturned to get him justice. He appealed to the Governor; he saw to the publication of the articles, which Kroeger wrote in jail, so that his wife and children might not want. As late as 1876 he had to pay a note for $100 with interest, which he had signed with Kroeger, the latter being unable to pay.

OF MORE PERSONAL CONCERN

At the formal installation of the Rev. Dr. William Greenleaf Eliot as Chancellor of Washington University at the
Annual Alumni meeting on February 29th, 1872, Harris
was guest of honor, adding his toast to those of other distinguished gentlemen.

Mrs. Ednah D. Cheney, of Boston, widow of Seth Cheney,
visited the city in the fall of 1873, staying with John L. Dear-
born. To the reporters she confessed, after having toured
the St. Louis schools with her fellow Yankee, Harris, that
the East had taken notice of his work and that it was "rare
that they put a man of such ability, of such literary power,
in that position."

There were some, of course, who found fault with Harris'
style and his philosophical vocabulary, and they attributed
it to his heavy diet of German philosophy. Were those who
charged that he was unable to write United States English,
that his style was long-drawn out, not pithy nor epigramatic,
aiming at the truth or mere literary effect? A man who had
the moral responsibility for tens of thousands of children,
could he be reproached for not indulging in vagaries and in
the light-hearted ramblings of pup journalists? Men rose
sincerely to his defence, as, for example, the author of the
following comment on "The Readjustment of Vocation":

> Like all his writings, it is instructive, elevating and in-
> spiring. It seems to be Mr. Harris' forte to enunciate
> grand principles so plainly, and in a manner so forcible
> and simple, that any earnest mind can comprehend
> them; and no one can thus comprehend them without
> being helped and instructed. Amid the confused
> thoughts and feelings and doubts which an awakened
> mind feels when contemplating or seeking to learn the
> principles of human progress, one of Mr. Harris' essays
> drops like a foundation crystal. Around it facts arrange
> themselves naturally, methodically and harmoniously,

and conviction takes shape and form where before was confusion and doubt.

His association with the Germans had nothing to do with any cumbersomeness of style. To be sure, he freely mingled with them socially. He became a member of the Germania Club,[7] attended their Christmas celebrations and may have sat in the large beer gardens to hear famed brass-bands produce the strains of Strauss and Weber and the rest while even the most distinguished among them would get up to dance and enjoy their stein. At the Polytechnic Hall he presided over the celebration of the Alexander von Humboldt Centennial, on the evening of September 14th, 1869. Present were the Mayor, the Hon. N. Cole, Carl Schurz, H. Block, Louis Spies, Isidor Busch and other well-known citizens. The afternoon before they had witnessed an impressive concert in Lafayette Park amid surroundings befitting the work and thought of that great scholar. Harris' views of the establishment of the German Empire after the Franco-Prussian War were tinged with Hegelian ideas without compromising his Americanism. Once more, in 1878,[8] he officiated at a von Humboldt affair, this time as *Festredner* in the English language at the unveiling of the Humboldt monument in Tower Grove Park. His popularity with the Germans, despite their unequivocal and complete rejection of the textbook method which he advocated, is plain from the occasional cartoons in the German papers. Thus, the *Laterne*[9] brought a frontpage cartoon showing him wielding the rod in a classroom and bearing the title: *Ich will Euch lehren Eingesandt schreiben!* ("I'll teach you to write letters to the Editor!"). When he was ready to resign, one of the papers carried an 11x15-inch cartoon representing him in the garb of an acrobat on a tight rope with the heading "No wonder he got enough!" On his back he carried a basket full of the sisters, cousins, and aunts of the School Board; from the ends of his balancing rod were suspended pans containing the Democrats on one side and the Republicans on the other, while to his one foot was tied a basket of heavy Germans singing the *Wacht an Rhein,* and to the other a basket full of Irish singing *Erin go bragh.* His acquaintance with editors of the German papers, such as Emil Pretorius of the *Westliche Post* and Friedrich Münch of the *Anzeiger des Westens,* was none other than pleasant, not to mention his intimate association with Charles Louis Bernays, a journalist of wide repute and a member of the editorial staff of the *Missouri Republican.* In 1879 it was his sad duty, to read the eulogy, as his dead friend had requested; he called Bernays a "paragon of friends" and a "hero of the heart." Indeed, this *Eulogy* of Bernays[10] ranks among the finest pieces Harris ever penned. He only once offended the Germans, particularly the farmers, unconsciously, by lumping them together with all the poor, illiterate and a-social immigrants from Europe who had no conception of American democracy. He duly and publicly apologized for this seeming aspersion.

Academic honors began to be heaped upon Harris, Yale giving him the M.A. *h.c.* in 1869. The Missouri State University, at Columbia, conferred on him the LL.D. on June 30th, 1870. The U.S. Government recognized him when Charles Sumner, Chairman of the Foreign Relations Committee, referred the request of the Japanese Embassy for information bearing on their study of American civilization, to him.

James M. Barnard, of Boston, while travelling in Europe, noticed the extent of Harris' fame as author of the *Annual Reports* of the St. Louis Schools and editor of the *Journal of Speculative Philosophy.* From Rome, Miss Anne Brewster wrote him about the Royal Museum of Instruction which was created by the Italian Minister of Public Instruction in 1875. Professor Dalla Vedova was anxious to get in touch with Harris.[11] Letters were exchanged with Eduard von

Hartmann, the author of the *Philosophie des Unbewussten,* and with Johann Karl Friedrich Rosenkranz, who addressed him *Verehrtester Herr und Freund* and closed one of his letters[12] by observing, how Hegel would have rejoiced over him! Hans Vaihinger, the author of the *Philosophy of As If,* also corresponded with Harris, and so did the great theologian Otto Pfleiderer. With J. Hutchinson Stirling an extensive exchange of thought was carried on.

But to return to St. Louis. On July 25th, 1879, Hinton Rowan Helper, of the city, addressed a very long letter to the Hon. Thomas Allen, Carlos S. Greeley, and Harris, in which he outlined a proposed contest and requested the three to act as a Committee of the Three Americas Railway to examine and select the five most persuasive and convincing essays in advocacy of the construction of a double-track longitudinal steel railway through North, Central and South America. A check for $5000 was enclosed, to be used as prizes. The scheme was to arouse such an enthusiasm "throughout all the countries from Alaska to Patagonia, inclusive, as will lead to the granting of all the requisite governmental guarantees and privileges and charters, by or before the 14th of October, 1892." This date marked, of course, the 400th Anniversary of the discovery of America.[13] Harris' enthusiasm and somewhat visionary interpretation of the mission and destiny of St. Louis and the Mississippi Valley, made him a staunch supporter of Helper's scheme. Helper was an author, had travelled extensively, had been a consul at Buenos Aires, and was an advocate of many other schemes such as to run a first-class line of American steamers regularly along both coasts of the Americas, and the cutting of a canal through Tehuantepec, or Nicaragua, or the Isthmus of Darien.

In home affairs, Harris was exceedingly public spirited. He would not hesitate to lend his name in support of any petition that might result in civic benefit. Thus he signed the petition to have the City of St. Louis separated from the County of St. Louis in the interest of better government.[14] Be it meetings, dinners, toasts, Harris stood ever ready to be on hand. St. Louis University called on him to join them in celebrating their Fiftieth Anniversary or Golden Jubilee, on June 24th, 1879, and the Knights of St. Patrick had him as guest at their annual gathering and lavish Grand Banquet on March 17th, 1880, at the Laclede Hotel. It was incumbent on him to respond to the fourth regular toast to American genius in literature and philosophy. He pointed out that the first great impulse to modern thought was given by a son of Ireland, in the person of Johannes Scotus Erigena, John the Scot, born in Ireland who, in 843, was called to Paris by Charles the Bold to found Scholasticism. To the Irish he attributed warmth of coloring, enthusiastic tone, and moving eloquence in American literature. The "volcanic fires of Celtic nature" thaws the cold and stern impassivity of the Anglo-Saxon and Norman disposition.

If Harris had had to choose between John Greenleaf Whittier and Walt Whitman he would have taken the former. Yet, when Whitman came to St. Louis to visit his brother Jefferson[15] and recuperate from an illness contracted in Kansas, Harris made his acquaintance either at the brother's home or at the lecture he gave, consisting of personal recollections of Abraham Lincoln.[16] From time to time, the poet sent him some of his publications.

Speculative philosophy came in for a bit of unwanted publicity when Emma M. McClellan sued for divorce from her husband, George B., who was a school teacher, but also a student of Kant. If his interest had remained solely in the Koenigsberger, it would have been all right; but there was another female teacher who also liked philosophy. The good wife tried to implicate Harris who summarily dismissed the matter and would not "dance attendance on the courts."

Unruffled by praise or blame, Harris worked on under circumstances where others have prepared for retirement, having accomplished a good life's work. But two more fruitful periods should follow the St. Louis episode. From the beginning, when Remington typewriters appeared on the market, Harris was interested and began to have machines of his own to speed up his literary production. He knew no such thing as "ghost writing." Writing confessedly with a nervous drive and making "a very wretched scrawl of any manuscript," he became fascinated with the typewriter which enabled him to write like copper-plate. He used his own system of hitting the keys.

When not at his office or on the speaker's platform he could be seen at his desk at home which, during the last years at St. Louis, was at 1116 Second Carondelet Avenue. The walls of every room were lined with books except where some old engraving was hung or a piece of statuary stood to remind him of the genius that could give tangible expression to a higher theme.

It was now near the end of his work in St. Louis, and he was looking forward to a little respite by undertaking a trip to Europe. Was he thinking of returning to St. Louis, or was he making other arrangements? At Montesano Springs, about 20 miles South of St. Louis, a company had formed to establish a summer resort that was to rival in scenery the Hudson Valley and balneotherapeutically Saratoga Springs. John Monteith, the former State Superintendent of Education, had invited him to join in this venture which he described as one that would please him in that he would be in congenial, intellectual and liberal-minded company. But Harris did not invest . . .

Part Three
BETWEEN WEST AND EAST

CHAPTER FOURTEEN

THE TRANSCENDENTAL LINK

PEDLAR AND BRAHMIN ON THE MISSISSIPPI

THE roots of William Torrey Harris were in the East. However much he was impressed with the important destiny of the Mississippi Valley and devoted himself to its furtherance, he was a Yankee at heart. Amos Bronson Alcott above all, and Emerson secondarily, were the ties that bound him to the East spiritually. And whenever Alcott appeared in the West, it was a silent confirmation of the homing instinct of Harris. The period of transition from life in the West to life in the East, had thus properly its symptoms in the appearance of Alcott and Emerson in St. Louis, events that were in every case inspired and engineered by Harris.

There never was, perhaps, a stranger team than Alcott and Harris, whose attachment was almost like that of father and son. In his youth, Harris had been deeply interested in some of the less orthodox ideas of spiritualism and the entire run of occult sciences, which interest eventually became sublimated in the devotion to Hegelianism and in his ability to enjoy the Neo-Platonism of Alcott. The association with the older man was, in a sense, Harris' protracted period of "ante-mundane soulwandering." Alcott represented the link between the unsystematic thinking of his youth and the rigor of logic which he practiced in his later years. Symbolically, a quotation from Alcott appeared at the head of the first number of the *Journal of Speculative Philosophy*. Long after Alcott's death, Harris acknowledged that his first acquaintance with the sage marked an important turning point in his history.[1]

Ever since he had heard and met Alcott in New Haven in 1857,[2] it had been Harris' intention not only to entertain close spiritual contact with him, but to help him whenever he could. Even while earning his meagre $50 a month during his first year at St. Louis, he was promoting Alcott conversations. Hopefully he wrote to Alcott, who had already embarked on a Western tour, in November, 1857, and Alcott replied from Buffalo:[3]

> DEAR SIR,
>
> Your letter of 26 November from St. Louis finds me here. Yes, I remember the stranger who waited at the New Haven Station to express his interest in my thoughts and Conversations; and am now pleased to hear from him again, and from the lands of free and formidable thinking, of strong heads and brave hearts. I am here spending a season in these wild parts, pausing a little while at the cities as I go along — at Cleveland presently, and expecting to reach Cincinnati sometime in January. If the way were fairly opened for me, as yourself and friends — "the young men" intimated in your letter — have meditated as possible, I might perhaps extend my jaunt as far as St. Louis, and spend some weeks with you, *before* turning my face Eastwards. If you think the adventure compassable and likely to prove profitable to all parties interested . . .

Harris, of course, had counted on the St. Louis Literary and Philosophical Society, as well as on the influence of Andrew Jackson Davis whom he had urged to make an announcement at his lectures (which was, however, never made) to enlist the necessary support for having Alcott come to St. Louis. He felt obliged to write Alcott in January, 1858, that due to the fact that the expense would be considerable and he was neither known by anyone except himself and could not be appreciated by the masses, it would be best if he did not come.[4]

Having become a teacher, Harris again tried to interest a group of people in Alcott, but unsuccessfully,[5] at least for the moment. Alcott was in Chicago, in December, 1858, when Harris went East to marry. However, in January, 1859, Alcott appeared in St. Louis at the suggestion and request of Harris.[6] The conversations were public, but there were also some intimate ones with Harris, Brokmeyer, Stedman, Hayden, H. M. Jones, Childs and Dr. J. H. Watters, a former Professor in St. Louis Medical College, all men who, in Harris' phraseology, were "possessed with a sort of philosophical fury, that made life for" them "not worth living unless consecrated to the study of Philosophy." Alcott entrusted Harris with an "inventory of his spiritual real estate" in case he should ever want to write his biography. Harris took it down in shorthand.[7]

The next meeting between Alcott, Harris, Brokmeyer and the rest occurred in 1866 during which year Alcott visited St. Louis twice. It was at the third meeting of the St. Louis Philosophical Society on February 2nd that the fact was brought up that Alcott would be visiting the city and that the Society would adjourn for a week to await him. Harris, to be sure, had sent Emerson and Alcott letters notifying them of their election as "Auxiliaries" to the Society; but it seems that the Society as such was not directly responsible for Alcott's visit, even though individual members were, notably Harris. The Manuscript of the *Record Book of the St. Louis Philosophical Society* has this to say regarding the first visit of Alcott:

Mr. A. Bronson Alcott was introduced to the Society and plans were discussed for the improvement of his stay with us to the best advantage. Society resolved to meet frequently during the two weeks coming and to admit to these meetings such persons, not members as were interested in the discussions or conversations of Mr. Alcott.

Many informal meetings were held afterwards. From Alcott's own diary[8] we learn that he was put up at Harris' residence, on Salisbury, between Ninth and Tenth Streets, and that he met with a hearty reception from his friend and family. Although Alcott carried away rheumatism from St. Louis, his mind became rejuvenated. When he paused, as he usually did, after one of his mystic statements and queried: "What say you to it, gentlemen?" there was at first silence among the philosophic group instead of the mellifluous flow of comment that he was used to back East. But when they did react, they spoke their mind and drove hard at truth, sparing no one. He experienced a freshness of spirit that he eventually grew to like. When they told him that he was a Hegelian in disguise, he was pleased, because he held admiration for those who could cast in logical language what he felt and passed on in veiled sentences. He did not "click" with Snider who could never wholly forgive either Harris or Alcott for being Yankees, even though they later took him into the Concord circle. He was a rustic and a *Biedermeier,* the one quality attracting him to Brokmeyer, the other rendering him more individual. When Alcott reached home after a somewhat prolonged stay in those "wild parts," he received a check from Harris to the amount of $200, which the Philosophical Society had raised for him, besides paying for his railroad trip to Terre Haute. To Harris he wrote:[9] "I am recruiting from the fearful waste of that six weeks in your parts. Had I stayed much longer, talking at the rate required, I should have spent myself entirely . . . It was a clean taking of flesh from my bones and left but little of me to find. But now I am replenishing wasted spirits and clothing and spring has come to help."

Alcott advertised Harris in the East. "Emerson and

Sanborn inquire often about you," he wrote in the same letter. He urged Harris to write books and to publish his translations. The *Radical Review* and the *North American* were deemed fit channels to popularize Harris. To Kroeger he wrote that he had recovered from the stroke of meeting the St. Louis friends in debate and that he knew now how to parry should he visit the group again, which he would gladly do. Indeed, a new subscription was taken up by the members of the Society, netting $220 from 26 persons and a ticket to Cincinnati. Eagerly, Alcott responded and the Society met once again in Extra Session on Sunday, December 2nd, 1866, at Mr. Hill's. Harris kept faithful records of all the conversations. Unfortunately, another attack of rheumatism set in so that Alcott "ran home not a day too soon," for Harris' comfort and his own, as he wrote from Concord in February.[10]

Between the third and fourth visit of Alcott's to the philosophical group lay Ralph Waldo Emerson's visit to St. Louis. Harris' attempts to bring Emerson out West date back to 1866.[11] On February 10th, Harris received a telegram from the bard: HAVE HEARD NOTHING. MISS ALCOTT SAYS YOU EXPECT ME. R. W. EGERSON [*sic*]. On the back Harris wrote the reply: COME, HALL ENGAGED FOR 7 & 8 & 10TH OF MARCH. To this message of the 21st, Emerson replied on the 24th: DO NOT EXPECT ME HAVE WRITTEN YOU YESTERDAY. R. W. EMERSON. A letter of Alcott's to Harris[12] discloses that Emerson, probably in apology for his failure to come to St. Louis, assured him nevertheless that they could depend upon him for lectures. There was, apparently a misunderstanding.[13] Plans concerning the public appearance of Emerson did not materialize until Wednesday, March 6th, 1867, when Emerson spoke under the auspices of the Public School Library.

From Harris' manuscript record we know definitely that

Emerson came at the invitation of the Philosophical Society.[14] Under March 4th we read:

Mr. Harris from the lecture Committee reported that Mr. Emerson had been engaged to lecture before the Philosophical Society on March 12th. A committee of arrangements was appointed to decide upon the proper form of the meeting, committee consisting of Messrs. Homer, Jones, Morgan, Snider, Watters, and Harris.

Harris also invited Emerson privately to his home and read him one or another of his papers, including his notes on Raphael's "Transfiguration" which appealed to the sage more than pure logic.[15] Psychologically and historically interesting was the observation of Denton J. Snider who felt compelled to remark on the New England kinship which, subtly, drew Harris and Emerson together, despite their difference in genius, and marked them off from the rest of the philosophic group who had none of the Yankee temperament and background.

Emerson read to the Society "Inspiration." "The singular and surprising lights" in the Philosophic Society definitely proceeded to dethrone him after the reading, to put truth and Hegel in his place. That was a distinctly new experience to Emerson who heretofore, wherever he went, had been the centre of attention. "They did not wish to see or hear me at all, but that I should see and hear them," he wrote to the elder James.[16] Though he mentioned the "German atheists" — knowing that this would please James — among whom Harris was active, he never spoke otherwise than tenderly of Harris, not only in his correspondence, but also in public.[17]

Emerson visited St. Louis again on December 16th, 1867, when he read his essay to a spell-bound audience at Philharmonic Hall. It was under the auspices of the Public School Library Society, with Harris as the guiding spirit. The bard stayed at the "Southern Hotel" which he pronounced superb. The members of the Philosophic Society who were represented in a body at the lecture, called on him there to renew their acquaintance.

Alcott put forth feelers again from Concord, near the end of 1868.[18] "I cannot ask of you," he wrote to Harris, "to make inquiries and gather companies for conversations. But if any of your friends feel disposed, shall gladly meet them on any reasonable terms. . ." Though the letter alludes to other engagements, he had apparently counted heavily on St. Louis, and when nothing developed in that quarter, he did not go West at all that winter. He would "willingly try the West once more"[19] a year later, and pleaded with Harris that in the event of his coming to St. Louis, he should let him have as much of himself as he could give him.[20] The Western trip materialized, but he did not see Harris for he was called back East sooner than he had anticipated.

Harris was in New England in the fall of 1870, and a letter by Alcott enquired anxiously whether he would be back in St. Louis when he expected to arrive there. A fresh course of conversations was arranged in December that year which, as Snider somewhat maliciously said, enabled "the aged Alcott to say over again and again what the repeating sayer of the said had already better said." He returned East "in the best of spirits." Another visit to St. Louis occurred in February, 1873. It was cut short by a summons from home because of the illness of his daughter, Mrs. Pratt, the mother of the "Little Men." But by now he was thoroughly "sold" on the West. A press release quoted him as saying:

> For conversation, I prefer a western company before an eastern. There appears a disposition to deal with things at first hand, a certain robust handling, rough perhaps, but ready and respectful, that more than compensates for the daintier and more decorous book-training common to eastern people.

Having been called away prematurely, he was not able

to speak to the fashionable audience of Rev. J. C. Learned, in the cozy little church of the Unity, at Park and Armstrong Avenues. But he returned in October, 1874, and spoke to the crowded pews. In preparation for this visit, Harris had even gone a step further than his elaborate preparations for earlier visits. He had given Alcott hints on what the public wanted and had suggested a departure from his conversational style, and Alcott lent a ready ear.[21] Harris had drawn up a little announcement of "Mr. Alcott's Conversations, including Readings, Lectures and Discourses, for 1874-5," bearing the date, Concord, September, 1874, and this note: "Address to the care of Prof. Wm. T. Harris, St. Louis, Mo." He gave four conversational evenings, apart from the church readings of the Scriptures and selections from Hermes Trismegistus. These engagements opened up a most successful touring season in the West. Another tour was planned for 1879-80, but did not materialize until the following season.

THE CONCORD TEMPTATION

It was Alcott's fatal attachment that eventually guided New England transcendentalism away from inspiration to speculative philosophy. And the temptation to fall heir to the traditions of the world-famous Concord group was too great for Harris to resist, particularly toward the end of his career in St. Louis.

Alcott had made heroic efforts to comprehend Hegelianism. He had protested against the inclusion of his fragments in the *Journal of Speculative Philosophy* because they "do not seem fit to appear under the great name of *philosophy*."[22] He was looking for a methodization of "loose and inconsequent thinking" as a result of Harris' writings in that *Journal*.[23] It appeared as if Harris and Alcott pooled their resources, the one with his wealth of logical thought, the other with his treasures of intuitions, to corner American idealism. Hegelianism was "Pure Idealism" to Alcott,[24] while Alcott's writings hinted at the very core of wisdom. "I am not philosopher enough," Alcott admitted, "to know whether I am philosopher in the strictest sense of pursuing a methodical habit of thinking. But if so competent a judge of method as Harris finds a logic in it, calls it 'dialectic' or by any name known to philosophy, then I suppose I am entitled to the praise which he bestows on my thinking."[25] Alcott's way of thinking was but another phase of the method which General Hitchcock used and which Harris appreciated so deeply during his symbolic period. But, more than that, the two had profound educational interests. Harris admired Alcott's practical wisdom, while the latter was anticipating a "better education and culture" through the efforts of Harris and his friends.[26] Yet nothing in Alcott's letters, full of the sincerest admiration though they are, conveyed so graphically his esteem of Harris as these lines:

> Interpreter of the Pure Reason's laws,
> And all the obligations Thought doth owe
> These high ambassadors of her great cause;
> Philosopher! Whose rare discernments show
> Apt mastery of her surpassing skill,
> And why each thought and thing is inly so
> Conceived and fashioned in the plastic Will;
> Thou Reason's canons dost so well maintain,
> With such adhesive and sincere regard,
> That every deviator seeks in vain
> To escape thy apprehension; evil-starred,
> With Dante's sophisters they writhe in pain.
> Then from thy judgment-seat, dismissed with ruth,
> Thou lead'st the stumblers in the way of truth.

Such admiration could but lead to strenuous efforts on the part of Alcott to have the philosopher near him in those parts that seemed to be the natural *locus* of the intellectual life. He held out inducements, including a professorship at Harvard.

> Mr. Emerson read me your letter of some weeks since in which you mention your promotion to the Head Superintendence of the schools. I fear for you. And have written to Davidson to persuade you to come East with him and Kroeger. Can you not spare yourself the time, and give us the pleasure of seeing you here? . . .[27]

Harris would come at least during the summer, duties permitting, and thus he wrote Alcott about a house, and the sage replied:[28] "Your inquiry about a house inspired the hope that you may yet be a neighbor of mine. It is too much to hope for, 'my cup would overflow.' . . . There are so many things in prospect that *with you here in Concord, I should live out my century . . .*" Nearly every letter broached the subject and held out new inducements. "Others are interested in yourself and future plans. Emerson, Hedge, Prof. Everett, should see you."[29] Harris' "proper home and seat of philosophy" was, in Alcott's conception, Concord and none other. There were several houses available, Hawthorne's among them, and half of the Alcott house. But Harris did not decide till the end of his term of Superintendency. Even then it was a struggle to tear himself from St. Louis. Almost with tears in his eyes he assured the St. Louisians that had been good to him, that he would retire in their midst.

To the people in the East, even to Emerson, it became more and more apparent that the spirit of transcendentalism was fleeing. In a letter to Harris he compared the men of might in St. Louis with the "debility of scholars in Massachusetts." Alcott was afraid that being too much absorbed in pedagogical matters, Harris might be spoiled for the higher life of philosophy, and thus he continued to urge him to forsake the West. He made good his promise to introduce his friend and protegé to all the notables in the East. As a token he got him an invitation to speak at the Chestnut Street Club, in Boston. To be admitted there at the parlor of the Rev. John T. Sargent, at 13 Chestnut, and that of Rev. Dr. Cyrus A. Bartol, at Number 17, was considered the highest honor Bostonians and New England intellectual circles in general could confer on a scholar.[30] Harris spoke in Sargent's parlor after he had attended the 42nd Annual Meeting of the American Institute of Instruction, at Fitchburg, Mass., and it was the 31st of July, 1871. Among the 20 persons present were Alcott, Elizabeth Palmer Peabody, Rev. Dr. F. H. Hedge, Professor Wm. P. Atkinson, David Atwood Wasson, C. K. Whipple,[31] Miss Mary Grew of Philadelphia, Mrs. Diaz of Plymouth, Mass., Mrs. Goddard of Boston, and the Misses Brackett and Eliot who had accompanied Harris from St. Louis. Harris read his essay "The Function of Education in its Relation to Government, Society, and the Individual." Alcott, who, as usual, praised Harris, and Miss Peabody who was most critical, monopolized the discussion, to the regret of some.

It was on another occasion that Harris addressed the Club on Goethe's *Faust*. He broached the subject of co-education, a thing permissible at the Radical Club but not in Boston society at large which expressed great consternation when they read in the papers the next day that the Superintendent from St. Louis would allow such a thing in his schools as co-education of the sexes "in the same building."

ORIGINS OF THE CONCORD SCHOOL OF PHILOSOPHY

"Can't we find the way for concentrating the forces of thought in an Academy or College wherein young men and women may gain command of their gifts for the high uses and ends of life?" wrote Alcott to Harris in 1869.[32] This was by no means the origin of the idea of a School of Philosophy at Concord. F. B. Sanborn, in his *Recollections of Seventy*

Years, has traced it to a common thought of Emerson and Alcott, as is evident from a letter of Emerson to Margaret Fuller of August, 1840. Besides the two, George Ripley, Henry Hedge and Theodore Parker were to form the puissant faculty of the university that was to be at Concord or Hyannis and would "anticipate by years the education of New England." And, again, in 1849, a formidable project was under way, but shortlived or practically still-born, the "Town and Country Club," the printed circular of which listed 54 names, headed by R. Waldo Emerson, and including besides Alcott, Garrison, Theodore Parker, Wendell Phillips, Drs. Howe and Hedge, Thoreau, Ellery Channing, J. Russell Lowell and other well-known personages.

Franklin Benjamin Sanborn returned to Concord in 1870, and Harris expressed his desire to come East, if but for a visit. "With Sanborn and Harris as neighbors, what might I not hope for! . . . Concord is the proper seat for an Academy of Philosophy, Literature and Religion."[33]

With marvellous persistence, Alcott pursued the idea of a School. In 1872 he wrote [34] to Harris:

> We had a great talk (private) at Bartol's lately. Emerson read a paper on "Influence," and Bartol, Hedge, Cabot, Weiss, gave their views. Had you been there the circle would have been full and round. Plato, Jesus, Swedenborg, Shakespeare, Goethe, Hegel, all came into the conversation.
>
> Cabot spoke to me afterwards of his appreciation of the Journal [of Speculative Philosophy] and particularly of your School Syllabus, etc. I wish we had a university waiting for a Head, and pair of Hands, I should know the man to recommend. Emerson read me your recent letter about Stirling. Things ripen as ideas attain ascendancy . . .

And again some months later: [35]

Sanborn has returned to Concord to reside permanently. And I do not surrender my hope that some day you are to make our little town your home also. A new spirit is awakening here and only the taking things at the turn is wanting to make it a literary and philosophical centre in the future as well as the present. So you see I dream on still as of yore.

From year to year, the dream seemed to take on more bodily shape. In 1876 he wrote in a letter to Harris:[36]

. . . I learn you are to be at the Centennial, and so cannot fail to ride into Massachusetts before you return. I wish it may happen that you and our Jacksonville and Quincy friends might meet in Concord. Our "Fortnightly Club" would have high designs upon you and Dr. Jones. Concord has at last its Club and actually sits fortnightly. Emerson and Sanborn are members.

"New lights" arose, such as the Rev. Joseph Cook and Porter C. Bliss, Editor of *The Literary Table,* and Alcott attached much significance to them in his scheme, as to Wm. Henry Channing and some others. Dr. Hiram K. Jones, the Platonist, was taken into the circle with open arms. When he arrived a second time in Concord, every afternoon and evening opportunities were "extemporized" for him and his party to meet people socially or "Platonically" at Alcott's, Emerson's, Sanborn's or Judge Hoar's. It was the closest approximation to Alcott's School idea. Yet, Harris was missing. "It may be the dream of an ancient, but not the less for that possible and desirable . . ." he confided to Harris,[37] and, "we shall expect you to join us next summer in our 'Concord Summer Symposium' which was so successfully inaugurated by Dr. Jones and his party last summer . . ."[38]

The time seemed auspicious now, and preparations for

the 1879 Concord Summer School of Philosophy and Literature were made in earnest. The first draft of the prospectus, confidential in nature, was sent to Harris and listed, as regular Professors, Alcott on Christian Theism; Harris on Speculative Philosophy; H. K. Jones, of Jacksonville, Ill., on Platonic Philosophy; David A. Wasson, of Medford, on Political Philosophy; and Mrs. Ednah D. Cheney, of Boston, on The History and Moral of Art; as Special Lecturers, F. B. Sanborn on Philanthropy and Social Science;T. W. Higginson, of Cambridge, on Modern Literature; Thomas Davidson, of Boston, on Greek Life and Literature; and George H. Howison, of Boston, on Philosophy from Leibniz to Hegel. In the final draft, the regular professors remained the same, with a slight modification in subjects, but Prof. B. Peirce, of Cambridge, on Physical Philosophy; Wendell Phillips, of Boston, on Public Eloquence; and Rev. C. A. Bartol, of Boston, on Pulpit Eloquence, were substituted for Sanborn, Higginson and Howison.

Alcott was visibly rejuvenated, and his letters reflected his enthusiasm. Still, Harris was a bit reticent and wavering in his decision. Perhaps excessive duties prevented his wholehearted devotion. At last he committed himself definitely "for most of the month of July." The School opened on July 15th, and Harris was present, a bit surprised when instead of the 30 or 40 persons he had expected, more than 200 appeared. Besides, a great many people attended the meetings in the hall down in the village. The romantic old Orchard House, then two centuries old, did not hold the crowds. In spite of the profound logic and abstruseness of Harris' lectures, his audiences increased daily. It was evident that he was the strongest man of the group, from the first. He lectured on psychological problems, methods of study, personality and immortality. Even Emerson turned out and sat at the feet of the American Hegel, wondering what strange twists had been given his transcendentalism.

CHAPTER FIFTEEN

CALLS AND TRIBUTES

THE EYES OF THE WORLD ON HARRIS' SCHOOLS

THE St. Louis schools under Harris' administration
came into the international spotlight at famous expositions.
After the Paris Expositions of 1855 and 1867, and the
London one of 1862, educational subjects began to attract
the attention of the public. To the Vienna Exposition of
1873, Harris sent a statistical chart covering the St. Louis
school system, also architectural drawings of model school
houses and a set of the *Annual Reports* of the Board during
his Superintendency. Since these were also printed in German for the benefit of the St. Louis Germans, they were
very acceptable to the educational representatives of the
various commissions meeting at Wien.

Great efforts were made for adequate representation at
the Centennial Exposition of Philadelphia in 1876. L. U.
Reavis, the great booster of St. Louis, anticipated great
things, but Harris was very skeptical. After all, the country
was in a tremendous depression. Because of political corruption "a wide-pervading sense of humiliation was felt
in this nation on the eve of our centennial birthday," he
wrote, after events showed his pessimism unjustified, "and
under the circumstances of so much dismay at crashing
fortunes, paralyzed industries, corporations bankrupt, corrupt legislators and executives, and the dread of a return to
party power of those who were lately vanquished in the

373

than $400, for which we have the money at hand, and more for other purposes when needed.

I wish you to occupy the Orchard House, and at a reasonable rent, as I have intimated to you. And now, as the season approaches for spring and summer movements, I wish to learn of your plans and prospects particularly as regards Concord. I wish the Orchard House occupied. The Estate will probably be purchased and dedicated to "The School of Philosophy." And when that takes effect, you certainly should not be away. And where else if not in Concord, can a "Summary of Thought" be reasonably planted? . ..

Please write in reply, *at once.*

Yours truly,

A. BRONSON ALCOTT

73. The Conspectus of the Committee had provided for, or envisaged, a most interesting exhibit of all phases of education, rural and city, White and Negro, primary and secondary, parochial and non-denominational, public and private, with photographic records of schools held in log cabins, mud huts and stately buildings. But the meagre $5000 appropriation of the State had gone for exhibiting "the vast resources of Missouri, vegetable, animal, and mineral, commercial and manufacturing," leaving nothing for educational documentation. The Committee was thus left to its own resources, relying heavily on the St. Louis members and Harris, their Chairman. Four public concerts netted the sun of $1588.20, which was sufficient for packing and repacking the exhibit and paying the attendant. The Railroads donated their services. Mrs. Ione H. Evans took charge in Philadelphia. The exhibit stayed nearly six months. The Kindergarten exhibit was arranged entirely at the expense of Miss Susan Blow. It was so successful that the St. Louis Board of Education received an award from the U. S. Centennial Commission "for excellence of work and for the establishment of Kindergartens as a part of the public school system."

An International Educational Conference was held beginning July 17th, first in the Hall of the Judges Pavilion, then in Pennsylvania Educational Pavilion, giving an opportunity to every nation to present a picture of its educational system. Harris was among the eager listeners and at the second meeting presented and read the Report of the Committee on Course of Study from Primary Schools to University.[1] He also spoke at one of the meetings of the Centennial National Institute, at Educators' Headquarters, at the Atlas Hotel, on the Centennial grounds. His confreres, the spelling reformers, also seized upon the opportunity to get up enthusiasm for removing the incubus of English spelling.

bloody field — who could have expected a grand result from a national exposition under such auspices?"

"Reposing special trust and confidence in the integrity and abilities of William T. Harris of the County of St. Louis," the Governor of the State of Missouri, Charles H. Hardin, appointed him an Honorary Member of the Board of State Centennial Managers on June 12th, 1875. By this very ornamental office, Harris was entitled to be a representative of the State of Missouri at Philadelphia.

About a hundred committees were formed, all working, as the advertisement suggested, rather than standing. Harris was in charge of Educational Statistics, and his official position was Chairman of the State Centennial Educational Committee. Preparations, all made from St. Louis, were by no means easy as the State had set aside nothing for its educational exhibit. A tremendous machinery was set in motion to procure funds and assistance of public spirited citizens. St. Louis had its own "Centennial Spell," a real spelling match which, unfortunately, left the Board of Public Schools "holding the bag." In all, 4480 pupils of from five to eight years' tutelage in the Public Schools participated, with teachers, parents and friends present. The responsible persons for the "Spell" were Harris, Edward Wyman, and J. L. Tracy who had instigated it. All would have been well if the latter had not given Harris and the Board to understand that the medals to be distributed and the cost of putting on the "Spell" was to be met either by donations or State contribution. Of the total of $1191 expenditure, only $725 could be found, and thus most of the pupils went without medals.

This unpleasantness aside, the work of the Executive Committee progressed and bore fruit in good exhibits, after all. The apathy of the Missourians on the whole in educational matters was, however, deplorable, but understandable in view of the after-effects of the panic of 1872.

73. The Conspectus of the Committee had provided for, or envisaged, a most interesting exhibit of all phases of education, rural and city, White and Negro, primary and secondary, parochial and non-denominational, public and private, with photographic records of schools held in log cabins, mud huts and stately buildings. But the meagre $5000 appropriation of the State had gone for exhibiting "the vast resources of Missouri, vegetable, animal, and mineral, commercial and manufacturing," leaving nothing for educational documentation. The Committee was thus left to its own resources, relying heavily on the St. Louis members and Harris, their Chairman. Four public concerts netted the sun of $1588.20, which was sufficient for packing and repacking the exhibit and paying the attendant. The Railroads donated their services. Mrs. Ione H. Evans took charge in Philadelphia. The exhibit stayed nearly six months. The Kindergarten exhibit was arranged entirely at the expense of Miss Susan Blow. It was so successful that the St. Louis Board of Education received an award from the U. S. Centennial Commission "for excellence of work and for the establishment of Kindergartens as a part of the public school system."

An International Educational Conference was held beginning July 17th, first in the Hall of the Judges Pavilion, then in Pennsylvania Educational Pavilion, giving an opportunity to every nation to present a picture of its educational system. Harris was among the eager listeners and at the second meeting presented and read the Report of the Committee on Course of Study from Primary Schools to University.[1] He also spoke at one of the meetings of the Centennial National Institute, at Educators' Headquarters, at the Atlas Hotel, on the Centennial grounds. His confreres, the spelling reformers, also seized upon the opportunity to get up enthusiasm for removing the incubus of English spelling.

Generally speaking, Harris was not entirely satisfied with the educational exhibit as a whole, nor the part that Missouri played in it.[2] The national vanity had been gratified, and the esthetic effect of the display was stupendous. He was delighted when he reflected on the rôle of education in the general scheme of an industrial civilization. The third stage of civilization had been reached by a dialectic necessity out of the principles governing primitive society and the "divide and conquer" stage of division of labor. The new method of instruction by experiment and original investigation, came in for much praise and much censure. The textbook method seemed on the downward grade, and stuffed animals and bug collections, machines and drawing seemed to hold the stage; in brief, Kindergarten instruction rather than book-learning. Harris realized, of course, that the product of education, the cultured human being, could not be placed on exhibition, and thus the whole show labored under a serious handicap. The foreign educational exhibits he did not regard as of more value to America than to furnish comparisons.

The Paris Universal Exposition of 1878 was to bring fame and recognition to Harris even more abundant than that of the other Expositions. The importance of Harris was fully recognized when the first meeting was called to the Director's room of the Columbia Life Insurance Company to consider how Missouri might best be represented. Harris made every effort to gather up a fine collection of educational items. The Kindergarten display made one of the most favorable impressions. John E. Bradley, Commissioner of Education of New York State, was not stingy in his praise and in his statement to the Legislative Assembly admitted that "no European city has school reports which compare with those of Boston and St. Louis."

Among the five American educators to receive decorations at that Exposition was Harris, to whom was awarded the

Silver Palm.³   St. Louis was awarded the Silver Medal in Primary Education, which was a further recognition of the work of Harris.⁴   The *Annual Reports* were subsequently placed in the Pedagogical Library which was in process of organization in the Palais Bourbon.   And another sequel to Harris' efforts in behalf of education was his election, by the French Minister of Public Instruction, as "Officer of the Academy."⁵

In 1866, the Superintendent of Public Education in the State of Missouri, T. S. Parker, on a special mission to St. Louis, asked Harris to meet him at the Planters House in order to discuss important business.   Harris, however, was not available.   In a letter,⁶ Parker disclosed that he had wanted to get him appointed Assistant State Superintendent. Unlike his predecessor in office, Harris did not covet the clergy-ridden State Superintendency of Missouri, and he declined.

Next door, in Kansas, Harris was known from the first as "one of the finest educators of this or any other age." When, in 1868, they were casting about for a Superintendent at Leavenworth City, they were thinking strongly of him, as may be seen by a letter of J. L. Wever, a member of the Board of Education.⁷   The sentiment in the West was strongly against experimentalism in education, as W. H. V. Raymond wrote to Harris from Alton, Illinois:⁸ "If more thinkers and fewer empiricists could get hold of our educational interests I think the country might soon look on more rational spectacles of mental cultivation throughout the land than we now see." Harris, however, likewise declined the Kansas offer.

In the early part of 1878, the question of a new State Superintendent of Public Schools came up in Missouri. *The Weekly Mail*, strong in its denunciation of the Missouri School Laws, believed that Harris' services, being those of a profound scholar and practical educator, would be inestimable in value, for he was "universally known as the man that has brought the public schools of St. Louis to their present high degree of perfection."[9] Mr. Kidd nominated Harris "with eulogy" at the State Convention of the Republican Party at St. Louis, but withdrew his nomination in favor of R. Baldwin, Editor of the Warrensburg *Standard*. When this candidate failed to be nominated by acclamation, Harris was renominated, but after a discussion it was held improbable that he would accept; St. Louis could not spare him anyway. Baldwin was then nominated by acclamation. All this only contributed to fanning Harris' popularity and reputation in St. Louis itself.

In philosophy also, recognition was not slow in coming. Alcott informed Harris that he was being considered for a chair in Philosophy at Harvard:[10]

. . . I enclose President Eliot's advertisement of the new courses of lectures at Harvard College . . . You will perceive there are two vacancies yet to be filled in the Philosophy course. Prof. Fisher of Yale is named for the one, and Stirling for the other. He has been written to. Besides this, he is offered the Lowell course, and the prospect of a permanent professorship. As he had cherished a wish to come to this country, it is not unlikely he may avail of this opportunity. Your name has also been suggested. Emerson I know favors your classes. I wish it might be. Between Stirling and yourself we should stand the best chance of learning "The Secret of Hegel." I hope you will consider the matter. If not in this year's course, your turn should come, before all others, in the next. . .

In March, 1873, Alcott called on President Eliot and intimated possibilities for Harris.[11] Some professor seemed to stand in the way, although Eliot appeared "very desirous" to have Harris connected with the College. A year later,

Alcott wrote:[12] "Harvard may be slow to find out and seat the American Hegel in its philosophic Chair. But there are those who think he should have the widest opportunities our country has to offer for teaching both by tongue and pen . . ." Also at the University of Michigan, Alcott reported, there was interest in Harris, and the Professor of Modern Languages and Literatures, Edward Payson Evans, wanted to know Harris personally, and it was through him that Alcott learned that they had considered securing Harris for the Presidency of the University.[13]

In Boston, Superintendent John Dudley Philbrick had resigned as early as 1874, alleging ill health, but had stayed on as no effort was made to look about for a new Superintendent. However, in 1876, the question of a successor became acute. Philbrick had been in office for 18 years under most trying circumstances. Harris' friends immediately became active. Newspapers supported his nomination, the *Worcester Spy*, the *Springfield Republican*, the *Boston Globe*, and even the *Christian Register* among them. They were looking for new blood. The Boston School Committee was referred to as "that embodiment of dulness." And Harris was, after all, a New Englander, who could infuse new vigor into the system. Philbrick was his friend, and when Harris learned about the wrangles, he was displeased that he should have been pitted against Philbrick as if he approved the derogatory criticism. On the whole, religionists opposed Harris' nomination who, for a long time, had been blissfully ignorant of the fact that he was the center of contention in the intellectual acropolis of America. Harris' friends, however, rose in his defence against the false accusation. Harris was pictured as a monster of unbelief whose personal influence would probably be very injurious to Boston children. They hurled the epithets of philosophical dreamer, speculator, German rationalist, free-thinker and skeptic against him. People that were not even thoroughly acquainted with him, published protests against such slander.[14]

Harris remained entirely passive. He had been named for the position without his knowledge. When Alcott pressed him for permission to further his claims to the office, he declined all assistance.[15] Robert R. Bishop, his long-time friend, also asked for a statement. He had vigorously opposed any criticism of Harris' religious views, and for that Harris was thankful, but he informed him that he could not accept even if elected.[16] He asked him to extricate him from the candidateship. Now even Philbrick wrote Harris a very friendly letter in which he discountenanced all "objectionable epithets" which appeared in articles written by people in his own camp. George H. Howison counselled Harris[17] not to interfere in any way in his nomination. The movement in his behalf he described as "entirely spontaneous," and he should not say that he would not be a candidate.

When election came around, 11 of the 24 Board members voted for Harris, 12 for Philbrick. For election, 13 votes were necessary. Another vote was called for and Philbrick was re-elected by only a small majority. Harris' friends, including Mrs. Julia Ward Howe, regretted that they had not been more insistent in their campaign. The inside story was told by Mrs. Harriet L. F. Walcott, of Boston, at a meeting of the Women's Club in Chicago. Harris' friends had considered his election a foregone conclusion, and thus did not counteract the whispers too strenuously. Finally, on the morning of the election, there appeared simultaneously in a number of Boston papers an article declaring that Harris was an infidel. An appeal was made to parents, asking them whether they were ready to assume the responsibility of giving the control of their schools into the hands of a man who did not believe in religion. There was no time now to refute the libel. The writer who signed himself "Christian Parent" won. The last sentence of his letter read: "Give us an educated Catholic, an educated Hebrew, — anyone but an infidel."

Now, Harris' friends wanted him in the post of Secretary of the Board of Education of the State of Massachusetts,[18] but Harris remained cool. The close call to Boston had, however, certain healthy reverberations in St. Louis itself. They knew now that the American Athens was defective in several respects, and that their own city had the ablest Superintendent of any.

In 1879, Harris came close to being called to New York City where Henry Kiddle, who had been Principal, Assistant Superintendent, and Superintendent of Schools for more than 25 years, had incurred the displeasure of the Board by adding to the *Cyclopaedia of Education* and the 1878 *Year Book of Education* which he had edited, a 354 page book on *Spiritual Communications* in which he had committed himself to a belief in spiritual phenomena and particularly the appearance, mostly through the medium of his daughter, Mrs. L. F. Weismann, of famous characters, from Archbishops to New York's political bosses, and from Moses to Wm. Cullen Bryant. Commissioner William Dowd was among the first to think of Harris for the post, and so was Commissioner Samuel G. Jelliffe even though he was a home-ruler. But Harris did not make application . . .

THE REWARD OF FAITHFUL SERVICE

At the close of the *Quarterly Report* which Harris offered to the Board of the St. Louis Public Schools, on January 13th, 1880, he wrote these paragraphs:

Next May will complete my twelfth year in the office of Superintendent, and thirteen and one half years as Superintendent and Assistant Superintendent. The same date also completes my twenty-second year's connection with the schools under your charge. As it has been my intention to close my career with these schools at that time, I owe it to you as a duty, as well as an act of courtesy, to notify you in this manner that I shall not be a candidate again for the position I now hold, and to which I have been so many times elected by your kind partiality or by your patient forbearance.

As my whole practical career since arriving at manhood has been spent in the St. Louis Public Schools, you can imagine better than I can find words to describe the feeling with which I shall part from them and you next May.

I'm conscious of a gradual but constant enfeeblement of health, which will not permit me to do what I conceive to be my duty by a school system which has grown from 15,000 pupils twelve years since to 50,000 the present year, and which deserves the ablest talents and most persistent industry on the part of its supervision.

Harris had not resigned, he had merely notified the Board that he would not be a candidate for election. The "dumb ague" which, as he told a reporter, attacked him in the afternoons, left him in an enfeebled condition, incapacitating him for night work. He sought relief by taking a rest and a change of climate. At another occasion he divulged that the city of St. Louis was on the threshold of a new era of growth and that he did not feel equal to the task of guiding its educational interests through it, having done that for another era. Sometime he would mention a literary task which he wanted to devote himself to, apart from or in addition to the cause of education. He bluntly denied all rumors that he was going to look after D. Appleton and Co's interests in the West.

When Jas. Stanton, a member of the Board, called on him in person in order to influence him to reverse his decision, he was persuaded that he needed rest badly. He had worked regularly 12 hours daily in the pursuit of his educational duties alone, sometimes 17, when the *Annual Reports* went to press. Denton J. Snider once confessed that had he worked as Harris did, it would have killed him in a year, if not sooner, and Snider, with more than fifty books to his credit, was not exactly one who took life easy. Personally, Harris never mentioned the fact that he felt his health failing, but he did speak of a certain nervousness that made itself manifest in his writing. It became a family reputation that his hand was peculiarly hard to read. One time the mother of a pupil rushed into his office with a note in her hand which she thought had been written by one of the Principals and wildly protested the "gross insult" the man had offered her. Harris looked at the note and recognized it as his. — It dealt with the transfer of her son from one school to another.[19]

Among professionals, Harris was known as the pet-Superintendent of the West. Indeed, among the great quartette of Harris-Pickard-Hancock-Rickoff, who annually met to discuss their views, he stood out like a giant. He had been re-elected to the Superintendency consistently with a very large majority, sometimes unanimously. The stormiest year he had encountered was 1878 when, as an aftermath of the textbook scandal, H. M. Tallman, a late "Book Agent" for the House of A. S. Barnes and Company, was nominated. Harris, however, received 18 votes, against 6 for Tallman, and elections were held behind closed doors. But at the May 13 meeting of the Board in 1879, Harris was splendidly acquitted by receiving the only nomination of the Board and being re-elected without opponent. Nobody, with the possible exception of Harris himself, had any doubt that he would also be re-elected in 1880.

Harris had been through a difficult era, the Civil War period and the depressions following it. The trials of his office would have crushed an irresolute man. Political control of the Board was growing; it was threatening to become a "ring." Since he regarded the education of the young as a sacred trust, the introduction of politics into school government was abhorrent to Harris. He had warded it off as long as he could; but now he did not feel quite so spry. Attacks upon his person, especially by religious groups and publishing interests, began to wear on him. Fictitious charges also were made, probably at the instigation of these interests, that he had issued instructions relative to the improvement of teachers' minds. The Hon. Robert M. Foster, tried to introduce a bill into the State Legislature, beginning 1879, proposing to oust the School Board and substitute a political body for it which would have left the schools in a pitiful condition, like "the poverty-stricken knight," as Harris phrased it, "who was dressed in a pair of spurs and a high standing dickey," alluding to the abolition of all High Schools in the State, possibly including the State University also. It would have destroyed by the stroke of a pen what Harris had built up. He could not quite shake off his disgust, though he submitted to the dictum of his own philosophy which he had expounded from a hundred rostrums and which affirmed his faith in democracy and hence the masses. If they had not been educated to the point where their decisions would be wise and just, the more effort would have to be put forth to educate them while those who had attained the stage of wisdom would have to suffer from their ignorance. He was looking forward to serving education even better by being untrammelled by an office.

For April 20th, 1880, Harris had requested a special meeting of the St. Louis Teachers' Association which was to become a memorable occasion quite to his own surprise. A chorus of 600 boys and girls selected from every Public School of the city, was gotten together and sang more or less in farewell of Harris. In all, 700 teachers were present and some three to four hundred parents and friends who heard Harris' farewell address. When in the course of his speech he mentioned the fact that in the examinations that had been given throughout the nation, the famous Quincy schools near Boston had scored 82%, but St. Louis 85.5%, or 3.5% higher than the best in the country, and that this had been achieved by supervision and that St. Louis schools thus "could challenge comparison in intellectual culture with any school in the United States, and probably the world," the audience rose to a spontaneous applause, the teachers waved their handkerchiefs and the pupils got up from their seats and danced. After he had finished his talk, there was again hearty applause and, quite impromptu, the boys and girls gave three grand rounds of applause, stamping their feet and clapping their hands shouting "Hurrah for Harris."

Now, Dr. Hill, President of the Board, addressed the children and, expressing the hope that Harris, though retiring, would keep up his interest in them and become no stranger to them nor the teachers or directors, asked who would second that hope. At once, hundreds of hands were extended at arm's length while the audience applauded. The impressive event ended by singing the "Star Spangled Banner."

A Committee, headed by John E. Kimball and representing Principals and teachers, drew up, on May 12th of the same year, resolutions embodying their esteem for their Superintendent. These resolutions were first printed, but then engrossed on fine card board, and the signatures of each one of 1100 teachers were written on similar paper, a leaf being assigned to everyone of the 80 schools. The whole was bound in morocco. The informal presentation was made through Francis E. Cook, on June 27th.

The Board adopted on May 11th the most cordial resolutions drawn up by F. N. Judson unanimously and under applause. Their formal presentation in a rich frame, was made later on in the presence of active as well as retired members. Leo Rassieur, Attorney of the Board, made the presentation speech and among other things said of the

385

schools, addressing Harris: "The proud position attained for them throughout the world is largely owing to the grand reputation as an educator, which you deservedly gained in consequence of your success in our midst, as well as by your general efforts in the cause of education."

In reply, Harris said that, as a reasonable man, he could not acknowledge the justice of so much praise as had been given him. For twenty years he had felt, and it had been his boast, that the St. Louis Public Schools had had a most admirable School Board.

On May 12th, Harris, not yet 45 years old, inducted Edward H. Long into the office of Superintendent. Long had been his Assistant for six years and had run against him in the 1875 elections but received only three votes as compared with Harris' 23. He was 40 years of age, a native of New York State. He had the highest regard for Harris and cherished his philosophy.

In complete secrecy, a circular letter had been sent to a number of friends and acquaintances of Harris, asking for a testimonial and a contribution. There were 157 contributors, including some of the first citizens of St. Louis. Among bankers there was James E. Yeatman, President of the Merchants' National Bank, who headed the Committee and entertained most cordial relations with Harris; Jno. C. H. D. Block, President of the Fourth National Bank; T. B. Edgar, President of the Continental Bank; and Jno. D. Perry, President of the Banking House of Bartholow, Lewis and Company. The railroads were represented by Thos. Allen, President of the St. Louis, Iron Mountain and Southern Railroad Company, and S. D. Barlow, the Secretary. Noted attorneys and lawyers also joined in the written expressions of their esteem. They praised his faithful service and devotion and acknowledged the debt that the city of St. Louis owed him. Even the Catholic opposition, though withholding signature of the testimonial, acknowledged in

Archbishop P. J. Ryan that Harris was "an able scholar with some most admirable philosophic principles, calculated to do much good in this unbelieving age" . . .

The reception took Harris entirely by surprise. Merely a brief note of Yeatman's, such as he would habitually receive from him to come for dinner, asked him to be present at a "meeting of citizens" at the St. Louis Club, on June 26th. When he arrived, he found most distinguished citizens waiting for him. Yeatman called the meeting to order, and Dr. William Greenleaf Eliot was elected Chairman. Thereupon Mr. J. C. Orrick presented Harris with a gold medal, three inches in diameter and a quarter of an inch in thickness.[20] One side had an allegorical representation of Education, surrounded by the names of Plato, Socrates, Aristotle, Pestalozzi, Hegel, Froebel, Arnold, and Horace Mann. The representation was a female figure seated on a bench, with opened books on her lap and closed ones piled up at the end of the bench. In front of her were two children with books under their arms walking toward her as though anxious to receive instruction. Under the figures was to be read in Roman letters EDUCATION. The reverse had a laurel wreath encircling this engraved inscription:

FROM CITIZENS OF ST. LOUIS TO
WILLIAM T. HARRIS,
IN GRATEFUL RECOGNITION OF TWENTY-THREE
YEARS OF FAITHFUL AND DISTINGUISHED
SERVICE AS TEACHER, PRINCIPAL, ASSISTANT
SUPERINTENDENT, AND SUPERINTENDENT
OF ST. LOUIS PUBLIC SCHOOLS.
1857-1880

Harris was visibly embarrassed. For a few seconds after Mr. Orrick had handed him the 24 carat gold medal, weighing eleven ounces, and stating, among other things, that St. Louis took just pride in pointing to him — educator, scholar, philosopher — "as one of the realized possibilities of this free West, in the Valley of the Mississippi," he stood fixed and motionless. Only with difficulty words came to him. At last he made, trembling, a little speech touching upon the education of the people and the principle which seemed to him to be true that the average of the community is the rule and that we must submit to it. At the same time we must provide the means of lifting up the average of the people by making the schools good enough for all, so as to elevate the lowest and strengthen the highest.

He said he had not been conscious that such feelings existed toward him among the citizens of St. Louis as he had just heard expressed, since he was aware of his own shortcomings and many bitter struggles. He thanked the citizens with his whole heart.

When he had seated himself amid the applause of his friends and admirers, Dr. Eliot rose and announced that they had come together for something additional. Personally, he regarded Harris' resignation as a calamity, and it was on his suggestion that Harris should, while travelling abroad, as he had planned, visit Scotland, England, Germany, and France, to investigate the respective educational systems, prepare his deductions, and make recommendations applicable to the United States, embodying them in a series of lectures under the auspices of Washington University. For this purpose the citizens had purchased for him a letter of credit in the amount of $1000. This he handed to him partly as a recognition of past services, and partly to be, assured of his return to St. Louis. The sentiment of gratitude resolved itself, as he jokingly put it, into a hope of favors expected, rather than of favors conferred, and he should therefore consider himself as a Professor of Washington University.

That was too much for Harris. He wanted to speak, but could not. Only after a long tear-choked silence he began inaudibly and falteringly. His interests had always been with St. Louis, he confessed — he did not intend to leave the city — he wanted to make it his home — he would return from Europe within half a year to publish his findings, then go back once more — the purse would enable him to carry out his design, and he thanked them heartily, one and all. Then all came up to him to congratulate him and bid him Godspeed. . . .

CHAPTER SIXTEEN

FIRST TRIP TO EUROPE

H ARRIS' last lecture at Washington University in a series of ten dealing with the History of Philosophy, was particularly well attended. Over a hundred persons heard him speak for an hour and a half on the life of his idol, Georg Wilhelm Friedrich Hegel. He was in the best of form, and it was a fine tribute to the man whose thought he and Brokmeyer had planted in the great American Bottom whence it was to spread all over the country. It was also a farewell address, for, on Saturday, August 14th, 1880, he sailed from New York on the White Star Screw Steamship Britannic. With Chas. Wynertt he occupied an inside cabin in the aft part of the boat.

THE HUNDRED INTRODUCTIONS

In his suitcase he carried a hundred letters of introduction to persons in Germany, Austria, Hungary, England, France, Italy, Switzerland, Belgium, Holland and Denmark. It is doubtful whether the majority of diplomats have had as many letters to their credit. In fact, he would not have needed them, for, a prominent merchant who was travelling in Europe at the time related the following story. When he was introduced to an assembly of distinguished persons and had acknowledged that his home was in St. Louis, he received the reply: "St. Louis . . . let me see; that is where the *Journal of Speculative Philosophy* is published and an excellent flour product is made, is it not?"

It would be interesting to list the introductions, but a few names may suffice. From German friends in St. Louis, from Susan Blow and others, he received thirteen letters to University professors and others. The U. S. Bureau of Education gave him introductions to the Minister of Public Instruction in every country he contemplated visiting, as well as to other prominent persons. Friends and acquaintances supplied him with many letters to persons residing in England and Scotland. Some names, however, should be noted: Hermann von Helmholtz in Berlin, Ernst Haeckel in Jena; John Tyndall, Thomas Henry Huxley, Herbert Spencer, Matthew and Edwin Arnold, and Cardinal John Henry Newman in England. Such men as the Cardinal, Spencer and Haeckel represented views diametrically opposed to those of Harris', but it seems he was willing and eager to make their personal acquaintance.

With Edwin Arnold, Harris had, strange to say, grave differences. His poem "Light of Asia" appeared in 1879, and Alcott was one of the first in the United States to hear about it through Rev. William Henry Channing, the poet's father-in-law.[1] The book came too late to have it discussed at the Concord Summer School of 1879. However, Harris studied it rather critically later and attributed its popularity to the formless first principle which it sets forth, while F. B. Sanborn was more nearly right when he maintained against this that it was due to its philanthropic attitude and idea of self-sacrifice set forth in a somewhat florid and fluent rhythm.

How many of these introductions Harris actually used, cannot be ascertained; but so far as is known, he visited only Belgium, England and Scotland, probably contemplating a visit to the oher counrties on a trip following this one. On the voyage across, he made some eight or ten worthwhile acquaintances and kept log faithfully until they docked at Liverpool, England, on August 22nd.

LACE, LANGUAGE AND EDUCATION

The Belgian Educational Congress was held at Brussels from August 22nd to the 29th. Harris arrived a bit late. Though an official representative of the U. S. Bureau of Education, the announcement of his coming was probably made too late, since only Henry Barnard and Alexander Delmar, *"ingénieur, ancien directeur du bureau de statistique,"* were mentioned as members of the Comité Générale from the U. S.

The occasion of the Congress was the 50th anniversary of Belgian independence. Harris had prepared himself well in the historic background of the nation. The manufacture of lace as the principal industry to him, as an "inhabitant of this hasty and impatient Western world,"[2] was "one of the most astonishing things." It seemed to him to require "an altogether different spiritual organization from that possessed by our people," the "type of inanimate patience" which he thought prevalent among the Hindu weavers.

Again, it was a source of marvel and speculation to him that the language and literature of the nation was French in form, but Teutonic in spirit, thus representing "a union of two principles utterly hostile to each other," each modifying the other and producing a compromise. The language line from Liège to Calais, dividing the Flemish speaking people from the French speaking people, also gave him occasion for comment. Thus, the people of Belgium, her industry, energy, prosperity, illiteracy, pauperism, government, religion, and liberalism, all seemed to him "a mass of contradictions, a puzzle rather than a problem that could be solved rationally."

The discussions at the Congress were often heated and marked by oratory. He found French and German views dominant. He took particular note of the prominence of women in the primary departments; the discussion of culture versus vocation studies; co-education; the liberty of opinion permitted the teachers; the general application of Froebel's methods to education higher than the Kindergarten; and the emphasis on scientific over against literary courses.

To friends in Ohio he wrote that the Congress was a great success, "surprising everyone." The delegates were very animated and nearly everyone spoke in the French language. He had difficulty in understanding it when it was spoken rapidly. Still, he managed to put in "now and then a word for our American experience on educational subjects."

He followed many of the invitations to attend institutions and model schools, the university, libraries, and the pedagogic museum. A special train took the members of the Congress to a fête with fire works at Antwerp, which was enjoyed from a special steamer. There was a great reception at the Hôtel de Ville in Brussels and, to crown it all, the gala reception with orchestral presentations in an enormous building decorated with pictures illustrating the history of Belgium. The King and Queen appeared late in the evening with their retinue.

'MONGST COLLEGERS, OPPIDANS AND OTHERS

From Belgium, Harris returned to England without visiting any of the other states on the continent. In London he was particularly interested in the grade schools. He visited the Ben Johnson Schools and attended some of their functions, such as concerts. He drew comparisons of the School Board meetings with those he knew so well from St. Louis, and noted the caste system generally prevailing in England. In the course of his stay he became acquainted with the aims of the Education Society and the Society for the Development of the Science of Education.

There was also a Froebel Society for the Promotion of the Kindergarten System, and he inspected the Kindergarten in connection with the Kindergarten Training College that was under the patronage of H. I. H. the Crown Princess of Germany. Above all, he manifested much interest in the Workmen's Social Educational League, with offices in London, which had been established, due to advanced thinking, for the purpose of promoting the formation of Public Opinion in reference to capital and labor, trade and technical education, finance, cooperation, land, colonies, government, law and national well-being generally, upon the basis of history.

At Birmingham, he studied in detail the High School which was founded in 1552 by King Edward the Sixth, and noted their system of admission upon payment of fees and on Foundation Scholarship. He also visited the Common and Lower Middle Schools, and Bath Row Girls' School. At Liverpool, the School Board's treatment of juvenile offenders interested him in particular, and he went to see the Protestant Section of the Truants' Industrial School and the South Corporation Certified Day Industrial School At Manchester he had himself guided through Owens College. He visited Eton College and Harrow, as well as Oxford and Cambridge which were contrasted with the universities of Scotland, Edinburgh and Glasgow to which he made a pilgrimage. The Scotch system of schools impressed him especially.

With such an itinerary, there was, indeed, little time for visits or genealogical explorations of which he was so fond, in later years. John Fiske and Thomas Davidson, both his friends, were in Europe in the same year, but indulged in more sightseeing than did Harris who confined himself strictly to collecting data on the school system, the published intention of his trip . . .

CHAPTER SEVENTEEN

RETURN TO ST. LOUIS

THE BUST THAT WAS NEVER MADE

DURING Harris' absence in Europe, to make their expression of devotion complete, the teachers of St. Louis contributed each a small gratuity of 5 or 10 cents toward a marble bust of Harris for the library, and appointed a Committee consisting of Messrs Kimball and Cook, Mrs. Fanning, and Miss Fruchte, to secure it. They had collected about $400 and expected a few hundred dollars more from former teachers and students and friends of their former Superintendent. But the bust was never ordered. Finally, they agreed on a picture of Harris enlarged to life-size and done in oil by a Mrs. Russell of St. Louis. The remainder of the money, some $300, they made up into a purse which, together with the portrait and an autograph album, was presented to Harris on his return from Europe. The entire teaching staff turned out for the occasion, yet few could actually witness the presentation by Cook in the meeting room of the Board. Harris was very touched and said that the names and the circumstances would forever burn in his memory.

There was good reason for their gratitude. As H. T. Bailey said, every man who had taught under Harris when he was Superintendent, was made over by him and became famous afterwards . . .

395

The Washington University Professorship

Soon afterwards, Harris set himself to the task of preparing his series of five lectures for Washington University on his experience abroad. He delivered them every Friday, beginning February 25th, 1881.

Now, Harris was no stranger to Washington University whose history was intimately connected with William Greenleaf Eliot, who may rightly be called the Father of the University; he was Harris' personal friend and an admirer of his scholarship and character. Not unlike Harris, he had left the East without completing his studies at Cambridge, was at first denounced as an infidel because, as a Unitarian minister, he interpreted the Bible by the light of reason. He served as a member on the Board of Public Schools and as its President, and engineered the Charter for Washington University which, for a time, was called Eliot Seminary. Most of the opportunities which the University afforded Harris, were due to Eliot.

It was in 1858 that Harris had substituted for Sylvester Waterhouse, as we have seen; but his subsequent connection with Washington University was to be more pleasant. As he rose in importance in the Public Schools, his opinion and advice were sought on frequent occasions. On June 1st, 1863, for example, he was invited to visit the final examinations of the Senior Class in Comparative Philology. The University was then under William Chauvenet who had succeeded Chancellor Joseph G. Hoyt who died in 1862. When Ex-Chancellor Chauvenet died, Harris was one of the pall-bearers. As early as 1866 he was invited to the meetings of the Board of Directors of Washington University "for the purpose of social intercourse, at the houses of the respective members." His invitation came through Yeatman. Harris made modest but pertinent remarks when called upon, in 1870, to give his opinion on a lecture by Rev. Dr. T. M. Post on "Methods of History for Americans."

In 1873, Eliot accepted the Chancellorship of the institution that called itself too grandiloquently, in his opinion, a university. However, under his leadership the school gained rapidly in standing. Through the medium of the High School, there was a constant exchange of students between the Public Schools and Washington University. This was intensified by the new administration of O'Fallon Polytechnic. Influenced by reading Goethe's *Wilhelm Meister*, Madame de Staël on German philosophy, and Fichte's *Bestimmung des Menschen* and his "sunclear statement" while at Cambridge, Eliot shared Harris' idealism. Many a time he invited the younger man to lecture. Thus, "Raphael's Transfiguration" was given by Harris in 1866 and repeated with a showing of autotypes twelve years later to quite a large audience. The public lectures sponsored by the University were regularly advertised to the Principals and Assistants of the Public Schools by circulars which Harris had printed or heliographed. Somewhat earlier than 1880, Harris began to serve in some sort of directorial capacity, for he was invited to sit in on meetings in which the condition and prospects of the University were being discussed.

Most important, however, Harris was a member of the faculty, as his name appeared in the catalogs from 1876-77 to 1891-92 inclusive, as "University Professor of the Philosophy of Education." He had no regular duties except lecturing from time to time "as may be specially arranged and announced." So far as is known, in January and February, 1877, he delivered three Smith lectures on "Education." In the spring of 1880, he gave a series of four upon "Educational Psychology," the first one just ten days after he had received the invitation from Eliot. Just before leaving for Europe and after his course at the Concord Summer School of Philosophy, he delivered the series of lectures on the "History of Philosophy," mentioned before. The latter he probably gave as a token of gratitude for receiving the professorship at the testimonial given him.

It was December when he submitted to Eliot a list of ten lectures to be given the following year, half of them dealing with education outside the United States, while four of them summarized the experiences he had gathered in Belgium and England. The other half dealt with problems of School management and the school as a social and moral influence in the community. Apart from these, there were three other lectures on "Literary Themes," treating the Norse Edda, Goethe's *Faust* and Dante's *Divine Comedy*, and four or five dealing with Hegel and his work. Harris, thus, contributed abundantly to Washington University in the city of St. Louis.

Ties With the West

Indirectly the University Club of St. Louis was connected with Washington University in that many of the university staff belonged to it. But beyond that, it reached other people also who had college or university training. It was founded in 1872,[1] and in 1874 Harris had given a talk on "The Relation of Philosophy to Society, Art and Religion," which was essentially identical with that given before the Chicago Philosophical Society.[2] It was rather important and created almost as great a sensation as his lecture on "The Relation of Church and State"[3] in which he had presented the issues very precisely. Religion, assuming a negative attitude toward the real world in time and peace, the State assuming a positive one, both have spheres of their own which they may not overstep under penalty of chaos to society. Yet they may exist side by side in harmony.

Another lecture before the University Club was given on February 25th, 1875, on the topic "The Relation of the Philosophy of Art to the Philosophy of History."[4] It was lectures of this type that Lilian Whiting rated as of great importance to the cultural life of St. Louis. She even traced direct influences of Harris' inspiring interpretations of art subjects in the life and work of some individuals and cited[5] as a typical instance John Hemming Fry, the artist, an Indiana youth of Virginian ancestry, "born and bred in that Middle West where he had, to be sure, some good books in his father's house, but no Art! Under Dr. Harris' tuition the world of art was revealed."

Through his associations at the University Club, Harris had created many friends in academic and other circles in St. Louis who missed his inspiring presence when he left the city, but who rallied as soon as he made his appearance again in St. Louis. In tribute to his practical business sense which he had demonstrated in all relations with the School Board, he was offered a Vice-presidency in the Collier White Lead Company which he, however, refused.

With the Public Schools Harris had not severed his connection entirely upon his resignation, for he acted still in an advisory capacity after his return from Europe. When visitors arrived who wanted to make a tour of inspection of the schools, he kept himself in readiness and would, in company with his successor in office, act as Cicerone to the delegation of Spaniards and others that arrived while he was still in the city.

After he had changed his residence definitely to Concord, Mass., early in 1880, he made it his habit to read the St. Louis daily papers, although he never was a good newspaper reader. When in the neighborhood of St. Louis on a lecture tour, or en route to an educational meeting, he would stop off, as he could not very well escape the importunity of his St. Louis associations. Thus, upon their request he would come and invariably he would have to lecture. As examples, we note his lecture on Christian Art, his talk in the parlor of Col. Thos. Richeson in 1882, and a series of lectures in the following year. Particularly in 1885 his friends made a concerted effort to have him back in St. Louis. However, the climate in Massachusetts he found much more conducive to his health, and his visits became fewer. At the Liberal Union Club meeting late in December he spoke on "The Bible in the Public Schools," joining in a panel discussion of the relation between Church and State.

Part Four
CONCORD PERIOD

CHAPTER EIGHTEEN

THE CONCORD SUMMER SCHOOL OF PHILOSOPHY

ORGANIZATION AND MANAGEMENT

T HOUGH Harris was not the originator of the Concord Summer School of Philosophy which operated from 1879 to 1888, he quickly became the pivotal figure in it. His activity was not confined to lecturing. A major portion of the correspondence with members of the faculty, and some business correspondence also, lay on his shoulders. Once he told a reporter in Indianapolis, in his modest way, that Mr. F. B. Sanborn was the business man and that he himself could be called chief consultant. The whole tenor of the School, the type of programs offered, with emphasis on Hegel, Kant, problems of immortality, the history of philosophy and the spiritual interpretation of Dante and Goethe, reflected his mode of thinking. All the faculty members were his personal friends, and so were large numbers of the attending pupils.

Tickets were handled by Sanborn, by H. L. Whitcomb, the Postmaster of Concord, and by A. Williams & Co., at Boston. Single admission was fixed at 50c, six tickets sold for $2.50 and twelve for $4.00. Advertisements appeared in the Boston dailies, in the Boston *Traveller*, the *Journal of Speculative Philosophy* and many other publications, solicited as well unsolicited. The receipts were such that they could adhere to their agreement of meeting all expenses of the lecturers and give them a small fee. The surplus was always small. And if the "business managers" had operated more with emphasis on cash profits than on intellectual returns, the School might have been a pecuniary success as well in the beginning. For attendance was always good.

According to Harris' own figures, attendance at the School during four years was as follows. The actual number of individuals registering during the season is not reflected in the table.

YEAR	TOTAL	AVERAGE ATTENDANCE PER LECTURE OR CLASS
1881	3008	64
1882	1288	35
1883	1711	47½ counting all
1884	1668	92 2/3 counting all

At least 18 States of the Union were represented by the persons that flocked to the 1879 session, and the picture did not change too markedly during the six or seven years that followed. Apart from Massachusetts, the West was particularly in evidence. Women were in the majority, and they were mostly teachers. It was commented upon that the School was an experiment in co-education. "The wife of a Western judge" would sit "side by side with a young graduate of Johns Hopkins University, both so intent upon their work that the question of sex is forgotten." Young ladies, "not many years in long dresses" listened to deep philosophy next to graybeards and men "bald on that part of the head supposed to be nearest the organ of thought," as the *New York Observer* reporter had it, who marvelled at the gathering of philosophers not all of whom were winged or full fledged. Many a romance started there, of course. Lucia Ames Mead, for instance, met her husband Edwin D. Mead at the lectures, but they did not get married until many years later.[1]

CONCORD SUMMER SCHOOL OF PHILOSOPHY

There were "orthodox Congregationalists, Baptists, Episcopalians, Unitarians, Hicksite Quakers, Swedenborgians, Free-religionists, Pantheists and nondescript" among the students, but the School furnished also "an Elysium, an Utopia, an Ultima Thule for all good suffragists." Yet, it was notably free of the "mongrel tribe of free-lovers, new lights and persons half insane, who prowl around every movement that holds out the least promise of giving them an entering wedge." As Geo. W. Cooke said, "fanatics of every sort seemed to shun the place."

The town of Concord was hospitable to the influx of strangers. Luxuriously shaded, it impressed the students as utterly free from wordly rivalry. Peacefully it lay there along the drowsy Concord River, the meadows studded with charming flowers. The homes, including Emerson's, were open to the visitors who came filled more with admiration than curiosity. The rooms of some of these remarkable Americans, as those of Mrs. Edward Hoar, "were bright with the faces of the Concord women, who looked so intelligent that" the out-of-town reporter "felt half-afraid to speak lest he might say what would strike them as foolish." There were no vices in the town, except conversation. The only indulgence and fun was the Annual Regatta on the river, held in July. In 1885, the town celebrated its 250th year of existence.

The old historic Orchard House served, in 1879, as a place of meeting in "a singular atmosphere of cheerful antiquity, or venerable youth." The furniture was plain, the floor was covered with rush matting. A picture of the famous school at Athens hung over the mantel suggesting high aims for the Concord venture. There were portraits of Emerson, Alcott, Walt Whitman, Pascal and Shakespeare, busts of Plato and Pestalozzi, a mask of Homer, a Cherub in bas-relief. Bookcases lined the walls. Outside stood rustic chairs with backs and arms made of apple and pine boughs, and rustic settees had been placed in the shade of the Yellow Pine. On the slope to the rear, paths had been made and steps cut into the hillside to permit *inter silvas academe querere verum.*

In 1880, the School opened in the new Hillside Chapel built with part of the fund of $1000 given by Mrs. Elizabeth Thompson of New York City for the general use of the School. The Orchard House, next to which the lecture hall was erected, was leased and later bought by Harris from Alcott. The atmosphere in Hillside Chapel was equally unaffected, and the only luxury was the bowl on the speaker's table that was always filled with flowers, be they from the meadow or the fragrant lily patches in the river. Behind the table sat the faculty, Sanborn to the left. Alcott himself would lecture sitting. Off in the corner, watch in hands, sat S. H. Emery, the unassuming presiding officer who had left Quincy, Illinois, and his lucrative stove business to devote himself to the furtherance of the literary and spiritual life. We do not know who said it, that the gift of silence is a mark of profundity and that Mr. Emery carried off the palm because he knew better than anyone else when not to speak.

The students filled the room quickly and quietly and took their places which they were expected to keep during the course. The hour had struck, but, following the academic custom, five minutes of grace were extended to the tardy ones. At the expiration of this period, Mr. Emery would rise and say simply, addressing the speaker: "The time for beginning has come, Mr. . . ." Instantly, silence fell and the lecture began.

The School suffered much from certain buffoons like Wilson Flagg, the reporter who wrote against the School, but understood nothing. The *Independent* refused to report the lectures, believing them to be humbug, tomfoolery or commonplace, covered up by an affected jargon; but it did publish Harris' articles. Harris called what a few papers reported about the School good-natured sport. They professed to be sending intelligent reporters, but when even these failed to catch the spirit and meaning and were unsuccessful in digesting long papers, the faculty wrote the abstracts themselves, which then were published in Boston, New York, St. Louis and Chicago, and many times in papers of other cities.

As an intellectual leaven in American life, the Concord School of Philosophy can hardly be over-estimated. It was so recognized in the early 80ies. Without a doubt, there was no university at the time that could have been more serious in its attempt to expound sound philosophy. American philosophy received a powerful impetus. It introduced the deepest thoughts to young students and to the serious-minded laity. Even the *New York Times* acknowledged in 1880 that Concord had become the trysting place of eminent thinkers who, it must be owned, had given transcendentalism a new turn.

In the first enthusiasm, there was talk of making the School an all-around institution. The attendance seemed to hold promise enough, while the following summer appeared to assure the permanence of the School. So successful were the courses that Dr. Noah Porter, President of Yale, who himself had lectured before the School, together with Dr. Deems, started a rival institution, "A School of Christian Philosophy," in the year 1881, and many a school afterwards modelled itself upon the Concord venture, benefitting by its mistakes as well as its successes. Had Harris and the rest paid less heed to religious pressure groups to give the School a definitely theistic leaning, and had the concession to scientific trends come earlier than it did, obsequies would probably not have been published as early as 1884 by those who saw symptoms of an early death. Indeed, the fullness and vigor of the programs were declining markedly by 1886, while with the demise of Alcott in 1888, it was felt that the School had come to its natural end with him.

CHARACTERS OLD AND NEW TO CONCORD

The Concord Summer School of Philosophy was, in the words of John Albee, the legacy of the old age of several of Concord's wise men. The academic and administrative duties devolved almost from the beginning, on younger men. They all did well and would have been an ornament to any of the foremost universities. There was no shamming in their work, as someone said; it was of the first order and was given from a full mind. It was highly original.

There was Alcott, the Dean of the School, the patriarch, with nimbus of white hair. His spiritual Don Quixotism delighted and fascinated all. During the first years he was ever "on top," the phrase a wealthy host once used in Detroit which, savoring of the saloon, hit off the loquacity of the sage. But in November, 1882, he had an apoplectic shock and Harris, much concerned, sought counsel among his friends. Dr. Hiram K. Jones, however, entertained no expectation, "nor even rational hope of his restoration to any use of his faculties, mental or physical — beyond that of a mere temporary subsistence of his frame."[2] He had attained his dream, and his blessing rested on the School. Yet, none of the members felt that the course of study was complete before he had given as much of his Valedictory address as he was able to.

The Director of the School, S. H. Emery, Jr., was a young man, self-effacing and polished in his manners. He lectured but a few times. F. B. Sanborn, the Secretary, tall, slight and dark, with keen dark eyes, was ever alert in discussion. His lectures were appreciated for their factual content and choice wording.

The man adored by all, he who seemed ever in the presence of a divinity which he could not express but which expressed him, — Ralph Waldo Emerson, was seen at the School during its early existence. When he gave his essay on "Memory" in 1879, he was in better form than he had been for years, although he had to ask his daughter Ellen for assistance. He regaled the members with his talks on "The True Gentleman" and "Aristocracy" during 1880, but before the fourth season of the School could get under way, he had joined the immortals. Indeed, the last time he left his home in 1882 it was, as Edwin D. Mead alleged,[3] "to hear an essay by Dr. Harris of the Concord School, and then his neighbor, on Carlyle's 'Sartor Resartus'."

Hiram K. Jones, the Platonist, was a physician from Jacksonville, Illinois, one of the finds of Alcott. Gray of hair, "of rather full build," he always said "distinctly and decidedly" what he thought, and no one could shake him in his conviction of right. He spoke often and fluently on Plato, extemporaneously and otherwise. On one occasion — it was in 1881 — Dr. Jones had gone a little too far in his denunciation of evolution, at which Harris came to the rescue of the evolutionists. The discussion became somewhat heated and Alcott, fearing that something might go wrong, began to deprecate any misunderstanding between the gentlemen. "Whereupon," as the writer for the *Free Religious Index*[4] continued, "Dr. Jones, looking surprised, exclaimed, 'I don't know what you mean, Mr. Alcott.' 'Nor I either,' echoed Professor Harris. Then the philosopher, discerning his native *Concord* again, smiled, and said as he subsided into his seat, 'Well, I don't know as I know what I mean myself,' adding, as a laugh rippled over the audience, 'I am a "Mystic," you know,' on which the merriment became general."

A welcome speaker and debater was Harris' close friend Thomas Davidson. In the early days of the School, just back from Greece, he would lecture on Attica with an intonation described as a very pretty Doric burr which was superimposed on his own Scotch burr. The pictures he threw on the sheet were out of focus and dim, due to the "astral oil" he used in the lamp. Occasionally, a profile, not classic at all, appeared incongruously displayed against a pediment in the crowded Orchard House, or the field of Marathon was thrown on a young woman's white waist. In later years this Scot of sandy hair and beard would shock the unsuspecting audience with some remarks reeking of socialism or a eulogy of the usually excoriated Emile Zola. "Tom," however, was a valiant defender of the School against the scorn of worldlings, despite what he acknowledged to be some crude and ill-delivered essays.[5] He would help out by reading Professor Luigi Ferri's paper in the liquid translation of Mrs. Helen Campbell, of Orange, N. J., or thrill the audience with an essay on smiling Sappho. Treading on delicate ground, he nevertheless "hid nothing that was pure and sweet in its nudity."

Harris' long-time acquaintance, Denton J. Snider, still active in the West at the time, was also harnessed to the School which liked him well enough as a speaker and a person, though he himself felt out of place among the Yankees. Like Davidson, he took his pupils on the screen to Aulis and Chalcis and gave them of his rich and long experience with Shakespeare's writings.

Until John Albee, another of Harris' close friends, gave his imaginary conversations in 1880, the visitors to the School had heard only elaborate and erudite productions. These conversations presented a new feature that was both restful and pleasing, while scholarly at the same time. The accomplished litterateur and keen, but charming critic once characterized himself as "too philosophical to succeed in literature, and too literary for a complete philosopher."[6]

As lecturers somewhat in the same category of literary and poetic interests should be mentioned the poet Edmund C. Stedman, Julian Hawthorne of New York, and H. G. O.

Blake. Frequent lectures were heard from Mrs. Ednah D. Cheney, a lady of high culture who, with her "gray crowned face" presented "the picture of beaming benevolence upon all mankind," and Julia Ward Howe, "brilliant leader of society, preacher, reformer, essayist, poet." James Elliot Cabot, with whom Harris had had correspondence regarding Hegel as early as 1865, also was a lecturer. René de Poyen Belleisle spoke in French on Emerson in July, 1884. Dr. Rowland G. Hazard, of Peace Dale, R. I., accomplished in literature and philosophy, spoke well and was enjoyed by the audience, and so was Dr. Edmund Montgomery, gentleman scholar and philosopher from Scotland and Texas.

The number of clergymen who were lecturers exceeded that of others, and their discourses were often more wordy than wise. Their "gigantic rhetoric" seemed somewhat out of place. There was the picturesque Rev. Dr. C. A. Bartol; Rev. W. H. Channing; the venerable Rev. Dr. Andrew P. Peabody; the Rev. Dr. J. S. Kedney; Rev. Dr. Elisha Mulford from Pennsylvania, who was a political philosopher in his own right; the Rev. W. R. Alger of Boston whose discourse "seemed to enlist the keenest interest of 'the one' (i.e. the few), while 'the many' wanly smiled in despair"; Rev. George Willis Cook of Dedham, Mass; the Rev. Dr. F. H. Hedge who spoke on Kant; the Reverends Robert A. Holland, Episcopalian Rector of St. Louis and Chicago, and David A. Wasson, a Unitarian of Massachusetts, who were known to Harris intimately for years; the Rev. Brother Azarias, President of Rock Hill College, Md., a Catholic; and, if he had been able to come in time for the session of 1884, Protap Chunder Mozoomdar of Calcutta, the Hindu. A good number of creeds and denominations were thus represented by the clergymen that have been named, not to speak of others among them and the laity whose names have not been given in this brief sketch.

Scientific interests were not entirely unrepresented. Pro-

411

fessor John Fiske of Cambridge, for whom Harris had high personal regards although he was in the Herbert Spencer camp, spoke on "The Origin and Destiny of Man," giving a rather exhaustive exposition of the theory of evolution. Professor John Watson of Queen's University, Kingston, Canada, lectured ably, but not in the accustomed Concord tone. Among persons with academic backing should further be mentioned Prof. Benjamin Peirce of Harvard, Prof. C. C. Everett of Harvard, Prof. T. Sterry Hunt of Montreal, Professors H. S. White, W. T. Hewett and C. C. Shackford of Cornell, and Prof. J. W. Mears of Hamilton College. George H. Howison was invited to speak in 1882 after his return from an extended sojourn in Germany. University Presidents likewise appeared on the programs of the sessions, including Noah Porter of Yale, and James McCosh of Princeton.

It was much to the credit of Harris whose own experience had made him appreciative of such consideration, that young men were given a chance to express themselves. Thus, Charles E. Garman of Amherst College, and young, handsome and pleasant H. N. Gardiner, Professor in Smith College, an "ideal instructor for young ladies," were asked to lecture.

The relation of William James to Harris and the Concord School was peculiar. The up and coming psychologist had been in correspondence with Harris since 1878.[7] There was a tension at first, due to the fact that James did not realize that the *Journal of Speculative Philosophy* was, after all, Harris', for, as sole person responsible for meeting the deficits, he surely had a voice in its policies. But Harris, in his inimitable fashion, won James over completely, though the latter professed repeatedly to his inability to follow him in his abstractions. However, William James was seen in the audience at the Concord School in 1882, asking many a curious question. The following year he lectured on psychology. He was also slated to speak on "Aristotle's Theory of Sense Perception in the Light of Recent Psychology" in the summer of 1887, but his lecture was cancelled.

Of course, James knew of Harris' contempt for empiricism. Harris would, without hurting anyone's feeling, "comment with grim humor" upon the "brilliant vagaries" and "shallow infelicities" of the new set of American thinkers, as Dr. Nicholas Murray Butler later so aptly stated. Harris, and the thinkers about him, may not have been wiser, but they were possibly more reverent. It would be a mistake to say that in the war between fixity and fluidity, Harris made his stand with the abiding, rigid Absolute in defiance of mobility and flexibility. The Hegelian doctrine itself, with its dialectic, militated against it, and the spirit of science to which he was by no means averse so long as it acknowledged the supremacy of ideas.

As composite as was the staff of the School which has been partially named, was the audience. However, it was not motley, for it was the serious student and people who cared for the School's message that made their way to Concord. During seasons in which a variety of lectures was offered, the school population changed, new faces replacing old. The intellectual coterie of Concord was strongly represented at all times, with Boston a close second. Miss Elizabeth Peabody, aside from lecturing and debating, sat in the audience, all attention, "rumpling her bonnet and white curls without the least consciousness of her movements." Mr. J. B. Hill, of Mason, N. Y., a vigorous old gentleman and one of Emerson's classmates, listened with seeming delight. George Parsons Lathrop, the editor of the *Boston Sunday Courier*, who had married Rose, the youngest daughter of Hawthorne, came over from Hawthorne's "Wayside" which he owned and occupied. Then there were Chief Justice Durfee, of Providence, R. I.; the Hon. George H. Calvert of Newport, a former Mayor of Baltimore and a gentleman of literary reputation; Edward Potter, son of Bishop Potter of New York; ex-Attorney General Hon. E. Rockwood Hoar; Courtland Palmer, President of the Nineteenth Century Club, and what their names might be.

In 1884, Harris invited J. C. Bundy, the editor and publisher of the *Religio-philosophical Journal* and an avowed Spiritualist. He came and joined the discussion after a paper of Dr. Holland's. He also urged — and this is interesting in view of Harris' early leanings — the establishment of a Psychical Research Society at Concord, while Harris praised him as a representative of "clean spiritualism."

Among Harris' faithful disciples let us name but Lilian Whiting, Anna Tolman Smith, and Mrs. Harriette R. Shattuck. His friends came from as far as St. Louis, Minnesota and California, while his own family and in-laws took a special pride in the School and made it a point to be present, even if only for a day, during the sessions.

In all, the roster of the speakers and listeners at the nine or ten summer sessions of the Concord School of Philosophy included a remarkably large number of persons who have since attained fame and distinction in the field of American letters, philosophy and public life, so that it is proper to speak of it as of a real influence whose value, because of its fundamentally idealistic and occasionally theological drift, may, of course, be open to dispute. None of the ventures copied after it during the School's existence could, however, compare in righteous enthusiasm and aspiration to a real philosophical faculty with such widely acknowledged talent.

HE OF HEAVENLY EARNESTNESS

"A square-shouldered gentleman, with a somewhat pale and very earnest face, lecturing to the company assembled there, partly from manuscript and in part extemporaneously. He wears spectacles, has a high forehead and thin, dark hair, a short, slightly grizzled beard, and speaks with remarkable clearness and precision in a pleasant, not very loud, voice, the modulations of which express great patience and amiability. His whole aspect denotes intense intellectual activity; the broad chest and shoulders indicating a strong physical basis which has enabled him to sustain that activity." — That is how William Torrey Harris appeared to George Parsons Lathrop at the Concord School in the summer of 1880.[8]

Unquestionably, Harris was, for erudition and philosophy, the strongest man in the School. After Emerson and Alcott, he was the commanding figure, the ablest and most popular speaker, also the most distinguished one. To these claims all writers bear witness. It was not merely a woman's admiration that elicited the remark: "Socrates himself could scarcely have set before you a grander sweep of thought."[9] His "heavenly earnestness" impressed all because he was also unaffected and modest. Often he would sit and talk with eyes closed. There was no one less dictatorial as a speaker. He would be large in his thoughts, yet hold with tenacity to a principle.

All his lectures at the School were specially prepared and came to the audience "like buckwheats fresh from the griddle."[10] The School was a school of *philosophy*, a fact too often forgotten by the critics. Harris never opposed science. In one of his 1881 lectures he stated unequivocally that one must be very much behind the age and times not to see that natural science elevates the mind above nature. In 1882, he reverted somewhat to his earlier views when lecturing on symbolism in art. But this time it was not General Hitchcock who listened appreciatively, but General Daniel Pratt, G.A.T., a blustering crank from Boston.

Harris avoided, as Sanborn stated correctly, both "the ecstasy of the Neo-Platonism" and pragmatism. It seems that all adverse criticism of the School was directed against everyone but Emerson and Alcott. In these, as also in Harris, Sanborn and Emery, everyone acknowledged a towering personality and deep font of knowledge. The *Index* was typical of most papers and journals that sneered and fumed: They would publish Harris' lectures or essays despite their criticism of the School.[11]

Harris' lecture on Emerson's relation to Goethe and Carlyle in the 1884 Emerson Symposium was regarded by many as his best. In 1887, Harris had worked out, in philosophic form, an insight which he had gained three or four years before to the effect that the mind acts in the form of syllogisms, in any act of sense-perception. This he elaborated in his lecture on "Aristotle's Theory of the Syllogism, compared with that of Hegel."[12] He regarded it at the time as his best contribution to philosophy. In all, he gave some 62 lectures during the School's existence, exclusive of the numerous discussions and extended remarks.

It was his method at the beginning of each of his lectures to sum up his previous one and to present the conclusions anew. His lectures, though long at times, were never "roundabout or prolix." His branching out into other fields when talking extemporaneously could be not only forgiven, but enjoyed. He was "extraordinarily quick and keen." One woman student said that he was excellent in the "conversations," "taking your poor little silly remark and unwinding a wise conclusion from it with an air of such grace that you feel for a moment as if you had really suggested all that yourself."

"His addresses were notable for their beauty of feeling and finish of expression."[13] Yet, they could not be called liquid, as his movements could not be called smooth. He was not an orator and anyone having heard him merely on the platform might have carried away disappointment.[14] Scholarship and oratory rarely mix. When his thoughts were crowding thick, the clarity of his exposition was liable to suffer, and occasionally he would fail to make complete sentences. Nevertheless, he drew his hearers to him, as it were, like a magnet. Hearing him, said Henry Ridgely Evans, was like sitting at the feet of Plato.

Harris did not escape the ridicule of the light-hearted and irresponsible press entirely. He himself took it graciously and in the spirit of fun. Not to be understood simply meant being ahead of the times, and in a democracy you must have infinite patience. James Jeffrey Roche wrote a poem entitled "A Concord Love Song" over which Harris heartily laughed. With allusions to the abstract in Thingness, Hereness, Ifness, Whichness, Meness, Theeness, it wound up in Usness.[15]

"When we used to speak of him before he became generally known as 'Professor Harris'," Sanborn wrote, "the skeptical philistinism of Boston and Harvard would ask with smooth malice what college gave him his title. It needed none, although he had the evidence of it . . ." He was "a doctor, indeed, a teacher of truth and of attainment, long before some university honored itself by conferring the titular degree." The phrase "dear Doctor Harris" had a peculiar pregnancy with many.

Charles Franklin Thwing once remarked that he had "never known a man who could so talk about himself as a third person. He was egoistic without being egotistic, and self-ward without a tinge of selfishness." A "marvelously clear-headed, deep-sighted, simple man," was the judgment of H. T. Bailey, another of his educational friends and admirers. If the hearer in the back row requested him to speak louder so that he could get his own full share of wisdom, Harris retorted that if he had to pay attention to how he spoke he feared that he would have nothing at all to say.

Charles H. Ames said about Harris that "his soul seemed to be not only absolutely devoid of envy, but absolutely inspired by love for mankind." Half seriously and half in jest, Tom Davidson wrote him in one of his letters in which he asked some favors:[16] "This is asking a good deal; but then you live to do good." Nothing truer could have flowed from his pen. Harris was, indeed, a large and good man.

His real enemies were not real people; they were ideas, wrong and mistaken to his way of thinking, and men like the Atomists, Sophists, Brahmans, Eleatics, Spinoza, Hamilton, Hume, Rousseau, Mill, Comte, Haeckel, and Herbert Spencer held them. He never fought the man, he waged relentless war against materialism, pantheism, agnosticism, and atheism. He was a friend to William James, but he was a foe of Pragmatism.

The erroneous impression was created that his Hegelianism, in which he is supposed to have penetrated deeper than either Kuno Fischer or Erdmann, alone made him tolerant. To err is human and folly and error are necessary factors in the dialectic of experience, without which there would be no development, no movement. Harris granted every man "freedom to err," as an inherently democratic principle. He thus was charity personified. Withall, he did not shrink from criticism; but when he gave it, he made another friend, or made the old one dearer to him.

Harris did not need apologists; he was a master in explaining his own position. The kind lady in the audience who was impressed by the denunciation of materialism but was not quite free of untutored sentimentalism, did him no kindness when she summed up Concord philosophy approvingly in the question: "Don't you think it much more elevating to regard the universe from within rather than from without . . .?"

At the end of the 1881 session, an able paper on Schopenhauer's philosophy was read by Mrs. Amalia J. Hathaway of Michigan, a German by birth. Harris, who did not approve of the arch-pessimist, was requested to make a statement.

He said, when pressed, that Schopenhauer's ideas reminded him very much of Mr. Alcott's views on instinct, but that he regarded Schopenhauer who had advanced nothing beyond the Oriental, as a case of arrested development, at which Alcott, amidst general mirth, asked him whether he considered him in this light.

Harris was kind, but he also was a Yankee and shrewd. His success cannot be understood without this. Some described him as a typical, refined New England scholar whose speech bore the stamp of New England, "even to the gentle, nasal shading." Never did he push himself to the fore as a speaker; he needed not, for he was always invited to contribute his thought. That he was known as a reconciler was due to his own philosophy which he formulated tersely as: "We can do nothing without the consent of our fellowmen." His method of reconciliation was, as Sanborn said who witnessed it so many times, not to withhold his own view, but to see "all that was good in the view of the others."

Lilian Whiting[17] recalled in the Concord School lectures "how, after one from Dr. Harris, some one would rise — in discussion — or controversy — and make a most blundering repetition of what he had heard, or thought he had heard! and Dr. Harris — with the patience of an angel, (while all the rest of us longed to see the blunderer thrown out of the window!) — (or appropriately consigned to the depths of the river!) — Dr. Harris would say, 'I think Mr. . . . means to say etc. etc.' and then he would translate the blunderer into coherence — and explain — and elucidate — with his clearness — his brilliancy — and his supreme kindness. . . "

Denton J. Snider who was Harris' great friend but also his critic when he seemed to discern his Yankee nature and could not follow his deepest abstract thoughts, once bemeaned himself and complimented Harris, saying, "he is too great for any praise of mine." It was this remark which gave Lilian Whiting the cue for her poem on Harris entitled

"An Impromptu,"[18] which is a beautiful tribute to the master.

THE END OF THE DREAM

When Alcott died on March 4th, 1888, Harris was in Chicago, and he was deeply moved when he read of it in the papers. He had been very close to Alcott despite the fact that the texture of their minds differed. They aspired to the best and highest, each in his own way, and they had a great mutual regard and respect.

Alcott's health had been failing for some time, — and with him the Concord School of Philosophy. Accordingly, the 1888 session of the Summer School was confined to a one day Alcott Memorial Service on June 16th. That Saturday was one of Lowell's "perfect days." Among those present were Mrs. Ralph Waldo Emerson, Miss Elizabeth Peabody, William Ellery Channing, Frederick Pratt, the grandson of Mr. Alcott, and his wife, Mrs. D. Lothrop, and Mrs. Harriett R. Shattuck.

Many paid tribute to Alcott, and there was a forenoon and an afternoon session. The biographical address was given by F. B. Sanborn, while Harris spoke on the philosophy of the sage that had passed away. He made the tribute an occasion to expound briefly the history of thought, especially the interesting speculations of gnostics and Neoplatonists. He showed the development from the conception of an "empty Absolute" to the Absolute Reason which knows and creates. Alcott's dogma of the lapses from the Absolute he characterized as repugnant to the present age, but pointed out its value in reminding us of spirituality. He quoted a number of Alcott's sayings appreciatively and almost reverently. Some twelve others gave their reminiscences of Alcott, and the Rev. Dr. Bartol as one of them, summed up his tribute beautifully by saying that Alcott was a born

420

Saint. "He was all evangel, and had no back door." "He was not angular, but circular," the most modest of men.

It is not quite certain whether the School was then intended to close forever. The program of the Memorial Service spoke only of the "present Summer." Events, however, soon took such a shape that it seemed wise to close the School for good. Sanborn might have acknowledged its failure to draw speakers and audiences in late years, but he graciously put it as if the step had been taken partly for the purpose of giving Harris "an opportunity to visit Europe more at leisure than he had formerly done." The School had not been exactly a financial failure, for its net income after ten years of functioning was 31 cents which Sanborn pocketed as his treasurer's salary. The dream of Alcott was finished. . . .

Harris' finest tribute, however, constituted his contributions to the two volumes brought out jointly with F. B. Sanborn, and entitled *A. Bronson Alcott, His Life and Philosophy.*

He had purchased Orchard House.

Louisa May died 2 days later.

CHAPTER NINETEEN

FURTHER SERVICE TO EDUCATION

PRESIDENTIAL OFFERS

H ARRIS was so popular in the West that in all the leading towns through which he happened to pass en route to an educational meeting, his friends would flock to the depots to pay him their personal respects.[1] It was thus only natural that after his retirement from Public School life they considered him for important positions.

At Indiana State University it had been proposed as early as the summer of 1875 to offer Harris the Presidency, while Adelbert University, now Adelbert College for men within Western Reserve University, at Cleveland, Ohio, made a similar offer to him in 1881. But Harris declined to have his name mentioned. During that year a movement was on foot to invite him to accept the Presidency of Missouri State University at Columbia, Mo., though he had already declined it in 1875; the hope was that he would make it famous among the institutions of the country. Under Dr. Samuel Spahr Laws, it had become notorious politically for its revival of the obsolete heresies of secession and State sovereignty, and as popular sentiment was decidedly against him, it was certain Dr. Laws would have to leave. But it was not until 1889 that he resigned under compulsion.[2]

Nebraska State University would also have welcomed Harris as its head. The letter of Rev. Dr. Robert A. Holland gives a graphic account:

3412 CALUMET AV. (CHICAGO) *June 26th,* (1882)

DEAR MR. HARRIS

Bishop Clarkson of Nebraska was with me yesterday. He is the mover in the effort of the regents of the State University to get you to take its Chancellorship. Clarkson is the most influential man in Nebraska. He begs me to urge you to accept. He says you can make your own terms. *You* shall be the University. You can appoint your own faculty, *three now,* the others in time. The means of the University will be ample for *all* ends you may contemplate. All possibilities are in it which your powers can organize. There will be no limit but your own. So Clarkson says. He is a man of big ideas, wants a big university, knows that the university is in the man, not in bricks — knows that you are the man and that you must be the university if you have anything to do with it or it is to get any adequate benefit from your headship. Bishop Clarkson doesn't exaggerate. He is thoroughly practical. He is bent on having you for this work. As he describes it, it looks to me like the grandest promise for an ideal university in America. Take Davidson, Snider, and Soldan and go. Don't refuse until you see Bishop Clarkson. He will be in Concord the last of July. Remember — you can dictate own terms. This last is confidential. But I know what I say. *Clarkson is the regency.*

Yours,

HOLLAND.

The official notification came through C. A. Holmes, President of the Board of Regents, in June, 1882, more than a week before Dr. Holland's letter, but Harris declined.

Of all offers the most enticing to Harris was, however, the Presidency of the University of Texas which was in the process of being formed in 1881, with an endowment of several million dollars. Harris was approached by O. N. Hollingworth, the Secretary of the State Board of Education in Texas. A paragraph from his first letter throws light on the universal acclaim that Harris had won in the educational field: "It is needless for me to indicate to you the vastness of the field to which,if you will pardon me for saying, you could dedicate your great powers, greater in my humble opinion than can be claimed for any other man in America."[3]

Until the university was properly established, they offered Harris charge of the Sam Houston State Normal Institute. Harris declined,[4] without, however, flatly rejecting the offer. In the meantime, his St. Louis friends prodded him on to accept. L. S. Holden, General Agent for D. Appleton and Co's Educational Department for Missouri Territory, with Headquarters at St. Louis, assured him that his going to Texas was "the universal sentiment of all classes, from the Principals of the schools to the Governor of the State."[5] Among other things he said:

... I am fully aware that your health demands quiet, but your organization is such that while life lasts your brain will be active and would it not be better to have some settled position where you can work out what providence has so eminently fitted you for, a system in Texas where the people await you with outstretched arms. You will find efficient co-laborers to aid you in all your plans, men who will approve your every plan, men who will aid you in all your efforts to make Texas schools the most perfect in the land from the Dist. school to the Public, the Normal and up to the university.

Can you not go?

Is it not possible for you to this year begin a yet greater work than you ever yet accomplished.

To day your name is more honored in this country

and abroad than that of any educator living or dead, but there is yet an opportunity for you to win new laurels and accomplish for Texas what your labors did _for St. Louis_, make for a state what you constructed for a city, the best educational system in the land.

Harris had made some kind of promise to help out in Texas during 1882, and everyone, including the Governor, was disappointed that he had not moved. He was urged repeatedly to send his suggestions on Normal Schools, which Texas was in the process of establishing in large numbers, to write articles for their *Journal of Education,*[6] and, if he preferred anonymity in respect of words of guidance, he was invited to furnish such matter as editorials.

When the ground for the State University was broken in Spring, 1882, Hollingworth again approached Harris and offered him a $4000 Professorship, as it now seemed clear that he did not care for the Presidency, and there were certain legal complications having to do with residency, preventing the immediate installation of Harris. The Chair was in Moral Philosophy, and was to be Harris' stepping stone to the presidency. A letter by Joseph Baldwin described the position more in detail;

SAM HOUSTON NORMAL INSTITUTE

HUNTSVILLE, TEXAS, *August* 19, 1882

DR. W. T. HARRIS
  Concord.

Esteemed Friend:

The regents of our university have carved out a department to suit you — Philosophy, Educational Psychology, and Political Economy — and elected you. Your work will be light — one hour a day, for a few months annually. You will have no care or responsibility. By your councils you can mould the University and largely the educational system of this wonderful state. It is immense—I have just completed a canvass of the state, giving a course of lectures in each of the fifteen State Normal Institutes. The educational outlook is most cheering. I made two speeches to the Regents in favor of making you the central man in the University. I assured them that you was [sic] the ablest educator and the best organizer on the continent, and that while you would not accept the Presidency, I believed you would accept the chair of Philosophy.

In the name of the great cosmopolitan state and the 20,000,000 citizens it is to have in the near future, I entreat you to accept. Austin is one of the most healthy cities on the continent. You can spend eight months in Austin and four in Concord.

Accept! Accept!! Accept!!!

Your sincere friend,

J. BALDWIN

Still, Harris preferred his Concord retirement and said nothing. This evoked a strong letter from Holden[7] in which he said:

DEAR MR. HARRIS,

Pardon my frequent epistles, but I have you and your affairs so much in my mind that I can not help writing when matters of moment come up.

I have received letters from Texas saying that Coln. Ashbel Smith, Cedar Bayou, and Prof. Wooldridge, Austin, Texas, were indignant that you did not respond to their letters.

You know a Southerner expects personal attention and feels a seeming slight, which I know you did not intend, but through great pressure of other matters forgot.

Readers are selling exceedingly well this Fall.

Yours Respfly.

L. S. HOLDEN

At last, Harris made answer to everyone concerned and gave them the real reason for his negative decision. His duties as Superintendent in St. Louis had exhausted him physically and his whole system was permeated by malaria. As a matter of fact, the course of ten lectures which he had just finished giving at the Concord Summer School had made such heavy claims on his strength that he had to take a brief vacation. He could not, in justice to the new Texas University, accept such a responsible position.

But, a more tempting offer was to come a few years later. When Edward S. Holden, President of the University of California, wrote Harris a letter on January 28th, 1887, he did so as a friend and follower of his educational theories. Having no ambition to be President, he was only waiting for Lick Observatory to be organized to assume directorship of it. It was he who made the suggestion to the trustees of the University to get Harris as his successor as President. Unfortunately, the trustees had not met Harris on his short visit to the West, but, with the exception of one, Hon. Judge Jno. S. Hager, who was noted for attaching large importance to personal documents, were very favorably disposed to call Harris. Harris himself cherished the idea, for he not only conveyed this impression to Holden himself, but, at his suggestion, got together quite a number of letters from persons in St. Louis who knew of his work and character. These he sent to Holden, and they included probably some of the strongest and best letters of recommendation ever written for any educator. A list of writers may suffice: General Jno. Pope; General John W. Noble; Dr. Robert A. Holland of St. George's Rectory; Rev. John Snyder, a Unitarian minister; Jno. B. Johnson; Isaac H. Sturgeon; Brandt V. B. Dixon; Morris J. Lippman; Superintendent Edward H. Long; Attorney-at-Law John C. Orrick; F. Louis Soldan; Susan V. Beeson; and Jas. E. Yeatman, President of the Merchants' National Bank, who apparently had caused most of the above to write their letters. From John C. Orrick, in particular, he got an excellent description of his executive abilities such as are most desirable in the President of a large university. Said he in his letter in reference to the Board of Public Schools at St. Louis:

The Board of Directors of Public Schools was quite a large body, representing various interests, many of the members being unreasonable; some ignorant and willful; others with peculiar hobbies, making it difficult to tolerate or manage them, and with all this to deal with, Mr. Harris was able to carry out his policy of establishing upon a broad and solid basis, the splendid system of Public Schools which this city is now enjoying. He found it in a low condition, but he left it one of the best systems in the Country. I think he has a peculiar faculty for getting along with people, and oftentimes managing them without their knowledge. He is not irascible — naturally of a tranquil temperament — firm in his purposes, and generally carried his point in his action as Superintendent of our Public Schools.

Unfortunately, nothing came of the position. Beginning 1888, Holden was anxious to assume duties at Lick Observatory, and the election of a President became urgent. The trustees looked in other directions. But Holden continued to persuade Harris to come out West to California where, if he were once seated there, he said, he could do incalculable good. Even as late as 1892, a letter written by George H. Howison to Harris on November 10th, enquired confidently whether he could be induced to consider the office of President of the University of California . . .

NOT TOO PROUD TO SERVE

Having been at the helm of one of the largest Public School systems in the United States, Harris, in his retirement at Concord, was not too proud to accept the Superintendentship in that little town. He held the position from 1882 to 1885. Unfortunately the service of this distinguished man is now completely forgotten.

The notebook which Harris kept is filled with details, such as the fact that the new curtains did not roll up properly, or that a certain Mabel Jones was not of sound mind, striking her fellow pupils habitually. When she finally knocked a little girl down the cellar stairs, Harris recommended her withdrawal from school.

The experience he had gained at St. Louis he now applied at Concord. He was for rapid advancement of the pupils and frowned upon keeping them back to go over and over the same studies. He laid out various forms, such as the ones for the Monthly Payroll of the Schools, the Programme Reports for every school, Teachers' Absences, and the like. By 1884, he had effected a re-arrangement of the course of study, and had re-issued the School Rules and Regulations. In compliance with State Laws he had to allow the reading of the Bible, although it was against his theory of religious tolerance which he expounded while in St. Louis.

In the handbill on "Discipline and Management, for the Consideration of Teachers", which he had issued, he warned the teachers not to inflict unusual punishment. He endeavored to foster the development of a sense of honor to replace the need for corporal punishment which was more widely resorted to in the East than in the West. His treatment of the matter of punishment in his 1884-85 *Report to the School Committee* is, indeed, classic. It discusses tersely retributive, corrective and other forms of punishment.

While re-writing and revising the School Laws he integrated them with the State School Laws. He revised the selection of textbooks and the procedure for having them approved. The *Syllabus of Lessons in Natural Science* which he had used in St. Louis for more than twelve years, he introduced at Concord, and urged the instructors to register in the Teacher's School of Science which the Boston Society of Natural History sponsored at no expense to the registrants. And in this connection it may be noted that in 1887 the American Association for the Advancement of Science elected him a Fellow.

During his tenure of office, Harris persuaded the School Committee for the Town of Concord to build up a "really good high school" so that pupils from the neighborhood would flock to Concord. He would not exclude himself from some of the social activities, the May Festival, for instance, which he attended in 1883, and he was a friend of the teachers. In his reports to the Committee he never failed to give full and specific credit to any of the teachers or supervisors. It must be said in justice to the School Committee at that time that it was aware of the great value which Harris was to them. They recorded in their *Annual Reports* their indebtedness to him.

OFFICIAL VISITOR

The Board of Official Visitors of the College of Liberal Arts, Boston University, chose Harris at the end of 1882[8] as a member. He continued in this capacity till Spring, 1892, and during the tenure of this office he served faithfully, marking the classes on the horaria as he visited them. The official notifications disclose that he listened to classes in the Philosophy of Ethics, Psychology, Theism, History, English Literature, Rhetoric, Anglo-Saxon, Philology, Sanskrit, German, French, Spanish, Italian, Romance Philology, and Biology, and possibly some others. He was beyond doubt the most versatile member of the Board.

On November 14th, 1883, it was voted by the Board of Overseers of Harvard College, Hon. E. R. Hoar presiding, that he be added to the Visiting Committee on Languages.

T. Cushing, Jr., expressed the belief that no one was so good a judge of methods and results as he.[9] He was supplied with a schedule of language classes and, later, one professor in the Classical Department was assigned to him in particular. In February, 1886, they asked him to devote more of his time to German than to the ancient tongues.[10] In the report which Harris furnished in November of that year, he considered above all Professor Bartlett's classes very meritorious. In 1887,[11] they assigned Harris to the Departments of Italian and Spanish in addition to the others.

As Chairman of the Sub-Committee on Modern Languages, composed of Henry Cabot Lodge who was called away to the U. S. House of Representatives, J. S. Perry who spent his time in France, and Russell Gray and W. J. Rolfe who never did any visiting, Harris presented, in 1888, to Solomon Lincoln, Chairman of the (General) Committee on Languages, his views on the conduct of classes in German, Spanish and Italian, also French. He considered it a matter of great good fortune in a youth to belong to Professor Norton's class in Dante, noted good results in German and expressed pleasure over the emphasis, generally, on philology.

As early as 1874 he had received an appointment from the Indiana State Board of Education to serve on the Board of Visitors to the State Normal School at Terre Haute. The occasions of his visit, particularly during 1875, were always taken advantage of by the teachers there to hear him talk on various subjects of pedagogical interest. Even while he was in Concord, they called him to Terre Haute, and in 1885 made him chairman of the Board of Visitors, paying all his expenses.

MASTER OF SCHOOLMASTERS

Harris' advice was sought by many quarters. *The Critic and Good Literature, The North American Review,* and *The Atlantic Monthly* solicited manuscripts. Martha's Vineyard Summer Institute, at Cottage City, invited him. Franklin W. Hooper urged him to sponsor his project for an institution in New York City devoted to Liberal Education and aiming at character and not knowledge for its own sake as the final end of education.[12] Dr. Hiram K. Jones enrolled him in the Book of the Constitution and By-Laws of the American Akádêmê,[13] while Harris contributed at least two items to its *Journal*.[14]

One of the distinct honors conferred on him was his election to membership in the Massachusetts Schoolmasters' Club, to its Presidency in 1884-85, and honorable membership later. It was this Boston club which, perhaps, had the fullest appreciation of Harris' pedagogical philosophy. In their *In Memoriam* to him (1909), they stressed the fact that he magnified on all occasions the superlative importance, in public school work, of "the conventionalities of intelligence" and that he resented all efforts to substitute for them instruction for bread winning pursuits. At the Hartford meeting of the State Teachers Association in December 1882, Harris had dealt pertinently with the problem of whether our public schools educate children beyond the position they must occupy in life. The school was to open all "windows of the soul" to the light of the universe.[15] All school problems he saw in world-wide and age-long perspectives. He addressed the Club at intervals of several years.[16]

TALKS TO TEACHERS AND OTHERS

Harris never was in retirement properly speaking, for he held himself in readiness at all times to speak and to write — not for pecuniary ends, but because he loved to be of service. A typical case was the Pennsylvania State Teachers' Association Meeting at Scranton, in 1888, where he talked and donated not only the amount he was to receive for the lecture, but his expenses as well. Particularly during 1882 and 1883, and again in 1885, and from 1887 to 1888 he unfolded an astonishing activity. Leaving for the present out of account his thorough devotion to the National Educational Association, the American Social Science Association, the American Institute of Instruction, and his Kindergarten interests during the Concord period, he contributed liberally to the cause of education. Each month, beginning in October, 1881, for nine months, appeared his articles on "Christianity in Art" in the *Chautauquan,* and for the same duration in the following season his lectures on "The History and Philosophy of Education". The latter corresponded in a sense to a course he gave at Boston University in November, 1882, while the former was continued in three installments as "Religion in Art", in 1886. In that year he contributed his "Philosophy made Simple." Again, in the summer of 1891 he developed much literary activity in connection with Chautauqua where he spoke at the Sunday Vespers. This continued through 1892 and was revived in 1903 when the Chautauqua Literary and Scientific Circle celebrated its 25th Anniversary. Professor Shumway read to the Chautauqua Circle in 1883 Harris' paper on "The Place of the Study of Latin and Greek in Modern Education" as an antidote to the "crude theories of the so-called practical men, like Charles Francis Adams, Jr."

Teachers in Massachusetts, Connecticut, Maine and New York City were addressed during the years 1881 to 1883. In August, 1881, Harris spoke at Greenville, S. C.; in October, 1883, at an Inter-State Educational Convention at Louisville, Ky. But he also was heard in Indiana during 1881 in six University Lectures at the State University, at Indianapolis and Terre Haute on education and art subjects, and in private parlors again at Terre Haute in 1882 and 1883, and at Indianapolis once more in December, 1888. His art lectures were often illustrated. About the time of his removal to Washington he bought a new magic lantern as the old one proved quite unsatisfactory.

An intense lecturing activity was unfolded also at Boston where, in addition to the ten lectures already mentioned for 1882 and the one on the "Philosophy of Religion" in 1884, a number of other addresses were given. The Trustees of Boston University invited him for the Commencement Exercises in Music Hall, on June 6th, 1883. During 1885 to 1886 he drew up, for the University, the Pedagogical and Art Examinations. A noteworthy address to a Boston audience was that on "The Church and the State in Relation to the School", at the Congregational Club, on October 20th, 1887, evoked by the reviving militancy of the Catholic Church. In the same year he was interested in the Hermetic Society, reading a sketch of its aims and taking notes on a talk about it by Mohini M. Chatterji. The five Boston University lectures delivered on December 5th, 7th, 12th, 14th and 19th, 1888, on "Educational Psychology" were, it is alleged, suggested by Harris himself, when he noticed that Dr. G. Stanley Hall had lectured publicly on pedagogy with much success. By having his name definitely linked with Boston University, Harris gained added prestige, which was one of the circumstances leading to his appointment as U. S. Commissioner of Education.

Many more lecture engagements could be mentioned; the following were among the more important: his lecture at Parkersburg in February, 1883, on "The Philosophy of Art versus the Isms of Aesthetes"; his talk at the Educational Convention at Hyde Park, Mass., of May, 1885; his address on the subject of "Compulsory Education in Relation to Crime and Social Morals" at the 12th Annual Conference of Charities and Correction at Washington, in 1885; his address at the Phillips Academy Alumni Association Meeting at Parker House, Boston, on March 24th, 1886; and his New Haven Address of May 7th, 1888, on "The Problem of Philosophy and its Method."

Periodic fluctuations may be noted in Harris' activity as

a speaker and writer: 1884 to 1885 and 1886 to 1887 were quiet periods and indicated that ill health was checking his prolific activity, though he continued to publish and write for his *Journal of Speculative Philosophy,* to contribute to numerous periodicals, and to manifest an active interest particularly in the National Educational Association and the American Social Science Association, the regular annual meetings of which he never missed and from which he rarely returned without having made a significant address.

CHAPTER TWENTY

THE BIG THREE

LEAVING out of account for the present Hegel, whom Harris continued, with only slight abatement, to study during his Concord days, the great minds who claimed most of his attention were Kant, Goethe and Dante. Perhaps we should also include Shakespeare, for Harris was much interested in him also. As early as 1873 he had written an article on Shakespeare's historical plays for *The Western*, which was published the following year, while for Denton J. Snider's Shakespeare School, held in Chicago in 1889, he wrote more or less a continuation of the theme under the title of "Shakespeare as an Epic Poet". As in the case of other scholars in the last century, Harris' attention was drawn to the great bard particularly through German criticism, and it reflected no doubt his own experience when he wrote in his paper for Snider's School that "probably we all remember the feelings of astonishment and curiosity with which we came first upon the mention of Shakespeare in reading Goethe's *Wilhelm Meister*." However, Shakespeare was never present to the same degree in his mind as were the other three geniuses mentioned, nor did he allow for him the same place on Olympus.

THE KOENIGSBERGER

While Harris resided in St. Louis he organized, in 1874, a Kant Club; the St. Louis Philosophical Society was gradually dispersing, since many of its members sought fields of work outside St. Louis.[1] Members of the Kant Club included besides himself D. J. Snider, E. H. Long, F. E. Cook, T. R. Vickroy, G. H. Howison, Rev. Dr. Robert A. Holland, W. M. Bryant, James Garland, Lyman Whitney Allen, Grace C. Bibb, William Schuyler, Scott H. Blewett. It was this Kant Club which met half the expense of publishing Harris' translation of the Second Part of Hegel's *Larger Logic,* "Essence," with the assistance of James S. Garland.

Harris gave many interesting talks, some of a very personal nature, as the one dealing with his impression of his visit to Brokmeyer when the latter was living in Warren County, Missouri. The Kant Club continued to meet even after Harris' departure for Concord and whenever he returned to St. Louis it received a fresh impulse through him until it died a natural death about 1889 when his visits to St. Louis became fewer. It was especially active in 1881, when the Centennial of the publication of Kant's *Kritik der Reinen Vernunft* was celebrated. Already during the previous year Harris had lectured on Kant at the Concord Summer School, but in 1881, the School devoted a whole week in August to the great Koenigsberger.

Whether the Concord School's celebration was suggested by Professor Dr. John W. Mears of Hamilton College is not certain; but it was he who had engineered the celebration in the parlor of "Temple Grove" in Saratoga, July 6th, 1881. For this very successful meeting a number of prominent speakers had been invited, among others, Harris, George S. Morris, Josiah Royce, President Bascom of the University of Wisconsin, and Lester F. Ward of the U. S. Geological Survey. Harris spoke on "Can the 'Kritik' be fairly treated from the Ground of Hegelianism?"[2] and on "Kant and Hegel in the History of Philosophy."

The Concord celebration also went off well, and Mears "of genial face" spoke. Other lecturers were Mrs. Julia

Ward Howe, Rev. F. H. Hedge, J. Elliot Cabot, President Noah Porter, and Professor George S. Morris who took the place of Professor Carroll C. Everett.[3] Furthermore, in 1881 Harris brought out his article on "Centennial of Kant's Kritik";[4] published his review of John Watson's *Kant and his English Critics;* and in at least two articles in the *Journal of Speculative Philosophy* called particular attention to the problems raised by Kant and their historical settings.[5] He was always rather critical of Kant and was at odds with him on several counts, such as, the limits he assigned to knowledge, his rejection of St. Anselm's proof of the existence of God, and others.

One of the members of the Kant Club in St. Louis, Dr. Robert A. Holland, whom Harris had slated for a number of lectures in Concord, was one of the most active Kantians in the diaspora. A minister, he was a keen thinker and interested in things philosophical in a genuine way, not merely with an object to religious exploitation. In St. Louis he was known as "the most actively helpful" of their divines and had been invited to give lectures at Washington University, and when he moved to Chicago he carried with him the torch of the St. Louis Philosophical Society. In a letter, in 1882, to Harris[6] he wrote: "We are going to remove the western headquarters of Hegelian study from St. Louis to Chicago." He had founded Kant and Hegel Clubs and was apt in discovering talent, such as Lewis J. Block, Bierbower, and Tuthill; the last named with his own hand copied the entire manuscript of Hegel's *Larger Logic* in three volumes and made a number of translations. Holland called him a trump.

Thus had Harris' work in St. Louis borne fruit. But it was not only in Chicago that philosophical clubs modelled upon the St. Louis Society were founded. They sprang up everywhere, and we find them as far as Denver, Colorado.

ALSO FORTNIGHTLY 438

i'vs CHICAGO + DENVER

THE WEIMAR SAGE

A constant spiritual companion of Harris' was Goethe who had proven such a friend to him in his pioneering days in St. Louis. The prolonged association with Brokmeyer had only intensified his admiration for the genius to whom the deepest mysteries of man were like an open book which Harris likewise aspired to read in virtue of his philosophic insight. Much of the Goethean theory of pedagogy had been absorbed by the Connecticut Yankee and passed unnoticed into the School plan.

The very first volume of the *Journal of Speculative Philosophy* gave space to Goethe's theory of colors, and numerous were the occasions in the St. Louis Philosophical Society at which the Weimar sage was discussed. Harris' talk at the Boston Chestnut Street Club in 1881 was on *Faust*.[7] Publicly and in private parlors in many States[8] he contributed to the wave of Goethe enthusiasm that gripped America in the 80's. The 1885 season at Concord was given over almost completely to Goethe whose personality and work were discussed most ably by the majority of speakers, although some apparently had not grasped the Titan, for which they were flayed by Thomas Davidson, who knew no mercy in such matters. Harris spoke on *Faust* and the novelettes in *Wilhelm Meister,* the book he had always loved so well because it seemed to address itself to him especially.

The Milwaukee Literary School was almost wholly inspired by the St. Louis Movement in Philosophy and the Concord Summer School of Philosophy. During its first term, from August 23rd to the 28th, 1886, all lectures were given over to Goethe and held at Milwaukee College. Snider, Harris, Sanborn and Professor Hewett met together on this occasion. It almost was a reunion in the name of Goethe, with President John Johnston presiding.[9]

Goethe talks were given by Harris also at St. Louis, but

in December, 1888, ten Goethe lectures were offered in the Madison Street Theatre in Chicago by the Goethe Literary Club, with Denton J. Snider conducting the School. Again it was a meeting of old friends, with Davidson and Harris and Mrs. Caroline K. Sherman of Chicago as speakers, not to forget Professor Calvin Thomas of Michigan University who was a great student and teacher of *Faust*. Chicago really had made an effort to "get culture" in those pre-University days, and the discussions, with all of the speakers in splendid form, were befitting the proverbial rough and ready West. On one occasion, Davidson cast oil on troubled waters when the audience was decidedly in a skirmish to determine which of the women depicted by Goethe was the greatest and most commendable one. Harris urged not to judge the work of poets and artists by their biography for that would be misleading and mischievous. He himself spoke on "Faust" and "Goethe's Ideal of Man as Inculcated in Wilhelm Meister."

Essentially the same lectures were given less than a week later at St. Louis, which city had, under the leadership of Professor F. Louis Soldan, dedicated itself in pursuance of the ideals of Harris and the other St. Louis philosophers to the continuation of cultural studies. The lectures were given under the auspices of the Goethe School in the Guild Room of St. George's Church, which was Dr. Robert A. Holland's. The speakers all were old friends: Harris, Snider, Holland, Wm. M. Bryant, Soldan and Mrs. Sherman. Harris contributed four lectures, one being on "Goethe as a Scientist." Every talk he gave was to a crowded audience among whom could be discerned General and Mrs. John W. Noble, Judge Woerner and his daughters, Professor F. N. Judson, Major J. B. Merwin, and others who knew Harris intimately since the days of his Superintendency.

Once again in Chicago — it was in March, 1894, and the 7th Annual Meeting — the Literary School under Snider as Director, offered ten lectures on Goethe under the auspices of the Chicago Kindergarten College, the proceeds of which were to be donated to the work of establishing and maintaining Kindergartens in the poorest district of the city. Harris had become U. S. Commissioner of Education in the meantime and was attending to urgent duties, but on the 28th he contributed a lecture on "Goethe's Pedagogical Ideas," and on the 30th one on "Goethe's Sociology." In fact, he never relinquished his interest in Goethe, publishing an article on "Goethe's 'World Spirit' and Vishnu of the Bhagavad Gita," and one on "The Lessons of Goethe's Faust." Both were reprinted a number of times and when, in 1902, he talked before the Twentieth Century Club in Boston[10] on "Goethe's World View" and "Goethe's Solution of Twentieth Century Problems," he was interpreting Goethe's message even to us today.

THE GREAT FLORENTINE

Every time Harris spoke of Dante Alighieri, his face would brighten and his eyes shine. So his friends related. His interest was part of a general revival of interest in Dante not only in his native country, but in Germany and England as well, and it was beginning to spread to the great liberals in America, Emerson, Longfellow, Norton and Lowell.

It was in August, 1860, that Harris had begun his Dante study. Daily he read at least one Canto of the *Purgatorio*, discovering deep meanings as he proceeded. He found that Dante grew more interesting the farther he pried into the pure regions of paradise. He would read portions of the work with his friend Childs, and the two then revelled evening after evening in the great poem. At last, on September 17th, the final portions were finished and their mysticism noted.[11] General Ethan Allen Hitchcock had been gathering *Notes on the Vita Nuova and Minor Poems of Dante*, and from a letter to him we gather that he communicated to Harris some of his insights.[12] The book was published eventually and appreciatively referred to in the second volume of the *Journal of Speculative Philosophy*. The "skyey influence" of the General should not be forgotten as a real factor in Harris' Dante interpretation.

This Dante interest gradually led to a somewhat close relationship with scholars in Italy. When Joseph Defonfride, Harris' close friend in St. Louis who, under his guidance, had become an avowed Hegelian, had gone to France in 1867, he virtually had to flee that country as the "vain French are hostile to everything which is not French" and he was under suspicion because of his American citizenship and of what they called his *idées allemandes*.[13] This Defonfride met the Italian Hegelian A. Vera, a Professor of Philosophy in the University of Naples who at one time had held the same post in the University of France, and made him acquainted with the St. Louis Movement in Philosophy. After a few years of acquaintance by correspondence, Harris was able to afford Vera an opportunity to have his *Introduction to Speculative Logic and Philosophy* published.[14]

And again, it was Thomas Davidson who, in his Rosmini phase during his prolonged stay among the Italians at Domodossola and elsewhere, brought Harris together with scholars in Italy who were Dante enthusiasts. N. R. d'Alfonso, one among many, sent Harris his writings, while Harris, in turn, invited the Italian to contribute to the spread of Dante study by writing for the *Journal of Speculative Philosophy* and lecturing *in extenso,* at Concord. The Summer School did full justice to Dante in 1886 when the majority of lectures was given over to the interpretation of Dante and his works. It was in that session that Harris, forgetting his past experience with the Catholic opposition, invited Brother Azarius to speak on "The Spiritual Sense of the Divina Commedia," with the result that his tolerance and broadness were severely criticised in some quarters of the press. Although many of the speakers slated for the Dante program could not or did not want to appear, those that were present, like Edwin D. Mead, spoke in glowing terms about it.

Already in St. Louis Harris had created disciples for Dante, among them Susie Blow who wrote a book on Dante's work and lectured frequently on *Il Paradiso*, which she favored. Denton J. Snider established a Dante School in St. Louis during 1893, to which Harris contributed some essays. At the Literary School in Chicago, during the holidays at the end of 1887, some of the erstwhile members of the St. Louis Philosophical Society, Harris, Davidson, F. Louis Soldan and Miss M. E. Beedy, came together under the Directorship of Snider to present a program of ten lectures in the Art Institute in which many interesting phases of the great Italian's work were discussed.

Harris' book on *The Spiritual Sense of Dante's Divina Commedia*, first published in 1889 by D. Appleton & Co., was later brought out also by Houghton Mifflin Co., and Kegan Paul, Trench, Trübner & Co. in London. His essay on "Dante's Doctrine of Sin" was published in the 1890-91 *Yearbook of the American Dante Society*. In 1892, he was presented, as "the true interpreter of the Italian genius," by A. Oldrini with a bronze medal cast in the material of the monument to Giordano Bruno erected in the Campo di Fiori at Rome.

The Società Dante Alighieri in Washington had Harris lecture at the Royal Italian Embassy on "What Dante has done for other Nations." In recognition of the service Harris had thus rendered throughout the years to Italian literature, S. M. Umberto I, King of Italy, conferred upon him the title of Commander of the Order of St. Maurice and Lazarus, on August 4th, 1894. But Harris had also had conferences with his Majesty's Privy Councilor, Signor Bodio, in 1893, on the formation of statistical tables of education with a view to throwing the most light on a nation's statistics of education.

CHAPTER TWENTY-ONE

PRIVATE AND SOCIAL LIFE AT CONCORD

THE SPIRIT OF ORCHARD HOUSE

WHEN Harris lectured at the 1879 Summer School of Philosophy at Concord, he was the guest of S. H. Emery, Jr., and his brother-in-law, Edward McClure, at the Orchard House from which Alcott had moved in 1877 to take up residence at the Thoreau house on Main Street. The following year, Harris moved his belongings to Concord during the month of May, but did not break entirely with St. Louis until 1881. In 1884, he acquired Orchard House by purchase.

Now this house had a long history behind it. Quaint and low-studded, it was situated next to Hawthorne's "Wayside." During 1879, the School was held in its rooms, but with the erection of the Hillside Chapel next door on the vacant lot, the Harris family had the house entirely to itself. Over the mantelpiece stood a plaster of paris bust of the Juno Ludovisi, and next to it hung photographs of the statues of Pericles and Aspasia. At one side was placed a huge easy chair provided with a bookrest. The walls were concealed by rows upon rows of bookshelves which extended into the adjoining room, except where some engraving was hung. Pamphlets, loose and in covers, filled all the spaces not taken up by books. In the centre of the large room stood the writing desk with a typewriter to which was attached a large tray. The desk had two large folding wings equipped with pigeon holes and compartments of various shapes, while more pigeon holes crammed with letters, writing materials, papers and memos rose above the writing top. To the left, a dictionary, the edges of which Harris had lettered himself, swung conveniently into place on an arm extending from the desk. The whole desk presented such a formidable sight that it might well have been compared to a little fortress.

The Orchard House had atmosphere enough. The spirit of Amos Bronson Alcott hovered about, but above all it had been the home of the "Little Women," Jo, Meg, Amy and Beth. Only two of the four were still alive, Beth, or Elizabeth, having died when she was 14, and Amy, or May, having died in Paris after her marriage. Meg, or Anna, had married John Pratt and was destined to outlive her whole family. Jo, or Louisa May, was the one whom Harris had met on his first visit to the Alcott home in 1865. Harris never knew Hawthorne who was their neighbor, nor Henry David Thoreau.

At home, when visitors called, Harris would devote his time to them, no matter how busy he was. He never monopolized the conversation although he was bristling with ideas and eager to contribute his thoughts. His cordiality was genuine, but was never over-solicitous. Occasionally he would be full of fun and responsive to witticisms, buoyant and of exuberant spirit. His was a fine and unobtrusive wit, and a pleasing sense of humor that was as mellow as Mark Twain's who, by the way, was born in the same year as he.

His cheerfulness and kindliness attracted all to him, be they scholars or children. The latter were very fond of him. Professor James Hayden Tufts used to recall particularly his simplicity in expression, despite the fact that he was so steeped in the terminology of Hegelianism. Writing of a somewhat later period, but in spirit applicable to the present one, Professor Tufts said:[1] "As a visitor to the Deweys' home he was in high favor with the children because in conversation he never left them out, but would manage very skilfully to intersperse his conversation with such illustrations and paraphrases as to make even seemingly difficult subjects interesting to the younger members of the circle at the dinner table."

SOME INTIMATE GLIMPSES

Harris loved his family, but his studies at home consumed the major portion of the day and sometimes of the night. His son Theodore, who became a lawyer in San Antonio, Texas, commented on his very uneventful life as a scholar, "without incident or dramatic sequence," and yet, his career had more brilliancy than that of most scholars. He was in the lime-light of teachers and philosophers often enough while his family knew him merely as the patient, kind, retired student that he was. Hardly ever do we meet a man who so overshadowed his wife and children, who loved him self-effacingly. A book rested on a special tray on the arm-chair which was meant for relaxation, a book lay on the table while he ate his meal, a book stuck out of his pocket while he made his way to the station. Yet, he had his own inimitable way of showing his devotion. He easily accomplished the transition from the life of ideas to that of attentiveness to everyday affairs, and was always approachable and considerate.

In New England he felt very much at home. Intellectually and emotionally he was rooted there. He always retained a New England gait and manner of speech. He loved his old home and visited it, as well as the burial places of his ancestors. Even while at Washington later on he had water from Connecticut — from a spring locally famous in the town of his birth — sent to his house.

Early in January, 1881, he was present at the wedding of his sister Sarah Lydia to Andrew J. Morey, of Strafford, Vt., which took place at Putnam Heights. His brother Edward Mowry Harris had also come from Providence where he had attained prominence. Republican by persuasion, he was a Royal Arch Mason, a member of the What Cheer Lodge, A.F. & A.M., and organizer and President of the Providence Whist and Chess Club, himself the chess champion of the State for some time. In the same year that their sister married, Charles Joseph, who resided in Denver, Colorado, took Florence Rust to wife. Sister Mary Jane married in 1886, brother Edward Mowry in 1887, the year in which their sister Ellen Elizabeth passed away.

William Torrey's first grandchild, Ethan Torrey Harris, was born in 1881 in St. Louis, but died a year later in Concord. The second one was a girl, Florence Albee Harris. Born in 1883 at Concord, she died in North Carolina not quite eight years of age. However, three more grandchildren, Arthur Lines Harris, Edith Harris and Amy Harris made their appearance in later years and raised families, but their children never knew their great grandfather Harris. A sixth grandchild arrived shortly before the turn of the century, but died young.

Harris' mother lived in her own house in Putnam, occasionally visiting with the Danielson's. She could, indeed, be proud of her William's attainments while he, in turn, bore the name of Harris and of Torrey with pride. Ever and anon he discovered branches of his family tree that had, like himself, become of note. Thaddeus William Harris, the entomologist, he found, was related to him, and likewise Daniel L. Harris who was Mayor of Springfield, Mass., and Senator Ira Harris, of Albany, N. Y. Attorney General of the U. S., Alphonso Taft of Cincinnati, whom he met on several occasions and who came to listen to his lectures at Concord, was a relative through the Torrey line. And in this way, Harris was related to President Taft who was the son of the Attorney General.

Yet a more modest and frugal man than Harris never lived. He was not averse to the use of alcohol, but seldom indulged. Only very rarely, when social duty required it, he smoked a cigar. For his own very private enjoyment he played the violin, the flute and the cabinet organ and is said to have had a good baritone and tenor voice.

When jotting down ideas or taking lecture notes, he was offhand, and his writing would never suggest methodical-ness. Still, he was animated by a desire to have things per-fect or at least clear and transparently logical. Hence the many drafts of important letters, the corrections and addi-tions in the final machine-written letter or the proof. His letters had not only postscripts, but footnotes. He kept care-ful accounts of his personal expenditures and of every enterprise in which he was interested or with which he had to do. But more often than not, such records were only for him to decipher. He checked himself in speaking and in writing as he did in spending, but he did spend lavishly on books.

He became economical to the point of stinginess, so far as his own use of the minutes was concerned. He had all the time in the world to talk philosophy with an earnest student, debating with him, drawing him out, reaching for the book on the shelf and reading the pertinent paragraph. But with himself he was severe. From Goethe he had learned to apply reflection systematically to practical af-fairs. He laid out his work for the day, not merely with an eye to efficiency, but with a view to its fitness in the order of things.

The leisure he had sought at Concord would, in the words of Sanborn, have seemed the height of activity. Inspiration was at his side, especially when he lectured, while he worked assiduously over his manuscripts. Most of his literary productions are polished and not without a certain amount of literary flourish and flashes of brilliancy. He found that close application, followed by a period of "soaking," and a final period of intensive work without change of subject, accomplished the most difficult task for him.

There were some sayings that he liked which were original with him and reflected his outlook on life. Some are: "Every man has a match with which he can light his own hell." "Insight is the key of life." "Beauty is the splendor of truth." "Each knowledge you acquire opens up a new window of the soul."

THE SMALLER SOCIAL CIRCLE

"The few superior persons in each community are so by their steadiness to reality and their neglect of appearance," said Emerson, and he might have applied it directly to Harris. For, he was not given to making friends by crowds, but by ones and twos, as Dr. Elmer E. Brown wrote, who knew him well.

Harris took a moderate part in the social life of Concord, such as it was. Congregational services he attended rather regularly, presumably for his own satisfaction or for the sake of his family. He was elected to membership in the Social Circle of Concord, a rather exclusive club which celebrated its Sesquicentennial in 1932. His membership lasted from 1883 to 1894, long after he had taken up residence in Washington, D. C., and until his stay there was assured for an indefinite period.

Among a small circle of friends, Harris could forget all formality and air his personal views. But even then he would never attack a person; it was the thought that he criticized, while personal enmity never entered his mind. By virtue of this disposition, he would ever make new friends and never lose the old ones, except by death. Nor did he ever forget his friends. For instance, when traveling West, he would make it a point to stop off to see his publisher, C. W. Bardeen, at Syracuse, N. Y., or Susan Blow, at Cazenovia. No matter what the difficulties, he kept his appointments, and when inadvertently he had to let his host wait, he would make it up by cheerfulness, frankness and almost boyish friendliness which won everyone over and redeemed the day for his host.[2]

A PHILOSOPHER ATINKERING

At St. Louis, Harris took occasion to do gymnastics and thus kept fit. As a matter of fact, he had done so well for himself that a palmist once told him he should enter the prize ring and, with a month's training knock out Mike McCoole. Some unruly boys whom he asked to lug a pair of heavy dumbbells into his office, submitted to him with respect and admiration when he held the dumbbells out at arm's length as if they were feathers. His physical exercises were somewhat curtailed in his later busy years as Superintendent, while at Concord he confined himself to rowing, and walking, which latter sport the Concord wise men had developed into a fine art. He also constructed a craft, generally described as odd, which he floated on Concord River. He calculated in detail the effect of varying loads on another boat which he intended to construct and which seemed to have the unconventional design of a barge wedded to a canoe.

As much as he loved the river, he loved the mountains more. With his telescope under his arm, he would climb the hills, but the mere enjoyment of the scenery was not enough. Out of his coat pockets he pulled the maps he had collected and proceeded to identify every peak he could spy. And he did not rest until he had identified all and, perchance, discovered a mistake in the maps which some Club had issued. So fond was he of looking for mountains through his telescope that he built himself, near his Concord home, in the midst of a grove of pines, a tower fifty

451

feet in height from which he could scan the horizon in all directions. The tower consisted of a spiral stairway built around an especially tall pine.

The devices he had invented in his youth he was still tinkering with. Bookcases had to be made every so often for his library which had now reached the 5000 volume mark or over. He made them in sections. Bookrests on chairs, swinging tables or trays, all these things were designed to aid him in study and scholarship. Every new invention and practical device he would try to copy if he thought it useful, or he would try to acquire it and not rest satisfied till he had it. It was a Connecticut trait, as he himself acknowledged. And it was good so, for it afforded him a diversion and a creative release of which he stood in need.

Withall, he had more the mind of an engineer than that of a natural scientist. For he did not love nature in any romantic sense; he did not collect beetles or fossils or plants. Museum specimens did not mean very much to him. He knew their names better than anyone else not in the field. But only if they could be made to throw light on an idea, let us say that of dialectic development, or could be understood as playing an important role in the development affecting man, would he have studied them in detail.

CHAPTER TWENTY-TWO

TWO CALIFORNIA TRIPS

Studyng the Zuñi Pueblo at First-Hand

IN the summer of 1887, Mrs. Mary Hemenway, a wealthy lady of Boston who had frequently consulted with Harris about many of her philanthropic and educational interests, took him and his family with her in her private car to California. The trip she undertook in connection with her work for the Zuñi Indians.

She was both a friend and a helper to John Fiske, the noted historian. Harris became intensely interested in these Indians and the evidences of the red man in New Mexico and Arizona where Mrs. Hemenway was gathering data. He would theorize on the connection of these pueblos and their civilization with European and Asiatic history, and became so absorbed in the idiosyncrasies of the race and its institutions that he sent a long letter to John Fiske[1] who was also his personal friend, in which he set forth his ideas which, he made it clear, needed, of course, archaeological support. Here again it was the meaning that interested him most, as well as the significance the findings might have for understanding American history.

Philosopher and Charming Travelling Companion

Another trip to California occurred in the following summer. The 27th Annual Meeting of the National Educational Association was to be held at San Francisco. The Concord School of Philosophy had closed after the Alcott Memorial, leaving Harris free to undertake the trip which meant once more a change of scenery for him, as he was going out this time by a different route. Late in July, the train carried him West. He was not alone, for others were going to the meeting, among them Henry Turner Bailey, editor of the *School Arts Book* and sometime Director of the Chautauqua School of Arts and Crafts. On the homeward trip, Professor Langdon Thompson of Purdue University, and Hon. Adlai Stevenson, afterwards Vice President of the United States, joined the little party. They were travelling together in the Pullman and Harris had the table before him spread over with papers and a memorandum pad, his fountain pen being "at hand upon a little cardboard rest he had invented."

Every so often, discussion of a formidable nature arose which developed into lectures. For instance, when they stopped at Livingston, Montana, for supper, Harris delighted his travelling companions with a conversation on art which some thought more illuminating than any they had heard before. Another time he talked on eternal life. And again he would spend all day unfolding to his friends some of the secrets of symbolism. A chance quotation which Charles H. Ames had made from Dante's Inferno, had started him off. Bailey kept a close diary of the trip which proved to him exceedingly profitable in that it represented his initiation into philosophy. As a matter of fact, Harris persuaded him to study Hegel, which he did later, getting up at 5 o'clock every morning to be with Hegel for two hours before breakfast. He did not hesitate to call Harris his intellectual godfather. His notes are certainly interesting as throwing light on Harris at ease.[2]

"The Wasach Range from Denver; Grand Caverns; Manitou; Garden of the Gods; Grand Cañon of the Gunnison; Marshall Pass; Salt Lake; Cape Horn; Oakland; The Crystal Palace; the Great [National Educational Association] Convention; Chinatown; The Cliff House; The Golden Gate;

Shasta; Rogue River Valley; the view from Markham Hill, Portland; Yellowstone National Park; the Dakota Wheat Fields; — all worth the time and money the views cost me, ten times over. But it is not primarily for these that I rejoice and give thanks; it is for an acquaintance with a man, an acquaintance I could not possibly have acquired had I not attended the convention."

"Those were red-letter days! The Doctor gave new and amusing names to the geysers, recounted the geologic history of the Park, lamed us with laughter by reading and commenting upon a dime novel he found in a Hotel bedroom, a lurid 'life' of Jesse and Frank James; quoted from memory and interpreted a half-dozen of Emerson's poems, reviewed Dante, revealed the meaning of the second part of *Faust*, beat us all at trout fishing, told us the names of all the flowers and birds we found, and upon challenge called the names of 'a hundred English poets as great as Longfellow or greater'!"

At the convention, Harris contributed to five departments of the National Educational Association and was one of the most popular speakers.

CHAPTER TWENTY-THREE

"BUT, MR. PRESIDENT, I VOTED
FOR CLEVELAND"

W HILE Harris was closing the affairs of the Concord Summer School of Philosophy, the country was deeply embroiled in the issues of civil service, Tammany Hall, and the tariff. Harris, though a Republican at heart, sided with the Democrats in their renomination of Grover Cleveland at the party convention in St. Louis, June 5th, 1888.

PAVING THE WAY FOR THE NEW COMMISSIONER
OF EDUCATION

Late in November, 1888, Harris received a letter from William A. Bell, editor of the *Indiana School Journal*, Indianapolis, informing him that several of his friends had been talking of the next School Commissioner, because the victory of Benjamin Harrison had made a change in administration necessary or desirable from a party point of view, and they had decided that he was "the best man in the United States for the place".[1] The first question put to him was whether he had voted Republican. Although it would not have made any difference to the educators which way he had voted, Bell thought it would with the appointing power. Only in the second place did he ask Harris whether he would accept the place if it were tendered him. Harris took a week to think it over and wrote Bell[2] that while he was flattered by their confidence, he had not been able to see his way "to the point of saying yes" to the ques-

456

tion as to whether he could accept the position of United States Commissioner of Education if it were offered to him. Harris' friends, of course, had assumed that he had voted the Republican ticket.[3]

In the meantime, more than one group of educational interests anticipated a change in the Commissionership as a corollary to the change in administration, and Harris came prominently into the picture. Thus, the Boston University lectures which he had given and which, apparently, had been arranged by A. E. Winship, the editor of the *Journal of Education* and *The American Teacher*, with the co-operation of Dean Huntington and President Warren, and which, moreover, were well-attended and well-spoken of in the press, had put the thought of Harris strongly in the minds of a number of persons as a possible candidate. Charles H. Ames, the Secretary of the Prang Educational Company and a man of some influence in educational circles, apprised Harris, his very good friend, of the fact that inasmuch as General Noble seemed to be booked for a Cabinet position, he might have an influence on the appointment of the Commissioner of Education.[4] Then too, Senator Hoar, who was favorably impressed with the report of Harris' lectures in the *Boston Daily Advertiser*, suggested the appointment of Harris.

James M. Greenwood, representing still another interest, told the Missouri State Teachers' Association meeting at St. Louis on December 28th, 1909, the following. It was during the week of President Harrison's inauguration that the Department of Superintendence of the National Educational Association was convening in Washington, D. C. Knowing that an appointment was to be expected soon, "several city and state superintendents had their political lightning rods stuck up hoping lightning would strike". But all, with one exception, agreed that Harris was the man, and Greenwood broached the subject at a private luncheon with Harris. The latter expressed willingness to accept the office if tendered him, but he thought it unlikely in view of the Democratic vote he had cast and his open opposition to the high tariff on works of art. If nothing else, this frank discussion with Greenwood shows that the superintendents the country over as a block were behind Harris, and their combined opinion must have weighed heavily with the President in his decision to offer Harris the Commissionership.

An inside story is offered us by Dr. Nicholas Murray Butler who has given an interesting account of his connection with the appointment of Harris in his autobiography *Across the Busy Years*.[5] The Office of Commissioner of Education was first offered to Dr. Butler, a very young man then, when he was sent for by President Harrison shortly after his inauguration on March 4th, 1889. Dr. Butler thanked the President most warmly for the compliment but could not be persuaded to deviate from the course he had set for himself, and suggested Harris as a candidate, referring the President to the Secretary of the Interior, General Noble, who had known Harris intimately in that he had served on the Board of Public Schools in the city of St. Louis.

General Thomas J. Morgan, Principal of the State Normal School at Providence, R. I., was also thought of by many as the most likely candidate for the position, and he received strong support, in fact, his name seems to have been under actual consideration for a time; but President Harrison apparently was awaiting developments. Early in May, 1889, he called upon his friend General Morgan to express his opinion of Harris as possible Commissioner of Education. Then, finally, in June, Morgan was summoned to choose between the Educational Bureau and the Indian Bureau in Washington, and he took the latter at the suggestion of the President and probably also because of other considerations, such as the higher salary and the fact that the work was much more to his liking. He notified Harris of his decision[6] and at the same time told him of the President's enquiries about him. He assured Harris that it would afford him "the highest possible satisfaction" to see him in that office and as a token of sincerity he enclosed the signed copy of his letter of May 7th, 1889, addressed to "Gen. Benjamin Harrison, My Dear Friend" in which he said:

On Sunday you asked me my opinion of Dr. Harris as Comm. of Education. As I look the field over I do not know of any man in the country who is, on the whole, so well qualified for the office as he is. He is a strong, noble, christian gentleman, has the most accurate acquaintance with our school system, is a deep and clear thinker, very forcible writer, is more widely known among educational men than any other educator, and is universally esteemed for his character, talents, and attainments. I think his appointment would give great satisfaction.

In the meantime, also, Col. Francis W. Parker, Principal of the Cook County (Illinois) Normal School, addressed a letter to the President of the United States, written June 28th, 1889, urging Harris' appointment as Commissioner of Education and stating that "Dr. Harris is the acknowledged head of educational affairs in the United States. By officially recognizing the leadership you [meaning President Harrison] would receive the profound thanks of 400,000 teachers."

FACT AND FANCY ABOUT THE APPOINTMENT

Now, the stories which Winship published in the *Journal of Education*[7] are a bit jumbled in that he was over-anxious to bring out the fact that he had much to do with the appointment of Harris. After discounting the fanciful in his accounts, the fact remains that he had backed Morgan very strongly at first, but, when he was no longer a candidate, went out equally strongly in support of Harris. His campaign for Harris, first by editorials in the Boston press and then throughout the country in Republican papers, may, as he claimed, have been instituted at the suggestion of President Harrison himself. He thus did contribute to overcoming any prejudices among politicians against Harris whom they had scored as a Mugwump. And it is also true, no doubt, that Harris spent some anxious months in waiting for the appointment that was felt would come with certainty.

On June 11th, 1889, Winship wrote Harris in joyful tones about the withdrawal of Morgan, adding: "I hope each day to see your appointment as Commissioner of Education", and asking him for photographs of himself "right away" for publication in the *Journal of Education,* as soon as the news should break. Two days later he informed Harris that he had "what seems to be pretty reliable information" that he would be invited to enter upon the duties as Commissioner the first of August.

Harris in the meantime had made an enquiry of General John W. Noble, Secretary of the Interior, regarding the rumors involving him, especially in view of the fact that he was planning his trip to Europe and the Paris Exposition. On June 14th, the Secretary was not yet able to give him the desired information, but on the 18th he wrote another letter stating that he had not learned "whether that promise or expression of intention has been made", but that Harris "of course understands" General Noble's desires which "have long since been expressed" and "may be working out." He should not wait to sail to Europe; he would cable him if anything came up.

THE CANDID INTERVIEW

Things came quickly to a head after this. Harris was called to Washington by telegram and the famous interview in the White House took place. When President Harrison offered him the Commissionership, Harris protested that, he did not believe in the high tariff on works of art the Republicans had adopted and that he, although a Republican, had voted in the last elections for Grover Cleveland. Indeed, Harris had written some articles for the *New York Independent*, championing Grover Cleveland and denouncing Republican politics. To this, the President replied: "That makes no difference; the educators of the country want you as Commissioner of Education."

The appointment, however, was still uncertain when Harris, with his wife and daughter Edith, sailed on July 27th for Europe. It had been Harris' intention to spend three months abroad with his family. But they had hardly arrived in Paris when a cable was received in care of Hottinguer, 38 Rue de Provence, apprising him of the appointment:

APPOINTED COMMISSIONER EDUCATION SALARY THREE THOUSAND COMMENCE SEPTEMBER THIRD COUNTRY MUCH PLEASED ACCEPT.
JOHN W NOBLE SECRETARY INTERIOR

On August 6th, Secretary Noble also dispatched a letter to Harris transmitting his commission from the President, notifying him that Nathaniel H. R. Dawson's resignation would take effect September 3rd, 1889, and urging him to enter on duty, if he accepted the appointment, as soon after that date as convenient. It was a great disappointment to Mrs. Harris that her first trip to Europe was so shortened to six weeks.

At the Exposition, Harris was joined by a certain Mr. Clark of Keokuk, an editor and a "cultivated gentleman" who, being a close friend of Secretary Noble, had been given the chance to go to Europe because of his ill health.[8] Harris was to bring back the official report on education for the Bureau of Education, upon the invitation of Col. Dawson.[9] The French bestowed on Harris a second title for his efforts in behalf of education, that of *Officier de l'Instruction Publique.*

When the public learned of the appointment of Harris as Commissioner of Education, many were the well-wishers and congratulations began to pour in from various sources. Some revealed their contribution toward the appointment; Massachusetts claimed credit, so did St. Louis, also the friends that Harris had in Indianapolis and in Chicago. Every Republican paper lent him support, except the *New York Tribune* and the Chicago *Inter-Ocean,* while the Democrats, naturally, were delighted over their victory. The educational press was solidly behind the appointment.

On the day that Col. Dawson received his notification of the acceptance of his resignation and confirmation of the report that Harris was to be his successor, the Commissioner sent Harris a letter of congratulation.[10] However, his intention to welcome him to the Bureau and to see him enter upon its duties, was not carried out. For, he wrote him later from Selma, Alabama, that he would be unable to be in Washington to receive him, but commended the office staff of clerks to his consideration and wished him well in his new position.[11]

On September 12th, 1889, Harris assumed office, being the fourth United States Commissioner of Education.

Part Five

WASHINGTON PERIOD

CHAPTER TWENTY-FOUR

SEVENTEEN YEARS AT THE HEAD OF
THE NATION'S SCHOOLS

THE OFFICE AND THE MAN

HARRIS' hair was now turning gray. He was, as Dr. Elmer E. Brown said, the acknowledged leader of Public School Education in the United States and none better than he could have been offered the post as United States Commissioner of Education. As a matter of fact, his appointment "brought great prestige to the Bureau of Education because of his distinction". When Harris received his LL.D. from Yale, the President said it was more an honor to the college than to the man; the case was similar in regard to the Bureau. The office had been held in respect, to be sure, before Harris, but it was considered generally as implying the publication of educational literature and drawing a comfortable salary, both of which, it was hinted, Harris would do "with as much dignity as any man that could have been selected". Those who wrote this and characterized the office as one of innocent idleness, little realized the amount of labor Harris was prepared to do.

Harris was a man from the ranks of the American people. He really was the first to hold office without benefit of aristocratic background, except, of course, in a spiritual sense. He was preceded by Henry Barnard who had served from March 14th, 1867, till his resignation in 1870. It was he who had created the Office of Education out of thin air, as it were. He was succeeded by General John Eaton who served

465

from March 17th, 1870, till 1886. Harris at one time had signed with Philbrick and seven others a petition to E. P. Seaver to retain John Eaton in office. The immediate predecessor of Harris, N. H. R. Dawson, was a Colonel and a Southerner from Alabama, who was not a teacher by profession. While he emphasized particularly higher education, General Eaton had established the routine of reports and the methods of gathering information regarding education in the United States, generally. These three represented, according to T. B. Ford,[1] the formative period of the Bureau. Harris represented the period of transformation. He gave the broad scope that it has maintained ever since in its present scientific period.

Harris had never entered politics directly, except to write some articles of a partisan nature. The politicians often had some goodnatured fun with him. He needed coaching, for now he dealt not with a city board but with the intricacies of national government. The "Bureau" had grown out of the National Educational Association whose Department of Superintendence, in February, 1866, had memorialized Congress regarding the formation of a clearing house of educational information. Even though President Johnson had signed the bill on March 2nd, 1867, to establish a "Department of Education", it was abolished on July 22nd of the following year, and the Office of Education, later known also as the Bureau of Education, was established instead in the Department of the Interior. All that was required by law of the Bureau, was "to collect statistics and facts showing the condition and progress of education in the several States and Territories, and to diffuse such information respecting the organization and management of schools and school systems, and methods of teaching, as shall aid the people of the United States in the establishment and maintenance of efficient school systems, and otherwise promote the cause of education throughout the country". The Commissioner was to incorporate his findings and recommendations in a report. The Bureau did not exercise any direct control over schools, except those in Alaska. Thus, it will be seen that the educational field under the supervision and scope of the Bureau was decidedly limited, perhaps due to a distrust in political efficiency and in part due to the belief in local self-government. As evidence of the first might be cited the fact that the management of the schools in the Philippines was awarded to the War Department, that of agricultural schools to the Department of Agriculture, and that of the Indian schools to the Indian Bureau.

Harris imparted to the Bureau its deeper meaning as a center of information and recommendation in conformity with democratic ideals that call for a sharing of knowledge and the passing on of profitable experience to those who care to have it, for the benefit of all. No other man was, indeed, better qualified to do this than our philosopher who, more clearly than anyone before or possibly since, had rationalized the democratic outlook so thoroughly and had applied it so successfully in education as well as in his dealings with people. Just as he maintained that in the five coordinate branches taught in the public schools, the windows of the soul are opened and the pupil may share in the experience of the race, so the Office of Education opened wide its files so that each school, college and university might see and profit by the experience of all, saving untold trouble and expense involved in individual effort. Thus, Harris' work consisted in answering enquiries about educational matters, sending out documents, filing news and reports, recording and classifying information, tabulating data, collecting statistics, distributing literature, indexing, reading, clipping, making schedules, editing, furnishing reports and summaries, issuing bulletins and bibliographies, making out vouchers, and receiving visitors. Even long before he became Commissioner, he was, in a way, unofficially connected with the Bureau. For, on several occasions he had been asked to represent the Bureau and to write circulars of information for which he received an honorarium.[2]

The home of the Bureau remained, during the 17 years of Harris' administration, in the Wright Building, a brick structure at the corner of Eighth and G Streets, opposite the Patent Office Building, and it occupied three floors. Harris had his office in the corner room on the second floor, with windows on both streets. A bust of Plato was placed in the lobby of the second floor. Immediately upon taking office, Harris co-ordinated all the information that had been gathered by his predecessors and made it available for ready reference. He established permanent contact with more than 20,000 educational centers in the States and kept accurate records. One of his concerns, as it had been in St. Louis, was the library which became a most valuable adjunct to the Bureau. He introduced into it the system that Melvil Dewey had made famous, a modification of his own.[3] The number of books alone grew from 100 under Barnard to 18,000 under Eaton and 23,000 under Dawson, to 86,000 under Harris. The number of pamphlets exceeded this figure by 11,000, bringing the total number of items close to 200,000. A number of specialists were attached to the Bureau under his administration, such as a specialist each in foreign educational systems, city school systems, art education, historical research and statistics, agricultural colleges, and Alaskan education. A specialist in charge of Land Grant College statistics was also added. The work was organized further into editorial, statistical, correspondence and record. The Division of International Exchange was added to the Bureau "for the comparative study of national school systems". A great deal of attention was paid by Harris to the museum which was with the foreign section of the library, but which never had adequate space for display. The whole Bureau remained cramped. Rather late, Harris was authorized to publish educational bulletins,[4] but the first one did not come out until 1906.

"Frank", a colored boy, served Harris as messenger. Dr. Henry Ridgely Evans, before becoming librarian, acted as his private secretary for three years; then his place was taken by Charles E. Waters. Mr. Lovick Pierce, the son of Bishop Pierce of the Southern Methodist Church of Georgia, was chief clerk. This Lovick Pierce, as M. Stevens related, had inherited a bishop's relish for a joke and carried a certain military precision into his multifarious duties. Miss Anna Tolman Smith, who had already been in the Bureau under General Eaton, now had charge of foreign and editorial work.

Harris' salary was fixed at $3000, the same as for Henry Barnard beginning with his second year in office, and the lowest of any Commissioner or Director in the National Government. Yet, he never asked for a raise. All the employees of the Bureau were likewise underpaid, and not until it became certain that Harris was not able to keep his specialists of ability, did he ask for a proportional increase in their salaries.[5] He brought out the fact that it was "quite difficult to get the attention of Congress to the salaries of this small Bureau". Wm. H. Sims, First Assistant Secretary, took up the matter of Harris' salary and made a very strong plea in his letter[6] to the Secretary of the Interior of December 7th, 1896. He stressed the fact that Harris, with a national and international reputation "both as an educator and a man of letters" drew for his services a salary "but equal to that received by many subordinate school officials in the large cities of the country". "No bureau of this Department", he added, "is, in my judgment, doing better or more useful work than the Bureau of Education. Under the present Commissioner the foundations laid are philosophic, unsectional, and statesmanlike. With rare tact and with modest appreciation of the delicate functions of his Bureau, he endeavors to avoid friction with the State and local systems of education, and yet to point them to the way and stimulate each community to higher and broader work." The Secretary of the Interior, D. R. Francis, was wholly in accord and made his plea on the strength of preserving and raising the dignity of the Bureau of Education. When Harris learned that his own salary was to be raised, he asked that the increase contemplated be distributed equally among the employees of the Bureau. President Theodore Roosevelt was very much surprised when Dr. Nicholas Murray Butler brought it to his attention that none of the salaries in the Bureau were higher than $1800.[7]

As to the budget of the Bureau, Harris has been severely criticised in that he did not ask often enough for an increase in appropriations. The total amount for the Bureau in 1897, for instance, was only $52,000, plus $42,000 for education in Alaska. Perhaps he deserved criticism for this failure, but we must also remember that, especially during 1892-93, there lay a depression over the country, and he knew that it would be futile to ask for more funds.

During his administration, the Bureau of Education was, as one of his successors, Dr. Philander Priestley Claxton, once pointed out, really a one-man office. He and Barnard were called to the office strictly on merit, while Eaton and Dawson entered through politics. Harris continued in office till 1906, when he requested that his resignation be accepted. He was appointed by a Republican President when he voted for a Democratic one, re-appointed by Grover Cleveland when he had returned to the Republican fold, and retained in office by both McKinley and Theodore Roosevelt, irrespective of his political views. In 1897, a Committee headed by State Superintendent Charles R. Skinner, of New York, the president of the National Educational Association, and Professor Nicholas Murray Butler, of Columbia University, called upon President McKinley by appointment to urge the retention of Harris in office, presenting documents to him by such prominent educators as Charles W. Eliot, James B. Angell, and many others; stronger and more representative documents, they believed, had never been presented to any President of the United States. Thus, throughout his tenure of office, Harris had the full support of American educators, no matter in what field of education they labored.

SOME OF MANY PROBLEMS

It was Ossian Lang who regretted that the Bureau of Education was, through "jealously guarded local prerogatives" prevented from becoming "a powerful lever for educational improvement throughout the United States". If we judge such leverage by its limitations in a democratic nation, it would seem that under Harris the Bureau was of considerable influence. In one of the discussions of De-Garmo's articles, Harris stated, perhaps more clearly than anywhere else, not only his position in regard to Herbartianism and the flowerpot theory of education, but revealed very strikingly the prime motivation in all his educational endeavors:

> the pride and glory of human nature,
> the freedom of the will,
> the independence of the ego, and
> the moral as the form of freedom.[8]

Harris is best characterized as a conservative progressive, as regards his work in the Bureau. In a letter to Dr. Nicholas Murray Butler[9], after asking for positive suggestions, he confessed that he was not wedded to the present system but wished "to see how the Office could be increased in usefulness by the addition of new functions". Dr. Butler shared Harris' view that under President Theodore Roose-

velt's administration and "with such a commission" as had
been appointed "to inquire and report upon the work of
the Scientific Bureaus", something definite would be accomplished for the Bureau.[10] He never slackened in thinking up new ways in which to extend the usefulness of the
Bureau. As an example, he contemplated, as late as 1905,
installing in the museum in the top of the Bureau "a really
good educational exhibit."[11]

So many were the problems that came to Harris' attention and the solutions offered by him that only a few can
be considered. The Land Grant Colleges were Harris'
concern and he agitated in 1895 for the establishment of
an office in the Bureau which should deal exclusively with
these problems.[12] Previous to that, in 1891, he had drawn
up a bill "to establish an educational fund to aid in the
support of public schools in the several States and Territories." In 1900 he came out with the idea of giving Civil
Service Examinations to teachers. In 1903 he prepared a
report on dental practitioning.[13] In 1905 he suggested
Presidential action in appointing a Committee of University Presidents to draft a law preventing the issuing of
bogus diplomas in medicine, dentistry and other fields.

Problems of freedom, individualism, over-education, hygiene, physical exercise, arrested development in children,
the workshop in common schools, the monitorial system,
nationalization in education, reared their heads and now
called for advice that would benefit not merely a city school
system, but the nation. With the little red school house in
mind, which had meant so much in his own education, he
brought about, as Dr. Elmer E. Brown has put it so well,
the "widely shared conviction among our people that the
little schools and the largest ideas belong together and are
not to be put asunder". He held on to the conviction
gained in practical experience that promotion was more apt
to be beneficial when quarterly instead of yearly. With

472

eminent educators he discussed publicly the difficulties involved in the grading of country schools. Throughout, he favored the six grade system over the seven, eight or nine grade systems. Already at St. Louis, when Principal of Clay School, he had to make concessions in this respect at the special request of Ira Divoll.[14]

In accord with his idea of stimulating the pupil to higher ideas, he favored covering the walls of the school room with replicas of the masters. Having been one of the first to introduce the study of nature into a public school system, he supported endeavors in that direction. No subject escaped his scrutiny, from teaching cookery in the schools to the place of the YMCA in education. He continued to speak on one of the most formidable problems throughout his career, the separation of the church from the school supported by public taxes. He spoke in favor of teaching music at school, believing in the saying "Let me make the songs of a people and I care not who makes their laws". With particular interest he followed the development of the High School which he considered, since early days, an integral part of the public school system, a sort of substitute for college, a "Peoples' College". He contributed much to the revamping of the teaching of geography, by sitting in on national and other committees, and aided Col. Parker in revolutionizing the teaching of this fundamental subject.[15] He was instrumental in shortening the time of learning at school and gaining, in consequence, time in the curriculum for teaching other subjects that help the pupil in broadening his horizon. And yet, he never exercised dictatorial powers or overstepped the boundaries of his office. But so universal was his prestige that whatever he suggested was looked upon with favor in educational circles. Especially through the medium of the National Educational Association and its various departments that took in the whole range of educational subjects and methods and reached every teacher, principal and superintendent in the country, did he exert a powerfully suggestive influence. It was not strange, then, that the educational thinking in the eighties and nineties of the past century was largely governed by the same trend of thought that Harris knew so well how to convey.

Nevertheless, new ideas were pressing to the fore, and there were clashes. With remarkable dexterity and insight Harris was able to discern the valuable in the new from the fads. Perhaps nothing was criticized by him so severely as the idea of a school city. To train a child in the ways of those who are responsible for the type of government we have, not the type we wish for, seemed utterly preposterous to him and diametrically opposed to the meaning of education. Then the cry "ambidexterity" was raised; but Harris again saw through the unfertile nature of such a concept. Again, "no recess" became the watchword for many teachers, yet it proved too ephemeral to even draw forth much discussion from Harris. Such suggestions, to his mind, did not touch the core of education at all.

But there was one educational idea against which he fought less successfully, that of overemphasizing manual training. He feared that too much "training" would war against the purpose of education in a democracy where care must be exercised not to limit a person's capacities for experience, but to give him as much opportunity as possible to explore and understand and thus find the place for which his individuality prepared him. He wanted the manual training school separate from the common school which he regarded as an "unmixed good"; for it gave to the youth "a greater amount of directive power than any other equal expenditure of effort can possibly do". The common school to him offered a sort of labor-saving machinery for the acquisition of knowledge. "The illiterate works with the unaided hand." Not so the educated man who has been reinforced, as it were, by the intelligence of the race.[16]

The matter of teaching Latin and Greek assumed larger importance with Harris the more he occupied himself with it. Some time in 1908 or '09 he wrote out the whole development of his thought, compiling a fairly complete list of the papers he had contributed to the subjects of the educational value of these ancient languages. When he wrote his letter, "A Brief for Latin and 'Christian Brother' Schools in the U.S.", to the Secretary of the Interior in 1898, and talked to the National Association of Faculties of the Agricultural and Mechanical Colleges that met at Washington in December, 1906, he had departed radically from the convictions that had made him leave Yale. He confessed in that informal talk that since three quarters of the words in the English dictionary are composed of Latin derivatives, he had gained a tremendous advantage over his friends and associates at St. Louis by his knowledge of Greek and Latin which were called the "college fetich" by Charles Francis Adams, Jr. He cited the Shakespearean phrase "the multitudinous seas incarnadine", in which the last word is usually understood as an adjective instead of a verb which it is. Latin, he thought, belongs definitely to the vestibule of education.

Dr. James T. Jardine, Chief, Office of Experiment Stations, United States Department of Agriculture, referred on one occasion[17] to the interest which Harris manifested in the development of agricultural education, and that this interest was "a very helpful factor in the progress that was made. His cooperation with the land-grant institutions in various ways, but specifically in helping them to reduce the teaching of agriculture to concrete pedagogical form was timely and fruitful, and this phase of his activities should not be overlooked in an appraisement of his unique services to education". Thus, he lent his support to the founding of the Farmers' Educational Association, addressed various bodies, such as the Association of American Agricultural Colleges and Experiment Stations in 1894 on "Teaching of Agriculture", or wrote personal letters and messages to persons prominent in the field of training in agriculture.[18]

While his *Reports,* which he transmitted by letter to the Secretary of the Interior annually, were of even greater importance than his famous St. Louis reports and carried great weight with the persons in responsible positions, his personal influence was extended in lectures, of course, and conversations, but also in a voluminous correspondence which often found its way into print. It covered a wide selection of subjects, and only a few may be named among the ones that were made public. There is a letter on corporal punishment addressed to I. H. Sturgeon (1891); a letter to Rhoden Mitchell, Principal of Rankin Richards Institute, North Carolina (1891); another to E. P. Dahlgren on Catholics and Protestants in the Public Schools (1892); a letter on the "Separation of Institutions forming State University of Montana, or their Concentration into one Institution" (1892); an epistle on art education to John S. Clark (1893); one to J. G. Harris, State Superintendent of Education on the educational campaign in the State of Alabama (1893); there are letters to Charles Wm. Eliot, as Chairman of the Committee of Ten (1903), George Pliny Brown, Henry Sabin, and many others.

In answer to an inquiry by Dr. Charles Franklin Thwing, then President of Western Reserve University[19] as to what he regarded "as among the greater worths of the work of the Bureau", Harris made jottings on the letter which reveal that he did not regard the collecting of statistics alone as of prime importance, but their interpretation as well. It may not be too exaggerated what J. M. Greenwood once stated, that there were perhaps not ten men in the U. S. who could interpret statistics in an intelligible manner, but Harris was one of them. Indeed, Harris made very extensive use of statistics; he was even fond of them, yet he was level-headed and philosophical and saw them in proper perspectives. He refused to be misled by what he called "hysterical statistics" which aided rather in garbling truth than in revealing it. He campaigned for "sound and health-giving statements of fact" and on one occasion flayed the neophyte in statistics on crime and religion as one who would compare only numerators but omit the denominator.

The emphasis on "moral education" which was characteristic of Harris, had nothing of the schoolmastery, moralizing, and Philistine about it. "The idea of regularity, punctuality, silence and industry as the cardinal school virtues, and relation of these virtues to the others" — that was what Harris understood by morality in the schools.[20] But, further than that, he made a most remarkable contribution in building up, within the Bureau, the Department of Education as a Preventive of Pauperism and Crime. It was he who memorialized Congress on this and Congress acted favorably in 1891, and, in consequence, Dr. Arthur McDonald was appointed specialist.

For the 52nd Congress, the Secretary of the Interior, John W. Noble, transmitted Harris' significant report on the city schools of the District of Columbia, in which he urged particularly a system of Kindergartens to "reach the spoiled child of the rich" who is wont to rule and dominate by virtue of his education under nurses and governesses, and "gather in the children of the slum at a sufficiently early age to cure them". Thus, more than a problem of pedagogy, the Kindergarten to him became an unqualified good in society, for without it the children of the rich produce "as much injury to the community as the criminals of the slums". He never tired in crusading for the Kindergarten and wrote much in its defence and spoke oftener, in New York, Chicago, St. Louis, Pittsburgh and the West, and being Commissioner of Education he gave to his statements the weight of title and position.

One of the significant testimonies which Harris gave as Commissioner was at the meeting of the Industrial Commission at its offices in Washington, D. C., on January 11th, 1899, with Vice-Chairman Phillips presiding. The 52-page pamphlet incorporating this report, valuable in itself for the statistics, is of special importance in that it summarizes his stand in regard to education, capital, labor and production, and bears witness to his unbounded faith in the American experiment over against any of the European ones.

Most of the enquiries concerning matters under the jurisdiction of the Bureau, were addressed to Harris directly. It could almost be said that educators knew Harris better than they did the Bureau of Education. In his career he had spoken to tens of thousands and by his articles he had reached many more. His principle of self-estrangement, as the basis of all education, may not have been understood by all, but it was the most fruitful single idea which he put to work in whatever he wrote, for it explained to him, steeped as he was in the Hegelian dialectic, the many processes and facts of education. Some of his most important writings, as "The Isolation of the School: Its Educational Function," contain as nucleus this thought. The business of the school he interpreted not as a "raising" and "training", but as "education", which has to do, on the one hand, with the subsumption of the pupil to his species and environment, but, on the other, strives to emancipate that individual to the worth-while and higher things in life, in brief, the eternal values. For that reason he could not view the problems of the Kindergartens, the grade schools, the high schools, the colleges and universities, in isolation.

He strove to articulate the entire education that is being offered through public agencies, and it was during his administration that this big undertaking was beginning to take shape. The work could not have been started from the top, by adjusting the curricula of the higher educational institutions; it had to start from below, with helping public school education to achieve that form and content which would ease and encourage the educational venture of the individual at a later date, be that education gotten at university or in the school of life itself. We cannot help but feel that the vision of Harris will yet be more fully appreciated when we are able to gain the proper distance and perspective in surveying the mushroom growth of American education. It is that vision, that may not always have been transparent in the conservatism which Harris seemed to favor unduly, which made him, nevertheless, easily the foremost figure among educators everywhere. Harris was not a teacher of the young merely, he was a teacher of teachers who could imbue them with a sense of the dignity of their profession and inspire belief in the ideals of education and thus, to speak with Josiah Royce, through compelling loyalty to a cause, help them in achieving the supreme thing in life.

Reindeer and Education

The visitor to the Bureau of Education during Harris' Commissionership would have been struck by a room on the first floor of the Wright Building whose walls were concealed by huge maps and an assortment of implements of primitive tribes, while a totem pole added to the picturesqueness. It was the Alaskan room in which the Alaskan Division of the Bureau carried on its functions of administering the education of that territory. If Harris had been guiding the visitor, he would have told him jokingly that one of his principal duties as Commissioner of Education consisted in counting and protecting herds of reindeer in Alaska.

The schools of Alaska were charged to the Office of Education during 1884 when General Eaton was Commissioner. But it was not until Col. Dawson's term that Rev. Dr. Sheldon Jackson, who for years had been active as a Presbyterian missionary in the great American West and of late among the tribes of the new territory, was appointed General Agent of Education in Alaska. He was serving on the slender salary of $1200, but had a desk in the Bureau of Education, and his travelling expenses were paid. Harris became intensely interested in the activity of this vigorous man and his important work, and a deep friendship resulted.

It was on December 26th, 1890, that Harris, realizing with much sympathy the plight of the natives of Alaska, forwarded a letter to the Secretary of the Interior in which he reminded him of a report from Dr. Jackson which described the dire condition of the Eskimos of arctic Alaska who had been driven to the verge of starvation because of the depletion of the whale, the walrus, the seal, the sea-lion, and the sea-otter upon which these people had depended for food. The situation was brought about by the wholesale slaughter of these animals by the whalers and the hunters for ivory, while the ever increasing canning industry had almost wholly depleted the fish supply, thus leaving the Eskimo without any food whatsoever. Whole villages were dying out as a consequence. As an alternative to shipping food to the natives, a costly and inexpedient way of keeping them alive, Jackson suggested the introduction of domesticated reindeer from Siberia, the reindeer being "food, clothing, house, furniture, implements and transportation to the people". The extensive tundras in Alaska being covered with a long, fibrous white moss, *Cladonia rangiferina*, might provide natural food for the animals, while artesian wells also abounded. The government would realize its portion by taxing the industry.

Harris was strongly in favor of the whole scheme and recommended the purchase of a herd of Siberian domesticated reindeer, their transportation to Alaska and instruction of the natives in the care and management of these animals. Mr. McComas, of the Committee of Education, sent his report[21] on January 9th, 1891, to the whole House, urging on the basis of Harris' and Jackson's recommendations, that the stock raising of reindeer be made "the great industrial feature" of the arctic regions of Alaska. At the meeting of that Committee, Dr. Jackson was present and gave a graphic account of his experiences in Alaska since 1885, the year in which the appropriation allowed by Congress in 1884 for "making needful and proper provision for the education of the children in Alaska without distinction of race" could be used in a practical way. Next to nothing was known at the time about the inhabitants of that territory, nor its agricultural possibilities. There was but one regular steamer a year. Harris was likewise invited to make a statement at that meeting. He took this occasion to plead for an increase in appropriations, from $50,000 *per annum* to $70,000, proposing also a separate fund for the purchase of reindeer.

Owing to the short term of Congress, the resolution of the Committee was not reached. Hon. Henry M. Teller then tried to tap another source, but failed. Now, Jackson made an appeal through the newspapers for a fund to purchase reindeer and succeeded in collecting $2,146. In the summer of 1891, he undertook, accordingly, with Capt. Healy in the *Bear*, a voyage to the Siberian coast, cultivated the good-will of the Siberians and brought back 16 live animals with Siberian reindeer keepers. In the fall of that year Hon. Teller introduced a bill, on December 17th to be exact, calling for an appropriation of $15,000 for the purchase and maintenance of herds of reindeer for the benefit of the Alaskans. The first big herd of domesticated reindeer was landed by Jackson at Port Clarence, July 4th, 1892. In 1896, Harris prevailed upon the Secretary of the Interior to persuade the government of the Czar of Russia to permit the establishment of a station in Siberia for the purpose of purchasing reindeer[22]. That permission was granted.

Sheldon Jackson appealed urgently to Harris for an increase in the educational facilities for the Eskimos as a sequel to providing a means of sustenance and industry. Harris was whole-heartedly for it. He favored giving the oversight of the schools to missionary Boards. As the most successful in that region, the Moravians were approached who, like the mission Boards of the Presbyterian, Congregationalist, Methodist and Baptist Churches, declined regretfully on the ground that they were already overloaded with work or could not see their way clear financially. However, through the efforts of Jackson, individual schools were taken over by some of these denominations and the Protestant Episcopal Church. The reason why Harris leaned so heavily on the missions despite his lifelong protestation against mixing educational with religious interests was, that the missions were the only ones in close contact with the natives; they knew them well, their modes of living, means of livelihood, character, families and attitudes. Thus, in the matter of distributing the herds of reindeer, Harris likewise looked to the Missionary Societies for co-operation and assistance. In 1896 he proposed to loan small herds to them. The Moravian Missionary Society, the Presbyterian head organization, and the American Missionary Association were particularly interested and co-operative, with the result that, in time, one could distinguish Congregational, Episcopalian, and other herds.

The funds for education in Alaska were under the direct

control of the Alaskan Division whose office was increased in 1891 by the appointment of an Assistant Agent of Education in Alaska. Since the funds were thus in the hands of a separate Division, the Division forming part of the Bureau of Education, this phase of education lay outside any sphere of influence which might not have accrued to the best interests of education. Around 1905, the schools of Alaska were put in charge of the Governor of Alaska who acted *ex officio* as Superintendent of Education.

As is so often the case, the one who brings about a good thing with self-sacrifice is being maligned at last when the thing is taken over by others who have watched and benefitted by past failures. This happened also to Sheldon Jackson who was, at the turn of the century, accused of having misappropriated government funds. But Harris stood staunchly by him and valiantly defended his friend against such slander. He was supported in this by many in the government service who had been with Jackson on his trips and cruises in Alaskan and Siberian waters. When, not long before Harris' death, Jackson presented him with two valuable volumes of photographs and Robert Laird Stewart's *Life* of himself, Harris wrote him[23] that he had not waited for the presentation copy but had purchased one on its first announcement and sent it to his son and grandchildren in Texas

as a valuable souvenir of a part of the life of their father and grandfather, lived through by me with deep interest and unwavering confidence in what I have thought to be of national importance in its results — namely, the reindeer movement —, and with pride in my association with Reverend Doctor Sheldon Jackson in a work so full of unusual and unexpected demands upon one's best efforts, in season and out of season, and for a constant faith in the goodness of the cause — involving as it does the civilizing of the natives

483

of Alaska and the utilizing of the resources of Alaska by the reindeer industry —, and a steadfast confidence in the general wisdom of the plans adopted in the management of that industry.

This letter, with New Year's wishes to Dr. Jackson and his daughters from the writer and his wife shows that Harris ever held Jackson in the highest esteem, while the Alaskan Division in the Bureau was a source of pride and satisfaction to him. Especially during the Klondike excitement, at the end of the century, the Alaskan room was the busiest place in the Bureau, as people swamped it with requests for information.

EDUCATING FOR CIVILIZATION

The reindeer project was so fascinating an issue, apart from its humanitarian aspect of providing a livelihood for natives starving to death as a result of the greed of the white man, because it meant a real venture in civilizing the "barbarous", as Harris, following nineteenth century ideas, called the backward races. By introducing the reindeer and thus helping the Eskimo to help himself, Harris could watch a significant transformation that had taken place more than once in the history of mankind, of how a tribe passes from the primitive stage of hunter and nomad to that of the pastoral stage which is more sedentary and makes possible the accumulation of wealth and property and the acquisition of culture through schooling and book-learning. The education of the Eskimo, a subject on which he liked to talk and write[24], thus proved to him many a truth in the philosophy of history to which he was partial.

His dictum was that we are educating other races so that they may participate in our civilization. This was, for instance, the burden of his talk at one time in Detroit to Indian teachers. While concerned about the education of the Indians in the States, he did not care too much to be in

484

charge of it, since Indian problems were deeply involved in political issues. Nevertheless, he dealt on various occasions with education among the red men, approving, for instance, Hailmann's *Syllabus* on arithmetic and the one on language, for teachers in Indian schools;[25] discussed at the Lake Mohonk Indian Conference of 1895 the relation of school education to the work of civilizing other races; and presented papers to the National Educational Association, Department of Indian Education, on "Civilization and Higher Education" and "Newspapers in Indian Schools".[26] When Carlisle Indian School, a U.S. Indian Industrial and Training School at Carlisle, Penna., celebrated its 20th year of founding in 1899, Harris gave the address on "What is Civilization?" He was no stranger there, for three years before he had visited the school at Commencement and given a talk.

The Commissionership of Harris happened to fall in a period of great political expansion of the United States at the end of the century and embraced the period of the war with Spain and the acquisition of Puerto Rico, the Philippines, the Hawaiian Islands, Guam, Wake Island and the Samoans. Harris knew personally many of the men who shaped the destiny of the nation, to name but William H. Taft who was rising swiftly to prominence at that time, and President Schurman of Cornell University who headed the Philippine Commission in 1899. It was in that year that Harris read at the National Educational Association his paper on "An Educational Policy for our New Possessions," and in the *San Juan News* during the same year appeared his letter to Gen. John Eaton, first American Superintendent of Schools in Puerto Rico, on Puerto Rican Schools.

When, in 1889, there was brought before Congress the Blair Bill which proposed to set apart a portion of the national income for the direct aid of States in supporting their common school system, Harris, though conscious of the fact that, as Commissioner, he was not authorized to support any bill, expressed privately his sympathy with it. In a letter to Hon. J. R. Preston, State Superintendent of Education, Jackson, Miss.,[27] which was later made public in the papers, he called it an entirely salutary measure which in no wise would infringe on the rights of the States. He pointed to Europe where, since the Franco-Prussian War, every nation recognized the need of universal education and no effort or outlay was spared to bring it about. He could foresee that such spread of education would ultimately undermine the central national authority in the European nations and bring them closer to democracy due to the fact that the greater the number of educated people, the more clamor for popular representation in the government. Harris wished the passage of the Bill particularly because he was familiar with education in the South which had to fight many odds, political as well as economic and racial.

It was characteristic of Harris' thinking that he was interested not only in education, but in educating for a purpose. Hence, the title of his address at the National Congress of Education, at Atlanta, Ga., on October 26th, 1895: "What the South is doing for Education and what Education is doing for the South." The answer to the second question he found in the fact that the productive power of the individual had been increased by nearly 50%, and a skilled laboring class had developed in virtue of progressive industrialization. Education "puts alertness and versatility in place of mere brute strength and persistency," "lifts the veil of distance in time and place" and imparts "aspiration and ambition." Primitive society can spare but one man to manufacture ornaments for the tribe, all the rest are needed to supply food and clothing of the plainest sort. In modern civilization with its railroads, the daily newspapers, and schools, we can release more and more people from the farm to give culture to the rest in the cities. However, those employed in this enterprise need greater skill and hence more education. "The work of education is the direct work of helping individuals to help themselves." In the testimony before the Industrial Commission he stressed that special pains be taken to encourage industrial training throughout the South, in Colored as well as White schools.

He always showed a remarkable understanding for the problems of the Negro in the South. Col. Dawson, his predecessor, had displayed little sympathy with the black man; he came from the gentry in Alabama. But Harris would address the Colored Conference, at Lincoln Memorial Chapel, Washington, D. C., on "Higher Education";[28] discuss normal school training for the Negroes and allied problems at the 1890 and 1891 Lake Mohonk Conferences; speak to the Colored teachers at Richmond, Va., and the Colored students at Atlanta University; and was present at the inauguration of Rev. John Gordon as President of Howard University; not to mention the number of articles and addresses dealing with education in the South. It is noteworthy in this connection that Harris was a guest gladly seen in the South, and invitations came from Columbia and Charleston, but most frequently from Atlanta.

Harris' personal relations to Negroes should also be noted. Dr. Elmer E. Brown told the story of how, when he went to see him at his home, he found him engaged in conversation with a young Colored man, a teacher in the public schools. This man had come to him for advice, and Harris was ever ready to give it to anyone. In taking over the Bureau of Education, Harris inherited B. Frank Morrison who had served Col. Dawson as office boy, and continued to act as special messenger under Harris who also brought him home. "Frank" lived with the Harrises during their stay in Washington, waiting on the table, taking care of the furnace, and doing many of the household errands for his board and room. He is remembered by Miss Edith Davidson Harris as intelligent, very capable and reliable, and faithful in all his tasks through the years, both in the Bureau and in the home. He continued in the Bureau under Dr. Brown, married and died, but his widow still thinks of the Harrises affectionately.

"There doubtless are many that would sympathize with me; but there is only one man I feel, that would, if he could, extend a helping hand — that is Dr. Harris. . . " Thus wrote Edward W. Williams, a Negro who was arrested, apparently unjustly, on charges of vagrancy and instead of having been given a fair trial at court at whose session Harris was to appear, was put into the workhouse, in a dark cell, with the "most vulgar" of his own kind. The letter was written for him and addressed to a Mr. Thorn, to be shown to Harris from whom he expected action in his behalf. On the envelope in which Harris kept the letter, is written in Harris' hand, with blue pencil: "Edw. W. Williams, Colored man. Philosopher persecuted by police. Befriended by Senator Hoar, W. T. Harris, J. W. Powell . . . "

CHAPTER TWENTY-FIVE

LIFE AT WASHINGTON AND IN THE ADIRONDACKS

At Home in the Nation's Capital

O N September 12th, 1889, Harris moved with his wife and daughter Edith from Concord to Washington. Here they changed residence several times. At first they lived at 914-23rd Street, N. W., which was not a healthy location because of the vicinity of the Potomac swamps. They therefore moved in 1895 to 1303 P. Street, N.W., and from there in 1902 to 1360 Yale Street, N.W., which was later re-named Fairmont Street, on Columbia Heights, on the "wholesome hills overlooking our grand Capital City." Son Theodore had long since gone to San Antonio, Texas, but would come on, with his family, for a visit on occasion, or, what happened more rarely, his father would visit him over the Christmas holidays. Theodore, who had taken to the profession of law, had risen rapidly to prominence. During 1900-02 he served as Texas State Senator, was a member of the San Antonio School Board from 1902 to 1908, and a member of the Executive Board of the Texas State Conference for Education during 1907-1910. At home, daughter Edith groomed herself to act more or less as her father's private secretary, and towards the end of her father's life a good deal of his extensive correspondence devolved upon her.

Now and then, Harris would visit with his brother Charles Joseph and his family in Asheville, N. C., and it was on one of these visits which he also utilized for gathering information on the schools, that Dr. Philander Priestley Claxton, then Superintendent of Schools, met him and learned to look on him with awe and reverence. As time went on, he relied more and more upon his brother Edward Mowry, who had become a well known physician in Providence, R. I. Their mother died in 1899, and their sister Mary Jane followed her in 1908. William was fond of all his family, especially his grandchildren who, in turn, liked him immensely. When his granddaughter, on one of her visits to Washington, complained that she did not like a house that had books for wall-paper, he was highly amused. He cared much for the judgment of his family. When Rose Peckham finally satisfied her long harbored curiosity to hear a talk by her famous cousin, William said after the lecture that he had felt all through the lecture Rose's eye on him and how she had weighed every word he spoke.[1]

Studying the genealogical history of his family, was one of Harris' chief relaxations. He utilized to the full the facilities of the Congressional Library, and daughter Edith aided him in ferreting out the records of their ancestry. But his real hour of relaxation came evenings when Mrs. Harris would read aloud, just as she had done in St. Louis, from the works of Balzac, Victor Hugo, Walter Scott and other men of eminence in the world of letters. Harris enjoyed, above all, the novels of Walter Scott, all of which were read and re-read a number of times. Carlyle's *Sartor Resartus*, principally the chapter on "Natural Supernaturalism," Emerson's "Experience" with its "globular thought," Juliana Horatia Ewing's *Story of a Short Life*, Kingsley's *Water Babies*, Frances Hodgson Burnett's *Little Lord Fauntleroy*, were among the more modern productions to be thoroughly enjoyed during these evening hours. Mrs. Harris is remembered by her children as very quiet and domestic, interested in her home and family.

Interest in music and the great works of art were

another source of relaxation to Harris who did not tire studying the beauty in Greek sculpture and the paintings of the Italian renaissance. Both his love for the Church Fathers and his fondness of liturgical music had earned him the nickname "Doctor Domine" long since. When Dr. Cecil Reddie, Head Master of Abbotsholme School, Derbyshire, England, who later came to La Porte, Indiana, where the Interlaken School was modelled after his school, similarly to the schools at Ilsenburg, Haubinda and Bieberstein in Germany, and Glarisegg in Switzerland, sent him a copy of *Gregorian and Anglican Chants for use in Abbotsholme School Chapel*, Harris was delighted, picked out the "arias of the ten tones and the thirty-seven Anglican chants," and wrote the donor a long and interesting letter.[2]

Harris' chief and almost only social relaxation outside the family circle were the meetings of The Literary Society. This intellectual group went back to the early days of Washington society. During Harris' time it met once or twice a month in the evening. As Miss Edith recollects,[3] its entertainment included one or two musical selections, an address by a member, followed by some discussion, perhaps, while refreshments were served by the hostess of the evening. The membership included such well-known persons as Dr. Gallaudet, Head of the Deaf and Dumb College in Washington; Dr. Burnett, a scientist in his own right, but best known as the husband of Frances Hodgson Burnett, the story writer mentioned above; John W. Foster, Secretary of State, 1892-93; General Greely, the Arctic explorer; George Kennan, traveller and writer on Russian topics; A. R. Spofford, Librarian of Congress for many years, and his daughter; John G. Nicolay, one of Lincoln's secretaries, and his daughter, an authoress; Alexander Graham Bell, inventor of the telephone, and many others prominent in the literary and artistic world of the Washington of that period.

It was a habit with Harris to overwork himself. The

malaria which he had contracted in St. Louis, never left him. When the humidity of the air was great, he would suffer very much, but get relief as soon as the first frost set in. Sometimes, returning from prolonged lecture tours, as the one to California in the winter of 1896, he broke down completely in the following spring and summer and had to recuperate from a state that was bordering on distraction. When going into retirement for a few weeks in summer to his camp in the Adirondacks, he took along piles of papers, manuscripts and books. In fact, wherever he travelled he took along his notes, hoping for a few quiet days or hours on the way, perhaps at the hotel, perhaps on the train. This avidity for knowledge was never stilled. His big arm chair in his study, into which he sank when returning from the Bureau, was clustered about with the day's mail, manuscripts, letters, papers, and books. Although a great advocate of the newspaper which, as a medium of public opinion to be heeded by popular government, he regarded as contributing toward the realization of Christianity,[4] he seldom read it, for, as he once told Fred A. Emery,[5] so many are the subjects discussed in it that he could not concentrate his mind on any single theme.

He made it his practice, after 1896, to get up at three or four o'clock in the morning and write his "day's task" before breakfast. But, during the night, he had probably awakened several times, reached for the pencil and paper by his bed, and jotted down his thoughts in the dark in both longhand and shorthand. These memoranda, often intelligible only to himself, he would pick up from the floor in the morning and file away according to a system of his own.

Nevertheless, Harris never lost his sense of humor, for humor he regarded as important for the preservation of sanity.[6] His disposition to be helpful also never changed. Ossian Lang once wrote in the *Nation*[7] that he had in his possession the copy of a long letter written by Harris to a small boy who had written to him as Commissioner of Education "to find out what stories would be most interesting for boys to read." The Commissioner took time out to tell him about the stories he himself had liked best, and mentioned above all those of Walter Scott.

Harris could be severe, but only as a father would be. When someone had made a blunder that would reflect on either himself or his office, he took it very much to heart. On one occasion he confessed to the blunderer that his act, unintentional though it was and done in good faith, had so sickened him that he had scarcely been able to visit the Bureau for days. But his anger would die down in due time and he might, in the end, even take the blame upon himself. Over the silly and absurd statements and misquotations of some reporters he would be very much concerned. Indeed, he had to suffer much at the hands of the stenographic reporters whose imperfect transcription would be further garbled by the type-setter who was incapable of following the thought.

Many were the students that called from far and near. Harris was able to entertain them all from the rich storehouse of his memory, be they students of philosophy, teachers or persons interested in literature. Theodore remembered one of the minor Indian princes that came to their home and enjoyed a conversation with his father. Two Norwegian gentlemen, who once called, were very much amazed that Harris knew more about the Edda than they did. The only times he became impatient were when uninformed persons made demands upon his time. Then he felt like the Buddhist monks who would confine the one found lacking in the library. It was his habit, at the Bureau and at home, to call for a volume which he needed for quick reference by designating it by the color of its binding. The librarian in the Bureau despaired over such an unscientific description, but Dr. Evans was quite proficient in procuring the right volume when Harris, for instance, would call for "Shaler's yellow book."

The Harris home was always open to friends, whether for an hour or to stay for the night. An often seen guest was Dr. Nicholas Murray Butler and the hospitality was reciprocal. For, when Harris came to New York on his frequent trips, he would put up at the Butler residence on 119 East 30th Street. "His circle of friends was notable," wrote Lilian Whiting,[8] "his own genius for friendship,—for coming into easy and sympathetic relations with the widest variety of people, was a very rare and very remarkable trait; he, the peer of the choicest scholarship, the most distinguished culture, could yet come into a sympathetic and infinitely helpful companionship with those who had no share in this lofty atmosphere . . ."

A STRANGE FRIENDSHIP

The friendship between Harris and Thomas Davidson began in St. Louis and continued till Tom's death. But there were abysmal differences in the views of the two as thinkers, and philosophers. Harris was steeped in German idealism, but Tom professed to thoughts like these, that Kant must be forgotten,[9] that "since the world began there never was such a piece of huge, solemn humbug as German philosophy. The land of beer never did produce but one great thinker and that was Leibniz,"[10] The systems of Schelling and Hegel he called "hollow schemes" "which for half a century deluded the world, and to some extent delude it still."[11] It would also seem as if Harris associated himself so clearly with Davidson in order to negate the negation. At the Concord Summer School of Philosophy, the Scot had shocked the audience when he ascribed irony to Christ and compared it with that of Zola.[12] These and many other statements by Davidson ill accord with the first principles of

494

his New Fellowship which he himself had drawn up. How much grander does the thought and personality of Harris appear in contrast with such untutored thinking and intellectual vehemence! Of course, allowance must be made for some genius that was undoubtedly Davidson's.

Harris had many an intellectual squabble with him. He knew his shortcomings only too well and charged him with solipsism when he tried to establish in several of his writings the doctrine that man is principally feeling, that "the world is at bottom a democracy of feeling, or, more strictly, of desiderant feelings." Had he maintained such a theory consistently, which Davidson, true to his native changeableness, did not, he would have been obliged, according to Harris, to deny morality, for it would have made him abandon belief in basic duties. That would have been an absurd position for Davidson himself, who was crusading for the good life. Witness his Fabian Society, which he abandoned, or which abandoned him, and the fate of the New Fellowship.

When the Concord School of Philosophy was waning, Davidson saw his opportunity to establish a similar school and profit by the failures and shortcomings of the work of Alcott, Harris and the rest. Farmington, Ct., the "quaint, old, shady New England town, overlooking the Farmington and Pequabuck rivers," some ten miles from Hartford, was calculated to attract a number of scholars and friends that he had met in his ubiquitous existence, and for three years he offered in his Summer School a noteworthy series of courses, well-organized and diversified enough to please varied tastes. He gathered to himself some that had gone to Concord to lecture or to listen. Among those lecturing were H. N. Gardiner of Smith College, Percival Chubb of London, and John Dewey. Harris also was harnessed, and during each of its three summer sessions he gave a lecture: on June 29th, 1888, on "Goethe's Ethics and

Pedagogics"; July 16th, 1889, on "Athanasius"; June 27th, 1890, on "The Historical-Philosophical View," in a course on the Relation of Church and State.

THE COTTAGE ON MT. HURRICANE

Three years was too long a time for Tom to devote himself to one undertaking. The summer session in 1889 was still going on at Farmington when he journeyed forth in search of another place which he found at the Northern end of Keene Valley in the Adirondacks and which, no doubt, reminded him of his native land. There he bought himself a farm of 167 acres for the sum of $1500. On September 13th, he wrote to Harris that he was "having a glorious time up here in the mountains. My farm is a complete success in every way. There is no finer place in all the Adirondacks."

Now the School was transplanted there, and in April, 1890, Harris wrote him[13] praising the "wonderfully rich repertoire of lectures" planned by Davidson on the side of Mt. Hurricane, and promising to visit it in the summer for a day or two, if possible. It is not certain whether this visit was made. However, in January, 1891, Tom again urged Harris to come to "Glenmore" (the name he had given to his farm) for a week in the summer, to give two evening and two morning lectures and bring Mrs. Harris and Edith along to stay all summer. He wanted Harris to see the place in early summer, for then he thought he would be sure to buy the lot next to him and put up a shanty. Harris replied[14] that he was going to Chautauqua on July 17th, but would come from there to Glenmore on the 22nd.

This plan was carried out. With his wife and daughter Edith he took the train up the scenic and historic route to Fort Ticonderoga and Crown Point on Lake Champlain. At Westport a three-seated mountain stage sent down from Harvey Willey's House on Mt. Hurricane was waiting and took them up the road to the West, stopping at Elizabeth-

496

town for a snack, and then climbing further till they reached Mt. Hurricane where they swung around to the West and then in a Northerly direction catching sight of a cluster of buildings on the slope. There Tom was in his weather-beaten Scotch habit, running down the hill with beaming countenance and hands outstretched for greeting long before he reached the coach.

The "Glenmore School for the Culture Sciences" had been running for a year, the members learning and laboring. And among one of the tangible evidences of the labor, there was a cottage, better a hut, built by one of the members on the North side of a hill, in a clearing, of the simplest construction of rough boards, unfinished inside, containing two rooms, with a piazza across the front, overlooking the group of houses — lecture-hall, dining-hall and farmhouse— that formed Glenmore below. Beyond ranged the higher Adirondack mountains on the horizon. This "wooden tent," as Harris called the structure which he acquired by purchase,[15] grew in the course of years to a seven room cottage, large enough to take in children and grandchildren. Year after year, the Harris family repaired to this spot, and Harris spent there what he called his vacation. Lectures were always part of the vacation, as were the many talks with Davidson and his philosophical friends that gathered during the summer. There were informal teas, given by the members of the School in their individual cottages; bonfires by the brook on an occasional evening not taken up with lectures; sometimes a climb of a thousand feet or two on a clear day up Mt. Hurricane; sometimes a day's excursion to the Ausable Lakes in Keene Valley, where William James had his summer camp; sometimes dramatic evenings at Glenmore gotten up by the members of the community for their own amusement, Harris doing his part, or Davidson contributing a rare treat in reciting selections from Scotch poetry.[16]

The camp was about 2000 feet above sea level. Many of

the guests and members stayed at the Willey House, which they reached by a path of half a mile through dense forest, carrying their lanterns by night. The lecture hall was at the top of a hill, and pious wishes were often heard that Davidson had put it at the foot of the hill instead.[17]

Davidson had a genius for arranging lecture continuities and selecting speakers to take part in the symposiums. In 1892, for instance, Prof. John Clark Murray of McGill University spoke in three lectures on Kant, Evolution, and Social Morality; Harris spoke on Alcott, Emerson and the New England Transcendentalists; John Dewey on the tendencies of English thought during the 19th century; Josiah Royce on recent tendencies in ethical doctrine; Dr. Max Margolis on Jewish literature; Dr. A. J. Leon (Ibn Abi Sulaiman) on Islam and Eastern customs; Davidson on Greek philosophy and Christianity; Louis J. Block, of Chicago, on the philosophy of literature. After Davidson's death in 1900, courses of lectures were continued for a time during July and August under the management of Stephen F. Weston of Antioch College. John Dewey owned a summer cottage in the woods beyond Davidson's property and gave his share of lectures, entering with his family the social life of the community as well. Harris now spoke more freely his convictions at Glenmore, as may be seen by the titles of his talks given July 27th to 29th, 1902: "The Theodicy of Human History," "Hegel's Doctrine of the Idea," and "The World View of Reason."[18] Professor James B. Pratt of Williams College, who also came to Glenmore, always remembered Harris "with a kind of *thrill,* so contagious was his enthusiasm over scholarship,"[19] although he told Harris[20] that he was still in the "gall and bitterness of empirical thinking."

Harris' broadness and tolerance was brought out not only in his friendship with the Hegel-despising Davidson, his utter impartiality to Protestants, Catholics, and Jews which he had shown already in his St. Louis days[21] and in his sympathy with the Negro, but in his association, at Glenmore, with the Semitic scholars mentioned and the young Jews from New York's Eastside whom Davidson had befriended and organized into the Breadwinners' College.[22] Some of these young men he would invite to spend a week or longer at Glenmore. When not in New York, Davidson had been in the habit of keeping in touch with the group by letter. After his death, Harris continued this custom of writing letters on philosophical topics. His personal friendship with several of these young men should be noted. There was, for instance, Edward Endelman who visited with the Harrises in the Adirondacks as well as in Washington and later became a prominent Attorney and Counselor-at-Law in New York; another was Morris R. Cohen, the well-known philosopher who became Professor of Philosophy in the University of Chicago; a third was Louis I. Dublin, the Statistician in the Metropolitan Life Insurance Company; and there was Joseph Kahn.

As chairman, for a time, of the classes that continued Davidson's work in New York, Endelman kept Harris informed about the progress of the "college." He was endeavoring to collect a small library for his fellow-students, and Harris sent him many of his own books and pamphlets as well as bundles of back-numbers of his *Journal of Speculative Philosophy*. Sometimes, the correspondence was long, as when Endelman criticised on twelve sheets Vera's logic and the problem of the freedom of the will. Harris' replies were equally long or longer. Sometimes, Harris' answer would take the form of a suggestion as this one jotted down in shorthand on the envelope:"If you read any puzzling arguments against self-activity, let me know them. Get all your pupils to read over and over again the 10th book of the *Laws* and you and Kahn work on Aristotle's XI.7—Compare my translation with Davidson's."

Morris R. Cohen likewise communicated to Harris the problems of the class, especially those that arose in the study of Aristotle and Plato, as suggested by Harris, and told him about the difficulties he himself as well as the class encountered. Harris' reply would then be read to the class for

ιainted with another young man, Bernard Sexton, a teacher, and the personal relationships here also were typical of his attitude of helpfulness to youthful seekers of the truth. He supplied him with books and eventually succeeded in making him a student and admirer of Hegel, Goethe and Dante.

CHAPTER TWENTY-SIX

HIGHLIGHTS OF A GREAT PUBLIC SPEAKING CAREER

AS in the past, and perhaps with greater vigor now, Harris devoted himself, apart from his official duties as Commissioner, to the cause of education, by visiting educational congresses, conventions and expositions. His connection with the National Educational Association was so important that it merits separate treatment later.

A GLORIOUS CRUISE TO EUROPE

In 1891, North Carolina held an exposition at Raleigh, and Harris delivered the address on Educational Day. The following year, he was engaged chiefly in the preparation of the International Congresses of Education which were to be held in Chicago, in July of 1893, in connection with the World's Columbian Exposition. The work was planned and executed by the National Educational Association of the United States, with Harris in general charge. The meetings, as those of the World's Parliament of Religions, which Harris likewise attended and addressed on "The Proofs of the Existence of God," were of the highest type.[1] In the same year, Harris delivered an address at Clark University.

The year 1895 was marked by the inauguration of Willimantic, Ct., Normal School and the National Congress of Education in October, held at the Exposition in Atlanta, Ga., at which Harris gave an address and discussed Henry

George, socialism and allied issues after the presentation of a paper by E. B. Andrew. But it was also the year in which he joined with his wife and daughter Edith the summer vacation party to Europe, organized by Frank C. Clark and composed of an exceptionally large number of persons of education and standing, teachers, lecturers, authors, and scientists. J. M. Greenwood from Kansas City, was in the party, and so were W. F. Bradbury, the Harvard mathematician, Hon. A. H. Byington and Hon. E. J. Hill, and the families of three U. S. Senators, besides a number of Reverends. They were sailing on the "City of Rome", and it turned out to be one of the original universities afloat, for Harris yielded to the unanimous request to entertain his fellow passengers by sharing with them some of his knowledge. He talked to them on the land of Scott, on Dante, Michael Angelo, Grecian and Roman architecture, and Emerson.

At Rome, Harris noted the fact that, with its antiquities, its face was turned toward the past. Perhaps he also joined those whom Pope Leo received in audience and witnessed the mass celebrated in the Pope's private chapel which, for the occasion, was decorated with a large American flag at either side of the papal throne.

" . . . It was a glorious contrast to come to Paris," Harris wrote later. Paris,

the city of the freshest modern ideals with its face turned toward the future. Then came the metropolitan city of the world, London, the city of our Anglo-Saxon forefathers, a city unique in itself. But one has only to name the localities of our visits from day to day to make clear the pleasant contrasts furnished us: After Glasgow the Highlands of Scotland; after these, Edinburgh and then the antiquarian visit to Melrose Abbey and the home of Scott. Then York with its impressive minster; then in succession the voyage across the North

Sea, the Antwerp Cathedral, the journey up the Rhine with glimpses of more than a hundred ancient castles, the city of Baden, the castle of Heidelberg, the Black Forest, the falls of the Rhine, the ascent of the Righi, a visit to the most wonderful mountains in the world at Grindelwald, three or four days' stay about the Lake of the four Cantons, a journey into Italy through the St. Gothard [sic] tunnel and a return through the Mt. Cenis tunnel: in succession Milan, Venice, Florence, Rome, Pisa and Genoa, then Geneva and Paris. After London, the home of Shakespeare, Warwick Castle, the town of Chester and then Glasgow again.

At Florence, Harris was assigned the famous parlors of Lorenzo the Magnificent, and it was there that he delivered a superb lecture to the group on the immortal Florentine whom the Medici had driven from this his native city.

On the way, he gathered up souvenirs, a scarf or two from Scotland, lace, umbrellas, a rug, glass from Venice, a pin for Edith, a ring, a letter case for himself, a portmanteau, and, of course, books. At Paris he went to the Opera. At London he had some dental work done for Edith because of an accident on the English Channel. At Edinburgh he received a telegram from Denver, Colorado, signed (N. M.) Butler President:

ASSEMBLED REPRESENTATIVES OF FOUR HUNDRED THOUSAND TEACHERS GREET YOU OUR HONORED LEADER AND ASK FOR YOU AND YOUR COMPANION OUR TREASURER GREENWOOD HEALTH AND SAFE RETURN.

On the trip he also visited Combe St. Nicholas in Somersetshire, England, where the first American ancestors of the Torrey family were born, and in the church that had stood six centuries and a half he pondered over the inscriptions and the ways of providence.

A Christmas in California

Maryland State Normal School held its commencement on May 28th, 1896, and Harris was asked to deliver the address, which he did. The Home Congress met at Boston on October 5th, and Harris again gave the address. However, the most significant event in that year was his trip to California in December. To understand the background of this trip it is necessary to say something about Harris' acquaintance with George Holmes Howison.[2] It dated back to St. Louis in the early sixties and had ripened into a solid and affectionate friendship, despite differences in point of view, which at first were not obvious.

Howison had left St. Louis and was teaching at Massachusetts Institute of Technology, but in the Spring of 1879 he was "all up" there and began casting about for another position. When, in 1883, something seemed to develop in the University of California, Harris sent a strong letter of recommendation to President W. T. Reid,[3] and in July, 1884, Howison was on his way to California. From Albany, N. Y., he dropped a letter to Harris saying that he regretted not having seen him again and added: "I need not say to you, after these long years of mutual intercourse, how much I value you. I hope to have the pleasure and profit of a long-lasting correspondence with you, now that so many thousand miles are to divide us and our work." And a voluminous correspondence it turned out to be.

Removal from New England to the West and away from Harris had an effect on Howison's thought. He became absorbed in work and worries at Berkeley, and became for a time an invalid. His letter to Harris of June 3rd, 1891, tells the sum and substance of the intellectual dispute that was taking shape between the friends. He feared that he had unconsciously but surely grown away from Hegel's way of viewing many things. He now extolled Leibniz as the one who had gained the most important insights in all philosophy. After the publication of Harris' book on Hegel's *Logic* and Howison's acceptance of the invitation of Professor Schurman of Ithaca to engage with Harris in a discussion in the *Philosophical Review,* the differences with Harris became more pronounced. Howison wrote from Berkeley under date of May 30th, 1892:

Now, if you prefer that we shall not go into this, you have only to say so, and I will cheerfully "inhibit." Of course, my review will be mainly antagonistic, and it cannot be altogether pleasant, either for you or for me. But I think I have so cordial a regard for your mind, despite our great divergencies, that I shall avoid the unhappiness into which your youthful friend Royce fell in attempting to overhaul Abbot. If I were not sure of being able to treat your book and, above all, yourself, with deep respect I feel, while reviewing it never so severely, I would not begin.

While thus things were shaping themselves, an invitation was tendered Harris in 1896 by the Executive Council of the Philosophical Union of which Howison was President, to address its members the following January, while the California Teachers' Association had already invited Harris for December-January. All arrangements for Harris' appearance before the philosophical and educational groups were made by the faithful Howison. As scheduled, Harris entered California from the South, stopping off at Los Angeles where he addressed the teachers of Los Angeles and vicinity according to plans made by Superintendent James A. Foshay. Then he moved North and made Howison's residence his own. In the evening of December 7th, the two friends dined with the Berkeley Club in Oakland and Harris read a paper.

Harris' public address in Berkeley before the Philosophical Union was scheduled for the following evening. In its Bulletin No. 17,[4] the Union had outlined fully its "Programme for a Critique of Hegelianism, based on Writings by Dr. W. T. Harris, chiefly his Book on Hegel's Logic." The Union was thus prepared when Harris arrived and delivered his lecture on "The Nature of the Divine Personality" at Stiles Hall. The Governor and Lt. Governor, the Speaker of the Assembly, the Archbishop of the Catholic Church, the Bishops of the Episcopal and Methodist Churches, the judges of the Supreme and Superior Courts, college professors, eminent clergymen, regents of the University, lawyers, doctors and other professional men, were among the invited guests. The auditorium was crowded beyond its doors long before Howison, the President of the Union, called the assemblage to order. Harris prefaced his lecture by saying that he was looking to California for a new revival of philosophic thought and he had the highest regards for Professor Howison in whose thinking he took more interest than in that of any other living philosopher.

On Saturday followed a luncheon at Professor Elmer Ellsworth Brown's, and in the evening a dinner was given at President Martin Kellogg's residence to which important guests had been invited. As a matter of fact, Harris had been asked to stay at Mr. and Mrs. Kellogg's. Then followed a joint discussion with Howison before the Presbyterian Ministers' Union at San Francisco in which the friends discussed the future of Christian theology. The same day, Professor C. M. Gayley gave a dinner in honor of Harris and after it Harris delivered his Congregational Club address.

In the evening following, there was an informal meeting with the Philosophical Union. In this and a subsequent meeting interesting problems were aired. In the afternoon of December 23rd, Harris addressed the Sorosis Society, composed of "women of education and fashion, the leaders

506

of San Francisco Society." Mrs. William B. Carr, the President, introduced Harris in a few happy remarks. He spoke on "Faust," offering a running comment. The officers and invited guests were ranged in a semicircle around the platform, and when Harris had done after an hour he was warmly applauded and "held quite a levee on the stage after the lecture."

The University Club tendered a dinner to Harris in the evening of the same day, James E. Tucker introducing the guest of honor. For Christmas Eve no engagements or dinners were scheduled, but the 25th was spent with the Howisons who had a few friends in for dinner as well as supper. The days after Christmas were taken up by a visit to Dr. Edward S. Holden's home at Mt. Hamilton; it had been Holden as President of the University and before he had become Director of Lick Observatory, who had made great efforts to get Harris as his successor in office. From December 28th to the 30th, Harris and Howison were at the 13th Annual Meeting of the State Teachers' Association at San Jose, a most successful meeting.

Howison and Harris joined in discussions on child study at the round table in the morning, both stressing character rather than interest in education. After a general session in the afternoon, Harris delivered his address on "Moral Education and School Discipline" in the evening. In the morning of the 30th, he spoke at the Kindergarten round table in a light vein on the "Organic Connection of the Kindergarten and Primary School," and the reporters noted his not too high opinion of the children of the *parvenu* whom he considered a danger to society. In the afternoon Howison gave an exposition of the famous conclusions arrived at by the Committee of Fifteen on which Harris had served. When he came "out of the depths," as one reporter had it, one thousand people gasped for breath. "Then the versatile Dr. Harris made a simple, popular little address . . ."

His topic was the one that Howison had suggested, "The Windows of the Soul."

The whole meeting of the teachers was conducted in great seriousness, so much so that one of the addresses, that by Professor Oliver Peebles Jenkins, was a relief for the audience because it was full of witticisms. "The people in the audience laughed," wrote Harr Wagner in the *Western Journal of Education*, "and those on the platform looked so serious. Brown looked at Bailey, Bailey looked at Harris, Harris looked at Linscott, as much as to say: 'Is he making fun of us?' and the humor of it all is that no one but Professor Jenkins knows whether he was serious or not."

Harris' visit to the West was a complete success. The cordial reception accorded him everywhere was a fine tribute to his ability and personal qualities. The *Journal* just mentioned came out with his portrait in a wreath of yew as a frontispiece, bearing the message below: "The West's Christmas Welcome to Hon. W. T. Harris, U. S. Commissioner of Education."

The Philosophical Union kept in close touch with Harris for some time afterwards, a number of members sending him their papers for criticism. The discussions with Howison were to be published in book form. But when Harris had not sent in his contribution by the end of 1897, Howison thought Harris was shunning a public discussion. That was, however, not the case at all, inasmuch as Harris had nearly broken down after his return, had been swamped by important work in the Bureau and was working on earlier commitments. When his book on the *Psychologic Foundations of Education* came off the press, Howison was, to an extent, reconciled over the delay and expressed sympathy with Harris "in the great main fibres" of his contention, however much he differed regarding "certain eminent details, e.g. the solution of the problem of freedom."[5]

As time passed, the differences in opinion between the

two friends became shallower once more. Nothing illustrates this better than a paragraph from Howison's letter of February 18th, 1902, after the former's publication of *The Limits of Evolution* which had caused Harris to write long letters in criticism:[6]

In fact, dear friend, as I read and reread your greater writings, which deal in detail with these great matters [God, creation and the individual souls], I am at a loss to tell what you do intend by your teaching, unless it is just this which I feel called upon to say in another way, — a way which seemed to me at once franker and more perspicuous. I should be glad to feel that we do agree in this bottom matter after all, that our differences are merely in expression, argumentation, and external form. But this would be at the expense of taking you quite out of the School of Hegel. Perhaps, though you wouldn't really mind that.

WITH MCKINLEY IN OMAHA

During the year 1897, Harris addressed the Educational Club of Philadelphia on "Herbert Spencer and What Knowledge is of the Most Worth," and the Vermont State Teachers' Association at Woodstock, on "The Rural School Problem." Over the Christmas holidays he undertook a trip to Nebraska and Iowa, besides his other engagements to speak which taxed his strength almost to the breaking point. He rallied, however, somewhat in 1898, when he delivered the Convocation address on "Higher Education, its Function in Preserving and Extending our Civilization" at the Quarter Centennial of Boston University, at the end of May; dedicated the Normal School at Providence and delivered his address on "The Future of the Normal School"; and spoke in praise of Wm. Henry Maxwell who was made Superintendent of the schools in Greater New York. When President McKinley made up his official party that year to visit the Transmississippi Exposition at Omaha, Nebraska, Mr. and Mrs. Harris were included. However, it seems to have been one of those rare occasions when Harris had to make no speeches nor attend educational conferences. In 1899 he buried his friend Andrew J. Rickoff whom, together with his wife who had of late assisted him enthusiastically, he esteemed highly as a friend and educational organizer.

We have omitted, of course, the occasional speeches Harris made throughout the years, such as the one in April, 1900, at the Missionary Ecumenical in New York City, or the one at a Kindergarten meeting in Brooklyn at about the same time, as well as his responses to welcome at the National Educational Association meetings at which he was seen every year.

On January 11th, 1900, he delivered the address at the unveiling of the statue erected to Edward Austin Sheldon by the school children of New York State in the Assembly Chamber of the State Capitol at Albany. It was Sheldon who had been instrumental in introducing Pestalozzianism English style in the U. S. and had done much good as Superintendent of Schools at Oswego, N. Y. Five months later, on June 30th, Harris delivered his address at the University of Rochester Semi-Centennial Day, on "The Past and Future of the University in America."

ANOTHER PARIS EXPOSITION

For more than a year past, Harris had again been very busy in preparation for an exhibit. This time it meant the proper representation of the United States, in particular the Bureau of Education, at the Paris Exposition of 1900. The ground was laid as early as December, 1898, with a banquet to F. N. Peck, U. S. Commissioner General to the exposition, in the city of Chicago, at which Harris responded to the toast "Education and the Paris Exposition." A monograph, later translated into French and bearing the title *Elementary Education in the United States,* was contributed by him for the series edited by Dr. Nicholas Murray Butler and offered to the U. S. educational exhibit by the State of New York.

A letter sent to Harris by Lovick Pierce, Chief Clerk in the Bureau, but Acting Commissioner in Harris' absence, throws a flood of light on the personal relation within the Bureau of Education under Harris. It reads:

Dear Dr. Harris:—

We have by mail, today, your parting salutation by way of the Pilot-boat off Sandy Hook, and make haste to express our appreciation of your kindness in think-ing of us among the last of the places and people you left in your native land. We are luxuriating in balmy breezes to-day and hope that you, and your companions in travel are getting in full the exhilaration of an open sea and air unconfined.

Most cordially,

LOVICK PIERCE. .

Acting Commissioner

Added to this were several postscripts. One by H. F. Hovey, that is, Mrs. Hovey, mother of Richard Hovey, the poet: "The Correspondence Division send kindly greetings to you and yours, wishing you a pleasant voyage, and a hope for a safe return. Missing you sadly." Eleanor T. Chester, a member of the Correspondence Division, added another line, while Florence K. Evans, the wife of Dr. Henry Ridgely Evans and the stenographer who took down many of Harris' letters, penned: "Book in hand, waiting for the '8o' letters." In jest, Mrs. C. Gordon Forbes, another member of the Cor-respondence Division wrote: "Did you say send all of your pamphlets?" Mrs. Emily Van Dorn Miller, assistant to Pierce, gave the thermometer reading of 83° at 10 a.m.

in the Chief Clerk's room. William Hamilton, member of the Alaskan Division, wrote a piece of news, "Small pox at Nome!" and "Frank" added affectionately: "Your lunch is ready Dr.; everything at the house is all right."

The Paris exposition put Harris strongly in memory of his esteemed friend John Dudley Philbrick who had informed him of the decorations the French were contemplating giving him back in 1878. He knew Philbrick as far back as 1852, and though he had never been officially connected with him, he revealed at the time of his death in 1886 that he had belonged to the inner circle of his friends.

ALMA MATERS REMEMBER A FAMOUS ALUMNUS

Yale was to come prominently into the picture once again in 1901, for in October she observed with pomp and pride the 200th Anniversary of the founding of the College. Among those present were the President of the United States, the Governor, representatives of foreign and American universities and representatives of the principal learned societies. Harris was in the procession. His class had met in 1898, and it was to meet again in 1908, and both times Harris was present. His attachment to Yale college was well brought out in an earlier after-dinner speech at a banquet in January, 1890, in which he alluded to the central thought of his philosophy of education: "Our first birth gave us life, feeling and locomotion — gave us individuality, all good things. Our second birth gave us community of thought and the heritage of the wisdom of the race — it gave us in short personality in place of mere individuality. For personality may be taken to signify individuality raised into a higher potency — an individuality that combines with other individualities and reenforces its single weight by the weight of all."[7] This second birth is, of course, the result of education, and in his own case it was Yale who was his spiritual mother.

The attachment to Yale had gone further. For, together with his brothers Edward Mowry and Charles Joseph he had established on December 13th, 1889, a small fund for the administration of the library with a donation of $500, to which he had added another $500 in 1898, and a third gift in 1901 of a like amount, to which his brother Charles Joseph, as a member of the class of '74, had added his check in the amount of $1500, thus bringing up the whole fund by May, 1901, to $3000. He left it at the discretion of his class-mate Van Name, the distinguished Librarian of Yale, to indicate the purpose of the fund to the Treasurer.

On August 9th, 1901, the celebration of another *alma mater* was witnessed by Harris; in fact, he delivered the address. The occasion was the 100th anniversary of the founding of Woodstock Academy. Only two years before he had attended commencement exercises at Phillips Academy, of which institution he became a Vice President in 1903. Worcester Academy, likewise, had not forgotten him. They asked him to speak on Latin and Greek in 1897.

THE MOST DISTINGUISHED FRIEND

The year 1902 witnessed the inauguration of Dr. Nicholas Murray Butler as President of Columbia University, in April. Harris was present, making his shorthand notes all the while Dr. Butler delivered his address.

The friendship between Harris and Dr. Butler dates back to Dr. Butler's postgraduate student days when he, much interested in philosophy and pedagogy, organized a Columbia College Philosophical Society and asked Harris' advice, and eventually offered him his articles for the *Journal of Speculative Philosophy*. Later, as has already been mentioned, Dr. Butler refused the office of Commissioner of Education in favor of Harris. It seems, the only time Harris ever failed to do a favor for his friend was when the latter asked him to write a volume on Rousseau.[8] To the delight, and doubtless with the support of Harris, Dr. Butler was made President of the National Educational Association, and it was then that Harris wrote him on September 25th, 1895:[9] "I am sure you are the man of men for the position and I wish you could have the job for ten years." He advised him further in every way possible so that any action or step he might take, would accrue to his benefit, watching over his career like a father. On several occasions he asked Dr. Butler to straighten out some tangles which the latter, with his native consummate skill and tact, was able to do to the great satisfaction of Harris. The fact that Dr. Butler was the editor of the *Educational Review*, occasioned considerable correspondence between the two scholars. They saw eye to eye on educational issues, and shoulder to shoulder they fought what they chose to call the forces of darkness in the educational system, particularly in the city schools of New York. They would support each other on the platform and in print. Upon receipt of a letter by Harris, expressing joy over some of President Theodore Roosevelt's speeches in 1902, Dr. Butler sent it on to the White House, for he was sure that Harris' opinion would please the President greatly.[10]

However, the mutual interests did not extend merely over the field of education. They included philosophy and the whole range of domestic and foreign policies. Together they would travel to the conventions of the National Educational Association, meeting on the train, whether en route to Florida, Louisiana or Illinois. They would visit each other at their respective homes in Washington and New York, to have some hours in which, as Dr. Butler phrased it in one of his letters to Harris,[11] "to settle on sound philosophical principles all questions regarding the universe which remain open at that time." While Harris would supply Dr. Butler with statistical and other information, Dr. Butler would keep Harris apprised of happenings in the political sphere with which he was familiar as close confidant of the Presidential circle. The invitation of Harris to have Dr. Butler stay a day or so with him would take the form of asking him to reconsecrate the prophet's chamber.[12]

When Dr. Butler accepted the presidency of Columbia University, he regretted keenly "that the old opportunities of spending a day or two every few months going over common ground" seemed no longer to exist.[13] In fact, when Dr. Butler at one time late in April, 1904, called at the White House, he was so rushed that he had to leave Washington without calling Harris. However, there was still a lively exchange of letters and journals and books, and much information, often confidential, passed between them. Through introductions of mutual friends they also kept in touch with each other, and Harris was invited to join the academic procession of Columbia University at commencement time. When the publishing firm of D. Appleton and Company acquired a new president in Mr. Sears, in 1904, Dr. Butler solicited the interest of the new management in a book by Harris on *The Course of Study in the Elementary Schools,* one of those projects that remained unfinished.

Harris entertained the highest regard for Dr. Butler, and after listening to his oration in commemoration of the 150th anniversary of the founding of King's College, delivered at Columbia University on October 31st, 1904, he wrote him:[14]

. . . I made the remark to some of our friends who had noticed the same thing to the same effect, that you belong to the race of Homer who could tell the story of the catalogue of the ships in such a way that it has a perennial interest to old and young. . . The device of giving the names of old heroes of the early history of the college to its professorships of the present day struck everybody as a happy thought which we could not help placing to your credit. Besides the catalogue of the ships part of the address which was so admirable, there were great suggestions as to the future policy of higher education, and you must bear patiently the congratulations which will come in to you from all quarters on the excellence of your address . . .

And, on October 13th, 1905, Harris wrote again to Dr. Butler:

You are always in my thoughts and give me courage for my own work and confidence in my fellow men as a social whole — as to its capacity to furnish men for emergency.

The regard, however, was entirely mutual, and Dr. Butler never withheld words of sincere admiration and almost filial piety for Harris. His often-quoted words written in a letter to the late Prof. Charles M. Perry, may stand here also: "I measure my words when I say that in my judgment Dr. Harris had the one truly great philosophical mind which has yet appeared on the western continent." In fact, his educational confession, to which he has held all his life and which has built itself a monument in the University which he has so ably governed,[15] coincides remarkably with the ideals of American education which Harris likewise upheld and defended on philosophical grounds.

The Louisiana Purchase Exposition

Col. Francis W. Parker had passed on in 1902, and Harris wrote a tribute to the man with whom he had differed "materially in regard to the theory of education," the man who had slighted him and indulged in personal criticism. Nevertheless, Harris believed him to be a first class educator. The Colonel, who had peculiar ways of his own, had, in spite of his show to the contrary, likewise esteemed Harris, as may be judged by the letter he wrote to President Harrison in 1889. But Harris had never been fully aware of his real feelings.

516

The year 1903 was filled, as were the preceding years, with routine matters connected principally with the Bureau which, it might be noted, was maliciously charged at that time with having established a laboratory for the study of abnormal classes. Harris found it necessary to refute these allegations. There was, in addition, the customary quota of articles for the journals and important addresses, among them the one given at the dedication of the McKinley Manual Training School at Washington, on January 29th; that on "The Kindergarten as a Preparation for the Highest Civilization," delivered before the International Kindergarten Union in Pittsburgh; and the address at the laying of the cornerstone of the Chicago Normal School on November 21st, at which he once again spoke good words about Colonel Parker.

The Southern Education Association met at Atlanta, Ga., and on the first of January Harris read his paper to which the Southern educators listened intently. He also spoke at the dedication of St. Patrick's Church School, The Carroll Institute, at Washington, and introduced his friend, Bishop Spalding of Peoria. While at the dedication of the new Central High School buildings at Philadelphia he made the response to the toast at the Alumni Banquet, speaking on "Public High Schools in the United States." But the most important event was the Louisiana Purchase Exposition at St. Louis, where he met many of his friends, including F. Louis Soldan, William H. Maxwell, Michael E. Sadler, William Rainey Harper, and many others. Being officers and speakers at the Congress of Arts and Science which was held in connection with the Exposition, they dined together at the "German Tyrolean Alps." Harris delivered his address on "Social Culture in the Form of Education and Religion." His own comment on this paper is interesting as revealing both his method and the point of view which he had reached:[16]

517

. . . I spent a great deal of time on the paper and remained in Washington all summer in order to do my best on the important question of religion as the fundamental educator giving to the people as a whole the insight which the social whole arrives at by a sort of institutional thinking — a partially sub-conscious thinking which divines the nature of the ultimate cause of man and nature and furnishes to its people a fundamental basis, so to speak, for their civilization.

In a similar vein he had written to W. H. Ward, of the New York *Independent*,[17] saying that in this paper he had tried "to reduce to its lowest terms the speculative thought at the bottom of Christian theism," a subject which had occupied his thoughts more than anything else for the past twenty-five years and longer.

A Notable Trip to Oregon

"The necessity of the study of history and literature is greater than ever before in our colleges and universities by reason of the fact that mechanical views of the universe sometimes assume too prominent a place in the mind of the youth." This was one of the central thoughts Harris brought out in his commencement address on "The Future of the State College and the State University," at Pennsylvania State College, on June 14th, 1905, when that institution celebrated its Semi-Centennial Jubilee.[18]

Harris had carried this address in his mind for longer than usual. President George W. Atherton had made certain definite suggestions, and Harris was striving to please him. A paragraph from one of his letters to the president[19] illustrates well his method of work: ". . . I always take a long time to think out an address and I seek always to get a unity of sufficient importance to justify and explain the different discussions which I insert in the address." It seemed as if Atherton was prescribing the course of his thinking, but in the end he modified his strictures by saying that he wanted Harris to give "the authoritative word that will serve to crystallize opinion for the next fifty years at least."[20]

Two months before this address, Harris was present at the celebration of the Centennial of the New York Public Schools, at which occasion he also delivered an address. Again apart from his activity in the National Educational Association which had now changed its name by special act of Congress to the National Education Association of the United States, and some minor talks like that to the State Teachers at Moberly, Missouri, in December, 1906, on "The Transient and Permanent in Education," Harris may be said to have closed his illustrious public speaking career with his convocation address at the Lewis and Clark Educational Congress at Portland, Oregon.

In Spring, 1905, Rev. W. G. Eliot, Jr., as Secretary of the Committee of the Lewis and Clark Centennial Exposition, sent Harris an invitation to attend the congresses and conferences that were to be held in August in connection with it. Harris suspected that the writer was the grandson of the William Greenleaf Eliot of St. Louis whom he had known so well. This proved to be correct, and in another letter Eliot stated that he remembered Harris well in the days of his boyhood. The invitation to attend was followed by one to deliver the Convocation Address. At first, Harris was a bit hesitant, but at last gave in. His letter of acceptance[21] was typical of his utter lack of vanity or desire to be "out in front." The last paragraph read:

I will try to work up a speech that will give a setting to the present problems, all along the line, in education. I will try to count up the "sphinx riddles" of education now confronting us, nationally and internationally, because we are trying to lift savage, barbarous, and semi-civilized peoples up to a point of cooperation with us industrially and politically. This is our greatest problem, and like unto it, if less formidable, is the problem of eradicating the slums of our cities.

On August 21st, Harris left Washington, and arrived at St. Paul two days later, only to find out that the sleeping car arrangements which he had made with the Canadian Sleeping Car Company were not to be honored. When he threatened to take an American road, he was finally accomodated and later did not regret having come by way of the Canadian Rockies to Portland. To Charles H. Ames he wrote on the way from Banff to Glacier.[22]

DEAR C. H. A.,

"You ought to be here"; "Well," say you, "I *have bean* there." "I have bean at Bannf and 'glacier,' at Medicine Hat and Field and Calgary and Winnipeg and thro' the hull Canadian Pacific route." I am at "Laggan" now, having passed Bannf at breakfast . . . I believe that Whymper was half right when he praised these mountains as compared with the Alps — I should not do such a thing, but if they were twice as great as they are we could say, as Whymper is reported as saying, "The Canadian Rockies are fifty or sixty Switzerlands rolled into one." But these mountains should be at least twice as high to warrant me to say what Whymper says. I will grant at the outset that these mountains beat the U. S. Rockies all to pieces . . . Do you know that I get a mountain effect from Mt. Washington that I prefer to all effects of the kind except the Alps?

There is one deep difference between your esthetique and mine — I want history intermingled with my geography — the human element must be there and I wish it to be world-historical and not merely "of yesterday" . . .

There were three postscripts appended to this letter. A letter to the "Folkses" at home also told, more geologically than lyrically, of the beauty of the Rockies and made comparisons with the scenery around Grindelwald. The close of the letter[23] may follow:

Toward night: We have come nigh thro' the mountains and seen by far the most wonderful ones since I wrote the foregoing.

Tomorrow I cross over into the U. S. again and perhaps will reach Portland at midnight.

All the rivers here have the appearance of glacial streams of a pea green color. All the rains of the Pacific winds rain out before they get across this mountain system and the consequence is a great growth of forests on the west side of the range and next to none on the east side.

Affectionately

PAPA

At Portland, Harris delivered his address on the 28th of August. On the sixth of September he was back home in Washington once again, "used up pretty effectively," to quote his own phrase.

CHAPTER TWENTY-SEVEN

MORE CONTRIBUTIONS TO AMERICAN EDUCATION

THE NATIONAL EDUCATIONAL ASSOCIATION

ANY history of the National Education Association of the United States, faithfully written, will reveal the great service that Harris rendered to it throughout his career as the most distinguished and most widely known educator of his day. Only some highlights, not elsewhere touched upon, may, therefore be presented here.

If we glance through the history as published in 1892, we find that Harris had delivered, since 1870, when he joined the organization, 44 addresses, or as many as five in a single year. Next in quantity of contributions was W. E. Sheldon with his 15 addresses. From this alone, not mentioning the numerous discussions which Harris participated in, his importance within the Association may fairly be measured. His activity after 1891 was equally as great if not greater. Dean John W. Withers, in the tribute of the Department of Superintendence of the Association to William Torrey Harris at St. Louis, March 24th, 1936, quoted President William Lowe Bryan on Harris' commanding influence: "He knew how to deal with men in the interests of his high purposes as effectively as the shrewdest Yankee, for he was Yankee before he was philosopher. He used to control the decisions of the National Education Association year after year. When he said 'thumbs up' on any proposal, it was adopted. When he said 'thumbs down,' that idea was dead as a dodo. They always thought that he must be right whether they understood what he was saying or not." However, Harris was not so dictatorial as it may seem from this quotation. He was, to be sure, "Iconoclast to little gods of clay,"[1] but his methods were gentle and persuasive, never sardonic. A. E. Winship spoke about the "almost idolatrous worship of America's public school men which he received during the years in which he was the official professional leader of the school people of the United States." He gave himself freely, as Bardeen wrote, and, we might add, he exercised the power which he held over his associates by virtue of his kindness and lack of presumption. Though speaking innumerable times he never developed oratorical powers that might influence the audience by suggestion. He always read from manuscript. When listening to another's address, he would sit quietly on the platform, a stiff notebook cover on his knees and some odd sheets of paper on which he scribbled his shorthand notes. But when he rose to speak, his words revealed the depth of his thought, which no one would have suspected to have any possible relation to the hastily penned notes. So gladly was he seen at the meetings, that in his later years he was obliged to make a speech in response every time a welcome was tendered him.

Harris had a hand in formulating the policies of the Association, and also in establishing some of its departments, such as the Elementary Department. He became president of the Department of Superintendence in 1873, and president of the Association in 1875. The circumstances of the meeting that was held in that year in Minneapolis, have been discussed earlier. He was active in the Normal Department and the Higher Department, and in the Spelling Reform Association, and made contributions to the Art, Music, Industrial and Kindergarten Departments. When T. W. Bicknell, in 1880, suggested the organization of a National

Council of Education for the purpose of "a more careful and deliberate examination of educational questions by a body of experts in the science and art of education," Harris was for it, but warned that the American people are jealous of any tendency to authority, and wanted to make sure that the work of such a council was wholly advisory. He served on the Committee of Eleven to consider the formation of such a body. His later work in the National Council of Education is well-known. His influence in that body has been ably described by J. M. Greenwood who attributed to him the quality of "complacency of waiting." He related how, when the majority seemed to be swept off their feet by some momentary current, he remarked to him with a half-quiet chuckle: "We can afford to wait."

In 1885, Harris made a confession[2] in regard to the Association which is worth quoting:

> I have regarded the meetings of the National Educational Association as precious opportunities for meeting prominent persons engaged in the work of education. Interesting questions have been discussed at every session; but I have never thought that the specially professional papers and discussions, though most numerous, were most profitable. Papers stimulating to broader views, or deeper culture, or greater enthusiasm have seemed to be of greater service. To me the sight of large numbers of representative teachers and superintendents has proved the attractive feature of the annual meeting — I should say the sight and the friendly greeting, the opportunity for comparison of views on matters of practical and speculative interest . . .

At the meeting of the Department of Superintendence in March, 1889, the advocates of manual training were in the great majority and argued for special proficiencies and subjects without reference to the effect upon the whole of education and its objectives. In contrast, Harris contended with Goethe that education must offer the pupil a "seed corn which is the possibility of countless harvests," while the educative effect of excessive manual training he compared to offering a piece of bread which nourishes only for a day.

At St. Paul, in 1890, he spoke before 2000 members of the Association. They gave him an ovation exceeding all previous ones, for he had become in the meantime Commissioner of Education of the United States. It was at that meeting that he recommended the publication of an annual report "giving an outline of the educational progress made in psychological and pedagogical observation" during the past year. Many were his significant utterances at different meetings and they were quoted the country over. Thus, at Philadelphia, in February, 1891, he said: "We wish to produce as many growing teachers as possible, as many as possible who each year have found fresh leads and have distanced their former selves."

There was also a great deal of good-natured fun, and many anecdotes have been told about Harris. Thus Dr. Edward Brooks once crossed the path of Harris in a discussion, and Brooks later said complacently in answer to an enquiry: "I think I rather had the best of him," which remark, however, only occasioned a good laugh, for everyone knew better. Many a time Harris would come to the rescue when things were not going too well at the meetings, and opposing interests and ideas came to a deadlock. Then he would get up, as at that Toronto meeting of 1891, and make a popular speech which made everyone forget the seriousness of the issue. Quietly determined in his views, he was also big-hearted.

With much glee the Harris-Maxwell incident has been often repeated, but it is so good that it bears re-telling.[3] The scene was the Richmond, Va., meeting of the Department of Superintendence. Harris had extolled the value of Greek and Latin, when Wm. H. Maxwell got up and spoke wholly in favor of English. Having done, Harris was asked by formal vote to make reply. "He was at his best, and so was the audience. He began his hilarious dance over the prostrate form of him who had played the re-enthronement act" of the Teuton queen. "It was not only irresistibly amusing, but it was every-way classic humor. It was wholly good-natured. There was not the shadow of suspicion of viciousness in it; pure classic mischief, with an educational purpose, — that was all. To report it is impossible. Every point that Mr. Maxwell had innocently presented merely furnished coloring for the vivifying of the historic painting by Dr. Harris." "When Dr. Harris was through, Mr. Marble, in his inimitable manner, coolly moved that Mr. Maxwell be invited to ask Dr. Harris another question. But Mr. Maxwell was silent, impressively silent. Judge Draper, who sat behind him, nudged him repeatedly, and said so as to be heard far and near, 'Get up, Maxwell, get up. Ask him another question.' To this Mr. Maxwell replied, 'Get up yourself.' 'Ah, I have a wife and children at home,' replied the judge. The most vivid imagination cannot portray the condition of that audience of dignitaries . . . "

It was Winship again who said that someone ought to print "as a beautiful memorial" Harris' two most famous utterances at the meetings of the Department of Superintendence at Richmond and at Cleveland, for these were the great flashes of his genius. One of the many pioneering jobs which the Department took upon itself for American education, was the sponsoring of the Committee of Fifteen in February, 1893, after the success of the Committee of Ten which had functioned so well in determining the content of intermediate education. The Committee of Fifteen, which was concerned with elementary education, reported in February 1895, at the Cleveland meeting, and Harris as Chairman presented the report of the subcommittee on the mutual relationship of the studies in the grades. The members of the committee were J. M. Greenwood, C. B. Gilbert, L. H. Jones, and W. H. Maxwell, and though the report voiced entirely the opinion of Harris, they fully subscribed, while disagreeing in details, to the soundness of the recommendations. The report occasioned much praise and much criticism, and it will forever clearly fix Harris' position in the history of pedagogy as the most consistent and influential exponent of the view that civilization must be interpreted first in order to find the values toward the realization of which we are engaged in the business of educating. Child-study does not reveal these values, but it is an important branch of pedagogy, along with the study of the educative process. Harris never denied the appearance of new values, but he did deny that they appear with the untutored child for whom an opportunity has never been provided to master or to know, through education, all his possibilities as a human being. Harris contended that the child is a mere possibility, like an acorn; only the oak reveals what is truly in the acorn. "Man has revealed what he is, not in the cradle, but in the great world of human history and literature and science." The plan of study in the school is to be laid out accordingly.

Through mathematics, man may master the universe about him. The quantitative study of nature is thus the first step in education to manhood. A qualitative study of nature cannot be the first step, for that is exactly the level of the primitives and "the superstitious savage" who "substitutes for mathematics the principle of life, and looks in the movement of inanimate things for an indwelling soul." The study of organic nature must likewise be based on the major premise and thus form a subsidiary to geography.

Next in importance is literature as a branch of study, which reveals man's ideas and emotions. But it needs another, the fourth branch, consisting in grammar and language, with the allied studies of logic and psychology. These cultivate the twofold attitude of the mind, "one toward the sign and one toward the signification." The fifth branch should acquaint the child with man as a member of the social organism and "looks to the formation of the state as the chief of human institutions." This is realized in the study of history. Harris also visualized a sixth branch of study, religion, but was aware that it implies a method totally different from the others, all of which are to be considered in co-ordination. Such studies as drawing, manual training and physical culture, were in his view not really co-ordinate, but "intellectual co-efficients." Drawing, for instance, is partly a skill, partly an art, and partly a mathematical branch. The purpose of the articulation was to show to the pupil at all times human achievement at every stage of development. The different branches open up the windows of the soul and give the child insight into the world of man and of nature.

The child-study faction did not relish this theory at all and made light of the five "co-ordinate" branches. But for years afterwards, the report was hailed as a master-piece and Harris was never deemed clearer, brighter and more forcible than when he spoke on this topic. In 1902, when the National Council of Education met in Minneapolis, Harris gave another notable address which was calculated to give education a philosophic basis. The title was: "The Difference between Efficient and Final Causes in Controlling Human Freedom."

One of the great occasions in his life, and a fitting tribute to his work in the Association, was the banquet tendered him by the Department of Superintendence at the Plankinton House, Milwaukee, Wis., on March 1st, 1905. Probably more educators of note were gathered there than at any time previously. The best description of this event has been given by Bardeen. Those assembled there, in their speeches, did not dwell so much on the scholar and the author and the leader as on the personal tribute of gratitude, what he had done for me, and me, and me. This modest, unassuming, almost shy man had wrought himself into the lives of so many who spoke that it was easy to see he had become a working force in hundreds who did not speak, and that far beyond what he is credited with in "Who's Who" is the silent influence that has gone out all these years in his personal influence over men and women . . . It is something to be a great man, it is much to be a useful man, it is a great deal to be a beacon, guiding to sanity and warning against pitfalls, but on that Milwaukee evening he must have felt most of all the triumph of Mary, Queen of Scots, *"Ich bin viel geliebt"*.

Harris was visibly moved by all the words that were spoken in affection. But he remained himself, the kind and humble philosopher. He was now nearly seventy, and confessed that he was just becoming able to apply his heart unto wisdom. On the car back to Chicago where he caught the train to Washington, he was conversing with a friend about the Logos. . .

UNIVERSITY EXTENSION AND CORRESPONDENCE UNIVERSITIES

The National Educational Association eclipsed every other teachers' organization by virtue of its ability to absorb the different interests into departments and holding their meetings in widely scattered places through the country. The American Institute of Instruction had been the only rival in its early days. But since it confined itself to the New England area, its activity and influence became more and more limited. Its greatest glory it achieved perhaps in 1883 at Fabian's in the beautiful White Mountains. But there were meetings as late as 1889, 1891 and 1906 which Harris attended and addressed.

On November 29th and 30th, 1889, there was a Conference in the Interest of Physical Training, called by the Massachusetts State Board of Education and held at Huntington Hall, in the Massachusetts Institute of Technology, with exhibitions and class exercises, illustrating German, Swedish and American methods. The conference was presided over by Harris who had always taken a keen interest in physical culture. He introduced the various speakers, including a number of physicians and men prominent in reformatory work and education. On May 26th, 1890, he addressed the Spencerian Business College in Washington.

The problem of university extension, and his activity in connection with it, Harris always rated as of some importance.[4] Through the efforts of Seth T. Stewart, School Principal of Brooklyn, N. Y., a Committee on the Promotion of University and School Extension was founded in 1889, and President Timothy Dwight of Yale had accepted the presidency of the University Extension Division and the chairmanship of the executive committee of the whole movement. Three public meetings were called for 1889-90. The second of them, held in the Spring of 1890, discussed what the universities and schools can do for the people, and Harris presented his views in a paper of that title. He spoke on the topic at Princeton, N. J., as well as at the National Educational Association meeting at St. Paul, Minn., in July, 1890. The following year he gave an address on "The Place of University Extension in American Education," which was incorporated in the *Proceedings of the First Annual Meeting of the National Conference on University Extension.*

The International Correspondence University had been founded in 1893, but at first specialized in Civil Service Extension Courses. It was one of the original ventures to offer education through the mails. In October, 1904, Channing Rudd had resigned his professorship and registrarship in the Columbian University to accept the presidency of this correspondence school.[5] Harris was asked to serve as Chairman of the Advisory Faculty. It seemed that the only correspondence the president had with him was to mail him his monthly check for $150, with kind regards, excusing his brevity by "the enormous amount of work necessary in perfecting the general organization."[6]

When the issues of *Leslie's Magazine*, the *Literary Digest*, the *Saturday Evening Post* and other journals began carrying large spread advertisements of the International Correspondence University of Washington, with portraits of Harris and ten other men of note whose careers did not seem to be in harmony with the rather unacademic message and the high pressure salesmanship, letters poured into Harris' office enquiring whether the "university" had his sanction and support. He could not do differently than acknowledge his connection and reiterate his belief in the sincerity of the men connected with it. But he seems to have terminated his connection with this venture soon after this rather unwelcome publicity.

THE BARNARD SOCIETY

It was at the April 9th, 1868, meeting of the Missouri State Teachers' Association in St. Louis, with Harris present, that a hearty approbation of Barnard's appointment as United States Commissioner of Education was given in a resolution of the body.[7] What Harris had done for American philosophy in his *Journal of Speculative Philosophy*, that Henry Barnard had done for pedagogy in his *American Journal of Education*. Soon after assuming, in 1889, the office in the Bureau of Education, Harris directed the preparation of a general index to Barnard's journal. Both he and Barnard had reached down into their own pockets to keep their respective journals alive, only with this difference that Barnard had been reduced to penuriousness.

Since 1878, there was in existence at Providence, R. I., an association of pedagogs which after its reorganization in 1882 called itself the Barnard Club. Harris spoke on the Kindergarten at one of its meetings in February, 1889, and later was elected an honorary member. His plans for a Henry Barnard Society and a Henry Barnard Publishing Company in both of which ventures Dr. Nicholas Murray Butler had likewise an interest, were, however, entirely thought up by himself.

Many were the letters which he received from Barnard and his daughters begging for advice and aid in working out their money problems. In response to these requests, he published a folder inviting educators to join his Barnard Society. The veteran educator was at the time in his 81st year. His work done, he found himself, in Harris' words, "embarrassed in his old age, by debts and mortgages, to a vexatious degree." Harris proposed to help him and render a service to American education at the same time, by forming a stock company for purchasing the plates of the *American Journal of Education,* thus securing "the two good results of relieving the noble man from the pinchings of poverty, and at the same time" "saving the stereotype plates of the thirty-one volumes of the journal from the melting pot." He was proposing to raise $25,000 by the sale, to members, of volumes of the journal already printed which Barnard had at his home in Hartford. There were to be membership certificates to the amount of $1, $5, $50 and $100, to the last attaching special privileges in the management of the Henry Barnard Publishing Company, but all entitling the holder to special discounts. The four-page folder was issued over Harris' signature and dated March, 1891. It was one of those friendly gestures of Harris, who was ever ready to help a friend in need.

MORE CONTRIBUTIONS TO EDUCATION

THE PSYCHOLOGIC FOUNDATIONS OF EDUCATION

It has often been said that one of the main contributions of Harris to the cause of education in its professional aspects was the *International Education Series*, published by D. Appleton & Co., and Winship thought that fifteen or twenty of the 57 volumes edited and prefaced by Harris might be issued as a "Memorial William T. Harris Edition." Now, the 37th volume was by Harris' own hand and bore the title *Psychologic Foundations of Education; an Attempt to Show the Genesis of the Higher Faculties of the Mind.* It appeared in 1898 and had been hanging fire for three years, in fact, had been advertised for two years till the publisher suggested taking it off the list. Since 1879, Harris had spoken a number of times on the subject, most noteworthy being his lectures on "Educational Psychology" at Sleeper Hall, in the University of Boston at the end of 1888, and his 1891 lecture on "Psychology for Teachers" at Henderson, Kentucky. Articles by his hand on educational psychology appeared in print as far back as 1869-70 and 1873-74.

With the appearance of the book, Harris, as Dr. B. A. Hinsdale of the University of Michigan wrote, placed himself in a position where he could easily be criticised. Until then, his thought was bared, to be sure, in numerous discussions; but by giving educators something as unalterable as a book, he had committed himself. The book sealed his fate as an educational thinker. Paradoxical as it may seem, having published the sum and substance of his educational wisdom which he had given so freely and with so much personal success, Harris was on the road to being forgotten, for he was not the spokesman for the trend of the times. Criticism was kind, forebearing, for Harris had been kind and forebearing, and his towering knowledge could not be assailed. Even John Dewey, his very good friend, could not help placing him publicly on the side of conservatism,

533

yes, even reactionism. Had Harris published the book twenty years earlier, the judgment of a later day, as of his day, might have been different. But it made its appearance too late in the history of American education.

None would deny that Harris had displayed a remarkable ability in practical education despite his speculative bias. But what they objected to was that he took away, as it were, the very desire to buttress educational measures and recommendations by testing the forces and reactions that come into play in the educative process. His approach was hampered, so it was believed, by his speculative ideas and his attitude that demanded an answer to what we are educating *for*. The book, however, is a monument — and about this there can be no doubt — to the point of view which prevailed during the height of his career and of which he was the acknowledged protagonist. It is historic now, but being historic should not be relegated to oblivion. As revealing the contrast between the speculative emphasis and the emphasis on investigation, between co-ordination and a budding consciousness of integration, between reason and enquiry with suggestion, between knowledge and an ever increasing doubtfulness and faltering certainty, between inwardness and dissipation of thought in activity, between values or qualities and fact or quantity, the book fairly epitomized the last stand of educational thinking against pragmatism and experimentalism. It did not help Harris when he rationalized so-called progress or waxed enthusiastic about the modern age. The spirit in which he viewed things was not identical with the spirit that motivated the civilization of his day. It is quite beside the point whether the title of the book, as some have held, was ill-chosen or misleading. To choose it was his privilege. Psychology did not have the same connotation in his vocabulary as it had in that of other educators. The same was the case with the concepts of history, development and evolution, which latter concept is even now undergoing reformulation. The book only helped to throw into high relief all these discrepancies. But by the same token, if ever educational thinking should wish to re-orient itself, it might find new inspiration in Harris' work. He himself considered it of great importance.

The book widened the gap between empiricists and idealists, and in this respect it came at a decisive moment in the intellectual history of America. Many were the letters that were received by him and which spoke in terms of high praise of his work, yes, even placed it on an equal footing with "the treatises of Aristotle which will live through the centuries and work human good." But we shall refrain from citing names lest some may be embarrassed who now hold different views. However, friend and foe acknowledged that the book bore testimony to great analytic power and held many significant thoughts. In this work more than in any other of his writings, Harris echoed less slavishly the views of Hegel or of Fichte or of Rosenkranz. He definitely expounded his own rational psychology which he now had to defend. It was during this period that there appeared his "Rational Psychology for Teachers" in the *Journal of Pedagogy* and elsewhere, and his educational creed, contributed to Ossian H. Lang's *Educational Creeds of the 19th Century*.[8] In the Chicago Kindergarten College lecture of 1899, he contrasted the two kinds of psychology and developed his thesis of how symbolic thinking grows into logical thinking, how imitation becomes originality, and how the feelings and emotions may be educated through the intellect and the will.

Rudolf Eucken, for one, praised Harris for his work because it offered a psychology which, with due respect to empirical fact, staunchly maintained the great principles of self-activity and freedom and developed them strictly scientifically.[9] It was only a few years before the publication of the *Foundations* that Harris had raised the problem as to whether education is possible without freedom of the will, and had taken a stand against John Dewey's doctrine of interest as related to will.

This fateful book on the *Psychologic Foundations of Education* marked perhaps the zenith of Harris' career as an educational philosopher. The University of Jena made him Doctor of Philosophy *honoris causa in* 1899.[10] Eucken, in congratulating him on this singular honor, pointed out in his letter that the award was made because Harris had been fighting valiantly for a philosophical foundation of pedagogy. Harris, in his reply, said that he had never known of an instance in which a German university had conferred a degree *causa honoris,* and the German philosopher's kind letter had quite overcome him. This was the last of the honorary degrees conferred on Harris, beginning with the M.A. from Yale and the LL.D. from the University of Missouri. In rapid succession had followed the Ph.D. from Brown University in 1893, the LL.D. from the University of Pennsylvania in 1894, the LL.D. from Yale in 1895, and the LL.D. from Princeton University in 1896. The Ph. D. from Jena was significant to Harris as a philosopher also because that university had played an important rôle during the flowering of speculative philosophy.

CHAPTER TWENTY-EIGHT

VARIED SOCIAL AND POLITICAL PROBLEMS

AMERICAN FIRST

DURING the Civil War, Harris had been on the side of the Union as a matter of course, during the expansion of America internationally, he was on the side of those who envisaged a greater America. As Commissioner of Education, he stood four square behind the national policies which the four Presidents under whom he served, pursued. His admiration for German philosophy and pedagogical ideas only served to add fuel to his ardor for an America strong and vigorous in the pursuit of an idealism and sound educational methods, and as autonomous as possible, free from outside influences. He praised President Harrison's political wisdom;[1] his faith in Grover Cleveland he had demonstrated long before; his enthusiasm for national expansion under William McKinley mounted, because it meant the triumph of civilization; and throughout Theodore Roosevelt's administration he sustained this enthusiasm. "It is grand for us friends of Mr. Roosevelt and of his personal methods to read of the 'great landslide' in this morning's paper, for it is not only a victory of the party (the G.O.P.) but especially our endorsement of the man Roosevelt himself and it warms one's heart to discover that the American people are up to seeing and appreciating a great man while he is yet living."[2] Harris may have been an isolationist before the Spanish-American War, as Dr. John J. Tigert, one of his distinguished successors in office believed, and become a staunch advocate of a rapprochement between

America and Europe after the event, but it is certain that his political outlook was more nearly that of Woodrow Wilson, whom he knew, than that of any other president.

Education at public expense, he said, "demands for its justification the existence of some political necessity which it provides for, or the existence of a general want in society for the supply of which the system of education serves a useful purpose."[3] It is thus clear, that education, with Harris, possessed political expediency. He furthermore stated[4] that "the ultimate significance of German thought in the history of the world is this: It will compel all other nations to adopt the same system of exhaustive specialization in the study of practical details, the same exhaustive preparation of its soldiers and materials of war, the same education of all its people. The history of Austria since Sadowa, and of France since Sedan, illustrate this trend of events." But he also said that "the philosophy of education in the deepest sense is yet to be made over into English." How prophetic and how true!

As the best-known American educator, it was a stroke of singular political wisdom that made him a member and chairman of the Board of Civil Service Examiners for Promotions in the Interior Department, for which office he was designated February 15th, 1897. His ability to view education as one of the fundamentals of civilization and the presence or lack of it as influencing the political and social structure of a nation, soon made his services in the national government invaluable, and he was consulted on many issues. He expressed his opinion on patriotism; he discussed the Postal Savings Banks; investigated the nature of compulsory laws; and revived his interest of long ago in the railroads.[5] At Baltimore, he gave an address before the National Conference of Charities, at Philadelphia he delivered one on immigration before the American Defence Association, at Cincinnati he spoke on the philosophy of crime and punishment before the National Prison Association. More than one article was written by him on the single tax.

THE NEWSPAPER, EDUCATION AND WISDOM

The newspaper as an instrument of education probably never had nor ever will have a more sincere friend and advocate than Harris. Scholars and philosophers on the whole, have never spoken in faintest praise of this product of civilization. Differently Harris. To the foreigner who criticised the American press for its proneness to sacrifice truth for publicity and scandal, he would point out while apologizing for the all-too frequent mistaking of licence for freedom, how much of real information is contained even in its daily gossip. By bringing information on politics and scientific events down to the level on which the intelligence of the greatest number may benefit by it, the newspaper was, according to him, the most effective educational agent in American democracy. He maintained that the English papers served up information "in the form of elaborate articles, as if written for encyclopaedias," employing a style that studiously excludes the people from the attainment of knowledge.[6]

Moreover, he recommended reading of the newspapers to young girls and argued with somewhat philosophic detachment, if not blindness, that they would thus improve their morals. The young girl sees in the paper the moral spectacle of sinners pursued by avenging demons of the law and public opinion. If she contemplates too steadily the picture of degradation and begins to be fascinated by it, she betrays the tendency to her mother, or to some member of the family, and a counter-influence begins its healing work at once. If she should grow up in ignorance until she encounters the vicious reality in later life, she is not prepared for it and falls an easy victim to the allurements of sin.[7] Harris thus advocated what Walter B. Pitkin urged nearly half a century later amid the most vigorous protests of parents and the church.

Nor was this point of view ever given up by Harris. At the celebration of the beginning of the second century of the American patent system, at Washington, D.C., in April, 1891, Harris delivered his address on "The Relation of Invention to the Communication of Intelligence and the Diffusion of Knowledge by Newspaper and Book"; and at Knoxville, Tenn., during June, 1902, he gave a series of four lectures on "The Newspaper as an Educator and its Relation to the School," using his article of 1881 on "The Printing Press as an Instrument of Education" as a basis. The newspaper he took also as an instrument of school extension and "a sort of national council by which contradictory feelings and prejudices become purified and adjusted into wisdom."

AT ODDS WITH MARX AND HENRY GEORGE

Harris subscribed to the fundamentals of political economy as enunciated by Henry Carey, of Philadelphia, that we need more commerce and less trade. More and more he leaned toward the idea that we are growing better and better — the old adage: From barbarism to civilization! He distinguished three classes of weaklings in society: The weakling in thrift who produces pauperism; the weakling in morals who is responsible for the production of crime; and the weakling in intellect who fills the asylums of the insane and feeble-minded.

He found himself at odds with Henry George's doctrine of the ownership of land. Socialism and George's work he had studied for about two years rather intensely and found weak spots in his doctrine. In that property in land was increasing only one third as fast as property of other kinds, and "the total production of the nation amounted to forty cents a day for each man, woman and child, the total expenses of land to each individual afforded only two and one-

fifth cents a day or one-eighteenth of the total production."
This fact he considered an objection to Henry George which
had never been set aside.[8]

He was looking forward to an era when all the resources
of the world would be capitalized. By that he meant that
"all sources of wealth are to be rated in the world market."
The "obvious advantage" which he thought would be
gained by this was the stimulation of industrial production
in the form of manufacturing by machinery.[9] At the headquarters of the National Education Association are preserved some Harris manuscripts that bear the title of "Looking backward to Socialism" (which is a first draft of another
one on "Socialism, Anarchy, and Free Competition" dating
from the year 1889) and "Why Should we not Adopt a
Form of Government Socialism in order to Save Ourselves
from the Evils of Competition?"[10] He did not go into print
with these manuscripts when he went to Washington, but
he had spoken freely on Henry George before, and in October, 1897, contributed to *The Forum* "Statistics versus
Socialism."[11]   Harris had *Das Kapital* in his library and
probably studied it in the period of his articles on Socialism,
realizing in the doctrines of Marx, who represented the reverse form of Hegelianism, decided dangers. In his 1882
paper on "Do the Public Schools educate Children beyond
the Position which they must occupy in Life?", which was
republished ten years later,[12] he maintained that if you exclude the humanities in the schools, you invite socialism and
communism and allow the mind to become "fly-blown with
crazy political and social theories destructive of the state."
It has been pointed out in an earlier chapter, how sympathetic Harris was toward giving the workers the best possible education in as well as out of school.

Meanwhile, capital and labor were edging more and
more toward violent clashes by virtue of their incompatibili-
ties, and labor was by far the more alert and informed about

economic and social problems. Capitalism was at a decided disadvantage because of its complacency and false sense of security. When it realized that the jig was up, it hurled only generalizations and arguments against the disciples of Marx for which the latter were prepared long in advance or which they regarded as primitive and had transcended in their dialectic. Now there was a certain faction which saw an opportunity in Harris' sociological and political views to deal the forces that were stirring a sound blow, and they approached him through persons of influence to persuade him to turn his skill in couching difficult thoughts in simple language to the cause of averting the dangers of a social revolution. Harris was to write tracts or pamphlets, three, ten, a dozen, or as many as he could or would, which were to be distributed by the tens of thousands among the working people. But it was already too late. The year was 1908, and Harris had nearly served out his time.[13]

FREE SILVER

In a very long letter of July 28th, 1899, Harris dilated upon the topic of free silver to his son Theodore who was grooming himself for the State Senatorship in Texas. He recalled the dreadful waste of a "wild-cat currency" in the period of 1857-61, when he was establishing himself in St. Louis.

> Every dealer in market had to own a "bank note detector" and consult it constantly — the latest edition of it — consuming fifty per cent more time in effecting purchases. Even peanut stands had to have the weekly issues of the bank-note detector. A pocketful of bills would include some that were 10% discount, some 25% and some 40% or even 75% discount. The small dealers had to run to the brokers and get rid of their bills from a distance at once or next week they might find them worth nothing.

The fact that a great nation could be forced by a popular vote into such an experiment as the unlimited expansion of its money by free coinage of an inferior precious metal in a forced ration to the most precious metal would be a fact sufficient to destroy our boasted Republic. The disorganization and suffering that we should cause in Europe would warrant Europe in a united effort to subdue us . . . "You cannot fool all the people all the time," — but we should have to admit that all the people, or a ruling majority of them, could be fooled into doing things that they could not undo again.

In July, 1896, Harris allowed himself to be interviewed on the silver strike while he was passing through Buffalo, N. Y. But at the time of his writing the letter to Theodore, he envisaged, as an aftermath of "free silver," riots and bloodshed and wanton destruction of property and, in the end, attempts at socialistic solution terminating in "communistic committees of citizens." On several occasions he concerned himself with the money question and the theory of property. One of his last manuscripts to go to press was written for the *Washington Star* on how to make the national currency elastic, and was printed in January, 1908. His plan consisted in government-issued, interest-bearing, convertible bonds purchasable for currency, a measure that would forestall the possibility of hoarding money.

SOCIOLOGY AND SUFFRAGE

The interest which Harris had in the American Social Science Association has already been alluded to. This organization, founded in 1865, was, during Harris' time, distinctly the ward of Frank B. Sanborn, his close friend, who served as third secretary and had much correspondence and verbal consultation with Harris who often advised on points of policy, speakers and the like. The Department of Education in which Harris acted as chairman, was understood by him as merely one aspect of the general work of the Association, dealing with "all phases of combination of man with his fellow-men — all kinds of associated effort wherein the might of the individual is reinforced by the might of the species."[14] Religious papers in particular acknowledged the progressive thought of Harris in the matter of female education,[15] which was one of his main concerns. His annual papers before the Association until 1884 confined themselves to pedagogical issues. From then on—and he spoke as late as 1900—his addresses assumed more and more socio-political aspects: The growth of cities in 1885, the right of property and the ownership of land in 1886, profit-sharing in 1888, the single tax in 1890. In 1898 and 1900 he discussed education again, but this time from the vantage-point of his position as the head of the nation's schools.

In view of the fact that woman suffrage was not granted in the U. S. until 1920, it is remarkable that as early as his principalship in St. Louis Harris was strongly in favor of giving women a free reign in education, politics, law and all the other phases of public life. He was for co-education from the start, and promoted the suffrage movement. Julia Ward Howe, one of the most prominent suffragettes, was his life-long friend. It was not merely his kindness, his "readiness to yield and to explain" where women were concerned, as Sanborn once remarked; he saw a cultural necessity in the service women might render to society. Thus, he never failed them when they appealed to him for lectures. Whether the request came from the Woman's Educational Association of Boston, [16] from Hardin College, "a first class School for Young Ladies" at Mexico, Mo.,[17] the St. Louis division of the American Suffrage Association,[18] the National Woman Suffrage Association of Massachusetts,[19] a college for women in Baltimore,[20] or the Woman's

Anthropological Association,[21]—Harris was ever ready to promote the cause of woman's education and advancement.

In his St. Louis reports he had pointed out the basis of the woman movement in politics, industry and education.[22] The Women's Education Union in England took an interest in his paper on "Latin and Greek in Modern Education" and printed extracts in the February, 1880, issue of their *Journal*.

Harris had personal concern in the New York State Women's Social Science Association which was organized January 21st, 1880, and re-organized the 31st of March following, and had as object suggesting and developing plans "for the advancement in industrial, intellectual, social, educational, philanthropic and moral interests". Miss Marion Talbot, daughter of Mrs. Emily Talbot, Secretary of the Education Department of the American Social Science Association, co-worker and admirer of Harris, was guided by Harris on several occasions after she had helped in founding the Association of Collegiate Alumnae at Boston, on January 14th, 1882, a somewhat broader organization than the Massachusetts Society for the University Education of Women, with which she was connected in an executive capacity. Harris obliged Miss Talbot by giving a course of four lectures during November and December, 1881, on the subject of education for the Massachusetts organization meeting in Boston. Mrs. Talbot had created quite a stir with a circular in which she asked mothers to keep a register of the physical and mental development of their babies on the theory that "to study the natural development of a single child is worth more than a Noah's Ark full of animals". It was the type of psychological research which Harris subscribed to. He may have drawn up or, at least, inspired the questionnaire himself. At any rate, he based some statistical observations on the returns.

For the National Educational Association Harris furnished

in 1885 a report on the higher education of women. His reception at the meeting of the Massachusetts Woman's Suffrage Association on May 1st of the same year, at Concord, was interesting. Attendance was poor because of the inclement weather and because, as one of the ladies said, and F. B. Sanborn repeated, the people of Concord were so good that they did not wish to be better. Harris attacked the problem from the standpoint of social science and the ever-increasing tendency to divided labor which gave rise to the great epochs of productive industry. Woman at first limited herself to the sphere of the family, but with the increase in labor-saving devices, she demanded her entrance upon the sphere of productive industry and education as well. The rôle of woman in all departments, "even to the exercise of the law-making power", he regarded as "a necessity of the near future". In a republic, each is his brother's keeper, and since "a government of the average is unpleasant for the higher strata of society", woman must be allowed to do her share in elevating the lower strata.

This philosophic approach to woman suffrage was quite acceptable to the good town of Concord whose weekly printed Harris' talk almost in full, but under the pretext of lack of space did not even bother to brief the talk of Rev. Anna Shaw who made a glowing appeal for the cause. Harris' speech was merely a cautious variation of the theme he had repeatedly set before women's organizations, particularly the Missouri Woman's Suffrage Association which he had addressed twice, and the last time only a year before the meeting of the Concord group.[23] The spirit of the times he interpreted as in the direction of emancipation, be it that of caste, age, race, climate, season, inherited wealth, locality or sex. His special appeal went out to women to enter the sphere of public life in order to eliminate the rigors of law and the corruption of politics.

Thus, in 1899, he introduced Bishop Spalding at the Catholic University at Washington, who delivered his address on "Higher Education of Women". The book by Fräulein Helene Lange, in its American translation as *The Higher Education of Women in Germany,* to which Harris had written a preface in 1890, was circulating well. To the Woman's Congress of the 1900 Paris Exposition, Harris sent an article on "The Relation of Women to the Trades and Professions," and when Smith College celebrated its 25th Anniversary on October 2nd and 3rd, 1900, he was one of seven speakers — the others were Dean LeBaron Russell Briggs of Harvard, and the Presidents of Yale, Columbia, Vassar, Wellesley and Bryn Mawr — at the Educational Conference that convened on the second day, and his brief address on "Higher Education for Women" was later printed as a tract in the *Political Equality Series* of the National American Woman Suffrage Association. In the *Ohio Educational Monthly* for 1901 appeared his article on "Why Many Women should Study Law," being another cast of his address entitled "Women in the Legal Profession" delivered at the third annual commencement of the Washington College of Law, on May 22nd, 1901.

CHAPTER TWENTY-NINE

FRUITS OF PHILOSOPHY

THE LAST THROES OF HEGEL

IN order not to delay any longer making the message of Hegel available to the public in a form that seemed acceptable to the thinkers in the St. Louis Movement in Philosophy, Harris brought out, in 1890, his volume of over 400 pages, entitled *Hegel's Logic. A Book on the Genesis of the Categories of the Mind. A Critical Exposition.* It was published in *Grigg's Philosophical Classics,* under the editorial supervision of Professor George S. Morris. A second edition was necessary five years later. The book was the fruit of Harris' life-long study of Hegel which began in his pioneering days in St. Louis. Its history thus went back more than 25 years when, on April 10th, 1864, he started to write what purported to be a textbook of logic, to which he intended to give the title of

LOGIC OR PURE SCIENCE

as

developed by Wm. T. Harris from
studies on Hegel and his expositors
Rosenkrantz [sic], Brokmeyer, Vera,
and others.

This proposed book was carried out for only 19 pages in a notebook, and on page 22 of the same, dated 1866, August 12th, we find the beginning of the *Prima Philosophia* which runs for five pages to stop with the word "Hence," while the following page has only a four-line entry under date of 1872, December 22nd. However, further back there are two chapters with "Remarks," finishing the "first series" of "Lectures on Logic," running over 25 pages and bearing at the head the date October 27th, 1865.

Harris had worked on the published volume about eight years. Henry C. Brokmeyer did not finish his translation of Hegel's *Logic* until summer or fall, 1895. He then turned his attention to the *Phaenomenologie* and could report to Harris on June 7th, 1897, that he was dictating the last nine pages of the Introduction. "This completes the work" he wrote, and added, "and I will have before me the Phenomenology, the Logic, and the Psychology in the language of *my life,* from Alpha to Omega, and A to Izzard . . . " These dates are important in view of the appearance of Harris' book. Doubtless, Brokmeyer had recast his earlier translations which Harris had taken down in shorthand and which had been transcribed in longhand by himself and possibly by his wife and sister Sarah, and which had been objected to by the publisher because they *liessen sich nicht lesen.* However, the statement that all the translations werē finished, proved illusory, for Brokmeyer was working on the notes as well as the translation for years afterwards. Nothing came of this translation, and it was thus a good thing that Harris' book appeared as a symbol and sign of the activity of the Hegel group. Brokmeyer died in 1906, his manuscript passed into the hands of Harris' brother David Henry; the two brothers together with Denton J. Snider, Eugene C. Brokmeyer (the translator's son), Lewis J. Block and others planned to publish it by donation and subscription. Harris was to write the introduction and assist in editing, but his illness intervened and only notes were gathered, oddly enough for four prefaces, but none was finished, while a general pessimism overtook the St. Louis group who had tried their best to collect sufficient funds for publication. Snider was among the first to realize that it was too late to publish anything on Hegel. The manuscript of Brok-. meyer's translation of the *Logik* which saw many vicissitudes during Harris' lifetime, has not yet finished its career.[1]

As a side-light on the fortunes of the *Logic* we might note that in 1907 Harris wrote to the widow of his friend Judge H. M. Jones[2] who was under the impression that her husband owed Harris a sum for having the "400,000 words for the three volumes of Hegel's *Large Logic*" and the "nearly one hundred and forty thousand words for the part of the Phenomenology — a total of 540,000 words in all, copied in hand-writing at something less than 5c. a folio of one hundred words." The judge had paid $100, which represented one half of the bill, while Harris had taken care of the rest and would not accept any further payment from Mrs. Jones.

It has been the contention of some that Harris, throughout his lecturing career, had stated Hegel's message and philosophy better and in clearer terms than Hegel himself had done, at least so far as the English speaking world was concerned. His influence on the St. Louis group has been indicated sufficiently, but beyond this it is almost impossible to trace it. All those who heard Harris' lectures, and they numbered tens of thousands throughout the breadth of the land, were exposed to Hegelian thinking. Add to this the readers of Harris' numerous articles, and it may well be said that Hegel, through Harris alone, influenced American thought in the last quarter of the 19th century appreciatively and decisively. Even such typical Americans as Walt Whitman took Hegel as their authority, and the influence in professional educational and philosophical circles began to fade only when, true to the dialectic, the erstwhile American Hegelians became the well-known and celebrated champions of pragmatism and its allies, which earned the recognition of being the American philosophy.

One reviewer of Harris' book called it "Hegel himself

reproduced, or as the theosophists say, 're-incarnated' in America, thinking his own thought over again, freshly, with a certain American terseness, forthrightness, board-of-trade rapidity of transaction — thinking it too with the illustrations of an American environment, large, dry-aired, crisp, clear, hopeful. No tobacco smoke about his head this time. Nor is he sedentary and professional, with long, many-coiled sentences that hang thoughts by the tail like possums. He thinks on his feet. He is a man of affairs . . ." [3]

"The best book on Hegel in any language," was the general verdict which even William James might have conceded had he taken the time and trouble to read no more than preface and last chapter, as he was wont to. George H. Howison was most enthusiastic, voicing his sincere approval in Latin and Greek with a bit of fun interspersed.[4] Professor Dr. Karl Hegel commented on Harris' *lichtvolle Klarheit* with which he had been able to present his father's philosophy that was losing ground rapidly in Germany.[5]

Shadworth Hollway Hodgson wrote from London[6] that he expected to find the want of a clear and condensed account of Hegel's master-thought in the English language filled by Harris' volume. Professor David George Ritchie, writing from Oxford[7] to Rev. R. A. Holland, confided that Harris' book was a valuable commentary especially "in the account given of the Phaenomenologie" and confirmed this judgment also to Harris.[8] Richard Lewis Nettleship, the editor of Thomas Hill Green, remarked that it was the work "of one to whom the Logic is a reality."[9]

In 1896-97, the Council of the Philosophical Union in California adopted, as we have seen, the book as its regular text for study and discussion. Years later, at Columbia University, Dr. Nicholas Murray Butler, as Professor in the Department of Philosophy and Education, based his examination questions on paragraphs from Harris' book. Now, all the Hegel students, in large part the legacy of the

St. Louis Movement in Philosophy, had their text, and seminars were founded in St. Louis, in Faribault, Minn., in Washington, in fact all over the country where Hegelians met.

Harris' debt to Hegel was now paid in large part. However, to the *Library of the World's Best Literature*, edited by Charles Dudley Warner, he contributed the section on Georg Wilhelm Friedrich Hegel, with extracts from his works.

THE MEMORY CLUB

Most great men have been credited with an astounding memory, and many are the statements by educators and philosophers which bear testimony to the fact that Harris likewise possessed a remarkable gift of retention and recall. In an argument, for instance, he would be able to name not only the book and the chapter to which he was referring, but also the page on which the statement in question occurred. However, it is not often that we get from a competent judge as candid a self-analysis of the mental processes involved in retention and recall, as we have it from Harris who founded what he called "The Memory Club. An Association formed for the Purpose of Experimental Studies in the Psychology of the Memory of Words." The mimeographed prospectus which he sent out in 1892, is so unique and interesting, that we cannot do better than to reproduce it in part. Though he mentioned Larkin Dunton, Principal of the Normal School at Boston, Mass., as co-founder, the circular was written entirely on the basis of his own experience. Of late he had found his memory for words and especially proper names growing weaker year by year. Said he:

... I suppose that there may be some connection between this decay of memory and some sort of arrested growth in a convolution of the brain — perhaps the

FRUITS OF PHILOSOPHY

Broca convolution. Believing that the will, the spiritual power in man, controls the intellectual activity and develops portions of the brain as instruments for its purpose, I think that an attention to verbal memory will restore vital activity to portions of the brain which have been allowed to dwindle through lack of use . . .

I have already myself experimented somewhat in memorizing the exercises given by Robertson in his French method. In 1880 I memorized the first fourteen exercises. In 1889 I relearned these exercises which had in the meantime become quite dim in my memory and went on learning the other exercises up to number 20. During the past year, 1891-92, I have memorized the succeeding twenty exercises (21-40) and have found to my gratification that my ability to memorize such word exercises has increased threefold over what it was in 1880. Meanwhile I am more pleased to find that the poetry and prose which I memorized when a boy comes back to me with a freshness which it has not possessed since my twentieth year.

The study of philosophy and of works of reflection necessarily leads to the neglect of mechanical details and especially tends to the disuse of verbal memory. In my seventeenth year I became much interested in the cultivation of memory and having a poor memory of dates I especially cultivated this species of faculty by memorizing important dates in English history.

The best result from this is that I find my memory has grown to be reasonably good in regard to dates and rather improves as I grow older. It is now forty years since I commenced that experiment in regard to the memory of numbers.

With regard to mnemonic systems as they exist and have existed one would say truly that they lay stress, one and all, upon the principle of association. They

553

require the student to hunt up fanciful relations between the matter to be remembered and other matters familiar to the individual but possessing only unessential relations of cause and effect and the relation of individual and species is undoubtedly useful in the way of cultivating thought but the search for unessential relations is on the other hand injurious to habits of logical thinking. The mechanical memory including the memory of dates and words and isolated items is to a certain extent indifferent to the other power of thinking and not positively injurious to it as is the mnemonic method of association with what is unessential.

It seems to me therefore that a person should to a certain extent cultivate the mechanical memory by itself so far at least as is useful to prevent aphasia, and torpidity in the other forms of mechanical memory.

Now it is held by certain psychologists (see Prof. James's recent "Principles of Psychology") that there are close and hard limits in this matter of memory cultivation. It is my belief that this opinion is not well founded. The experiments of our club may do something to settle the question.

The members were to get a copy of Robertson's *The Whole French Method* in two volumes, published by A. Derache, in Paris, 1854, and start in by learning by heart the story of *Le Jeune Alexis Delatour*. Date, number of minutes of study and number of words memorized were to be recorded faithfully, as well as "the amount of time taken to recover on subsequent days what has been forgotten of the exercises already learned". In this way, it was intended to prove his own theory that it is the will that acts the major rôle in memory, rather than the factors which the physiological psychologists presuppose.

Quite apart from this desire and ability in Harris to acquire and retain much knowledge, our philosopher noticed

554

an even more important thing in his mental growth: An increase in wisdom with the years. While his body was slowly succumbing to the ravages of malaria, pneumonia and heart disease, his mind became clearer all the while. It was on July 14th, 1908, that he wrote to his son Theodore:

I am every day surprised at myself. Because in questions and points in philosophy, especially in the erudition that relates to the Greek philosophy and to its continuation in the later history in Alexandria and Rome, I have no difficulty in getting hold of very important points which enable me to solve things which gave me trouble all the years. I spent the best hours of my thinking and reading for about three years on Aristotle, and later for two years on Plato in order to be able to be a critical judge with regard to all fine points in the definition of words that have been the despair of dictionaries . . .

Some Old Leanings

The more Harris progressed in his grasp of fundamental problems in philosophy — and there is no end to gaining fresh insights — the more he became convinced that philosophy has practical implications for life. In "What the Universities can do for the People" he brought out this fact in a plain statement: "The most practical of all instruction is that which finds the unity of all branches of knowledge, and teaches their human application. Ethics is certainly the most practical of all branches of human learning." Such discoveries as he made from time to time, as that of the significance of the three figures of the syllogism in psychology (1888-89) or the ten insights published in the ten chapters to an *Introduction to Philosophy* in his *Journal of Speculative Philosophy*[10] were important, of course. But that the business of philosophy relates to practical issues of life, was the major insight by which already the early St. Louis group lived through the ante-bellum and Civil War period. As early as February, 1866, Harris published in the *St. Louis Commercial Advertiser* an article on "Abstraction considered to its Practical Relation to Life", while in 1896 he addressed the 20th Century Club at Boston on "The Practical Side of Philosophy". It was thus *a propos* a suggestion he had made earlier, namely, that if we have to go back to Kant, we might again go forward to Fichte.

Ever and anon the tendency to symbolize, which had drawn him so close to General Hitchcock, would have an occasion to assert itself. Thus, in 1896, he was asked to describe and name some of the paintings in the pavilions of the Congressional Library,[11] each of which seemed in a triangular, synthetic arrangement to convey the nature of the elements in their relation to man. In the notes for a letter to Miss Fanny Bacon of St. Louis, dating from the year 1903, he discussed Emerson's reluctance, which he shared with the Neo-Platonists, in giving a name to God lest one become self-satisfied with the name and dispense with exploring the reality behind it. But he also dwelt at some length on his poem "The Lords of Life" which he deemed the sublimest poem that he knew of. "It says that the inventor of the game of life, in which we meet with that great series of events which we call our experience, is 'omnipresent without name.'" But Harris went on, as he had done several decades before in front of Church's painting "Heart of the Andes", to philosophize and symbolize in connection with Emerson's conception of Monadnock. Apparently a discussion of the theme of the "berry blue and gold," contained in a communication from Miss Bacon, had occasioned this dilatation; for he called her attention to Emerson's poem "Bacchus" which describes what kind of grape the blue and gold berry is.

The year 1903 marked the 100th birthday of the Concord bard, and all over the country people met in commemoration of Emerson. At Washington, tributes to the poet were paid at All Souls' Church, under the auspices of the Unitarian Club, and Harris spoke on Emerson as an Orientalist. At Boston, the Unitarians held a mass meeting at Symphony Hall. At New York, the Society of American Authors arranged an elaborate dinner at the Waldorf Astoria on May 25th, to which Harris was invited. With him, at the guest table, sat, among others, Dr. Jacob G. Schurman, Edwin Markham, Hon. S. J. Barrows, Rev. Moncure D. Conway, and Dr. MacCracken, Chancellor of the University of New York. That "grand old woman", Mrs. Julia Ward Howe, or, as she called herself, member of the octogenarian phalanx, could not be present. Erastus Ransom was toastmaster, and Harris responded to the toast "The Emersonian Philosophy". Conway had at the exhibit in connection with this function, the picture of the Summer School of Philosophy at Concord, with Alcott and Harris and his daughter Edith in the foreground.

At Concord, the Free Religious Association of America had organized an Emerson Memorial School. There were present many of Harris' friends and associates in the Concord School of Philosophy who had commemorated Emerson as early as 1882, when Harris gave what in the opinion of the papers was one of the best estimates of the bard, both just and reverent; now Harris remained strangely silent at his summer home in the Adirondacks. Perhaps he needed a rest, perhaps he wished to remain in the background, for he would have been sure to have become the subject of undue publicity with the sightseers and strangers as one of those who had been rather closely associated with Emerson and Alcott.[12] The topic he might have selected, that of the Philosophy of Emerson, was treated by President Schurman in Huntington Hall at Boston and by Hugo Muensterberg at Harvard University.

For long, Harris had shown a deep interest in all of Emerson's writings,[13] including his poems with a Hindu background, and had made it his special concern to dig out the sources upon which Emerson relied. He had corresponded with Dr. Edward W. Emerson, the poet's son, whom Henry T. Bailey[14] quoted as having said about Harris: "What a mind that man has! He is one of the most delightful men I know, and the most scholarly. That is all very interesting, but my Father never thought of one tenth of all that! He was not a philosopher in any sense, nor a mystic; he was a poet, and grasped ideas as poets do. He gave a volume by some philosopher to a friend once, and admitted to him afterwards that he had not read it, and that the quotations from Plato which the volume contained, were, after all, what he cared for."

One November morning in 1904, Harris' long harbored interest in psychic research was roused by an article in the *Educational Review,* and he made haste to write to Dr. Nicholas Murray Butler about it:[15]

The chief great article in the whole magazine is the article of Barrett on the result of psychical research. That is the best thing ever written on the subject and is not only the most scientific and candid but it is also the most judicious. I was surprised to find that he understood exactly the limitations of hypnotism which (hypnotism) he was one of the first to suggest as an object of psychical research. I have been so afraid of hypnotism that I have not taken any pleasure in hearing it discussed, and especially as a therapeutic agency. I have an idea that the hypnotizing of a person means that the subject hypnotized becomes a parasite, so to speak, of the hypnotizer, and that he loses individuality. The hypnotic state is therefore to me a degenerate state, a falling back into perhaps what might be called the foetal stage of the human animal. The descent into the hypnotic state of course makes subsequent lapses of the same kind easier and easier. This is a terrible disease of the mind. Now I see that Mr. Barrett explains in other ways the danger of hypnotism so that he seems to understand the situation exactly. On the other hand I admit that in cases of dipsomania and the like, hypnotism is a warrantable cure and that the higher suggestion of hypnotism may be of great use in cases of that kind where the individual has fallen under the influence of some ruling suggestion. Perhaps the tobacco habit could be cured that way, and I think that it has been cured in that way. But the article is a very important article and I am glad that you saw fit to select it for reproduction in your valuable journal.

When his old friend, Denton J. Snider, sent him his book on *Feeling, Psychologically Treated, and Prolegomena to Psychology,* he wrote him a lengthy letter[16] in which occur the following paragraphs which are of importance in gauging Harris' philosophical thinking:

This book, I saw at once, is the book for me. I have been interested ever since 1873 or 4 in the relation of feeling on the one hand to plant life, and on the other hand to sense-perception, and I have written that subject over three times and the last time I wrote it for my "Psychologic Foundations"; it is really the chief point in the second part of that book. It is a kind of furnishing of bridges and tunnels for the Aperçus expounded by Aristotle in his "De Anima".

Vegetation contains the real causal influence which acts upon an environment and reveals itself on it. It carries its revelation so far that it takes this environment and strips off the determination already formed on it, substituting its own determinations, making it into vegetable cells, not in general but of the specific kind which belong to the plant itself and not in general even

559

then but specifically according to the peculiarities and idiosyncracies of the particular plant that is growing. Feeling goes through the same activity that digestion (THREPTIKON) but with an additional reflection upon it, that is to say the content is omitted and the form of the action of digestion is reproduced in the mind and made an object. That is to say in real digestion the self-activity acts upon an environment and reproduces itself in it. In feeling the self-activity goes through the form of digestion without the content and perceives the form.

EMPTY ABSOLUTES AND THE BARE IDEA OF GOD

By virtue of his many critical talks on the Oriental attitude toward life in which he brought out the contrast with the Christian outlook, as well as by virtue of his philological interests which led him to investigate the origin of words, Harris came into the repute of being a great Oriental scholar having few equals in the mastery of Sanskrit and some other Eastern tongues. Harris himself never made such a claim, which would have been hard to substantiate. It is true that he studied Sanskrit, and there are many notes which bear witness to his endeavors in this direction. He possessed a number of etymological works, such as Kluge and Lutz's *English Etymology*, William Dwight Whitney's *Oriental and Linguistic Studies*, John Stuart Blackie's *Etymological Geography*, S. S. Haldane's *Outline of Etymology*, and many others. In his library he also had not a few of Max Müller's books, including volumes of the *Sacred Books of the East*. Books and pamphlets were sent him by some Hindu acquaintances, especially after the Parliament of Religion meetings. They kept him informed on Raja Ram Mohan Roy, the Prathana Samaj, the Brahmo Samaj, and other movements. He had in his possession such magazines as *The Indian Social Reformer* and *New India*. Particularly in the Brahmo Samaj he manifested great interest inasmuch as it represented the theistic version of Hindu beliefs. There are extensive notes in his own hand on the Vedas and the Vedanta, shorthand notes on a lecture by Chakravarti given at Washington in 1893, and many other pertinent items, including a correspondence with Bipen Chandra Pal and Professor S. S. Langley for whom he made copies of passages relating to the twelve *nidanas* of the Buddhists.

Harris' interpretation of the Orient was colored entirely by the Hegelian concept of history in which Oriental thinking figured as a necessary stage in the development of mind. He called Eastern thought "precocious wisdom" and a "kind of pre-historic adumbration of European thought". He could not see any positive values accruing to the study of Indian philosophy and religion except in so far as they would eventually reveal the superiority of the Christian point of view. In this sense it would be "a sort of cathartic for the imagination". At a rather early date he had attained what he called an insight, that the East generally, and India in particular stands for nihilism, abstractionism and negative absolutism against which the West must assert the positive virtues and attitudes growing out of an understanding of Christianity. With reservations, he had high regard for the *Bhagavad Gita* whose central thought was brought home to him by Emerson's poetic restatement. He also acknowledged worth in the ethics of Buddhism and the intellectual features of Vedantism. But he favored the Sankhya because it represents a species of dualism and thus falls, to all appearance, outside the speculations that drive at "negative unity". With concepts like *maya* he had no sympathy whatever.[17]

The Orient is the great antithesis to Western thinking, whether expressed in the ethical code of the Chinese who do not know of the social combination of men in a modern state, or in Hindu metaphysics which is allegedly ignorant of the fullness of God as portrayed in Hegel's philosophy.

His philosophy of history was, to Harris, "a theodicy, a justification of the ways of God to man — an exhibition of
the manifestation of Reason in the movements of human
history".[18]

Harris did not tire of stating and restating the conflict
between East and West, and it was his belief that Christianiy
must triumph because civilization is identical with Christianity. While serving the Public Schools in St. Louis, he
had been exposed to many an uncalled-for criticism on account of his interest in German philosophy which was alleged to be devoid of belief in God and antagonistic to the
Christian endeavor. He even had to defend himself publicly
and stated in a letter to L. S. Holden which was circularized
in August, 1879, that he was not an atheist and that "now"
he was "the farthest possible removed from a doubt of the
existence of a personal first cause". His Christian conviction was thus philosophically grounded and unshakable.
During his Concord intermezzo, he was once asked by a
minister to define Christianity because it was noticed that he
was studying the sacred writings of the East, and he retorted,
no doubt to the utter gratification of the Reverend, but still
giving leeway to interpretation: "It is absolute truth fighting
against error, and always has been." Was the querying gentleman aware what idealistic and Hegelian twist Harris had
imparted to Christianity? What significance could be imparted to "always has been" in the face of the time-bound
gospel record and biblical revelation? Thus, when Harris
spoke of Christianity he meant the interpretation that we
have given the original Christian message in order to make
it conform to our ideals and justify our practical, if not utili-
tarian ways to God. Christianity, he once said in Concord,
is the goal toward which we may advance indefinitely and
never surpass. It supplies the principle by which we criti-
cize ourselves and our institutions.

But it was not the Christianity of Christ, it was Christianity as inspired by theology and the interpretation of the Church Fathers and above all by Hegel. The Trinity is not the object of worship and prayer, and God is Reason more than he is Love; the proof of the existence of God is more significant than unquestioning devotion. To Julia Ward Howe Harris wrote on October 5th, 1901:[19]

. . . It has been for many years with me a paradox in the history of philosophy that Anselm and Descartes had put forward a proof of God which had for its basis the bare existence of the idea of God in the mind. It was unthinkable to me that the bare existence of an idea in the mind should be a proof of the objective existence corresponding to the idea. I was reflecting one day upon the basis of philosophical knowledge as presented by Plato in the Tenth Book of the "Laws", and of Aristotle in the Eleventh Book of the Metaphysics when I seemed to see the real thought of Anselm which had been unfortunately stated. Perhaps it would be better to say that we had outgrown his form of statement but had not outgrown the thought which lay in his mind.

In the year 1858 I came to what seemed to me to be a real philosophical insight and all of my subsequent life has served to make me more certain of the validity of that insight. It amounted to seeing that self-activity or self-determining is presupposed by all dependent being, and even by time and space themselves as well as by all of their contents. This insight recognized the activity of the first principle of the universe, and I could seem to see quite clearly that its activity must take the form of intellect and will, or else lose its independence and therefore come into the condition of presupposing another principle beyond it. One could not get rid of the first principle in any event because the result of disproving a principle as original and primordial would be to place or presuppose another first principle above it.

These arguments were more fully set forth in his article entitled "Faith and Knowledge: Kant's Refutation of the Ontological Proof of the Being of God" in the fifteenth volume of his *Journal of Speculative Philosophy*. Harris' Christianism was, in the last analysis, a justification of Western civilization which acknowledges reason and the various aspects of human personality as driving forces in the world toward something better, something bigger, something more fully integrated, something more perfect in form and content. At the same time, the Orient had to provide the necessary antithesis, even if it meant the garbling of its outlook on life. This garbling, however, was pardonable and perhaps inevitable since the transcription and translation of philosophical Oriental ideas was furnished by men who were not able to acquire real understanding through the veil of language and thought steeped in theological thinking. *Nirvana* to *them did* spell *nothing* or the *void;* the words in which the Hindu couched his thought about the deity in order to convey something of the grandeur of its being, *did* suggest formlessness and the absence of positive features. In a way, not only all Christian interpreters, but all Hegelians, more unconsciously than intentionally, offered up the Orient as a sacrifice to their own systems.

Few are the references to the Bible in Harris' lectures, and fewer still were the lectures dealing with Bible problems. When he spoke, as he did on April 24th, 1895, in Calvary Baptist Church at Washington, on "The Bible and Sociology",[20] it was on the Bible as a book of historical-sociological consequences, rather than a book containing the revelation for all time. Accordingly, the agencies of religion, more than the revealed word, were his concern as evidences of the workings of Providence. Hence these titles of his addresses: "The Educative Work of Missions", "The Separation of the Church from the School Supported by Public Taxes", "University and School Extension as Supplemented by the Churches" and "Beginning, Growth and Effect of Christianity". Here Harris was dealing with history and the illustrations of the work of Reason which takes Christianity for its vehicle.

SOME OF THE NEWER ISMS

If Harris was responsible for any movement it was the "back to Hegel". For, while the St. Louis Movement in Philosophy was, in a sense, just that, it still rode in the wake of a current that was sweeping many countries. But in the late 90's and the beginning of the 20th century, both the New England transcendentalism and the enthusiasm for Hegel were practically dead, and positivism, realism and naturalism and their allies reared their heads in pragmatism and experimentalism.

Harris still corresponded with the friends he had made in St. Louis, Concord and other places. Mutually enlightening letters passed between them and the Harris-Howison disputes were referred to them. Thus, Harris circularized them in 1891-92 in regard to the eternal nature of the soul, sin, imperfection and similar problems. S. H. Emery, Jr., who had returned to Quincy, Ill., and there associated himself with the American Straw Board Company, came out with opinions which he had apparently suppressed in Concord. He was typical of others who also had been dominated by the kind personality of Harris; but in the more impersonal attitude of composing a letter behind a desk they were able to give free rein to their thoughts. Emery, for instance, divulged that he had always experienced difficulties with Harris' interpretation of the Trinity and the category of quantity in regard to the Absolute.[21] But Harris, used

565

to the brusqueness of a Thomas Davidson, endeavored to clear up any misunderstandings. Without yielding he was still persuasive in these words of his letter: "I am not at all certain that you have not made a good and valid statement."

More and more Harris leaned toward Plato and Aristotle in his own thinking. Especially when, in connection with editing Webster's dictionary he felt that better definitions might be made of certain philosophical terms on the basis of a study of the originals, he delved deeply into the works of these ancients. His first Plato studies, reaching back to 1858,[22] were rather unyielding in that he found "everlasting diffuseness and commonplaceness of thought". When he read Hegel's *History of Philosophy* about the year 1863, he became aware that he had missed much, that Plato was speaking from a different plane of mind and from different presuppositions. From then on he realized, and experience with many thinkers bore him out,

> that there are two attitudes of mind, the one which looks out upon the objects of experience in space and time and finds them always in the form of things and even each with its environment . . . The other view is the one taken first by Plato as a conscious thinker, but long before by the religious thinkers and by the artists and literary writers of the world, namely the view from the standpoint of introspection. We perceive in consciousness three kinds of activities, that is to say they are determinations of a self by a self. This kind of being is totally different from that kind of being which is always dependent on an environment and which therefore shares its being with the environment.[23]

These statements point out the basis of the dialectic that developed between Harris and some of his unphilosophical friends. They explain the tussle he had with religious thinkers, such as Rev. James McCosh over the concept of reality,[24] and pragmatic thinkers whose acknowledged leader was William James. In a letter to George H. Howison,[25] Harris was less reserved in his personal opinion about William James than ordinarily:

> . . . William James delights to appeal to the pit and top gallery now and then by making mouths at what all the rest of us reverence as gods. His ridiculous attack on Hegel in his book "The Will to Believe" shows that he wishes to keep as his own the gallery and the pit among the readers of philosophical literature. He has a species of ethical conscience in this matter, having persuaded himself that he is to be so frank with his readers that he not only tells them all that he does know but takes great pains to tell them what he does not know. For surely William James has not arrived at that sublime pitch of egotism which enables him to feel sure that his insight into Hegel is the utmost possible insight . . .

But the progress of pragmatism was not to be impeded. And, similarly, in the philosophy of education, Herbart's doctrine gained the ascendency. Harris himself had been instrumental in encouraging students and incipient pedagogs to go to Germany for further study and background. But he was not fully aware that independent minds had forged ahead and recast almost the entire mental picture, and Hegel was now only a name. It is interesting to note that Dr. Elmer E. Brown whom Harris himself had suggested as his successor in office, came to prominence in the very Herbartian movement which Harris largely disapproved of. These young students who had gone to Germany returned steeped in the new ism, and another dialectic developed between them and Harris who, to be sure, conceded many points to Herbart, but could not subscribe to his psychology. Particularly during 1893-95, he came out with a number of papers against Herbartianism, notably the one on "Herbart's Unmoral Education". There were disputes with DeGarmo and the other representatives of the new thinking in education who rallied around the National Herbart Society, later organized as the National Society for the Scientific Study of Education. Many were the ones who applied to Harris for clarification of the issues that had become acute between the followers of Froebel and Pestalozzi and the apperception group. Particularly on his California trip in 1896-97, Harris made enlightening remarks to the groping and bewildered teachers.

THE SOCIETY FOR PHILOSOPHICAL INQUIRY

The Society for Philosophical Inquiry at Washington, D. C., was founded, according to the history which Kepler Hoyt presented to the members in 1918,[26] on January 20th, 1893, and first met in the old Columbian University building and later in the public library. There is every reason to believe that Harris was instrumental in launching this society, as he presided at the first meeting and served, together with Rev. Dr. Frank Sewall, a Swedenborgian, and Dr. L. D. Lodge, on the Committee on Constitution and By-Laws. Rev. Dr. James MacBride Sterrett, an Episcopalian and at that time a professor of philosophy at the Columbian University, was elected President. In the beginning, the members came together weekly. The tone was idealistic and the early clashes with realism, positivism and pragmatism were remembered well by the older members. Harris had good tussles, to the delight of all, with Major John W. Powell, a geologist and anthropologist of note, Professor Lester F. Ward, the sociologist and likewise avowed champion of empiricism, and Dr. James C. Welling. President of the Columbian University, with whom he clashed on the topic of metaphysical reals.[27] Major Powell, who had been a member of the expedition surveying the Grand Cañon, was wont to put algebraic equations all around the black-board of the room in which they were meeting, starting in one corner and finishing in the same. All during this performance Harris would sit twiddling his thumbs, eyes closed. As soon as Powell was done, he started to tear into him and rip his propositions to pieces.[28]

Harris spoke and debated on numerous occasions, but there is no full record of the meetings. In 1896 or thereabouts, he unfolded more than ordinary activity. In 1904, he gave a significant talk on John Locke. Several typewritten copies of a paper on "John Locke as a Metaphysician" have been discovered among his remains, and since with it were notes on Locke's treatment of space, it may well be the paper he presented on that occasion. The *Popular Science Monthly*, with J. McKeen Cattell as editor, requested an article at that time, and since he was in the Locke mood he intended to send in a paper on "Locke and Toleration."

One of the last meetings of the Society which Harris attended fell on November 7th, 1905. After the lecture of Dr. Sterrett's who blessed the Catholics "for the religious life they nurture in our citizens," but anathemized "their efforts at ecclesiastical world power," and in answer to Rabbi Abram Simon who asked whether pragmatism was not somewhat like utilitarianism, Harris remarked on the resemblance of the former to the Scottish Common Sense philosophy. But at the meeting three weeks later, Mr. E. S. Steele thought such a comparison incorrect. The last meeting at which Harris was seen was that in commemoration of Professor Edward Farquhar, the historian, who had served as secretary from the date of founding till his death.

At George Washington University, where the meetings were later held, the Society met on May 3rd, 1910, in commemoration of Harris himself who doubtless had been the most distinguished member of the circle. Seven members did him honor in their talks. Previously, at their November 16th, 1909, meeting, they had set down in the minutes their "grateful appreciation of the valuable service to the world of the deeper thought by its recently deceased member, Dr. William Torrey Harris, whose contributions to Philosophy constitute one of the most conspicuous and valuable of America's gifts to the progress of learning, and whose participation during many years in the discussions of this Society were an inspiration and a service to be held in grateful and delightful memory."

Distinguished men and women have belonged to this society or lectured before it, including Governor John W. Hoyt, Dr. Nicholas Murray Butler, Paul Carus, Dr. Elmer E. Brown, Dr. S. P. Langley, Secretary of the Smithsonian Institution, and C. H. Hinton, the mathematician. Dr. Brown, a pragmatist who was tempered by his study in Germany, attested to the largeness of Harris not only in his own case, but in the discussions at these and other meetings when some particularly sharp remark roused Harris "from the calm of academic exposition and he became in a moment transformed into the powerful debater, with 20 centuries of philosophic thought at his command." And Dr. Sterrett acknowledged in his memorial speech entitled "The Genesis of the Philosopher" that Harris had been for years the leader and master of the society.

TEACHER OF PHILOSOPHY

Rev. Dr. Edward Elliott Richardson, Elton Professor of Philosophy at George Washington University, and a member of the Society of Philosophical Inquiry, related at the Commemoration of the 100th Anniversary of Harris' birth by the U. S. Office of Education, how he, as a young man, called on Harris one evening because he had heard that he liked to converse on philosophy with anyone who showed an interest in the subject. Although, at the door, he made the casualness of his visit quite clear to the maid, Harris, when told of the stranger — and he could be seen through the opening sitting at dinner — rose immediately and spent an entire hour in conversation. He would, indeed, rather talk philosophy than eat. Later, Dr. Richardson met Harris again in a crowded street car and, strap-hanging, they philosophized.

Stories like these could be multiplied. The humblest beginner, as soon as he manifested a desire to learn about philosophical problems, would be engaged by Harris in conversation and one more friend was won for the cause. Harris did not make any display of learning on such occasions, but treated the tyro with perfect equality. While in Concord, Marietta Kies, who was a Professor of Philosophy at Mt. Holyoke Seminary, came to him for lessons in philosophy for a year or two and then compiled a book of extracts from his writings which were published under the title of *Introduction to the Study of Philosophy by William Torrey Harris*, the first book that presented his philosophy in a somewhat coherent and systematic form. It appeared in 1889.

Howard Sandison, a teacher in the State Normal School Department of Psychology and Methods, Terre Haute, Ind., was typical of many young men who were helped by Harris in the pursuit of their profession. The impulse to study philosophy and psychology was awakened in him by reading Harris' introduction to philosophy, as published in the *Journal of Speculative Philosophy*.[29] He adopted Harris' *Psychologic Foundations of Education* in his classes.

At his home on Fairmont Street in Washington, Harris would hold, Sundays, philosophy classes for a limited number of Kindergartners. Thus, at the end of March, 1904, he had some ten or eleven at his house, talking to them on psychology and explaining the difference between concepts and percepts. Regular classes in philosophy were also given by him to university students and others. His ten lectures

on "The Philosophy of History" which he had given in
1904 at the Columbian University[30] and which represented
an expansion of the six-lecture course offered in the same
university during March and April, 1896, under the title
of "Practical Lessons of History,"[31] had become very well-
known in Washington and elsewhere. They were most in-
formative and inspiring, for he treated the problems from
the point of view that "philosophy is found in the history
of philosophy." Those who were acquainted with these
lectures would tell their friends and urge their own students
to take lessons from Harris. Thus, Dr. James McBride
Sterrett at one time sent him a class of four: Dr. U. G. B.
Pierce, the Unitarian Minister of All Souls' Church; Rev.
J. W. Smith of Epworth Methodist Church; Oscar H. W.
Carlson, a young Swede; and Alberto Nin-Frias, Premier
Secrétaire of the Legation of Uruguay. The latter wrote
Harris later that he had "often thought of the *serene* moments of pure speculation" in those classes and that if there
was something missing in his intellectual joys of late it was
the Monday class. For two weeks the only books he had
read were Hegel's *History* and *Logic,* but, without probably
realizing the gulf that separated their thinking, he wanted
Harris to give greater weight to the French philosophers,
particularly Henri Hypolite Taine who had had a large
influence on his Latin compatriots.[32] Carlson, who aspired
likewise to a diplomatic career, was also very grateful to
Harris for having been taught to see history through Hegel's
eyes.

Harris kept himself well-informed about what the colleges
and universities were doing in philosophy. This is proven
by his address at the National Educational Association meeting in 1888 at San Francisco. His personal contacts with
the universities, and particularly the young students of
philosophy, increased with the years. It was Wilbur L.
Cross, Governor of Connecticut, who recollected the fol-

572

lowing incident at the occasion of the Harris Centenary at Putnam, Ct.:[33]

I was once in company with Mr. Harris on an afternoon and evening in the late eighties. This was the year before he became United States Commissioner of Education. At that time I was secretary to a philosophical club at Yale University presided over by Professor Ladd. Mr. Harris accepted an invitation to address us. He liked young men and young men liked him. We were struggling with Hegel whose philosophy we had difficulty in understanding, so we asked Mr. Harris, as the leading Hegelian scholar of the period, to come to New Haven to shed a little light on a very abstruse philosophy. In his exposition there was both light and enthusiasm. As I remember the address, Mr. Harris emphasized the idealistic aspect of the Hegelian philosophy beyond what was usual with other interpreters.

The *Deutsche Verein* at Harvard likewise asked Harris about this time to speak and he chose as topic "What has Modern German Thought done for us?" Wellesley College appointed him a member of the Committee of Visitors to the Department of Philosophy and Pedagogics, and he served in that capacity for several years, beginning December, 1893. At the opening of the Jones Memorial Symposium of Philosophy, at Illinois College, on June 3rd, 1897, Dr. Hiram K. Jones of Jacksonville presided in the morning, while Harris did so at the afternoon session and in the evening talked on "The Fruits of Philosophy."

Miss Lilly Lindquist, Supervisor of Foreign Languages in the Detroit public schools, told the story[34] of how she remembered Harris from her undergraduate days at Smith College. When she was president of the Philosophical Society on the campus, she invited him to lecture on Hegel. Nothing of the lecture was recalled, but her memory of how "his charming simplicity" made the college girls forget his great erudition and important position remained vivid with her.

Dr. Nicholas Murray Butler, while a Professor at Columbia University, asked Harris on several occasions to meet his classes in philosophy and to elucidate such problems as the relation between Kant and Hegel. It was Dr. Butler who built up the Department of Philosophy and Psychology at Columbia, and called John Dewey to the university. With justifiable pride he wrote Harris:[35] "I do not know where else in the world there is such an array of scholars of high rank and promise in the field of philosophy and psychology."

In December, 1907, Harris accepted the invitation to address the Philosophical Society at Ithaca, N. Y., and spoke on the pragmatism of William James and the Common Sense philosophy of Thomas Reid and Dugald Stewart. Not enough of his notes has been preserved, but from what there is we can infer that he criticised among other things James' conception of the flow of consciousness. In this connection, a pocket memo of his, dated April 5th, 1909, probably one of the last that he carried around with him, is interesting. It states that "Wm. James' Pragmatism has a menagerie of ideas, a dramatic assemblage whose interaction amaze[s] us and interest[s] us."

The Aristotelian Society of England elected Harris at their December 19th, 1881, meeting Corresponding Member, and through this connection he became widely known in professional circles in England. On one of his visits to England he addressed them, according to Percival Chubb. His address on "Kant's Third Antinomy and his Fallacy Regarding the First cause," given at the Philosophical Congress at Chicago in 1893, not to mention his other activities in connection with the World's Columbian Exposition, likewise earned him international fame among philosophers who already were well acquainted with him as the editor of the *Journal of Speculative Philosophy*. The Southern Society for Philosophy and Psychology which, for their first annual meeting in 1904, met at Baltimore and Philadelphia in conjunction with the American Association for the Advancement of Science, of which Harris had been a member as early as August, 1878, extended an invitation to him.

At the meetings of the American Philosophical Association he spoke at least three times. At the Princeton, N. J., meeting on December 29th, 1903, he presented his paper to which he gave this lengthy title which is in the nature of an abstract: "A Thesis. Hegel's Voyage of Discovery reaches as its goal an insight into the necessity of goodness and righteousness in an absolute being and into the consequent necessity that the absolute has the form of personality." It was at this gathering that he enjoyed a discussion with George Santayana and met President and Mrs. Woodrow Wilson who received the members of the Association. At the Philadelphia meeting in 1904, Harris presented "Primary and Secondary Phases of Causality;" at the Cambridge, Mass., meeting of 1905, "God as Regulative Idea and God as the Absolute." The Western Philosophical Association, contemplating for Easter, 1909, a meeting at Washington University, commemorating the fiftieth anniversary of the coming together of the Harris-Brokmeyer group in St. Louis for the systematic study of philosophy, sent a formal request to Harris to be present. The letter by their President, Professor Arthur Oncken Lovejoy, addressed to the man who had done so much to promote idealism and the study of philosophy in America, came a little too late, for it was already close to the end of Harris' allotted span of time. Educators had recognized Harris' contributions earlier and more fully than the philosophers and teachers of philosophy. . .

CHAPTER THIRTY

THE LAST RETIREMENT

RESIGNATION AND A PRESIDENT'S APPRECIATION

A great good fortune came to Harris at the end of May, 1906. From Dr. Henry S. Pritchett, President of the Carnegie Foundation for the Advancement of Teaching, he received a delicately phrased letter dated May 26th, offering him the highest retiring allowance that the Foundation was able to award. The letter intimated that the grants of the Foundation were made in recognition of honorable service, not as acts of charity. Dr. Pritchett wrote that it had seemed to the trustees of the Foundation that

> they could best serve this purpose by tendering to a few men who have rendered great service to education, places at the head of what they wish to make a roll of honor. There is naturally no other name connected with American education which is so identified with its progress for the last thirty years as yours. We should like in the best way possible to show our appreciation of what you have done for education and philosophy. If it be agreeable to you, therefore, we should be glad to confer on you, as the first man to whom such recognition for meritorious service is given, the highest retiring allowance which our rules will allow, an annual income of $3,000, of which, under the rules, one-half would be paid to Mrs. Harris should she survive you.

576

Harris was overcome, for he had long contemplated resigning his Commissionership to devote his time to the writing of books and articles he had long planned. His health was beginning to fail him for the arduous duties of the office and his outside activities, while his salary had never permitted him to think of the future as carefree. At the same time, the pension system in those days was not sufficiently understood to regard it as an unqualified good and due. The Carnegie Foundation for the Advancement of Teaching which had been incorporated by Act of Congress as late as February, 1906, had among its corporate members many friends of Harris. Dr. Pritchett himself had been a Professor of Mathematics at Washington University, St. Louis, and was called to the Presidency of Massachusetts Institute of Technology. Among the others were Nicholas Murray Butler, Charles William Eliot, Jacob G. Schurman, Woodrow Wilson, and Charles F. Thwing, all friends and admirers of the man whom they wanted to honor. But it was Dr. Butler who was principally responsible for the Foundation's action. His letter leaves no doubt about it:

(Personal)   MAY 28, 1906
DR. WILLIAM T. HARRIS
   1360 *Yale Street, N. W.*
   Washington, D. C.

My dear Dr. Harris:

Before this you will perhaps have heard from President Pritchett, of the Carnegie Foundation for the Advancement of Teaching, and as I am a Trustee of that foundation and a member of the Executive Committee, I want to add a personal letter to whatever he may have written. For two or three years past I have been worrying a good deal about you in a filial sort of way and fearing lest the increasing burden of routine work at the Bureau would not only wear out your strength, but also interfere to prevent the accomplishment of those literary and philosophical tasks that you have planned for yourself and that so many of us want to see you finish. I am particularly anxious to have you complete for publication those lectures on the philosophy of history, and then to make a book which shall, in encyclopaedic form, however brief, present an organized outline of your philosophical system and teachings.

So soon as the Carnegie Foundation was organized, the idea occurred to me — and I was delighted to find that it had also occurred to others — that nothing would so fix the high purpose and aim of the Foundation in the minds of the teachers of the country as by making its first act one to place at your disposal, if you saw fit to accept it, the maximum retiring allowance named in the rules, in order that you might be free for the rest of your life to work quietly at literary and philosophical studies, free from the wear and tear incidental to the operation of the Bureau. Sorry as I should be, personally, to see you withdraw from the Bureau, and serious as would be my misgivings about the possibility of securing a successor at all adequate to the tasks which you have set, nevertheless I honestly believe that you have done for the Bureau your greatest work and that no field of usefulness remains at all comparable to that of literary and philosophical activity. To be drawn off day by day and hour by hour to write little reports, to keep up routine correspondence, and to collect this and that piece of information for some inquirer, is bound to interfere with the consecutive thought and composition which means so much to you.

Personally, I believe that if you should feel that you could be the first American teacher to receive a retiring allowance from the Foundation, it would add immensely to its prestige and dignity, and it would fix, once for all, in the minds of the teachers of the country, the fact that there was now in existence a means by which teachers themselves were able, as administrators of this great trust, to make some provision for those distinguished members of their profession who had great service to render by thought and by pen.

I am writing off what you sometimes call the "top of my mind" and should have been glad if it were possible for me to talk about the matter with you in Washington. Unfortunately, however, I am very busy here until June 21st, when I am sailing for Europe to pass the summer in Germany.

With warmest regards,
I am,
Always faithfully yours,
NICHOLAS MURRAY BUTLER

In the last paragraph of his letter of acceptance to Dr. Pritchett,[1] Harris. with characteristic modesty expressed his personal feelings: "Permit me to say that I have never in my life before been so completely taken by surprise nor have I ever before received so high an honor — an honor that I must feel to be completely beyond my deserts." And to Dr. Butler he wrote:

DEAR DR. BUTLER: *June* 12/06

I saw at once your thoughtfulness of me in the Carnegie retirement pension foundation.

But I had never tho't such a thing possible until it occurred. It accomplishes what I really needed to lift me above all worry in financial matters for the rest of my life. And the continuance of the moiety to Mrs. Harris is particularly useful & appreciated as a removal of worry for those one leaves behind him.

579

I wish that I c'd come to New York and have one or two hours of your time sometime between now and next Sunday evening 17th or whatever other time wd be possible for you to arrange.* I wish to speak to you about arrangements for my resignation and cannot write what I want to say.

Very sincerely and gratefully yours,

W. T. Harris

*by telegram
I can reach you at any time you may appoint.

It had been Harris' intention to resign upon reaching his 70th birthday, but many factors had prevented him from doing so. Now there was no longer any need of delay. The conference with Dr. Butler resulted in a definite course of action, and in less than a week he sent this letter to President Theodore Roosevelt:

To the President of the United States
Sir:

I have the honor to offer herewith my resignation as Commissioner of Education, the same to take effect at your convenience.

Permit me to acknowledge in this place with gratitude your constant kindness to me throughout the period in which I have held office under your administration.

With expressions of distinguished respect and esteem, your obedient servant.

W. T. Harris
Commissioner of Education

June 18, 1906

The following day, President Roosevelt accepted his resignation by letter:

THE LAST RETIREMENT

THE WHITE HOUSE
WASHINGTON

June 19, 1906

MY DEAR DR. HARRIS:

In accepting your resignation as Commissioner of Education it is due to you to express not merely my regret at your feeling obliged to leave the service of the Government but my keen realization of the gain that has come to the United States from your presence in Washington and from your identification with the cause of education. I think it is a safe thing to say that all the people of our country who are most alive to the need of the real and thorough system of education have felt a peculiar pride and confidence in you.

With hearty good wishes, believe me,

Sincerely yours,

(Signed) THEODORE ROOSEVELT

DR. W. T. HARRIS,
Commissioner of Education,
Washington, D. C.

It was "a sad day for all" when Harris left the Bureau, wrote Mrs. Emily Van Dorn Miller, one of the secretaries.[2] The resignation came as a surprise only to those who had not been in constant touch with Harris and hence could not gauge his slowly failing health, which seemed to make such a step necessary. Actually, he had told beforehand of his resignation only to few in the Bureau, Mr. Upton, his editor, and Miss Smith. Later he feared he might have hurt some by having kept them in ignorance.

The papers carried the formal announcement, an Associated Press release, on June 19th. Now, letters in great numbers were received at the Bureau and at Harris' home. Almost everyone expressed regret over his resignation, his old friends of many ventures, Holland, Johnson, Howison,

Bigelow, Thwing, and others. The educational journals all over the country gave notice of the change in the Commissionership because it was felt to be a major event in the history of American education which had, up till then, been dominated by the name of Harris. They sensed that one of the epochs in pedagogy, fruitful and prosperous beyond compare, had come to a close and that now the torch was handed on to younger hands and men with different ideals. Andrew Sloan Draper telegraphed: "We all feel that we have lost much in your retirement." But those who knew how well Harris deserved a rest, shared the spirit of Edward S. Holden who wrote from the Library of the U. S. Military Academy at West Point: "Heaven knows that you have done enough work in all these years to break down any man — work extending from the Philippines and Alaska to Cuba and Porto Rico!"

Dr. Benjamin Ide Wheeler, President of the University of California, wrote[3] that he had always felt "that the larger view and all the better things were safe and sure" as long as Harris was on guard. Many Englishmen also remembered the kindnesses shown them while they were in the United States, Caroline Coignon, Foster Watson, Cloudesley Brereton and the others, expressing astonishment over his resignation. Others, like McClure, Sanborn and Garland welcomed the fact that he was now free of political ties. All agreed that he could devote himself henceforth to even greater literary activity. Mr. W. W. Appleton was looking forward to Harris' finishing his book on the course of study. Some voiced the view that he should not have been allowed to resign, but that, as in European countries, he should have been made a Counsellor. Many also were his friends and acquaintances who called in person to express their regrets and wish him well in his future work. Among them was Monsignor O'Connell, Rector of the Catholic University at Washington, D. C.

THE LAST RETIREMENT

Nicholas Murray Butler and Benjamin Ide Wheeler, and both Senators from California, recommended Dr. Elmer E. Brown who was Professor of the Theory and Practice of Education at the University of California, for the appointment as Harris' successor, and Harris himself had looked very much with favor on the appointment. He was anxious that Dr. Brown, who was at the time at Clifton Springs, come at once to Washington and take over. In fact, he was in a sort of nervous tension and counted the days since he had presented his resignation to President Roosevelt. Finally, on July 1st, Dr. Brown was installed as the fifth U. S. Commissioner of Education, and served for five years. When he took over the office of the man whom he admired greatly without sharing his educational views in their entirety, he made the statement that it was an extraordinary legacy that was left to the Bureau of Education by Harris. Although now few accepted Harris' philosophical point of view, and many were the persons who were looking forward to a change in administration to allow more pragmatic and what they called scientific views to prevail, Dr. Brown expected all educational systems and institutions throughout the land to renew their loyalty to that "massive and dominant moral purpose to which Dr. Harris gave his lifelong devotion".

"INSTEAD OF BEING IDLE . . ."

One of the first things that Harris did after his retirement became effective, was to make preparations for an increased literary activity, disencumbered by official duties. As a first step he prepared an inventory of his manuscripts and printed articles, classified them as educational, philosophical and art, and reviewed the projects that he had a mind to carry out. He also caught up on his reading and re-read the books that had meant so much to him. In 1908 he commenced reading Hegel's *Philosophy of History* for the 17th time. A

letter to his brother David Henry, of June, 1908, tells best of
his prodigious activity during his retirement:

When I left my office of Commissioner of Education,
I made a rough inventory of the work I had begun in
philosophy and sociology and literature and found that
I had between thirty and forty undertakings of my own
on hand which had received various amounts of work
during the past thirty years, some of them only two or
three weeks' work, some of them two or three months'
work, and some of the most important had received
studies extending all-told into twelve months to twenty-
four months. My studies in Aristotle taken up and
pursued over weeks together ever since 1870, have been
pursued with more vigor than ever before during the
past three years and my work in Plato has occupied me
nearly two years — of course not working all the time,
but intermittently as I had strength and was stimulated
by new ideas or by finding Plato's influence on thinkers
who had not been well understood by me in former
years. I will give an example. Plato uses the word idea
and the word eidos in the sense of species and then
works up the thought of vital creative power and in the
most important parts of his philosophy reads into the
word idea (eidos) this vital creative power signifying
very nearly the same as the English word soul. Aristotle
uses eidos in the same general sense as Plato and invents
other forms of expression, namely entelechy and ener-
geia, etc.

I mention this study of eidos and idea because it is
in a certain sense a key to Hegel's use of the word form
in the second volume of his Logic. It is difficult for the
student of Hegel to get hold of the thought of this part
of the Logic because he does not know the Greek
thought on this subject as it was developed by Aristotle
and Plato. Form (eidos) is Aristotle's "formal cause",

so-called, but it should be rendered in English by the words "form-making cause" and Aristotle's form-making cause is pretty nearly what Begriff is in Hegel and what Fichte found to be the nature of human personality, namely, that which polarizes itself as subject and object, the same self being both subject and object, but, Fichte calls it Subjektiv-Objektivität. In respect to my study of Plato and Aristotle I have got on the track of more ideas of Hegel than I ever supposed had been borrowed by him, notwithstanding Hegel, in his "History of Philosophy" is never tired of repeating his praises of Plato and Aristotle for their speculative insights.

I have made this digression to explain to you that instead of being idle and with spare time on my hands, I have done more work in reading and studying in important fields of investigation than I did in the whole twenty years previous to my coming to Washington. I have been making investigations which I had been obliged to postpone. And I can carry on investigations when I am sick better than not, because such investigations divert my mind from my malady . . .

Harris was not lonely in his retirement. It was for his 70th birthday that Wm. Geo. Bruce, Publisher of the *School Journal* in Milwaukee, had brought out a colored souvenir postcard which pictured him with blue eyes. Most educators kept it on their desks. Dr. Nicholas Murray Butler congratulated him on the birthday prior to his retirement "on having completed seventy of the fullest years that have yet been accomplished in human history."[4] Yet, his retirement added even more to this accomplishment, perhaps more in personal yield than in actual literary production.

Harris continued his fondness of medieval Latin hymns. "I live by them", he told a friend. His love for Eusebius and Iamblichus grew. He read up on science, interested himself in volcanic glass, gave Miss Sarah Eddy, of Providence, R. I., the dimensions of his head (which was narrow as compared with its length), so she could make a clay model of it from some pictures he sent her.[5] His daughter Edith lightened his correspondence by acting as his secretary. Quietly, on December 27th, 1908, he celebrated at Washington with Sarah who had so faithfully and self-effacingly stood by him as he climbed the ladder to success and fame, their golden wedding.

BOTTLING UP STRENGTH

Both he and Sarah had suffered for long years from malaria. The extra work in connection with the Bureau's educational exhibit at St. Louis, had prevented Harris' going up North in 1905 to the Adirondacks, and his 1906 visit there was cut short by attacks of malaria, grippe and neuralgia. Faithfully he took the medicines his brother Edward had prescribed, among them *Quina Laroche Ferugineux,* which relieved his malarial fever. Unable to stand low temperatures, he would sometimes have his room heated up to 99 degrees to avoid congestive chills. Often he would wear his overcoat at home. His early inclination toward unorthodox therapeutic measures re-asserted itself, and he conceived of several self-cures based upon spurious medical theory. While at Columbia University in fall, 1904, for instance, he could not resist spending some time in the gymnasium with the result that he returned to Washington with a severe cold. He tried "aerating" his blood by taking walks, but ended up by contracting pneumonia which affected his left side. He acknowledged that often he lived by sheer will-power, as he felt that he was "nearly broken to pieces". Still, he kept on working like a Titan after finding, as he used to say, "a little nucleus of vital strength" on which to build a cure.

Sick as he was, he would not forego his beloved National Education Association meetings. "The last time we saw Dr. Harris", wrote Bardeen, was

at the Cleveland meeting of 1908. On the first evening
we dined with him and Mr. Ames of Boston at an un-
disturbed little table away off somewhere in the café
downstairs. We sat there late, and Dr. Harris was never
more entertaining. He was in a reminiscent and anec-
dotal mood, and his stories were interesting not only
in themselves but for the revelation in himself of a
disposition more pronounced than we had before observed to throw a mantle of charity over those with
whom he had differed, and especially to recognize the
search for truth in men whose environment and training were against them.

To the "Folkses" at home, Harris wrote that this meeting
in Cleveland had used him up. The report he was to present
he had written between 4 a.m. and 10 a.m., and delivered at
10:30 a.m. On July 3rd, he returned to Washington, exhausted. He tried sleeping 12 hours a night in order, as
he said, to "bottle up" his strength for closing the house at
Washington. This done, he escorted his son's wife to the
S. S. United States of the Scandinavian-American Line on
which she was to sail from New York to Europe. She was
his son's second wife, a musician from Norway, Julie Bene-
dicite Plessner by name, whom he had married in 1903 after
the death, in San Antonio, of his first wife Florence Fairchild in 1901. After seeing that she was properly taken care
of, he started on his trip to his beloved Adirondacks where
his family was waiting for him. At the Pennsylvania Station in
New York he was suddenly seized by an attack of malarial
fever and was barely able "to crawl from the Penn station
to the ferry". From the ferry he changed to the Hudson
River boat. A night of fevers and biliousness followed. At
Albany he was assisted to carriage and depot. In Saratoga he
stopped four hours at a hotel, lying abed, then took the
Montreal express to Westport and drove ten miles by carriage to Elizabethtown, "not able to sit up in the carriage

except by clutching the framework of the sides of the covered wagon". Another feverish night passed at the hotel. By now he had fasted nearly 24 hours. After taking some nourishment in the morning he continued his journey in pretty much the same condition. On arrival at Hurricane, he took immediately to bed with a feeling that he had "no longer any necessity of living on pure will-power three or four hours at a time", but was in good care and nursing with his wife and daughter Edith.[6]

Brother Edward took a touching interest in William's welfare without, however, quite understanding that William had to devote himself to his work or perish for lack of interest in life. William was to eat raw eggs and malted milk, and as a tonic he was to continue with his quinine concoction. The packing and lifting and going up-hill had made the first days at Hurricane rather difficult. There was the usual summer school at Glenmore, and William had himself put down for a week's course of lectures. But Edward advised strongly against such an exertion, especially in view of the fact that William was also working on Webster's dictionary. "You and I must remember", he wrote, "that we are growing old and cannot do the work of our younger days".[7] However, William was not so easily to be dissuaded from his intention. His condition improved and he was able to send his brother, at his request, a telegram stating that he was "growing more comfortable and not any weaker".[8]

HOME — HOSPITAL AND STUDIO

When Edward came to Hurricane to examine William he found that his right lung was hepatized "or perhaps full of dropsical fluid". A similar condition prevailed in regard to the cavity of the chest. The details were described by Harris in a long letter to his good friend Charles H. Ames.[9] Edward had brought a cardiac specialist by automobile from Lake Placid who had discovered five deposits of serum of the blood separated from the fibrin, or red corpuscles, and found that the chief valve of the heart had been strained and weakened and was working intermittently with the result of separating the serum, which by effusion escaped through the surrounding tissues and settled in the lungs and stomach and gradually moved down to the lower parts of the body. "Of course", said the expert, "it is an incurable disease, but medical science has many ways of mitigating the consequences by the use of violent medicines, strychnine, nitroglycerine and especially digitalis, which is the most wonderful of all specifics discovered in modern times for this disease". "But", he said, "the chief difficulty will be the difficulty of getting you to obey the prescriptions of the doctor and keep in bed; you may read and write and sit up a little in bed, if properly propped up by pillows, or perhaps in an easy rocking-chair." I replied that I supposed I had done my work, but that I should be glad to save all the pieces that could be saved by medicine and obedience to the directions of the physician, hoping that I could get together enough strength to permit me to print two or three books which I had long projected and for which I had the materials together and all ready.

To tell the truth, it had never occurred to me that heart failure was involved in this breakdown, but it gave me a great deal of light on the nature of dropsy which had been mysterious to me before. I saw that it was a disintegration of the vital bond that unites the essential principles of the blood and that any continuation of weakness in the mitral valve would be sure to be fatal. I commenced taking the violent medicines under the care of a local physician who came to see me daily and sometimes twice a day. My brother returned again after another eight days with an expert, this time from the sanitarium at Saranac Lake who made a new examination, quite as thorough as the previous one, and he expressed surprise that he found that the diagnosis of the previous week as reported to him could not be verified this time. It had become evident to him that the violent medicines produced extraordinary and favorable effects on me. The effusion of serum had stopped and the dropsical deposits had nearly disappeared and the regularity of the pulse had returned and things looked favorable.

By this time the month of September had begun and my brother began to be anxious about moving me out of the mountains in time to escape cold snaps that might be expected, which would make it dangerous to move me. He would return after another week and if I could stand the journey, would accompany me south—he hoped that I would stop at some place like Lakewood, New Jersey. But I was stubbornly determined to return to Washington, as the basis of all my supplies. My house was carefully adapted by me for a hospital as well as a studio with an express design of making a comfortable place to live in no matter what should happen. I had expended more than five hundred dollars connecting bedrooms with bathrooms, and with similar improvements, the very month before I moved into the house. It is, as you know, Mrs. Harris' house, purchased with the legacy from her brother. It has been made so convenient that I cannot rest anywhere else so comfortably. Then all my books and manuscripts and typewriters and desks are there and at least two of us, Edith and her mother, know where to find nearly every book that is needed for use.

I made so comfortable a journey, taking it in stages; first day to Elizabethtown and night's rest on the Hudson River steamer, reaching Desbrosses Street Ferry at

New York next morning; and on the third day a journey to Washington in the morning, reaching the house a little after one o'clock. I placed myself under my family physician and have visited him every week, twice a week, since the eleventh of September, for diagnosis and prescription, and he reports "continued progress"; although I have found September and October very malarious months here and I have seemed to myself very miserable from day to day, excepting the three or four days last week in which we have had a black frost which is fatal to microbes; but when I am in my own house with all my resources, I manage to keep myself amused and delighted, as, for instance, this morning I am reading William James's "Hegel and his Method", the most remarkable article that he, William James, has ever written. He undertakes in the Hibbert Journal for October 1908 to give a positive explanation of what he accredits to Hegel as really worth while: "from the center in Hegel come those towering sentences of his that are comparable only to Luther's, as where, etc." Were you present at my lecture on William James at Glenmore this summer? You will remember that I treated his savage attacks, two of them on religion, and one of them on Hegel, as mere bluffs, or challenges to his theological or Hegelian opponents to draw and defend themselves. He is tired of waiting any longer for their response and accordingly takes up himself the defence of Hegel and probably will take up the cause of religion in the same way.

I have amused myself two or three days with the attack on common schools by Prof. Larned of West Point and am in correspondence with Supt. Aldrich of Brookline on the subject, being about to write him a long letter on the subject.

I have also been obliged to spend some days on the

new pamphlet published by the Bureau of Education, giving the bibliography of all my writings as far as the library division of the Bureau is able to complete such a list. I shall send you with this a copy of that pamphlet.

In the meantime I hope to get up to my brother's in Providence as usual for Thanksgiving. I am making it the first object of my life to keep out of exposures to weather or fatigue or broken rest at night or climbing stairs or walking in the malarious air (that prevails here or even in Mass., more or less till snow flies). If you would be at home in West Newton it is possible that I might see you some forenoon in Providence, (the day after Thanksgiving?) in which case my brother would telephone you, but it is impossible now to tell whether or when.

Harris had rallied sufficiently to enable him to make a trip to Springfield, Mass., to see the publisher in regard to some problems connected with Webster's Dictionary, and later spend Thanksgiving, as planned, with his brother and family at Providence.[10] When it became known that he was very ill, letters with all good wishes for a speedy recovery poured in. Mr. O. M. Baker, President of the G. & C. Merriam Company asked him to "take good care of the animal". Cheering letters arrived from his disciple and friend, Dr. Holland. Even unknown friends and admirers wrote to him. The Department of Superintendence of the National Education Association formally expressed their regrets over his illness and let him know that they missed his presence and his counsel.[11] From the general meeting at Denver, Colo., in July, 1909, Dr. Nicholas Murray Butler kept him apprised of the proceedings. A telegram of greetings was also sent, and Harris' reply well reflects his feelings toward the Association:

THE LAST RETIREMENT

DOCTOR NICHOLAS MURRAY BUTLER
C/O NATIONAL EDUCATION ASSOCIATION

MY HEARTFELT THANKS FOR THE KIND WORDS
OF REMEMBRANCE FROM YOU AND ALL THE
DEAR OLD FRIENDS. GIVE MY LOVE TO THE
NATIONAL EDUCATIONAL ASSOCIATION COR-
PORATELY AND INDIVIDUALLY.

W. T. HARRIS

Ben Blewett dispatched a telegram of greetings and best
wishes for health and strength from the principals, teachers
and superintendents of the St. Louis Public Schools who
were meeting in annual assembly.[12] Not one of his friends
forgot him . . .

GIVE ME BOOKS OR I SHALL DIE

During the winter of 1908-09, brother Edward made
several trips to Washington to look after William who, in
turn, kept him informed of any major changes in his condition. Long and detailed histories of his case were
periodically written to Providence. In March, 1909, William noted the return of his normal appetite. He wished
for fried eggs, Beechnut bacon and baked potatoes, which
combination from then on formed his regular breakfast.
His dropsical condition   disappeared gradually.   In the
meantime, plans had been made for him to live at Providence to be more directly under the care of his brother. But
his chief concern was books. He had 12,000 of them, and
planned on moving them in their boxes, each two feet long,
which served for shelves. They were simply to be crated,
but he needed a floor plan of the house into which he was
to move in Providence, so the boxes could be labelled and
put right-away into their proper places, without disturbing
the books at all, and he directing the transfer from his easy-
chair. He wrote more than a thousand words about his

books to Edward in one of his letters[13] which has these autobiographical paragraphs at the close:

I do not think that you quite understand what books
are to me. If I were to go to live in a hotel or to live
in any private house of a relative or friend I should die
in a few weeks from starvation for the lack of certain
mental food which I get in some fourteen varieties of
books and researches that I am carrying on and which
enable me to forget my bodily pains and my mental sorrows. I have during my life utterly lost my possibility
of being amused even by climbing mountains, or visiting art galleries, or by attending lectures or by hearing
music, and I have settled down into grooves which
give me consolation and amusement, but not of such
a kind that other people can share it with me. This will
seem a dark saying and I will illustrate it: I am interested to the full in new studies in Aristotle and Plato
which I have been making for four years, and in the old
Persian-Bactrian sacred books, the Zend-Avesta and have
been rewarded by discoveries which grow more and more
numerous as time goes on. I have been interested, as
you know, since 1860 in the study of Hegel and Kant
and other German philosophers, and also in German
students of comparative religion and comparative art
developments of nations and in the philosophy of history and things of that kind. I have had great consola-
tions this winter in new studies in the philosophy of
history. You see that I am sort of a secular clergyman
interested in the great "literary bibles," as Snider calls
them. I have been reading Snider's book on Herodotus
within the last month and found it a tremendous book
throwing a blaze of light on the history of ancient nations as seen by the Greeks in the fifth century B.C.
Last year I studied up Arrian's history of Alexander the
Great, a wonderful book for showing us glimpses of

India and Persia in the fourth century B.C. I find my-self getting more interested in the hard or dry puzzles of history and literature; they become juicy and nutri-tive to me.

Now you see that I must have access to my fountains from which I draw not only information but also get access to the thoughts of the greatest thinkers along these lines and a hotel or a boarding-house life could not pos-sibly be endured by me for any considerable length of time. I think you noticed what kind of books I took up with me to the Adirondacks last summer — The Sacred Books of the East, and my dictionaries of Oriental lan-guages and various books of philosophy. With these I was able to take refuge whenever I was overcome by loneliness. These are peculiarities of mine and I do not recommend them for anybody else, but something like them, or as a substitute for them must be had by old people to make life worth living from day to day. With a background of these things one can interest his friends and be interested in what they are doing, and if one does not have some literary or scientific pursuits he has to find his consolation in making money and investing it and I am certain that making money and investing it is better than sailing yachts.

Why should you not pack your valise and come down here to Washington when Amy and James come and we can talk over things more at length and you may notice the improvement in my pulse which is at present the best pulse I have ever had in my life and you may also by percussion and auscultation take a new diagnosis of the mitral valve. Bring along with you the plan of the house unless you can send it to me by return mail.

Affectionately your brother,

W. T. HARRIS

DEPARTURE FROM WASHINGTON

The wisdom of moving from Washington to Providence might be disputed. It was solely dictated by brotherly feelings, and William's overestimation of his strength. Brother Edward had already made the suggestion in his letter of May 12th, 1908, but at that time William had not seen his way clear to leaving the capital where he had planned on staying the rest of his life. Concord might have been a place equally as good as Providence, and not too far from there. But Harris had confided in Sanborn that there were too many ghosts there. Not one of the old bards was left, while the place was full of the memories of Alcott, Emerson, Channing and the rest who had either died or moved away.

Sentiment might have had something to do with the decision to move to Providence, apart from the benefits to be derived from being near his brother physician. The town was rich in memories of the fate of the first Harrises. Thomas Harris, with twelve other families, had there "incorporated together into a town of fellowship" in the year 1637, had drawn up with 38 others a form of government in 1640, become a prominent citizen and public officer, and died in peace in 1686. Thomas Harris Jr., who had taken Elnathan Tew for wife, had likewise spent his life at Providence.

The last day in Washington drew near. On the eve of his departure, Dr. Henry Ridgely Evans, his erst-while private secretary in the Bureau, called on him. It was he who had compiled *A List of Writings of William Torrey Harris* that was published as chapter II of the *Report of the Commissioner of Education*. In one of his letters to his class-mate Col. Wm. Plumb Bacon,[14] Harris had characterized this bibliography done at the suggestion of the new Commissioner "a sort of compliment to an old man." Dr. Evans always entertained the highest regard for Harris, and that

596

evening, as he sat in Harris' study, he listened to a detailed scientific description of what Harris was suffering from. It amounted to "a learned lecture on the physiology of the heart and the particular organic disease" he was afflicted with. "His poise and serenity at the time were remarkable."[15]

THE NUMBERED DAYS OF PROVIDENCE

It was a warm July day when the Harris family moved to Providence and took up residence at 535 Broadway, adjacent to the residence of Dr. Edward Mowry Harris and his family at 4 Bell street. At first, Harris was very tired, and the task of seeing to it that his library of 12,000 volumes was arranged properly was threatning to exhaust his energy. However, after a few days he was strong enough to visit his brother. Old friends called on him and he would even feel up to lecturing to them on such topics as Beethoven's music. F. B. Sanborn visited him occasionally and they reminisced about their Concord days, about Theodore Parker, the freeing of the slaves, and the historic periods they had been through.

His health, however, did not improve in the long run. The dropsical condition returned, his heart weakened more and more, Medical science could do little at his age. He passed his 74th birthday comfortably. Gaining all the while in philosophic composure, he lost his grip on life. There was no abating of the virility of his mind, and he faced the inevitable placidly and with benignity, as befits the idealist that he was.

He went on reading and writing and ordering books as if he had an eternity to complete his work. On October 25th, he sent for his copy of MacKenzie's *Hegel's Educational Theory,* eager to know how the professor had treated the subject. Calmly he sent for Edward Endelman who had become a prominent lawyer in the meantime, to come to see

597.

him.   The message went astray and when a second one reached Endelman, it was too late.   A finished copy of Webster's *New International Dictionary,* with Harris' name on the title page, came shortly before his death, — in time for him to see it in its final form and to order copies sent to his relatives and friends.   At a quarter to two, in the afternoon of November 5th, 1909, with his wife and daughter Edith, his brother Edward and his family about, he passed on . . .

CHAPTER THIRTY-ONE

WORK AND MEMORIES

THE MONUMENT ON PUTNAM HEIGHTS

W HEN the news of Harris' death came out, few knew that he had changed residence to Providence. The funeral was held at Bell Street Chapel. His book on *The Spiritual Sense of Dante's Divine Comedy* was placed in his hands. A large photograph of him was arranged amid flowers on the casket. Miss Laura J. Pratt gave the organ recital, a mixed quartet sang several of his favorite selections. Rev. Antone G. Singsen offered the prayer and read the Beatitudes and the 23rd Psalm, and selections from one of the public school readers edited by Harris, and Tennyson's "Crossing the Bar," while Dr. Elmer E. Brown and Frank B. Sanborn made brief addresses. The City of Providence ordered all flags on the public buildings and schools to fly half mast for more than a day.

The remains were interred at Putnam Heights, in Connecticut, near where he was born. He was the third most famous man to come out of Windham County, the other two were General Israel Putnam and General Nathaniel Lyon, hero of the battle of Wilson's Creek. But Harris' had been a gentler art than that of war, for he had enriched his countrymen by planting the love of wisdom in them and given them the magic wand of education that unlocks all that is worth-while in life and thought. On the tombstone in the little cemetery on the hill we read:

YANKEE TEACHER

WILLIAM TORREY HARRIS, PH.D., LL.D.
BORN IN NORTH KILLINGLY, CONN.
SEPTEMBER 10, 1835
DIED IN PROVIDENCE, R. I.
NOVEMBER 5, 1909

FOUNDER AND EDITOR
OF THE
JOURNAL OF SPECULATIVE PHILOSOPHY

UNITED STATES COMMISSIONER OF EDUCATION
1889—1906
A RARE SCHOLAR WHOSE LIFE WAS ZEALOUSLY
AND UNTIRINGLY DEVOTED TO PHILOSOPHY AND
EDUCATION.

HIS RELATION TO THE WORLD IS THAT OF A
SUPERIOR SPIRIT. ALL THAT HE UTTERS HAS
REFERENCE TO SOMETHING COMPLETE, GOOD,
TRUE, BEAUTIFUL, WHOSE FURTHERANCE HE
STRIVES TO PROMOTE IN EVERY BOSOM.
GOETHE'S TRIBUTE TO PLATO.

THEY THAT ARE WISE SHALL SHINE AS THE BRIGHT-
NESS OF THE FIRMAMENT; AND THEY THAT TURN
MANY TO RIGHTEOUSNESS AS THE STARS FOREVER
AND EVER. DANIEL XII.

WEBSTER'S NEW INTERNATIONAL DICTIONARY

It was on the first of July, four months before he died, that Harris set his hand to the preface of eight pages of the 1910 edition of Webster's which appeared in the fall of 1909 and which, though based on the editions of 1890 and 1900, had become practically a new book under his editorship, with 2700 pages and 400,000 title words in the vocabulary. The proof-sheets were stamped August 20th, 1909, and it was one of those gratifying experiences when Harris was yet able to lay his eyes on them and see a copy of this monu-

600

mental work which, in its title: *Webster's New International,* suggested its world-wide scope, continuous with the English language itself.

Harris had acted as Editor-in-Chief and F. Sturges Allen as General Editor. It was the 10th *Webster* and *Merriam-Webster Dictionary,* and nearly thirty office editors, a very large number for that day, had collaborated. It stayed on the market for 25 years, till it was superseded by the second edition of the *New International.* The edition for which Harris had been responsible, was well characterized by President William A. Neilson, in the preface to the 1934 edition, as "the most radical of all the revisions thus far." No comparison could be made between it and earlier editions. The Merriam-Webster Company had achieved a complete triumph. It was the last great literary labor of Harris, and a fitting close to his career. From Florida to Maine, and from there around the world, the *New International* was hailed as the greatest of the *Websters,* and Harris became now known not only to every educator and philosopher, but to every lover of the English word.

In the 1900 edition, full credit had been tendered Harris "who not only gave his judgment and study to the perfection of the main outlines of the work, but closely revised the whole Supplement, line by line, first in the copy and again in the proofs." The Supplement here referred to had been worked out by Harris and Allen. It was embodied in the vocabulary of the 1910 edition.

Harris' articles in *Johnson's Cyclopaedia* had given him, as he himself was aware, a reputation "for the ability to hit the nail on the head in philosophical articles and get together the erudition or learning on the subject, but also to sift and winnow the unimportant from the deep and essential ideas that had lain at the root of philosophical discussions."[1] Of course, there was a difference between an encyclopaedia and a dictionary article. He took great pride, however, in his own devices and the fact that even though his own articles in the new *Webster* would never become popular because of their subject-matter, "they may get famous at some time when some competent person, or a number of competent persons, explain the completeness with which encyclopedia articles have been replaced by dictionary articles, only one-fifth in length."[2]

He had made a thorough examination of all the philosophical and psychological terms. Under the letter A alone he had examined 227 words. He was extremely conscientious in his definitions. As a matter of fact, he had devoted many months of study of Plato and Aristotle in the original Greek simply preparatory to writing on such topics as "idea" and the like. As an example of his meticulousness may be cited corrections in the entry "cyclic" which, under the third meaning, was discussing and illustrating the use of the word in classical prosody. In the department of philosophy he had contributed modifications of the terms in metaphysics, logic, psychology, ethics and esthetics which Professor Hartley B. Alexander of the University of Nebraska had either edited or defined. Such "modifications" amounted not seldom to new definitions, which, in that case, were signed by Harris. There were some 55 such items which he re-wrote; less than a third bear his signature. Among these we note "Aristotelianism," "Hegelianism," "Kantianism," "Herbartianism," "Fichteanism," "Leibnizianism," "apperception," "essence," "energy," "entelechy," and "realism," His article on "Plato" pleased him most and he rated it as one of his most important contributions. His notes on the transliteration of Greek names are still extant.

There was much correspondence also. For instance, his definition of "Katharsis" drew forth some criticism from Mr. Sheffield who leaned heavily on Professor Butcher's translation, while Harris supported himself by Hermann

Bonitz, Jacob Bernays and other German scholars. Between Springfield, Mass., Washington, D. C., and Hurricane, N. Y., there was a lively exchange of letters for many years.

However, Harris' practical suggestions in the making of the dictionary were, also from a business point of view, singularly important, and well illustrate his native Yankee inventiveness. Already in 1878, he had made a suggestion to the publishers, in his review of a *Webster*, to mark the places where the letters begin, either by bits of leather or heavier paper, or by staining the edges of all pages belonging to a certain letter with black ink for a space half an inch in length, beginning at the top with the first letter.

In the letter to his son, extracts from which have already been quoted, Harris hinted at a secret in connection with the publication of the 1910 edition of *Webster's*. Soon after the 1900 edition had come out in which he had added 25,000 words, the Merriam Company was contemplating a far greater dictionary than had ever been published before. And Harris discovered "pretty soon," i.e., around 1900 or 1901, "a device, which, though very simple, had apparently not been seen by any of the publishers, nor by G. & C. Merriam Co. themselves. This device was adopted after two or three years of discussion by the firm and is a secret of the firm . . . " What the device was, he did not divulge in the letter, nor, as he phrased it, had he "ever told it in any letter, or verbally, to any mortal being, relative, or friend or foe" and enjoined upon his son not even to make mention to anyone that there was a secret connected with the next edition in order to forestall curiosity and copying. The letter also alluded vaguely to certain other devices which he had "conceived of from the beginning" and which he had never been sure of being able to carry out. The big secret, however, was the divided page, and Harris was the originator of it, despite all assertions to the contrary.

Mr. O. M. Baker, President of the Merriam Company, in a letter to Harris' daughter[3] stated:

> I note in one of your letters that you expressed great pleasure in seeing references to the divided page. I don't wonder at that because your good father had a great fight with all of us before we consented to adopt it. We have yet to find anyone who refers to it at all but who commends it — and a good many educators speak of it . . . But you must not forget that is only one of the elements for which we give your good father credit, and notably his insistence upon the encyclopedic character of the work, which has been universally commended. There are many other features, but as you had the correspondence at the time you must be familiar with them.

The divided page, with the less common and obsolete words in fine print at the bottom of the page, made it possible to incorporate in the dictionary an amount of words which otherwise would have encumbered the handiness of the volume, or made a second volume necessary, or else would have precluded the feasibility of including words which nevertheless belong in a dictionary. When the tome appeared, the divided page was hailed immediately as a stroke of genius. In the resolutions[4] passed by the publishers on the death of Harris, the Company officials stated expressly in regard to the "great revision of 1910":

> His service to that work was especially marked in drawing its ground lines, and to his ingenious invention and persuasive advocacy was due the adoption of the divided page, a device which went far to make possible the advance of the book above its predecessors. Succeeding to a line of illustrious lexicographers — Webster, Goodrich, and Porter — his name will always be associated with the crowning of their work by the New International Dictionary.

In a way, his work on the *Webster* closed a cycle of his development which started with his early interest in phonography and linguistics, leading him, on the one hand, to a study of meanings, and, on the other, to his spelling reform tendencies. He had been in many ventures and conventions of the spelling reformers together with Melvil Dewey and others. He had never gone to excesses because of his appreciation of the historical and etymological elements reflected in English spelling which preserve the continuities.

In a letter to E. O. Vaile, editor of *Intelligence*,[5] he wrote:

Reforms like the spelling reform, or like temperance, or tree-planting, have no chance when the mind of the people is feverish to the point of revolution. I have often thought of the sudden collapse which all reforms met at the time of our civil war*. They were simply dropped out of sight and hearing.

That footnote in the letter just quoted must not be taken to mean that he never returned to his interest in reforming English spelling. In 1896 he entertained such strong doubts as to its success because the country was in the midst of the discussions of the silver standard and, being an economic problem, claimed priority over such seemingly unimportant questions as the spelling of words. Spelling reformers were active not only in America, but in England as well, and in 1901 made a formidable showing in the Department of Superintendence in the National Educational Association. The University of Chicago brought out in that year the discussions by Vaile, Slosson Thompson, Emerson E. White, Harris and others. We also have an unfinished manuscript by Harris,[6] representing an address at the Simplified Spelling Board meeting in New York, in 1907.

---

* I was a spelling reformer before the Civil War.

605

For his participation in the "new creation" of the G. & C. Merriam Company, the authorities of the Panama Pacific Exposition at San Francisco awarded Harris, posthumously, a diploma and a medal in 1917.[7]

IRONS THAT STAYED IN THE FIRE

In his letter of April 6th, 1909, to his brother Edward in which he touched upon the suggestion, preposterous to him, to store his library, Harris gave an indication of what he yet intended to do: "And if I should recover and get some strength I could do nothing [without my books] in the way of putting together and completing scores of literary enterprises that are begun and many of them nearly finished."

During his illness he had definitely planned to apply what he called a "new device" to his philosophical and educational writings, and had actually spent many hours and days in whipping his manuscripts into shape. He had acted on his own impulse as well as at the repeated urgings of his friends, particularly Dr. Nicholas Murray Butler. All during his life he had carried more topics in his mind than he was able to write on. During September-October, 1906, he had made a little catalog of projects, comprising 37 items, which he called "Irons in the Fire." They included at least 10 books, one each on Dante, Goethe, Emerson and Carlyle, one on Hegel's *Philosophy of Religion,* treatises on Art for Teachers, Wordsworth's Ode, on Wundt and Furtwangler, and some other topics to be mentioned presently. The book on *The Course of Study in the Elementary Schools,* which he also listed, was to be ready in the fall of 1904 for publication by D. Appleton & Co., but was never finished. Three books, however, he nearly completed. The first was the volume of *Practical Lessons of History,* or, *The Evolution of Civilization.*

The objectives of the book were to impart political wisdom by presenting "the spectacle of the experiments of mankind in the matter of learning how to govern themselves." Seeing the failures and successes should save us from the mistakes and errors of the past. Twenty-two chapters of this are in typewritten form, tracing history from tribal government through the Orient, Greece and Rome, the rise of Christianity and Mohammedanism and reformations and revolutions down to government by public opinion. As a possible 23rd chapter Harris had contemplated using his *Andover Review* article of 1886 on "English and German. A Study in the Philosophy of History." The 15th chapter, bearing the tentative title of "Philosophy vs. Science" seems, in the opinion of Miss Edith Davidson Harris, not to have been written or at least not completed or included. He did incorporate, however, the six lectures he had given at St. Louis during February and March, 1885, and which were still available to him in notes taken by pupils in the class;[8] in addition, the four lectures on "The Spiritual Lesson of History, or, What does History Teach?" given at the Old South Church in Boston during April-May, 1889; the address on "The Philosophic Aspects of History" delivered on December 31st, 1890, before the American Historical Association; the four lectures on "The Practical Lessons in History," delivered at the Old South Meeting House at Boston,[9] during November-December, 1890;[10] the ten lectures of 1893-94 at Johns Hopkins University on "The Philosophy of History"; the Old South Lectures, expanded to six, before the Columbian University in 1896 under the same title as that of the proposed book; the five lectures on history, beginning with the "Defects of Tribal Government" and ending with "The Age of Revolutions and the Outcome of History" delivered in 1901 at the Phebe A. Hearst Kindergarten Training School at Washington, D. C.; and, finally, the revised version of the Johns

Hopkins lectures in the series of ten delivered before the Columbian University in 1904.

Harris intended, moreover, to utilize the lecture he gave at the Milwaukee Summer School in August, 1886, which was rated a masterly analysis and comparison of the Teu-tonic and Anglo-Saxon genius, as well as his Chautauqua articles on "The History and Philosophy of Education,"[11] and the lecture by the same title at Boston, in 1882, and printed in the *New England Journal of Education*. He also was thinking of using some of the papers in his *Journal of Speculative Philosophy*. The bulk of the material for the proposed book was composed of lecture notes, fragments of manuscripts, clippings, drafts and quotations from educational and philosophical works, some done in the hand of his son and some in that of his daughter, all of which were to be integrated.

There was another major work which was planned by Harris in the evening of his life: *A History and Philosophy of Education*. Much preliminary work had been done, and the whole project resolved itself into revising and expanding the lectures he had given on numerous occasions, principally those at Indiana University during February, 1881, and at Boston and Chautauqua during 1882, his talks at the Pedagogical Conference at Johns Hopkins University in 1891, and the course on the "History of Education" at the same institution in the fall of 1892. In the first lecture of this last mentioned course, Harris had dealt with the literature of the history of education with which he was, of course, exceedingly well acquainted. Every seat was filled in the lecture hall of the university's Physical Laboratory, and it was the success he earned there that determined him in large part to undertake the writing of a work on the subject. The impression he had created among the graduate students of history and politics, who were his principal listeners, was distinctly favorable, not to say delightful, as the reporters had it.[12]

In many ways the subject was interrelated with his other favorite theme, the philosophy of history, and some chapters he conceived as interchangeable. His six chapters on education in the United States which he contributed in 1894 to Shaler's *The United States,* no doubt formed part of the plan. At all events, this project did not progress so rapidly as the *Practical Lessons of History,* mainly because he had said too much extemporaneously in the pertinent lectures, and fewer abstracts had appeared in print.

A third book that he carried in his mind and toward which some progress was made, was that on *School Management,* comprising sections on teaching, salaries, grading, and classification. His experience in St. Louis had, of course, been particularly rich along these lines, not to mention his connection with the Concord schools. A start in the direction of writing this book was made by gathering up some of his publications, including his National Educational Association address at Nashville, Tenn., in 1889, on "Art Education the True Industrial Education — A Cultivation of Aesthetic Taste of Universal Utility"; that of 1899 at Columbus, Ohio, on "How to make Good Teachers out of Poor Ones"; some of his work as Commissioner, e.g., "The Study of Arrested Development in Children, as Produced by Injudicious School Methods"; the answers to his 1893 questionnaire to 827 school superintendents regarding "Class Intervals in City Public Schools," and his 1906 address before the American Institute of Instruction. He also planned on giving some space to a discussion of the School City: a scheme which he criticized in no uncertain terms: "If I wanted a child to be taught the tricks of the demagogue and the devices of the unscrupulous politicians, I should by all means place him in a 'school city' as organized on Mr. Gill's plan, and expect that the child would learn how to bribe his superiors and to undervalue honest and truthful straight-forwardness of conduct."¹³ With all his idealism and the faults he may have possessed in common with all philosophers and theorists, Harris had never been blind to some of the sterner realities of our economic, social and political life. His books, thus, would have been of considerable practical value for his time.

TIME AND MEMORY

"When the true teacher dies, the guardian spirits of a true humanity weep over his departure," said C. F. Childs, that gentle teacher who was Harris' close friend in the early days of St. Louis. Childs had departed while young, Harris was not allotted his full four score. But he had been, in a sense, the personification of American education and philosophical thinking in its conservative tendencies during the period in which he lived and worked. Those of a like mind with him, felt keenly that the ideals they had cherished had no longer that staunch support in a universally acclaimed and respected person such as Harris. It was not sentiment, it was confession that appeared in *The Nation*: "All of us who knew him hope that to some degree we too were edited and amended and enlarged by him. . ." For its Christmas number in 1909, *The School Board Journal* published an impressive frontispiece with the caption "Education's Loss," representing Education, as a robed woman, leaning in rueful posture over the portrait of Harris.

Scores of resolutions were adopted by different societies and bodies after his death had become known to them, — just one indication of the sweep of his influence. Some recalled the service he had done in their particular field, others mingled with detached appraisals personal memories. In terseness and comprehensiveness perhaps this sentence in the resolution of the College Entrance Examination Board of New York, of January, 1910, surpassed them all:

"American Schools, from the University to the Kindergarten, are the richer for his service as scholar, educational administrator and critic."

On July 23rd, 1909, Harris had been elected a Vice President of the International Institute of Sociology at their meeting in Bern, but the news of this honor apparently had never reached him.[14] St. Louis attached his name to one of their Teachers' Colleges. Friends wrote kind letters to his wife and daughter who were left behind and remained in Providence for many years. Mrs. Harris lived till her 84th year and died, after an illness of some five years, on September 21st, 1920. Miss Edith Davidson Harris took charge of the literary remains in a spirit of unselfish devotion and has since assisted most liberally all those who have sought information about her illustrious father.

Prophetically, Susan Blow, the devoted disciple of Harris, said back in 1910: "We shall hear more of the great leader now that his leadership has ceased." Yet, her words remained substantially unfulfilled till 1935, when the Western Division of the American Philosophical Association at its 36th Annual Meeting at St. Louis commemorated the one hundredth anniversary of his birth, and the United States Department of the Interior, Office of Education, gave, on December 9th, at Washington, a reception and dinner honoring his memory with the co-operation of the National Council of State Superintendents and Commissioners of Education, American Council on Education, and National Education Association. On May 29th, 1936, in his native town, North Killingly, Ct., now Putnam Heights, the State Board of Education presented a program at his grave, at the little school house he attended, and at the church, a program in which very appropriately the school children took an active part.

The memory of Harris that threatened to fade out in the first third of the century, thus has become brighter with the years. And, as the nation becomes ever more appreciative of her past, people will have no longer any ground to ask: "Who was Harris?" but they will have been taught to know and recognize him as one of the wisest and greatest of America's educators and thinkers.

HARRIS ADDRESSES OUR TIME

In proof of the contention that Harris' thinking was not ephemeral, the address of welcome which he gave at the Washington, D. C., meeting of the National Educational Association in the month of July, 1898, may close this book.[15] This was the setting: In Manila Bay, the fleet of the Spaniards was destroyed, the Marines had just landed at Guantánamo Bay, and Guam was to be seized . . .

It is fitting that you hold this annual session at the capital of the nation. You meet here at an important epoch in the history of the country. The annual census of the United States in 1880 showed for the first time an aggregate of over fifty millions of inhabitants. It was a true remark, then made by one of us in a session of the Department of Superintendents, that America had now, for the first time, ascended above the horizon of Europe. We had become visible to Great Britain and its peers on the continent as a nation of equal rank, and to be taken account of in future adjustments of the powers of the world. In that year we had reached the full stature of national manhood, and were as strong as the strongest nations of Europe in numbers and wealthproducing power.

After another ten years, in 1890, we found that, in effective size and strength, we surpassed in wealth-producing power and in numbers the largest of them.

It has been only a question of time when we should take our place among the nations as a real power in the management of the affairs of the world; when we should be counted with the great powers of Europe in the government of Asia, and the isles of the sea. It was a moment to be postponed rather than hastened by the patriotic citizen. When our power of producing wealth is increasing out of proportion with the rest of the world, and when our population is swelled by waves of migration from Europe, why should we be in a feverish haste to precipitate the new era — the era of close relationship with the states of Europe? For here is the parting of the ways, and the beginning of an essentially new era. Most of what is old and familiar to us must change and give place to new interests. Once the United States enters upon this career, all its powers and resources must be devoted to adapting it to the new situation and defending its line of advance. For it cannot move back without national humiliation.

And it is this very summer that the hand of the dial of our destiny has pointed at twelve, and for better or worse we have now entered upon our new epoch as an active agent in the collected whole of great powers that determine and fix the destiny of the peoples on the planet. This new era is one of great portent to the statesmen of America. All legislation hereafter must be scrutinized, in view of its influence upon our international relations. We cannot any longer have that smug sense of security and isolation which has permitted us to legislate without considering the effect on foreign nations. Hereafter our foremost national interest must be the foreign one, and consequently our highest studies must be made on the characters, inclinations, and interests of foreign peoples. It is obvious that this study requires a greater breadth of education, more specializing in history, and in the manners and customs of European nations; their methods of organizing industries, as well as their methods of organizing armies and navies. We must even master foreign literatures and see what are the fundamental aspirations of the people. This points to the function of the system of education in the future of this country. This indicates the vocation of the schoolmaster in the coming time.

The new burden of preparing our united people for the responsibilities of a closer union with Europe, and for a share in the dominion over the islands and continents of the Orient, this new burden will fall on the school systems in the several states, and more particularly on the colleges and universities that furnish higher education. For it is higher education that must furnish the studies in history and in the psychology of peoples which will provide our ministers and ambassadors abroad with their numerous retinue of experts and specialists, thoroughly versed in the habits and traditions of the several nations. The knowledge required by our members of Congress and our executive departments will make a demand upon higher education for post-graduate students who have concentrated their investigations upon points in international law and the philosophy of history. Diplomacy will become a great branch of learning for us.

This has been felt for sometime, altho it has not been consciously realized . . .

The education of the elementary school fits the citizen for most of his routine work in agriculture, manufactures, commerce, and mining. But the deeper problems of uniting our nation with the other great nations, and harmonizing our unit of force with that greater unit, must be solved by higher education, for it alone can make the wide combinations that are necessary. Shallow elementary studies give us the explanation of that which lies near us. They help us to understand our immediate environment, but for the understanding of deep national differences, and for the management of all that is alien to our part of the world, deeper studies are required. The student must penetrate the underlying fundamental differences of the world history in order to see how such different fruits have grown on the same tree of humanity. We must look to our universities and colleges for the people who have learned to understand the fashions and daily customs of a foreign people, and who have learned to connect the surface of their everyday life with the deep national principles and aspirations which mold and govern their individual and social action. Hence the significance of this epoch in which you are assembled to discuss the principles of education and its methods of practice. There have been great emergencies, and great careers have opened to American teachers, in our former history; but you stand today on the vestibule of a still more important age, the age of the union of the new world with the old world.

NOTES

NOTES

Most of the correspondence referred to in this biography is in private hands and unpublished. Unless otherwise indicated, the originals are in possession of Miss Edith Davidson Harris. There are deposits of unpublished material at the Jefferson Memorial, Missouri Historical Society, St. Louis, Mo., at Headquarters, National Education Society of the United States, Washington, D.C., and at Concord Public Library, Concord, Mass. Quotations from Harris' writings have been made in almost every case from the original manuscript, although the printed documents have been referred to when generally accessible.

INTRODUCTION

1 Nicholas Murray Butler, "William Torrey Harris", in *Educational Review*, 38, p. 534-535 (Dec., 1909), repr. in *J. of Ed.*, 82 p. 596 (Dec. 16, 1905) and C. M. Perry, *The St. Louis Movement in Philosophy*, p. 67-68.

2 References to this and other pronouncements may be consulted in the articles listed in Kurt F. Leidecker, "Bibliography: William Torrey Harris in Literature", *William Torrey Harris* 1835-1935, a Collection of Essays, including Papers and Addresses presented in Commemoration of Dr. Harris' Centennial at the St. Louis Meeting of the Western Division of the American Philosophical Society. Edited by Edward L. Schaub (The Open Court, 1936).

CHAPTER I

1 This section is based on the genealogical notebooks, clippings, and letters, many in the handwriting of his daughter, systematically arranged and considerably expanded. All footnotes mine.

2 Of the numerous writings on this branch of the Harris family, cf. especially Albert Hutchinson, *A Genealogy and Ancestral Line of Bethuel Harris* (Keene, N.H., 1907), pp. 1 ff.

3 Cf. Henry E. Whipple, *A Brief Genealogy of the Whipple Families* (Providence, 1873), pp. 6-14, and Charles H. Whipple, *Genealogy of the Whipple-Wright, Wager, Ward, Pell, McLean-Burnet Families* (Los Angeles, 1917), pp. 11-13.

4 Cf. Avery F. Angell, *Genealogy of the Descendants of Thomas Angell* (Providence, 1872), pp. 9-12. Through this Angell line Harris is linked closely with the ancestors of Dr. James R. Angell, President of Yale University, who himself has, on occasion, proudly called attention to this fact.

5 Cf. the vivid description in Col. J. T. Holmes, *The American Family of Rev. Obadiah Holmes* (Columbus, O., 1915), pp. 18 ff.

6 Mrs. Jennie (Henderson) Porter, *Hannah Johnson and Polly Palmer with some of her Kinsfolk* (Kansas City, Mo., 1930), p. 9.

7 Cf. L. Smith Hobart, *William Hobart, his Ancestors and Descendants* (Springfield, Mass., 1886), pp. 1-52.

8 Cf. John Adams Vinton, The Symmes Memorial (Boston, 1873).

9 Cf. Henry E. Turner, *Greenes of Warwick in Colonial History* (Newport, R. I., 1877), pp. 5 ff.

10 Cf. a paper by Judge Bullock on "Some Incidents in the Life and Times of Stukeley Westcote, one of the Twelve Associates of Roger Williams", read at one of the meetings of the Rhode Island Veteran Citizens' Historical Association.

11 *New England Historical and Genealogical Register*, vol. 21, pp. 12 ff. and Edwin Eugene Towne, *The Descendants of William Towne* (Newtonville, Mass., 1901), pp. 15-25.

12 See Roscoe Conkling Fitch, *History of the Fitch Family*, A.D. 1400-1930, vol. 2, chapter 1.

13 Cf. Hon. Ralph D. Smith, *History of Guilford, Conn.* (Albany, N. Y., 1877).

14 Cf. Frank Farnsworth Starr, *The Edward Jackson Family of Newton, Mass.* (Hartford, Ct., 1895), pp. 5-27.

15 Cf. for details Samuel W. Reed, "Sketch of the Life of Capt. Wm. Torrey", *Magazine of New England History*, July, 1892. See also *id.* vol. 3, pp. 198-199.

16 Cf. Frederic C. Torrey, *The Torrey Families and their Children in America*, vol. 1, pp. 348-349, where the title page and the first page are reproduced. The discourse appeared in print 70 years after it was written, with a preface by the Rev. Mr. Prince, who lived in the family for a good number of years.

17 Cf. a paper read before the Weymouth Historical Society, April 7, 1880, by H. A. Newton.

18 Samuel Forbes Rockwell, *Davis Families of Early Roxbury and Boston* (North Andover, Mass., 1932), chapter 2.

19 Rev. Israel Wilkinson, *Memoirs of the Wilkinson Family in America* (Jacksonville, Ill., 1869), pp. 32-46. For controversial data with reference to Samuel Wilkinson, son of Lieut. Laurance Wilkinson, through whom Harris descended, cf. p. 47.

20 Cf. Browning's *Colonial Dames of Royal Descent*.

21 Cf. Elias Child, *Genealogy of the Child, Childs and Childe Families* (Utica, N. Y., 1881), pp. 67 ff.

22 Cf. E. E. and E. McC. Salisbury, *Family-Histories and Genealogies*, vol. 1, Part 2 (1892), pp. 473 ff.

23 Cf. Brookline Historical Publication Society, Publication No. 14: Susan Vining Griggs, *The Devotion Family of Brookline*.

CHAPTER II

1 Cf. William A. Mowry, "The First American Public School", *Education*, 21 (1901), pp. 535 ff. Cf. also Bernard C. Steiner, *The History of Education in Connecticut* (Bureau of Education, Circular of Information, No. 2, 1893, Washington, 1893).

2 Cf. especially the issue of July, 1840.

3 *Connecticut Common School Journal*, 3, p. 187-188.

4 Figures for 1839, but essentially unchanged in 1847. The medium salary of one-room school teachers in 1937 was $517 a year.

5 New York had 44,452 of them, Virginia 58,732, North Carolina 56,609, Tennessee 58,531. Connecticut had the lowest number of any State in the Union.

6 Miss Catherine Davison Torrey who shortly after married Dr. Fenner Harris Peckham. Women teachers were usually employed in summer and then they lasted ordinarily only one term.

7 It is no longer standing.

8 The following description has been carefully compiled from W. T. Harris, "Recollections of a Red Schoolhouse", in *Youth's Companion*, Nov. 21, 1901, and "How I was Educated", in *Forum* for August, 1886, as well as contempor-

NOTES

ary documents and information kindly supplied by relatives of the biographee.

9 Average pupil attendance in all schools of Connecticut was 52.

10 This description is furnished by Miss Edith Davidson Harris who has vague recollections which, she says, may not be altogether correct. When she saw the house first, it had already begun to crumble, and so she brought away as souvenirs a door-latch and a bit of wall-paper.

11 Even Hartford did not possess a daily paper, and for daily news people relied on New York.

12 Cf. a letter by James S. (?) Copp, 1871, in possession of Miss Frances Zilpah Torrey Benner, complimenting mother Harris on her children and her eagerness to give them an education.

13 This and other quotations relative to school methods are from W. T. Harris' own writings as given in Henry Ridgely Evans, "A List of the Writings of William Torrey Harris", *Advance Sheets, U. S. Bureau of Education,* chapter 2 of the *Report of the Commissioner of Education for* 1907. Though listing 479 items, this bibliography is by no means complete. A new list is in preparation.

CHAPTER III

1 Cf. Austin Francis Munich, *The Beginnings of Roman Catholicism in Connecticut* (New Haven, Ct., 1935).

2 Their names, in 1835, were: Elisha Atkins, Roswell Whitmore, William Bushnell, Alvin Underwood, Congregationalist; Calvin Cooper, Jonathan Oatley, Daniel Smith, Baptist.

3 Cf. Clive Day, *The Rise of Manufacturing in Connecticut,* 1820-1850 (New Haven, Ct., 1935); Jarvis Means Morse, *A Neglected Period of Connecticut's History,* 1818-1850 (New Haven, Ct., 1933).

4 Cf. Jabez H. Hayden, *Historical Sketches* (Windson Locks, Ct., 1900), pp. 63-69.

5 Cf. Sidney Withington, *The First Twelve Years of Railroads in Connecticut* (New Haven, Ct., 1935).

6 These stories according to Edward Mowry Harris.

CHAPTER IV

1 See *The Putnam Patriot* (Putnam, Ct.), for Thursday, June 4th, 1936, p. 3, for a description of the ceremonies.

2 *Forum,* 1, p. 557.

3 The function of Academies was to supplement the education received in deficient public schools.

4 William's brother Edward went to Danielson Academy, Danielson, Ct., and Nicholas Academy, Dudley, Mass., and it is just a guess that William went to one or the other of the two also.

5 In "Our most Honored Alumnus", *Woodstock Academy Gleaner,* August, 1906.

6 As Commissioner of Education he no longer felt proud of this early production.

7 Cf. George Otis Ward, *The Worcester Academy, its Location and its Principals* (Worcester, Mass., 1918).

8 Cf. the first section of the By-Laws of the elaborate Constitution. The motto of the society was *Haec studia adolescentiam accuunt.* President at the time was Rollin N. Hill, as Mrs. Gertrude L. Houlihan, Alumni Office Secretary, informs me.

9 Miss Katherine Fenner Peckham, who died at Putnam Heights, Ct., April 1st, 1939.

621

10 Told by Miss Katherine Fenner Peckham.

11 The quoined structure with its belfry was erected in 1818 according to the plans of Elias Carter, opposite the Sampson Howe Tavern which antedated it by 30 years.

12 There are two compositions from that period which show a budding imagination and a growing mastery of style. They are in manuscript, also in shorthand among a later collection of early writings. "The Permanence of Fame" dates from the Spring of 1851. In shorthand Harris later inserted, perhaps erroneously, the remark that this was the first piece he ever wrote and that it was delivered at an exhibition in Woodstock, in the Spring term of 1851. But we know that the title of his essay then was "The Faculties of the Mind". Whether written in Woodstock or Worcester, it remains an interesting document. "Astronomy" was written in the fall of 1852.

13 Cf. *The 20th Annual Report of the Board of Directors of the St. Louis Public Schools*, p. 135, and *Forum*, 1, p. 559.

14 Cf. Claude M. Fuess, *An Old New England School* (Boston and New York, 1917).

15 Cf. the letters to George T. Eaton, Secretary of the Alumni Association at Andover, Mass., under date of December 23rd, 1899, and May 18th, 1904, in possession of the Academy.

16 Dr. McKenzie says of him: "That great, strong, Scotch-Irish heart, the best blood the world has seen up to this day; that firm inflexible purpose, gentle as a woman of heart, stern as commander in hand . . . If I have ever seen anywhere any semblance of despotism and absolute monarchy, it was Phillips Academy under Samuel H. Taylor." *The Phillipian*, June 30th, 1903.

17 Fuess, *ib.*, p. 308.

18 Cf. *Speeches at the First Dinner of the Phillips Academy Alumni Association*, March 24th, 1886, pp. 52-53.

19 Andover, Mass., July 18th, 1853.

20 William kept among his papers his literal translation of a part of the ninth book of Virgil's *AEneid*, as well as that of the first ten lines of the same author's first eclogue.

CHAPTER V

1 For this description cf. chiefly his letter of September 18th, 1854, to grandmother Torrey.

2 Matriculation did not take place before six months of residence, but the parents or guardians were required to deposit a bond of $200. William was thus only on probation.

3 Cf. a letter dated Nov. 6th, 1854, to his sister Sarah which closes with a Latin salutation and signature.

4 The second term began on January 3rd, 1855, and ended April 10th, the third lasted from May 2nd to July 26th. Spring vacation lasted three weeks, summer vacation seven weeks.

5 Cf. William's letter from New Haven, dated August 21st, 1855, to his sister Sarah Lydia, then 16 years of age. In possession of Miss Frances Zilpah Torrey Benner. The end is missing.

6 Cf. his letter of September 1st, 1855.

7 She was born October 29th, 1836.

8 From a letter to his mother, presumably written in 1856.

9 *Forum*, 1, p. 558.

10 This paragraph I take from a letter to me of Profesor Edward Parmalee Morris, under date of April 30th, 1937.

NOTES

11 A marginal note in the scrap-book which contains this letter to the editor says that it was "written to call attention to spiritualism". Note the neutral phrasing! Mr. H. N. Goodman, at whose request he had written the article, replied the following day with an article entitled "Miracles—Old and New", in which he criticised the skepticism which would reject any objective manifestation of spiritualism which he considered similar to Bible miracles, and substitute for it a psychological explanation or one that does not take recourse to anything but what the human frame itself contains, such as "nervous fluids", Baron von Reichenbach's "odylic forces", mesmeric and electric forces and the like.

12 Born in Cohocten, N. Y., October 11th, 1809.

13 Later, I have been informed by Professor Andrew Keogh, Librarian at Yale University, "the wooden spoon man was elected by his class and the spoon was the symbol of the highest elective honor in the Junior class". Now the wooden spoon seems to be the symbol of the chairman of the Junior prom committee, to judge by occasional pictorial releases of the press, e.g., March, 1940.

14 One Yale man, in the June, 1857, *Yale Literary Magazine*, described this burial of Euclid as "an institution which might be venerated for its age, were it not an outrage execrable in proportion to its years. Night is made hideous, by a grand burlesque of the most solemn of human experiences. Respectable men are ashamed to be present at the performance, undisguised".

15 Anson Phelps Stokes, *Memorials of Eminent Yale Men* (1914), pp. 273-74.

16 *Ib.*, pp. 278-79.

17 The indenture was made between him and a Samuel N. Rowell on May 17th, 1856, retroeffective apparently to September of the previous year. It was also stipulated that the lessee had the privilege of leasing the gymnasium for two years more for a yearly rent of not more than $300.00.

18 The receipts from various individuals, mostly his class-mates, but also from a German club, do not quite total $200.00, while expenses for coal, gas, fixtures, plumbing, equipment and the like reached more than $150.00. The business end of this venture came up once more in an unpleasant way while Harris was in St. Louis, the leaseholder unjustifiably demanding once more to see the receipts.

19 Cf. "Our Most Honored Alumnus", *Woodstock Academy Gleaner*, August, 1906.

20 There are also two shorthand copies in the notebooks of early writings. Date of delivery: January 4th, 1857.

21 Except for the hoop-skirts, the picture represents a modern aspect with the young ladies practicing with bow and arrow on the lawn of this castle-like structure. Sarah's niece, Elizabeth Dorrance Bugbee (the daughter of her brother James Bugbee) who was born just a year before Sarah, had been in Oread the same year but unlike her remained through 1855. The reason for Sarah's short stay was illness.

22 Cf. the letter to his father form New Haven, April 10th, 1857.

23 This was a change which has sometimes been described as opposed by the professor of moral philosophy and the classical scholars, but which, Professor emer. Edward Parmalee Morris informs me, was adopted nearly unanimously by the faculty.

24 Cf. his letter to him of July 18th, 1853.

25 These chapters are almost exclusively based on the diary which W. T. Harris kept in shorthand. Miss Edith Davidson Harris used much time and patience in making accurate transcriptions, and my sincere thanks are due her for graciously putting the transcription at my disposal.

26 The first stimulus to read this book may have come through his classmate Chauncy Saymour Kellogg, who had presented a dissertation by this title at the Junior Exhibition on April 7th.
27 Sarah figures very frequently in the diary as S. T. B.
28 At this second place they paid $3.00 a person per week for room and board, while they would have saved only $1.00 had they made their meals in the room.
29 In meeting women, he would always make comparison with his own Sarah. For instance, Mrs. Hayden whom he came to know he called "a pretty woman with black eyes", but not so refined as Sarah.

CHAPTER VI

1 Cf. also a letter by Dr. F. H. Peckham, an uncle by marriage (he had married Catherine D. Torrey), written from Providence, R. I., October 11th, 1857, and a letter to his grandmother, dated September 10th, 1857. He had considered going to Illinois and perhaps teaching there in the public schools.
2 *The Phonographic Magazine,* May, 1890. For details about this top-notch journalist, cf. Wm. Hyde, *Missouri Historical Society,* Bull. No. 12 (St. Louis, 1896), p. 9-10, also Walter B. Steven's biography of Joseph B. McCullagh, in vol's 25 ff. of the *Missouri Historical Review* (1930 ff.).
3 It was the firm Boggs and Grant, "General agents for selling, bartering real or personal property, notes, bonds and other securities; borrowing or loaning of money on real estate or other good security; collecting of rents, renting of homes, collecting of notes, bills, accounts, or other demands", as a half-inch advertisement in *The Weekly Telegraph* of March 12, 1859, has it.
4 In unfinished state in the shorthand Book of Early Writings, 1851-1859. It is dated December 27th, 1857. A separate study of this Philosophic Society has been made by the writer.
5 Again, I am indebted to Miss Edith Davidson Harris for transcribing the shorthand diary.
6 Cf. Taylor and Crooks, *Sketch Book of Saint Louis* (St. Louis, 1858); Adolphus M. Hart, *Life in the Far West; or The Adventures of a Hoosier in the Mound City* (St. Louis, 1853); E. D. Kargau, *St. Louis in früheren Jahren. Ein Gedenkbuch für das Deutschtum* (St. Louis, 1893).
7 As late as 1890, he told a reporter: "Phonography was a thing that I went into *con amore.* I cared a great deal more about the art than I did about making money by it . . . I was enamored with the philosophic basis of the Pitman alphabet, as thousands have been. Even if it was a slower system people would be attracted to it because it has such a philosophical analysis of sounds. I was always interested in philology, and the phonographic alphabet, being a correct analysis of sounds, assisted me in those studies. It is the only shorthand alphabet that is founded on a scientific analysis of sound." *Phonographic Magazine,* May, 1890, p. 137.
8 Yale College and the St. Louis Public Library got most of these.
9 Miss Edith Davidson Harris, in deciphering this diary and other matter, used a dictionary and a small *Manual* of the Isaac Pitman system, together with a small textbook of the Graham reporting terms. Her experience leads her to think that he wrote a "sort of a combination of the Isaac Pitman and Graham systems at that time and sometimes invented his own reporting abbreviations" (letter to me, dated Walpole, N. H., August 16th, 1936). A good many "Phonography Devices" of his are preserved, showing how he sought to improve consistently throughout the years his shorthand characters, taking hints and suggestions wherever he found them. In 1890 he made the statement in

NOTES

the *Phonographic Magazine* that he had always been interested in all new systems of shorthand, but that he had looked in vain for any improvement over the Pitman system.

10 Col. O'Fallon played an important rôle in starting the Pacific Railroad, was a large real estate owner who had given the grounds for St. Louis University and Washington University, and had endowed O'Fallon Polytechnic Institute. Cf. J. T. Scharf, ed., *History of Saint Louis, City and County* (1883), vol. 1, pp. 343-354. See also the personal sketches of John F. Darby, in his *Personal Recollections* (St. Louis, 1880).

11 St. Louis, Mo., March 31st, 1858.

12 January 29th, 1858.

13 Jones' Commercial College was a creditable institution which though for four months after opening in 1841 had not received a single pupil, was now thriving at the Southeast corner of Third Street and Washington Avenue. Jonathan Jones was president.

14 March 29th, 1858. Neither books nor pens were returned.

15 March 30th, 1858.

16 April 13th, 1858.

17 The apple theory may not have been altogether original with William. It has been advanced frequently, witness the recent slogan "An apple a day keeps the doctor away". Odell Shepard, in his biography of Alcott, *Pedlar's Progress*, tells of some young man who came to Fruitlands from Brooks Farm and had lived on apples alone for a year. The apple theory was evidently in the air at that period also.

18 April 8th, 1858.

19 March 27th, 1858.

20 For a detailed description of the St. Louis *Turnvereine* cf. E. D. Kargau, *op. cit.*, pp. 293-309.

21 April 10th, 1858.

22 April 13th, 1858.

23 January 17th, 1858.

24 April 10th, 1858.

25 Letter from Putnam, Ct., December 20th, 1857.

26 Father Harris had acquired land in Missouri when he had been out West, but had encountered difficulty with it. At one time, William intended to use Moore to locate some land in the South of the State and start with buying 320 acres for about $60. This was to be an arrangement for re-paying his father a loan of $55 made the previous fall. An interesting side-light on the land sales of those times is given in a passage of the diary under March 16th. Land deals are mentioned frequently throughout the journal and the letters. Cf. also William's letter to his father of March 31st, 1858. It mentions good land at 12½¢ West of the Iron Mountain Railroad, and taxes on 320 acres of Missouri land to the amount of $2.40.

27 January 31st, 1858.

28 February 26th, 1858.

29 January 29th, 1858; similarly, February 2nd.

30 February 13th, 1858.

31 February 20th, 1858.

32 March 21st, 1858.

33 He had seen an article in *The Phrenological Journal* on pure reason which he thought could have been much better written by himself; cf. also an article on "Relations of Phrenology and Spiritualism" in Buchanan's *Journal of Man* for 1856.

34 January 19th, 1858.

35 January 24th, 1858.
36 March 8th, 1858.
37 February 22nd, 1858.
38 Eventually, Moore of the same class of '58 as William, entered the class of '59 at Yale and graduated. For two or three years afterwards he lived in New York, engaged in phonographic writing and reporting. From the *Second Biographical Record of the Class of Fifty-Eight* we learn that "in 1864, or thereabouts, he went to Sacramento, Cal., where he taught phonography and was engaged in reporting. In 1865 he was engaged in reporting in San Francisco, where he continued until the summer of 1866, when his health failed very rapidly and he came East, reaching New York in August. From there he went to Trenton, N. J., quite ill, and on the morning of October 17, 1866, he died . . ."
39 January 22nd. 1858.
40 The clippings from the *New York Times* and other papers regarding this affair are found in William's first and second scrap books. He also received the mournful notices of the drowning of his class-mate, George Elliot Dunham.
41 March 31st, 1858.
42 January 15th, 1858.
43 March 23rd, 1858. Now and then Albee sent pieces he had published which were immediately put into the scrapbook. There we find "The Omen", "Sonnet", "Pre-existence", "Les Bords du Rhin", "My Dead Cousin", "The Wreck". In 1858, John graduated from Harvard Divinity School and preached his first sermon. His dissertation on "Matter and Spirit" was noted for its evident love of beauty and the sympathy with the general literary spirit of Transcendentalism.
44 Etta C. Sperry, of Woodbridge, Ct.
45 March 2nd, 1858.
46 March 6th, 1858.
47 In March, an acquaintance of Rev. Storer, a bachelor, showed up in St. Louis, and William assisted him in solving some problems in geometry.
48 February 20th, 1858.
49 March 4th, 1858.
50 March 29th, 1858. Cf. also his affectionate letter to his grandmother, of same date.
51 March 9th, 1858.
52 Letter of March 31st, 1858.
53 March 29th, 1858.
54 February 11th, 1858.
55 January 19th, 1858.
56 February 1st, 1858.
57 February 7th, 1858.
58 March 13th, 1858.
59 April 3rd, 1858.
60 *From its Origin in Greece down to the Present Day*. Library Edition (N. Y., D. Appleton & Co., 1857).
61 February 1st, 1858.
62 March 12th, 1858.
63 This book is No. 333 in his catalog of books.
64 This set comprises No's 339-341.
65 January 6th, 1858. Lewes' *History of Philosophy*, appropriately called *die trübe Quelle . . . aus der Spencer seine philosophiegeschichtlichen Kenntnisse*

NOTES

schöpfte (Dr. Ludwig Stein, *Philosophische Strömungen der Gegenwart*, Stuttgart, 1908, p. 215).
66 February 21st, 1858.
67 February 26th, 1858.
68 Cf. Wilkin, *Charles Dickens in America*, and C. H. Jones, "St. Louis, Missouri", in *The Land We Love* (Charlotte, N. C.), December, 1868.
69 April 10th, 1858.
70 February 12th, 1858.
71 February 15th, 1858.
72 February 23rd, 1858.
73 March 8th, 1858.
74 March 10th, 1858.
75 Cf. his letter to S. S. McClure, the publisher, under date of Concord, Mass., September 7th, 1887, and "Books that have helped me", reprinted, N. Y., 1888, from *Forum* for April 1887.
76 March 11th, 1858.
77 March 14th, 1858.
78 Published by D. Appleton & Co.
79 March 26th, 1858.
80 March 26th, 1858.
81 April 13th, 1858.
82 It is interesting to note that the classification of books and of knowledge engaged Harris at such an early date.
83 The 1857-58 journals of Harris and his scrap books make it possible for us to reconstruct a considerable portion of the activity of the society.
84 William's letter to his brother Edward, September 30th, 1858.
85 Cf. George P. Bond, *An Account of Donati's Comet of 1858* (Cambridge, 1858), p. 7. In Harris' 2nd Scrap Book we find a clipping (from the U. S. Gazette?) relative to the discovery of Donati's Comet.
86 Joliet, Illinois, 1858.
87 Stuttgart und Tübingen, 1858.
88 April 12th, 1858.
89 Sometimes S. T. or George B. Hayden. We are dealing no doubt with the same person, only the shorthand reading presenting this difficulty.
90 March 12th, 1858.
91 Cf. his Commonplace Book for 1864.
92 April 6th, 1858.
93 April 10th, 1858.
94 His other interests were financial and sociologico-economical. He wrote *The Resources of Missouri* (St. Louis, 1867), and later Harris followed his columns in *The Missouri Republican* on "St. Louis, the Commercial Centre of North America".
95 March 15th, 1858.
96 March 18th, 1858.
97 March 26th, 1858.
98 I am quoting from his letter to me of February 25th, 1938.

CHAPTER VII

1 Cf. the *Daily Records of the Official Transactions of the Superintendent of the St. Louis Public Schools,* in manuscript. There were four other appointments besides Harris'. One was that of Emeretta A. Waters who served him a year later as Second Assistant.

2 Third standing Resolution, signed by Mr. C. P. E. Johnson, Secretary of the Board of Public Schools, and dated 1859.

3 The dimensions were 74½ feet by 56 feet, with two wings 30 feet by 9 feet each. The height of the stories varied, the first being 9 feet, the second 12 and third 14 feet. Each story had four rooms (30x26½), two wardrobes in the wings, and a hall 11½ feet in width.

4 *Fifth Annual Report*, p. 24.

5 To a large extent it was relieved by the expansion programs of the years 1853, '55, '57, '58, and particularly 1859, when nine schools had been constructed with a total capacity, for that year at least, of about 3000 pupils.

6 *Personal Recollections* (St. Louis, 1880), p. 14 ff. For the history of education in the State of Missouri cf. also Perry S. Rader, *School History of the State of Missouri* (Brunswick, Mo., 1891), and an article by C. A. Phillips, "A Century of Education in Missouri" in *Missouri Historical Review*, 15, 298 ff.

7 In the 1864 *Reports*.

8 Divoll's *Daily Records* for 1858, however, show that sometimes the third Saturday was the day of meeting.

9 An interesting history has been given by John E. Kimball, a teacher in the High School, and a one-time Secretary of the St. Louis Teachers' Association, in the Appendix to the *Thirteenth Annual Report*, on pages xxxiii-xxxix. The origin of the Association goes back to 1850, but the first definite date traceable is November 27th, 1852. In 1867, the teacher body having become too large, the Association was split up into several groups.

10 *Fifth Annual Report*, p. 47.

11 The specimen abstract of the exercises of December 11th, 1858, may be found in the Appendix, p. lxi, of the *Seventh and Eighth Annual Reports*. The essay, dated December 10th, is preserved.

12 Cf. Barth's letters to Harris of September 3rd, 1862, and May 16th, 1863 (?).

13 *A Border City during the Civil War*, p. 255.

14 Those of male Principals by $200, of female Principals by $100, that of female Assistants by $50 per year.

15 Principal of the High School, left to assume the duties of a Professor at Washington University.

16 Principal of the Normal School, became Head of Illinois State Normal University.

17 He assumed, before leaving St. Louis, the offices the two aforementioned ones had held.

18 Quotation from C. F. Childs.

19 *Report* for 1861-62.

20 Till then, Negroes paid the school tax, but did not share in educational privileges. Now their children were taught in five different schools under control of a "Board of Education for Colored Schools" composed of Negroes, counselled by Whites, particularly members of the Western Sanitary Commission.

21 Diary of 1866.

22 In the paper entitled "Education".

23 From the 1860 Diary.

24 Was in possession of Dr. Walton C. John, Senior Specialist in Higher Education, U. S. Office of Education, a sincere admirer of Harris.

25 Harris once said of Divoll that he was a man rather of practical power than of deep cognition. Cf. "The New England Heritage of Missouri", *Missouri Historical Review*, 27 (1932), pp. 64-69.

26 February 7th, 1868.

NOTES

27 February 13th, 1868.

28 St. Louis was often called the Mound City, and the big mounds in East St. Louis are still a great attraction for tourists.

CHAPTER VIII

1 The following poem is Essay No. 21, in Harris' Book of Early Writings, comprising the years 1851 to 1859.

2 September 30th, 1860.

3 Letter dated St. Louis, September 30th, 1858.

4 Cf. the letter to his grandmother Torrey, St. Louis, September 16th, 1859.

5 Cf. letter of June 15th, 1861.

6 June 26th, 1861.

7 Letter dated St. Louis, Mo., August 19th. Internal evidence reveals that the year must be 1861.

8 September 12th, 1861.

9 When the road was first laid through Jefferson Barracks, where at that time they had established the largest military hospital, the Secretary of War was insistent that the trains pass through on horse power. Cf. *Missouri Historical Review*, 15 (1920), p. 148.

10 Under June 12th, 1862. Sarah Lydia herself had been teaching as early as 1858 at Putnam, Ct. Equipped with a fine knowledge of Latin and French and a love of algebra, she entered St. Louis Normal School in the fall. In 1863, she taught in Irondale, Mo., but when in the first half of 1864 the demand for teachers was very great in St. Louis, due to the lifting of tuition fees in the Public Schools, she returned and assumed duties in Webster School without having graduated from Normal School. She returned to Putnam for reasons of health. but we find her back again soon and teaching also Evening School when this branch flourished once more in the St. Louis educational system. In August, 1868, she resigned from duties in Washington School.

11 A copy of the speech may be consulted in Harris' second Scrap Book. It is unsigned, but we gather from *The Phonographic Magazine*, 4 (1890), p. 137, that he was the reporter.

12 Cf. Carl Schurz, *Reminiscences* (N. Y., 1908), 2, p. 200.

13 Cf. the short-hand copy of a letter he sent to Dr. Peckham on June 26th, 1861.

14 The following outline of how the war affected St. Louis is based on the volumes of Moore's *Rebellion Record*, various histories of the Civil War and W. T. Harris' clippings. Cf. Walter B. Stevens, *Missouri* (Chicago etc., 1915), 1, pp. 239-362, also the centennial edition of 1921; Floyd C. Shoemaker, *A History of Missouri and Missourians* (Columbia, Mo., 1927); pp. 244-258; Menra Hopewell, *Camp Jackson History of the Missouri Volunteer Militia of St. Louis* (St. Louis, 1861); Robert J. Rombauer, *The Union Cause in St. Louis in 1861* (St. Louis, 1909); Prof. C. M. Woodward, "The City of St. Louis". Brenda Elizabeth Richard offered in 1934 a M. A. Thesis at Washington University under the title of *St. Louis During the Civil War* (in MS). Cf. also Col. Wm. M. Wherry, "The Campaign in Missouri, and Battle of Wilson's Creek, 1861", a paper read before the U. S. Military Service Institute, West Point, N. Y., May 23, 1878 and printed in *Western*, n. s., 6 (1880), pp. 177-195; Denton J. Snider, *The St. Louis Movement* etc. (St. Louis, 1920), pp. 53-59; John Fiske, *The Mississippi Valley in the Civil War* (Boston & N. Y., 1900); *War of Rebellion, Official Records of Union and Confederate Armies*, Series I, vol. 2.

15 Col. Keller Anderson.

16 Cf. letter of Edwin H. Bugbee, December 1st, 1861.

17 Rev. George Miller.

18 Cf., e.g., Edward Channing, *A History of the United States*, vol. 6 (N. Y., 1925).

19 He repeated more or less what he had said in the 1873 Peace Society address.

20 The following sketch is condensed from Bvt. Maj.-Gen. George W. Cullum's *Biographical Register of the Officers and Graduates of the U. S. Military Academy at West Point, N. Y.*, 1, pp. 167-179; H. E. Robinson, "General Ethan Allen Hitchcock, some account of a Missouri author somewhat neglected but whose Writings will live when more popular writers are forgotten", *Missouri Historical Review*, 2 (April, 1908), pp. 173-187.

21 A St. Louis German paper (date unknown) printed an article in which the writer alleged having seen a translation by Hitchcock of Spinoza's *Ethics* from a German version.

22 Letter of his grandmother Torrey, St. Louis, September 16th, 1859.

23 Letter of November 21st, 1863, copied in shorthand into the unfinished 1858 *Journal*, p. 326.

24 Letter of December 20th, 1864. Shorthand copy in the incomplete 1860 *Diary*. Outlines may also be found in the *Common Place Book* begun in 1864.

25 March 16th, 1864.

26 On p. 64.

27 In a letter to S. S. McClure, September 7th, 1887.

28 Cf. the document: War Department, Adjutant General's Office, Washington, July 30, 1862; *General Orders, No. 250*.

CHAPTER IX

1 June 19th, 1865. This whole section retold from the *Diary*. The shorthand of the *Diary* is concerned mainly with expenses.

2 By the name of Diver (?).

3 Published at Putnam, at the time. Copy of speech preserved in Harris' *General Scrapbook No. 6*, p. 15-16.

4 The *Diary* stops abruptly with the 4th of July celebration and resumes with the 7th of July. This date, however, should be changed to the 17th, to bring it in line with the dates in Alcott's *Journals*. The interruption in the *Diary* is taken up with seven snake stories in shorthand and by a little essay on "Politics of the Present", written July 20th.

5 The rate on the Fitchburg Railroad was 65¢ for 20 miles.

6 I am indebted for this information to Mr. Richard G. Hensley, Chief Librarian of the Reference Division, The Public Library of the City of Boston. This book of 367 pages was published in Boston, 1864. Cf. below for more details concerning Harris' criticism which was written during February, 1865. The *Diary* contains the draft, on pages 6-21.

7 These letters are preserved and may be consulted in Ralph L. Rusk, *The Letters of Ralph Waldo Emerson* (N. Y., 1939), 5, p. 421-422. Professor Rusk, in his footnote No. 95, is correct in interpreting the date on these notes of introduction as 1865, but Harris himself was in error when he later wrote in F. B. Sanborn and Harris, *A. Bronson Alcott, His Life and Philosophy* (Boston, 1893), 2, p. 593, that his visit to Alcott occurred on July 8th. To be sure, the date in his diary is also corrected from the 18th of July to the 8th, but from internal evidence and the corroborating date on Emerson's notes which are apparently clear and indisputable, we must conclude that July 18th, 1865, is the correct date of Harris' visit to Emerson's house and the latter's notes to Cabot and Hedge.

NOTES

[8] The Journals of Alcott, as published by Professor Odell Shepard (Boston, 1938), contain a reference to Harris' visit. Cf. July 17, 1865, entry. Alcott was mistaken about William's age. He was only 29, and he did not graduate from Yale.

[9] From the *First Biographical Record of the Class of Fifty-Eight*, p. 91.

[10] A draft may be consulted in the 1865 *Diary*. It was composed March 22nd, 1865.

[11] In her letter of October 18th, 1856.

[12] The following letter is a transcript from the shorthand copy in the 1866 *Diary*.

[13] Edward Mowry was educated first in the Putnam, Ct., public schools, then at the Academies mentioned, at Yale and Harvard Medical College. He established his practice at Providence and was elected President of the Providence Medical Association in 1882. His medical practice netted him a comfortable income, but most of his money came from the management of his wife's estate after he married, and his successful investments in real estate in Putnam, Providence, and later Pasadena, California. Like William, he was interested in art, as well as music, and was something of a painter himself. He was fond of travel and was quite a noted chess player in Rhode Island.

[14] Childs was born January 17th, 1831, in Steuben County, N. Y. Before coming to St. Louis he had graduated from Antioch College and spent three years at Oberlin.

[15] Cf. Harris' *Diary*, Friday, September 7th, 1860.

[16] A good description of the city in the grip of cholera, though of the year 1844, may be consulted in Taylor and Crooks, *Sketch Book of Saint Louis* (St. Louis, 1858), pp. 23 ff.; the cholera of 1849 in Friedrich Schnake, "*Geschichte der deutschen Presse und Bevölkerung von St. Louis und Umgegend*", *Der Deutsche Pionier*, June, 1873.

[17] Letter of February 22nd, 1870.

[18] Monteith came from the ministry, and his administration is not noted for outstanding measures.

[19] *Commonwealth*, vol. 4, No. 39, Saturday, May 26th, 1866, p. 1, col's 1-6. This information I also owe to Mr. Richard G. Hensley of the Boston Public Library.

CHAPTER X

[1] Cf. the *Thirteenth Annual Report*, p. 8.

[2] For education in St. Louis cf. Ira Divoll, "Historical Sketch of the St. Louis Public Schools", 13*th Ann. Rep. of the Board of Directors of the St. Louis Public Schools* (St. Louis, 1867), pp. 98-127; bird's eye view of the history and workings of the Public School system by Harris in the 25*th Ann. Rep.*, pp. 252-264; Wm. Hyde and Howard L. Conard, *Encyclopedia of the History of St. Louis* (N. Y., 1899), 4, pp. 2011 ff.; Nathan H. Parker, *Missouri as it is in* 1867 (Philadelphia, 1867), pp. 53-56; J. A. Dacus and James W. Buel, *A Tour of St. Louis* (St. Louis, 1878), pp. 81-107; *Switzler's Illustrated History of Missouri from* 1541 *to* 1877 (St. Louis, 1879), pp. 292-294; S. Waterhouse, *The Resources of Missouri* (St. Louis, 1867), pp. 54-56; an article in the *St. Louis Globe-Democrat* for June 18, 1875; "Sidney", letter to the editor of the *St. Louis Evening Post*, dated St. Louis, Aug. 5, 1878; J. Bittman, "*Historische Uebersicht des Schulwesens in St. Louis*", *Westliche Post*, Nov. 15 (?), 1877, a translation and recast from the School Reports; Charlotte E. Eliot, *William Greenleaf Eliot, Minister, Educator, Philanthropist* (Boston & N. Y., 1904), pp. 66-79, 93-94, 98; Walter B. Stevens, *St. Louis, the Fourth City*, 1764-1909 (St. Louis & Chicago 1909), 1, chapter 24; *id., Missouri*

(Centennial ed., 1921), 2, chapter 31; Floyd C. Shoemaker, *A History of Missouri and Missourians* (Columbia, Mo., 1927), pp. 362-372; *St. Louis Globe-Democrat*, March 29, 1931, reprinted in *Missouri Historical Review*, 26, p. 220-221; Frederic L. Billon, *Annals of St. Louis in its Territorial Days from 1804 to 1821* (St. Louis, 1888), pp. 78-81; *Edward's Great West* (1860), p. 324; *Thoughts about the City of St. Louis, her Commerce and Manufactures, Railroads, etc.* (St. Louis, Mo., 1854), pp. 20-22, 25, 49 ff.

3 *Thirteenth Annual Report*, p. 11.

4 Cf. further, *Missouri Historical Society Collections*, 3 (1908-1911), p. 95-96.

5 Letter of July 24th, 1870.

6 Letter of June 24th, 1871.

7 Letter of July 4th, 1871.

8 As they did in Boston, Cincinnati and Chicago.

9 Cf. the *Fifteenth Annual Report*, and a letter to the Board under date of December 8th, 1868.

10 The decisive report which brought about these reorganizations was requested by the Board themselves, and was presented by Harris on July 19th, 1872. It is a manuscript of 13 pages, legal size, which has been preserved. In it are given explanations which were deemed necessary to a full understanding "of the Administrative Department's working and of the reasons for a change".

11 A bird's eye view of the St. Louis Public School System was given by Harris also in the *Eighteenth Annual Report*, pp. 160-165; cf. his history in the *Twenty-first Annual Report*, pp. 161-184.

12 The *Boston Sunday Herald*, August 19th, 1877.

13 In 1869.

14 Dr. Philander Priestley Claxton, U. S. Commissioner of Education, 1911-1921, President, Austin Peay Normal School, Clarksville, Tenn. Cf. his statement in the U. S. Department of the Interior, Office of Education, *Bulletin*, 1936, No. 17, p. 24.

15 The quotation is from his review of the Centennial Exposition.

16 May 8th, 1875.

17 Monographs on the various phases treated in this section are in manuscript or print.

18 This was, in essence, the 1873 formulation of the Course of Study. Cf. also p. 84 of the *Nineteenth Annual Report*.

19 Cf. the *Twentieth Annual Report*, p. 71 ff.

20 Quoted from a short survey of the history of St. Louis schools written in 1875.

21 In 1869-70.

22 The topic of the lecture was "The Education of Women", the time, April, 1872, the auspices those of the Association for the Better Education of Women.

23 Cf. Kurt F. Leidecker, "The Education of Negroes in St. Louis, Missouri, during William Torrey Harris' Administration", *The Journal of Negro Education*, 10 (October, 1941), pp. 643-649.

24 Cf. the Fifteenth Annual Report, p. 56.

25 *School Board Journal*, New York City, September, 1903. Cf. also U. S. Department of the Interior, Office of Education, *Bulletin* 1936, No. 17, p. 10.

26 These quotations from the *Seventeenth Annual Report*, p. 66. Cf. the *Fifteenth Annual Report*, p. 18; *Eighteenth Annual Report*, p. 76; the little known article "Some Thoughts on the Hamlet Problem in the School-Room" (1874); etc.

NOTES

27 Monographs on the phases treated in this chapter will discuss the problems raised more fully on the basis of documentary evidence.
28 Letter to Professor Will S. Monroe, October 12th, 1896.
29 Cf. Kurt F. Leidecker, "The 101st Year of the Kindergarten", *The American-German Review*, 7, No. 5, pp. 6-8 (June, 1941).
30 Cf. the *Twenty-second Annual Report*, section on the Kindergarten.
31 A complete history of teaching German in St. Louis public schools has been written by J. C. Christin, for the *Twenty-first Annual Report*, pp. 114-130; by L. Wm. Teuteberg for the *Twenty-fourth*, p. 66 ff., and the *Twenty-fifth*, pp. 97-115. Cf. also the *Twenty-third Annual Report*, pp. 164-177, where the arguments for and against German instruction are discussed.
32 We are speaking only of the German language group, not of courses offered in the High School, for instance, for those of other national extraction willing to learn the German language.
33 He was born in Switzerland, settled in Ohio in 1847, and was Professor of Languages at Miami College, Oxford, O. He stayed at Cincinnati a short while before coming to St. Louis.
34 Cf. the *Seventeenth Annual Report*, p. 185.
35 Born in Germany, May 4th, 1830, died November 26th, 1878. He distinguished himself as teacher and composer. Cf. Ernst C. Krohn, *A Century of Missouri Music* (St. Louis, 1924), pp. 13-14, 125, *et al. loc.*; Walter B. Stevens, *St. Louis, The Fourth City, 1764-1909*, 1, p. 949-950. At one time he criticised music teaching in the schools severely and was censored by the Board.
36 Especially in 1862 and again in 1864, Divoll made strenuous efforts to establish his library. Cf. Kurt F. Leidecker, "The Debt of Melvil Dewey to William Torrey Harris", *The Library Quarterly*, 139-142 (April, 1945), 15, pp. 139-142.
37 Given in February, 1865, in the Mercantile Library Hall, under direction of F. C. Childs. The profits amounting to $5726.65 were turned over to the library fund.
38 The *Twenty-first Annual Report*, p. 60-61. The problem of tying up education at school and education for life has been discussed somewhat in Kurt F. Leidecker, "William Torrey Harris' Theory of Culture and Civilization", *International Education Review*, 4 (1935), pp. 266-278.
39 Thus, in his address before the 4th Annual Convention of the German Teachers' Association in St. Louis, 1875. First used in the *Nineteenth Annual Report* (written between 1872-73).
40 Cf. the *Seventeenth Annual Report*.
41 In 1878. Much of Harris' connection with the American Social Science Association may be reconstructed from letters and his scrapbooks, as well as other sources.
42 In the *Twenty-second Annual Report*, p. 115.
43 Spoken at the Detroit meeting, August 5th, 1874, of the National Educational Association.
44 Cf. the *Thirteenth Annual Report*, (1867), p. 72.
45 Fuller treatments of the topics discussed are in manuscript.
46 *A Forgotten Obligation* (St. Louis, 1926).
47 The whole controversy into which we cannot enter here, had many very interesting phases.
48 Cf. the summary of his impressions at the Centennial Exposition.
49 The collected articles appeared as *Letter on Public Schools with Special Reference to the System as Conducted in St. Louis* (St. Louis, 1870). The St. Louis Public Schools are called a "stupendous swindle and fraud".

50 We have to forego in this place the details of Harris' and the opposition's arguments which are most instructive.

51 In a letter to Robert R. Bishop.

52 August, 1876: "The Division of School Funds for Religious Purposes."

CHAPTER XI

1 In connection with this cf. Kurt F. Leidecker, "Harris and Indian Philosophy", *William Torrey Harris*, 1835-1935, a Collection of Essays etc., ed. by Edward L. Schaub (Open Court, Chicago & London, 1936), pp. 81-122. The problems involved here will be discussed once more in a later chapter.

2 Language and reading were subjects of first rate importance in St. Louis and Missouri generally. For the language difficulties in St. Louis cf. Allen Walker Read, "Attitudes toward Missouri Speech", *Missouri Historical Review*, 29, pp. 259-271.

3 Limited space forbids more details.

4 The history of the AII may be consulted in *Lectures read before the American Institute of Instruction, at Town Hall, Saratoga, N. Y., July 6*, 1880. *With the Journal of Proceedings* (Boston, 1880), p. 22 ff.

5 A good survey of the interdependence of the National Teachers' Association and the NEA, as well as the AII is given in *National Educational Association, Addresses and Journal of Proceedings, Sessions of the Year* 1879, in the Inaugural Address of President John Hancock.

6 This discussion of Harris' affiliation with the three or four educational associations mentioned in this section, had to be necessarily brief and does not adequately suggest the amount of service he rendered as an administrator or speaker.

7 Harris defined an autotype as a system of photography in carbon which has the advantage of reproducing every line or dot of the original, without exaggeration.

8 The School of Design was closed when it became known that Wayman Crow had donated a building to Washington University for art purposes. It had not been a great financial success, yet the indebtedness equalled the assets left.

9 Cf. the *Nineteenth Annual Report*, p. 164.

10 Cf. his article on "Home Culture in Art Studies".

11 Letter to Professor Will S. Monroe, October 12th, 1896. In this connection must be mentioned another factor which aided art-appreciation in St. Louis, the publication of *The Western*, to which Harris referred in rather personal terms as "our" publication. The treatment of Harris' influence on St. Louis art life could not be made exhaustive in the available space.

12 Cf. letter of January 14th, 1863.

13 We mention this as one of the curiosities. Much more could be said about the rôle which Harris played in supporting the cause of music in St. Louis, without even touching upon the part which music played in the public schools under his guidance.

14 For this I have the authority of Professor Howard G. Carragan, of Rensselaer Polytechnic Institute, Troy, N. Y., who was kind enough to study the pertinent manuscript and published material. Harris himself was convinced of his priority in the description, and a search in the historical literature thus far has borne him out.

15 In a November number of the year 1873.

16 Cf. also the *Twenty-fourth Annual Report*, p. 203.

NOTES

[17] A fine, illustrated description of Shaw's Missouri Botanical Garden may be consulted in the *Western Education Review* for October, 1871.

[18] The departments of knowledge to be covered by the Society's intentions were: Art, Literature, Science, Theology, Philosophy, Education, Domestic Economy, Law, and Medicine, to which was added Mechanics. There was to be a co-operation with the libraries. Membership was $2. Information was given to non-members, according to Article III of the By-Laws, for a fee of 25 cents. A. H. Blaisdell acted as General Secretary, from 3037 Pine Street; the President was Mrs. John W. Noble; Vice-President, Miss Sue V. Beeson. Harris' friends and acquaintances were thus in key positions, with H. H. Morgan, Denton J. Snider, J. H. Hosmer and others as co-Secretaries.

[19] Even though there are some discussions in literature about both ventures, there is room for a great many monographs on the St. Louis Movement in Philosophy. I refer merely to the items under Perry, Harris, Dodson, Forbes, Schuyler, Muirhead, Riley, Snider, Whiting and Morgan in Kurt F. Leidecker, "Bibliography: William Torrey Harris in Literature" at the end of the Centennial volume *William Torrey Harris*, 1835-1935, edited by Edward L. Schaub. See note 1 above.

[20] Cf. William Schuyler, "German Philosophy in St. Louis", *Bulletin of the Washington University Association*, 1904, p. 66.

[21] Harris' characterization, written about March, 1878, as Miss Edith Davidson Harris concludes from matter filed with the sketch of Brokmeyer's biography.

[22] Geo. C. Stedman, in a letter to Harris of January 1st, 1860.

[23] Cf. Harris' letter to his uncle, Dr. Peckham, dated June 26th, 1861.

[24] Cf. his shorthand letter to Harris, November 2nd, 1860.

[25] Cf. his letter to Harris under date of February 16th, 1862. Most of the Brokmeyer letters are fast fading, having been written either with pencil or with poor ink on poor paper.

[26] Cf. letter of October 20th, 1864.

[27] Cf. letter of October 9th, 1863.

[28] Cf. an autobiographical note prepared for a Mr. Ripley.

[29] Cf. Denton J. Snider, *The St. Louis Movement in Philosophy, Literature, Education and Psychology; with Chapters of Autobiography* (1920), especially p. 269.

[30] Edward L. Schaub, "Harris and the Journal of Speculative Philosophy", in the memorial volume edited by him (see note 1), p. 51.

[31] From the *Record Book*, p. 63-64.

[32] In the year 1875.

CHAPTER XII

[1] Denton J. Snider, *A Writer of Books in his Genesis*, p. 308-309.

[2] Cf. H. H. Morgan, "The St. Louis Society of Pedagogy", *Western*, n.s., vol. 3, pp. 737-750 (December, 1877).

[3] June 22nd, 1871.

[4] In 1873.

[5] February 7th, 1880.

[6] In March, 1874.

[7] July 10th to 12th, 1876, during a very hot season.

[8] On May 7th, 1880.

[9] On August 28th, 1874 or 1875.

[10] June 22nd, 1875.

[11] In December, 1879. Susan Blow was invited at that occasion.

12 Held December 31st, to January 3rd.
13 June 7th, 1875.
14 Meeting September 1st to 3rd.
15 June 5th.
16 June 9th; the place, Alton, Illinois.
17 June 17th.
18 December 29th.
19 December 13th.
20 December 26th, 1878.
21 On May 7th.
22 December 26th, 1876.
23 July 10th.
24 This was the only year in the period in question, as Mr. Richard G. Hensley, Chief Librarian, Reference Division, Public Library of Boston, wrote me (June 3rd, 1940), that Charles Eliot was President of the Festival. It was held on May 27th.
25 In the preparation of this biography it has been necessary to consult so many documents that I feel that nearly all the items written and published by Harris have been consulted. It was at first intended to append a full bibliography of both the writings of Harris and the writings about him, but space does not permit.
26 Mr. W. J. S. Bryan, of St. Louis, a devoted Harris student who has pleasant recollections of him, has endeavored to gather all of Harris' printed articles and books.
27 Largely placed by Miss Edith Davidson Harris with the National Education Association in Washington, D. C., and the Missouri Historical Society of St. Louis.
28 Cf. the *Yale Biographical Record.*
29 Letter of May 20th, 1873, by a certain Mr. W. M. Soper (Loper?).
30 Letter from Harrisburg, May 13th, 1875.
31 Letter of C. W. Brown, November 3rd, 1876.
32 Cf. Bailey's letter to Harris, April 6th, 1877.
33 February 24th, 1877. The shorthand copy may be consulted in the 1866 *Diary* of Harris. Even though there is some doubt as to the reading of the shorthand, the tone of the paragraph is such that our conclusion seems fully justified.
34 Letter of June 30th, 1878.
35 September 5th, 1878.
36 Cf. page 109 ff. See especially the *Sixteenth Annual Report*, p. 134, for a very explicit statement.
37 Vol. 4 (1870), pp. 114-129.
38 Letter dated Amherst, Mass., May 9th, 1873.
39 *A Classification and Subject Index for Cataloguing and Arranging the Books and Pamphlets of a Library* (Amherst, Mass., 1876), p. 3.
40 For the full justification of this view cf. Kurt F. Leidecker, "The Debt of Melvil Dewey to William Torrey Harris", *The Library Quarterly*, 15, p. 139-142 (April, 1945).
41 Grosvenor Dawe, *Melvil Dewey. Seer: Inspirer: Doer.* 1851-1931 (Library ed., 1932), p. 48.
42 On October 26th.
43 On Bailey's alleged unjust treatment by the library authorities, cf. *Library Journal*, 1, p. 221 (February 28th, 1877); cf. also 5, pp. 106 and 139, respecting Crunden's administration.

NOTES

44 On April 7th, 1871, for instance.
45 In February, 1875, speaking on "The Facts and Ideas that Underlie our Civilization".
46 On May 30th, 1884, lecturing on "The Philosophy of Religion". Cf. *The Index*, Boston, June 19th, 1884, pp. 605-610.
47 May 14th.
48 Cf. his *Personal Scrapbook No. 3*, p. 28-29 for the proof entitled "A Visit to Eastern Schools". It was probably intended for Merwin's *Journal of Education*.
49 General Sherman invited the visitors for dinner in order to share with them his war experiences.
50 Shortly before his death, Bernays wrote a fine, appreciative biography of Harris for *Der Westen*.

CHAPTER XIII

1 July 29th, 1870.
2 Appeared in the *Missouri Republican* during July, 1879.
3 In the same paper and same month. "A Divine Retribution" appeared in the same paper on August 8th, 1880. The *Journal of Speculative Philosophy*, in its April, 1882, and July, 1883, numbers contains poems by Theodore.
4 Dr. J. Haynes author of *Threads of Philosophy, Moral Mirror, Manipulations on Various Heads, Poems*, etc. Date of chart listing 50 items, unknown.
5 An 1880 quotation from Harris' writings by the *Minneapolis* (Minn.) *Tribune* to the effect that he was a palmistry enthusiast, is probably spurious.
6 June 16th, 1869.
7 Probably in 1872. He received his invitation in September from Hermann Eisenhardt, the Secretary.
8 On November 24th.
9 *Jahrgang* 2, No. 22 (December 2nd, 1877).
10 Given on June 25th, 1879. Bernays died June 22nd.
11 Cf. her letter of January 15th, 1876.
12 November 26th, 1873.
13 In this connection cf. also Enrique Parmer, "To Mexico and Isles of the Pacific", *Western*, n.s., vol. 5 (1879), pp. 56-68.
14 In 1876.
15 Jefferson Whitman lived at 2316 Pine Street. The time was October, 1879.
16 Cf. Walt Whitman, *Memoirs of President Lincoln and other Lyrics of the War* (Portland, Me., 1906); William E. Barton, *Abraham Lincoln and Walt Whitman* (Indianapolis, 1928).

CHAPTER XIV

1 In a letter to Professor Will S. Monroe, October 12th, 1896.
2 Cf. Odell Shepard, *Pedlar's Progress. The Life of Bronson Alcott* (Boston, 1937), p. 467.
3 Letter of December 22nd, 1857.
4 Cf. Harris' shorthand *Diary* of 1858, under January 17th.
5 Cf. Alcott to Harris, Letter of November 15th, 1858.
6 Cf. F. B. Sanborn and William T. Harris, *A. Bronson Alcott* (Boston, 1893), 2, p. 552-553. See also *Pedlar's Progress*, pp. 472-477, and Odell Shepard, *The Journals of Alcott*, pp. 311-313.
7 Miss Edith Davidson Harris found the original of the "real estate" in the *Commonplace Book* for 1857, vol. 1, p. 95. It was dictated by Alcott and signed by him after Harris had read back his notes.

637

8 *The Journals of Alcott*, pp. 378-382.
9 Letter of April 17th, 1866, from Concord.
10 Cf. letter dated February 10th, 1867.
11 Cf. Ralph L. Rusk, *Letters of Ralph Waldo Emerson*, 5, p. 456.
12 June 17th, 1866.
13 The letter promised by Emerson in the telegram is referred to in Rusk, *op. cit.*, vol. 5, p. 458. It is dated Concord, February 23rd, 1866.
14 Cf. also Rusk, *op. cit.*, vol. 5, p. 514, n. 140, and reference to *The Commonwealth*, March 30th 1867.
15 Cf. his letter of June 28th, 1867; Rusk, *op. cit.*, p. 521.
16 Letter of April 4th, 1867.
17 As in a speech he gave sometime in July, 1872. The source of the clipping cannot be ascertained.
18 Letter to Harris, November 22nd, 1868.
19 Letter to Harris of November 6th, 1869.
20 Letter of December 17th, 1869.
21 Cf. his letter of September 27th, 1874.
22 Alcott's letter to Harris, March 11th, 1872.
23 Letter of February 7th, 1874.
24 Letter of September 22nd, 1868.
25 *The Journals of Alcott*, p. 428.
26 Letter of September 19th, 1872.
. 27 Letter of July 7th, 1868.
28 Letter of May 20th, 1870.
29 Letter of July 29th, 1870.
30 The Club was in existence from about 1867 to 1880. Cf. Mrs. John T. Sargent, *Sketches and Reminiscences of the Radical Club of Chestnut Street, Boston* (Boston, 1880).
31 He wrote reviews of the event for the *National Standard* and the *Springfield Republican*.
32 Letter of June 6th, 1869.
33 *The Journals of Alcott*, p. 408 (May 3rd, 1870).
34 Letter of February 6th, 1872.
35 Letter of September 19th, 1872.
36 Letter of May 8th, 1876.
37 Letter of August 15th, 1878.
38 Letter of October 5th, 1878.

CHAPTER XV

1 Substantially the same paper he gave at the National Educational Institute Convention at Baltimore.
2 The educational exhibits were scattered throughout several buildings. A detailed catalog of items exhibited by St. Louis is given in the January 9, 1877, Report of the Committee to the Board. A general description of the foreign educational exhibits may be found, apart from the catalogs of the nations themselves, in an Extra of the *New York Tribune*, No. 35, "Guide to the Exhibition" (September, 1876), p. 6. Descriptions of U. S. Exhibits by States may be consulted in the various State Education Journals, such as Indiana, Michigan, Virginia, Iowa, Ohio, beginning with August, 1876, but particularly in the *Pennsylvania School Journal*. The Missouri exhibit was discussed very appreciatively by W. E. Crosby, Editor of *The Common School* (Iowa). Science instruction was criticised in the article, but Harris' reports were characterized as "surpassing in value, perhaps, any other educational matter of the kind".

NOTES

[3] The Gold Palm of the University of France went to John Eaton, the Cross of the Legion of Honor and the Gold Palm to John D. Philbrick, the two other Silver Palms to Henry Kiddle, of New York, and J. Ormond Wilson, of Washington.

[4] Cf. the letter of John D. Philbrick, Director of the American Section of Education, dated Paris, October 19th, 1878.

[5] Cf. Philbrick's letter of December 5th, 1878.

[6] August 2nd, 1866.

[7] Written January 15th, 1868.

[8] April 20th, 1868.

[9] The writer was Thos. M. Johnson.

[10] Letter dated Concord, July 24th, 1869.

[11] Cf. Alcott's letter to Harris, Concord, April 14th, 1873, and *The Journals of Alcott*, under March 18th, 1873. Possibly it was Samuel Longfellow who went with Alcott to call on President Eliot.

[12] Letter to Harris, Boston, February 7th, 1874.

[13] Cf. Alcott's letter to Harris, dated Ann Arbor, February 9th, 1870.

[14] Cf., e.g., a note of F. P. Stearns to Harris, of February 20th, 1876.

[15] Cf. Alcott's letter of December 3rd, 1875, and Harris' memorandum on it: "Declined all assistance, December 8/75".

[16] Cf. the scribbled draft of a telegram on the program of the Grand Farewell Matinee for Dr. Hans von Bülow, at Mercantile Library Hall, February 12th, and the letter to R. R. Bishop.

[17] In a letter of February 26th, 1876.

[18] Cf. letter of Alcott to Harris, Concord, May 8th, 1876.

[19] This story was told by J. B. Merwin, managing editor of the *American Journal of Education*.

[20] It was designed by Professor Carl Gutherz, of Washington University, and made by Mermod, Jaccard & Co.

CHAPTER XVI

[1] He wrote from London under date of August 4th, 1879.

[2] This and the following quotations are from his article in *Education*: *An International Magazine*, 1 (1881), p. 623-632.

CHAPTER XVII

[1] Cf. a history of the club by James S. Garland, in *Western*, n.s., vol. 1, pp. 519-526 (August, 1875). See also Denton J. Snider, *The St. Louis Movement* etc., pp. 179-181. Many of the lectures were printed in the *Western*.

[2] Cf. letter of Alcott to Harris, dated Boston, January 27th, 1874.

[3] Delivered in St. Louis on December 16th, 1873.

[4] The MS, No. 652, is in the NEA collection in Washington, D. C.

[5] In a letter to Miss Edith Davidson Harris, March, 1937.

CHAPTER XVIII

[1] Cf. her letter to me of August 28th, 1935, written from Brookline, Mass. The quotations in this and the following paragraphs are taken from newspaper clippings mainly from the years 1879-1881.

[2] Letter to Harris, dated Jacksonville, Ill., November 9th, 1882.

[3] Cf. *The Influence of Emerson* (1903), p. 205.

[4] Boston, August 18th, 1881.

[5] Cf. his review "The Concord Philosophical School", *Town Topics*, August 22nd, 1885, p. 7.

6 Writings under "Meister Junior" in the *Arkansas Ladies' Journal*, August 15th, 1885.

7 The correspondence is interesting from several points of view, for instance that of Wm. James' impetuosity, Harris' reconciliatory attitude, and the development of American philosophy in general.

8 From a clipping from the *Boston Sunday Herald*, August 1st, 1880, unsigned, but with the notation by Harris that it was written by Lathrop.

9 Anna Tolman Smith.

10 *Boston Herald*, July 23rd, 1887.

11 *The Index* was the organ of the Free Religious Association.

12 Delivered July 22nd, 1887.

13 *Yale Bulletin*.

14 Ossian Lang.

15 The poem appeared in the *Boston Evening Transcript*, and was reprinted in *The Index*, August 14th, 1884, p. 82.

16 Letter to Harris, August 27th, 1894.

17 Letter to Miss Edith Davidson Harris, April 9th, 1936.

18 Published in her volume of poems entitled "From Dreamland Sent" (1895).

CHAPTER XIX

1 Cf. *American Journal of Education* (Texas ed.), February 9th, 1886.

2 Cf. letter to me of Miss Maurine Woolf, Secretary to the President of the University of Missouri, December 12th, 1944.

3 Letter to Harris, dated Austin, Texas, May 19th, 1881.

4 Letter of June 14th, 1881.

5 Letter to Harris, dated June 27th, 1881.

6 Cf. the letter on the duty of a town to establish a High School, in *Texas Journal of Education*, March, 1882.

7 Dated St. Louis, September 8th, 1882.

8 Cf. letter of November 15th, 1882.

9 Cf. his letter to Harris, December 3rd, 1883.

10 Cf. letter of Theodore Lyman to Harris, February 15th, 1886.

11 Cf. letter of H. C. Lodge to Harris, January 27th, 1887.

12 That was in 1882.

13 Cf. his letter from Jacksonville, Ill., September 28th, 1883.

14 One in 1886, the other in 1891.

15 Cf. Harris' address at the meeting of the State Teachers' Association at Indianapolis in 1888 on "The Windows of the Soul; or, What Shall the Common Schools Teach?" Cf. *The Indianapolis Journal*, December 28th, 1888.

16 In 1883 (cf. his *Personal Scrapbook No. 5*, p. 171). In 1888 he spoke on "Excessive Helps in Education" (MS of 44 pages at NEA headquarters in Washington). In 1895 he spoke on "The Old Psychology vs. the New" (MS in same place).

CHAPTER XX

1 This was the reason Harris assigned to the dwindling of the society. Cf. a blue-pencil note on a query submitted to him by William Schuyler.

2 Cf. his *Personal Scrapbook No. 5*, p. 204.

3 Cf. the programs of 1881; *Personal Scrapbook No. 5*, p. 14-15; *Personal Scrapbook* (unnumbered), p. 28-31; *General Scrapbook No. 14*, p. 85-87.

4 Saratoga and Concord, 1881.

5 Interesting publications on Kant were brought out by him in 1887, 1888 and 1896. Cf. list of MSS in NEA headquarters, No's 195, 360, 389, 413, 705, 706, 786.

NOTES

6 Chicago, February 27th, 1882.
7 Cf. *Personal Scrapbook No. 5*, p. 143 and 155-156.
8 As in the parlor of Mrs. George W. Fisher, at Rochester, N. Y., in November, 1882. Cf. *Personal Scrapbook No. 5*, p. 126-128.
9 Cf. Marion V. Dudley, *Poetry and Philosophy of Goethe* (Chicago, 1887), which also contains the Harris contributions.
10 November 15th and December 6th.
11 Cf. Harris' 1860 *Diary*, entries under August 26th, 27th, September 3rd, 6th, 9th, 13th, 15th and 17th.
12 Cf. Harris' letter to Hitchcock, December 20th, 1864.
13 Cf. his letter to Harris, dated Florence, Italy, February 23rd, 1868.
14 It appeared in 1873, largely with the subsidy of members of the St. Louis Philosophical Society.

CHAPTER XXI

1 In a letter to me dated Santa Barbara, California, May 22nd, 1935.
2 According to a story told by Dr. Elmer E. Brown.

CHAPTER XXII

1 Draft dated January 15th, 1887. The letter was probably sent two days later.
2 Cf. *School Arts Book X*, pp. 989-993 (June, 1911), and his *Yankee Notions* (Cambridge, 1929), pp. 96-108.

CHAPTER XXIII

1 Letter of November 24th, 1888.
2 Letter of December 3rd, 1888, from shorthand copy.
3 Cf. letter of Mary E. Nicholson to Harris, dated Indianapolis, November 29th, 1888.
4 Letter to Harris of March 2nd, 1889.
5 Vol. 1 (1939), pp. 189-190.
6 Cf. letter dated Providence, June 13th, 1889.
7 April 7th, 1910, and May 28th, 1925.
8 Cf. Secretary Noble's letter to Harris of June 18th, 1889.
9 Cf. his letter to Harris, dated May 28th, 1889.
10 August 6th, 1889.
11 Cf. his letters of September 9th, 10th and 13th.

CHAPTER XXIV

1 Cf. his thesis entitled *The Education Contributions of the U. S. Commissioners of Education, 1867-1928.* Doctor's Dissertation of George Washington University, 1933. Pp. 53-68 deal with Harris.
2 Cf. Col. Dawson's letters to him of May 4th, April 5th, and July 11th, 1889.
3 Cf. above, Chapter 12, note 40.
4 Cf. 29 Stat. L. 140, 171.
5 Cf. his letter to the Department of the Interior, December 5th, 1896.
6 Cf. 54th Congress, 2nd Session, House of Representatives, Document No. 95.
7 Cf. letter of Dr. Butler to Harris, November 21st, 1904. The Butler-Harris correspondence remains unedited and unpublished.
8 Cf. *Education*, January, 1896: "Is Education possible without Freedom of the Will?"
9 March 31st, 1903.

10 Cf. Dr. Butler's letter to Harris of April 1st, 1903.

11 Cf. his letter to Dr. Butler, November 4th, 1904.

12 Cf. the House of Representatives Document.

13 Cf. Butler-Harris correspondence of October, 1903.

14 Cf. Harris' letter to Hon. J. M. Greenwood, Superintendent of Schools, Kansas City, Mo., dated April 11th, 1903, in which he reiterated his original conviction.

15 Cf. in this connection Harris' discussion of the Report on Geography of the New England Association of School Superintendents (1901) and his address in New York City on March 1st, 1889, on "History in Schools".

16 Cf. his article on "Industrial Education in the Common Schools", *Education*, for June, 1886. See also his letter to Professor Henry H. Belfield on the relation of manual training schools to common schools.

17 In his message to the Commissioner of Education at a celebration at Washington, commemorating the 100th anniversary of Harris' birth; cf. Office of Education, *Bulletin*, 1936, No. 17, p. 54.

18 Cf., e.g., his letter to C. D. Woods of the Agriculture Experiment Station, Orono, Maine, 1897, on "Indian Corn".

19 Letter of October 17th, 1906; cf. his *A History of Education in the United States since the Civil War* (Boston & N. Y., 1910), pp. 309-313.

20 Cf. his letter to Professor Will S. Monroe, October 12th, 1896, in which he lists this as one of his most important discoveries in education. See also the *Christian Register Tract Series*, No. 12, by him, entitled "Morality in the Schools"; and his lecture on "Moral Education" at Buffalo High School, in 1896.

21 No. 3414, to accompany H. Res. 258.

22 Cf. his letter of November 7th.

23 Letter to Jackson, January 6th, 1909.

24 Cf. his discussion in the *Bureau of Education Report* of 1896-97; his article in *Ainslee's Magazine*, 6, pp. 172-180 (September, 1900); his notes on textbooks for Alaska, No. 404 among the MSS at NEA headquarters.

25 In 1894; cf. MS No. 526 in the NEA collection.

26 The former, offered in 1901, is MS No. 749 in the NEA collection; the latter may be consulted in *NEA Journal of Proceedings and Addresses*, 1902, pp. 875-877.

27 November 16th, 1889.

28 Cf. his notes forming deposit No. 230 of the NEA collection. The date was March 25th, 1890.

CHAPTER XXV

1 Remembered by Miss Katherine Peckham.

2 The year was 1907.

3 Letter to me of January 16th, 1945.

4 Cf. *The School Journal*, April 29th, 1899, p. 489.

5 Cf. *Records of the Columbian Historical Society*, 35-36, p. 251.

6 Cf. his letter to C. W. Bardeen, December 21st, 1901.

7 July 5th, 1906.

8 Letter to Mrs. Edward M. Harris, dated Boston, June 19th, 1925.

9 See William Knight, *Memorials of Thomas Davidson, The Wandering Scholar* (Boston & London, 1907), p. 38.

10 *Ib.*, p. 124.

11 *Ib.* p. 149; cf. p. 109.

12 *Ib.* p. 47.

13 Letter of April 4th, 1890.

NOTES

Letter of February 4th, 1891.
15 Letter to Davidson, August 23rd, 1892.
16 The description of the camp was kindly furnished the author by Miss Edith Davidson Harris.
17 Cf. the excellent description by A. M. Kellogg in *The School Journal*, August 20th, 1892, p. 103-104: cf. further *The Scottish Review*, January, 1892, with Murray's article on "A Summer School of Philosophy", also William Knight's volume referred to above.
18 On the 30th he participated in a symposium. The notes are preserved.
19 Letter to me of April 6th, 1937.
20 Letter to Harris upon reading his book on Hegel's *Logic*, May 14th, 1909.
21 Cf. his notes, dated October 12th, 1877, MS 49 W, First Series, under III.
22 Cf. *The Education of the Wage-Earners*, ed. by Charles M. Bakewell, 1904.
23 A correspondence of some volume between Harris and the Breadwinner College remains unedited.

CHAPTER XXVI

1 His MS, representing reports and the like in connection with the Congresses of Education, may be consulted as No's 313, 321, 341, 358 and 399 of the material deposited with the NEA at Washington.
2 An extensive Howison-Harris correspondence of considerable philosophical interest has been preserved and is in preparation for publication.
3 June 4th, 1883.
4 Berkeley, September 21st, 1896.
5 Letter to Harris, dated Berkeley, March 7th, 1898.
6 Cf. two long letters to Howison under date of December 23rd, 1901.
7 Quoted from MS No. 416.
8 Cf. letters by Dr. Nicholas Murray Butler of March 5th, April 15th and 22nd, 1890.
9 This and other correspondence quoted by permission of Dr. Nicholas Murray Butler.
10 Cf. letter of Dr. Butler to Harris, July 1st, 1902.
11 December 31st, 1901.
12 E.g., in Harris' letter to Dr. Butler of November 21st, 1901.
13 Letter of Dr. Butler to Harris, October 7th, 1903.
14 Letter of November 3rd, 1904.
15 See the *New York Times Magazine*, January 3rd, 1937.
16 From letter to Dr. Butler, November 9th, 1904.
17 February 4th, 1905.
18 This college was established by Act of February 22nd, 1855, as "Farmers' High School of Pennsylvania" and became a little later known also as Agricultural College of Pennsylvania.
19 Dated May 20th, 1905.
20 Letter of May 24th, 1905.
21 Dated May 20th, 1905.
22 Letter of August 25th, 1905.
23 Of same date as the preceding.

CHAPTER XXVII

1 George Pliny Brown, from a poem reprinted in *School and Home Education*, March, 1910.
2 In a letter to F. Louis Soldan, June 23rd, 1885.
3 From *Journal of Education*, March 8th, 1894.

4 Cf. his notes written during the last year of his life, MS 628, 2nd Series, from which we are taking some of the data.
5 The home office was located in the ICU Building, 1100-1106 Fourteenth Street, N. W., Washington, D. C.
6 Letter of Channing Rudd to Harris, dated October 31st, 1904.
7 Cf. Harris' *General Scrapbook No. 6*, p. 49.
8 Cf. his earlier "My Pedagogical Creed", *School Journal* for 1897.
9 Letter of Rudolf Eucken to Harris, dated Jena, April 8th, 1898.
10 Cf. Kurt F. Leidecker, "An Eucken-Harris Correspondence", *International Education Review*, vol. 7, pp. 286-289 (1938).

CHAPTER XXVIII

1 Cf. his article by that title in the *Independent* for November, 1892.
2 Letter of November 9th, 1904. For a discussion of Harris' theory of Culture and Civilization, cf. Kurt F. Leidecker's article in *International Education Review*, 4, pp. 266-278 (1935).
3 "German Instruction in American Schools and the National Idiosyncrasies of the Anglo-Saxons and the Germans", an address before the National German-American Teachers' Association at Cleveland, O., July 16th, 1890.
4 *Ib.*
5 Cf. his letter to Professor Alexander Hogg, Fort Worth, Texas, 1893, MS 314 in NEA collection. Also for some of the other items cf. this collection.
6 Cf. p. 5-6 of *Industrial Commission. Education. Testimony of Dr. William T. Harris* (January 11, 1899).
7 We quote from a newspaper clipping, the *Evening Record,* probably of San Francisco, November 20th, 1888.
8 Cf. his letter to Professor Will S. Monroe, October 12th, 1896.
9 Cf. his notes dated April, 1903.
10 Cf. MSS 835, 243, 837 and 589.
11 *Forum*, 24, pp. 186-199.
12 In *U. S. Bureau of Education. Art and Industry.* Part 2.
13 A feeble attempt at dealing with these vital sociological problems was already made by *The Radical Review* whose publisher, Benj. R. Tucker, invited Harris to subscribe and contribute as early as December 25th, 1876. Cf. his letter of that date.
14 From MS, dated September 3rd, 1881. For a full discussion of Harris' sociological views, cf. Frances B. Harmon, *The Social Philosophy of the St. Louis Hegelians* (N. Y., 1943).
15 Thus *The National Baptist,* September 14th, 1882.
16 He spoke on "The Education of Women" on April 18th, 1872.
17 Cf. letter by the President, A. W. Terrill, January 8th, 1877.
18 Talks in 1881, 1883, 1884.
19 Address of May 30th, 1889.
20 Address of 1891.
21 Address of February 12th, 1891.
22 Cf. especially his *Annual Report* for 1872-73.
23 February 8th, 1884.

CHAPTER XXIX

1 The fate of the MS has occupied several scholars of late.
2 Letter of February 5th, 1907.
3 *The Living Church,* May 16th, 1891, vol. 14, p. 114.
4 Letter dated Berkeley, February 12th, 1891.

NOTES

5 Cf. his letter dated Erlangen, April 19th, 1891.
6 May 2nd, 1891.
7 Jesus College, March 31st, 1891.
8 Letter to him of same date.
9 Letter to R. A. Holland from Balliol College, Oxford, March 25th, 1891.
10 Cf. letter to Professor Will S. Monroe, October 12th, 1896.
11 Probably those in the Southeast pavilion on the second floor.
12 Cf. also the Procopeia Club meeting in Concord in April, 1896, at which Sanborn regaled the members with reminiscences.
13 Cf. items 185, 338, 594, 766, 767 and 867 in the NEA collection, and index of Evans' *List*.
14 Letter to Harris of March 21st, 1898, from North Scituate, Mass.
15 Letter of November 4th, 1904.
16 December 18th, 1905.
17 Cf. my article referred to in note 1, chapter XI.
18 Cf. Harris' letter to S. S. McClure, Concord, Mass., September 7th, 1887.
19 From a carbon copy corrected in Harris' handwriting, in possession of Dr. Henry Ridgely Evans.
20 In a course of lectures sponsored by the American Society of Religious Education.
21 Cf. Emery's letter of January 23rd, 1892, and Harris' of January 26th.
22 Cf. his letter to D. P. Jenkins, author of "The Passing of Plato", January 8th, 1898.
23 *Ib.*
24 Cf. Harris' letter to McCosh of January 23rd, 1891.
25 January 4th, 1898.
26 Cf. the *Memoirs of the Society for Philosophical Inquiry of Washington, D. C.,* Fourth Series (1909-1927), p. 230 ff.
27 Meeting of April, 1893. Cf. shorthand-longhand notes of Harris' under that date.
28 As recollected by Dr. Henry Ridgely Evans.
29 Cf. his letter to Harris of April 24th, 1907. Sandison corresponded with Harris from 1886 till 1908.
30 On February 6th, 13th, 20th, 27th, March 5th, 12th, 19th, 26th and April 2nd.
31 March 11th, 18th, 25th, April 1st, 8th and 15th. At the same time also an art lecture was announced under the auspices of the Columbian College.
32 Cf. his letter to Harris of May 4th, 1909.
33 From *The Putnam* (Connecticut) *Patriot,* June 4th, 1936.
34 In a letter to me of March 14th, 1940. The lecture was probably identical with the one Harris gave in March, 1898, at Smith College.
35 Letter of Dr. Butler to Harris of November 21st, 1904.
36 Cf. Lovejoy's letter to Harris of October 21st, 1908.

CHAPTER XXX

1 Cf. Harris' letter of May 29th, 1906.
2 Letter to Harris, August 7th, 1908.
3 Letter to Harris of July 21st, 1906.
4 Letter to Harris of October 17th, 1905.
5 Cf. his letter to Miss Sarah Eddy of December 12th, 1908.
6 This description from a letter to his son Theodore, July 14th, 1908.
7 Letter of Edward Mowry Harris from Putnam Heights, Ct., July 21st, 1908.
8 Telegram of July 24th, 1908.

9 Letter of November 10th, 1908.
10 Cf. Harris' letter to Col. Bacon, of December 5th, 1908.
11 Cf. letter of W. S. Sutton, University of Texas, to Hon. Theodore Harris, February 24th, 1909, with copy of resolutions.
12 September 7th, 1909.
13 These and the following quotations from his letter to Edward Mowry Harris, April 6th, 1909.
14 Letter of December 5th, 1908.
15 In his talk given in Washington, December 9th, 1935.

CHAPTER XXXI

1 Letter to his son Theodore, July 14th, 1908.
2 From the same letter.
3 Letter to Miss Edith Davidson Harris, April 13th, 1911.
4 Passed November 23rd, 1909.
5 Letter of June 4th, 1896, in possession of Dr. Nicholas Murray Butler.
6 Cf. MS 799 in the NEA collection.
7 Cf. letter to Miss Edith Davidson Harris, July 10th, 1917, notifying her of the award.
8 The titles are variously given as "The Spirit of World History", or "The Progress of Man into a Conscious Realization of True Freedom", which may represent titles of individual lectures.
9 As part of the series of Old South Lectures in History.
10 November 21st was given the first lecture on "Oriental History". The titles of the others were "Greece", "Rome" and "Modern Civilization".
11 Cf. the abstracts printed in the *New England Journal of Education*.
12 Cf. also Harris' "The Philosophy of Education", printed in *Johns Hopkins University Studies*, 2, Pt. 5-6, pp. 269-277 (Baltimore, 1893), as well as separately.
13 Cf. *The School Bulletin*, 32, No. 379 (March, 1906).
14 Cf. letter of Professor Lester Frank Ward to Miss Edith Davidson Harris, March 16th, 1910.
15 Quoted with permission of the National Education Association.

ADIRONDACK CAMP 492

EUROPE TRIP 502

SYRACUSE P. 450 - 1
CAZENOVIA

Syllogism 416

CPSIA information can be obtained at www.ICGtesting.com
Printed in the USA
BVOW042024100512

289781BV00001B/134/A